To Valerie, Nina, and Nicholas
With love and affection

—Sam Alapati

To Heidi, Brandi, and Lisa

—Darl Kuhn

To Oyuna and Evan for putting up with me and all the evenings and
weekends spent with my computer instead of with them!!

To Carol, Gerry, Susan, Doug, Scott, Chris, Jaimie, Katie, Jenny, Jeremy, and Sean. I love my family!

—Bill Padfield

D1438462

Contents at a Glance

Contents

About the Authors

Sam R. Alapati is an Oracle ACE and an experienced Oracle database administrator (OCP Oracle Database 11g). Sam is currently the senior technical director for Miro Consulting, Inc., in Woodbridge, New Jersey, and regularly consults with Fortune 500 companies in the areas of Oracle Database, Oracle E-Business, and Oracle Fusion Middleware technology. Sam has written several books on Oracle database management, including *Expert Oracle Database 11g Administration, Oracle Database 11g: New Features for DBAs and Developers* (with Charles Kim), and *RMAN Recipes for Oracle Database 11g* (with Darl Kuhn and Arup Nanda), all published by Apress. Sam lives in Dallas, Texas with his wife, Valerie, and children Shannon, Nina and Nicholas.

Darl Kuhn is a senior database administrator working for Oracle. He handles all facets of database administration from design and development to production support. He also teaches advanced database courses at Regis University in Colorado. Darl does volunteer DBA work for the Rocky Mountain Oracle Users Group. He has a graduate degree from Colorado State University and lives near Spanish Peaks, Colorado with his wife, Heidi, and daughters, Brandi and Lisa.

Bill Padfield is an Oracle Certified Professional, working for a large telecommunications company in Denver, Colorado as a lead database administrator. Bill helps administer and manage a large data warehouse environment consisting of more than 75 databases. Bill has been an Oracle Database administrator for more than 14 years, and has been in the IT industry since 1985. Bill also teaches graduate database courses at Regis University and currently resides in Aurora, Colorado with his wife, Oyuna, and son, Evan.

About the Technical Reviewer

 **Surachart Opun** was born in Phetchabun, Thailand. He graduated with a bachelor's degree in computer engineering. He has worked in the Internet service provider business over eight years. He has a lot of experience with Oracle Database and Linux. He has worked with Oracle Database and Oracle Real Applications Cluster over six years. He is an Oracle Certified Professional 10g and 11g. He is also an Oracle Certified Expert RAC. He is interested in Oracle Database technology and spends a lot of time on it. His blog is http://surachartopun.com. He has spent a lot of time sharing his Oracle knowledge and helping people with Oracle technology. In 2010, he became an Oracle ACE and developed the Oracle User Group in Thailand, to which he is a contributor.

Acknowledgments

The authors owe thanks to the great publishing team at Apress for helping them throughout the writing process. Jonathan Gennick, senior acquisitions editor, helped significantly in outlining the topics (recipes) for this book, and helped us produce the best book we possibly could, by nudging us along with incisive comments/suggestions/criticisms, all of which have tremendously increased both the presentation style of the book as well as the quality of the contents. Jonathan is that rare editor who is not only technically proficient, but also a consummate editor of books, in the traditional sense of the term. Thank you, Jonathan, for your patience and hard work throughout this project! All three of us are beneficiaries of your sagacious advice and continual encouragement over the past few months.

The authors would like to thank the tremendous work done by the technical editor of the book, Surachart Opun, senior analyst at True Internet, who somehow found time from his prolific blogging and other work to perform a marvelous review of our draft chapters. Surachart not only caught several mistakes in code and elsewhere, but also made numerous suggestions to improve the presentation of the various recipes. Thank you, Surachart, for all your painstaking and cheerful work in helping us out with the book. Anita Castro, coordinating editor, has superbly guided us throughout this project, and helped keep things on schedule. Managing a three-author project isn't a piece of cake by any means, but Anita sure makes it seem that way! Mary Ann Fugate copyedited the chapters with great skill, and we appreciate her contributions toward improving the quality of this book.

Personal Acknowledgments

First of all, my heartfelt thanks to the great help and cooperation from my two co-writers—Darl Kuhn and Bill Padfield—it sure was great working with you, Darl and Bill—I've enjoyed every minute of it! I'd like to acknowledge the support and encouragement of my company, Miro Consulting Inc., Woodbridge, New Jersey, whose CEO, Scott Rosenberg, is not only a great leader but also an enthusiastic promoter of Oracle technology with our many clients across the United States. Miro's president, Eliot Colon, its vice president of technical services, Wayne Federico, and its vice president, Bob Kinkade, have always been supportive of my work at Miro, and I've learned a lot from working with each of them.

I'd like to express the generosity and help offered by my friends Kishore Rachamalla, Praveen Katapally, and Sreeny Chinta during my tenure at ERCOT in Taylor, Texas, where I started initial work on this and another book. I'm grateful for the kindness and show of support by Sam Nataros, whose gift from the heart I'll always cherish—thank you, Sam, your gesture inspires me every single day!

My family, of course, has sacrificed the most in making this book possible, and thus I'm grateful to Valerie, Shannon, Nicholas, and Nina for their help and support over the past few years while I was working on this and another book. Last but not least, I'd like to acknowledge my debt to my other family—my mother, Swarna Kumari, my father, Appa Rao, and my brothers, Hari Hara Prasad and Siva Sankara Prasad, Aruna, Vanaja, Ashwin, Teja, Aparna, and Soumya, for their abiding love and faith in me.

Sam Alapati

Thanks to fellow co-authors Sam Alapati and Bill Padfield, and also thanks to the numerous DBAs and developers from whom I've learned performance tuning techniques over the years: Dave Jennings, Bob Suehrstedt, Scott Schulze, Pete Mullineaux, Janet Bacon, Sue Wagner, Mohan Koneru, Arup Nanda, Charles Kim, Bernard Lopuz, Barb Sannwald, Tim Gorman, Shawn Heisdorffer, Doug Davis, Sujit Pattanaik, Ken Roberts, Roger Murphy, Mehran Sowdaey, Kevin Bayer, Dan Fink, Guido Handley, Margaret Carson, Nehru Kaja, Tim Colbert, Glenn Balanoff, Bob Mason, Shari Plantz-Masters, Mike Nims, Denise Duncan, Brad Blake, Ravi Narayanaswamy, Abid Malik, Abdul Ebadi, Kevin Hoyt, Trent Sherman, Sandra Montijo, Jim Secor, Maureen Frazzini, Sean Best, Stephan Haisley, Geoff Strebel, Patrick Gates, Krish Hariharan, Buzzy Cheadle, Mark Blair, Gary Dodge, Karen Kappler, Mike Hutchinson, Liz Brill, Ennio Murroni, Mike O'Neill, Beth Loker, Mike Eason, Greg Roberts, Debbie Earman, Tom Wheltle, Ken Toney, Gabor Gyurovszky, Scott Norris, Joey Canlas, Eric Wendelin, Gary Smith, Mark Lutze, Kevin Quinlivan, Dave Bourque, Roy Backstrom, Larry Carpenter, Joe Meeks, Ashish Ray, John Lilly, Dave Wood, Laurie Bourgeois, Steve Buckmelter, Casey Costley, John DiVirgilio, John Goggin, Brett Guy, Simon Ip, Pascal Ledru, Kevin O'Grady, Peter Schow, Todd Sherman, Jeff Shoup, Mike Tanaka, Todd Wichers, Doug Cushing, Will Thornburg, Steve Roughton, Ambereen Pasha, Dinesh Neelay, Kye Bae, Thom Chumley, Jeff Sherard, Dona Smith, Erik Jasiak, Gary Schut, Don Gritzmacher, Aaron Isom, Kristi Jackson, Karolyn Vowles, Amin Jiwani, Paula Still, K. P. Muthe, Joe Pinkerton, Arvin Kuhn, Darin Christensen, Terry Roam, Doug Drake, Marilyn Wenzel, Doc Heppler, Mert Lovell, Carl Beasly, Brian Beasly, Odean Bowler, and Jim Stark.

Darl Kuhn

I'd like to thank my gracious co-authors, Sam Alapati and Darl Kuhn, for all of their help and support, and for taking on a rookie for this project. I couldn't have made it without their help.

There are so many people I can thank that have helped me over the years in my career, so please know that I appreciate every single individual who has encouraged and helped me along. First of all, I'd like to thank Bob Ranney for giving me the opportunity to be a DBA. I also would like to thank some of my key managers over the years that have helped me, including Beth Bowen, Larry Wyzgala, John Zlamal, Linda Scheldrup, Amy Neff, and Maureen Frazzini.

Of course, there are many DBAs, developers, system administrators, and architects that have helped me greatly in my career. First, I need to thank the DBAs on my current team who make the everyday grind a blast. These folks have helped me so much professionally and have become great friends over the many years we have worked together. This includes Dave Carter, Debbie Fitzgerald, Pankaj Guleria, Pete Sardaczuk, Brad Strom, and Rebecca Western.

Over the years, I've learned an awful lot from the following folks, who have always been generous with their time and help, and patient with my questions. This includes Mark Nold, Mick McMahon, Sandra Montijo, Jerry Sanderson, Glen Sanderson, Jose Fernandez, Mike Hammontre, Pat Cain, Dave Steep, Gary Whiting, Ron Fullmer, Becky Enter, John Weber, Avanish Gupta, Scott Bunker, Paul Mayes, Bill Read, Rod Ermish, Rick Barry, Sun Yang, Sue Wagner, Glenn Balanoff, Linda Lee Burau, Deborah Lieou-McCall, Bob Zumpf, Kristi Sargent, Sandy Hass, George Huner, Pad Kail, Curtis Gay, Ross Bartholomay, Carol Rosenow, Scott Richards, Sheryl Gross, Lachelle Shambe, John Piel, Rob Grote, Rex Ellis, Zane Warton, Steve Pearson, Jim Barclay, Jason Hermstad, Shari Plantz-Masters, Denise Duncan, Bob Mason, Brad Blake, Mike Nims, Cathie Wilson, Rob Coates, Shirley Amend, Rob Bushlack, Cindy Patterson, Debbie Chartier, Blair Christensen, Meera Ganesan, and Kedar Panda.

Bill Padfield

CHAPTER 1

Optimizing Table Performance

This chapter details database features that impact the performance of storing and retrieving data within a table. Table performance is partially determined by database characteristics implemented prior to creating tables. For example, the physical storage features implemented when first creating a database and associated tablespaces subsequently influence the performance of tables. Similarly, performance is also impacted by your choice of initial physical features such as table types and data types. Therefore implementing practical database, tablespace, and table creation standards (with performance in mind) forms the foundation for optimizing data availability and scalability.

An *Oracle database* is comprised of the physical structures used to store, manage, secure, and retrieve data. When first building a database, there are several performance-related features that you can implement at the time of database creation. For example, the initial layout of the datafiles and the type of tablespace management are specified upon creation. Architectural decisions instantiated at this point often have long-lasting implications.

A *tablespace* is the logical structure that allows you to manage a group of datafiles. Datafiles are the physical datafiles on disk. When configuring tablespaces, there are several features to be aware of that can have far-reaching performance implications, namely locally managed tablespaces and automatic segment storage–managed tablespaces. When you reasonably implement these features, you maximize your ability to obtain acceptable future table performance.

The *table* is the object that stores data in a database. Database performance is a measure of the speed at which an application is able to insert, update, delete, and select data. Therefore it's appropriate that we begin this book with recipes that provide solutions regarding problems related to table performance.

We start by describing aspects of database and tablespace creation that impact table performance. We next move on to topics such as choosing table types and data types that meet performance-related business requirements. Later topics include managing the physical implementation of tablespace usage. We detail issues such as detecting table fragmentation, dealing with free space under the high-water mark, row chaining, and compressing data. Also described is the Oracle Segment Advisor. This handy tool helps you with automating the detection and resolution of table fragmentation and unused space.

1-1. Building a Database That Maximizes Performance

Problem

You realize when initially creating a database that some features (when enabled) have long-lasting ramifications for table performance and availability. Specifically, when creating the database, you want to do the following:

- Enforce that every tablespace ever created in the database must be locally managed. Locally managed tablespaces deliver better performance than the deprecated dictionary-managed technology.

- Ensure users are automatically assigned a default permanent tablespace. This guarantees that when users are created they are assigned a default tablespace other than SYSTEM. You don't want users ever creating objects in the SYSTEM tablespace, as this can adversely affect performance and availability.

- Ensure users are automatically assigned a default temporary tablespace. This guarantees that when users are created they are assigned a temporary tablespace other than SYSTEM. You don't ever want users using the SYSTEM tablespace for a temporary sorting space, as this can adversely affect performance and availability.

Solution

Use a script such as the following to create a database that adheres to reasonable standards that set the foundation for a well-performing database:

```
CREATE DATABASE O11R2
   MAXLOGFILES 16
   MAXLOGMEMBERS 4
   MAXDATAFILES 1024
   MAXINSTANCES 1
   MAXLOGHISTORY 680
   CHARACTER SET AL32UTF8
DATAFILE
'/ora01/dbfile/O11R2/system01.dbf'
   SIZE 500M REUSE
   EXTENT MANAGEMENT LOCAL
UNDO TABLESPACE undotbs1 DATAFILE
'/ora02/dbfile/O11R2/undotbs01.dbf'
   SIZE 800M
SYSAUX DATAFILE
'/ora03/dbfile/O11R2/sysaux01.dbf'
   SIZE 500M
DEFAULT TEMPORARY TABLESPACE TEMP TEMPFILE
'/ora02/dbfile/O11R2/temp01.dbf'
   SIZE 500M
```

```
DEFAULT TABLESPACE USERS DATAFILE
'/ora01/dbfile/O11R2/users01.dbf'
   SIZE 50M
LOGFILE GROUP 1
        ('/ora01/oraredo/O11R2/redo01a.rdo',
         '/ora02/oraredo/O11R2/redo01b.rdo') SIZE 200M,
        GROUP 2
        ('/ora01/oraredo/O11R2/redo02a.rdo',
         '/ora02/oraredo/O11R2/redo02b.rdo') SIZE 200M,
        GROUP 3
        ('/ora01/oraredo/O11R2/redo03a.rdo',
         '/ora02/oraredo/O11R2/redo03b.rdo') SIZE 200M
USER sys    IDENTIFIED BY topfoo
USER system IDENTIFIED BY topsecrectfoo;
```

The prior **CREATE DATABASE** script helps establish a good foundation for performance by enabling features such as the following:

- Defines the **SYSTEM** tablespace as locally managed via the **EXTENT MANAGEMENT LOCAL** clause; this ensures that all tablespaces ever created in database are locally managed. If you are using Oracle Database 11g R2 or higher, the **EXTENT MANAGEMENT DICTIONARY** clause has been deprecated.

- Defines a default tablespace named **USERS** for any user created without an explicitly defined default tablespace; this helps prevent users from being assigned the **SYSTEM** tablespace as the default. Users created with a default tablespace of **SYSTEM** can have an adverse impact on performance.

- Defines a default temporary tablespace named **TEMP** for all users; this helps prevent users from being assigned the **SYSTEM** tablespace as the default temporary tablespace. Users created with a default temporary tablespace of **SYSTEM** can have an adverse impact on performance, as this will cause contention for resources in the **SYSTEM** tablespace.

Solid performance starts with a correctly configured database. The prior recommendations help you create a reliable infrastructure for your table data.

How It Works

A properly configured and created database will help ensure that your database performs well. It is true that you can modify features after the database is created. However, oftentimes a poorly crafted **CREATE DATABASE** script leads to a permanent handicap on performance. In production database environments, it's sometimes difficult to get the downtime that might be required to reconfigure an improperly configured database. If possible, think about performance at every step in creating an environment, starting with how you create the database.

When creating a database, you should also consider features that affect maintainability. A sustainable database results in more uptime, which is part of the overall performance equation. The **CREATE DATABASE** statement in the "Solution" section also factors in the following sustainability features:

- Creates an automatic UNDO tablespace (automatic undo management is enabled by setting the UNDO_MANAGEMENT and UNDO_TABLESPACE initialization parameters); this allows Oracle to automatically manage the rollback segments. This relieves you of having to regularly monitor and tweak.

- Places datafiles in directories that follow standards for the environment; this helps with maintenance and manageability, which results in better long-term availability and thus better performance.

- Sets passwords to non-default values for DBA-related users; this ensures the database is more secure, which in the long run can also affect performance (for example, if a malcontent hacks into the database and deletes data, then performance will suffer).

- Establishes three groups of online redo logs, with two members each, sized appropriately for the transaction load; the size of the redo log directly affects the rate at which they switch. When redo logs switch too often, this can degrade performance.

You should take the time to ensure that each database you build adheres to commonly accepted standards that help ensure you start on a firm performance foundation.

If you've inherited a database and want to verify the default permanent tablespace setting, use a query such as this:

```
SELECT *
FROM database_properties
WHERE property_name = 'DEFAULT_PERMANENT_TABLESPACE';
```

If you need to modify the default permanent tablespace, do so as follows:

```
SQL> alter database default tablespace users;
```

To verify the setting of the default temporary tablespace, use this query:

```
SELECT *
FROM database_properties
WHERE property_name = 'DEFAULT_TEMP_TABLESPACE';
```

To change the setting of the temporary tablespace, you can do so as follows:

```
SQL> alter database default temporary tablespace temp;
```

You can verify the UNDO tablespace settings via this query:

```
select name, value
from v$parameter
where name in ('undo_management','undo_tablespace');
```

If you need to change the undo tablespace, first create a new undo tablespace and then use the ALTER SYSTEM SET UNDO_TABLESPACE statement.

1-2. Creating Tablespaces to Maximize Performance

Problem

You realize that tablespaces are the logical containers for database objects such as tables and indexes. Furthermore, you're aware that if you don't specify storage attributes when creating objects, then the tables and indexes automatically inherit the storage characteristics of the tablespaces (that the tables and indexes are created within). Therefore you want to create tablespaces in a manner that maximizes table performance and maintainability.

Solution

When you have the choice, tablespaces should always be created with the following two features enabled:

- Locally managed

- Automatic segment space management (ASSM)

Here's an example of creating a tablespace that enables the prior two features:

```
create tablespace tools
  datafile '/ora01/dbfile/INVREP/tools01.dbf'
  size 100m                                   -- Fixed datafile size
  extent management local         -- Locally managed
  uniform size 128k                         -- Uniform extent size
  segment space management auto -- ASSM
/
```

■ **Note** As of Oracle Database 11g R2, the EXTENT MANAGEMENT DICTIONARY clause has been deprecated.

Locally managed tablespaces are more efficient than dictionary-managed tablespaces. This feature is enabled via the EXTENT MANAGEMENT LOCAL clause. Furthermore, if you created your database with the SYSTEM tablespace as locally managed, you will not be permitted to later create a dictionary-managed tablespace. This is the desired behavior.

The ASSM feature allows for Oracle to manage many of the storage characteristics that formerly had to be manually adjusted by the DBA on a table-by-table basis. ASSM is enabled via the SEGMENT SPACE MANAGEMENT AUTO clause. Using ASSM relieves you of these manual tweaking activities. Furthermore, some of Oracle's space management features (such as shrinking a table and SecureFile LOBs) are allowed only when using ASSM tablespaces. If you want to take advantage of these features, then you must create your tablespaces using ASSM.

You can choose to have the extent size be consistently the same for every extent within the tablespace via the UNIFORM SIZE clause. Alternatively you can specify AUTOALLOCATE. This allows Oracle to allocate extent sizes of 64 KB, 1 MB, 8 MB, and 64 MB. You may prefer the auto-allocation behavior if the objects in the tablespace typically are of varying size.

How It Works

Prior to Oracle Database 11g R2, you had the option of creating a tablespace as dictionary-managed. This architecture uses structures in Oracle's data dictionary to manage an object's extent allocation and free space. Dictionary-managed tablespaces tend to experience poor performance as the number of extents for a table or index reaches the thousands.

You should never use dictionary-managed tablespaces; instead use locally managed tablespaces. Locally managed tablespaces use a bitmap in each datafile to manage the object extents and free space and are much more efficient than the deprecated dictionary-managed architecture.

In prior versions of Oracle, DBAs would spend endless hours monitoring and modifying the physical space management aspects of a table. The combination of locally managed and ASSM render many of these space settings obsolete. For example, the storage parameters are not valid parameters in locally managed tablespaces:

- NEXT

- PCTINCREASE

- MINEXTENTS

- MAXEXTENTS

- DEFAULT

The SEGMENT SPACE MANAGEMENT AUTO clause instructs Oracle to manage physical space within the block. When you use this clause, there is no need to specify parameters such as the following:

- PCTUSED

- FREELISTS

- FREELIST GROUPS

The alternative to AUTO space management is MANUAL space management. When you use MANUAL, you can adjust the previously mentioned parameters depending on the needs of your application. We recommend that you use AUTO (and do not use MANUAL). Using AUTO reduces the number of parameters you'd otherwise need to configure and manage. You can verify the use of locally managed and ASSM with the following query:

```
select
 tablespace_name
,extent_management
,segment_space_management
from dba_tablespaces;
```

Here is some sample output:

```
TABLESPACE_NAME               EXTENT_MAN SEGMENT
----------------------------- ---------- -------
SYSTEM                        LOCAL      MANUAL
SYSAUX                        LOCAL      AUTO
UNDOTBS1                      LOCAL      MANUAL
TEMP                          LOCAL      MANUAL
USERS                         LOCAL      AUTO
TOOLS                         LOCAL      AUTO
```

■ **Note** You cannot create the SYSTEM tablespace with automatic segment space management. Also, the ASSM feature is valid only for permanent, locally managed tablespaces.

You can also specify that a datafile automatically grow when it becomes full. This is set through the AUTOEXTEND ON clause. If you use this feature, we recommend that you set an overall maximum size for the datafile. This will prevent runaway or erroneous SQL from accidentally consuming all available disk space. Here's an example clause:

```
SIZE 1G AUTOEXTEND ON MAXSIZE 10G
```

When you create a tablespace, you can also specify the tablespace type to be smallfile or bigfile. Prior to Oracle Database 10g, smallfile was your only choice. A smallfile tablespace allows you to create one or more datafiles to be associated with a single tablespace. This allows you to spread out the datafiles (associated with one tablespace) across many different mount points. For many environments, you'll require this type of flexibility.

The bigfile tablespace can have only one datafile associated with it. The main advantage of the bigfile feature is that you can create very large datafiles, which in turn allows you to create very large databases. For example, with the 8 KB block size, you can create a datafile as large as 32 TB. With a 32 KB block size, you can create a datafile up to 128 TB. Also, when using bigfile, you will typically have fewer datafiles to manage and maintain. This behavior may be desirable in environments where you use Oracle's Automatic Storage Management (ASM) feature. In ASM environments, you typically are presented with just one logical disk location from which you allocate space.

Here's an example of creating a bigfile tablespace:

```
create bigfile tablespace tools_bf
  datafile '/ora01/dbfile/O11R2/tools_bf01.dbf'
  size 100m
  extent management local
  uniform size  128k
  segment space management auto
/
```

You can verify the tablespace type via this query:

```
SQL> select tablespace_name, bigfile from dba_tablespaces;
```

Unless specified, the default tablespace type is smallfile. You can make bigfile the default tablespace type for a database when you create it via the SET DEFAULT BIGFILE TABLESPACE clause. You can alter the default tablespace type for a database to be bigfile using the ALTER DATABASE SET DEFAULT BIGFILE TABLESPACE statement.

1-3. Matching Table Types to Business Requirements

Problem

You're new to Oracle and have read about the various table types available. For example, you can choose between heap-organized tables, index-organized tables, and so forth. You want to build a database application and need to decide which table type to use.

Solution

Oracle provides a wide variety of table types. The default table type is heap-organized. For most applications, a heap-organized table is an effective structure for storing and retrieving data. However, there are other table types that you should be aware of, and you should know the situations under which each table type should be implemented. Table 1-1 describes each table type and its appropriate use.

Table 1-1. Oracle Table Types and Typical Uses

Table Type/Feature	Description	Benefit/Use
Heap-organized	The default Oracle table type and the most commonly used	Table type to use unless you have a specific reason to use a different type
Temporary	Session private data, stored for the duration of a session or transaction; space is allocated in temporary segments.	Program needs a temporary table structure to store and sort data. Table isn't required after program ends.
Index-organized (IOT)	Data stored in a B-tree index structure sorted by primary key	Table is queried mainly on primary key columns; provides fast random access
Partitioned	A logical table that consists of separate physical segments	Type used with large tables with millions of rows; dramatically affects performance scalability of large tables and indexes
Materialized view (MV)	A table that stores the output of a SQL query; periodically refreshed when you want the MV table updated with a current snapshot of the SQL result set	Aggregating data for faster reporting or replicating data to offload performance to a reporting database
Clustered	A group of tables that share the same data blocks	Type used to reduce I/O for tables that are often joined on the same columns

Table Type/Feature	Description	Benefit/Use
External	Tables that use data stored in operating system files outside of the database	This type lets you efficiently access data in a file outside of the database (like a CSV or text file). External tables provide an efficient mechanism for transporting data between databases.
Nested	A table with a column with a data type that is another table	Seldom used
Object	A table with a column with a data type that is an object type	Seldom used

How It Works

In most scenarios, a heap-organized table is sufficient to meet your requirements. This Oracle table type is a proven structure used in a wide variety of database environments. If you properly design your database (normalized structure) and combine that with the appropriate indexes and constraints, the result should be a well-performing and maintainable system.

Normally most of your tables will be heap-organized. However, if you need to take advantage of a non-heap feature (and are certain of its benefits), then certainly do so. For example, Oracle partitioning is a scalable way to build very large tables and indexes. Materialized views are a solid feature for aggregating and replicating data. Index-organized tables are efficient structures when most of the columns are part of the primary key (like an intersection table in a many-to-many relationship). And so forth.

■ **Caution** You shouldn't choose a table type simply because you think it's a cool feature that you recently heard about. Sometimes folks read about a feature and decide to implement it without first knowing what the performance benefits or maintenance costs will be. You should first be able to test and prove that a feature has solid performance benefits.

1-4. Choosing Table Features for Performance

Problem

When creating tables, you want to implement the appropriate data types and constraints that maximize performance, scalability, and maintainability.

Solution

There are several performance and sustainability issues that you should consider when creating tables. Table 1-2 describes features specific to table performance.

Table 1-2. *Table Features That Impact Performance*

Recommendation	Reasoning
If a column always contains numeric data, make it a number data type.	Enforces a business rule and allows for the greatest flexibility, performance, and consistent results when using Oracle SQL math functions (which may behave differently for a "01" character vs. a 1 number); correct data types prevent unnecessary conversion of data types.
If you have a business rule that defines the length and precision of a number field, then enforce it—for example, NUMBER(7,2). If you don't have a business rule, make it NUMBER(38).	Enforces a business rule and keeps the data cleaner; numbers with a precision defined won't unnecessarily store digits beyond the required precision. This can affect the row length, which in turn can have an impact on I/O performance.
For character data that is of variable length, use VARCHAR2 (and not VARCHAR).	Follows Oracle's recommendation of using VARCHAR2 for character data (instead of VARCHAR); Oracle guarantees that the behavior of VARCHAR2 will be consistent and not tied to an ANSI standard. The Oracle documentation states in the future VARCHAR will be redefined as a separate data type.
Use DATE and TIMESTAMP data types appropriately.	Enforces a business rule, ensures that the data is of the appropriate format, and allows for the greatest flexibility and performance when using SQL date functions and date arithmetic
Consider setting the physical attribute PCTFREE to a value higher than the default of 10% if the table initially has rows inserted with null values that are later updated with large values.	Prevents row chaining, which can impact performance if a large percent of rows in a table are chained
Most tables should be created with a primary key.	Enforces a business rule and allows you to uniquely identify each row; ensures that an index is created on primary key column(s), which allows for efficient access to primary key values
Create a numeric surrogate key to be the primary key for each table. Populate the surrogate key from a sequence.	Makes joins easier (only one column to join) and one single numeric key performs better than large concatenated columns.

Recommendation	Reasoning
Create a unique key for the logical business key—a recognizable combination of columns that makes a row unique.	Enforces a business rule and keeps the data cleaner; allows for efficient retrieval of the logical key columns that may be frequently used in WHERE clauses
Define foreign keys where appropriate.	Enforces a business rule and keeps the data cleaner; helps optimizer choose efficient paths to data; prevents unnecessary table-level locks in certain DML operations
Consider special features such as virtual columns, read-only, parallel, compression, no logging, and so on.	Features such as parallel DML, compression, or no logging can have a performance impact on reading and writing of data.

How It Works

The "Solution" section describes aspects of tables that relate to performance. When creating a table, you should also consider features that enhance scalability and availability. Oftentimes DBAs and developers don't think of these features as methods for improving performance. However, building a stable and supportable database goes hand in hand with good performance. Table 1-3 describes best practices features that promote ease of table management.

Table 1-3. Table Features That Impact Scalability and Maintainability

Recommendation	Reasoning
Use standards when naming tables, columns, constraints, triggers, indexes, and so on.	Helps document the application and simplifies maintenance
If you have a business rule that specifies the maximum length of a column, then use that length, as opposed to making all columns VARCHAR2(4000).	Enforces a business rule and keeps the data cleaner
Specify a separate tablespace for the table and indexes.	Simplifies administration and maintenance
Let tables and indexes inherit storage attributes from the tablespaces.	Simplifies administration and maintenance
Create primary-key constraints out of line.	Allows you more flexibility when creating the primary key, especially if you have a situation where the primary key consists of multiple columns
Create comments for the tables and columns.	Helps document the application and eases maintenance

Continued

Recommendation	Reasoning
Avoid large object (LOB) data types if possible.	Prevents maintenance issues associated with LOB columns, like unexpected growth, performance issues when copying, and so on
If you use LOBs in Oracle Database 11g or higher, use the new SecureFiles architecture.	SecureFiles is the new LOB architecture going forward; provides new features such as compression, encryption, and deduplication
If a column should always have a value, then enforce it with a NOT NULL constraint.	Enforces a business rule and keeps the data cleaner
Create audit-type columns, such as CREATE_DTT and UPDATE_DTT, that are automatically populated with default values and/or triggers.	Helps with maintenance and determining when data was inserted and/or updated; other types of audit columns to consider include the users who inserted and updated the row.
Use check constraints where appropriate.	Enforces a business rule and keeps the data cleaner; use this to enforce fairly small and static lists of values.

1-5. Avoiding Extent Allocation Delays When Creating Tables

Problem

You're installing an application that has thousands of tables and indexes. Each table and index are configured to initially allocate an initial extent of 10 MB. When deploying the installation DDL to your production environment, you want install the database objects as fast as possible. You realize it will take some time to deploy the DDL if each object allocates 10 MB of disk space as it is created. You wonder if you can somehow instruct Oracle to defer the initial extent allocation for each object until data is actually inserted into a table.

Solution

The only way to defer the initial segment generation is to use Oracle Database 11g R2. With this version of the database (or higher), by default the physical allocation of the extent for a table (and associated indexes) is deferred until a record is first inserted into the table. A small example will help illustrate this concept. First a table is created:

```
SQL> create table f_regs(reg_id number, reg_name varchar2(200));
```

Now query USER_SEGMENTS and USER_EXTENTS to verify that no physical space has been allocated:

```
SQL> select count(*) from user_segments where segment_name='F_REGS';
  COUNT(*)
```

```
----------
         0
SQL> select count(*) from user_extents where segment_name='F_REGS';
  COUNT(*)
----------
         0
```

Next a record is inserted, and the prior queries are run again:

```
SQL> insert into f_regs values(1,'BRDSTN');

1 row created.

SQL>> select count(*) from user_segments where segment_name='F_REGS';
  COUNT(*)
----------
         1

SQL> select count(*) from user_extents where segment_name='F_REGS';
  COUNT(*)
----------
         1
```

The prior behavior is quite different from previous versions of Oracle. In prior versions, as soon as you create an object, the segment and associated extent are allocated.

■ **Note**   Deferred segment generation also applies to partitioned tables and indexes. An extent will not be allocated until the initial record is inserted into a given extent.

How It Works

Starting with Oracle Database 11g R2, with non-partitioned heap-organized tables created in locally managed tablespaces, the initial segment creation is deferred until a record is inserted into the table. You need to be aware of Oracle's deferred segment creation feature for several reasons:

- Allows for a faster installation of applications that have a large number of tables and indexes; this improves installation speed, especially when you have thousands of objects.

- As a DBA, your space usage reports may initially confuse you when you notice that there is no space allocated for objects.

- The creation of the first row will take a slightly longer time than in previous versions (because now Oracle allocates the first extent based on the creation of the first row). For most applications, this performance degradation is not noticeable.

We realize that to take advantage of this feature the only "solution" is to upgrade to Oracle Database 11g R2, which is oftentimes not an option. However, we felt it was important to discuss this feature because you'll eventually encounter the aforementioned characteristics (when you start using the latest release of Oracle).

You can disable the deferred segment creation feature by setting the database initialization parameter DEFERRED_SEGMENT_CREATION to FALSE. The default for this parameter is TRUE.

You can also control the deferred segment creation behavior when you create the table. The CREATE TABLE statement has two new clauses: SEGMENT CREATION IMMEDIATE and SEGMENT CREATION DEFERRED—for example:

```
create table f_regs(
 reg_id number
,reg_name varchar2(2000))
segment creation immediate;
```

■ **Note** The COMPATIBLE initialization parameter needs to be 11.2.0.0.0 or greater before using the SEGMENT CREATION DEFERRED clause.

1-6. Maximizing Data Loading Speeds

Problem

You're loading a large amount of data into a table and want to insert new records as quickly as possible.

Solution

Use a combination of the following two features to maximize the speed of insert statements:

- Set the table's logging attribute to NOLOGGING; this minimizes the generation redo for direct path operations (this feature has no effect on regular DML operations).

- Use a direct path loading feature, such as the following:

  - INSERT /*+ APPEND */ on queries that use a subquery for determining which records are inserted

  - INSERT /*+ APPEND_VALUES */ on queries that use a VALUES clause

  - CREATE TABLE…AS SELECT

Here's an example to illustrate NOLOGGING and direct path loading. First, run the following query to verify the logging status of a table. In this example, the table name is F_REGS:

```
select
 table_name
,logging
from user_tables
where table_name = 'F_REGS';
```

Here is some sample output:

```
TABLE_NAME                     LOG
------------------------------ ---
F_REGS                         YES
```

The prior output verifies that the table was created with LOGGING enabled (the default). To enable NOLOGGING, use the ALTER TABLE statement as follows:

```
SQL> alter table f_regs nologging;
```

Now that NOLOGGING has been enabled, there should be a minimal amount of redo generated for direct path operations. The following example uses a direct path INSERT statement to load data into the table:

```
insert /*+APPEND */ into f_regs
select * from reg_master;
```

The prior statement is an efficient method for loading data because direct path operations such as INSERT /*+APPEND */ combined with NOLOGGING generate a minimal amount of redo.

How It Works

Direct path inserts have two performance advantages over regular insert statements:

- If NOLOGGING is specified, then a minimal amount of redo is generated.

- The buffer cache is bypassed and data is loaded directly into the datafiles. This can significantly improve the loading performance.

The NOLOGGING feature minimizes the generation of redo for direct path operations only. For direct path inserts, the NOLOGGING option can significantly increase the loading speed. One perception is that NOLOGGING eliminates redo generation for the table for all DML operations. That isn't correct. The NOLOGGING feature never affects redo generation for regular INSERT, UPDATE, MERGE, and DELETE statements.

One downside to reducing redo generation is that you can't recover the data created via NOLOGGING in the event a failure occurs after the data is loaded (and before you back up the table). If you can tolerate some risk of data loss, then use NOLOGGING but back up the table soon after the data is loaded. If your data is critical, then don't use NOLOGGING. If your data can be easily re-created, then NOLOGGING is desirable when you're trying to improve performance of large data loads.

What happens if you have a media failure after you've populated a table in NOLOGGING mode (and before you've made a backup of the table)? After a restore and recovery operation, it will appear that the table has been restored:

```
SQL> desc f_regs;
```

```
Name                                      Null?     Type
----------------------------------------- -------- ----------------------------
REG_ID                                              NUMBER
REG_NAME                                            VARCHAR2(2000)
```

However, when executing a query that scans every block in the table, an error is thrown.

```
SQL> select * from f_regs;
```

This indicates that there is logical corruption in the datafile:

```
ORA-01578: ORACLE data block corrupted (file # 10, block # 198)
ORA-01110: data file 10: '/ora01/dbfile/O11R2/users201.dbf'
ORA-26040: Data block was loaded using the NOLOGGING option
```

As the prior output indicates, the data in the table is unrecoverable. Use NOLOGGING only in situations where the data isn't critical or in scenarios where you can back up the data soon after it was created.

■ **Tip**   If you're using RMAN to back up your database, you can report on unrecoverable datafiles via the REPORT UNRECOVERABLE command.

There are some quirks of NOLOGGING that need some explanation. You can specify logging characteristics at the database, tablespace, and object levels. If your database has been enabled to force logging, then this overrides any NOLOGGING specified for a table. If you specify a logging clause at the tablespace level, it sets the default logging for any CREATE TABLE statements that don't explicitly use a logging clause.

You can verify the logging mode of the database as follows:

```
SQL> select name, log_mode, force_logging from v$database;
```

The next statement verifies the logging mode of a tablespace:

```
SQL> select tablespace_name, logging from dba_tablespaces;
```

And this example verifies the logging mode of a table:

```
SQL> select owner, table_name, logging from dba_tables where logging = 'NO';
```

How do you tell whether Oracle logged redo for an operation? One way is to measure the amount of redo generated for an operation with logging enabled vs. operating in NOLOGGING mode. If you have a development environment for testing, you can monitor how often the redo logs switch while the transactions are taking place. Another simple test is to measure how long the operation takes with and without logging. The operation performed in NOLOGGING mode should occur faster because a minimal amount of redo is generated during the load.

1-7. Efficiently Removing Table Data

Problem

You're experiencing performance issues when deleting data from a table. You want to remove data as efficiently as possible.

Solution

You can use either the TRUNCATE statement or the DELETE statement to remove records from a table. TRUNCATE is usually more efficient but has some side effects that you must be aware of. For example, TRUNCATE is a DDL statement. This means Oracle automatically commits the statement (and the current transaction) after it runs, so there is no way to roll back a TRUNCATE statement. Because a TRUNCATE statement is DDL, you can't truncate two separate tables as one transaction.

This example uses a TRUNCATE statement to remove all data from the COMPUTER_SYSTEMS table:

```
SQL> truncate table computer_systems;
```

When truncating a table, by default all space is de-allocated for the table except the space defined by the MINEXTENTS table-storage parameter. If you don't want the TRUNCATE statement to de-allocate the currently allocated extents, then use the REUSE STORAGE clause:

```
SQL> truncate table computer_systems reuse storage;
```

You can query the DBA/ALL/USER_EXTENTS views to verify if the extents have been de-allocated (or not)—for example:

```
select count(*)
 from user_extents where segment_name = 'COMPUTER_SYSTEMS';
```

How It Works

If you need the option of choosing to roll back (instead of committing) when removing data, then you should use the DELETE statement. However, the DELETE statement has the disadvantage that it generates a great deal of undo and redo information. Thus for large tables, a TRUNCATE statement is usually the most efficient way to remove data.

Another characteristic of the TRUNCATE statement is that it sets the high-water mark of a table back to zero. When you use a DELETE statement to remove data from a table, the high-water mark doesn't change. One advantage of using a TRUNCATE statement and resetting the high-water mark is that full table scan queries search only for rows in blocks below the high-water mark. This can have significant performance implications for queries that perform full table scans.

Another side effect of the TRUNCATE statement is that you can't truncate a parent table that has a primary key defined that is referenced by an enabled foreign-key constraint in a child table—even if the child table contains zero rows. In this scenario, Oracle will throw this error when attempting to truncate the parent table:

```
ORA-02266: unique/primary keys in table referenced by enabled foreign keys
```

Oracle prevents you from truncating the parent table because in a multiuser system, there is a possibility that another session can populate the child table with rows in between the time you truncate the child table and the time you subsequently truncate the parent table. In this situation, you must temporarily disable the child table–referenced foreign-key constraints, issue the TRUNCATE statement, and then re-enable the constraints.

Compare the TRUNCATE behavior to that of the DELETE statement. Oracle does allow you to use the DELETE statement to remove rows from a parent table while the constraints are enabled that reference a child table (assuming there are zero rows in the child table). This is because DELETE generates undo, is read-consistent, and can be rolled back. Table 1-4 summarizes the differences between DELETE and TRUNCATE.

If you need to use a DELETE statement, you must issue either a COMMIT or a ROLLBACK to complete the transaction. Committing a DELETE statement makes the data changes permanent:

```
SQL> delete from computer_systems;
SQL> commit;
```

■ **Note**   Other (sometimes not so obvious) ways of committing a transaction include issuing a subsequent DDL statement (which implicitly commits an active transaction for a session) or normally exiting out of the client tool (such as SQL*Plus).

If you issue a ROLLBACK statement instead of COMMIT, the table contains data as it was before the DELETE was issued.

When working with DML statements, you can confirm the details of a transaction by querying from the V$TRANSACTION view. For example, say that you have just inserted data into a table; before you issue a COMMIT or ROLLBACK, you can view active transaction information for the currently connected session as follows:

```
SQL> insert into computer_systems(cs_id) values(1);
SQL> select xidusn, xidsqn from v$transaction;
    XIDUSN     XIDSQN
---------- ----------
         3      12878
SQL> commit;
SQL> select xidusn, xidsqn from v$transaction;
no rows selected
```

Table 1-4. Comparison of DELETE and TRUNCATE

	DELETE	TRUNCATE
Option of committing or rolling back changes	YES	NO (DDL statement is always committed after it runs.)
Generates undo	YES	NO
Resets the table high-water mark to zero	NO	YES
Affected by referenced and enabled foreign-key constraints	NO	YES
Performs well with large amounts of data	NO	YES

■ **Note** Another way to remove data from a table is to drop and re-create the table. However, this means you also have to re-create any indexes, constraints, grants, and triggers that belong to the table. Additionally, when you drop a table, it's temporarily unavailable until you re-create it and re-issue any required grants. Usually, dropping and re-creating a table is acceptable only in a development or test environment.

1-8. Displaying Automated Segment Advisor Advice

Problem

You have a poorly performing query accessing a table. Upon further investigation, you discover the table has only a few rows in it. You wonder why the query is taking so long when there are so few rows. You want to examine the output of the Segment Advisor to see if there are any space-related recommendations that might help with performance in this situation.

Solution

Use the Segment Advisor to display information regarding tables that may have space allocated to them (that was once used) but now the space is empty (due to a large number of deleted rows). Tables with large amounts of unused space can cause full table scan queries to perform poorly. This is because Oracle is scanning every block beneath the high-water mark, regardless of whether the blocks contain data.

This solution focuses on accessing the Segment Advisor's advice via the DBMS_SPACE PL/SQL package. This package retrieves information generated by the Segment Advisor regarding segments that may be candidates for shrinking, moving, or compressing. One simple and effective way to use the DBMS_SPACE package (to obtain Segment Advisor advice) is via a SQL query—for example:

```
SELECT
  'Segment Advice --------------------------'|| chr(10) ||
  'TABLESPACE_NAME  : ' || tablespace_name   || chr(10) ||
  'SEGMENT_OWNER    : ' || segment_owner      || chr(10) ||
  'SEGMENT_NAME     : ' || segment_name       || chr(10) ||
  'ALLOCATED_SPACE  : ' || allocated_space    || chr(10) ||
  'RECLAIMABLE_SPACE: ' || reclaimable_space  || chr(10) ||
  'RECOMMENDATIONS  : ' || recommendations    || chr(10) ||
  'SOLUTION 1       : ' || c1                 || chr(10) ||
  'SOLUTION 2       : ' || c2                 || chr(10) ||
  'SOLUTION 3       : ' || c3 Advice
FROM
TABLE(dbms_space.asa_recommendations('FALSE', 'FALSE', 'FALSE'));
```

Here is some sample output:

```
Segment Advice --------------------------
TABLESPACE_NAME  : USERS
SEGMENT_OWNER    : MV_MAINT
SEGMENT_NAME     : F_REGS
ALLOCATED_SPACE  : 20971520
RECLAIMABLE_SPACE: 18209960
RECOMMENDATIONS  : Perform re-org on the object F_REGS, estimated savings is 182
09960 bytes.
SOLUTION 1       : Perform Reorg
SOLUTION 2       :
SOLUTION 3       :
```

In the prior output, the F_REGS table is a candidate for the shrink operation. It is consuming 20 MB, and 18 MB can be reclaimed.

How It Works

In Oracle Database 10g R2 and later, Oracle automatically schedules and runs a Segment Advisor job. This job analyzes segments in the database and stores its findings in internal tables. The output of the Segment Advisor contains findings (issues that may need to be resolved) and recommendations (actions to resolve the findings). Findings from the Segment Advisor are of the following types:

- Segments that are good candidates for shrink operations

- Segments that have significant row chaining

- Segments that might benefit from OLTP compression

When viewing the Segment Advisor's findings and recommendations, it's important to understand several aspects of this tool. First, the Segment Advisor regularly calculates advice via an automatically scheduled DBMS_SCHEDULER job. You can verify the last time the automatic job ran by querying the DBA_AUTO_SEGADV_SUMMARY view:

```
select
 segments_processed
,end_time
from dba_auto_segadv_summary
order by end_time;
```

Here is some sample output:

```
SEGMENTS_PROCESSED END_TIME
------------------ ----------------------------
                 9 30-JAN-11 02.02.46.414424 PM
                11 30-JAN-11 06.03.44.500178 PM
                17 30-JAN-11 10.04.35.688915 PM
```

You can compare the END_TIME date to the current date to determine if the Segment Advisor is running on a regular basis.

■ **Note**   In addition to automatically generated segment advice, you have the option of manually executing the Segment Advisor to generate advice on specific tablespaces, tables, and indexes (see Recipe 1-9 for details).

When the Segment Advisor executes, it uses the Automatic Workload Repository (AWR) for the source of information for its analysis. For example, the Segment Advisor examines usage and growth statistics in the AWR to generate segment advice. When the Segment Advisor runs, it generates advice and stores the output in internal database tables. The advice and recommendations can be viewed via data dictionary views such as the following:

- DBA_ADVISOR_EXECUTIONS

- DBA_ADVISOR_FINDINGS

- DBA_ADVISOR_OBJECTS

There are three different tools for retrieving the Segment Advisor's output:

- Executing DBMS_SPACE.ASA_RECOMMENDATIONS

- Manually querying DBA_ADVISOR_* views

- Viewing Enterprise Manager's graphical screens

In the "Solution" section, we described how to use the DBMS_SPACE.ASA_RECOMMENDATIONS procedure to retrieve the Segment Advisor advice. The ASA_RECOMMENDATIONS output can be modified via three input parameters, which are described in Table 1-5. For example, you can instruct the procedure to show information generated when you have manually executed the Segment Advisor.

Table 1-5. Description of ASA_RECOMMENDATIONS Input Parameters

Parameter	Meaning
all_runs	TRUE instructs the procedure to return findings from all runs, whereas FALSE instructs the procedure to return only the latest run.
show_manual	TRUE instructs the procedure to return results from manual executions of the Segment Advisor. FALSE instructs the procedure to return results from the automatic running of the Segment Advisor.
show_findings	Shows only the findings and not the recommendations

You can also directly query the data dictionary views to view the advice of the Segment Advisor. Here's a query that displays Segment Advisor advice generated within the last day:

```
select
  'Task Name       : ' || f.task_name   || chr(10) ||
  'Start Run Time  : ' || TO_CHAR(execution_start, 'dd-mon-yy hh24:mi') || chr (10) ||
  'Segment Name    : ' || o.attr2     || chr(10) ||
  'Segment Type    : ' || o.type      || chr(10) ||
  'Partition Name  : ' || o.attr3     || chr(10) ||
  'Message         : ' || f.message   || chr(10) ||
  'More Info       : ' || f.more_info || chr(10) ||
  '---------------------------------------------------' Advice
FROM dba_advisor_findings    f
    ,dba_advisor_objects     o
    ,dba_advisor_executions e
WHERE o.task_id   = f.task_id
AND   o.object_id = f.object_id
AND   f.task_id   = e.task_id
AND   e. execution_start > sysdate - 1
AND   e.advisor_name = 'Segment Advisor'
ORDER BY f.task_name;
```

Here is some sample output:

```
Task Name      : SYS_AUTO_SPCADV_53092205022011
Start Run Time : 05-feb-11 22:09
Segment Name   : CWP_USER_PROFILE
Segment Type   : TABLE
Partition Name :
Message        : Compress object REP_MV.CWP_USER_PROFILE, estimated savings is
 3933208576 bytes.
More Info      : Allocated Space:3934257152: Used Space:10664: Reclaimable Spa
ce :3933208576:
---------------------------------------------------
```

The prior output indicates that a table segment is a candidate for compression. The allocated, used, and reclaimable space numbers are displayed to help you determine the space savings.

You can also view Segment Advisor advice from Enterprise Manager. To view the advice, first navigate to the Advisor Central page. Next navigate to the Segment Advisor page. Then navigate to the Segment Advisor Recommendations. This page will display any recent Segment Advisor findings and recommendations.

1-9. Manually Generating Segment Advisor Advice

Problem

You have a table that experiences a large amount of updates. You have noticed that the query performance against this table has slowed down. You suspect the table may be experiencing poor performance due to row chaining. Therefore you want to manually confirm with the Segment Advisor that a table has issues with row chaining.

Solution

You can manually run the Segment Advisor and tell it to specifically analyze all segments in a tablespace or look at a specific object (such as a single table or index). You can manually generate advice for a specific segment using the DBMS_ADVISOR package by executing the following steps:

1. Create a task.

2. Assign an object to the task.

3. Set the task parameters.

4. Execute the task.

■ **Note** The database user executing DBMS_ADVISOR needs the ADVISOR system privilege. This privilege is administered via the GRANT statement.

The following example executes the DBMS_ADVISOR package from an anonymous block of PL/SQL. The table being examined is the F_REGS table.

```
DECLARE
  my_task_id    number;
  obj_id        number;
  my_task_name varchar2(100);
  my_task_desc varchar2(500);
BEGIN
  my_task_name := 'F_REGS Advice';
  my_task_desc := 'Manual Segment Advisor Run';
```

```
---------
-- Step 1
---------
  dbms_advisor.create_task (
  advisor_name => 'Segment Advisor',
  task_id      => my_task_id,
  task_name    => my_task_name,
  task_desc    => my_task_desc);
---------
-- Step 2
---------
  dbms_advisor.create_object (
  task_name   => my_task_name,
  object_type => 'TABLE',
  attr1       => 'MV_MAINT',
  attr2       => 'F_REGS',
  attr3       => NULL,
  attr4       => NULL,
  attr5       => NULL,
  object_id   => obj_id);
---------
-- Step 3
---------
  dbms_advisor.set_task_parameter(
  task_name => my_task_name,
  parameter => 'recommend_all',
  value     => 'TRUE');
---------
-- Step 4
---------
  dbms_advisor.execute_task(my_task_name);
END;
/
```

Now you can view Segment Advisor advice regarding this table by executing the DBMS_SPACE package and instructing it to pull information from a manual execution of the Segment Advisor (via the input parameters—see Table 1-6 for details)—for example:

```
SELECT
  'Segment Advice --------------------------'|| chr(10) ||
  'TABLESPACE_NAME   : ' || tablespace_name   || chr(10) ||
  'SEGMENT_OWNER     : ' || segment_owner     || chr(10) ||
  'SEGMENT_NAME      : ' || segment_name      || chr(10) ||
  'ALLOCATED_SPACE   : ' || allocated_space   || chr(10) ||
  'RECLAIMABLE_SPACE: ' || reclaimable_space || chr(10) ||
  'RECOMMENDATIONS   : ' || recommendations   || chr(10) ||
  'SOLUTION 1        : ' || c1                || chr(10) ||
  'SOLUTION 2        : ' || c2                || chr(10) ||
  'SOLUTION 3        : ' || c3 Advice
FROM
TABLE(dbms_space.asa_recommendations('TRUE', 'TRUE', 'FALSE'));
```

Here is some sample output:

```
Segment Advice --------------------------
TABLESPACE_NAME  : USERS
SEGMENT_OWNER    : MV_MAINT
SEGMENT_NAME     : F_REGS
ALLOCATED_SPACE  : 20971520
RECLAIMABLE_SPACE: 18209960
RECOMMENDATIONS  : Perform re-org on the object F_REGS, estimated savings is 182
09960 bytes.
SOLUTION 1       : Perform Reorg
SOLUTION 2       :
SOLUTION 3       :
```

You can also retrieve Segment Advisor advice by querying data dictionary views—for example:

```
SELECT
 'Task Name       : ' || f.task_name  || chr(10) ||
 'Segment Name    : ' || o.attr2      || chr(10) ||
 'Segment Type    : ' || o.type       || chr(10) ||
 'Partition Name  : ' || o.attr3      || chr(10) ||
 'Message         : ' || f.message    || chr(10) ||
 'More Info       : ' || f.more_info TASK_ADVICE
FROM dba_advisor_findings f
    ,dba_advisor_objects  o
WHERE o.task_id = f.task_id
AND o.object_id = f.object_id
AND f.task_name like 'F_REGS Advice'
ORDER BY f.task_name;
```

If the table has a potential issue with row chaining, then the advice output will indicate it as follows:

```
TASK_ADVICE
--------------------------------------------------------------------------------
Task Name       : F_REGS Advice
Segment Name    : F_REGS
Segment Type    : TABLE
Partition Name  :
Message         : Perform re-org on the object F_REGS, estimated savings is 182
09960 bytes.
More Info       : Allocated Space:20971520: Used Space:2761560: Reclaimable Spa
ce :18209960:
```

How It Works

The DBMS_ADVISOR package is used to manually instruct the Segment Advisor to generate advice for specific tables. This package contains several procedures that perform operations such as creating and executing a task. Table 1-6 lists the procedures relevant to the Segment Advisor.

Table 1-6. DBMS_ADVISOR Procedures Applicable for the Segment Advisor

Procedure Name	Description
CREATE_TASK	Creates the Segment Advisor task; specify "Segment Advisor" for the ADVISOR_NAME parameter of CREATE_TASK. Query DBA_ADVISOR_DEFINITIONS for a list of all valid advisors.
CREATE_OBJECT	Identifies the target object for the segment advice; Table 1-7 lists valid object types and parameters.
SET_TASK_PARAMETER	Specifies the type of advice you want to receive; Table 1-8 lists valid parameters and values.
EXECUTE_TASK	Executes the Segment Advisor task
DELETE_TASK	Deletes a task
CANCEL_TASK	Cancels a currently running task

The Segment Advisor can be invoked with various degrees of granularity. For example, you can generate advice for all objects in a tablespace or advice for a specific table, index, or partition. Table 1-7 lists the object types for which Segment Advisor advice can be obtained via the DBMS_ADVISOR.CREATE_TASK procedure.

Table 1-7. Valid Object Types for the DBMS_ADVISOR.CREATE_TASK Procedure

Object Type	ATTR1	ATTR2	ATTR3	ATTR4
TABLESPACE	tablespace name	NULL	NULL	NULL
TABLE	user name	table name	NULL	NULL
INDEX	user name	index name	NULL	NULL
TABLE PARTITION	user name	table name	partition name	NULL
INDEX PARTITION	user name	index name	partition name	NULL
TABLE SUBPARTITION	user name	table name	subpartition name	NULL
INDEX SUBPARTITION	user name	index name	subpartition name	NULL
LOB	user name	segment name	NULL	NULL

Object Type	ATTR1	ATTR2	ATTR3	ATTR4
LOB PARTITION	user name	segment name	partition name	NULL
LOB SUBPARTITION	user name	segment name	subpartition name	NULL

You can also specify a maximum amount of time that you want the Segment Advisor to run. This is controlled via the SET_TASK_PARAMETER procedure. This procedure also controls the type of advice that is generated. Table 1-8 describes valid inputs for this procedure.

Table 1-8. Input Parameters for the DBMS_ADVISOR.SET_TASK_PARAMETER Procedure

Parameter	Description	Valid Values
TIME_LIMIT	Limit on time (in seconds) for advisor run	N number of seconds or UNLIMITED (default)
RECOMMEND_ALL	Generates advice for all types of advice or just space-related advice	TRUE (default) for all types of advice, or FALSE to generate only space-related advice

1-10. Automatically E-mailing Segment Advisor Output

Problem

You realize that the Segment Advisor automatically generates advice and want to automatically e-mail yourself Segment Advisor output.

Solution

First encapsulate the SQL that displays the Segment Advisor output in a shell script—for example:

```
#!/bin/bash
if [ $# -ne 1 ]; then
  echo "Usage: $0 SID"
  exit 1
fi
# source oracle OS variables
. /var/opt/oracle/oraset $1
#
BOX=`uname -a | awk '{print$2}'`
#
sqlplus -s <<EOF
mv_maint/foo
spo $HOME/bin/log/seg.txt
```

```
set lines 80
set pages 100
SELECT
 'Segment Advice -------------------------'|| chr(10) ||
 'TABLESPACE_NAME   : ' || tablespace_name   || chr(10) ||
 'SEGMENT_OWNER     : ' || segment_owner     || chr(10) ||
 'SEGMENT_NAME      : ' || segment_name      || chr(10) ||
 'ALLOCATED_SPACE   : ' || allocated_space   || chr(10) ||
 'RECLAIMABLE_SPACE: ' || reclaimable_space || chr(10) ||
 'RECOMMENDATIONS   : ' || recommendations   || chr(10) ||
 'SOLUTION 1        : ' || c1                || chr(10) ||
 'SOLUTION 2        : ' || c2                || chr(10) ||
 'SOLUTION 3        : ' || c3 Advice
FROM
TABLE(dbms_space.asa_recommendations('FALSE', 'FALSE', 'FALSE'));
EOF
cat $HOME/bin/log/seg.txt | mailx -s "Seg. rpt. on DB: $1 $BOX" dkuhn@oracle.com
exit 0
```

The prior shell script can be regularly executed from a Linux/Unix utility such as cron. Here is a sample cron entry:

```
# Segment Advisor report
16 11 * * * /orahome/oracle/bin/seg.bsh DWREP
```

In this way, you automatically receive segment advice and proactively resolve issues before they become performance problems.

How It Works

The Segment Advisor automatically generates advice on a regular basis. Sometimes it's handy to proactively send yourself the recommendations. This allows you to periodically review the output and implement suggestions that make sense.

The shell script in the "Solution" section contains a line near the top where the OS variables are established through running an oraset script. This is a custom script that is the equivalent of the oraset script provided by Oracle. You can use a script to set the OS variables or hard-code the required lines into the script. Calling a script to set the variables is more flexible and maintainable, as it allows you to use as input any database name that appears in the oratab file.

1-11. Rebuilding Rows Spanning Multiple Blocks

Problem

You have a table in which individual rows are stored in more than one block. That situation leads to higher rates of I/O, and causes queries against the table to run slowly. You want to rebuild the spanned rows such that each row fits into a single block.

For example, you're running the following query, which displays Segment Advisor advice:

```
SELECT
 'Task Name       : '  || f.task_name  || chr(10) ||
 'Segment Name    : '  || o.attr2      || chr(10) ||
 'Segment Type    : '  || o.type       || chr(10) ||
 'Partition Name  : '  || o.attr3      || chr(10) ||
 'Message         : '  || f.message    || chr(10) ||
 'More Info       : '  || f.more_info TASK_ADVICE
FROM dba_advisor_findings f
    ,dba_advisor_objects  o
WHERE o.task_id   = f.task_id
AND   o.object_id = f.object_id
ORDER BY f.task_name;
```

Here is the output for this example:

```
TASK_ADVICE
-----------------------------------------------------------------------------
Task Name        : EMP Advice
Segment Name     : EMP
Segment Type     : TABLE
Partition Name   :
Message          : The object has chained rows that can be removed by re-org.
More Info        : 47 percent chained rows can be removed by re-org.
```

From the prior output, the EMP table has a large percentage of rows affected by row chaining and is causing performance issues when retrieving data from the table. You want to eliminate the chained rows within the table.

Solution

One method for resolving the row chaining within a table is to use the MOVE statement. When you move a table, Oracle requires an exclusive lock on the table; therefore you should perform this operation when there are no active transactions associated with the table being moved.

Also, as part of a MOVE operation, all of the rows are assigned a new ROWID. This will invalidate any indexes that are associated with the table. Therefore, as part of the move operation, you should rebuild all indexes associated with the table being moved. This example moves the EMP table:

```
SQL> alter table emp move;
```

After the move operation completes, then rebuild any indexes associated with the table being moved. You can verify the status of the indexes by interrogating the DBA/ALL/USER_INDEXES view:

```
select
 owner
,index_name
,status
from dba_indexes
where table_name='EMP';
```

Here is some sample output:

```
OWNER                            INDEX_NAME                       STATUS
-----------------------------    -----------------------------    --------
MV_MAINT                         EMP_PK                           UNUSABLE
```

Rebuilding the index will make it usable again:

```
SQL> alter index emp_pk rebuild;
```

You can now manually generate Segment Advisor advice (see Recipe 1-9) for the segment and run the query listed in the "Problem" section of this recipe to see if the row chaining has been resolved.

How It Works

A certain amount of space is reserved in the block to accommodate growth within the row. Usually a row will increase in size due to an UPDATE statement that increases the size of a column value. If there isn't enough free room in the block to accommodate the increased size, then Oracle will create a pointer to a different block that does have enough space and store part of the row in this additional block. When a single row is stored in two or more blocks, this is called *row chaining*. This can cause potential performance issues because Oracle will have to retrieve data from multiple blocks (instead of one) when retrieving a chained row.

A small number of chained rows won't have much impact on performance. One rough guideline is that if more than 15% of a table's rows are chained, then you should take corrective action (such as moving the table to re-organize it).

The amount of free space reserved in a block is determined by the table's storage parameter of PCTFREE. The default value of PCTFREE is 10, meaning 10% of the block is reserved space to be used for updates that result in more space usage. If you have a table that has columns that are initially inserted as null and later updated to contain large values, then consider setting PCTFREE to a higher value, such as 40%. This will help prevent the row chaining.

Conversely, if you have a table that is never updated after rows are inserted, then consider setting PCTFREE to 0. This will result in more rows per block, which can lead to fewer disk reads (and thus better performance) when retrieving data.

You can view the setting for PCTFREE by querying the DBA/ALL/USER_TABLES view—for example:

```
select table_name, pct_free
from user_tables;
```

The move operation removes each record from the block and re-inserts the record into a new block. For chained rows, the old chained rows are deleted and rebuilt as one physical row within the block. If the table being moved has a low setting for PCTFREE, consider resetting this parameter to a higher value (as part of the move operation)—for example:

```
SQL> alter table emp move pctfree 40;
```

Another method for verifying row chaining (besides the Segment Advisor) is to use the ANALYZE TABLE statement. First you must create a table to hold output of the ANALYZE TABLE statement:

```
SQL> @?/rdbms/admin/utlchain.sql
```

The prior script creates a table named CHAINED_ROWS. Now you can run the ANALYZE statement to populate the CHAINED_ROWS table:

```
SQL> analyze table emp list chained rows;
```

Now query the number of rows from the CHAINED_ROWS table:

```
SQL> select count(*) from chained_rows where table_name='EMP';
```

If the issue with the chained rows has been resolved, the prior query will return zero rows. The advantage of identifying chained rows in this manner is that you can fix the rows that are chained without impacting the rest of the records in the table by doing the following:

1. Create a temporary holding table to store the chained rows.

2. Delete the chained rows from the original table.

3. Insert the rows from the temporary table into the original table.

Here's a short example to demonstrate the prior steps. First create a temporary table that contains the rows in the EMP table that have corresponding records in the CHAINED_ROWS table:

```
create table temp_emp
as select *
from emp
where rowid in
(select head_rowid from chained_rows where table_name = 'EMP');
```

Now delete the records from EMP that have corresponding records in CHAINED_ROWS:

```
delete from emp
where rowid in
(select head_rowid from chained_rows where table_name = 'EMP');
```

Now insert records in the temporary table into the EMP table:

```
insert into emp select * from temp_emp;
```

If you re-analyze the table, there should be no chained rows now. You can drop the temporary table when you're finished.

UNDERSTANDING THE ORACLE ROWID

Every row in every table has a physical address. The address of a row is determined from a combination of the following:

- Datafile number

- Block number

- Location of the row within the block

- Object number

You can display the address of a row in a table by querying the ROWID pseudo-column—for example:

```
SQL> select rowid, emp_id from emp;
```

Here's some sample output:

```
ROWID                 EMP_ID
------------------ ----------
AAAFWXAAFAAAAlWAAA          1
```

The ROWID pseudo-column value isn't physically stored in the database. Oracle calculates its value when you query it. The ROWID contents are displayed as base-64 values that can contain the characters A–Z, a–z, 0–9, +, and /. You can translate the ROWID value into meaningful information via the DBMS_ROWID package. For example, to display the file number, block number, and row number in which a row is stored, issue this statement:

```
select
 emp_id
,dbms_rowid.rowid_relative_fno(rowid) file_num
,dbms_rowid.rowid_block_number(rowid) block_num
,dbms_rowid.rowid_row_number(rowid)   row_num
from emp;
```

Here's some sample output:

```
    EMP_ID  FILE_NUM BLOCK_NUM   ROW_NUM
---------- ---------- ---------- ----------
      2960         4        144       126
      2961         4        144       127
```

You can use the ROWID value in the SELECT and WHERE clauses of a SQL statement. In most cases, the ROWID uniquely identifies a row. However, it's possible to have rows in different tables that are stored in the same cluster and so contain rows with the same ROWID.

1-12. Freeing Unused Table Space

Problem

You've analyzed the output of the Segment Advisor and have identified a table that has a large amount of free space. You want to free up the unused space to improve the performance queries that perform full table scans of the table.

Solution

Do the following to shrink space and re-adjust the high-water mark for a table:

1. Enable row movement for the table.

2. Use the ALTER TABLE...SHRINK SPACE statement to free up unused space.

■ **Note** The shrink table feature requires that the table's tablespace use automatic space segment management. See Recipe 1-2 for details on how to create an ASSM-enabled tablespace.

When you shrink a table, this requires that rows (if any) be moved. This means you must enable row movement. This example enables row movement for the **INV** table:

```
SQL> alter table inv enable row movement;
```

Next the table shrink operation is executed via an **ALTER TABLE** statement:

```
SQL> alter table inv shrink space;
```

You can also shrink the space associated with any index segments via the **CASCADE** clause:

```
SQL> alter table inv shrink space cascade;
```

How It Works

When you shrink a table, Oracle re-organizes the blocks in a manner that consumes the least amount of space. Oracle also re-adjusts the table's high-water mark. This has performance implications for queries that result in full table scans. In these scenarios, Oracle will inspect every block below the high-water mark. If you notice that it takes a long time for a query to return results when there aren't many rows in the table, this may be an indication that there are many unused blocks (because data was deleted) below the high-water mark.

You can instruct Oracle to *not* re-adjust the high-water mark when shrinking a table. This is done via the **COMPACT** clause—for example:

```
SQL> alter table inv shrink space compact;
```

When you use **COMPACT**, Oracle defragments the table but doesn't alter the high-water mark. You will need to use the **ALTER TABLE…SHRINK SPACE** statement to reset the high-water mark. You might want to do this because you're concerned about the time it takes to defragment and adjust the high-water mark. This allows you to shrink a table in two shorter steps instead of one longer operation.

1-13. Compressing Data for Direct Path Loading

Problem

You're working with a decision support system (DSS)-type database and you want to improve the performance of an associated reporting application. This environment contains large tables that are loaded once and then frequently subjected to full table scans. You want to compress data as it is loaded because this will compact the data into fewer database blocks and thus will require less I/O for subsequent reads from the table. Because fewer blocks need to be read for compressed data, this will improve data retrieval performance.

Solution

Use Oracle's basic compression feature to compress direct path–loaded data into a heap-organized table. Basic compression is enabled as follows:

1. Use the `COMPRESS` clause to enable compression either when creating, altering, or moving an existing table.

2. Load data via a direct path mechanism such as `CREATE TABLE...AS SELECT` or `INSERT /*+ APPEND */`.

■ **Note** Prior to Oracle Database 11g R2, basic compression was referred to as DSS compression and enabled via the `COMPRESS FOR DIRECT_LOAD OPERATION` clause. This syntax is deprecated in Oracle Database 11g R2 and higher.

Here's an example that uses the `CREATE TABLE...AS SELECT` statement to create a basic compression-enabled table and direct path–load the data:

```
create table regs_dss
compress
as select reg_id, reg_name
from regs;
```

The prior statement creates a table with compressed data in it. Any subsequent direct path–load operations will also load the data in a compressed format.

■ **Tip** You can use either the `COMPRESS` clause or the `COMPRESS BASIC` clause to enable the basic table compression feature. The `COMPRESS` clause and `COMPRESS BASIC` clause are synonymous.

You can verify that compression has been enabled for a table by querying the appropriate `DBA/ALL/USER_TABLES` view. This example assumes that you're connected to the database as the owner of the table:

```
select table_name, compression, compress_for
from user_tables
where table_name='REGS_DSS';
```

Here is some sample output:

```
TABLE_NAME                     COMPRESS COMPRESS_FOR
------------------------------ -------- ------------
REGS_DSS                       ENABLED  BASIC
```

The prior output shows that compression has been enabled in the basic mode for this table. If you're working with a table has that already been created, then you can alter its basic compression characteristics with the ALTER TABLE statement—for example:

```
SQL> alter table regs_dss compress;
```

When you alter a table to enable basic compression, this does not affect any data currently existing in the table; rather it only compresses subsequent direct path data load operations.

If you want to enable basic compression for data in an existing table, use the MOVE COMPRESS clause:

```
SQL> alter table regs_dss move compress;
```

Keep in mind that when you move a table, all of the associated indexes are invalidated. You'll have to rebuild any indexes associated with the moved table.

If you have enabled basic compression for a table, you can disable it via the NOCOMPRESS clause—for example:

```
SQL> alter table regs_dss nocompress;
```

When you alter a table to disable basic compression, this does not uncompress existing data within the table. Rather this operation instructs Oracle to not compress data for subsequent direct path operations. If you need to uncompress existing compressed data, then use the MOVE NOCOMPRESS clause:

```
SQL> alter table regs_dss move nocompress;
```

How It Works

The basic compression feature is available at no extra cost with the Oracle Enterprise Edition. Any heap-organized table that has been created or altered to use basic compression will be a candidate for data loaded in a compressed format for subsequent direct path–load operations. There is some additional CPU overhead associated with compressing the data, but you may find in many circumstances that this overhead is offset by performance gains due to less I/O.

From a performance perspective, the main advantage to using basic compression is that once the data is loaded as compressed, any subsequent I/O operations will use fewer resources because there are fewer blocks required to read and write data. You will need to test the performance benefits for your environment. In general, tables that hold large amounts of character data are candidates for basic compression—especially in scenarios where data is direct path–loaded once, and thereafter selected from many times.

Keep in mind that Oracle's basic compression feature has no effect on regular DML statements such as INSERT, UPDATE, MERGE, and DELETE. If you require compression to occur on all DML statements, then consider using OLTP compression (see Recipe 1-14 for details).

You can also specify basic compression at the partition and tablespace level. Any table created within a tablespace created with the COMPRESS clause will have basic compression enabled by default. Here's an example of creating a tablespace with the COMPRESS clause:

```
CREATE TABLESPACE comp_data
  DATAFILE '/ora01/dbfile/O11R2/comp_data01.dbf'
  SIZE 500M
  EXTENT MANAGEMENT LOCAL
  UNIFORM SIZE 512K
  SEGMENT SPACE MANAGEMENT AUTO
  DEFAULT COMPRESS;
```

You can also alter an existing tablespace to set the default degree of compression:

```
SQL> alter tablespace comp_data default compress;
```

Run this query to verify that basic compression for a tablespace is enabled:

```
select tablespace_name, def_tab_compression, compress_for
from dba_tablespaces
where tablespace_name = 'COMP_DATA';
```

Here is some sample output:

```
TABLESPACE_NAME                 DEF_TAB_ COMPRESS_FOR
------------------------------  -------- ------------
COMP_DATA                       ENABLED  BASIC
```

■ **Tip**   You cannot drop a column from a table created with basic compression enabled. However, you can mark a column as unused.

1-14. Compressing Data for All DML

Problem

You're in an OLTP environment and have noticed that there is a great deal of disk I/O occurring when reading data from a table. You wonder if you can increase I/O performance by compressing the data within the table. The idea is that compressed table data will consume less physical storage and thus require less I/O to read from disk.

Solution

Use the COMPRESS FOR OLTP clause when creating a table to enable data compression when using regular DML statements to manipulate data. This example creates an OLTP compression–enabled table:

```
create table regs
(reg_id   number
,reg_name varchar2(2000)
) compress for oltp;
```

■ **Note** Prior to Oracle Database 11g R2, OLTP table compression was enabled using the COMPRESS FOR ALL OPERATIONS clause. This syntax is deprecated in Oracle Database 11g R2 and higher.

You can verify that compression has been enabled for a table by querying the appropriate DBA/ALL/USER_TABLES view. This example assumes that you're connected to the database as the owner of the table:

```
select table_name, compression, compress_for
from user_tables
where table_name='REGS';
```

Here is some sample output:

```
TABLE_NAME                       COMPRESS COMPRESS_FOR
------------------------------ -------- ------------
REGS                             ENABLED  OLTP
```

If you've already created the table, you can use the ALTER TABLE statement to enable compression on an existing table—for example:

```
SQL> alter table regs compress for oltp;
```

When you alter a table's compression mode, it doesn't impact any of the data currently within the table. Subsequent DML statements will result in data stored in a compressed fashion.

If you want to enable OLTP compression for data in an existing table, use the MOVE COMPRESS FOR OLTP clause:

```
SQL> alter table regs move compress for oltp;
```

Keep in mind that when you move a table, all of the associated indexes are invalidated. You'll have to rebuild any indexes associated with the moved table.

If you have enabled OLTP compression for a table, you can disable it via the NOCOMPRESS clause—for example:

```
SQL> alter table regs nocompress;
```

When you alter a table to disable OLTP compression, this does not uncompress existing data within the table. Rather this operation instructs Oracle to not compress data for subsequent DML operations.

How It Works

OLTP compression requires the Oracle Enterprise Edition and the Advanced Compression Option (extra cost license). The COMPRESS FOR OLTP clause enables compression for all DML operations. The OLTP compression doesn't immediately compress data as it is inserted or updated in a table. Rather the compression occurs in a batch mode when the degree of change within the block reaches a certain threshold. When the threshold is reached, all of the uncompressed rows are compressed at the same time. The threshold at which compression occurs is determined by an internal algorithm (over which you have no control).

You can also specify OLTP compression at the tablespace level. Any table created in an OLTP compression–enabled tablespace will by default inherit this compression setting. Here's an example of tablespace creation script specifying OLTP compression:

```
CREATE TABLESPACE comp_data
  DATAFILE '/ora01/dbfile/O11R2/comp_data01.dbf'
  SIZE 10M
  EXTENT MANAGEMENT LOCAL
  UNIFORM SIZE 1M
  SEGMENT SPACE MANAGEMENT AUTO
  DEFAULT COMPRESS FOR OLTP;
```

You can also alter an existing tablespace to set the default degree of compression:

```
SQL> alter tablespace comp_data default compress for oltp;
```

You can verify the default compression characteristics with this query:

```
select tablespace_name, def_tab_compression, compress_for
from dba_tablespaces
where tablespace_name = 'COMP_DATA';
```

Here is some sample output:

```
TABLESPACE_NAME                 DEF_TAB_ COMPRESS_FOR
------------------------------- -------- ------------
COMP_DATA                       ENABLED  OLTP
```

1-15. Compressing Data at the Column Level

Problem

You're using the Oracle Exadata product and you want to efficiently compress data. You have determined that compressed data will result in much more efficient I/O operations, especially when reading data from disk. The idea is that compressed data will result in much fewer blocks read for SELECT statements.

Solution

To enable hybrid columnar compression, when creating a table, use either the COMPRESS FOR QUERY or the COMPRESS FOR ARCHIVE clause—for example:

```
create table f_regs(
 reg_id number
,reg_desc varchar2(4000))
compress for query;
```

You can also specify a degree of compression of either LOW or HIGH:

```
create table f_regs(
 reg_id number
,reg_desc varchar2(4000))
compress for query high;
```

The default level of compression for QUERY is HIGH, and the default level of compression for ARCHIVE is LOW. You can validate the level of compression enabled via this query:

```
select table_name, compression, compress_for
from user_tables
where table_name='F_REGS';
```

Here is some sample output:

```
TABLE_NAME                      COMPRESS COMPRESS_FOR
------------------------------- -------- ------------
F_REGS                          ENABLED  QUERY HIGH
```

If you attempt to use hybrid columnar compression in an environment other than Exadata, you'll receive the following error:

```
ERROR at line 1:
ORA-64307: hybrid columnar compression is only supported in tablespaces
residing on Exadata storage
```

How It Works

Exadata is Oracle's high-performance database machine. It is designed to deliver high performance for both data warehouse and OLTP databases. Exadata storage supports hybrid columnar compression and is available starting with Oracle Database 11g R2.

Hybrid columnar compression compresses the data on a column-by-column basis. Column-level compression results in higher compression ratios than Oracle basic compression (see Recipe 1-13) or OLTP compression (see Recipe 1-14). There are four levels of hybrid columnar compression. These levels are listed here from the lowest level of compression to the highest level:

- COMPRESS FOR QUERY LOW

- COMPRESS FOR QUERY HIGH

- COMPRESS FOR ARCHIVE LOW

- COMPRESS FOR ARCHIVE HIGH

COMPRESS FOR QUERY is appropriate for bulk load operations on heap-organized tables that are infrequently updated. This type of compression is optimized for query performance and is therefore more appropriate for DSS and data warehouse databases, whereas COMPRESS FOR ARCHIVE maximizes the degree of compression and is more appropriate for data that is stored for long periods of time and will not be updated.

■ **Note**   Refer to the Oracle Exadata Storage Server Software documentation for more information on hybrid columnar compression.

1-16. Monitoring Table Usage

Problem

You've recently inherited a database that contains hundreds of tables. The application is experiencing performance issues. As part of your overall tuning strategy, you want to obtain a better understanding of the application by determining which tables are being used by what types of SQL statements. Tables that aren't being used can be renamed and later dropped. By removing unused tables, you can free up space, reduce the clutter, and focus your performance analysis on actively used tables.

Solution

Use Oracle's standard auditing feature to determine which tables are being used. Auditing is enabled as follows:

1.   Set the AUDIT_TRAIL parameter.

2.   Stop and start your database to enable the setting of AUDIT_TRAIL.

3.   Use the AUDIT statement to enable auditing of specific database operations.

Oracle's standard auditing feature is enabled through setting the AUDIT_TRAIL initialization parameter. When you set the AUDIT_TRAIL parameter to DB, this specifies that Oracle will write audit records to an internal database table named AUD$. For example, when using an spfile, here's how to set the AUDIT_TRAIL parameter:

```
SQL> alter system set audit_trail=db scope=spfile;
```

If you are using an init.ora file, open it with a text editor and set the AUDIT_TRAIL value to DB. After you've set the AUDIT_TRAIL parameter, you'll need to stop and restart your database for it to take effect.

■ **Tip**   When first setting up a database, we recommend that you set the AUDIT_TRAIL parameter to DB. This way, when you want to enable auditing for a specific action, you can do so without having to stop and restart (bounce) the database.

Now you can enable auditing for a specific database operation. For example, the following statement enables auditing on all DML statements on the EMP table owned by INV_MGMT:

```
SQL> audit select, insert, update, delete on inv_mgmt.emp;
```

From this point on, any DML access to the EMP table will be recorded in the SYS.AUD$ table. Oracle provides several auditing views based on the AUD$ table, such as DBA_AUDIT_TRAIL or DBA_AUDIT_OBJECT. You can query these views to report on auditing actions—for example:

```
select
  username
 ,obj_name
 ,to_char(timestamp,'dd-mon-yy hh24:mi') event_time
 ,substr(ses_actions,4,1)  del
 ,substr(ses_actions,7,1)  ins
 ,substr(ses_actions,10,1) sel
 ,substr(ses_actions,11,1) upd
from dba_audit_object;
```

Here is some sample output:

```
USERNAME                     OBJ_NAME   EVENT_TIME            DEL INS SEL UPD
---------------------------- ---------- --------------------- --- --- --- ---
INV_MGMT                     EMP        05-feb-11 15:08       -   S   -   S
INV_MGMT                     EMP        05-feb-11 15:10       -   -   S   -
INV_MGMT                     EMP        05-feb-11 15:10       S   -   -   -
```

In the prior SQL statement, notice the use of the SUBSTR function to reference the SES_ACTIONS column of the DBA_AUDIT_OBJECT view. That column contains a 16-character string in which each character means that a certain operation has occurred. The 16 characters represent the following operations in this order: ALTER, AUDIT, COMMENT, DELETE, GRANT, INDEX, INSERT, LOCK, RENAME, SELECT, UPDATE, REFERENCES, and EXECUTE. Positions 14, 15, and 16 are reserved by Oracle for future use. The character of S represents success, F represents failure, and B represents both success and failure.

To turn off auditing on an object, use the NOAUDIT statement:

```
SQL> noaudit select, insert, update, delete on inv_mgmt.emp;
```

■ **Tip**   If you need to view the SQL_TEXT or SQL_BIND columns of the AUD$ table, then set the AUDIT_TRAIL initialization parameter to DB_EXTENDED.

How It Works

Sometimes it's handy when troubleshooting disk space or performance issues to know which tables in the database are actually being used by the application. If you've inherited a database that contains a large number of tables, it may not be obvious which objects are being accessed. Enabling auditing allows you to identify which types of SQL statements are accessing a table of interest.

Once you have identified tables that are not being used, you can simply rename the tables and see if this breaks the application or if any users complain. If there are no complaints, then after some time you can consider dropping the tables. Make sure you take a good backup of your database with both RMAN and Data Pump before you drop any tables you might have to later recover.

If you simply need to know whether a table is being inserted, updated, or deleted from, you can use the DBA/ALL/USER_TAB_MODIFICATIONS view to report on that type of activity. This view has columns, such as INSERTS, UPDATES, DELETES, and TRUNCATED, that will provide information as to how data in the table is being modified—for example:

```
select table_name, inserts, updates, deletes, truncated
from user_tab_modifications;
```

In normal conditions, this view is not instantly updated by Oracle. If you need to immediately view table modifications, then use the DBMS_STATS.FLUSH_DATABASE_MONITORING_INFO procedure to update the view:

```
SQL> exec DBMS_STATS.FLUSH_DATABASE_MONITORING_INFO();
```

CHAPTER 2

Choosing and Optimizing Indexes

An index is a database object used primarily to improve the performance of SQL queries. The function of a database index is similar to an index in the back of a book. A book index associates a topic with a page number. When you're locating information in a book, it's usually much faster to inspect the index first, find the topic of interest, and identify associated page numbers. With this information, you can navigate directly to specific page numbers in the book. In this situation, the number of pages you need to inspect is minimal.

If there were no index, you would have to inspect every page of the book to find information. This results in a great deal of page turning, especially with large books. This is similar to an Oracle query that does not use an index and therefore has to scan every used block within a table. For large tables, this results in a great deal of I/O.

The book index's usefulness is directly correlated with the uniqueness of a topic within the book. For example, take this book; it would do no good to create an index on the topic of "performance" because every page in this book deals with performance. However, creating an index on the topic of "bitmap indexes" would be effective because there are only a few pages within the book that are applicable to this feature.

Keep in mind that the index isn't free. It consumes space in the back of the book, and if the material in the book is ever updated (like a second edition), every modification (insert, update, delete) potentially requires a corresponding change to the index. It's important to keep in mind that indexes consume space and require resources when updates occur.

Also, the person who creates the index for the book must consider which topics will be frequently looked up. Topics that are selective and frequently accessed should be included in the book index. If an index in the back of the book is never looked up by a reader, then it unnecessarily wastes space.

Much like the process of creating an index in the back of the book, there are many factors that must be considered when creating an Oracle index. Oracle provides a wide assortment of indexing features and options. These objects are manually created by the DBA or a developer. Therefore, you need to be aware of the various features and how to utilize them. If you choose the wrong type of index or use a feature incorrectly, there may be detrimental performance implications. Listed next are aspects to consider before you create an index:

- Type of index
- Table column(s) to include
- Whether to use a single column or a combination of columns
- Special features such as parallelism, turning off logging, compression, invisible indexes, and so on

- Uniqueness

- Naming conventions

- Tablespace placement

- Initial sizing requirements and growth

- Impact on performance of SELECT statements (improvement)

- Impact on performance of INSERT, UPDATE, and DELETE statements

- Global or local index, if the underlying table is partitioned

When you create an index, you should give some thought to every aspect mentioned in the previous list. One of the first decisions you need to make is the type of index and the columns to include. Oracle provides a robust variety of index types. For most scenarios, you can use the default B-tree (balanced tree) index. Other commonly used types are concatenated, bitmap, and function-based indexes. Table 2-1 describes the types of indexes available with Oracle.

Table 2-1. Oracle Index Type Descriptions

Index Type	Usage
B-tree	Default, balanced tree index, good for high-cardinality (high degree of distinct values) columns
B-tree cluster	Used with clustered tables
Hash cluster	Used with hash clusters
Function-based	Good for columns that have SQL functions applied to them
Indexed virtual column	Good for columns that have SQL functions applied to them; viable alternative to using a function-based index
Reverse-key	Useful to balance I/O in an index that has many sequential inserts
Key-compressed	Useful for concatenated indexes where the leading column is often repeated; compresses leaf block entries
Bitmap	Useful in data warehouse environments with low-cardinality columns; these indexes aren't appropriate for online transaction processing (OLTP) databases where rows are heavily updated.
Bitmap join	Useful in data warehouse environments for queries that join fact and dimension tables

Index Type	Usage
Global partitioned	Global index across all partitions in a partitioned table
Local partitioned	Local index based on individual partitions in a partitioned table
Domain	Specific for an application or cartridge

This chapter focuses on the most commonly used indexes and features. Hash cluster indexes, partitioned indexes, and domain indexes are not covered in this book. If you need more information regarding index types or features not covered in this chapter or book, see Oracle's SQL Reference Guide at http://otn.oracle.com.

The first recipe in this chapter deals with the mechanics of B-tree indexes. It's critical that you understand how this database object works. Even if you've been around Oracle for a while, we feel it's useful to work through the various scenarios outlined in this first recipe to ensure that you know how the optimizer uses this type of index. This will lay the foundation for solving many different types of performance problems (especially SQL tuning).

2-1. Understanding B-tree Indexes

Problem

You want to create an index. You understand that the default type of index in Oracle is the B-tree, but you don't quite understand how an index is physically implemented. You want to fully comprehend the B-tree index internals so as to make intelligent performance decisions when building database applications.

Solution

An example with a good diagram will help illustrate the mechanics of a B-tree index. Even if you've been working with B-tree indexes for quite some time, a good example may illuminate technical aspects of using an index. To get started, suppose you have a table created as follows:

```
create table cust(
 cust_id number
,last_name varchar2(30)
,first_name varchar2(30));
```

You determine that several SQL queries will frequently use LAST_NAME in the WHERE clause. This prompts you to create an index:

```
SQL> create index cust_idx1 on cust(last_name);
```

Several hundred rows are now inserted into the table (not all of the rows are shown here):

```
insert into cust values(7, 'ACER','SCOTT');
insert into cust values(5, 'STARK','JIM');
insert into cust values(3, 'GREY','BOB');
```

```
insert into cust values(11,'KHAN','BRAD');
.....
insert into cust values(274, 'ACER','SID');
```

After the rows are inserted, we ensure that the table statistics are up to date so as to provide the query optimizer sufficient information to make good choices on how to retrieve the data:

```
SQL> exec dbms_stats.gather_table_stats(ownname=>'MV_MAINT', -
        tabname=>'CUST',cascade=>true);
```

As rows are inserted into the table, Oracle will allocate extents that consist of physical database blocks. Oracle will also allocate blocks for the index. For each record inserted into the table, Oracle will also create an entry in the index that consists of the ROWID and column value (the value in LAST_NAME in this example). The ROWID for each index entry points to the datafile and block that the table column value is stored in. Figure 2-1 shows a graphical representation of how data is stored in the table and the corresponding B-tree index. For this example, datafiles 10 and 15 contain table data stored in associated blocks and datafile 22 stores the index blocks.

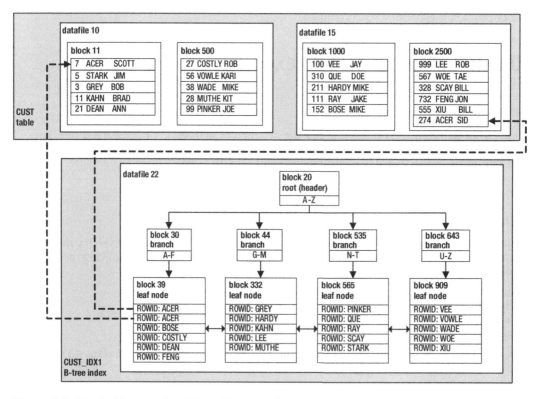

Figure 2-1. Physical layout of a table and B-tree index

There are two dotted lines in Figure 2-1. These lines depict how the ROWID (in the index structure) points to the physical location in the table for the column values of ACER. These particular values will be used in the scenarios in this solution.

When selecting data from a table and its corresponding index, there are three basic scenarios:

- All table data required by the SQL query is contained in the index structure. Therefore only the index blocks need to be accessed. The blocks from the table are never read.

- All of the information required by the query is not contained in the index blocks. Therefore the query optimizer chooses to access both the index blocks and the table blocks to retrieve the data needed to satisfy the results of the query.

- The query optimizer chooses not to access the index. Therefore only the table blocks are accessed.

The prior situations are covered in the next three subsections.

Scenario 1: All Data Lies in the Index Blocks

There are two scenarios that will be shown in this section:

- *Index range scan*: This occurs when the optimizer determines it is efficient to use the index structure to retrieve multiple rows required by the query. Index range scans are used extensively in a wide variety of situations.

- *Index fast full scan*: This occurs when the optimizer determines that most of the rows in the table will need to be retrieved. However, all of the information required is stored in the index. Since the index structure is usually smaller than the table structure, the optimizer determines that a full scan of the index is more efficient. This scenario is common for queries that count values.

First the index range scan is demonstrated. For this example, suppose this query is issued that selects from the table:

```
SQL> select last_name from cust where last_name='ACER';
```

Before reading on, look at Figure 2-1 and try to answer this question: "What are the minimal number of blocks Oracle will need to read to return the data for this query?" In other words, what is the most efficient way to access the physical blocks in order to satisfy the results of this query? The optimizer could choose to read through every block in the table structure. However, that would result in a great deal of I/O, and thus it is not the most optimal way to retrieve the data.

For this example, the most efficient way to retrieve the data is to use the index structure. To return the rows that contain the value of ACER in the LAST_NAME column, Oracle will need to read three blocks: block 20, block 30, and block 39. We can verify that this is occurring by using Oracle's Autotrace utility:

```
SQL> set autotrace on;
SQL> select last_name from cust where last_name='ACER';
```

Here is a partial snippet of the output:

```
--------------------------------------------------------------------
| Id | Operation        | Name      | Rows | Bytes | Cost (%CPU)| Time     |
--------------------------------------------------------------------
|  0 | SELECT STATEMENT |           |  101 |  808  |  1   (0)| 00:00:01 |
|* 1 |  INDEX RANGE SCAN| CUST_IDX1 |  101 |  808  |  1   (0)| 00:00:01 |
--------------------------------------------------------------------
```

The prior output shows that Oracle needed to use only the CUST_IDX1 index to retrieve the data to satisfy the result set of the query. *The table data blocks were not accessed;* only the index blocks were required. This is a particularly efficient indexing strategy for the given query. Listed next are the statistics displayed by Autotrace for this example:

Statistics
```
------------------------------------------------------------
       1  recursive calls
       0  db block gets
       3  consistent gets
       0  physical reads
```

The consistent gets value indicates that three blocks were read from memory (db block gets plus consistent gets equals the total blocks read from memory). Since the index blocks were already in memory, no physical reads were required to return the result set of this query.

Next an example that results in an index fast full scan is demonstrated. Consider this query:

```
SQL> select count(last_name) from cust;
```

Using SET AUTOTRACE ON, an execution plan is generated. Here is the corresponding output:

```
--------------------------------------------------------------------
| Id | Operation           | Name      | Rows | Bytes | Cost (%CPU)| Time     |
--------------------------------------------------------------------
|  0 | SELECT STATEMENT    |           |   1  |   8   |  3   (0)| 00:00:01 |
|  1 | SORT AGGREGATE      |           |   1  |   8   |         |          |
|  2 |  INDEX FAST FULL SCAN| CUST_IDX1 | 1509 | 12072 |  3   (0)| 00:00:01 |
--------------------------------------------------------------------
```

The prior output shows that only the index structure was used to determine the count within the table. In this situation, the optimizer determined that a full scan of the index was more efficient than a full scan of the table.

Scenario 2: All Information Is Not Contained in the Index

Now consider this situation: suppose we need additional information from the CUST table. This query additionally selects the FIRST_NAME column:

```
SQL> select last_name, first_name from cust where last_name = 'ACER';
```

Using SET AUTOTRACE ON and executing the prior query results in the following execution plan:

```
--------------------------------------------------------------------------------
| Id | Operation                   | Name     | Rows | Bytes | Cost (%CPU)| Time     |
--------------------------------------------------------------------------------
|  0 | SELECT STATEMENT            |          |  101 |  1414 |    3  (0)| 00:00:01 |
|  1 |  TABLE ACCESS BY INDEX ROWID| CUST     |  101 |  1414 |    3  (0)| 00:00:01 |
|* 2 |   INDEX RANGE SCAN          | CUST_IDX1|  101 |       |    1  (0)| 00:00:01 |
--------------------------------------------------------------------------------
```

The prior output indicates that the CUST_IDX1 index was accessed via an INDEX RANGE SCAN. The INDEX RANGE SCAN identifies the index blocks required to satisfy the results of this query. Additionally the table is read by TABLE ACCESS BY INDEX ROWID. The access to the table by the index's ROWID means that Oracle uses the ROWID (stored in the index) to locate the data contained within the table blocks. In Figure 2-1, this is indicated by the dotted lines that map the ROWID to the appropriate table blocks that contain the value of ACER in the LAST_NAME column.

Again, looking at Figure 2-1, how many table and index blocks need to be read in this scenario? The index requires that blocks 20, 30, and 39 must be read. Since FIRST_NAME is not included in the index, Oracle must read the table blocks to retrieve these values. Oracle knows the ROWID of the table blocks and directly reads blocks 11 and 2500 to retrieve that data. That makes a total of five blocks. Here is a partial snippet of the statistics generated by Autotrace that confirms the number of blocks read is five:

```
Statistics
----------------------------------------------------------
          1  recursive calls
          0  db block gets
          5  consistent gets
          0  physical reads
```

Scenario 3: Only the Table Blocks Are Accessed

In some situations, even if there is an index, Oracle will determine that it's more efficient to use only the table blocks. When Oracle inspects every row within a table, this is known a *full table scan*. For example, take this query:

```
SQL> select * from cust;
```

Here are the corresponding execution plan and statistics:

```
--------------------------------------------------------------------------------
| Id | Operation           | Name | Rows | Bytes | Cost (%CPU)| Time     |
--------------------------------------------------------------------------------
|  0 | SELECT STATEMENT    |      | 1509 | 24144 |   12  (0)| 00:00:01 |
|  1 |  TABLE ACCESS FULL  | CUST | 1509 | 24144 |   12  (0)| 00:00:01 |
--------------------------------------------------------------------------------
Statistics
----------------------------------------------------------
          0  recursive calls
          0  db block gets
        119  consistent gets
          0  physical reads
```

The prior output shows that a total of 119 blocks were inspected. Oracle searched every row in the table to bring back the results required to satisfy the query. In this situation, all blocks of the table must be read, and there is no way for Oracle to use the index to speed up the retrieval of the data.

■ **Note** For the examples in this recipe, your results may vary slightly, depending on how many rows you initially insert into the table. We used approximately 1,500 rows for this example.

How It Works

The B-tree index is the default index type in Oracle. For most OLTP-type applications, this index type is sufficient. This index type is known as B-tree because the ROWID and associated column values are stored within blocks in a *balanced* tree-like structure (see Figure 2-1). The B stands for balanced.

B-tree indexes are efficient because, when properly used, they result in a query retrieving data far faster than it would without the index. If the index structure itself contains the required column values to satisfy the result of the query, then the table data blocks need not be accessed. Understanding these mechanics will guide your indexing decision-making process. For example, this will help you decide which columns to index and whether a concatenated index might be more efficient for certain queries and less optimal for others. These topics are covered in detail in subsequent recipes in this chapter.

ESTIMATING THE SPACE AN INDEX WILL REQUIRE

Before you create an index, you can estimate how much space it will take via the DBMS_SPACE.CREATE_INDEX_COST procedure—for example:

```
SQL> set serverout on
SQL> exec dbms_stats.gather_table_stats(user,'CUST');
SQL> variable used_bytes number
SQL> variable alloc_bytes number
SQL> exec dbms_space.create_index_cost( 'create index cust_idx2 on cust(first_name)', -
                :used_bytes, :alloc_bytes );
SQL> print :used_bytes
```

Here is some sample output for this example:

```
USED_BYTES
----------
    363690
```

```
SQL> print :alloc_bytes
```

Here is some sample output for this example:

```
ALLOC_BYTES
-----------
    2097152
```

The used_bytes variable gives you an estimate of how much room is required for the index data. The alloc_bytes variable provides an estimate of how much space will be allocated within the tablespace.

2-2. Deciding Which Columns to Index

Problem

A database you manage contains hundreds of tables. Each table typically contains a dozen or more columns. You wonder which columns should be indexed.

Solution

Listed next are general guidelines for deciding which columns to index.

- Define a primary key constraint for each table that results in an index automatically being created on the columns specified in the primary key (see Recipe 2-3).

- Create unique key constraints on non-null column values that are required to be unique (different from the primary key columns). This results in an index automatically being created on the columns specified in unique key constraints (see Recipe 2-4).

- Explicitly create indexes on foreign key columns (see Recipe 2-5).

- Create indexes on columns used often as predicates in the WHERE clause of frequently executed SQL queries.

After you have decided to create indexes, we recommend that you adhere to index creation standards that facilitate the ease of maintenance. Specifically, follow these guidelines when creating an index:

- Use the default B-tree index unless you have a solid reason to use a different index type.

- Create a separate tablespace for the indexes. This allows you to more easily manage indexes separately from tables for tasks such as backup and recovery.

- Let the index inherit its storage properties from the tablespace. This allows you to specify the storage properties when you create the tablespace and not have to manage storage properties for individual indexes.

- If you have a variety of storage requirements for indexes, then consider creating separate tablespaces for each type of index—for example, INDEX_LARGE, INDEX_MEDIUM, and INDEX_SMALL tablespaces, each defined with storage characteristics appropriate for the size of the index.

Listed next is a sample script that encapsulates the foregoing recommendations from the prior two bulleted lists:

```
CREATE TABLE cust(
 cust_id     NUMBER
,last_name  VARCHAR2(30)
,first_name VARCHAR2(30));
--
ALTER TABLE cust ADD CONSTRAINT cust_pk PRIMARY KEY (cust_id)
USING INDEX TABLESPACE reporting_index;
--
ALTER TABLE cust ADD CONSTRAINT cust_uk1 UNIQUE (last_name, first_name)
USING INDEX TABLESPACE reporting_index;
--
CREATE TABLE address(
 address_id NUMBER,
 cust_id    NUMBER
,street      VARCHAR2(30)
,city        VARCHAR2(30)
,state       VARCHAR2(30))
TABLESPACE reporting_data;
--
ALTER TABLE address ADD CONSTRAINT addr_fk1
FOREIGN KEY (cust_id) REFERENCES cust(cust_id);
--
CREATE INDEX addr_fk1 ON address(cust_id)
TABLESPACE reporting_index;
```

In the prior script, two tables are created. The parent table is CUST and its primary key is CUST_ID. The child table is ADDRESS and its primary key is ADDRESS_ID. The CUST_ID column exists in ADDRESS as a foreign key mapping back to the CUST_ID column in the CUST table.

How It Works

You should add an index only when you're certain it will improve performance. Misusing indexes can have serious negative performance effects. Indexes created of the wrong type or on the wrong columns do nothing but consume space and processing resources. As a DBA, you must have a strategy to ensure that indexes enhance performance and don't negatively impact applications.

Table 2-2 encapsulates many of the index management concepts covered in this chapter. These recommendations aren't written in stone: adapt and modify them as needed for your environment.

Table 2-2. *Index Creation and Maintenance Guidelines*

Guideline	Reasoning
Add indexes judiciously. Test first to determine quantifiable performance gains.	Indexes consume disk space and processing resources. Don't add indexes unnecessarily.
Use the correct type of index.	Correct index usage maximizes performance. See Table 2-1 for more details.
Use consistent naming standards.	This makes maintenance and troubleshooting easier.
Monitor your indexes, and drop indexes that aren't used. See Recipe 2-15 for details on monitoring indexes.	Doing this frees up physical space and improves the performance of Data Manipulation Language (DML) statements.
Don't rebuild indexes unless you have a solid reason to do so. See Recipe 2-17 for details on rebuilding an index.	Rebuilding an index is generally unnecessary unless the index is corrupt or you want to change a physical characteristic (such as the tablespace) without dropping the index.
Before dropping an index, consider marking it as unusable or invisible.	This allows you to better determine if there are any performance issues before you drop the index. These options let you rebuild or re-enable the index without requiring the Data Definition Language (DDL) index creation statement.
Consider creating concatenated indexes that result in only the index structure being required to return the result set.	Avoids having to scan any table blocks; when queries are able to use the index only, this results in very efficient execution plans.
Consider creating indexes on columns used in the `ORDER BY`, `GROUP BY`, `UNION`, or `DISTINCT` clauses.	This may result in more efficient queries that frequently use these SQL constructs.

Refer to these guidelines as you create and manage indexes in your databases. These recommendations are intended to help you correctly use index technology.

INDEXES WITH NO SEGMENTS

You can instruct Oracle to create an index that will never be used and won't have any extents allocated to it via the `NOSEGMENT` clause:

```
SQL> create index cust_idx1 on cust(first_name) nosegment;
```

Even though this index will never be used, you can instruct Oracle to determine if the index might be used by the optimizer via the `_USE_NOSEGMENT_INDEXES` initialization parameter—for example:

```
SQL> alter session set "_use_nosegment_indexes"=true;
SQL> set autotrace trace explain;
SQL> select first_name from cust where first_name = 'JIM';
```

Here's a sample execution plan showing the optimizer would use the index (assuming that you dropped and re-created it normally without the NOSEGMENT clause):

```
------------------------------------------------------------------------------
Id  | Operation          | Name      | Rows | Bytes | Cost (%CPU)| Time      |
------------------------------------------------------------------------------
  0 | SELECT STATEMENT   |           |    1 |    17 |    1  (0)| 00:00:01 |
* 1 |   INDEX RANGE SCAN | CUST_IDX1 |    1 |    17 |    1  (0)| 00:00:01 |
------------------------------------------------------------------------------
```

That begs the question, why would you ever create an index with NOSEGMENT? If you have a very large index that you want to create without allocating space, to determine if the index would be used by the optimizer, creating an index with NOSEGMENT allows you to test that scenario. If you determine that the index would be useful, you can drop the index and re-create it without the NOSEGMENT clause.

2-3. Creating a Primary Key Index

Problem

You want to enforce that the primary key columns are unique within a table. Furthermore many of the columns in the primary key are frequently used within the WHERE clause of several queries. You want to ensure that indexes are created on primary key columns.

Solution

When you define a primary key constraint for a table, Oracle will automatically create an associated index for you. There are several methods available for creating a primary key constraint. Our preferred approach is to use the ALTER TABLE...ADD CONSTRAINT statement. This will create the index and the constraint at the same time. This example creates a primary key constraint named CUST_PK and also instructs Oracle to create the corresponding index (also named CUST_PK) in the USERS tablespace:

```
alter table cust add constraint cust_pk primary key (cust_id)
using index tablespace users;
```

The following queries and output provide details about the constraint and index that Oracle created. The first query displays the constraint information:

```
select
 constraint_name
,constraint_type
from user_constraints
where table_name = 'CUST';
```

```
CONSTRAINT_NAME                  C
------------------------------   -
CUST_PK                          P
```

This query displays the index information:

```
select
 index_name
,tablespace_name
,index_type
,uniqueness
from user_indexes
where table_name = 'CUST';
```

```
INDEX_NAME       TABLESPACE_NAME INDEX_TYPE       UNIQUENESS
---------------  --------------- ---------------  ---------------
CUST_PK          USERS           NORMAL           UNIQUE
```

How It Works

The solution for this recipe shows the method that we prefer to create primary key constraints and the corresponding index. In most situations, this approach is acceptable. However, you should be aware that there are several other methods for creating the primary key constraint and index. These methods are listed here:

- Create an index first, and then use `ALTER TABLE...ADD CONSTRAINT`.
- Specify the constraint inline (with the column) in the `CREATE TABLE` statement.
- Specify the constraint out of line (from the column) within the `CREATE TABLE` statement.

These techniques are described in the next several subsections.

Create Index and Constraint Separately

You have the option of first creating an index and then altering the table to apply the primary key constraint. Here's an example:

```
SQL> create index cust_pk on cust(cust_id);
SQL> alter table cust add constraint cust_pk primary key(cust_id);
```

The advantage to this approach is that you can drop or disable the primary key constraint independently of the index. If you work with large data volumes, you may require this sort of flexibility. This approach allows you to disable/re-enable a constraint without having to later rebuild the index.

Create Constraint Inline

You can directly create an index inline (with the column) in the `CREATE TABLE` statement. This approach is simple but doesn't allow for multiple column primary keys and doesn't name the constraint:

```
SQL> create table cust(cust_id number primary key);
```

If you don't explicitly name the constraint (as in the prior statement), Oracle automatically generates a name like SYS_C123456. If you want to explicitly provide a name, you can do so as follows:

```
create table cust(cust_id number constraint cust_pk primary key
using index tablespace users);
```

The advantage of this approach is that it's very simple. If you're experimenting in a development or test environment, this approach is quick and effective.

Create Constraint Out of Line

You can also define the primary key constraint out of line (from the column) within the CREATE TABLE statement:

```
create table cust(cust_id number
,constraint cust_pk primary key (cust_id)
using index tablespace users);
```

The out-of-line approach has one advantage over the inline approach in that you can specify multiple columns for the primary key.

All of the prior techniques for creating a primary key constraint and corresponding index are valid. It's often a matter of DBA or developer preference as to which technique is used.

2-4. Creating a Unique Index

Problem

You have a column (or combination of columns) that contains values that should always be unique. You want to create an index on this column (or combination of columns) that enforces the uniqueness and also provides efficient access to the table when using the unique column in the WHERE clause of a query.

■ **Note**   If you want to create a unique constraint on the primary key column(s), then you should explicitly create a primary key constraint (see Recipe 2-3 for details). One difference between a primary key and a unique key is that you can have only one primary key definition per table, whereas you can have multiple unique keys. Also, unique key constraints allow for null values, whereas primary key constraints do not.

Solution

This solution focuses on using the ALTER TABLE...ADD CONSTRAINT statement. When you create a unique key constraint, Oracle will automatically create an index for you. This is our recommended approach for creating unique key constraints and indexes. This example creates a unique constraint named CUST_UX1 on the combination of the LAST_NAME and FIRST_NAME columns of the CUST table:

```
alter table cust add constraint cust_ux1 unique (last_name, first_name)
using index tablespace users;
```

The prior statement creates the unique constraint, and additionally Oracle automatically creates an associated index. The following query displays the constraint that was created successfully:

```
select
 constraint_name
,constraint_type
from user_constraints
where table_name = 'CUST';
```

Here is a snippet of the output:

```
CONSTRAINT_NAME                 C
------------------------------  -
CUST_UX1                        U
```

This query shows the index that was automatically created along with the constraint:

```
select
 index_name
,tablespace_name
,index_type
,uniqueness
from user_indexes
where table_name = 'CUST';
```

Here is some sample output:

```
INDEX_NAME           TABLESPACE INDEX_TYPE UNIQUENESS
-------------------- ---------- ---------- ---------
CUST_UX1             USERS      NORMAL     UNIQUE
```

How It Works

Defining a unique constraint ensures that when you insert or update column values, then any combination of non-null values are unique. Besides the approach we displayed in the "Solution" section, there are several additional techniques for creating unique constraints:

- Use the CREATE TABLE statement.

- Create a regular index, and then use ALTER TABLE to add a constraint.

- Create a unique index and don't add the constraint.

These techniques are described in the next few subsections.

Use CREATE TABLE

Listed next is an example of using the CREATE TABLE statement to include a unique constraint.

```
create table cust(
 cust_id number
,last_name varchar2(30)
,first_name varchar2(30)
,constraint cust_ux1 unique(last_name, first_name)
 using index tablespace users);
```

The advantage of this approach is that it's simple and encapsulates the constraint and index creation within one statement.

Create Index First, Then Add Constraint

You have the option of first creating an index and then adding the constraint as a separate statement—for example:

```
SQL> create unique index cust_uidx1 on cust(last_name, first_name) tablespace users;
SQL> alter table cust add constraint cust_uidx1 unique (last_name, first_name);
```

The advantage of creating the index separate from the constraint is that you can drop or disable the constraint without dropping the underlying index. When working with large indexes, you may want to consider this approach. If you need to disable the constraint for any reason and then re-enable it later, you can do so without dropping the index (which may take a long time for large indexes).

Creating Only a Unique Index

You can also create just a unique index without adding the unique constraint—for example:

```
SQL> create unique index cust_uidx1 on cust(last_name, first_name) tablespace users;
```

When you create only a unique index explicitly (as in the prior statement), Oracle creates a unique index but doesn't add an entry for a constraint in DBA/ALL/USER_CONSTRAINTS. Why does this matter? Consider this scenario:

```
SQL> insert into cust values (1, 'STARK', 'JIM');
SQL> insert into cust values (1, 'STARK', 'JIM');
```

Here's the corresponding error message that is thrown:

```
ERROR at line 1:
ORA-00001: unique constraint (MV_MAINT.CUST_UIDX1) violated
```

If you're asked to troubleshoot this issue, the first place you look is in DBA_CONSTRAINTS for a constraint named CUST_UIDX1. However, there is no information:

```
select
  constraint_name
from dba_constraints
where constraint_name='CUST_UIDX1';
no rows selected
```

The "no rows selected" message can be confusing: the error message thrown when you insert into the table indicates that a unique constraint has been violated, yet there is no information in the constraint-related data-dictionary views. In this situation, you have to look at DBA_INDEXES to view the details of the unique index that has been created—for example:

```
select index_name, uniqueness
from dba_indexes where index_name='CUST_UIDX1';

INDEX_NAME                     UNIQUENESS
------------------------------ ----------
CUST_UIDX1                     UNIQUE
```

2-5. Indexing Foreign Key Columns

Problem

A large number of the queries in your application use foreign key columns as predicates in the WHERE clause. Therefore, for performance reasons, you want to ensure that you have all foreign key columns indexed.

Solution

Unlike primary key constraints, Oracle does not automatically create indexes on foreign key columns. For example, say you have a requirement that every record in the ADDRESS table be assigned a corresponding CUST_ID column that exists in the CUST table. To enforce this relationship, you create a foreign key constraint on the ADDRESS table as follows:

```
alter table address add constraint addr_fk1
foreign key (cust_id) references cust(cust_id);
```

▪ **Note** A foreign key column must reference a column in the parent table that has a primary key or unique key constraint defined on it. Otherwise you'll receive the error "ORA-02270: no matching unique or primary key for this column-list."

You realize the foreign key column is used extensively when joining the CUST and ADDRESS tables and that an index on the foreign key column will dramatically increase performance. You have to manually create an index in this situation. For example, a regular B-tree index is created on the foreign key column of CUST_ID in the ADDRESS table:

```
SQL> create index addr_fk1 on address(cust_id);
```

You don't have to name the index the same as the foreign key name (as we did in the prior lines of code). It's a personal preference as to whether you do that. We feel it's easier to maintain environments when the constraint and corresponding index have the same name.

How It Works

Foreign keys exist to ensure that when inserting into a child table, a corresponding parent table record exists. This is the mechanism to guarantee that data conforms to parent/child business relationship rules. From a performance perspective, it's usually a good idea to create an index on foreign key columns. This is because parent/child tables are frequently joined on the foreign key column(s) in the child table to the primary key column(s) in the parent table—for example:

```
select
 a.last_name, a.first_name, b.state
from cust a
     ,address b
where a.cust_id = b.cust_id;
```

In most scenarios, the Oracle query optimizer will choose to use the index on the foreign key column to identify the child records that are required to satisfy the results of the query. If no index exists, Oracle has to perform a full table scan on the child table.

If you've inherited a database, then it's prudent to check if columns with foreign key constraints defined on them have a corresponding index. The following query displays indexes associated with foreign key constraints:

```
select
  a.constraint_name cons_name
 ,a.table_name   tab_name
 ,b.column_name cons_column
 ,nvl(c.column_name,'***No Index***') ind_column
from user_constraints  a
     join
     user_cons_columns b on a.constraint_name = b.constraint_name
     left outer join
     user_ind_columns  c on b.column_name = c.column_name
                      and b.table_name  = c.table_name
where constraint_type = 'R'
order by 2,1;
```

If there is no index on the foreign key column, the ***No Index*** message is displayed. For example, suppose the index in the "Solution" section was accidentally dropped and then the prior query was run. Here is some sample output:

```
CONS_NAME          TAB_NAME                CONS_COLUMN               IND_COLUMN
-----------------  ----------------------  ------------------------  --------------------
ADDR_FK1                   ADDRESS                    CUST_ID                ***No Index***
```

2-6. Deciding When to Use a Concatenated Index

Problem

You have a combination of columns (from the same table) that are often used in the WHERE clause of several SQL queries. For example, you use LAST_NAME in combination with FIRST_NAME to identify a customer:

```
select last_name, first_name
from cust
where last_name = 'SMITH'
and first_name = 'STEVE';
```

You wonder if it would be more efficient to create a single concatenated index on the combination of LAST_NAME and FIRST_NAME columns or if performance would be better if two indexes were created separately on LAST_NAME and FIRST_NAME.

Solution

When frequently accessing two or more columns in conjunction in the WHERE clause, a concatenated index is often more selective than two single indexes. For this example, here's the table creation script:

```
create table cust(
 cust_id number primary key
,last_name varchar2(30)
,first_name varchar2(30));
```

Here's an example of a concatenated index created on LAST_NAME and FIRST_NAME:

```
SQL> create index cust_idx1 on cust(last_name, first_name);
```

To determine whether the concatenated index is used, several rows are inserted (only a subset of the rows is shown here):

```
SQL> insert into cust values(1,'SMITH','JOHN');
SQL> insert into cust values(2,'JONES','DAVE');
..........
SQL> insert into cust values(3,'FORD','SUE');
```

Next, statistics are generated for the table and index:

```
SQL> exec dbms_stats.gather_table_stats(ownname=>'MV_MAINT',-
        tabname=>'CUST',cascade=>true);
```

Now Autotrace is turned on so that the execution plan is displayed when a query is run:

```
SQL> set autotrace on;
```

Here's the query to execute:

```
select last_name, first_name
from cust
where last_name = 'SMITH'
and first_name = 'JOHN';
```

Listed next is an explain plan that shows the optimizer is using the index:

```
---------------------------------------------------------------------
| Id | Operation        | Name      | Rows | Bytes | Cost (%CPU)| Time     |
---------------------------------------------------------------------
|  0 | SELECT STATEMENT |           |   13 |   143 |    1   (0)| 00:00:01 |
|* 1 |  INDEX RANGE SCAN| CUST_IDX1 |   13 |   143 |    1   (0)| 00:00:01 |
---------------------------------------------------------------------
```

The prior output indicates that an INDEX RANGE SCAN was used to access the CUST_IDX1 index. Notice that all of the information required to satisfy the results of this query was contained within the index. The table data was not required. Oracle accessed only the index.

One other item to consider: suppose you have this query that additionally selects the CUST_ID column:

```
select cust_id, last_name, first_name
from cust
where last_name = 'SMITH'
and first_name = 'JOHN';
```

If you frequently access CUST_ID in combination with LAST_NAME and FIRST_NAME, consider adding CUST_ID to the concatenated index. This will provide all of the information that the query needs in the index. Oracle will be able to retrieve the required data from the index blocks and thus not have to access the table blocks.

How It Works

Oracle allows you to create an index that contains more than one column. Multicolumn indexes are known as *concatenated indexes*. These indexes are especially effective when you often use multiple columns in the WHERE clause when accessing a table. Here are some factors to consider when using concatenated indexes:

- If columns are often used together in the WHERE clause, consider creating a concatenated index.

- If a column is also used (in other queries) by itself in the WHERE clause, place that column at the leading edge of the index (first column defined).

- Keep in mind that Oracle can still use a lagging edge index (not the first column defined) if the lagging column appears by itself in the WHERE clause (see the next few paragraphs here for details).

In older versions of Oracle (circa v8), the optimizer would use a concatenated index only if the leading edge column(s) appeared in the WHERE clause. In modern versions, the optimizer uses a concatenated index even if the leading edge column(s) aren't present in the WHERE clause. This ability to use an index without reference to leading edge columns is known as the *skip-scan* feature. For example, say you have this query that uses the FIRST_NAME column (which is a lagging column in the concatenated index created in the "Solution" section of this recipe):

```
SQL> select last_name from cust where first_name='DAVE';
```

Here is the corresponding explain plan showing that the skip-scan feature is in play:

```
-----------------------------------------------------------------------
| Id | Operation        | Name      | Rows | Bytes | Cost (%CPU)| Time     |
-----------------------------------------------------------------------
|  0 | SELECT STATEMENT |           |   38 |   418 |    1   (0)| 00:00:01 |
|* 1 |  INDEX SKIP SCAN | CUST_IDX1 |   38 |   418 |    1   (0)| 00:00:01 |
-----------------------------------------------------------------------
```

A concatenated index that is used for skip-scanning is more efficient than a full table scan. However, if you're consistently using only a lagging edge column of a concatenated index, then consider creating a single-column index on the lagging column.

2-7. Reducing Index Size Through Compression

Problem

You want to create an index that efficiently handles cases in which many rows have the same values in one or more indexed columns. For example, suppose you have a table defined as follows:

```
create table cust(
 cust_id number
,last_name varchar2(30)
,first_name varchar2(30)
,middle_name varchar2(30));
```

Furthermore, you inspect the data inserted into the prior table with this query:

```
SQL> select last_name, first_name, middle_name from cust;
```

You notice that there is a great deal of duplication in the LAST_NAME and FIRST_NAME columns:

```
LEE          JOHN         Q
LEE          JOHN         B
LEE          JOHN         A
LEE          JOE          D
SMITH        BOB          A
SMITH        BOB          C
SMITH        BOB          D
SMITH        JOHN         J
SMITH        JOHN         A
SMITH        MIKE         K
SMITH        MIKE         R
SMITH        MIKE         S
```

You want to create an index that compresses the values so as to compact entries into the blocks. When the index is accessed, the compression will result in fewer block reads and thus improve performance. Specifically you want to create a key-compressed index on the LAST_NAME and FIRST_NAME columns of this table.

Solution

Use the COMPRESS N clause to create a compressed index:

```
SQL> create index cust_cidx1 on cust(last_name, first_name) compress 2;
```

The prior line of code instructs Oracle to create a compressed index on two columns (LAST_NAME and FIRST_NAME). For this example, if we determined that there was a high degree of duplication only in the first column, we could instruct the COMPRESS N clause to compress only the first column (LAST_NAME) by specifying an integer of 1:

```
SQL> create index cust_cidx1 on cust(last_name, first_name) compress 1;
```

How It Works

Index compression is useful for indexes that contain multiple columns where the leading index column value is often repeated. Compressed indexes have the following advantages:

- Reduced storage

- More rows stored in leaf blocks, which can result in less I/O when accessing a compressed index

The degree of compression will vary by the amount of duplication in the index columns specified for compression. You can verify the degree of compression and the number of leaf blocks used by running the following two queries before and after creating an index with compression enabled:

```
SQL> select sum(bytes) from user_extents where segment_name='&&ind_name';
SQL> select index_name, leaf_blocks from user_indexes where index_name='&&ind_name';
```

You can verify the index compression is in use and the corresponding prefix length as follows:

```
select index_name, compression, prefix_length
from user_indexes
where index_name = 'CUST_CIDX1';
```

Here's some sample output indicating that compression is enabled for the index with a prefix length of 2:

```
INDEX_NAME                      COMPRESS PREFIX_LENGTH
------------------------------- -------- -------------
CUST_CIDX1                      ENABLED              2
```

You can modify the prefix length by rebuilding the index. The following code changes the prefix length to 1:

```
SQL> alter index cust_cidx1 rebuild compress 1;
```

You can enable or disable compression for an existing index by rebuilding it. This example rebuilds the index with no compression:

```
SQL> alter index cust_cidx1 rebuild nocompress;
```

■ **Note** You cannot create a key-compressed index on a bitmap index.

2-8. Implementing a Function-Based Index

Problem

A query is running slow. You examine the WHERE clause and notice that a SQL UPPER function has been applied to a column. The UPPER function blocks the use of the existing index on that column. You want to create a function-based index to support the query. Here's an example of such a query:

```
SELECT first_name
FROM cust
WHERE UPPER(first_name) = 'DAVE';
```

You inspect USER_INDEXES and discover that an index exists on the FIRST_NAME column:

```
select  index_name, column_name
from user_ind_columns
where table_name = 'CUST';
```

```
INDEX_NAME            COLUMN_NAME
-------------------- --------------------
CUST_IDX1            FIRST_NAME
```

You generate an explain plan via SET AUTOTRACE TRACE EXPLAIN and notice that with the UPPER function applied to the column, the index is not used:

```
---------------------------------------------------------------------------
| Id  | Operation          | Name | Rows  | Bytes | Cost (%CPU)| Time     |
---------------------------------------------------------------------------
|   0 | SELECT STATEMENT   |      |     1 |    17 |     2  (0)| 00:00:01 |
|*  1 |   TABLE ACCESS FULL| CUST |     1 |    17 |     2  (0)| 00:00:01 |
---------------------------------------------------------------------------
```

You need to create an index that Oracle will use in this situation.

Solution

There are two ways to resolve this issue:

- Create a function-based index.

- If using Oracle Database 11g or higher, create an indexed virtual column (see Recipe 2-9 for details).

This solution focuses on using a function-based index. You create a function-based index by referencing the SQL function and column in the index creation statement. For this example, a function-based index is created on UPPER(name):

```
SQL> create index cust_fidx1 on cust(UPPER(first_name));
```

To verify if the index is used, the Autotrace facility is turned on:

```
SQL> set autotrace trace explain;
```

Now the query is executed:

```
SELECT first_name
FROM cust
WHERE UPPER(first_name) = 'DAVE';
```

Here is the resulting execution plan showing that the function-based index is used:

```
--------------------------------------------------------------------------------
| Id  | Operation                    | Name      | Rows | Bytes | Cost (%CPU)| Time     |
--------------------------------------------------------------------------------
|   0 | SELECT STATEMENT             |           |    1 |    34 |    1   (0)| 00:00:01 |
|   1 |  TABLE ACCESS BY INDEX ROWID | CUST      |    1 |    34 |    1   (0)| 00:00:01 |
|*  2 |   INDEX RANGE SCAN           | CUST_FIDX1|    1 |       |    1   (0)| 00:00:01 |
--------------------------------------------------------------------------------
```

■ **Note**   You can't modify a column that has a function-based index applied to it. You'll have to drop the index, modify the column, and then re-create the index.

How It Works

Function-based indexes are created with functions or expressions in their definitions. Function-based indexes allow index lookups on columns referenced by SQL functions in the WHERE clause of a query. The index can be as simple as the example in the "Solution" section of this recipe, or it can be based on complex logic stored in a PL/SQL function.

■ **Note**   Any user-created SQL functions must be declared deterministic before they can be used in a function-based index. *Deterministic* means that for a given set of inputs, the function always returns the same results. You must use the keyword DETERMINISTIC when creating a user-defined function that you want to use in a function-based index.

If you want to see the definition of a function-based index, select from the DBA/ALL/USER_IND_EXPRESSIONS view to display the SQL associated with the index. If you're using SQL*Plus, be sure to issue a SET LONG command first—for example:

```
SQL> SET LONG 500
SQL> select index_name, column_expression from user_ind_expressions;
```

The SET LONG command in this example tells SQL*Plus to display up to 500 characters from the COLUMN_EXPRESSION column, which is of type LONG.

2-9. Indexing a Virtual Column

Problem

You're currently using a function-based index but need better performance. You want to replace the function-based index with a virtual column and place an index on the virtual column.

■ **Note**   The virtual column feature requires Oracle Database 11g or higher.

Solution

Using a virtual column in combination with an index provides you with an alternative method for achieving performance gains when using SQL functions on columns in the WHERE clause. For example, suppose you have this query:

```
SELECT first_name
FROM cust
WHERE UPPER(first_name) = 'DAVE';
```

Normally, the optimizer will ignore any indexes on the column FIRST_NAME because of the SQL function applied to the column. There are two ways to improve performance in this situation:

- Create a function-based index (see Recipe 2-8 for details).

- Use a virtual column in combination with an index.

This solution focuses on the latter bullet. First a virtual column is added to the table that encapsulates the SQL function:

```
SQL> alter table cust add(up_name generated always as (UPPER(first_name)) virtual);
```

Next an index is created on the virtual column:

```
SQL> create index cust_vidx1 on cust(up_name);
```

This creates a very efficient mechanism to retrieve data when referencing a column with a SQL function.

How It Works

You might be asking this question: "Which performs better, a function-based index or an indexed virtual column?" In our testing, we were able to create several scenarios where the virtual column performed better than the function-based index. Results may vary depending on your data.

The purpose of this recipe is not to convince you to immediately start replacing all function-based indexes in your system with virtual columns; rather we want you to be aware of an alternative method for solving a common performance issue.

A virtual column is not free. If you have an existing table, you have to create and maintain the DDL required to create the virtual column, whereas a function-based index can be added, modified, and dropped independently from the table.

Several caveats are associated with virtual columns:

- You can define a virtual column only on a regular heap-organized table. You can't define a virtual column on an index-organized table, an external table, a temporary table, object tables, or cluster tables.

- Virtual columns can't reference other virtual columns.

- Virtual columns can reference columns only from the table in which the virtual column is defined.

- The output of a virtual column must be a scalar value (a single value, not a set of values).

To view the definition of a virtual column, use the DBMS_METADATA package to view the DDL associated with the table. If you're selecting from SQL*Plus, you need to set the LONG variable to a value large enough to show all data returned:

```
SQL> set long 10000;
SQL> select dbms_metadata.get_ddl('TABLE','CUST') from dual;
```

Here's a partial snippet of the output showing the virtual column details:

```
"UP_NAME" VARCHAR2(30) GENERATED ALWAYS AS (UPPER("FIRST_NAME"))
VIRTUAL VISIBLE) SEGMENT CREATION IMMEDIATE
```

You can also view the definition of the virtual column by querying the DBA/ALL/USER_IND_EXPRESSIONS view. If you're using SQL*Plus, be sure to issue a SET LONG command first—for example:

```
SQL> SET LONG 500
SQL> select index_name, column_expression from user_ind_expressions;
```

The SET LONG command in this example tells SQL*Plus to display up to 500 characters from the COLUMN_EXPRESSION column, which is of type LONG.

2-10. Avoiding Concentrated I/O for Index

Problem

You use a sequence to populate the primary key of a table and realize that this can cause contention on the leading edge of the index because the index values are nearly similar. This leads to multiple inserts into the same block, which causes contention. You want to spread out the inserts into the index so that the inserts more evenly distribute values across the index structure. You want to use a reverse-key index to accomplish this.

Solution

Use the REVERSE clause to create a reverse-key index:

```
SQL> create index inv_idx1 on inv(inv_id) reverse;
```

You can verify that an index is reverse-key by running the following query:

```
SQL> select index_name, index_type from user_indexes;
```

Here's some sample output showing that the INV_IDX1 index is reverse-key:

```
INDEX_NAME                      INDEX_TYPE
------------------------------  ---------------------------
INV_IDX1                        NORMAL/REV
USERS_IDX1                      NORMAL
```

■ **Note**   You can't specify REVERSE for a bitmap index or an index-organized table.

How It Works

Reverse-key indexes are similar to B-tree indexes except that the bytes of the index key are reversed when an index entry is created. For example, if the index values are 100, 101, and 102, the reverse-key index values are 001, 101, and 201:

```
Index value             Reverse key value
-------------           --------------------
100                     001
101                     101
102                     201
```

Reverse-key indexes can perform better in scenarios where you need a way to evenly distribute index data that would otherwise have similar values clustered together. Thus, when using a reverse-key index, you avoid having I/O concentrated in one physical disk location within the index during large inserts of sequential values. The downside to this type of index is that it can't be used for index range scans, which therefore limits its usefulness.

You can rebuild an existing index to be reverse-key by using the REBUILD REVERSE clause—for example:

```
SQL> alter index f_regs_idx1 rebuild reverse;
```

Similarly, if you want to make an index that is reverse-key into a normally ordered index, then use the REBUILD NOREVERSE clause:

```
SQL> alter index f_regs_idx1 rebuild noreverse;
```

2-11. Adding an Index Without Impacting Existing Applications

Problem

You know from experience that sometimes when an index is added to a third-party application, this can cause performance issues and also can be a violation of the support agreement with the vendor. You want to implement an index in such a way that the application won't ever use the index.

Solution

Often, third-party vendors don't support customers adding their own indexes to an application. However, there may be a scenario in which you're certain you can increase a query's performance without impacting other queries in the application. You can create the index as invisible and then explicitly instruct a query to use the index via a hint—for example:

```
SQL> create index inv_idx1 on inv(inv_id) invisible;
```

Next, ensure that the OPTIMIZER_USE_INVISIBLE_INDEXES initialization parameter is set to TRUE (the default is FALSE). This instructs the optimizer to consider invisible indexes:

```
SQL> alter system set optimizer_use_invisible_indexes=true;
```

Now, use a hint to tell the optimizer that the index exists:

```
SQL> select /*+ index (inv INV_IDX1) */ inv_id from inv where inv_id=1;
```

You can verify that the index is being used by setting AUTOTRACE TRACE EXPLAIN and running the SELECT statement:

```
SQL> set autotrace trace explain;
SQL> select /*+ index (inv INV_IDX1) */ inv_id from inv where inv_id=1;
```

Here's some sample output indicating that the optimizer chose to use the invisible index:

```
--------------------------------------------------------------------------
| Id | Operation        | Name     | Rows | Bytes | Cost (%CPU)| Time     |
--------------------------------------------------------------------------
|  0 | SELECT STATEMENT |          |    1 |    13 |    1   (0)| 00:00:01 |
|* 1 |  INDEX RANGE SCAN| INV_IDX1 |    1 |    13 |    1   (0)| 00:00:01 |
--------------------------------------------------------------------------
```

Keep in mind that an invisible index means only that the optimizer can't see the index. Just like any other index, an invisible index consumes space and resources when executing DML statements.

How It Works

In Oracle Database 11g and higher, you have the option of making an index invisible to the optimizer. Oracle still maintains invisible indexes but doesn't make them available for use by the optimizer. If you want the optimizer to use an invisible index, you can do so with a SQL hint. Invisible indexes have a couple of interesting uses:

- You can add an invisible index to a third-party application without affecting existing code or support agreements.

- Altering an index to invisible before dropping it allows you to quickly recover if you later determine that the index is required.

The first bulleted item was discussed in the "Solution" section of this recipe. The second scenario is discussed in this section. For example, suppose you've identified an index that isn't being used and are considering dropping it. In earlier releases of Oracle, you could mark the index as UNUSABLE and then later drop indexes that you were certain weren't being used. If you later determined that you needed an unusable index, the only way to re-enable the index was to rebuild it. For large indexes, this could take a long time and consume considerable database resources.

Making an index invisible has the advantage that it tells the optimizer only to not use the index. The invisible index is still maintained as the underlying table has records inserted, updated, or deleted. If you decide that you later need the index, there is no need to rebuild it. You simply have to mark it as visible again—for example:

```
SQL> alter index inv_idx1 visible;
```

You can verify the visibility of an index via this query:

```
SQL> select index_name, status, visibility from user_indexes;
```

Here's some sample output:

```
INDEX_NAME                     STATUS    VISIBILITY
------------------------------ --------- ----------
INV_IDX1                       VALID     VISIBLE
```

OLD SCHOOL: INSTRUCTING THE OPTIMIZER NOT TO USE AN INDEX

In the olden days, sometimes the rule-based optimizer (deprecated) would choose to use an index that would significantly decrease performance. In these situations, DBAs and developers would manually instruct the optimizer not to use an index on a numeric-based column as follows:

```
SQL> select cust_id from cust where cust_id+0 = 12345;
```

In the prior statement, the +0 adds nothing to the logic of the SQL statement (and therefore has no impact on the result set). In this scenario, the optimizer will automatically not use an index on a numeric column that has been modified with an arithmetic expression.

Similarly with character-based columns, indexes will be ignored for columns that have characters concatenated to them—for example:

```
SQL> select last_name from cust where last_name || '' = 'SMITH';
```

In the prior statement, the ||'' adds nothing to the logic of the SQL, but results in the optimizer not using an index on the LAST_NAME column (if one exists).

2-12. Creating a Bitmap Index in Support of a Star Schema

Problem

You have a data warehouse that contains a star schema. The star schema consists of a large fact table and several dimension (lookup) tables. The primary key columns of the dimension tables map to foreign key columns in the fact table. You would like to create bitmap indexes on all of the foreign key columns in the fact table.

Solution

You use the `BITMAP` keyword to create a bitmap index. The next line of code creates a bitmap index on the `CUST_ID` column of the `F_SALES` table:

```
SQL> create bitmap index f_sales_cust_fk1 on f_sales(cust_id);
```

The type of index is verified with the following query:

```
SQL> select index_name, index_type from user_indexes where index_name='F_SALES_CUST_FK1';
```

```
INDEX_NAME                      INDEX_TYPE
------------------------------- ---------------------------
F_SALES_CUST_FK1                BITMAP
```

How It Works

A bitmap index stores the `ROWID` of a row and a corresponding bitmap. You can think of the bitmap as a combination of ones and zeros. A one indicates the presence of a value, and a zero indicates that the value doesn't exist. Bitmap indexes are ideal for low-cardinality columns (few distinct values) and where the application is not frequently updating the table. Bitmap indexes are commonly used in data warehouse environments where you have star schema design.

A typical star schema structure consists of a large fact table and many small dimension (lookup) tables. In these scenarios, it's common to create bitmap indexes on fact table–foreign key columns. The fact tables are typically loaded on a daily basis and (usually) aren't subsequently updated or deleted.

You shouldn't use bitmap indexes on OLTP databases with high `INSERT`/`UPDATE`/`DELETE` activities, due to locking issues. Locking issues arise because the structure of the bitmap index results in potentially many rows being locked during DML operations, which results in locking problems for high-transaction OLTP systems.

■ **Note** Bitmap indexes and bitmap join indexes are available only with the Oracle Enterprise Edition of the database.

2-13. Creating a Bitmap Join Index

Problem

You're working in a data warehouse environment. You have a fairly large dimension table that is often joined to an extremely large fact table. You wonder if there's a way to create a bitmap index in such a way that it can eliminate the need for the optimizer to access the dimension table blocks to satisfy the results of a query.

Solution

Here's the basic syntax for creating a bitmap join index:

```
create bitmap index <index_name>
on <fact_table> (<dimension_table.dimension_column>)
from <fact_table>, <dimension_table>
where <fact_table>.<foreign_key_column> = <dimension_table>.<primary_key_column>;
```

Bitmap join indexes are appropriate in situations where you're joining two tables using the foreign key column(s) in one table that relate to primary key column(s) in another table. For example, suppose you typically retrieve the CUST_NAME from the D_CUSTOMERS table while joining to a large F_SHIPMENTS fact table. This example creates a bitmap join index between the F_SHIPMENTS and D_CUSTOMERS tables:

```
create bitmap index f_shipments_bm_idx1
on f_shipments(d_customers.cust_name)
from f_shipments, d_customers
where f_shipments.d_cust_id = d_customers.d_cust_id;
```

Now, consider a query such as this:

```
select
  d.cust_name
from f_shipments f, d_customers d
where f.d_cust_id = d.d_cust_id
and d.cust_name = 'Sun';
```

The optimizer can choose to use the bitmap join index and thus avoid the expense of having to join the tables.

How It Works

Bitmap join indexes store the results of a join between two tables in an index. Bitmap indexes are beneficial because they avoid joining tables to retrieve results. The syntax for a bitmap join index differs from a regular bitmap index in that it contains FROM and WHERE clauses.

Bitmap join indexes are usually suitable only for data warehouse environments where you have tables that get loaded and then are not updated. When updating tables that have bitmap join indexes declared, this potentially results in several rows being locked. Therefore this type of an index is not suitable for an OLTP database.

2-14. Creating an Index-Organized Table

Problem

You want to create a table that is the intersection of a many-to-many relationship between two tables. The intersection table will consist of two columns. Each column is a foreign key that maps back to a corresponding primary key in a parent table.

Solution

Index-organized tables (IOTs) are efficient objects when the table data is typically accessed through querying on the primary key. Use the ORGANIZATION INDEX clause to create an IOT:

```
create table cust_assoc
(cust_id number
,user_group_id number
,create_dtt timestamp(5)
,update_dtt timestamp(5)
,constraint cust_assoc_pk primary key(cust_id, user_group_id)
)
organization index
including create_dtt
pctthreshold 30
tablespace nsestar_index
overflow
tablespace dim_index;
```

Notice that DBA/ALL/USER_TABLES includes an entry for the table name used when creating an IOT. The following two queries show how Oracle records the information regarding the IOT in the data dictionary:

```
select table_name, iot_name
from user_tables
where iot_name = 'CUST_ASSOC';
```

Here is some sample output:

```
TABLE_NAME                      IOT_NAME
------------------------------  ------------------------------
SYS_IOT_OVER_184185             CUST_ASSOC
```

Listed next is another slightly different query with its output:

```
select table_name, iot_name
from user_tables
where table_name = 'CUST_ASSOC';
```

Here is some sample output:

```
TABLE_NAME                      IOT_NAME
------------------------------  ------------------------------
CUST_ASSOC
```

Additionally, DBA/ALL/USER_INDEXES contains a record with the name of the primary key constraint specified. The INDEX_TYPE column contains a value of IOT - TOP for IOTs:

```
select index_name, index_type
from user_indexes
where table_name = 'CUST_ASSOC';
```

Here is some sample output:

```
INDEX_NAME                   INDEX_TYPE
---------------------------- ---------------------------
CUST_ASSOC_PK                IOT - TOP
```

How It Works

An IOT stores the entire contents of the table's row in a B-tree index structure. IOTs provide fast access for queries that have exact matches and/or range searches on the primary key.

All columns specified up to and including the column specified in the INCLUDING clause are stored in the same block as the CUST_ASSOC_PK primary key column. In other words, the INCLUDING clause specifies the last column to keep in the table segment. Columns listed after the column specified in the INCLUDING clause are stored in the overflow data segment. In the previous example, the UPDATE_DTT column is stored in the overflow segment.

PCTTHRESHOLD specifies the percentage of space reserved in the index block for the IOT row. This value can be from 1 to 50, and defaults to 50 if no value is specified. There must be enough space in the index block to store the primary key. The OVERFLOW clause details which tablespace should be used to store overflow data segments.

2-15. Monitoring Index Usage

Problem

You maintain a large database that contains thousands of indexes. As part of your proactive maintenance, you want to determine if any indexes are not being used. You realize that unused indexes have a detrimental impact on performance, because every time a row is inserted, updated, and deleted, the corresponding index has to be maintained. This consumes CPU resources and disk space. If an index isn't being used, it should be dropped.

Solution

Use the ALTER INDEX...MONITORING USAGE statement to enable basic index monitoring. The following example enables index monitoring on an index named F_REGS_IDX1:

```
SQL> alter index f_regs_idx1 monitoring usage;
```

The first time the index is accessed, Oracle records this; you can view whether an index has been accessed via the V$OBJECT_USAGE view. To report which indexes are being monitored and have ever been used, run this query:

```
SQL> select index_name, table_name, monitoring, used from v$object_usage;
```

If the index has ever been used in a SELECT statement, then the USED column will contain the YES value. Here is some sample output from the prior query:

```
INDEX_NAME                      TABLE_NAME                      MON USED
------------------------------  ------------------------------  --- ----
F_REGS_IDX1                     F_REGS                          YES YES
```

Most likely, you won't monitor only one index. Rather, you'll want to monitor all indexes for a user. In this situation, use SQL to generate SQL to create a script you can run to turn on monitoring for all indexes. Here's such a script:

```
set pagesize 0 head off linesize 132
spool enable_mon.sql
select
  'alter index ' || index_name || ' monitoring usage;'
from user_indexes;
spool off;
```

To disable monitoring on an index, use the NOMONITORING USAGE clause—for example:

```
SQL> alter index f_regs_idx1 nomonitoring usage;
```

How It Works

The main advantage to monitoring index usage is to identify indexes not being used. This allows you to identify indexes that can be dropped. This will free up disk space and improve the performance of DML statements.

The V$OBJECT_USAGE view shows information only for the currently connected user. You can verify this behavior by inspecting the TEXT column of DBA_VIEWS for the V$OBJECT_USAGE definition:

```
SQL> select text from dba_views where view_name = 'V$OBJECT_USAGE';
```

Notice the following line in the output:

```
where io.owner# = userenv('SCHEMAID')
```

That line instructs the view to display information only for the currently connected user. If you're logged in as a DBA privileged user and want to view the status of all indexes that have monitoring enabled (regardless of the user), execute this query:

```
select io.name, t.name,
       decode(bitand(i.flags, 65536), 0, 'NO', 'YES'),
       decode(bitand(ou.flags, 1), 0, 'NO', 'YES'),
       ou.start_monitoring,
       ou.end_monitoring
from sys.obj$ io
    ,sys.obj$ t
    ,sys.ind$ i
    ,sys.object_usage ou
where i.obj# = ou.obj#
and io.obj# = ou.obj#
and t.obj# = i.bo#;
```

The prior query removes the line from the query that restricts output to display information only for the currently logged-in user. This provides you with a convenient way to view all monitored indexes.

2-16. Maximizing Index Creation Speed

Problem

You're creating an index based on a table that contains millions of rows. You want to create the index as fast as possible.

Solution

This solution describes two techniques for increasing the speed of index creation:

- Turning off redo generation
- Increasing the degree of parallelism

You can use the prior two features independently of each other, or they can be used in conjunction.

Turning Off Redo Generation

You can optionally create an index with the NOLOGGING clause. Doing so has these implications:

- The redo isn't generated that would be required to recover the index in the event of a media failure.
- Subsequent direct-path operations also won't generate the redo required to recover the index information in the event of a media failure.

Here's an example of creating an index with the NOLOGGING clause:

```
create index inv_idx1 on inv(inv_id, inv_id2)
nologging
tablespace inv_mgmt_index;
```

You can run this query to determine whether an index has been created with NOLOGGING:

```
SQL> select index_name, logging from user_indexes;
```

Increasing the Degree of Parallelism

In large database environments where you're attempting to create an index on a table that is populated with many rows, you may be able to reduce the time it takes to create the index by using the PARALLEL clause. For example, this sets the degree of parallelism to 2 when creating the index:

```
create index inv_idx1 on inv(inv_id)
parallel 2
tablespace inv_mgmt_data;
```

You can verify the degree of parallelism on an index via this query:

```
SQL> select index_name, degree1 from user_indexes;
```

■ **Note** If you don't specify a degree of parallelism, Oracle selects a degree based on the number of CPUs on the box times the value of `PARALLEL_THREADS_PER_CPU`.

How It Works

The main advantage of `NOLOGGING` is that when you create the index, a minimal amount of redo information is generated, which can have significant performance implications when creating a large index. The disadvantage is that if you experience a media failure soon after the index is created (or have records inserted via a direct-path operation), and subsequently have a failure that causes you to restore from a backup (taken prior to the index creation), then you may see this error when the index is accessed:

```
ORA-01578: ORACLE data block corrupted (file # 4, block # 11407)
ORA-01110: data file 4: '/ora01/dbfile/O11R2/inv_mgmt_index01.dbf'
ORA-26040: Data block was loaded using the NOLOGGING option
```

This error indicates that the index is logically corrupt. In this scenario, you must re-create or rebuild the index before it's usable. In most scenarios, it's acceptable to use the `NOLOGGING` clause when creating an index, because the index can be re-created or rebuilt without affecting the table on which the index is based.

In addition to `NOLOGGING`, you can use the `PARALLEL` clause to increase the speed of an index creation. For large indexes, this can significantly decrease the time required to create an index.

Keep in mind that you can use `NOLOGGING` in combination with `PARALLEL`. This next example rebuilds an index in parallel while generating a minimal amount of redo:

```
SQL> alter index inv_idx1 rebuild parallel nologging;
```

2-17. Reclaiming Unused Index Space

Problem

You have an index consuming space in a segment, but without actually using that space. For example, you're running the following query to display the Segment Advisor's advice:

```
SELECT
  'Task Name       : ' || f.task_name    || CHR(10) ||
  'Start Run Time  : ' || TO_CHAR(execution_start, 'dd-mon-yy hh24:mi') || chr (10) ||
  'Segment Name    : ' || o.attr2        || CHR(10) ||
  'Segment Type    : ' || o.type         || CHR(10) ||
  'Partition Name  : ' || o.attr3        || CHR(10) ||
  'Message         : ' || f.message      || CHR(10) ||
  'More Info       : ' || f.more_info    || CHR(10) ||
```

```
         '-------------------------------------------------' Advice
FROM dba_advisor_findings   f
    ,dba_advisor_objects    o
    ,dba_advisor_executions e
WHERE o.task_id   = f.task_id
AND    o.object_id = f.object_id
AND    f.task_id   = e.task_id
AND    e. execution_start > sysdate - 1
AND    e.advisor_name = 'Segment Advisor'
ORDER BY f.task_name;
```

The following output is displayed:

```
ADVICE
------------------------------------------------------------------------------
Task Name      : F_REGS Advice
Start Run Time : 19-feb-11 09:32
Segment Name   : F_REGS_IDX1
Segment Type   : INDEX
Partition Name :
Message        : Perform shrink, estimated savings is 84392870 bytes.
More Info      : Allocated Space:166723584: Used Space:82330714: Reclaimable S
pace :84392870:
------------------------------------------------------
```

You want to shrink the index to free up the unused space.

Solution

There are a couple of effective methods for freeing up unused space associated with an index:

- Rebuilding the index

- Shrinking the index

Before you perform either of these operations, first check USER_SEGMENTS to verify that the amount of space used corresponds with the Segment Advisor's advice. In this example, the segment name is F_REGS_IDX1:

```
SQL> select bytes from user_segments where segment_name = 'F_REGS_IDX1';

BYTES
----------
 166723584
```

This example uses the ALTER INDEX...REBUILD statement to re-organize and compact the space used by an index:

```
SQL> alter index f_regs_idx1 rebuild;
```

Alternatively, use the `ALTER INDEX...SHRINK SPACE` statement to free up unused space in an index—for example:

```
SQL> alter index f_regs_idx1 shrink space;
```

```
Index altered.
```

Now query `USER_SEGMENTS` again to verify that the space has been de-allocated. Here is the output for this example:

```
  BYTES
----------
    524288
```

The space consumed by the index has considerably decreased.

How It Works

Usually rebuilding an index is the fastest and most effective way to reclaim unused space consumed by an index. Therefore this is the approach we recommend for reclaiming unused index space. Freeing up space is desirable because it ensures that you use only the amount of space required by an object. It also has the performance benefit that Oracle has fewer blocks to manage and sort through when performing read operations.

Besides freeing up space, you may want to consider rebuilding an index for these additional reasons:

- The index has become corrupt.

- You want to modify storage characteristics (such as changing the tablespace).

- An index that was previously marked as unusable now needs to be rebuilt to make it usable again.

Keep in mind that Oracle attempts to acquire a lock on the table and rebuild the index online. If there are any active transactions that haven't committed, then Oracle won't be able to obtain a lock, and the following error will be thrown:

```
ORA-00054: resource busy and acquire with NOWAIT specified or timeout expired
```

In this scenario, you can either wait until the there is little activity in the database or try setting the `DDL_LOCK_TIMEOUT` parameter:

```
SQL> alter session set ddl_lock_timeout=15;
```

The `DDL_LOCK_TIMEOUT` initialization parameter is available in Oracle Database 11g or higher. It instructs Oracle to repeatedly attempt to obtain a lock for the specified amount of time.

If no tablespace is specified, Oracle rebuilds the index in the tablespace in which the index currently exists. Specify a tablespace if you want the index rebuilt in a different tablespace:

```
SQL> alter index inv_idx1 rebuild tablespace inv_index;
```

■ **Tip** If you're working with a large index, you may want to consider using features such as NOLOGGING and/or PARALLEL (see Recipe 2-16 for details).

If you use the ALTER INDEX...SHRINK SPACE operation to free up unused index space, keep in mind that this feature requires that the target object must be created within a tablespace with automatic segment space management enabled. If you attempt to shrink a table or index that has been created in a tablespace using manual segment space management, you'll receive this error:

ORA-10635: Invalid segment or tablespace type

As we've noted elsewhere in this chapter, we recommend that you use the ASSM feature whenever possible. This allows you to take advantage of all the Oracle segment management features.

The ALTER INDEX...SHRINK SPACE statement has a few nuances to be aware of. For example, you can instruct Oracle to attempt only to merge the contents of index blocks (and not free up space) via the COMPACT clause:

```
SQL> alter index f_regs_idx1 shrink space compact;
```

The prior operation is equivalent to the ALTER INDEX...COALESCE statement. Here's an example of using COALESCE:

```
SQL> alter index f_regs_idx1 coalesce;
```

If you want to maximize the space compacted, either rebuild the index or use the SHRINK SPACE clause as shown in the "Solution" section of this recipe. It's somewhat counterintuitive that the COMPACT space doesn't actually initiate a greater degree of realized free space. The COMPACT clause instructs Oracle to only merge index blocks where possible and not to maximize the amount of space being freed up.

CHAPTER 3

Optimizing Instance Memory

Optimizing the memory you allocate to an Oracle database is one of the most critical tasks you need to perform as a DBA. Over the years, Oracle DBAs were used to spending vast amounts of their time analyzing memory usage by the database and trying to come up with the best possible allocation of memory. In Oracle Database 11g, the burden of allocating Oracle's memory is shifted almost completely to the database itself. This chapter shows you how to take advantage of Oracle's automatic memory management feature, so you can leave the database to optimize memory usage, while you focus on more important matters.

This chapter starts off by explaining how to set up automatic memory management for a database. The chapter also shows you how to set minimum values for certain components of memory even under automatic memory management. It also includes recipes that explain how to create multiple buffer pools, how to monitor Oracle's usage of memory, and how to use the Oracle Enterprise Manager's Database Control (or Grid Control) tool to get advice from Oracle regarding the optimal sizing of memory allocation. You'll also learn how to optimize the use of the Program Global Area (PGA), a key Oracle memory component, especially in data warehouse environments.

In Oracle Database 11g, Oracle has introduced an exciting new result caching feature. Oracle can now cache the results of both SQL queries and PL/SQL functions in the shared pool component of Oracle's memory. We discuss that server result cache in this chapter. In addition, you'll also find a recipe that explains how to take advantage of Oracle's client-side result caching feature. Finally, we show how to use the exciting new Oracle feature called the Oracle Database Smart Flash Cache.

3-1. Automating Memory Management

Problem

You want to automate memory management in your Oracle database. You have both OLTP and batch jobs running in this database. You want to take advantage of the automatic memory management feature built into Oracle Database 11g.

Solution

Here are the steps to implement automatic memory management in your database, if you've already set either the `SGA_TARGET` or the `PGA_AGGREGATE_TARGET` parameters (or both). We assume that we are going to allocate 2,000 MB to the `MEMORY_MAX_TARGET` parameter and 1,000 MB to the `MEMORY_TARGET` parameter.

1. Connect to the database with the SYSDBA privilege.

2. Assuming you're using the SPFILE, first set a value for the MEMORY_MAX_TARGET parameter:

```
SQL> alter system set memory_max_target=2G scope=spfile;
System altered.
```

You must specify the SCOPE parameter in the alter system command, because MEMORY_MAX_TARGET isn't a dynamic parameter, which means you can't change it on the fly while the instance is running.

3. Note that if you've started the instance with a traditional init.ora parameter file instead of the SPFILE, you must add the following to your init.ora file:

```
memory_max_target = 2000M
memory_target = 1000M
```

4. Bounce the database.

5. Turn off the SGA_TARGET and the PGA_AGGREGATE_TARGET parameters by issuing the following ALTER SYSTEM commands:

```
SQL> alter system set sga_target = 0;
SQL> alter system set pga_aggregate_target = 0;
```

6. Turn on automatic memory management by setting the MEMORY_TARGET parameter:

```
SQL> alter system set memory_target = 1000M;
```

From this point on, the database runs under the automatic memory management mode, with it shrinking and growing the individual allocations to the various components of Oracle memory according to the requirements of the ongoing workload. You can change the value of the MEMORY_TARGET parameter dynamically anytime, as long as you don't exceed the value you set for the MEMORY_MAX_TARGET parameter.

■ **Tip** The term "target" in parameters such as memory_target and pga_memory_target means just that—Oracle will try to stay under the target level, but there's no guarantee that it'll never go beyond that. It may exceed the target allocation on occasion, if necessary.

You don't have to set the SGA_TARGET and PGA_AGGREGATE_TARGET parameters to 0 in order to use automatic memory management. In Recipe 3-3, we show how to set minimum values for these parameters even when you choose to implement automatic memory management. That recipe assumes you're implementing automatic memory management, but that for some reason, you need to specify your own minimum values for components such as the SGA and the PGA.

How It Works

In earlier releases of the Oracle database, DBAs used to set values for the various SGA components, or would specify values for the SGA and the PGA. Starting with the Oracle Database 11g release, Oracle enables you to completely automate the entire instance memory allocation, by just setting a single initialization parameter, MEMORY_TARGET, under what's known as automatic memory management. In this Recipe, we show you how to set up the automatic memory management feature in your database.

If you're creating a new Oracle database with the help of the Database Configuration Assistant (DBCA), you're given a choice among automatic memory management, shared memory management, and manual memory management. Select the automatic memory management option, and specify the values for two automatic memory-related parameters: MEMORY_TARGET and MEMORY_MAX_TARGET. The first parameter sets the current value of the memory allocation to the database, and the second parameter sets the limit to which you can raise the first parameter if necessary.

Oracle's memory structures consist of two distinct memory areas. The system global area (SGA) contains the data and control information and is shared by all server and background processes. The SGA holds the data blocks retrieved from disk by Oracle. The program global area (PGA) contains data and control information for a server process. Each server process is allocated its own chunk of the PGA. Managing Oracle's memory allocation involves careful calibration of the needs of the database. Some database instances need more memory for certain components of the memory. For example, a data warehouse will need more PGA memory in order to perform huge sorts that are common in such an environment. Also, during the course of a day, the memory needs of the instance might vary; during business hours, for example, the instance might be processing more online transaction processing (OLTP) work, whereas after business hours, it might be running huge batch jobs that involve data warehouse processing, jobs that typically need higher PGA allocations per each process.

In prior versions of the Oracle database, DBAs had to carefully decide the optimal allocation of memory to the individual components of the memory one allocated to the database. Technically, you can still manually set the values of the individual components of the SGA as well as set a value for the PGA, or partially automate the process by setting parameters such as SGA_TARGET and PGA_AGGREGATE_TARGET. Although Oracle still allows you to manually configure the various components of memory, automatic memory management is the recommended approach to managing Oracle's memory allocation. Once you specify a certain amount of memory by setting the MEMORY_TARGET and MEMORY_MAX_TARGET parameters, Oracle automatically tunes the actual memory allocation, by redistributing memory between the SGA and the PGA.

■ **Tip** When you create a database with the Database Configuration Assistant (DBCA), automatic memory management is the default.

Oracle Database 11g lets you automate all the memory allocations for an instance, including shared memory and the PGA memory, if you choose to implement automatic memory management by setting the MEMORY_TARGET and MEMORY_MAX_TARGET parameters. Under an automatic memory management regime, Oracle automatically tunes the total SGA size, the SGA component sizes, the instance PGA size, and the individual PGA size. This dynamic memory tuning by the Oracle instance optimizes database performance, as memory allocations are changed automatically by Oracle to match changing database workloads. Automatic memory management means that once you set the MEMORY_TARGET parameter, you can simply ignore the following parameters by not setting them at all:

- SGA_TARGET

- PGA_AGGREGATE_TARGET

- DB_CACHE_SIZE

- SHARED_POOL_SIZE

- LARGE_POOL_SIZE

- JAVA_POOL_SIZE

If you're moving from a system where you were using the SGA_TARGET and PGA_AGGREGATE_TARGET parameters, you can follow the procedures shown in the "Solution" section of this recipe to move to the newer automatic memory management mode of managing Oracle's memory allocation. Note that while setting the MEMORY_TARGET parameter is mandatory for implementing automatic memory management, the MEMORY_MAX_TARGET parameter isn't—if you don't set this parameter, Oracle sets its value internally to that of the MEMORY_TARGET parameter. Also, the MEMORY_MAX_TARGET parameter acts as the upper bound for the MEMORY_TARGET parameter. Oracle has different minimum permissible settings for the MEMORY_TARGET parameter, depending on the operating system. If you try to set this parameter below its minimum allowable value, the database will issue an error. Some of the memory components can't shrink quickly and some components must have a minimum size for the database to function properly. Therefore, Oracle won't let you set too low a value for the MEMORY_TARGET parameter. The following example shows this:

```
SQL> alter system set memory_target=360m scope=both;
alter system set memory_target=360m scope=both
*
ERROR at line 1:
ORA-02097: parameter cannot be modified because specified value is invalid
ORA-00838: Specified value of MEMORY_TARGET is too small, needs to be at least
544M

SQL> alter system set memory_target=544m scope=both;

alter system set memory_target=544m scope=both
*
ERROR at line 1:
ORA-02097: parameter cannot be modified because specified value is invalid
ORA-00838: Specified value of MEMORY_TARGET is too small, needs to be at least
624M

SQL>  alter system set memory_target=624m scope=both;

System altered.

SQL>
```

You'll notice that Oracle issued an error when we tried to set a very low value for the MEMORY_TARGET parameter. Note that Oracle took iterations to decide to let you know the minimum allowable level for the MEMORY_TARGET parameter.

How does one go about setting the value of the MEMORY_MAX_TARGET parameter? It's simple—you just pick a value that's high enough to accommodate not only the current workloads, but also the future needs of the database. Since the MEMORY_TARGET parameter is dynamic, you can alter it on the fly and if necessary, re-allocate memory among multiple instances running on a server. Just be sure that you set the value of the MEMORY_MAX_TARGET parameter to a size that's at least equal to the combined value of the present settings of the SGA_TARGET and the PGA_AGGREGATE_TARGET parameters (if you're migrating from the 10g release). Always make sure to check with your system administrator, so you don't allocate too high an amount of memory for your Oracle instance, which could result in problems such as paging and swapping at the operating system level, which will affect not only your Oracle database, but also everything else that's running on that server.

3-2. Managing Multiple Buffer Pools

Problem

You're using automatic memory management, but have decided to allocate a minimum value for the buffer pool component. You'd like to configure the buffer pool so it retains frequently accessed segments, which may run the risk of being aged out of the buffer pool.

Solution

You can use multiple buffer pools instead of Oracle's single default buffer pool, to ensure that frequently used segments stay cached in the buffer pool without being recycled out of the buffer pool. In order to implement multiple buffer pools in your database, you need to do two things: create two separate buffer pools—the KEEP buffer pool and the RECYCLE buffer pool. Once you do this, you must specify the BUFFER_POOL keyword in the STORAGE clause when you create a segment. For example, if you want a segment to be cached (or pinned) in the buffer pool, you must specify the KEEP buffer pool.

■ **Note** Neither the KEEP nor the RECYCLE pool is part of the default BUFFER CACHE. Both of these pools are outside the default buffer cache.

Here's how you create the two types of buffer pools.

In the SPFILE or the init.ora file, specify the two parameters and the sizes you want to assign to each of the pools:

```
db_keep_cache_size=1000m
db_recycle_cache_size=100m
```

Here's how you specify the default buffer pool for a segment:

```
SQL> alter table employees
     storage (buffer_pool=keep);

Table altered.
SQL>
```

How It Works

Configuring a KEEP buffer pool is an ideal solution in situations where your database contains tables that are referenced numerous times. You can store such frequently accessed segments in the KEEP buffer cache. By doing this, you not only isolate those segments to a specific part of the buffer pool, but also ensure that your physical I/O is minimized as well. How large the KEEP buffer pool ought to be depends on the total size of the objects you want to assign to the pool. You can get a rough idea by summing up the size of all candidate objects for this pool, or you can check the value of the DBA_TABLES view (BLOCKS column) to figure this out.

While we're on this topic, we'd like to point out the counterpart to the KEEP buffer pool—the RECYCLE buffer pool. Normally, the Oracle database uses a least recently used algorithm to decide which objects it should jettison from the buffer cache, when it needs more free space. If your database accesses very large objects once or so every day, you can keep these objects from occupying a big chunk of your buffer cache, and instead make those objects age right out of the buffer cache after they've been accessed. You can configure such behavior by allowing candidate objects to use the RECYCLED buffer pool either when you create those objects, or even later on, by setting the appropriate storage parameters, as shown in the following examples (note that you must first set the DB_RECYCLE_CACHE_SIZE initialization parameter, as shown in the "Solution" section of this recipe.

You can execute the following query to figure out how many blocks for each segment are currently in the buffer cache:

```
SQL> select o.object_name, count(*) number_of_blocks
     from dba_objects o, v$bh v
     where o.data_object_id = v.objd
     and o.owner !='SYS'
     group by o.object_name
     order by count(*);
```

When your database accesses large segments and retrieves data to process a query, it may sometimes age out other segments from the buffer pool prematurely. If you need these prematurely aged-out segments later on, it requires additional I/O. What exactly constitutes a large table or index segment is subject to your interpretation. It's probably safe to think of the size of the object you're concerned with by considering its size relative to the total memory you have allocated to the buffer cache. Oracle figures that if a single segment takes up more than 10% of (non-sequential) physical reads, it's a large segment, for the purpose of deciding if it needs to use the KEEP or RECYCLE buffer pools. So, a handful of such large segments can occupy a significant proportion of the buffer cache and hurt the performance of the database.

If you have other segments that the database accesses, let's say, every other second, they won't age out of the buffer pool since they are constantly in use. However, there may be other segments that will be adversely affected by the few large segments the database has read into its buffer cache. It's in such situations that your database can benefit most by devoting the RECYCLE pool for the large segments. Of course, if you want to absolutely, positively ensure that key segments never age out at all, then you can create the KEEP buffer cache and assign these objects to this pool.

3-3. Setting Minimum Values for Memory

Problem

You're using automatic memory management, but you think that the database sometimes doesn't allocate enough memory for the PGA_AGGREGATE_TARGET component.

Solution

Although automatic memory management is supposed to do what it says—automate memory allocation—there are times when you realize that Oracle isn't allocating certain memory components optimally. You can set a minimum value for any of the main Oracle memory components—buffer cache, shared pool, large pool, Java pool, and the PGA memory. For example, even after specifying automatic memory management, you can specify a target for the instance PGA with the following command, without having to restart the database:

```
SQL> alter system set pga_aggregate_target=1000m;
```

Oracle will, from this point forward, never decrease the PGA memory allocation to less than the value you've set—this value implicitly sets a minimum value for the memory parameter. The database will continue to automatically allocate memory to the various components of the SGA, but first it subtracts the memory you've allocated explicitly to the PGA—in this case, 1,000 MB, from the MEMORY_TARGET parameter's value. What remains is what the database will allocate to the instance's SGA.

How It Works

Ever since Oracle introduced the SGA_TARGET (to automate shared memory management) in Oracle Database 10g and the MEMORY_TARGET parameter (to automate shared memory and PGA memory management) in Oracle Database 11g, some DBAs have complained that these parameters sometimes weren't appropriately sizing some of the components of Oracle memory, such as the buffer cache.

There's some evidence that under automatic memory management, the database could lag behind an event that requires a sudden increase in the allocation to either one of the individual components of the SGA or to the PGA. For example, you may have a spurt of activity in the database that requires a quick adjustment to the shared pool component of memory—the database may get to the optimal shared pool size allocation level only after it notices the events that require the higher memory. As a result, the database may undergo a temporary performance hit. Several DBAs have, as a result, found that automatic memory management will work fine, as long as you set a minimum value for, say, the buffer cache or the PGA or both, by specifying explicit values for the SGA_TARGET and the PGA_AGGREGATE_TARGET initialization parameters, instead of leaving them at their default value of zero. The database will still use automatic memory management, but will now use the specific values you set for any of the memory components as minimum values. Having said this, in our experience, automatic memory management works as advertised most of the time; however, your mileage may vary, depending on any special time-based workload changes in a specific database. At times like this, it's perfectly all right to set minimum values that represent your own understanding of your processing requirements, instead of blindly depending on Oracle's automatic memory algorithms.

3-4. Monitoring Memory Resizing Operations

Problem

You've implemented automatic memory management in your database and would like to monitor how the database is currently allocating the various dynamically tuned memory components.

Solution

Under an automatic memory management mode, you can view the current allocations of memory in any instance by querying the V$MEMORY_DYNAMIC_COMPONENTS view. Querying this view provides vital information to help you tune the MEMORY_TARGET parameter. Here's how you execute a query against this view:

```
SQL> select * from v$memory_target_advice order by memory_size;

MEMORY_SIZE MEMORY_SIZE_FACTOR ESTD_DB_TIME ESTD_DB_TIME_FACTOR    VERSION
----------- ------------------ ------------ ------------------- ----------
        468                .75        43598              1.0061          0
        624                  1        43334                   1          0
        780               1.25        43334                   1          0
        936                1.5        43330               .9999          0
       1092               1.75        43330               .9999          0
       1248                  2        43330               .9999          0

6 rows selected.

SQL>
```

Your current memory allocation is shown by the row with the MEMORY_SIZE_FACTOR value of 1 (624 MB in our case). The MEMORY_SIZE_FACTOR column shows alternate sizes of the MEMORY_TARGET parameter as a multiple of the current MEMORY_TARGET parameter value. The ESTD_DB_TIME column shows the time Oracle estimates it will need to complete the current workload with a specific MEMORY_TARGET value. Thus, the query results show you how much faster the database can process its work by varying the value of the MEMORY_TARGET parameter.

How It Works

Use the V$MEMORY_TARGET_ADVICE view to get a quick idea about how optimal your MEMORY_TARGET allocation is. You need to run a query based on this view after a representative workload has been processed by the database, to get useful results. If the view reports that there are no gains to be had by increasing the MEMORY_TARGET setting, you don't have to throw away precious system memory by allocating more memory to the database instance. Oftentimes, the query may report that potential performance, as indicated by the ESTD_DB_TIME column of the V$MEMORY_TARGET_ADVICE view, doesn't decrease at a MEMORY_SIZE_FACTOR value that's less than 1. You can safely reduce the setting of the MEMORY_TARGET parameter in such cases.

You can also use the V$MEMORY_RESIZE_OPS view to view how the instance resized various memory components over a past interval of 800 completed memory resizing operations. You'll see that the database automatically increases or shrinks the values of the SGA_TARGET and PGA_AGGREGATE_TARGET parameters based on the workload it encounters. The following query shows how to use the V$MEMORY_RESIZE_OPS view to understand Oracle's dynamic allocation of instance memory:

```
SQL> select component,oper_type,oper_mode,parameter, final_size,target_size
     from v$memory_resize_ops

COMPONENT             OPER_TYPE   OPER_MODE   PARAMETER         FINAL_SIZE    TARGET_SIZE
--------------------  ----------  ---------   ---------------   -----------   -----------

DEFAULT buffer cache  GROW        DEFERRED    db_cache_size      180355072     180355072
shared pool           GROW        DEFERRED    shared_pool_size   264241152     264241152
...
20 rows selected.
SQL>
```

The OPER_TYPE column can take two values - GROW or SHRINK, depending on whether the database grows or shrinks individual memory components as the database workload fluctuates over time. It's this ability to respond to these changes by automatically provisioning the necessary memory to the various memory components that makes this "automatic" memory management. The DBA will do well by monitoring this view over time, to ensure that automatic memory management works well for his or her databases.

3-5. Optimizing Memory Usage

Problem

You've set up automatic memory management in your databases and would like to optimize memory usage with the help of Oracle's memory advisors.

Solution

Regardless of whether you set up automatic memory management (AMM) or automatic shared memory management (ASMM), or even a manual memory management scheme, you can use Oracle's Memory Advisors to guide your memory tuning efforts. In this example, we show how to use Oracle Enterprise Manager Database Control to easily tune memory usage. Here are the steps:

1. Go to the Database Home page in Database Control. Click Advisor Central at the bottom of the page.

2. In the Memory Advisors page that appears, click Advice next to the Total Memory Size box under Automatic Memory Management.

The Memory Size Advice graph appears in a separate window, as shown in Figure 3-1. In this graph, the improvement in DB time is plotted against the total memory that you've currently set for the MEMORY_TARGET parameter. The higher the value of improvement in DB time, the better off will be the performance. The graph shows how performance (improvement in DB time) will vary as you change the

`MEMORY_TARGET` parameter value. The total memory you allocate can't be more than the maximum allowed memory for this instance, which is indicated by the dotted straight line in the graph.

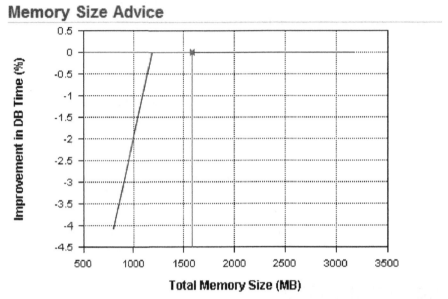

Figure 3-1. *The Memory Size Advice graph in Database Control*

How It Works

When you implement automatic memory management, Oracle automatically adjusts memory between the various components of total memory—the SGA and the PGA—during the course of the instance, depending on the workload characteristics of the instance. Instead of running queries using various views to figure out if your current memory allocation is optimal, you can follow a couple of easy steps to figure things out quickly. You can review the Automatic Database Diagnostic Monitor(ADDM) reports to see if they contain any comments or recommendations about inadequate memory. ADDM recommends that you add more memory to the MEMORY_TARGET parameter, if it considers that the current memory allocation is insufficient for optimal performance.

If the ADDM reports recommend that you increase the size of the MEMORY_TARGET parameter, the next question is by how much you should increase the memory allocation. Oracle's built-in Memory Advisors come in handy for just this purpose. Even in the absence of a recommendation by the ADDM, you can play with the Memory Advisors to get an idea of how an increase or decrease in the MEMORY_TARGET parameter will impact performance.

You can also choose to optimize your PGA memory allocation from the same Memory Advisors page by clicking PGA at the top of the page. In the case of the PGA, in the PGA Target Advice page, the graphs plots the PGA cache hit percentage against the PGA target size. Ideally, you'd want the PGA cache ratio somewhere upward of around 70%. The PGA Target Advice page will help you determine approximately what value you should assign to the PGA_AGGREGATE_TARGET parameter to achieve your performance goals.

3-6. Tuning PGA Memory Allocation

Problem

You've decided to set a specific minimum memory size for the PGA_AGGREGATE_TARGET parameter, although you're using Oracle's automatic memory management to allocate memory. You'd like to know the best way to figure out the optimal PGA memory allocation.

Solution

There are no hard and fast rules for allocating the size of the PGA_AGGREGATE_TARGET parameter. Having said that, if you're operating a data warehouse, you're more likely to need much larger amounts of memory set apart for the PGA component of Oracle's memory allocation. You can follow these basic steps to allocate PGA memory levels:

1. Use a starting allocation more or less by guessing how much memory you might need for the PGA.

2. Let the database run for an entire cycle or two of representative workload. You can then access various Oracle views to figure out if your first stab at the PGA estimation was on target.

How It Works

Although automatic memory management is designed to optimally allocate memory between the two major components of Oracle memory—the SGA and the PGA—it's certainly not uncommon for many DBAs to decide to set their own values for both the SGA and the PGA, either as part of the alternative mode of memory management, automatic shared memory management, wherein you set the SGA_TARGET and the PGA_AGGREGATE_TARGET parameters explicitly to manage memory, or even under the newer automatic memory management system. Unlike the SGA_TARGET parameter, where cache hit ratios could mislead you as to the efficacy of the instance, you'll find that an analysis of the hit ratios for the PGA_AGGREGATE_TARGET parameter are not only valid, but also highly useful in configuring the appropriate sizes for this parameter.

The Oracle database uses PGA memory to perform operations such as sorting and hashing. The memory you allocate to the PGA component is used by various SQL work areas running in the database (along with other users of the PGA memory such as PL/SQL and Java programs). Ideally, you'd want all work areas to have an optimal PGA memory allocation. When memory allocation is ideal, a work area performs the entire operation in memory. For example, if a SQL operation involves sorting operations, under optimal PGA allocation, all of the sorting is done within the PGA memory allocated to that process. If the PGA memory allocation isn't optimal, the work areas make one or more passes over the data—this means they have to perform the operations on disk, involving time consuming I/O. The more passes the database is forced to make, the more I/O and the longer it takes to process the work.

Oracle computes the PGA cache hit percentage with the following formula:

```
Bytes Processed * 100 /(Bytes processed + Extra Bytes Processed)
```

Bytes Processed is the total number of bytes processed by all the PGA memory using SQL operations since the instance started. You should seek to get this ratio as close to 100 as possible—if your PGA cache hit percentage is something like 33.37%, it's definitely time to increase PGA memory allocation by raising the value you've set for the PGA_AGGREGATE_TARGET parameter. Fortunately, the PGA_AGGREGATE_TARGET parameter is dynamic, so you can adjust this on the fly without a database restart, to address a sudden slowdown in database performance due to heavy sorting and hashing activity.

You can issue the following simple query to find out the PGA cache hit percentage as well as a number of PGA performance-related values.

```
SQL>select  * from v$pgastat;
NAME                                    VALUE          UNIT
--------------------------------------  -------------  ----------
aggregate PGA target parameter          570425344      bytes
aggregate PGA auto target               481397760      bytes
total PGA inuse                         35661824       bytes
total PGA allocated                     70365184       bytes
maximum PGA allocated                   195681280      bytes
over allocation count                   0              bytes processed
extra bytes read/written                0              bytes
cache hit percentage                    100            percent
SQL>
```

Since we're using our test database here, the cache hit percentage is a full 100%, but don't expect that in a real-life database, especially if it is processing a lot of data warehouse–type operations!

You can also use the V$SQL_WORKAREA_HISTOGRAM view to find out how much of its work the database is performing in an optimal fashion. If a work area performs its work optimally, that is, entirely within PGA memory, it's counted as part of the OPTIMAL_COUNT column. If it makes one or more passes, it will go under the ONEPASS_COUNT or the MULTIPASS_COUNT columns. Here's a query that shows how to do this:

```
SQL> select optimal_count, round(optimal_count*100/total, 2) optimal_perc,
  2  onepass_count, round(onepass_count*100/total, 2) onepass_perc,
  3  multipass_count, round(multipass_count*100/total, 2) multipass_perc
  4  from
  5  (select decode(sum(total_executions), 0, 1, sum(total_executions)) total,
  6  sum(OPTIMAL_EXECUTIONS) optimal_count,
  7  sum(ONEPASS_EXECUTIONS) onepass_count,
  8  sum(MULTIPASSES_EXECUTIONS) multipass_count
  9  from  v$sql_workarea_histogram
 10* where low_optimal_size > (64*1024))
SQL> /
```

OPTI_COUNT	OPTI_PERC	ONEPASS_CT	ONEPASS_PERC	MULTIPASS_CT	MULTIPASS_PERC
8069	100	0	0	0	0

One pass is slower than none at all, but a multi-pass operation is a sure sign of trouble in your database, especially if it involves large work areas. You'll most likely find that your database has slowed to a crawl and is unable to scale efficiently when the database is forced to make even a moderate amount of multi-pass executions that involve large work areas, such as those that are sized 256 MB to 2 GB. To make sure that you don't have any huge work areas running in the multi-pass mode, issue the following query:

```
SQl> select low_optimal_size/1024 low,
    (high_optimal_size+1)/1024 high,
    optimal_executions, onepass_executions, multipasses_executions
    from v$sql_workarea_histogram
    where total_executions !=0;
```

You can also execute simple queries involving views such as **V$SYSSTAT** and **V$SESSTAT** as shown here, to find out exactly how many work areas the database has executed with an optimal memory size (in the PGA), one-pass memory size, and multi-pass memory sizes.

```
SQL>select name profile, cnt, decode(total, 0, 0, round(cnt*100/total)) percentage
    from (SELECT name, value cnt, (sum(value) over ()) total
    from V$SYSSTAT
    where name like 'workarea exec%');
```

Remember that this query shows the total number of work areas executed under each of the three different execution modes (optimal, one-pass, and multi-pass), since the database was started. To get the same information for a specific period of time, you can use queries involving Automatic Session History (ASH).

You can also view the contents of the Automatic Workload Repository (AWR) for information regarding how the database used its PGA memory for any interval you choose. If you regularly create these reports and save them, you can have a historical record of how well the PGA allocation has been over a period of time. You can also view the ADDM report for a specific time period to evaluate what proportion of work the database is executing in each of the three modes of execution we discussed earlier. In a data warehouse environment, where the database processes huge sorts and hashes, the optimal allocation of the PGA memory is one of the most critical tasks a DBA can perform.

3-7. Configuring the Server Query Cache

Problem

You'd like to set up the server query cache that's part of Oracle's memory allocation.

Solution

You can control the behavior of the server query cache by setting three initialization parameters: RESULT_CACHE_MAX_SIZE, RESULT_CACHE_MAX_RESULT, and RESULT_CACHE_REMOTE_EXPIRATION. For example, you can use the following set of values for the three server result cache-related initialization parameters:

```
RESULT_CACHE_MAX_SIZE=500M        /* Megabytes
RESULT_CACHE_MAX_RESULT=20        /* Percentage
RESULT_CACHE_REMOTE_EXPIRATION=3600       /* Minutes
```

You can disable the server result cache by setting the RESULT_CACHE_MAX_SIZE parameter to 0 (any non-zero value for this parameter enables the cache).

If you set the RESULT_CACHE_MODE initialization parameter to FORCE, the database caches all query results unless you specify the /*+ NO_RESULT_CACHE */ hint to exclude a query's results from the cache. The default (and the recommended) value of this parameter is MANUAL, meaning that the database caches query results only if you use the appropriate query hint or table annotation (explained later).You can set this parameter at the system level or at the session level, as shown here:

```
SQL> alter session set result_cache_mode=force;
```

You can remove cached results from the server result cache by using the FLUSH procedure from the DBMS_RESULT_CACHE package, as shown here:

```
SQL> execute dbms_result_cache.flush
```

How It Works

The server result cache offers a great way to store results of frequently executed SQL queries and PL/SQL functions. This feature is easy to configure with the help of the three initialization parameters we described in the "Solution" section. However, remember that Oracle doesn't guarantee that a specific query or PL/SQL function result will be cached no matter what.

In some ways, you can compare the Oracle result cache feature to other Oracle result storing mechanisms such as a shared PL/SQL collection, as well as a materialized view. Note, however, that whereas Oracle stores a PL/SQL collection in private PGA areas, it stores the result cache in the shared pool as one of the shared pool components. As you know, the shared pool is part of the SGA. Materialized views are stored on disk, whereas a result cache is in the much faster random access memory. Thus, you can expect far superior performance when you utilize the result cache for storing result sets, as opposed to storing pre-computed results in a materialized view. Best of all, the result cache offers the Oracle DBA a completely hands-off mode of storing frequently accessed result sets—you don't need to create any objects, as in the case of materialized views, index them, or refresh them. Oracle takes care of everything for you.

The server query cache is part of the shared pool component of the SGA. You can use this cache to store both SQL query results as well as PL/SQL function results. Oracle can cache SQL results in the SQL result cache and PL/SQL function results in the PL/SQL function result cache. You usually use the server query cache to make the database cache queries that are frequently executed but need to access a large number of rows per execution. You configure the server query cache by setting the following initialization parameters in your database.

- RESULT_CACHE_MAX_SIZE: This sets the memory allocated to the server result cache.

- RESULT_CACHE_MAX_RESULT: This is the maximum amount of memory a single result in the cache can use, in percentage terms. The default is 5% of the server result cache.

- RESULT_CACHE_REMOTE_EXPIRATION: By default, any result that involves remote objects is not cached. Thus, the default setting of the RESULT_CACHE_REMOTE_EXPIRATION parameter is 0. You can, however, enable the caching of results involving remote objects by setting an explicit value for the RESULT_CACHE_REMOTE_EXPIRATION parameter.

Setting the three initialization parameters for the server result cache merely enables the cache. To actually use the cache for your SQL query results, or for PL/SQL function results, you have to either enable the cache database-wide, or for specific queries, as the following recipes explain.

Once the database stores a result in the server result cache, it retains it there until you either remove it manually with the DBMS_RESULT_CACHE.FLUSH procedure, or until the cache reaches its maximum size set by the RESULT_CACHE_MAX_SIZE parameter. The database will remove the oldest results from the cache when it needs to make room for newer results when it exhausts the capacity of the server result cache.

3-8. Managing the Server Result Cache

Problem

You've enabled the server result cache, but you aren't sure if queries are taking advantage of it. You also would like to find out how well the server result cache is functioning.

Solution

You can check the status of the server result cache by using the DBMS_RESULT_CACHE package. For example, use the following query to check whether the cache is enabled:

```
SQL> select dbms_result_cache.status() from dual;

DBMS_RESULT_CACHE.STATUS()
-------------------------------------------------------
ENABLED
SQL>
```

You can view a query's explain plan to check whether a query is indeed using the SQL query cache, after you enable that query for caching, as shown in the following example. The explain plan for the query shows that the query is indeed making use of the SQL query cache component of the result cache.

```
SQL> select  /*+ RESULT_CACHE */ department_id, AVG(salary)
    from hr.employees
    group by department_id;
.
.
.
```

```
-----------------------------------------------------------------
| Id | Operation            | Name                  |Rows
-----------------------------------------------------------------
|  0 | SELECT STATEMENT     |                       | 11
|  1 |   RESULT CACHE       | 8fpza04gtwsfr6n595au15yj4y |
|  2 |    HASH GROUP BY     |                       | 11
|  3 |     TABLE ACCESS FULL| EMPLOYEES             | 107
-----------------------------------------------------------------
```

You can use the MEMORY_REPORT procedure of the DBMS_RESULT_CACHE package to view how Oracle is allocating memory to the result cache, as shown here:

```
SQL> SET SERVEROUTPUT ON
SQL> execute dbms_result_cache.memory_report

R e s u l t   C a c h e   M e m o r y   R e p o r t
[Parameters]
Block Size = 1024 bytes
Maximum Cache Size = 950272 bytes (928 blocks)
Maximum Result Size = 47104 bytes (46 blocks)
[Memory]
Total Memory = 46340 bytes [0.048% of the Shared Pool]
... Fixed Memory = 10696 bytes [0.011% of the Shared Pool]
... State Object Pool = 2852 bytes [0.003% of the Shared Pool]
... Cache Memory = 32792 bytes (32 blocks) [0.034% of the Shared Pool]
....... Unused Memory = 30 blocks
....... Used Memory = 2 blocks
.......... Dependencies = 1 blocks
.......... Results = 1 blocks
.............. SQL = 1 blocks

PL/SQL procedure successfully completed.
SQL>
```

You can monitor the server result cache statistics by executing the following query:

```
SQL> select name, value from V$RESULT_CACHE_STATISTICS;

NAME                         VALUE
--------------------         ----------
Block Size (Bytes)           1024
Block Count Maximum          3136
Block Count Current          32
Result Size Maximum (Blocks) 156
Create Count Success         2
Create Count Failure         0
Find Count                   0
Invalidation Count           0
Delete Count Invalid         0
Delete Count Valid           0
SQL>
```

The `Create Count Success` column shows the number of queries that the database has cached in the server result cache, and the `Invalidation Count` column shows the number of times the database has invalidated a cached result.

How It Works

You can monitor and manage the server result cache with the `DBMS_RESULT_CACHE` package provided by Oracle. This package lets you manage both components of the server result cache, the SQL result cache and the PL/SQL function result cache. You can use the `DBMS_RESULT_CACHE` package to manage the server result cache memory allocation, as well as to bypass and re-enable the cache (when recompiling PL/SQL packages, for example), flush the cache, and to view statistics relating to the server query cache memory usage.

The server result cache is part of Oracle's shared pool component of the SGA. Depending on the memory management system in use, Oracle allocates a certain proportion of memory to the server result cache upon starting the database. Here are the rules that Oracle uses for deciding what percentage of the shared pool it allocates to the server result cache:

- If you're using automatic memory management by setting the `MEMORY_TARGET` parameter, Oracle allocates 0.25% of the `MEMORY_TARGET` parameter's value to the server result cache.

- If you're using automatic shared memory management with the `SGA_TARGET` parameter, the allocation is 0.5% of the `SGA_TARGET` parameter.

- If you're using manual memory management by setting the `SHARED_POOL_SIZE` parameter, the allocation is 1% of the `SHARED_POOL_SIZE` parameter.

In an Oracle RAC environment, you can size the server cache differently on each instance, just as you do with the `MEMORY_TARGET` and other instance-related parameters. Similarly, when you disable the server result cache by setting the `RESULT_CACHE_MAX_SIZE` to 0, you must do so on all the instances of the cluster.

The server result cache can potentially reduce your CPU overhead by avoiding recomputation of results, where data may have to be fetched repeatedly from the buffer cache, which results in a higher number of logical I/Os. When you opt to cache the results in the cache instead of pre-computing them and storing them in materialized views, you can also potentially reduce the database disk I/O as well. Just remember that the primary purpose of the result cache isn't to store just any results in memory—it's mainly designed to help with the performance of queries that involve static or mostly static data. Thus, a data warehouse or decision support system is likely to derive the greatest benefit from this new performance feature.

3-9. Caching SQL Query Results

Problem

You've configured the server result cache in your database. You would now like to configure a set of queries whose result you would like to be cached in the server result cache.

Solution

Set the RESULT_CACHE_MODE initialization parameter to the appropriate value for making queries eligible for caching in the server result cache. You can set the RESULT_CACHE_MODE to the value FORCE, to force all SQL results to be cached by the database. Oracle recommends that you set the RESULT_CACHE_MODE parameter value to MANUAL, which happens to be the default setting. The RESULT_CACHE_MODE parameter is dynamic, so you can set this parameter with the ALTER SYSTEM (or the ALTER SESSION) command.

When you set the RESULT_CACHE_MODE parameter to the value MANUAL, the database caches the results of only specific queries—queries that you enable for caching by using either a query hint or a table annotation. The following example shows how to use the query hint method to specify a query's results to be cached in the server result cache.

```
SQL> select /*+ RESULT_CACHE */ prod_id, sum(amount_sold)
     from  sales
     group by prod_id
     order by prod_id;
```

The query hint /*+RESULT_CACHE */ tells the database to cache the results of the previous query. You can turn off the result caching for this query by using the /+ NO_RESULT_CACHE */ hint, as shown in the following example.

```
SQL> select /*+ NO_RESULT_CACHE */ prod_id, SUM(amount_sold)
     from  sales
     group by prod_id
     order by prod_id;
```

When you run this query, the server won't cache the results of this query any longer, because you've specified the MANUAL setting for the RESULT_CACHE_MODE initialization parameter.

The alternative way to specify the caching of a query's results is to use the table annotation method. Under this method, you specify the RESULT_CACHE attribute when you create a table or alter it. You can annotate a CREATE TABLE or ALTER TABLE statement with the RESULT_CACHE attribute in two different modes: DEFAULT or FORCE, as shown in the following examples:

```
SQL> create table stores (...) RESULT_CACHE (MODE DEFAULT);
SQL> alter table stores RESULT_CACHE (MODE FORCE);
```

We explain the implications of setting the RESULT_CACHE_MODE initialization parameter to FORCE in the "How it Works" section.

How It Works

If you set the value of the RESULT_CACHE_MODE parameter to FORCE, Oracle executes all subsequent queries only once. Upon subsequent executions of those queries, the database retrieves the results from the cache. Obviously, you don't want to store the results of each and every SQL statement, because of the performance implications, as well as the fact that the server result cache may run out of room. Thus Oracle recommends that you specify the MANUAL setting for the RESULT_CACHE_MODE parameter.

If you can set the result caching behavior with the use of SQL hints, why use table annotations? Table annotations are an easy way to specify caching without having to modify the application queries directly by adding the SQL hints. It's easier to simply issue an ALTER TABLE statement for a set of tables, to enable the caching of several queries that use that set of tables. Note that when you annotate a table, those annotations apply to the entire query, but not for fragments of that query.

If you annotate a table *and* specify a SQL hint for query caching, which method will Oracle choose to determine whether to cache a query's results? Query hints are given precedence by the database over table annotations. However, the relationship between SQL hints and table annotations is complex, and whether the database caches a query's results also depends on the specific value of the table annotation, as summarized in the following discussion.

Table Annotations and Query Hints

As mentioned earlier, you can use both SQL hints and table annotations to specify which query results you want the result cache to store, with hints overriding annotations. Use either the ALTER TABLE or the CREATE TABLE statements to annotate tables with the result cache mode. Here's the syntax for a CREATE or ALTER TABLE statement when annotating a table or a set of tables:

```
CREATE|ALTER TABLE [<schema>.]<table> ... [RESULT_CACHE (MODE {FORCE|DEFAULT})]
```

Note the following important points about table annotations:

- The mode value DEFAULT is, of course, the default value, and this merely removes any table annotations you may have set and doesn't permit caching of results that involve this table.

- If you set at least one table to the DEFAULT mode, any query involving that table won't be allowed to store its results in the cache.

- If you set all the tables in a query to the FORCE mode, Oracle will always consider that query for caching—unless you turn off the caching with the NO_RESULT_CACHE hint within the query.

- If you set at least one table in a query to DEFAULT by annotating a CREATE TABLE statement, as shown here, Oracle caches results of this query only if you've either set the RESULT_CACHE_MODE parameter to FORCE or specified the RESULT_CACHE hint.

```
SQL> CREATE TABLE sales (id number) RESULT_CACHE (MODE DEFAULT);
```

Note that the previous statement is equivalent to the following statement, because the default value of the attribute RESULT_CACHE is DEFAULT.

```
SQL> CREATE TABLE sales (id number);
```

You can check that the database created the table SALES with the RESULT_CACHE attribute set to the value DEFAULT:

```
SQL> select table_name, result_cache from user_tables where table_name ='SALES';

TABLE_NAME                   RESULT_
---------------------------- -------
SALES                        DEFAULT

SQL>
```

If you specify the table creation statement with the RESULT_CACHE(MODE FORCE) option, this will prevail over the MANUAL setting of the RESULT_CACHE_MODE initialization parameter that you've set at the session level. The following example illustrates how this works.

1. First alter the table STORES to specify the RESULT_CACHE attribute with the MODE FORCE option:

   ```
   SQL> alter table stores result_cache (mode force);
   ```

2. Then ensure that you've set the RESULT_CACHE_MODE initialization parameter to the value MANUAL.

3. Then execute the following query:

   ```
   SQL> select prod_id, sum(amount_sold)
        from stores
        group by prod_id
        having prod_id=999;
   ```

On subsequent executions, the database will retrieve the results for the preceding query from the server result cache. The reason this is so is that when you specify the RESULT_CACHE (MODE FORCE) annotation, it overrides the MANUAL setting for the RESULT_CACHE_MODE parameter. Remember that when you set this parameter to the MANUAL mode, Oracle will cache query results only if you specify a query hint or annotation. The query shown here doesn't involve the use of a hint, but its results are cached because the RESULT_CACHE (MODE FORCE) annotation makes the database behave the same way as it does when the RESULT_CACHE_MODE parameter is set to FORCE—it caches the query results of all eligible queries.

Query hints, however, ultimately trump the RESULT_CACHE (MODE FORCE) annotation, as shown in the following example.

First alter the table STORES to specify the RESULT_CACHE attribute with the MODE FORCE option:

```
SQL> alter table stores result_cache (mode force);
```

Ensure that you've set the RESULT_CACHE_MODE initialization parameter to the value MANUAL.
Execute the following query:

```
SQL>select /*+ no_result_cache */ *
    from stores
    order by time_id desc;
```

In this example, even though you've annotated the STORES table to allow caching with the MODE FORCE option, the /*+ no_result_cache */ hint overrides the annotation and prevents the caching of the results of any query that involves the STORES table.

Requirements for Using the Result Cache

There are a few read consistency requirements that a query must satisfy, in order for the database to use the result cache:

- In cases involving a snapshot, if a read-consistent snapshot builds a result, it must retrieve the latest committed state of the data, or the query must use a flashback query to point to a specific point in time.

- Whenever a session transaction is actively referencing the tables or views in a query, the database won't cache the results from this query for read consistency purposes.

In addition to the read consistency requirements for result caching, the following objects or functions, when present in a query, make that query ineligible for caching:

- CURRVAL and NEXTVAL pseudo columns

- The CURRENT_DATE, CURRENT_TIMESTAMP, USERENV_CONTEXT, SYS_CONTEXT (with non-constant variables), SYSDATE, and SYS_TIMESTAMP

- Temporary tables

- Tables owned by SYS and SYSTEM

3-10. Caching Client Result Sets

Problem

You use a lot of OCI applications that involve repetitive queries. You would like to explore how you can cache the result sets on the client.

Solution

You can enable client-side query caching of SQL query results by enabling the client result cache. The client result cache works similarly to the server result cache in many ways, but is separate from the server cache. You set the client result cache by setting the following initialization parameters:

- CLIENT_RESULT_CACHE_SIZE: To enable the client result cache, set this parameter to 32 KB or higher, up to a maximum of 2 GB. By default, this parameter is set to zero, meaning the client query cache is disabled. Unlike in the case of the server result cache, the CLIENT_RESULT_CACHE_SIZE parameter value sets the maximum size of result set cache per process, not for the entire instance. Since this parameter isn't a dynamic one, a reset requires that you bounce the instance. You have to determine the size of this parameter based on the potential number of results that'll be cached, as well as the average size of the result set, which depends both on the size of the rows and the number of rows in the result set.

■ **Tip** Oracle cautions you not to set the CLIENT_RESULT_CACHE_SIZE during database creation, due to potential errors.

- CLIENT_RESULT_CACHE_LAG: This parameter lets you specify the maximum amount of time the client result cache can fall behind a change that affects the result set values. By default, the value of this parameter is set to 3,000 milliseconds, so you can omit this parameter if this time interval is adequate for you. Changes in this parameter also need a restart of the database, because it's a static parameter.

■ **Note**   You can use the client query cache with all OCI applications and drivers built using OCI.

In addition, you must specify the value of the initialization parameter `COMPATIBLE` at 11.0.0 or higher to enable the client result cache. If you want to cache views on the client side, the value of the `COMPATIBLE` parameter must be 11.2.0.0 or higher.

In addition to the initialization parameters you must set on the database server, Oracle lets you also include an optional client-side configuration file to specify values that override the values of the client query cache–related parameters in the initialization file. If you specify any of these parameters, the value of that parameter will override the value of the corresponding parameter in the server initialization file. You can specify one or more of the following parameters in the optional client configuration file, which you can include in the `sqlnet.ora` file on the client:

> `OCI_RESULT_CACHE_MAX_SIZE`: Maximum size (in bytes) for the query cache for each individual process
>
> `OCI_RESULT_CACHE_MAX_RSET_SIZE`: Maximum size of a result set in bytes in any process
>
> `OCI_RESULT_CACHE_MAX_RSET_ROWS`: Maximum size of the result set in terms of rows, in any process

You can't set any query cache lag–related parameters in the client-side file. Once you set the appropriate initialization parameters and the optional client-side configuration file, you must enable and disable queries for caching with either the `/*+ result_cache +/` (and the `/*+ no_result_cache +/`) hint, or table annotations. Once you do this, the database will attempt to cache all eligible queries in the client query cache.

How It Works

You can deploy client-side query result caching to speed up the responses of queries that your database frequently executes in an OCI application. The database keeps the result set data consistent with any database changes, including session changes. You can potentially see a huge performance improvement for repetitive queries because the database retrieves the results from the local OCI client process rather than having to re-access the server via the network and re-execute the same query there and fetch those results. When an OCI application issues an `OCIStmtExecute()` or `OCIStmtFetch()` call, Oracle processes those calls locally on the client, if the query results are already cached in the client query cache.

The big advantage of using a client-side query cache is that it conserves your server memory usage and helps you scale up your applications to serve more processes. The client query cache is organized on a per-process basis rather than a per-session basis. Multiple client sessions can share the same cached result sets, all of which can concurrently access the same result sets through multiple threads and multiple statements. The cache automatically invalidates the cached result sets if an OCI process finds significant database changes on the database server. Once a result set is invalidated, the query will be executed again and a fresh result set is stored in the cache.

■ **Tip**   Oracle recommends that you use client-side caching only for read-only or mostly read-only queries.

You can optionally set the RESULT_CACHE_MODE parameter (see Recipe 3-7) to control caching behavior, but by default, this parameter is set to the value MANUAL, so you can leave it alone. You really don't want to set this parameter to its alternative value FORCE, which compels the database to cache the results of every eligible SQL query—obviously, the cache will run out of room before too long! You can then specify either the appropriate query hint at the SQL level or table annotations at the table level to control the client-side result caching. What if you've already set up server-side result caching through the server query cache? No matter. You can still enable client result caching. Just remember that by default, client-side caching is disabled and server-side result caching is enabled.

When implementing client query caching, it's important that an OCIStmtExecute() call is made so a statement handle can match a cached result. The very first OCIStmtExecute() call for an OCI statement handle goes to the server regardless of the existence of a cached result set. Subsequent OCIStmtExecute() calls will use the cached results if there's a match. Similarly, only the first OCIStmtFetch() call fetches rows until it gets the "Data Not Found" error—subsequent fetch calls don't need to fetch the data until they get this error, if the call matches the cached result set. Oracle recommends that your OCI applications either cache OCI statements or use statement caching for OCI statement handles, so they can return OCI statements that have already been executed. The cached set allows multiple accesses from OCI statement handles from single or multiple sessions.

As with the server-side cache, you can set the RESULT_CACHE_MODE parameter to FORCE to specify query caching for all queries. Oracle recommends you set this parameter to the alternative value of MANUAL and use SQL hints (/*+ result_cache */) in the SQL code the application passes to the OCIStmtPrepare(), and OCIStmtPrepare2() calls. You can also use table annotations, as explained in Recipe 3-7, to specify caching when you create or alter a table. All queries that include that table will follow the caching specifications subsequently.

You can query the V$CLIENT_RESULT_CACHE_STATS view for details such as the number of cached result sets, number of cached result sets invalidated, and the number of cache misses. The statistic Create Count Success, for example, shows the number of cached result sets the database didn't validate before caching all rows of the result set. The statistic Create Count Failure shows the number of the cached result sets that didn't fetch all rows in the result set.

3-11. Caching PL/SQL Function Results

Problem

You've set up a server query cache in your database and would like to implement the caching of certain PL/SQL function results.

Solution

Oracle's server query cache (Recipe 3-7) helps you cache both normal SQL query results as well as PL/SQL function results. By using the server result cache, you can instruct the database to cache the results of PL/SQL functions in the SGA. Other sessions can use these cached results, just as they can use cached query results with the query result cache. Once you've configured the server query cache by setting the appropriate initialization parameters (please see Recipe 3-7), you are ready to make use of this feature.

You must specify the RESULT_CACHE clause inside a function to make the database cache the function's results in the PL/SQL function result cache. When a session invokes a function after you enable caching, it first checks to see if the cache holds results for the function with identical parameter values. If so, it fetches the cached results and doesn't have to execute the function body. Note that if you declare a function first, you must also specify the RESULT_CACHE clause in the function declaration, in addition to specifying the clause within the function itself.

Listing 3-1 shows how to cache a PL/SQL function's results.

Listing 3-1. Creating a PL/SQL Function with the /*+result_cache*/ Hint

```
SQL> create or replace package store_pkg is
       type store_sales_record is record (
       store_name stores.store_name%TYPE,
     mgr_name    employees.last_name%type,
     store_size  PLS_INTEGER
     );
     function get_store_info (store_id PLS_INTEGER)
      RETURN store_info_record
      RESULT_CACHE;
     END store_pkg;
     /
Create or replace package body store_pkg is
     FUNCTION get_store_sales (store_id PLS_INTEGER)
     RETURN store_sales_record
     RESULT_CACHE RELIES_ON (stores, employees)
   IS
     rec   store_sales_record;
   BEGIN
     SELECT store_name INTO rec.store_name
     FROM stores
     WHERE store_id = store_id;
     SELECT e.last_name INTO rec.mgr_name
     FROM stores d, employees e
     WHERE d.store_id = store_id
     AND d.manager_id = e.employee_id;
      SELECT COUNT(*) INTO rec.store_size
     FROM EMPLOYEES
     WHERE store_id = store_id;
      RETURN rec;
   END get_store_sales;
END store_pkg;
/
```

Let's say you invoke the function with the following values:

```
SQL> execute store_pkg.get_store_sales(999)
```

The first execution will cache the PL/SQL function's results in the server result cache. Any future executions of this function with the same parameters (999) won't require the database to re-execute this function—it merely fetches the results from the server result cache.

Note that in addition to specifying the RESULT_CACHE clause in the function declaration, you can optionally specify the RESULT_CACHE RELIES ON clause in the function body, as we did in this example. In this case, specifying the RESULT_CACHE_RELIES_ON clause means that the result cache relies on the tables STORES and EMPLOYEES. What this means is that whenever these tables change, the database invalidates all the cached results for the get_store_info function.

How It Works

The PL/SQL function result cache uses the same server-side result cache as the query result cache, and you set the size of the cache using the RESULT_CACHE_MAX_SIZE and RESULT_CACHE_MAX_RESULT initialization parameters, with the first parameter fixing the maximum SGA memory that the cache can use, and the latter fixing the maximum percentage of the cache a single result can use. Unlike the query result cache, the PL/SQL function cache may quickly gather numerous results for caching, because the cache will store multiple values for the same function, based on the parameter values. If there's space pressure within the cache, older cached function results are removed to make room for new results.

Oracle recommends that you employ the PL/SQL function result cache to cache the results of functions that execute frequently but rely on static or mostly static data. The reason for specifying the static data requirement is simple: Oracle automatically invalidates cache results of any function whose underlying views or tables undergo committed changes. When this happens, the invocation of the function will result in a fresh execution.

Whenever you introduce a modified version of a package on which a result cache function depends (such as in Listing 3-1), the database is supposed to automatically flush that function's cached results from the PL/SQL function cache. In our example, when you hot-patch (recompile) the package store_pkg, Oracle technically must flush the cached results associated with the get_store_info function. However, sometimes the database may fail to automatically flush these results. In order to ensure that the cached results of the function are removed, follow these steps whenever you recompile a PL/SQL unit such as a package that includes a cache-enabled function.

1. Place the result cache in the bypass mode.

   ```
   SQL> execute DBMS_RESULT_CACHE.bypass(true);
   ```

2. Clear the cache with the flush procedure.

   ```
   SQL> execute DBMS_RESULT_CACHE.flush;
   ```

3. Recompile the package that contains the cache-enabled function.

   ```
   SQL> alter package store_pkg compile;
   ```

4. Re-enable the result cache with the bypass procedure.

   ```
   SQL> execute DBMS_RESULT_CACHE.bypass(false);
   ```

■ **Tip**　If you're using both the SQL query cache and PL/SQL function result cache simultaneously, remember that both caches are actually part of the same server query cache. In cases such as this, ensure that you've sized the RESULT_CACHE_SIZE parameter high enough to hold cached results from both SQL queries and PL/SQL functions.

If you're operating in an Oracle RAC environment, you must run the cache enabling and disabling steps on each RAC instance.

Of course, when you bypass the cache temporarily in this manner, during that time the cache is bypassed, the database will execute the function, instead of seeking to retrieve its results from the cache. The database will also bypass the result cache on its own for a function if a session is in the process of performing a DML statement on a table or view that the function depends on. This automatic bypassing of the result cache by the database ensures that users won't see uncommitted changes of another session in their own session, thus ensuring read consistency.

You can use the V$RESULT_CACHE_STATISTICS, V$RESULT_CACHE_MEMORY, V$RESULT_CACHE_OBJECTS, and V$RESULT_CACHE_DEPENDENCY views to monitor the usage of the server result cache, which includes both the SQL result cache as well as the PL/SQL function result cache.

Important Considerations

While a PL/SQL function cache gets you results much faster than repetitive execution of a function, PL/SQL collections (arrays)–based processing could be even faster because the PL/SQL runtime engine gets the results from the collection cache based in the PGA rather than the SGA. However, since this requires additional PGA memory for each session, you'll have problems with the collections approach as the number of sessions grows large. The PL/SQL function is easily shareable by all concurrent sessions, whereas you can set up collections for sharing only through additional coding.

You must be alert to the possibility that if your database undergoes frequent DML changes, the PL/SQL function cache may not be ideal for you—it's mostly meant for data that never changes, or does so only infrequently. Even if you set the RESULT_CACHE_REMOTE_EXPIRATION parameter to a high value, any DML changes will force the database to invalidate the cached PL/SQL function cache result sets.

Oracle will invalidate result cache output when it becomes out of date, so when a DML statement modifies the rows of a table that is part of a PL/SQL function that you've enabled for the function cache, the database invalidates the cached results of that function. This could happen if the specific rows that were modified aren't part of the PL/SQL function result set. Again, remember that this limitation could be "bypassed" by using the PL/SQL function cache in databases that are predominantly read-only.

Restrictions on the PL/SQL Function Cache

In order for its results to be cached, a fuction must satisfy the following requirements:

- The function doesn't use an OUT or an IN OUT parameter.

- An IN parameter of a function has one of these types: BLOB, CLOB, NCLOB, REF CURSOR, Collection Object, and Record.

- The function isn't a pipelined table function.

- The function isn't part of an anonymous block.

- The function isn't part of any module that uses invoker's rights as opposed to definer's rights.

- The function's return type doesn't include the following types: BLOB, CLOB, NCLOB, REF CURSOR, Object, Record, or a PL/SQL collection that contains one of the preceding unsupported return types.

3-12. Configuring the Oracle Database Smart Flash Cache

Problem

Your AWR (Automatic Workload Repository) report indicates that you need a much larger buffer cache. You also notice that the shared pool is sized correctly, and so you can't set a higher minimum level for the buffer cache by reducing the shared pool memory allocation. In addition, you're limited in the amount of additional memory you can allocate to Oracle.

Solution

Depending on your operating system, you can use the new Oracle Database Smart Flash Cache feature, in cases where the database indicates that it needs a much larger amount of memory for the buffer cache. Right now, the Flash Cache feature is limited to Solaris and Oracle Linux operating systems.

Set the following parameters to turn the Flash Cache feature on:

- DB_FLASH_CACHE_FILE: This parameter sets the pathname and the file name for the flash cache. The file name you specify will hold the flash cache. You must use a flash device for the flash cache file, and it could be located in the operating system file system, a raw disk, or an Oracle ASM disk group—for example:

```
DB_FLASH_CACHE_FILE= "/dev/sdc"
DB_FLASH_CACHE_FILE = "/export/home/oracle/file_raw"      /* raw file
DB_FLASH_CACHE_FILE = "+dg1/file_asm"                     /* using ASM storage
```

- DB_FLASH_CACHE_SIZE: This parameter sets the size of the flash cache storage. Here's an example:

```
DB_FLASH_CACHE_SIZE = 8GB
```

You can toggle between a system with a flash cache and one without, by using the alter system command as shown here:

```
SQL> alter system set db_flash_cache_size = 0;      /* disables the flash cache
SQL> alter system set db_flash_cache_size = 8G;     /* reenables the flash cache
```

Note that although you can successfully enable and disable the flash cache dynamically as shown here, Oracle doesn't support this method.

■ **Note** If you're using Oracle RAC, in order to utilize the Flash Cache feature, you must enable it on all the nodes of the cluster.

How It Works

Oracle Database Smart Flash Cache, a feature of the Oracle Database 11.2 release, is included as part of the enterprise edition of the database server. Flash Cache takes advantage of the I/O speed of flash-based devices, which perform much better than disk-based storage. For example, small disk-based reads offer a 4-millisecond response, whereas a flash-based device takes only 0.4 milliseconds to perform the same read.

Note that Flash Cache is really a read-only cache—when clean (unmodified) data blocks are evicted from the buffer cache due to space pressure, those blocks are then moved to the flash cache. If they're required later on, the database will move transferred data blocks back to the SGA from the flash cache. It's not always realistic to assume that you and the Oracle database will have access to unlimited memory. What if you can allocate only a maximum of 12 GB for your Oracle SGA, but it turns out that if you have 50 GB of memory, the database will run a whole lot faster? Oracle Database Smart Flash Cache is designed for those types of situations.

Oracle recommends that you size the flash cache to a value that's a multiple of your buffer cache size. There's no hard and fast rule here: use a trial and error method by just setting it to anywhere between one and ten times the size of the buffer cache size and calibrate the results. Oracle also suggests that if you encounter the db file sequential read wait event as a top wait event and if you have sufficient CPU capacity, you should consider using the flash cache.

Once you enable the flash cache, Oracle moves data blocks from the buffer cache to the flash cache (the file you've created) and saves metadata about the blocks in the database buffer cache. Depending on the number of blocks moved into the flash cache, you may want to bump up the size of the MEMORY_TARGET parameter so the accumulated metadata doesn't impact the amount of memory left for the other components.

Oracle offers two devices for flash cache storage—Sun Storage F5100 Flash Array and the Sun Flash Accelerator F20 PCIe Card. Since you can specify only a single flash device, you will need a volume manager. It turns out that Oracle ASM is the best volume manager for these devices, based on Oracle's tests.

If you're using the flash cache in an Oracle RAC environment, you must create a separate flash cache file path for each of the instances, and you will also need to create a separate ASM disk group for each instance's flash cache.

Oracle testing of the Database Smart Flash Cache feature shows that it's ideally suited for workloads that are I/O bound. If you have a very heavy amount of concurrent read-only transactions, the disk system could be saturated after some point. Oracle Database Smart Flash Cache increases such a system's throughput by processing more IOPS (I/O per second). Oracle's testing results of this feature also show that response times increased by five times when Smart Flash Cache was introduced to deal with workloads facing significant performance deterioration due to maxing out of their disk I/O throughput. As of the writing of this book, Oracle makes these claims only for workloads that are exclusively or mostly read-only operations. While Oracle is still in the process of testing the flash cache for write-intensive workloads, note that even for read-only operations, the reduced load on your disk system due to using the flash cache will mean that you'll have more I/O bandwidth to handle your writes.

3-13. Tuning the Redo Log Buffer

Problem

You'd like to know how to tune the redo log buffer, as you've reviewed several AWR reports that pointed out that the redo log buffer setting for your production database is too small.

Solution

You configure the size of the redo log buffer by setting the value of the initialization parameter LOG_BUFFER. This parameter is static, so any changes to it require a restart of the database. You set the parameter in your init.ora file as follows:

```
log_buffer=4096000
```

You can also change the size of the log buffer, with the following ALTER SYSTEM statement:

```
SQL> alter system set log_buffer=4096000 scope=spfile;

System altered
SQL>
```

The default value of the LOG_BUFFER parameter is way too small for many databases. Oracle states that you don't normally need to set a value larger than 1 MB for this parameter. However, you shouldn't hesitate to raise it to a much larger amount, if it's warranted by circumstances.

How It Works

When the Oracle server processes change data blocks in the buffer cache, those changes are written to the redo logs in the form of redo log entries, before they are written to disk. The redo log entries enable the database to redo or reconstruct the database changes by using various operations such as INSERT, UPDATE, and DELETE, as well as DDL operations. The Oracle redo logs are thus critical for any database recovery, because it's these redo log entries that enable the database to apply all the changes made to the database from a point in time in the past. The changed data doesn't directly go to the redo logs, however; Oracle first writes the changes to a memory area called the redo log buffer. It's the value of this memory buffer that you can configure with the LOG_BUFFER parameter. The Oracle log writer (LGWR) process writes the redo log buffer entries to the active redo log file (or group of files). LGWR flushes the contents of the buffer to disk whenever the buffer is one-third full, or if the database writer requests the LGWR to write to the redo log file. Also, upon each COMMIT or ROLLBACK by a server process, the LGWR process writes the contents of the buffer to the redo log file on disk.

The redo log buffer is a re-usable cache, so as entries are written out to the redo log file, user processes copy new entries into the redo log buffer. While the LGWR usually works fast enough so there's space in the buffer, a larger buffer will always have more room for new entries. Since there's no cost whatsoever to increasing the LOG_BUFFER size, feel free to set it to higher than the suggested maximum of 1 MB for this parameter.

If your database is processing large updates, the LGWR has to frequently flush the redo log buffer to the redo log files even in the absence of a COMMIT statement, so as to keep the buffer no more than a third full. Raising the size of the redo log buffer is an acceptable solution in this situation, and allows the LGWR to catch up with the heavy amount of entries into the redo log buffer. This also offsets a slow I/O system in some ways, if you think the performance of the LGWR process is not fast enough. There are a couple of ways in which you keep the pressure on the redo log buffer down: you can batch COMMIT operations for all batch jobs and also specify the NOLOGGING option where possible, say during regular data loads. When you specify the NOLOGGING option during a data load, Oracle doesn't need to use the redo log files, and hence it also bypasses the redo log buffer as well.

It's fairly easy to tune the size of the LOG_BUFFER parameter. Just execute the following statement to get the current "redo log space request ratio":

```
SQL> select round(t.value/s.value,5) "Redo Log Space Request Ratio"
     from v$sysstat s, v$sysstat t
     where s.name = 'redo log space requests'
     and t.name = 'redo entries'
```

The redo log space request ratio is simply the ratio of total redo log space requests to redo entries. You can also query the V$SYSSTAT view to find the value of the statistic redo buffer allocation retries. This statistic shows the number of times processes waited for space in the redo log buffer:

```
SQL> select name,value from V$SYSSTAT
     where name= 'redo buffer allocation retries';
```

Execute this SQL query multiple times over a period of time. If the value of the "redo buffer allocation retries" statistic is rising steadily over this period, it indicates that the redo log buffer is under space pressure and as a result, processes are waiting to write their redo log entries to the redo log buffer. You must increase the size of the redo log buffer if you continue to see this.

CHAPTER 4

Monitoring System Performance

Monitoring system and database performance is a complex task, and there can be many aspects to managing performance, including memory, disk, CPU, database objects, and database user sessions—just for starters. This chapter zeroes in on using Oracle's Automatic Workload Repository (AWR) to gather data about the activities occurring within your database, and help convert that raw data into useful information to help gauge performance within your database for a specific period of time. Usually, when there are performance issues occurring within a database, it's easy to know when the performance problems are occurring because database activity is "slow" during that given time frame. Knowing this time frame is the starting point to perform the analysis using the AWR information.

The AWR is created automatically when you create your Oracle database, and automatically gathers statistics on the activities occurring within your database. Some of this data is real-time or very near real-time, and some of the data represents historical statistics on these activities. The most current data on active sessions is stored in the Active Session History (ASH) component of the performance statistics repository. The more historical snapshots of data are generally known as the AWR snapshots.

The AWR process captures hourly snapshots by default from Oracle's dynamic performance views, and stores them within the AWR. This gives the DBA the ability to view database activity over any period of time, whether it is a single-hour time frame, up to all activity that is stored within the AWR. For instance, if you have a period of time where your database is performing poorly, you can generate an AWR report that will give statistics on the database activity for only that specific period of time.

The ASH component of the AWR is really meant to give the DBA a more real-time look at session information that is not captured within the AWR snapshots. The session information stored within the ASH repository is data that is sampled every second from the dynamic performance views.

Oracle has had similar information within the database for many years with its predecessors UTLBSTAT/UTLESTAT and Statspack, but the report data hasn't been generated or saved automatically until AWR came along with Oracle 10g. This information can now help monitor your database performance much more easily, whether it be analyzing real-time data on activities currently going on within your database, or historical information that could be days, weeks, or even months old, depending on the configuration of the AWR within your database.

4-1. Implementing Automatic Workload Repository (AWR)

Problem

You want to store historical database performance statistics on your database for tuning purposes.

Solution

By implementing and using the Automatic Workload Repository (AWR) within your database, Oracle will store interval-based historical statistics in your database for future reference. This information can be used to see what was going on within your database within a given period of time. By default, the AWR should be enabled within your database. The key initialization parameter to validate is the STATISTICS_LEVEL parameter:

```
SQL> show parameter statistics_level

NAME                                 TYPE     VALUE
------------------------------------ -------- ------------------------------
statistics_level                     string   TYPICAL
```

This parameter can be set to BASIC, TYPICAL (which is the default), and ALL. As long as the parameter is set to TYPICAL or ALL, statistics will be gathered for the AWR. If the parameter is set to BASIC, you simply need to modify the parameter in order to start gathering AWR statistics for your database:

```
alter system set statistics_level=TYPICAL scope=both;
```

How It Works

The predecessor of AWR, which is Statspack, requires manual setup and configuration to enable the statistics gathering. As stated, there generally is no setup required, unless the STATISTICS_LEVEL parameter has been changed to the BASIC setting. By default, an AWR snapshot is taken every hour on your database, and is stored, by default, for eight days. These are configurable settings that can be modified, if desired. See Recipe 4-2 for information on modifying the default settings of the AWR snapshots.

In addition to simply seeing the value of the STATISTICS_LEVEL parameter, you can also view the V$STATISTICS_LEVEL view to see this information, which has information on the STATISTICS_LEVEL setting, as well as all other relevant statistical components within your database:

```
SELECT statistics_name, activation_level, system_status
FROM v$statistics_level;

STATISTICS_NAME                          ACTIVAT SYSTEM_S
---------------------------------------- ------- --------
Buffer Cache Advice                      TYPICAL ENABLED
MTTR Advice                              TYPICAL ENABLED
Timed Statistics                         TYPICAL ENABLED
Timed OS Statistics                      ALL     DISABLED
Segment Level Statistics                 TYPICAL ENABLED
PGA Advice                               TYPICAL ENABLED
Plan Execution Statistics                ALL     DISABLED
Shared Pool Advice                       TYPICAL ENABLED
Modification Monitoring                  TYPICAL ENABLED
Longops Statistics                       TYPICAL ENABLED
Bind Data Capture                        TYPICAL ENABLED
Ultrafast Latch Statistics               TYPICAL ENABLED
Threshold-based Alerts                   TYPICAL ENABLED
Global Cache Statistics                  TYPICAL ENABLED
Active Session History                   TYPICAL ENABLED
```

```
Undo Advisor, Alerts and Fast Ramp up    TYPICAL ENABLED
Streams Pool Advice                      TYPICAL ENABLED
Time Model Events                        TYPICAL ENABLED
Plan Execution Sampling                  TYPICAL ENABLED
Automated Maintenance Tasks              TYPICAL ENABLED
SQL Monitoring                           TYPICAL ENABLED
Adaptive Thresholds Enabled              TYPICAL ENABLED
V$IOSTAT_* statistics                    TYPICAL ENABLED
Session Wait Stack                       TYPICAL ENABLED

24 rows selected.
```

The type of information that is stored in the AWR includes the following:

- Statistics regarding object access and usage

- Time model statistics

- System statistics

- Session statistics

- SQL statements

The information gathered is then grouped and formatted by category. Some of the categories found on the report include the following:

- Instance efficiency

- Top 5 timed events

- Memory and CPU statistics

- Wait information

- SQL statement information

- Miscellaneous operating system and database statistics

- Database file and tablespace usage information

■ **Note** To use AWR functionality, the following must apply. First, you must be licensed for the Oracle Diagnostics Pack, otherwise you need to use Statspack. Second, the CONTROL_MANAGEMENT_PACK_ACCESS parameter must be set to DIAGNOSTIC+TUNING or DIAGNOSTIC.

4-2. Modifying the Statistics Interval and Retention Periods

Problem

You need to set an interval or retention period for your AWR snapshots to values other than the default.

Solution

By using the DBMS_WORKLOAD_REPOSITORY PL/SQL package, you can modify the default snapshot settings for your database. In order to first validate your current retention and interval settings for your AWR snapshots, run the following query:

```
SQL> column awr_snapshot_retention_period format a40
SQL> SELECT EXTRACT(day from retention) || ':' ||
        EXTRACT(hour from retention) || ':' ||
        EXTRACT (minute from retention)  awr_snapshot_retention_period,
        EXTRACT (day from snap_interval) *24*60+
        EXTRACT (hour from snap_interval) *60+
        EXTRACT (minute from snap_interval) awr_snapshot_interval
FROM dba_hist_wr_control;

AWR_SNAPSHOT_RETENTION_PERIOD   AWR_SNAPSHOT_INTERVAL
-----------------------------   ---------------------
8:13:45                                            60
```

The retention period output just shown is in day:hour:minute format. So, our current retention period is 8 days, 13 hours, and 45 minutes. The interval, or how often the AWR snapshots will be gathered, is 60 minutes in the foregoing example. To then modify the retention period and interval settings, you can use the MODIFY_SNAPSHOT_SETTINGS procedure of the DBMS_WORKLOAD_REPOSITORY package. To change these settings for your database, issue a command such as the following example, which modifies the retention period to 30 days (specified by number of minutes), and the snapshot interval at which snapshots are taken to 30 minutes. Of course, you can choose to simply set one parameter or the other, and do not have to change both settings. The following example shows both parameters simply for demonstration purposes:

```
SQL> exec DBMS_WORKLOAD_REPOSITORY.MODIFY_SNAPSHOT_SETTINGS(retention=>43200, interval=>30);

PL/SQL procedure successfully completed.
```

You can then simply rerun the query from the DBA_HIST_WR_CONTROL data dictionary view in order to validate that your change is now in effect:

```
SQL> /

AWR_SNAPSHOT_RETENTION_PERIOD              AWR_SNAPSHOT_INTERVAL
----------------------------------------   ---------------------
30:0:0                                                        30
```

How It Works

It is generally a good idea to modify the default settings for your database, as eight days of retention is often not enough when diagnosing possible database issues or performing database tuning activities on your database. If you have been notified of a problem for a monthly process, for example, the last time frame that denoted an ordinary and successful execution of the process would no longer be available, unless snapshots were stored for the given interval. Because of this, it is a good idea to store a minimum of 45 days of snapshots, if at all possible, or even longer if storage is not an issue on your database. If you want your snapshots to be stored for an unlimited amount of time, you can specify a zero value, which tells Oracle to keep the snapshot information indefinitely (actually, for 40,150 days, or 110 years). See the following example:

```
SQL> exec DBMS_WORKLOAD_REPOSITORY.MODIFY_SNAPSHOT_SETTINGS(retention=>0);

PL/SQL procedure successfully completed.

SQL> /

AWR_SNAPSHOT_RETENTION_PERIOD            AWR_SNAPSHOT_INTERVAL
---------------------------------------- ----------------------
40150:0:0                                                   30
```

The default snapshot interval of one hour is usually granular enough for most databases, as when there are more frequent or closer to real-time needs, you can use the Active Session History (ASH) information. By increasing the default snapshot interval to greater than one hour, it can actually make it more difficult to diagnose performance issues, as statistics for the increased window may make it harder to distinguish and identify performance issues for a given time period.

4-3. Generating an AWR Report Manually

Problem

You want to generate an AWR report, and know the time frame on which to gather information.

Solution

In order to generate an AWR report, run the `awrrpt.sql` script found under the `$ORACLE_HOME/rdbms/admin` directory. In this example, we needed to enter information for the following:

- Report type (text or html)

- Number of days you want displayed from which to choose snapshots

- The starting snapshot number for the period on which you want to generate a report

- The ending snapshot number for the period on which you want to generate a report

- The name of the report (enter a name if you do not want the default report name and location)

The lines in bold type here denote points where user input is required:

```
$ sqlplus / as sysdba @awrrpt

Current Instance
~~~~~~~~~~~~~~~~~
   DB Id    DB Name      Inst Num Instance
----------- ------------ -------- ------------
 2334201269 ORCL               1 ORCL

Specify the Report Type
~~~~~~~~~~~~~~~~~~~~~~~~~
Would you like an HTML report, or a plain text report?
Enter 'html' for an HTML report, or 'text' for plain text
Defaults to 'html'
Enter value for report_type: text

Type Specified:  text

Instances in this Workload Repository schema
~~~~~~~~~~~~~~~~~~~~~~~~~~~~~~~~~~~~~~~~~~~~~~

   DB Id     Inst Num DB Name      Instance     Host
----------- -------- ------------ ------------ ------------
* 2334201269        1 ORCL         ORCL         ora

Using 2334201269 for database Id
Using             1 for instance number

Specify the number of days of snapshots to choose from
~~~~~~~~~~~~~~~~~~~~~~~~~~~~~~~~~~~~~~~~~~~~~~~~~~~~~~~~~
Enter value for num_days: 7
Listing the last 7 days of Completed Snapshots

                                              Snap
Instance    DB Name       Snap Id   Snap Started       Level
----------- ------------ --------- ------------------ -----
ORCL        ORCL              257 28 May 2011 00:00      2

                              258 28 May 2011 13:39      2
                              259 28 May 2011 15:00      2
                              260 28 May 2011 16:00      2
                              261 28 May 2011 17:00      2
                              262 28 May 2011 18:00      2
                              263 28 May 2011 19:00      2
                              264 28 May 2011 20:00      2
```

```
265  28 May 2011 21:00      2
266  28 May 2011 22:00      2
267  28 May 2011 23:00      2
268  29 May 2011 00:00      2

269  29 May 2011 11:52      2
270  29 May 2011 13:00      2
271  29 May 2011 14:00      2
272  29 May 2011 15:00      2
273  29 May 2011 16:00      2
274  29 May 2011 17:00      2

275  30 May 2011 17:00      2
276  30 May 2011 18:00      2
277  30 May 2011 19:00      2
278  30 May 2011 20:00      2
```

Specify the Begin and End Snapshot Ids
~~~~~~
Enter value for begin_snap: 258
Begin Snapshot Id specified: 258

Enter value for end_snap: 268
End   Snapshot Id specified: 268

Specify the Report Name
~~~~~~~~~~~~~~~~~~~~~~~~~
The default report file name is awrrpt_1_258_268.txt. To use this name,
press <return> to continue, otherwise enter an alternative.

Enter value for report_name: /tmp/awrrpt_1_258_268.txt

Using the report name /tmp/awrrpt_1_258_268.txt

< Output of report is shown across the screen >

End of Report
Report written to /tmp/awrrpt_1_258_268.txt

How It Works

In the foregoing example, note that between some of the snapshots listed there is a blank line. Since we are getting information based on the dynamic performance views of the data dictionary, you cannot specify a snapshot period that spans bounces of the database instance, as all statistics in the dynamic performance views are lost when a database instance is shut down. Therefore, choose a snapshot period only for the life of an instance; otherwise you can experience the following error:

```
Enter value for begin_snap: 274
Begin Snapshot Id specified: 274

Enter value for end_snap: 275
End   Snapshot Id specified: 275

declare
*
ERROR at line 1:
ORA-20200: The instance was shutdown between snapshots 274 and 275
ORA-06512: at line 42
```

Although it is recommended to use the `awrrpt.sql` script to generate the desired AWR report, you can manually use the `AWR_REPORT_TEXT` or `AWR_REPORT_HTML` functions within the `DBMS_WORKLOAD_REPOSITORY` package to generate an AWR report, if needed. You need to also have your database's DBID and instance number handy as well when running either of these functions. See the following for an example:

```
SELECT  dbms_workload_repository.awr_report_text
        (l_dbid=>2334201269,l_inst_num=>1,l_bid=>258,l_eid=>268)
FROM dual;
```

4-4. Generating an AWR Report via Enterprise Manager

Problem

You want to generate an AWR report from within Enterprise Manager.

Solution

Within Enterprise Manager, depending on your version, the manner in which to generate an AWR report may differ. There is also generally more than one way to generate an AWR report. In Figure 4-1, this particular screen shows that you enter the beginning and ending snapshot ranges, and after you click the Generate Report button, an AWR HTML report will immediately be displayed within your browser window. A sample screen of the resulting AWR report is shown in Figure 4-2.

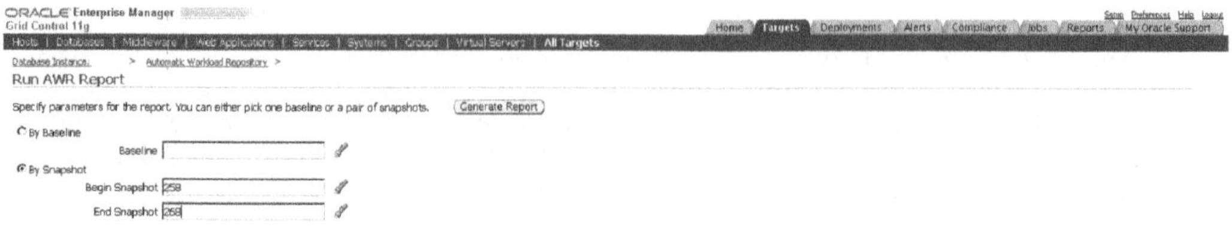

Figure 4-1. Generating an AWR report within Enterprise Manager

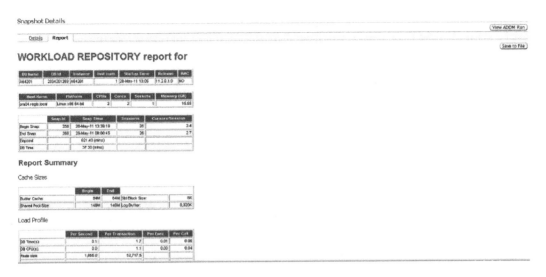

Figure 4-2. *HTML AWR report*

How It Works

The AWR report via Enterprise Manager can be generated if you have Database Control configured, or if you are using Grid Control. You need to be licensed for the Oracle Diagnostics Pack in order to be able to use this feature.

4-5. Generating an AWR Report for a Single SQL Statement

Problem

You want to see statistics for a single SQL statement, and do not want all other associated statistics generated from an AWR report.

Solution

You can run the `awrsqrpt.sql` script, which is very similar to `awrrpt.sql`. You will be prompted for all of the same information, except you will have an additional prompt for a specific SQL ID value—for example:

```
Specify the SQL Id
~~~~~~~~~~~~~~~~~~~
Enter value for sql_id: 5z1b3z8rhutn6
SQL ID specified:  5z1b3z8rhutn6
```

The resulting report zeroes in on information specifically for your SQL statement, including CPU Time, Disk Reads, and Buffer Gets. It also gives a detailed execution plan for review. See the following snippet from the report:

```
Stat Name                          Statement   Per Execution % Snap
---------------------------------  ----------  -------------- -------
Elapsed Time (ms)                     210,421       105,210.3    9.4
CPU Time (ms)                          22,285        11,142.3    1.6
Executions                                  2             N/A    N/A
Buffer Gets                         1,942,525       971,262.5   12.5
Disk Reads                          1,940,578       970,289.0   14.0
Parse Calls                                 9             4.5    0.0
Rows                                        0             0.0    N/A
User I/O Wait Time (ms)               195,394             N/A    N/A
Cluster Wait Time (ms)                      0             N/A    N/A
Application Wait Time (ms)                   0             N/A    N/A
Concurrency Wait Time (ms)                   0             N/A    N/A
Invalidations                                0             N/A    N/A
Version Count                                2             N/A    N/A
Sharable Mem(KB)                            22             N/A    N/A
```

Execution Plan

```
----------------------------------------------------------------------------------------------
| Id | Operation             | Name      | Rows  | Bytes | Cost (%CPU)| Time     |PQ Dis
----------------------------------------------------------------------------------------------
|  0 | SELECT STATEMENT      |           |       |       | 73425 (100)|          |
|  1 |  PX COORDINATOR       |           |       |       |            |          |
|  2 |   PX SEND QC (RANDOM)| :TQ10000   |     1 |    39 | 73425  (1)| 00:14:42 | P->S
|  3 |    PX BLOCK ITERATOR  |           |     1 |    39 | 73425  (1)| 00:14:42 | PCWC
|  4 |     TABLE ACCESS FULL| EMPPART    |     1 |    39 | 73425  (1)| 00:14:42 | PCWP
----------------------------------------------------------------------------------------------
```

Full SQL Text

```
SQL ID        SQL Text
------------  --------------------------------------------------------------------
5z1b3z8rhutn  /* SQL Analyze(98, 0) */ select * from emppart where empno > 12345
```

How It Works

Utilizing this feature is a handy way to get historical statistics for a given SQL statement. For current statements, you can continue to use other mechanisms such as AUTOTRACE, but after a SQL statement has been run, using the awrsqrpt.sql script provides an easy mechanism to help analyze past run statements and help retroactively tune poorly performing SQL statements.

4-6. Creating a Statistical Baseline for Your Database

Problem

You want to establish baseline statistics that represent a normal view of database operations.

Solution

You can create AWR baselines in order to establish a saved workload view for your database, which can be used later for comparison to other AWR snapshots. The purpose of a baseline is to establish a normal workload view of your database for a predefined time period. Performance statistics for an AWR baseline are saved in your database, and are not purged automatically. There are two types of baselines—fixed and moving.

Fixed Baselines

The most common type of baseline is called a fixed baseline. This is a single, static view that is meant to represent a normal system workload. To manually create an AWR baseline, you can use the `CREATE_BASELINE` procedure of the `DBMS_WORKLOAD_REPOSITORY` PL/SQL package. The following example illustrates how to create a baseline based on a known begin and end date and time for which the baseline will be created:

```
SQL> exec dbms_workload_repository.create_baseline -
    (to_date('2011-06-01:00:00:00','yyyy-mm-dd:hh24:mi:ss'), -
    to_date('2011-06-01:06:00:00','yyyy-mm-dd:hh24:mi:ss'),'Batch Baseline #1');

PL/SQL procedure successfully completed.
```

For the foregoing baseline, we want to establish a normal workload for a data warehouse batch window, which is between midnight and 6 a.m. This baseline will be held indefinitely unless explicitly dropped (see Recipe 4-7 for managing AWR baselines). Any fixed baseline you create stays in effect until a new baseline is created. If you want to have a set expiration for a baseline, you can simply specify the retention period for a baseline when creating it by using the `EXPIRATION` parameter, which is specified in days:

```
exec dbms_workload_repository.create_baseline( -
start_time=>to_date('2011-06-01:00:00:00','yyyy-mm-dd:hh24:mi:ss'), -
end_time=>to_date('2011-06-01:06:00:00','yyyy-mm-dd:hh24:mi:ss'), -
baseline_name=>'Batch Baseline #1', -
expiration=>30);
```

You can also create a baseline based on already created AWR snapshot IDs. In order to do this, you could run the `CREATE_BASELINE` procedure as follows:

```
exec dbms_workload_repository.create_baseline( -
start_snap_id=>258,end_snap_id=>268,baseline_name=>'Batch Baseline #1', -
expiration=>30);
```

Moving Baselines

Like the fixed baseline, the moving baseline is used to capture metrics over a period of time. The big difference is the metrics for moving baselines are captured based on the entire AWR retention period. For instance, the default AWR retention is eight days (see Recipe 4-2 on changing the AWR retention period). These metrics, also called adaptive thresholds, are captured based on the entire eight-day window. Furthermore, the baseline changes with each passing day, as the AWR window for a given database moves day by day. Because of this, the metrics over a given period of time can change as a database evolves and performance loads change over time. A default moving baseline is automatically created—the SYSTEM_MOVING_BASELINE. It is recommended to increase the default AWR retention period, as this may give a more complete set of metrics on which to accurately analyze performance. The maximum size of the moving window is the AWR retention period. To modify the moving window baseline, use the MODIFY_BASELINE_WINDOW_SIZE procedure of the DBMS_WORKLOAD_REPOSITORY package, as in the following example:

```
SQL> exec dbms_workload_repository.modify_baseline_window_size(30);

PL/SQL procedure successfully completed.
```

How It Works

Setting the AWR retention period is probably the most important thing to configure when utilizing the moving baseline, as all adaptive threshold metrics are based on information from the entire retention period. When setting the retention period for the moving baseline, remember again that it cannot exceed the AWR retention period, else you may get the following error:

```
SQL> exec dbms_workload_repository.modify_baseline_window_size(45);
BEGIN dbms_workload_repository.modify_baseline_window_size(45); END;
*
ERROR at line 1:
ORA-13541: system moving window baseline size (3888000) greater than retention
(2592000)
ORA-06512: at "SYS.DBMS_WORKLOAD_REPOSITORY", line 686
ORA-06512: at line 1
```

If you set your AWR retention to an unlimited value, there still is an upper bound to the moving baseline retention period, and you could receive the following error if you set your moving baseline retention period too high, and your AWR retention period is set to unlimited:

```
exec dbms_workload_repository.modify_baseline_window_size(92);
BEGIN dbms_workload_repository.modify_baseline_window_size(92); END;
*
ERROR at line 1:
ORA-13539: invalid input for modify baseline window size (window_size, 92)
ORA-06512: at "SYS.DBMS_WORKLOAD_REPOSITORY", line 686
ORA-06512: at line 1
```

For fixed baselines, the AWR retention isn't a factor, and is a consideration only based on how far back in time you want to compare a snapshot to your baseline. After you have set up any baselines, you can get information on baselines from the data dictionary. To get information on the baselines in your database, you can use a query such as the following one, which would show you any fixed baselines you have configured, as well as the automatically configured moving baseline:

```
SELECT baseline_name, start_snap_id start_id,
       TO_CHAR(start_snap_time, 'yyyy-mm-dd:hh24:mi') start_time,
       end_snap_id end_id,
       TO_CHAR(end_snap_time, 'yyyy-mm-dd:hh24:mi') end_time,
       expiration
FROM dba_hist_baseline
ORDER BY baseline_id;
```

BASELINE_NAME	START_ID	START_TIME	END_ID	END_TIME	EXPIRATION
SYSTEM_MOVING_WINDOW	255	2011-05-27:22:00	358	2011-06-08:22:00	
Batch Baseline #1	258	2011-05-28:13:39	268	2011-05-29:00:00	30

From the foregoing results, the moving baseline includes the entire range of snapshots based on the AWR retention period; therefore the expiration is shown as NULL. You can get similar information by using the SELECT_BASELINE_DETAILS function of the DBMS_WORKLOAD_REPOSITORY package. You do need the baseline_id number to pass into the function to get the desired results:

```
SELECT start_snap_id, start_snap_time, end_snap_id, end_snap_time,
       pct_total_time pct  FROM (SELECT * FROM
       TABLE(DBMS_WORKLOAD_REPOSITORY.select_baseline_details(12)));
```

START_SNAP_ID	START_SNAP_TIME	END_SNAP_ID	END_SNAP_TIME	PCT
258	28-MAY-11 01.39.19.296 PM	268	29-MAY-11 12.00.45.211 AM	100

To get more specific information on the moving baseline in the database, you are drilling down into the statistics for the adaptive metrics. For instance, to see an average and maximum for each metric related to *reads* based on the moving window, you could use the following query:

```
column metric_name format a50
SELECT metric_name, average, maximum FROM
(SELECT * FROM TABLE
(DBMS_WORKLOAD_REPOSITORY.select_baseline_metric('SYSTEM_MOVING_WINDOW')))
where lower(metric_name) like '%read%'
order by metric_name;
```

METRIC_NAME	AVERAGE	MAXIMUM
Average Synchronous Single-Block Read Latency	.159658155	53.8876404
Consistent Read Changes Per Sec	2.99232446	3984.11246
Consistent Read Changes Per Txn	117.812978	239485
Consistent Read Gets Per Sec	202.570936	64677.436
Consistent Read Gets Per Txn	3930.41373	372602.889
Logical Reads Per Sec	224.984307	64690.6884
Logical Reads Per Txn	4512.34119	840030
Logical Reads Per User Call	276.745756	135804
Physical Read Bytes Per Sec	1249601.48	528672777
Physical Read IO Requests Per Sec	6.44664078	2040.73828

```
Physical Read Total Bytes Per Sec                1272159.18  528699475
Physical Read Total IO Requests Per Sec          7.82238122  2042.31792
Physical Reads Direct Lobs Per Sec               .006030572  4.6953047
Physical Reads Direct Lobs Per Txn               .231642268        141
Physical Reads Direct Per Sec                    59.3280451  64535.1513
Physical Reads Direct Per Txn                    602.336945  371825.222
Physical Reads Per Sec                           152.539244  64535.2511
Physical Reads Per Txn                           2966.04803  371831.889
```

4-7. Managing AWR Baselines via Enterprise Manager

Problem

You want to create and manage AWR baselines using Enterprise Manager.

Solution

Using Enterprise Manager, you can easily configure or modify baselines. In Figure 4-3, you can see the window where you can establish or modify your existing baselines, including any fixed baselines, as well as the system moving baseline. To create a new fixed baseline, you would click the Create button, which would navigate you to the screen shown in Figure 4-4, where you can configure your new fixed baseline. Within this screen, you name your baseline, and choose between a snapshot-based or time-based baseline.

Figure 4-3. *Managing baselines within Enterprise Manager*

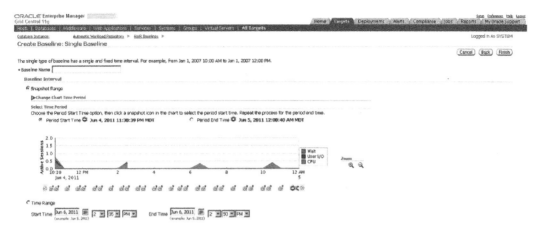

Figure 4-4. *Creating new fixed baseline within Enterprise Manager*

When deciding to modify your existing baselines, the screen options differ between modifying fixed baselines, and modifying the system moving baseline. Figure 4-5 shows the modifiable options for a fixed baseline. As you can see, the only real modification that can be made is the actual baseline name itself. Figure 4-6 shows how to change the moving baseline window within Enterprise Manager. As mentioned before, the actual screens may differ between versions of the Enterprise Manager tool.

Figure 4-5. *Modifying a fixed baseline within Enterprise Manager*

Figure 4-6. *Modifying the moving baseline within Enterprise Manager*

How It Works

For any fixed baseline created or the system moving baseline, you can also simply generate an AWR report based on a particular baseline. Figure 4-1 shows how to generate a snapshot-based AWR report by clicking the By Snapshot button. Using this same screen, you can also generate an AWR report for a baseline simply by clicking the By Baseline button.

If you want to delete a baseline from within Enterprise Manager, simply click the radio button of the baseline you wish to delete, and then click the Delete button, as depicted in Figure 4-7. Figure 4-8 shows how to actually delete the baseline. You can choose to keep or purge the baseline data by clicking the appropriate radio button.

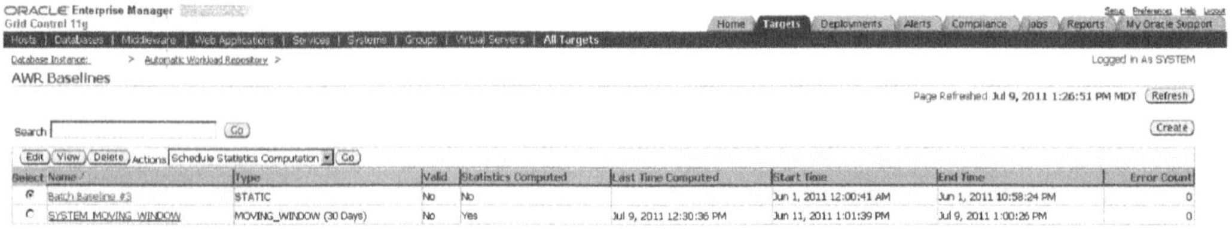

Figure 4-7. *Choosing a baseline to delete*

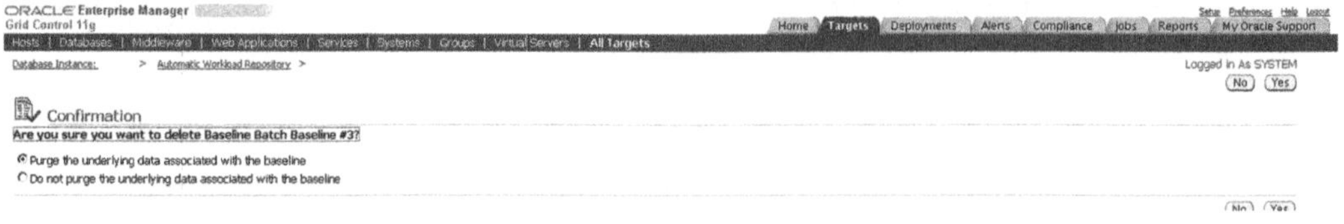

Figure 4-8. *Deleting a baseline*

> ■ **Note** You cannot delete the system moving baseline.

4-8. Managing AWR Statistics Repository

Problem

You have AWR snapshots and baselines in place for your database, and need to perform regular maintenance activities for your AWR information.

Solution

By using the `DBMS_WORKLOAD_REPOSITORY` package, you can perform most maintenance on your baselines, including the following:

- Renaming a baseline
- Dropping a baseline
- Dropping a snapshot range

To rename a baseline, use the `RENAME_BASELINE` procedure of the `DBMS_WORKLOAD_REPOSITORY` package:

```
SQL>  exec dbms_workload_repository.rename_baseline -
    ('Batch Baseline #9','Batch Baseline #10');

PL/SQL procedure successfully completed.
```

To drop a baseline, simply use the `DROP_BASELINE` procedure:

```
SQL> exec dbms_workload_repository.drop_baseline('Batch Baseline #1');

PL/SQL procedure successfully completed.
```

If you have decided you have AWR snapshots you no longer need, you can reduce the number of AWR snapshots held within your database by dropping a range of snapshots using the `DROP_BASELINE` procedure:

```
SQL>  exec dbms_workload_repository.drop_snapshot_range(255,256);

PL/SQL procedure successfully completed.
```

How It Works

In addition to the `DBMS_WORKLOAD_REPOSITORY` package, there are other things you can do to analyze your AWR information in order to help manage all of the AWR information in your database, including the following:

- Viewing AWR information from the data dictionary

- Moving AWR information to a repository in another database location

If you wanted to store AWR information for an entire grid of databases in a single database, Oracle provides scripts that can be run in order to extract AWR information from a given database, based on a snapshot range, and in turn, load that information into a different database.

To extract a given snapshot range of AWR information from your database, you need to run the `awrextr.sql` script. This script is an interactive script, and asks for the same kind of information as when you generate an AWR report using the `awrrpt.sql` script. You need to answer the following questions when running this script:

1. DBID (defaults to DBID of current database)

2. Number of days of snapshots to display for extraction

3. The beginning snapshot number to extract

4. The ending snapshot number to extract

5. Oracle directory in which to place the resulting output file holding all the AWR information for the specified snapshot range; the directory must be entered in upper case.

6. Output file name (defaults to `awrdat` plus snapshot range numbers)

Keep in mind that the output file generated by this process does take up space, which can vary based on the number of sessions active at snapshot time. Each individual snapshot needed for extraction can take up 1 MB or more of storage, so carefully gauge the amount of snapshots needed. If necessary, you can break the extraction process into pieces if there is inadequate space on a given target directory.

In addition, for each output file generated, a small output log file is also generated, with information about the extraction process, which can be useful in determining if the information extracted matches what you think has been extracted. This is a valuable audit to ensure you have extracted the AWR information you need.

Once you have the extract output file(s), you need to transport them (if necessary) to the target server location for loading into the target database location. The load process is done using the `awrload.sql` script. What is needed for input into the load script includes the following:

1. Oracle directory in which to place the resulting output file holding all the AWR information for the specified snapshot range; the directory must be entered in upper case.

2. File name (would be the same name as entered in number 6 of the extraction process (for the `awrextr.sql` script); when entering the file name, exclude the `.dmp` suffix, as it will be appended automatically.

3. Target schema (default schema name is `AWR_STAGE`)

4. Target tablespace for object that will be created (provides list of choices)

5. Target temporary tablespace for object that will be created (provides list of choices)

After the load of the data is complete, the AWR data is moved to the SYS schema in the data dictionary tables within the target database. The temporary target schema (for example, AWR_STAGE) is then dropped.

In order to generate an AWR report generated from one database that is then loaded into a different database, use the AWR_REPORT_TEXT function of the DBMS_WORKLOAD_REPOSITORY package. For example, let's say we loaded and stored snapshots 300 through 366 into our separate AWR database. If we wanted to generate an AWR report for the information generated between snapshots 365 and 366 for a given database, we would run the following command, with the DBID of the originating, source database, as well as the beginning and ending snapshot numbers as follows:

```
SELECT  dbms_workload_repository.awr_report_text
        (l_dbid=>2334201269,l_inst_num=>1,l_bid=>365,l_eid=>366)
FROM dual;
```

4-9. Creating AWR Baselines Automatically

Problem

You want to periodically create baselines in your database automatically.

Solution

You can create an AWR repeating template, which gives you the ability to have baselines created automatically based on a predefined interval and time frame. By using the CREATE_BASELINE_TEMPLATE procedure within the DBMS_WORKLOAD_REPOSITORY package, you can have a fixed baseline automatically created for this repeating interval and time frame. See the following example to set up an AWR template:

```
SQL> alter session set nls_date_format = 'yyyy-mm-dd:hh24:mi:ss';

SQL> exec DBMS_WORKLOAD_REPOSITORY.create_baseline_template( -
>       day_of_week           => 'WEDNESDAY', -
>       hour_in_day           => 0, -
>       duration              => 6, -
>       start_time            => '2011-06-14:00:00:00', -
>       end_time              => '2011-06-14:06:00:00', -
>       baseline_name_prefix  => 'Batch Baseline ', -
>       template_name         => 'Batch Template', -
>       expiration            => 365);

PL/SQL procedure successfully completed.
```

For the foregoing template, a fixed baseline will be created based on the midnight to 6 a.m. window every Wednesday. In this case, this template creates baselines for a normal batch window time frame.

If you are using Enterprise Manager, you can create a template using the same parameters. See Figure 4-9 for an example.

Figure 4-9. *Creating an AWR template*

How It Works

If you need to drop your template, you simply use the DROP_BASELINE_TEMPLATE procedure from the DBMS_WORKLOAD_REPOSITORY package. See the following example:

```
SQL> exec dbms_workload_repository.drop_baseline_template('Batch Template');

PL/SQL procedure successfully completed.
```

If you wish to view information on any templates you have created, you can query the DBA_HIST_BASELINE_TEMPLATE view. See the following sample query:

```
column template_name format a14
column prefix format a14
column hr format 99
column dur format 999
column exp format 999

SELECT template_name, baseline_name_prefix prefix,
to_char(start_time,'mm/dd/yy:hh24') start_time,
to_char(end_time,'mm/dd/yy:hh24') end_time,
substr(day_of_week,1,3) day, hour_in_day hr, duration dur, expiration exp,
to_char(last_generated,'mm/dd/yy:hh24') last
FROM dba_hist_baseline_template;


TEMPLATE_NAME  PREFIX         START_TIME  END_TIME    DAY  HR  DUR  EXP  LAST
-------------- -------------- ----------- ----------- ---  --- ---- ---- -----------
Batch Template Batch Baseline 06/14/11:00 06/14/11:06 WED   0    6  365 06/14/11:00
```

4-10. Quickly Analyzing AWR Output

Problem

You have generated an AWR report, and want to quickly interpret key portions of the report to determine if there are performance issues for your database.

Solution

The AWR report, like its predecessors Statspack and UTLBSTAT/UTLESTAT for earlier versions of Oracle, has a multitude of statistics to help you determine how your database is functioning and performing. There are many sections of the report. The first three places on the report to gauge how your database is performing are as follows:

1. DB Time

2. Instance Efficiency

3. Top 5 Timed Events

The first section displayed on the report shows a summary of the snapshot window for your report, as well as a brief look at the elapsed time, which represents the snapshot window, and the DB time, which represents activity on your database. If the DB time exceeds the elapsed time, it denotes a busy database. If it is a lot higher than the elapsed time, it may mean that some sessions are waiting for resources. While not specific, it can give you a quick view to see if your overall database is busy and possibly overtaxed. We can see from the following example of this section that this is a very busy database by comparing the elapsed time to the DB time:

```
               Snap Id      Snap Time     Sessions Curs/Sess
            --------- ------------------- -------- ---------
Begin Snap:    18033 11-Jun-11 00:00:43       59       2.3
  End Snap:    18039 11-Jun-11 06:00:22       69       2.4
  Elapsed:             359.66 (mins)
  DB Time:           7,713.90 (mins)
```

The instance efficiency section gives you a very quick view to determine if things are running adequately on your database. Generally, most percentages within this section should be above 90%. The Parse CPU to Parse Elapsd metric shows how much time the CPU is spending parsing SQL statements. The lower this metric is, the better. In the following example, it is about 2%, which is very low. If this metric ever gets to 5%, it may mean investigation is warranted to determine why the CPU is spending this much time simply parsing SQL statements.

```
Instance Efficiency Percentages (Target 100%)
~~~~~~~~~~~~~~~~~~~~~~~~~~~~~~~~~~~~~~~~~~~~~~~
            Buffer Nowait %:   99.64       Redo NoWait %:   99.99
            Buffer  Hit   %:   91.88   In-memory Sort %:   99.87
            Library Hit   %:   98.92        Soft Parse %:   94.30
           Execute to Parse %:  93.70        Latch Hit %:   99.89
  Parse CPU to Parse Elapsd %:   2.10     % Non-Parse CPU:   99.75
```

The third place to get a quick glance at your database performance is the Top 5 Timed Events section. This section gives you a quick look at exactly where the highest amount of resources are being consumed within your database for the snapshot period. Based on these results, it may show you that there is an inordinate amount of time spent performing full-table scans, or getting data across a network database link. The following example shows that the highest amount of resources is being used performing index scans (noted by "db file sequential read"). We can see there is significant time on "local write wait", "enq: CF - contention", and "free buffer waits", which gives us a quick view of what possible contention and wait events are for our database, and gives us immediate direction for investigation and analysis.

```
Top 5 Timed Foreground Events                      Avg
~~~~~~~~~~~~~~~~~~~~~~~~~~~~~~~                    wait   % DB
Event                        Waits    Time (s)    (ms)   Time Wait Class
---------------------------  -----------  -----------  ------  ------ ----------
db file sequential read      3,653,606     96,468       26    20.8   User I/O
local write wait                94,358     67,996      721    14.7   User I/O
enq: CF - contention            18,621     46,944     2521    10.1      Other
free buffer waits            3,627,548     38,249       11     8.3 Configurat
db file scattered read       2,677,267     32,400       12     7.0   User I/O
```

How It Works

After looking at the DB Time, Instance Efficiency, and Top 5 Timed Events sections, if you want to look in more detail at the sections of a given AWR report, refer to Recipe 7-17 in Chapter 7 for more information. Because the sheer volume of information in the AWR report is so daunting, it is strongly recommended to create baselines that represent a normal processing window. Then, AWR snapshots can be compared to the baselines, and metrics that may just look like a number on a given AWR report will stand out when a particular metric is significantly above or below a normal range.

4-11. Manually Getting Active Session Information

Problem

You need to do performance analysis on sessions that run too frequently or are too short to be available on available AWR snapshots. The AWR snapshots are not taken often enough to capture the information that you need.

Solution

You can use the Oracle Active Session History (ASH) information in order to get real-time or near real-time session information. While the AWR information is very useful, it is bound by the reporting periods, which are by default run every hour on your database. The ASH information has active session information, and is sampled every second from V$SESSION, and can show more real-time or near real-time session information to assist in doing performance analysis on your database. There are a few ways to get active session information from the database:

- Running the canned ASH report

- Running an ASH report from within Enterprise Manager (see Recipe 4-12)

- Getting ASH information from the data dictionary (see Recipe 4-13)

The easiest method to get information on active sessions is to run the `ashrpt.sql` script, which is similar in nature to the `awrrpt.sql` script that is run when generating an AWR report. When you run the `ashrpt.sql` script, it asks you for the following:

- Report type (text or HTML)

- Begin time for report (defaults to current time minus 15 minutes)

- End time for report (defaults to current time)

- Report name

There are many sections to the ASH report. See Table 4-1 for a brief description of each section. See the following snippet from many of the sections of the ASH report. Some sections have been shortened for brevity.

Top User Events   DB/Inst: ORCL/ORCL (Jun 18 12:00 to 12:45)

Event	Event Class	% Activity	Avg Active Sessions
CPU + Wait for CPU	CPU	35.36	1.66
db file scattered read	User I/O	33.07	1.55
db file sequential read	User I/O	21.33	1.00
read by other session	User I/O	6.20	0.29
direct path read temp	User I/O	2.59	0.12

Top Background Events   DB/Inst: ORCL/ORCL (Jun 18 12:00 to 12:45)

Event	Event Class	% Activity	Avg Active Sessions
Log archive I/O	System I/O	12.77	0.68
CPU + Wait for CPU	CPU	6.38	0.34
log file parallel write	System I/O	5.66	0.30
log file sequential read	System I/O	4.91	0.26
log file sync	Commit	1.06	0.06

Top Event P1/P2/P3 Values DB/Inst: ORCL/ORCL (Jun 18 12:00 to 12:45)

Event	% Event	P1 Value, P2 Value, P3 Value	% Activity
Parameter 1	Parameter 2	Parameter 3	
db file scattered read	17.30	"775","246084","16"	0.14
file#	block#	blocks	
Datapump dump file I/O	6.32	"1","32","2147483647"	6.32
count	intr	timeout	
RMAN backup & recovery I/O	5.83	"1","32","2147483647"	5.80
count	intr	timeout	

Top Service/Module   DB/Inst: ORCL/ORCL (Jun 18 12:00 to 12:45)

Service	Module	% Activity	Action	% Action
SYS$BACKGROUND	UNNAMED	31.00	UNNAMED	31.00
	DBMS_SCHEDULER	18.87	GATHER_STATS_JOB	18.87
	Data Pump Worker	18.87	APP_IMPORT	18.87
SYS$BACKGROUND	MMON_SLAVE	1.95	Auto-Flush Slave A	1.42

Top SQL Command Types   DB/Inst: ORCL/ORCL (Jun 18 12:00 to 12:45)

SQL Command Type	Distinct SQLIDs	% Activity	Avg Active Sessions
INSERT	2	18.88	1.00
SELECT	27	2.36	0.12

Top SQL Statements   DB/Inst: ORCL/ORCL (Jun 18 12:00 to 12:45)

SQL ID	Planhash	% Activity	Event	% Event
av2f2stsjfr5k	3774074286	1.16	CPU + Wait for CPU	0.80

```
 select a.tablespace_name, round(sum_free/sum_bytes,2)*100 pct_free from
(select tablespace_name, sum(bytes) sum_bytes from sys.dba_data_files group by t
ablespace_name) a, (select tablespace_name, sum(bytes) sum_free , max(bytes)
 bigchunk from sys.dba_free_space group by tablespace_name) b where a.table
```

Top Sessions   **DB/Inst: ORCL/ORCL** **(Jun 18 12:00 to 12:45)**

```
    Sid, Serial# % Activity Event                            % Event
--------------- ---------- ------------------------------- ----------
User                  Program                      # Samples Active    XIDs
------------------- ------------------------------ ------------------ --------
     365, 3613     18.87 CPU + Wait for CPU                  12.29
D_USER                oracle@oraprod (DW01)        1,755/2,700 [ 65%]     8

                      Datapump dump file I/O                 6.32
                                                   903/2,700 [ 33%]       8

     515, 8721     18.87 db file scattered read             17.26
SYS                   oracle@oraprod (J000)        2,465/2,700 [ 91%]     1
```

Top Blocking Sessions   **DB/Inst: ORCL/ORCL** **(Jun 18 12:00 to 12:45)**

```
   Blocking Sid % Activity Event Caused                     % Event
--------------- ---------- ------------------------------- ----------
User                  Program                      # Samples Active    XIDs
------------------- ------------------------------ ------------------ --------
     549,    1      2.09 enq: CF - contention                2.03
SYS                   oracle@oraprod (CKPT)        248/2,700 [  9%]       0
```

Top DB Objects   **DB/Inst: ORCL/ORCL** **(Jun 18 12:00 to 12:45)**

```
      Object ID % Activity Event                            % Event
--------------- ---------- ------------------------------- ----------
Object Name (Type)                                 Tablespace
---------------------------------------------------- ------------------------
      1837336       3.25 db file scattered read              3.25
STG.EMPPART.EMPPART10_11P (TAB EMP_S

      1837324       3.05 db file scattered read              3.05
STG.EMPPART.EMPPART10_10P (TAB EMP_S
```

Top DB Files   **DB/Inst: ORCL/ORCL** **(Jun 18 12:00 to 12:45)**

```
       File ID % Activity Event                             % Event
--------------- ---------- ------------------------------- ----------
File Name                                          Tablespace
---------------------------------------------------- ------------------------
         200       6.31 Datapump dump file I/O               6.31
/opt/vol01/ORCL/app_s_016.dbf                      APP_S

         ------------------------------------------------------------
```

```
Activity Over Time        DB/Inst: ORCL/ORCL  (Jun 18 12:00 to 12:45)

                          Slot                               Event
Slot Time (Duration)      Count Event                        Count % Event
-------------------       -------- --------------------------- -------- -------
12:00:00   (5.0 min)      2,672 CPU + Wait for CPU            1,789   12.52
                                db file scattered read          290    2.03
                                enq: CF - contention            290    2.03
12:05:00   (5.0 min)      2,586 CPU + Wait for CPU            1,396    9.77
                                RMAN backup & recovery I/O      305    2.14
                                db file scattered read          287    2.01
12:10:00   (5.0 min)      2,392 CPU + Wait for CPU            1,068    7.48
                                Log archive I/O                 423    2.96
                                RMAN backup & recovery I/O      356    2.49
...
                          ----------------------------------------------------------
```

Table 4-1. *ASH Report Section Information for the Specified Report Period*

Section Name	Description
General Report Information	Contains database name, reporting period, CPU and memory information
Top User Events	Displays the top run user events for the reporting period
Top Background Events	Shows the top wait events in the database
Top P1/P2/P3 Events	Lists top wait event parameter values based on highest percentages, ordered in descending order
Top Service Module	Displays the top services or module names
Top Client IDs	Shows the top users
Top SQL Command Types	Shows all the SQL commands run
Top SQL Statements	Displays the top consuming SQL statement text
Top SQL Using Literals	Shows SQL statements using literals; this can assist in determining offending SQL for shared pool contention.
Top PL/SQL Procedures	Displays the PL/SQL programs run
Top Sessions	Displays the top sessions within the database

Section Name	Description
Top Blocking Sessions	Sessions that are blocking other sessions
Top Sessions Running PQs	Sessions running parallel query processes
Top DB Objects	Objects referenced
Top DB Files	Files referenced
Top Latches	Latch information for the reporting period
Activity Over Time	Shows top three consuming events for each five-minute reporting period shown on report

How It Works

Retrieving ASH information is necessary if you need to get session information more current than you can retrieve from the AWR report. Again, AWR information is generated only hourly by default. ASH information is gathered every second from V$SESSION, and stores the most useful session information to help gauge database performance at any given moment.

The ASH information is stored within a circular buffer in the SGA. Oracle documentation states that the buffer size is calculated as follows:

```
Max [Min [ #CPUs * 2 MB, 5% of Shared Pool Size, 30MB ], 1MB ]
```

The amount of time that the information is stored within the data dictionary depends on the activity within your database. You may need to view the DBA_HIST_ACTIVE_SESS_HISTORY historical view in order to get the ASH information you need if your database is very active. For an example of querying the DBA_HIST_ACTIVE_SESS_HISTORY view, see Recipe 4-13. To quickly see how much data is held in your historical view, you could simply get the earliest SAMPLE_TIME from the DBA_HIST_ACTIVE_SESS_HISTORY view:

```
SELECT min(sample_time) FROM dba_hist_active_sess_history;

MIN(SAMPLE_TIME)
---------------------------------------------------------------------
20-MAR-11 11.00.27.433 PM
```

The MMON background process, which manages the AWR hourly snapshots, also flushes ASH information to the historical view at the same time. If there is heavy activity on the database, and the buffer fills between the hourly AWR snapshots, the MMNL background process will wake up and flush the ASH data to the historical view.

The V$ACTIVE_SESSION_HISTORY and DBA_HIST_ACTIVE_SESS_HISTORY views contain much more detailed information than just the samples shown within this recipe, and you can drill down and get much more information at the session level, if desired, including information regarding actual SQL statements, the SQL operations, blocking session information, and file I/O information.

4-12. Getting ASH Information from Enterprise Manager

Problem

You want to get to ASH information from within Enterprise Manager because you use Enterprise Manager for performance tuning activities.

Solution

The ASH report generated from within Enterprise Manager has the same sections as specified in Table 4-1 (see Recipe 4-11). To generate an ASH report from within Enterprise Manager, you generally need to be in the Performance tab, depending on your particular version of Enterprise Manager. As with running the `ashrpt.sql` script, you need to specify the beginning and ending time frames for the report period desired. See Figure 4-10 for an example of the screen used to generate an ASH report, and Figure 4-11 for a sample of the ASH report output:

Figure 4-10. *Generating ASH report from Enterprise Manager*

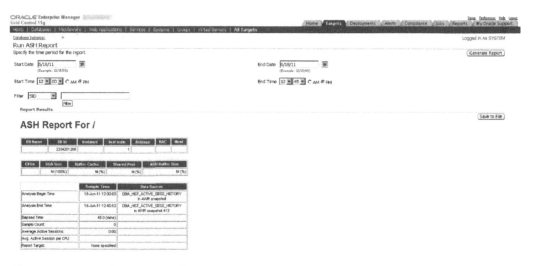

Figure 4-11. *Sample ASH report from Enterprise Manager*

How It Works

When generating an ASH report, you have the option to filter on specific criteria. In Figure 4-12, see the Filter drop-down menu. If you have a very active database, and already want to zero in on a specific SQL_ID, for example, you can choose the SQL_ID option from the Filter drop-down menu, and enter the SQL_ID value. The resulting report will show information based only on the filtered criteria.

The choices to filter on include the following:

- SID

- SQL_ID

- Wait Class

- Service

- Module

- Action

- Client

Many of the foregoing filters can be found in the V$SESSION view. For a list of the possible wait classes, you can query the DBA_HIST_EVENT_NAME view as shown in the following example:

```
SELECT DISTINCT wait_class FROM dba_hist_event_name;

WAIT_CLASS
------------------------------------------------------------
Concurrency
User I/O
Administrative
System I/O
Scheduler
Configuration
Other
Application
Cluster
Network
Idle
Commit
```

Figure 4-12. *Customizing ASH report by filter*

4-13. Getting ASH Information from the Data Dictionary

Problem

You want to see what ASH information is kept in Oracle's data dictionary.

Solution

There are a couple of data dictionary views you can use to get ASH information. The first, V$ACTIVE_SESSION_HISTORY, can be used to get information on current or recent sessions within your database. The second, DBA_HIST_ACTIVE_SESS_HISTORY, is used to store older, historical ASH information.

If you wanted to see all the events and their total wait time for activity within the past 15 minutes in your database, you could issue the following query:

```
SELECT s.event, sum(s.wait_time + s.time_waited) total_wait
FROM v$active_session_history s
WHERE s.sample_time between sysdate-1/24/4 AND sysdate
GROUP BY s.event
ORDER BY 2 desc;
```

```
EVENT                                                            TOTAL_WAIT
--------------------------------------------------------------- ----------
                                                                  20002600
db file scattered read                                            15649078
read by other session                                              9859503
db file sequential read                                             443298
direct path read temp                                               156463
direct path write temp                                              139984
log file parallel write                                              49469
db file parallel write                                               21207
log file sync                                                         11793
```

```
SGA: allocation forcing component growth                           11711
control file parallel write                                         4421
control file sequential read                                        2122
SQL*Net more data from client                                        395
SQL*Net more data to client                                           66
```

If you wanted to get more session-specific information, and wanted to see the top 5 sessions that were using the most CPU resources within the last 15 minutes, you could issue the following query:

```
column username format a12
column module format a30

SELECT * FROM
(
SELECT s.username, s.module, s.sid, s.serial#, count(*)
FROM v$active_session_history h, v$session s
WHERE h.session_id = s.sid
AND    h.session_serial# = s.serial#
AND    session_state= 'ON CPU' AND
       sample_time > sysdate - interval '15' minute
GROUP BY s.username, s.module, s.sid, s.serial#
ORDER BY count(*) desc
)
where rownum <= 5;
```

```
USERNAME    MODULE                           SID    SERIAL#   COUNT(*)
---------- ----------------------------- ---------- ---------- ----------
SYS        DBMS_SCHEDULER                    536          9         43
APPLOAD    etl1@app1 (TNS V1-V3)            1074       3588         16
APPLOAD    etl1@app1 (TNS V1-V3)            1001       4004         12
APPLOAD    etl1@app1 (TNS V1-V3)             968        108          5
DBSNMP     emagent@ora1 (TNS V1-V3)          524          3          2
```

The SESSION_STATE column has two valid values, ON CPU and WAITING, which denote whether a session is active or is waiting for resources. If you wanted to see the sessions that are waiting for resources, you could issue the same query as previously, with a SESSION_STATE of WAITING.

If you wanted to see the most heavily used database objects for a given sample period, you could join V$ACTIVE_SESSION_HISTORY to the DBA_OBJECTS view to get that information. In the following example, we are getting a list of the top 5 database objects in use, along with the event associated with that database object, over the past 15 minutes:

```
SELECT * FROM
(
SELECT o.object_name, o.object_type, s.event,
       SUM(s.wait_time + s.time_waited) total_waited
FROM v$active_session_history s, dba_objects o
WHERE s.sample_time between sysdate - 1/24/4 and sysdate
AND s.current_obj# = o.object_id
GROUP BY o.object_name, o.object_type, s.event
ORDER BY 4 desc
)
```

```
WHERE rownum <= 5;
```

```
OBJECT_NAME              OBJECT_TYPE       EVENT                      TOTAL_WAITED
------------------       ---------------   -------------------------  ------------
WRI$_ALERT_OUTSTANDING   TABLE             Streams AQ: enqueue block   110070196
                                           ed on low memory
APP_ETL_IDX1             INDEX             read by other session        65248777
APP_SOURCE_INFO          TABLE PARTITION   db file scattered read       33801035
EMPPART_PK_I             INDEX PARTITION   read by other session        28077262
APP_ORDSTAT              TABLE PARTITION   db file scattered read       15569867
```

How It Works

The DBA_HIST_ACTIVE_SESS_HISTORY view can give you historical information on sessions that have aged out of the V$ACTIVE_SESSION_HISTORY view. Let's say you had a day when performance was particularly bad on your database. You could zero in on historical session information for a given time frame, provided it is still held within the DBA_HIST_ACTIVE_SESS_HISTORY view. For instance, if you wanted to get the users that were consuming the most resources for a given day when performance was poor, you could issue the following query:

```
SELECT * FROM
(
SELECT u.username, h.module, h.session_id sid,
       h.session_serial# serial#, count(*)
FROM dba_hist_active_sess_history h, dba_users u
WHERE h.user_id = u.user_id
AND   session_state= 'ON CPU'
AND   (sample_time between to_date('2011-05-15:00:00:00','yyyy-mm-dd:hh24:mi:ss')
AND    to_date('2011-05-15:23:59:59','yyyy-mm-dd:hh24:mi:ss'))
AND u.username != 'SYS'
GROUP BY u.username, h.module, h.session_id, h.session_serial#
ORDER BY count(*) desc
)
where rownum <= 5;
```

```
USERNAME      MODULE                         SID     SERIAL#    COUNT(*)
------------  ------------------------  ----------  ----------  ----------
APPLOAD1      etl1@app1 (TNS V1-V3)           1047         317        1105
APPLOAD1      etl1@app1 (TNS V1-V3)           1054         468         659
APPLOAD1      etl1@app1 (TNS V1-V3)           1000         909         387
STG           oracle@ora1 (TNS V1-V3)          962        1707         353
APPLOAD1      etl1@app1 (TNS V1-V3)            837       64412         328
```

To then zero in on the database objects, you could issue the following query for the same time frame:

```
SELECT * FROM
(
SELECT o.object_name, o.object_type, s.event,
       SUM(s.wait_time + s.time_waited) total_waited
FROM dba_hist_active_sess_history s, dba_objects o
```

```
WHERE s.sample_time
between to_date('2011-05-15:00:00:00','yyyy-mm-dd:hh24:mi:ss')
AND    to_date('2011-05-15:23:59:59','yyyy-mm-dd:hh24:mi:ss')
AND s.current_obj# = o.object_id
GROUP BY o.object_name, o.object_type, s.event
ORDER BY 4 desc
)
WHERE rownum <= 5;


OBJECT_NAME                  OBJECT_TYPE     EVENT                     TOTAL_WAITED
---------------------------  --------------- ------------------------- ------------
EMPPART                      TABLE PARTITION PX Deq Credit: send blkd    8196703427
APPLOAD_PROCESS_STATUS       TABLE           db file scattered read      628675085
APPLOAD_PROCESS_STATUS       TABLE           read by other session       408577335
APP_SOURCE_INFO              TABLE PARTITION db file scattered read      288479849
APP_QUALITY_INFO             TABLE PARTITION Datapump dump file I/O      192290534
```

Minimizing System Contention

It's not uncommon for Oracle DBAs to field calls about a user being locked or "blocked" in the database. Oracle's locking behavior is extremely sophisticated and supports simultaneous use of the database by multiple users. However, on occasion, it's possible for a user to block another user's work, mostly due to flaws in application design. This chapter explains how Oracle handles locks and how to identify a session that's blocking others.

Oracle database can experience two main types of contention for resources. The first is contention for transaction locks on a table's rows. The second type of contention is that caused by simultaneous requests for areas of the shared memory (SGA), resulting in latch contention. In addition to showing you how to troubleshoot typical locking issues, we will also show how to handle various types of latch contention in your database.

Oracle Wait Interface is a handy name for Oracle's internal mechanism for classifying and measuring the different types of waits for resources in an Oracle instance. Understanding Oracle wait events is *the* key to instance tuning, because high waits slow down response time. We will explain the Oracle Wait Interface in this chapter and show you how to reduce the most common Oracle wait events that beguile Oracle DBAs. We will show you how to use various SQL scripts to unravel the mysteries of the Oracle Wait Interface, and we will also show how to use Oracle Enterprise Manager to quickly track down the SQL statements and sessions that are responsible for contention in the database.

5-1. Understanding Response Time

Problem

You want to understand what database response time is, and its relationship with wait time.

Solution

The most crucial performance indicator in a database is response time. Response time is the time it takes to get a response from the database for a query that a client sends to the database. Response time is simply the sum of two components:

```
response time = processing time + wait time
```

The foregoing relationship is also frequently represented as R=S + W, where R is the response time, S the service time, and W stands for the wait time. The processing time component is the actual time spent by the database processing the request. Wait time, on the other hand, is time actually wasted by the database—it's the time the database spends waiting for resources such as a lock on a table's rows, library cache latch, or any of the numerous resources that a query needs to complete its processing. Oracle has hundreds of official wait events, a dozen or so of which are crucial to troubleshooting slow-running queries.

Do You Have a Wait Problem?

It's easy to find out the percentage of time a database has spent waiting for resources instead of actually executing. Issue the following query to find out the relative percentages of wait times and actual CPU processing in the database:

```
SQL> select metric_name, value
  2 from v$sysmetric
  3 where metric_name in ('Database CPU Time Ratio',
  4 'Database Wait Time Ratio') and
  5 intsize_csec =
  6 (select max(INTSIZE_CSEC) from V$SYSMETRIC);

METRIC_NAME                        VALUE
-----------------------------      -----------
Database Wait Time Ratio           11.371689
Database CPU Time Ratio            87.831890
SQL>
```

If the query shows a very high value for the Database Wait Time Ratio, or if the Database Wait Time Ratio is much greater than the Database CPU Time Ratio, the database is spending more time waiting than processing and you must dig deeper into the Oracle wait events to identify the specific wait events causing this.

Find Detailed Information

You can use the following Oracle views to find out detailed information of what a wait event is actually waiting for and how long it has waited for each resource.

> V$SESSION: This view shows the event currently being waited for as well as the event last waited for in each session.

> V$SESSION_WAIT: This view lists either the event currently being waited for or the event last waited on for each session. It also shows the wait state and the wait time.

> V$SESSION_WAIT_HISTORY: This view shows the last ten wait events for each current session.

> V$SESSION_EVENT: This view shows the cumulative history of events waited on for each session. The data in this view is available only so long as a session is active.

V$SYSTEM_EVENT: This view shows each wait event and the time the entire instance waited for that event since you started the instance.

V$SYSTEM_WAIT_CLASS: This view shows wait event statistics by wait classes.

How It Works

Your goal in tuning performance is to minimize the total response time. If the Database Wait Time Ratio (in the query shown in the "Solution" section) is high, your response time will also be high due to waits or bottlenecks in your system. On the other hand, high values for the Database CPU Time Ratio indicate a well-running database, with few waits or bottlenecks. The Database CPU Time Ratio is calculated by dividing the total CPU used by the database by the Oracle time model statistic DB time.

Oracle uses *time model statistics* to measure the time spent in the database by the type of operation. Database time, or DB time, is the most important time model statistic—it represents the total time spent in database calls, and serves as a measure of total instance workload. DB time is computed by adding the CPU time and wait time of all sessions (excluding the waits for idle events). An AWR report shows the total DB time for the instance (in the section titled "Time Model System Stats") during the period covered by the AWR snapshots. If the time model statistic DB CPU consumes most of the DB time for the instance, it shows the database was actively processing most of the time. DB time tuning, or understanding how the database is spending its time, is fundamental to understanding performance.

The total time spent by foreground sessions making database calls consists of I/O time, CPU time, and time spent waiting for non-idle events. Your DB time will increase as the system load increases—that is, as more users log on and larger queries are executed, the greater the system load. However, even in the absence of an increase in system load, DB time can increase, due to deterioration either in I/O or application performance. As application performance degrades, wait time will increase and consequently DB time (that is, response time) will increase.

DB time is captured by internal instrumentation, ASH, AWR, and ADDM, and you can find detailed performance information by querying various views or through Enterprise Manager.

■ **Note** If the host system is CPU-bound, you'll see an increase in DB time. You must first tune CPU usage before focusing on wait events in that particular case.

The V$SESSION_WAIT view shows more detailed information than the V$SESSION_EVENT and the V$SYSTEM_EVENT views. While both the V$SESSION_EVENT and the V$SESSION_WAIT views show that there are waits such as the event db file scattered read, for example, only the V$SESSION_WAIT view shows the file number (P1), the block number read (P2), and the number of blocks read (P3). The columns P1 and P2 from this view help you identify the segments involved in the wait event that is currently occurring.

■ **Note** The Automatic Workload Repository (AWR) queries the V$SYSTEM_EVENT view for its wait event–related analysis.

You can first query the **V$SYSTEM_EVENT** view to rank the top wait events by total and average time waited for that event. You can then drill down to the wait event level, by focusing on the events at the top of the event list. Note that you can query the **V$WAITSTAT** view for the same information as well. In addition to providing information about blocking and blocked users and the current wait events, the **V$SESSION** view also shows the objects that are causing the problem, by providing the file number and block number for the object.

5-2. Identifying SQL Statements with the Most Waits

Problem

You want to identify the SQL statements responsible for the most waits in your database.

Solution

Execute the following query to identify the SQL statements that are experiencing the most waits in your database:

```
SQL> select ash.user_id,
  2   u.username,
  3   s.sql_text,
  4   sum(ash.wait_time +
  5   ash.time_waited) ttl_wait_time
  6   from v$active_session_history ash,
  7   v$sqlarea s,
  8   dba_users u
  9   where ash.sample_time between sysdate - 60/2880 and sysdate
 10   and ash.sql_id = s.sql_id
 11   and ash.user_id = u.user_id
 12   group by ash.user_id,s.sql_text, u.username
 13* order by ttl_wait_time
SQL>
```

The preceding query ranks queries that ran during the past 30 minutes, according to the total time waited by each query.

How It Works

When you're experiencing a performance problem, it's a good idea to see which SQL statements are waiting the most. These are the statements that are using most of the database's resources. To find the queries that are waiting the most, you must sum the values in the **wait_time** and the **time_waited** columns of the **V$ACTIVE_SESSION_HISTORY** for a specific SQL statement. In order to do this, you must join the **V$SQLAREA** view with the **V$ACTIVE_SESSION_HISTORY** view, using **SQL_ID** as the join column.

Besides the **SQL_ID** of the SQL statements, the **V$ACTIVE_SESSION_HISTORY** view also contains information about the execution plans used by the SQL statements. You can use this information to identify why a SQL statement is experiencing a high amount of waits. You can also run an Active Session History (ASH) report, using a SQL script or through Oracle Enterprise Manager, to get details about the top SQL statements in the sampled session activity. The Top SQL section of an ASH report helps you identify the high-load SQL statements that are responsible for performance problems. Examining the Top SQL report may show you, for example, that one bad query has been responsible for most of the database activity.

5-3. Analyzing Wait Events

Problem

You want to analyze Oracle wait events.

Solution

Several recipes in this chapter show you how to analyze the most important Oracle wait events. An overwhelming amount of wait time in a database is due to I/O–related waits, such as those caused by either full table scans or indexed reads. While indexed reads may seem to be completely normal on the face of it, too many indexed reads can also slow down performance. Therefore, you must investigate why the database is performing a large number of indexed reads. For example, if you see the `db file sequential read` event (indicates indexed reads) at the top of the wait event list, you must look a bit further to see how the database is accumulating these read events. If you find that the database is performing hundreds of thousands of query executions, with each query doing only a few indexed reads, that's fine. However, if you find that just a couple of queries are contributing to a high number of logical reads, then, most likely, those queries are reading more data than necessary. You must tune those queries to reduce the `db file sequential read` events.

How It Works

Wait events are statistics that a server process or thread increments when it waits for an event to complete, in order to continue its processing. For example, a SQL statement may be modifying data, but the server process may have to wait for a data block to be read from disk, because it's not available in the SGA. Although there's a large number of wait events, the most common events are the following:

- buffer busy waits
- free buffer waits
- db file scattered read
- db file sequential read
- enqueue waits
- log buffer space
- log file sync

Analyzing Oracle wait events is the most important performance tuning task you'll perform when troubleshooting a slow-running query. When a query is running slow, it usually means that there are excessive waits of one type or another. Some of the waits may be due to excessive I/O due to missing indexes. Other waits may be caused by a latch or a locking event. Several recipes in this chapter show you how to identify and fix various types of Oracle wait-related performance problems. In general, wait events that account for the most wait time warrant further investigation. However, it's important to understand that wait events show only the symptoms of underlying problems—thus, you should view a wait event as a window into a particular problem, and not the problem itself. When Oracle encounters a problem such as buffer contention or latch contention, it simply increments a specific type of wait event relating to that latch or buffer. By doing this, the database is showing where it had to wait for a specific resource, and was thus unable to continue processing. The buffer or latch contention can often be traced to faulty application logic, but some wait events could also emanate from system issues such as a misconfigured RAID system. Missing indexes, inappropriate initialization parameters, inadequate values for initialization parameters that relate to memory, and inadequate sizing of redo log files are just some of the things that can lead to excessive waits in a database. The great benefit of analyzing Oracle wait events is that it takes the guesswork out of performance tuning—you can see exactly what is causing a performance slowdown, so you can immediately focus on fixing the problem.

5-4. Understanding Wait Class Events

Problem

You want to understand how Oracle classifies wait events into various classes.

Solution

Every Oracle wait event belongs to a specific wait event class. Oracle groups wait events into classes such as `Administrative`, `Application`, `Cluster`, `Commit`, `Concurrency`, `Configuration`, `Scheduler`, `System I/O`, and `User I/O`, to facilitate the analysis of wait events. Here are some examples of typical waits in some of these classes:

> `Application`: Lock-related wait information
>
> `Commit`: Waits for confirmation of a redo log write after committing a transaction
>
> `Network`: Waits caused by delays in sending data over the network
>
> `User I/O`: Waiting to read blocks from disk

Two key wait classes are the `Application` and the `User I/O` wait classes. The `Application` wait class contains waits due to row and table locks caused by an application. The `User I/O` class includes the `db file scattered read`, `db file sequential read`, `direct path read`, and `direct path write` events. The `System I/O` class includes redo log–related wait events among other waits. The `Commit` class contains just the `log file sync` wait information. There's also an "idle" class of wait events such as `SQL*Net message from client` for example, that merely indicate an inactive session. You can ignore the idle waits.

How It Works

Classes of wait events help you quickly find out what type of activity is affecting database performance. For example, the `Administrative` wait class may show a high number of waits because you're rebuilding an index. Concurrency waits point to waits for internal database resources such as latches. If the Cluster wait class shows the most wait events, then your RAC instances may be experiencing contention for global cache resources (gc cr block busy event). Note that the System I/O wait class includes waits for background process I/O such as the DBWR (database writer) wait event db file parallel write.

The Application wait class contains waits that result from user application code—most of your enqueue waits fall in this wait class. The only wait event in the Commit class is the log file sync event, which we examine in detail later in this chapter. The Configuration class waits include waits such as those caused by log files that are sized too small.

5-5. Examining Session Waits

Problem

You want to find out the wait events in a session.

Solution

You can use the V$SESSION_WAIT view to get a quick idea about what a particular session is waiting for, as shown here:

```
SQL> select event, count(*) from v$session_wait
     group by event;
```

EVENT	COUNT(*)
SQL*Net message from client	11
Streams AQ: waiting for messages in the queue	1
enq: TX - row lock contention	1

```
...
15 rows selected.

SQL>
```

The output of the query indicates that one session is waiting for an enqueue lock, possibly because of a blocking lock held by another session. If you see a large number of sessions experiencing row lock contention, you must investigate further and identify the blocking session.

Here's one more way you can query the V$SESSION_WAIT view, to find out what's slowing down a particular session:

```
SQL> select event, state, seconds_in_wait siw
     from   v$session_wait
     where  sid = 81;
```

EVENT	STATE	SIW
enq: TX - row lock contention	WAITING	976

The preceding query shows that the session with the SID 81 has been waiting for an enqueue event, because the row (or rows) it wants to update is locked by another transaction.

■ **Note** In Oracle Database 11g, the database counts each resource wait as just one wait, even if the session experiences many internal time-outs caused by the wait. For example, a wait for an enqueue for 15 seconds may include 5 different 3-second-long wait calls—the database considers these as just a single enqueue wait.

How It Works

The first query shown in the "Solution" section offers an easy way to find out which wait events, if any, are slowing down user sessions. When you issue the query without specifying a SID, it displays the current and last waits for all sessions in the database. If you encounter a locking situation in the database, for example, you can issue the query periodically to see whether the total number of enqueue waits is coming down. If the number of enqueue waits across the instance is growing, that means more sessions are encountering slowdowns due to blocked locks.

The V$SESSION_WAIT view shows the current or the last wait for each session. The STATE column in this view tells you if a session is currently waiting. Here are the possible values for the STATE column:

> WAITING: The session is currently waiting for a resource.

> WAITED UNKNOWN TIME: The duration of the last wait is unknown (this value is shown only if you set the TIMED_STATISTICS parameter to false).

> WAITED SHORT TIME: The most recent wait was less than a hundredth of a second long.

> WAITED KNOWN TIME: The WAIT_TIME column shows the duration of the last wait.

Note that the query utilizes the seconds_in_wait column to find out how long this session has been waiting. Oracle has deprecated this column in favor of the wait_time_micro column, which shows the amount of time waited in microseconds. Both columns show the amount of time waited for the current wait, if the session is currently waiting. If the session is not currently waiting, the wait_time_micro column shows the amount of time waited during the last wait.

5-6. Examining Wait Events by Class

Problem

You want to examine Oracle wait event classes.

Solution

The following query shows the different types of wait classes and the wait events associated with each wait class.

```
SQL> select  wait_class, name
  2  from v$event_name
  3  where name LIKE 'enq%'
  4  and wait_class <> 'Other'
  5* order by wait_class
SQL> /

WAIT_CLASS                              NAME
--------------------                    -------------------------
Administrative                          enq: TW - contention
Concurrency                             enq: TX - index contention
...
SQL>
```

To view the current waits grouped into various wait classes, issue the following query:

```
SQL> select wait_class, sum(time_waited), sum(time_waited)/sum(total_waits)
  2  sum_waits
  3  from v$system_wait_class
  4  group by wait_class
  5* order by 3 desc;

WAIT_CLASS                     SUM(TIME_WAITED)              SUM_WAITS
------------------ ----------  -----------------         -----------------
Idle                                 249659211             347.489249
Commit                                 1318006             236.795904
Concurrency                              16126               4.818046
User I/O                                135279               2.228869
Application                                912                .0928055
Network                                    139                .0011209
...
SQL>
```

If you see a very high sum of waits for the Idle wait class, not to worry—actually, you should expect to see this in any healthy database. In a typical production environment, however, you'll certainly see more waits under the User I/O and Application wait classes. If you notice that the database has accumulated a very large wait time for the Application wait class, or the User I/O wait class, for example, it's time to investigate those two wait classes further. In the following example, we drill down into a couple of wait classes to find out which specific waits are causing the high sum of total wait time under the Application and Concurrency classes. To do this, we use the V$SYSTEM_EVENT and the $EVENT_NAME views in addition to the V$SYSTEM_WAIT_CLASS view. Focus not just on the total time waited, but also on the average wait, to gauge the effect of the wait event.

```
SQL> select a.event, a.total_waits, a.time_waited, a.average_wait
     from v$system_event a, v$event_name b, v$system_wait_class c
     where a.event_id=b.event_id
     and b.wait_class#=c.wait_class#
     and c.wait_class in ('Application','Concurrency')
     order by average_wait desc;
```

EVENT	TOTAL_WAITS	TIME_WAITED	AVERAGE_WAIT
enq: UL - contention	1	499	499.19
latch: shared pool	251	10944	43.6
library cache load lock	24	789	32.88

```
SQL>
```

■ **Tip**   Two of the most common Oracle wait events are the db file scattered read and the db file sequential read events. The db file scattered read wait event is due to full table scans of large tables. If you experience this wait event, investigate the possibility of adding indexes to the table or tables. The db file sequential read wait event is due to indexed reads. While an indexed read may seem like it's a good thing, a very high amount of indexed reads could potentially indicate an inefficient query that you must tune. If high values for the db file sequential read wait event are due to a very large number of small indexed reads, it's not really a problem—this is natural in a database. You should be concerned if a handful of queries are responsible for most of the waits.

You can see that the enqueue waits caused by the row lock contention are what's causing the most waits under these two classes. Now you know exactly what's slowing down the queries in your database! To get at the session whose performance is being affected by the contention for the row lock, drill down to the session level using the following query:

```
SQL> select a.sid, a.event, a.total_waits, a.time_waited, a.average_wait
    from v$session_event a, v$session b
    where time_waited > 0
    and a.sid=b.sid
    and b.username is not NULL
    and a.event='enq: TX - row lock contention';
```

SID	EVENT	TOTAL_WAITS	time_waited	average_wait
68	enq: TX - row lock contention	24	8018	298

```
SQL>
```

The output shows that the session with the SID 68 is waiting for a row lock that's held by another transaction.

How It Works

Understanding the various Oracle wait event classes enhances your ability to quickly diagnose Oracle wait-related problems. Analyzing wait events by classes lets you know if contention, user I/O, or a configuration issue is responsible for high waits. The examples in the "Solution" section show you how to start analyzing the waits based on the wait event classes. This helps identify the source of the waits, such as concurrency issues, for example. Once you identify the wait event class responsible for most of the waits, you can drill down into that wait event class to find out the specific wait events that are contributing to high total waits for that wait event class. You can then identify the user sessions waiting for those wait events, using the final query shown in the "Solution" section.

5-7. Resolving Buffer Busy Waits

Problem

Your database is experiencing a high number of buffer busy waits, based on the output from the AWR report. You want to resolve those waits.

Solution

Oracle has several types of buffer classes, such as data block, segment header, undo header, and undo block. How you fix a buffer busy wait situation will depend on the types of buffer classes that are causing the problem. You can find out the type of buffer causing the buffer waits by issuing the following two queries. Note that you first get the value of `row_wait_obj#` from the first query and use it as the value for `data_object_id` in the second query.

```
SQL> select row_wait_obj#
     from v$session
     where event = 'buffer busy waits';

SQL> select owner, object_name, subobject_name, object_type
     from dba_objects
     where data_object_id = &row_wait_obj;
```

The preceding queries will reveal the specific type of buffer causing the high buffer waits. Your fix will depend on which buffer class causes the buffer waits, as summarized in the following subsections.

Segment Header

If your queries show that the buffer waits are being caused by contention on the segment header, there's free list contention in the database, due to several processes attempting to insert into the same data block—each of these processes needs to obtain a free list before it can insert data into that block. If you aren't already using it, you must switch from manual space management to automatic segment space management (ASSM)—under ASSM, the database doesn't use free lists. However, note that moving to ASSM may not be easily feasible in most cases. In cases where you can't implement ASSM, you must increase the free lists for the segment in question. You can also try increasing the free list groups as well.

Data Block

Data block buffer contention could be related to a table or an index. This type of contention is often caused by right-hand indexes, that is, indexes that result in several processes inserting into the same point, such as when you use sequence number generators to produce the key values. Again, if you're using manual segment management, move to ASSM or increase free lists for the segment.

Undo Header and Undo Block

If you're using automatic undo management, few or none of the buffer waits will be due to contention for an undo segment header or an undo segment block. If you do see one of these buffer classes as the culprit, however, you may increase the size of your undo tablespace to resolve the buffer busy waits.

How It Works

A buffer busy wait indicates that more than one process is simultaneously accessing the same data block. One of the reasons for a high number of buffer busy waits is that an inefficient query is reading too many data blocks into the buffer cache, thus potentially keeping in wait other sessions that want to access one or more of those same blocks. Not only that, a query that reads too much data into the buffer cache may lead to the aging out of necessary blocks from the cache. You must investigate queries that involve the segment causing the buffer busy waits with a view to reducing the number of data blocks they're reading into the buffer cache.

If your investigation of buffer busy waits reveals that the same block or set of blocks is involved most of the time, a good strategy would be to delete some of these rows and insert them back into the table, thus forcing them onto different data blocks.

Check your current memory allocation to the buffer cache, and, if necessary, increase it. A larger buffer cache can reduce the waiting by sessions to read data from disk, since more of the data will already be in the buffer cache. You can also place the offending table in memory by using the KEEP POOL in the buffer cache (please see Recipe 3-7). By making the hot block always available in memory, you'll avoid the high buffer busy waits.

Indexes that have a very low number of unique values are called low cardinality indexes. Low cardinality indexes generally result in too many block reads. Thus, if several DML operations are occurring concurrently, some of the index blocks could become "hot" and lead to high buffer busy waits. As a long-term solution, you can try to reduce the number of the low cardinality indexes in your database.

Each Oracle data segment such as a table or an index contains a header block that records information such as free blocks available. When multiple sessions are trying to insert or delete rows from the same segment, you could end up with contention for the data segment's header block.

Buffer busy waits are also caused by a contention for free lists. A session that's inserting data into a segment needs to first examine the free list information for the segment, to find blocks with free space into which the session can insert data. If you use ASSM in your database, you shouldn't see any waits due to contention for a free list.

5-8. Resolving Log File Sync Waits

Problem

You're seeing a high amount of log file sync wait events, which are at the top of all wait events in your database. You want to reduce these wait events.

Solution

The following are two strategies for dealing with high `log file sync` waits in your database.

- If you notice a very large number of waits with a short average wait time per wait, that's an indication that too many commit statements are being issued by the database. You must change the commit behavior by batching the commits. Instead of committing after each row, for example, you can specify that the commits occur after every 500 rows.

- If you notice that the large amount of wait time accumulated due to the `redo log file sync` event was caused by long waits for writing to the redo log file (high average time waited for this event), it's more a matter of how fast your I/O subsystem is. You can alternate the redo log files on various disks to reduce contention. You can also see if you can dedicate disks entirely for the redo logs instead of allowing other files on those disks—this will reduce I/O contention when the LGWR is writing the buffers to disk. Finally, as a long-term solution, you can look into placing redo logs on faster devices, say, by moving them from a RAID 5 to a RAID 1 device.

How It Works

Oracle (actually the LGWR background process) automatically flushes a session's redo information to the redo log file whenever a session issues a `COMMIT` statement. The database writes commit records to disk before it returns control to the client. The server process thus waits for the completion of the write to the redo log. This is the default behavior, but you can also control the database commit behavior with the `COMMIT_WRITE` initialization parameter.

■ **Note** The `COMMIT_WRITE` parameter is an advanced parameter that has been deprecated in Oracle Database 11.2. Since it may have an adverse impact on performance, you may want to leave the parameter alone and rely on Oracle's default commit behavior.

The session will tell the LGWR process to write the session's redo information from the redo log buffer to the redo log file on disk. The LGWR process posts the user session after it finishes writing the buffer's contents to disk. The `log file sync` wait event includes the wait during the writing of the log buffer to disk by LGWR and the posting of that information to the session. The server process will have to wait until it gets confirmation that the LGWR process has completed writing the log buffer contents out to the redo log file.

The `log file sync` events are caused by contention during the writing of the log buffer contents to the redo log files. Check the `V$SESSION_WAIT` view to ascertain whether Oracle is incrementing the `SEQ#` column. If Oracle is incrementing this column, it means that the LGWR process is the culprit, as it may be stuck.

As the `log file sync` wait event is caused by contention caused by the LGWR process, see if you can use the `NOLOGGING` option to get rid of these waits. Of course, in a production system, you can't use the `NOLOGGING` option when the database is processing user requests, so this option is of limited use in most cases.

The `log file sync` wait event can also be caused by too large a setting for the `LOG_BUFFER` initialization parameter. Too large a value for the `LOG_BUFFER` parameter will lead the LGWR process to write data less frequently to the redo log files. For example, if you set the `LOG BUFFER` to something like 12 MB, it sets an internal parameter, `log_io_size`, to a high value. The `log_io_size` parameter acts as a threshold for when the LGWR writes to the redo log files. In the absence of a commit request or a checkpoint, LGWR waits until the `log_io_size` threshold is met. Thus, when the database issues a `COMMIT` statement, the LGWR process would be forced to write a large amount of data to the redo log files at once, resulting in sessions waiting on the `log file sync` wait event. This happens because each of the waiting sessions is waiting for LGWR to flush the contents of the redo log buffer to the redo log files. Although the database automatically calculates the value of the `log_io_size` parameter, you can specify a value for it, by issuing a command such as the following:

```
SQL> alter system set "_log_io_size"=1024000 scope=spfile;

System altered.

SQL>
```

5-9. Minimizing read by other session Wait Events

Problem

Your AWR report shows that the `read by other session` wait event is responsible for the highest number of waits. You'd like to reduce the high `read by other session` waits.

Solution

The main reason you'll see the `read by other session` wait event is that multiple sessions are seeking to read the same data blocks, whether they are table or index blocks, and are forced to wait behind the session that's currently reading those blocks. You can find the data blocks a session is waiting for by executing the following command:

```
SQL> select p1 "file#", p2 "block#", p3 "class#"
     from v$session_wait
     where event = 'read by other session';
```

You can then take the `block#` and use it in the following query, to identify the exact segments (table or index) that are causing the `read by other session` waits.

```
SQL> select relative_fno, owner, segment_name, segment_type
     from dba_extents
     where file_id = &file
     and &block between block_id
     and block_id + blocks - 1;
```

Once you identify the hot blocks and the segments they belong to, you need to identify the queries that use these data blocks and segments and tune those queries if possible. You can also try deleting and re-inserting the rows inside the hot blocks.

In order to reduce the amount of data in each of the hot blocks and thus reduce these types of waits, you can also try to create a new tablespace with a smaller block size and move the segment to that tablespace. It's also a good idea to check if any low cardinality indexes are being used, because this type of an index will make the database read a large number of data blocks into the buffer cache, potentially leading to the `read by other session` wait event. If possible, replace any low cardinality indexes with an index on a column with a high cardinality.

How It Works

The `read by other session` wait event indicates that one or more sessions are waiting for another session to read the same data blocks from disk into the SGA. Obviously, a large number of these waits will slow down performance. Your first goal should be to identify the actual data blocks and the objects the blocks belong to. For example, these waits can be caused by multiple sessions trying to read the same index blocks. Multiple sessions can also be trying to execute a full table scan simultaneously on the same table.

5-10. Reducing Direct Path Read Wait Events

Problem

You notice a high amount of the `direct path read` wait events, and also of `direct path read temp` wait events, and you'd like to reduce the occurrence of those events.

Solution

`Direct path read` and `direct path read temp` events are related wait events that occur when sessions are reading data directly into the PGA instead of reading it into the SGA. Reading data into the PGA isn't the problem here—that's normal behavior for certain operations, such as sorting, for example. The `direct path read` and `direct path read temp` events usually indicate that that the sorts being performed are very large and that the PGA is unable to accommodate those sorts.

Issue the following command to get the file ID for the blocks that are being waited for:

```
SQL> select p1 "file#", p2 "block#", p3 "class#"
    from v$session_wait
    where event = 'direct path read temp';
```

The column P1 shows the file ID for the read call. Column P2 shows the start BLOCK_ID, and column P3 shows the number of blocks. You can then execute the following statement to check whether this file ID is for a temporary tablespace tempfile:

```
SQL> select relative_fno, owner, segment_name, segment_type
    from dba_extents
    where file_id = &file
    and &block betgween block_id and block_id + &blocks - 1;
```

The direct read–type waits can be caused by excessive sorts to disk or full table scans. In order to find out what the reads are actually for, check the P1 column (file ID for the read call) of the V$SESSION_WAIT view. By doing this, you can find out if the reads are being caused by reading data from the TEMP tablespace due to disk sorting, or if they're occurring due to full table scans by parallel slaves.

If you determine that sorts to disk are the main culprit in causing high direct read wait events, increase the value of the PGA_AGGREGATE_TARGET parameter (or specify a minimum size for it, if you're using automatic memory management). Increasing PGA size is also a good strategy when the queries are doing large hash joins, which could result in excessive I/O on disk if the PGA is inadequate for handling the large hash joins. When you set a high degree of parallelism for a table, Oracle tends to go for full table scans, using parallel slaves. If your I/O system can't handle all the parallel slaves, you'll notice a high amount of direct path reads. The solution for this is to reduce the degree of parallelism for the table or tables in question. Also investigate if you can avoid the full table scan by specifying appropriate indexes.

How It Works

Normally, during both a sequential db read or a scattered db read operation, the database reads data from disk into the SGA. A direct path read is one where a single or multiblock read is made from disk directly to the PGA, bypassing the SGA. Ideally, the database should perform the entire sorting of the data in the PGA. When a huge sort doesn't fit into the available PGA, Oracle writes part of the sort data directly to disk. A direct read occurs when the server process reads this data from disk (instead of the PGA).

A direct path read event can also occur when the I/O subsystem is overloaded, most likely due to full table scans caused by setting a high degree of parallelism for tables, causing the database to return buffers slower than what the processing speed of the server process requires. A good disk striping strategy would help out here. Oracle's Automatic Storage Management (ASM) automatically stripes data for you. If you aren't already using ASM, consider implementing it in your database.

Direct path write and direct path write temp wait events are analogous to the direct path read and the direct path read temp waits. Normally, it's the DBWR that writes data from the buffer cache. Oracle uses a direct path write when a process writes data buffers directly from the PGA. If your database is performing heavy sorts that spill onto disk, or parallel DML operations, you can on occasion expect to encounter the direct path write events. You may also see this wait event when you execute direct path load events such as a parallel CTAS (create table as select) or a direct path INSERT operation. As with the direct path read events, the solution for direct path write events depends on what's causing the waits. If the waits are being mainly caused by large sorts, then you may think about increasing the value of the PGA_AGGREGATE_TARGET parameter. If operations such as parallel DML are causing the waits, you must look into the proper spreading of I/O across all disks and also ensure that your I/O subsystem can handle the high degree of parallelism during DML operations.

5-11. Minimizing Recovery Writer Waits

Problem

You've turned on the Oracle Flashback Database feature in your database. You're now seeing a large number of wait events due to a slow RVWR (recovery writer) process. You want to reduce the recovery writer waits.

Solution

Oracle writes all changed blocks from memory to the flashback logs on disk. You may encounter the `flashback buf free by RVWR` wait event as a top wait event when thie database is writing to the flashback logs. To reduce these recovery writer waits, you must tune the flash recovery area file system and storage. Specifically, you must do the following:

- Since flashback logs tend to be quite large, your database is going to incur some CPU overhead when writing to these files. One of the things you may consider is moving the flash recovery area to a faster file system. Also, Oracle recommends that you use file systems based on ASM, because they won't be subject to operating system file caching, which tends to slow down I/O.

- Increase the disk throughput for the file system where you store the flash recovery area, by configuring multiple disk spindles for that file system. This will speed up the writing of the flashback logs.

- Stripe the storage volumes, ideally with small stripe sizes (for example, 128 KB).

- Set the `LOG_BUFFER` initialization parameter to a minimum value of 8 MB—the memory allocated for writing to the flashback database logs depends on the setting of the `LOG_BUFFER` parameter.

How It Works

Unlike in the case of the redo log buffer, Oracle writes flashback buffers to the flashback logs at infrequent intervals to keep overhead low for the Oracle Flashback Database. The `flashback buf free by RVWR` wait event occurs when sessions are waiting on the RVWR process. The RVWR process writes the contents of the flashback buffers to the flashback logs on disk. When the RVWR falls behind during this process, the flashback buffer is full and free buffers aren't available to sessions that are making changes to data through DML operations. The sessions will continue to wait until RVWR frees up buffers by writing their contents to the flashback logs. High RVWR waits indicate that your I/O system is unable to support the rate at which the RVWR needs to flush flashback buffers to the flashback logs on disk.

5-12. Finding Out Who's Holding a Blocking Lock

Problem

Your users are complaining that some of their sessions are very slow. You suspect that those sessions may be locked by Oracle for some reason, and would like to find the best way to go about figuring out who is holding up these sessions.

Solution

As we've explained in the introduction to this chapter, Oracle uses several types of locks to control transactions being executed by multiple sessions, to prevent destructive behavior in the database. A blocking lock could "slow" a session down—in fact, the session is merely waiting on another session that is holding a lock on an object (such as a row or a set of rows, or even an entire table). Or, in a development scenario, a developer might have started multiple sessions, some of which are blocking each other.

When analyzing Oracle locks, some of the key database views you must examine are the V$LOCK and the V$SESSION views. The V$LOCKED_OBJECT and the DBA_OBJECTS views are also very useful in identifying the locked objects. In order to find out whether a session is being blocked by the locks being applied by another session, you can execute the following query:

```
SQL> select s1.username || '@' || s1.machine
  2  || ' ( SID=' || s1.sid || ' ) is blocking '
  3  || s2.username || '@' || s2.machine || ' ( SID=' || s2.sid || ' ) ' AS blocking_status
  4  from v$lock l1, v$session s1, v$lock l2, v$session s2
  5  where s1.sid=l1.sid and s2.sid=l2.sid
  6  and l1.BLOCK=1 and l2.request > 0
  7  and l1.id1 = l2.id1
  8  and l2.id2 = l2.id2 ;


BLOCKING_STATUS
--------------------------------------------------------------------

HR@MIRO\MIROPC61 ( SID=68 )  is blocking SH@MIRO\MIROPC61 ( SID=81 )

SQL>
```

The output of the query shows the blocking session as well as all the blocked sessions.

A quick way to find out if you have any blocking locks in your instance at all, for any user, is to simply run the following query:

```
SQL> select * from V$lock where block > 0;
```

If you don't get any rows back from this query—good—you don't have any blocking locks in the instance right now! We'll explain this view in more detail in the explanation section.

How It Works

Oracle uses two types of locks to prevent destructive behavior: exclusive and shared locks. Only one transaction can obtain an exclusive lock on a row or a table, while multiple shared locks can be obtained on the same object. Oracle uses locks at two levels—row and table levels. Row locks, indicated by the symbol TX, lock just a single row of a table for each row that'll be modified by a DML statement such as INSERT, UPDATE, and DELETE. This is true also for a MERGE or a SELECT … FOR UPDATE statement. The transaction that includes one of these statements grabs an exclusive row lock as well as a row share table lock. The transaction (and the session) will hold these locks until it commits or rolls back the statement. Until it does one of these two things, all other sessions that intend to modify that particular row are blocked. Note that each time a transaction intends to modify a row or rows of a table, it holds a table lock (TM) as well on that table, to prevent the database from allowing any DDL operations (such as DROP TABLE) on that table while the transaction is trying to modify some of its rows.

In an Oracle database, locking works this way:

- A reader won't block another reader.

- A reader won't block a writer.

- A writer won't block a reader of the same data.

- A writer will block another writer that wants to modify the same data.

It's the last case in the list, where two sessions intend to modify the same data in a table, that Oracle's automatic locking kicks in, to prevent destructive behavior. The first transaction that contains the statement that updates an existing row will get an exclusive lock on that row. While the first session that locks a row continues to hold that lock (until it issues a COMMIT or ROLLBACK statement), other sessions can modify any other rows in that table other than the locked row. The concomitant table lock held by the first session is merely intended to prevent any other sessions from issuing a DDL statement to alter the table's structure. Oracle uses a sophisticated locking mechanism whereby a row-level lock isn't automatically escalated to the table, or even the block level.

5-13. Identifying Blocked and Blocking Sessions

Problem

You notice enqueue locks in your database and suspect that a blocking lock may be holding up other sessions. You'd like to identify the blocking and the blocked sessions.

Solution

When you see an enqueue wait event in an Oracle database, chances are that it's a locking phenomenon that's holding up some sessions from executing their SQL statements. When a session waits on an "enqueue" wait event, that session is waiting for a lock that's held by a different session. The blocking session is holding the lock in a mode that's incompatible with the lock mode that's being requested by the blocked session. You can issue the following command to view information about the blocked and the blocking sessions:

```
SQL> select decode(request,0,'Holder: ','Waiter: ')||sid sess,
    id1, id2, lmode, request, type
    from v$lock
    where (id1, id2, type) in
    (select id1, id2, type from v$lock where request>0)
    order by id1, request;
```

The V$LOCK view shows if there are any blocking locks in the instance. If there are blocking locks, it also shows the blocking session(s) and the blocked session(s). Note that a blocking session can block multiple sessions simultaneously, if all of them need the same object that's being blocked. Here's an example that shows there are locks present:

```
SQL> select sid,type,lmode,request,ctime,block from v$lock;

        SID          TY          LMODE       REQUEST       CTIME        BLOCK
    --------------   --------   -----------  -----------   --------    -------
            127       MR           4             0         102870         0
             81       TX           0             6            778         0
            191       AE           4             0            758         0
            205       AE           4             0            579         0
            140       AE           4             0          11655         0
             68       TM           3             0            826         0
             68       TX           6             0            826         1
    ...
SQL>
```

The key column to watch is the BLOCK column—the blocking session will have the value 1 for this column. In our example, session 68 is the blocking session, because it shows the value 1 under the BLOCK column. Thus, the V$LOCK view confirms our initial finding in the "Solution" section of this recipe. The blocking session, with a SID of 68, also shows a lock mode 6 under the LMODE column, indicating that it's holding this lock in the exclusive mode—this is the reason session 81 is "hanging," unable to perform its update operation. The blocked session, of course, is the victim—so it shows a value of 0 in the BLOCK column. It also shows a value of 6 under the REQUEST column, because it's requesting a lock in the exclusive mode to perform its update of the column. The blocking session, in turn, will show a value of 0 for the REQUEST column, because it isn't requesting any locks—it's already holding it.

If you want to find out the wait class and for how long a blocking session has been blocking others, you can do so by querying the V$SESSION view, as shown here:

```
SQL> select  blocking_session, sid,  wait_class,
        seconds_in_wait
        from     v$session
        where blocking_session is not NULL
        order by blocking_session;

BLOCKING_SESSION        SID        WAIT_CLASS       SECONDS_IN_WAIT
-----------------     --------     -------------    -----------------
           68           81         Application                 7069

SQL>
```

The query shows that the session with SID=68 is blocking the session with SID=81, and the block started 7,069 seconds ago.

How It Works

The following are the most common types of enqueue locks you'll see in an Oracle database:

- TX: These are due to a transaction lock and usually caused by faulty application logic.

- TM: These are table-level DML locks, and the most common cause is that you haven't indexed foreign key constraints in a child table.

In addition, you are also likely to notice ST enqueue locks on occasion. These indicate sessions that are waiting while Oracle is performing space management operations, such as the allocation of temporary segments for performing a sort.

5-14. Dealing with a Blocking Lock

Problem

You've identified blocking locks in your database. You want to know how to deal with those locks.

Solution

There are two basic strategies when dealing with a blocking lock—a short-term and a long-term strategy. The first thing you need to do is get rid of the blocking lock, so the sessions don't keep queuing up—it's not at all uncommon for a single blocking lock to result in dozens and even hundreds of sessions, all waiting for the blocked object. Since you already know the SID of the blocking session (session 68 in our example), just kill the session in this way, after first querying the V$SESSION view for the corresponding serial# for the session:

```
SQL> alter system kill session '68, 1234';
```

The short-term solution is to quickly get rid of the blocking locks so they don't hurt the performance of your database. You get rid of them by simply killing the blocking session. If you see a long queue of blocked sessions waiting behind a blocking session, kill the blocking session so that the other sessions can get going.

For the long run, though, you must investigate why the blocking session is behaving the way that it is. Usually, you'll find a flaw in the application logic. You may, though, need to dig deep into the SQL code that the blocking session is executing.

How It Works

In this example, obviously, the blocking lock is a DML lock. However, even if you didn't know this ahead of time, you can figure out the type of lock by examining the TYPE (TY) column of the V$LOCK view. Oracle uses several types of internal "system" locks to maintain the library cache and other instance-related components, but those locks are normal and you won't find anything related to those locks in the V$LOCK view.

For DML operations, Oracle uses two basic types of locks—transaction locks (TX) and DML locks (TM). There is also a third type of lock, a user lock (UL), but it doesn't play a role in troubleshooting general locking issues. Transaction locks are the most frequent type of locks you'll encounter when troubleshooting Oracle locking issues. Each time a transaction modifies data, it invokes a TX lock, which is a row transaction lock. The DML lock, TM, on the other hand, is acquired once for each object that's being changed by a DML statement.

The LMODE column shows the lock mode, with a value of 6 indicating an exclusive lock. The REQUEST column shows the requested lock mode. The session that first modifies a row will hold an exclusive lock with LMODE=6. This session's REQUEST column will show a value of 0, since it's not requesting a lock—it already has one! The blocked session needs but can't obtain an exclusive lock on the same rows, so it requests a TX in the exclusive mode (MODE=6) as well. So, the blocked session's REQUEST column will show a value of 6, and its LMODE column a value of 0 (a blocked session has no lock at all in any mode).

The preceding discussion applies to row locks, which are always taken in the exclusive mode. A TM lock is normally acquired in mode 3, which is a Shared Row Exclusive mode, whereas a DDL statement will need a TM exclusive lock.

5-15. Identifying a Locked Object

Problem

You are aware of a locking situation, and you'd like to find out the object that's being locked.

Solution

You can find the locked object's identity by looking at the value of the ID1 (LockIdentifier) column in the V$LOCK view (see Recipe 5-13). The value of the ID1 column where the TYPE column is TM (DML enqueue) identifies the locked object. Let's say you've ascertained that the value of the ID1 column is 99999. You can then issue the following query to identify the locked table:

```
SQL> select object_name from dba_objects where object_id=99999;

OBJECT_NAME
------------
TEST
SQL>
```

An even easier way is to use the V$LOCKED_OBJECT view to find out the locked object, the object type, and the owner of the object.

```
SQL> select lpad(' ',decode(l.xidusn,0,3,0)) || l.oracle_username "User",
    o.owner, o.object_name, o.object_type
    from v$locked_object l, dba_objects o
    where l.object_id = o.object_id
    order by o.object_id, 1 desc;
```

```
User      OWNER     OBJECT_NAME     OBJECT_TYPE
------    ------    ------------    ------------
HR        HR        TEST            TABLE
SH        HR        TEST            TABLE

SQL>
```

Note that the query shows both the blocking and the blocked users.

How It Works

As the "Solution" section shows, it's rather easy to identify a locked object. You can certainly use Oracle Enterprise Manager to quickly identify a locked object, the ROWID of the object involved in the lock, and the SQL statement that's responsible for the locks. However, it's always important to understand the underlying Oracle views that contain the locking information, and that's what this recipe demonstrates. Using the queries shown in this recipe, you can easily identify a locked object without recourse to a monitoring tool such as Oracle Enterprise Manager, for example.

In the example shown in the solution, the locked object was a table, but it could be any other type of object, including a PL/SQL package. Often, it turns out that the reason a query is just hanging is that one of the objects the query needs is locked. You may have to kill the session holding the lock on the object before other users can access the object.

5-16. Resolving enq: TM Lock Contention

Problem

Several sessions in your database are taking a very long time to process some insert statements. As a result, the "active" sessions count is very high and the database is unable to accept new session connections. Upon checking, you find that the database is experiencing a lot of enq: TM - contention wait events.

Solution

The enq: TM - contention event is usually due to missing foreign key constraints on a table that's part of an Oracle DML operation. Once you fix the problem by adding the foreign key constraint to the relevant table, the enq: TM - contention event will go away.

The waits on the enq: TM - contention event for the sessions that are waiting to perform insert operations are almost always due to an unindexed foreign key constraint.. This happens when a dependent or child table's foreign key constraint that references a parent table is missing an index on the associated key. Oracle acquires a table lock on a child table if it's performing modifications on the primary key column in the parent table that's referenced by the foreign key of the child table. Note that these are full table locks (TM), and not row-level locks (TX)—thus, these locks aren't restricted to a row but to the entire table. Naturally, once this table lock is acquired, Oracle will block all other sessions that seek to modify the child table's data. Once you create an index in the child table performing on the column that references the parent table, the waits due to the TM contention will go away.

How It Works

Oracle takes out an exclusive lock on a child table if you don't index the foreign key constraints in that table. To illustrate how an unindexed foreign key will result in contention due to locking, we use the following example. Create two tables, STORES and PRODUCTS, as shown here:

```
SQL> create table stores
     (store_id      number(10)     not null,
     supplier_name     varchar2(40)      not null,
     constraint stores_pk PRIMARY KEY (store_id));
SQL>create table products
     (product_id     number(10)     not null,
     product_name    varchar2(30)    not null,
     supplier_id     number(10)     not null,
     store_id     number(10)     not null,
     constraint fk_stores
     foreign key (store_id)
     references stores(store_id)
     on delete cascade);
```

If you now delete any rows in the STORES table, you'll notice waits due to locking. You can get rid of these waits by simply creating an index on the column you've specified as the foreign key in the PRODUCTS table:

```
create index fk_stores on products(store_id);
```

You can find all unindexed foreign key constraints in your database by issuing the following query:

```
SQL> select * from (
     select c.table_name, co.column_name, co.position column_position
     from   user_constraints c, user_cons_columns co
     where  c.constraint_name = co.constraint_name
     and    c.constraint_type = 'R'
     minus
     select ui.table_name, uic.column_name, uic.column_position
     from   user_indexes ui, user_ind_columns uic
     where  ui.index_name = uic.index_name
     )
     order by table_name, column_position;
```

If you don't index a foreign key column, you'll notice the child table is often locked, thus leading to contention-related waits. Oracle recommends that you always index your foreign keys.

■ **Tip**   If the matching unique or primary key for a child table's foreign key never gets updated or deleted, you don't have to index the foreign key column in the child table.

Oracle will tend to acquire a table lock on the child table if you don't index the foreign key column. If you insert a row into the parent table, the parent table doesn't acquire a lock on the child table; however, if you update or delete a row in the parent table, the database will acquire a full table lock on the child table. That is, any modifications to the primary key in the parent table will result in a full table lock (TM) on the child table. In our example, the STORES table is a parent of the PRODUCTS table, which contains the foreign key STORE_ID. The table PRODUCTS being a dependent table, the values of the STORE_ID column in that table must match the values of the unique or primary key of the parent table, STORES. In this case, the STORE_ID column in the STORES table is the primary key of that table.

Whenever you modify the parent table's (STORES) primary key, the database acquires a full table lock on the PRODUCTS table. Other sessions can't change any values in the PRODUCTS table, including the columns other than the foreign key column. The sessions can only query but not modify the PRODUCTS table. During this time, any sessions attempting to modify any column in the PRODUCTS table will have to wait (TM: enq contention wait). Oracle will release this lock on the child table PRODUCTS only after it finishes modifying the primary key in the parent table, STORES. If you have a bunch of sessions waiting to modify data in the PRODUCTS table, they'll all have to wait, and the active session count naturally will go up very fast, if you've an online transaction processing–type database that has many users that perform short DML operations. Note that any DML operations you perform on the child table don't require a table lock on the parent table.

5-17. Identifying Recently Locked Sessions

Problem

A session is experiencing severe waits in the database, most likely due to a blocking lock placed by another session. You've tried to use the V$LOCK and other views to drill deeper into the locking issue, but are unable to "capture" the lock while it's in place. You'd like to use a different view to "see" the older locking data that you might have missed while the locking was going on.

Solution

You can execute the following statement based on ASH, to find out information about all locks held in the database during the previous five minutes. Of course, you can vary the time interval to a smaller or larger period, so long as there's ASH data covering that time period.

```
SQL> select to_char(h.sample_time, 'HH24:MI:SS') TIME,h.session_id,
    decode(h.session_state, 'WAITING' ,h.event, h.session_state) STATE,
    h.sql_id,
    h.blocking_session BLOCKER
    from v$active_session_history h, dba_users u
    where u.user_id = h.user_id
    and h.sample_time > SYSTIMESTAMP-(2/1440);
```

TIME	SID	STATE	SQL_ID	BLOCKER
17:00:52	197	116 enq: TX - row lock contention	094w6n53tnywr	191
17:00:51	197	116 enq: TX - row lock contention	094w6n53tnywr	191
17:00:50	197	116 enq: TX - row lock contention	094w6n53tnywr	191

...

```
SQL>
```

You can see that ASH has recorded all the blocks placed by session 1, the blocking session (SID=191) that led to a "hanging" situation for session 2, the blocked session (SID=197).

How It works

Often, when your database users complain about a performance problem, you may query the **V$SESSION** or **V$LOCK** views, but you may not find anything useful there, because the wait issue may have been already resolved by then. In these circumstances you can query the **V$ACTIVE_SESSION_HISTORY** view to find out what transpired in the database during the previous 60 minutes. This view offers a window into the Active Session History (ASH), which is a memory buffer that collects information about all active sessions, every second. The **V$ACTIVE_SESSION_HISTORY** contains one row for each active session, and newer information continuously overwrites older data, since ASH is a rolling buffer.

We can best demonstrate the solution by creating the scenario that we're discussing, and then working through that scenario. Begin by creating a test table with a couple of columns:

```
SQL> create table test (name varchar(20), id number (4));
Table created.
SQL>
```

Insert some data into the test table.

```
SQL> insert into test values ('alapati','9999');
1 row created.
SQL> insert into test values ('sam', '1111');
1 row created.
SQL> commit;
Commit complete.
SQL>
```

In session 1 (the current session), execute a SELECT * FOR UPDATE statement on the table TEST—this will place a lock on that table.

```
SQL> select * from test for update;

SQL>
```

In a different session, session 2, execute the following UPDATE statement:

```
SQL> update test set name='Jackson' where id = '9999';
```

Session 2 will hang now, because it's being blocked by the SELECT FOR UPDATE statement issued by session 1. Go ahead now and issue either a ROLLBACK or a COMMIT from session 1:

```
SQL> rollback;
Rollback complete.
SQL>
```

When you issue the ROLLBACK statement, session 1 releases all locks it's currently holding on table TEST. You'll notice that session 2, which has been blocked thus far, immediately processes the UPDATE statement, which was previously "hanging," waiting for the lock held by session 2.

Therefore, we know for sure that there was a blocking lock in your database for a brief period, with session 1 the blocking session, and session 2 the blocked session. You can't find any evidence of this in the V$LOCK view, though, because that and all other lock-related views show you details only about currently held locks. Here's where the Active Session History views shine—they can provide you information about locks that have been held recently but are gone already before you can view them with a query on the V$LOCK or V$SESSION views.

■ **Caution** Be careful when executing the Active Session History (ASH) query shown in the "Solution" section of this recipe. As the first column (SAMPLE_TIME) shows, ASH will record session information every second. If you execute this query over a long time frame, you may get a very large amount of output just repeating the same locking information. To deal with that output, you may specify the SET PAUSE ON option in SQL*Plus. That will pause the output every page, enabling you to scroll through a few rows of the output to identify the problem.

Use the following query to find out the wait events for which this session has waited during the past hour.

```
SQL> select sample_time, event, wait_time
     from v$active_session_history
     where session_id = 81
     and session_serial# = 422;
```

The column SAMPLE_TIME lets you know precisely when this session suffered a performance hit due to a specific wait event. You can identify the actual SQL statement that was being executed by this session during that period, by using the V$SQL view along with the V$ACTIVE_SESSION_HISTORY view, as shown here:

```
SQL> select sql_text, application_wait_time
     from v$sql
     where sql_id in ( select sql_id from v$active_session_history
     where sample_time =  '08-MAR-11 05.00.52.00 PM'
     and session_id = 68 and session_serial# = 422);
```

Alternatively, if you have the SQL_ID already from the V$ACTIVE_SESSION_HISTORY view, you can get the value for the SQL_TEXT column from the V$SQLAREA view, as shown here:

```
SQL> select sql_text FROM v$sqlarea WHERE sql_id = '7zfmhtu327zm0';
```

Once you have the SQL_ID, it's also easy to extract the SQL Plan for this SQL statement, by executing the following query based on the DBMS_XPLAN package:

```
SQL> select * FROM table(dbms_xplan.display_awr('7zfmhtu327zm0'));
```

The background process MMON flushes ASH data to disk every hour, when the AWR snapshot is created. What happens when MMON flushes ASH data to disk? Well, you won't be able to query older data any longer with the V$ACTIVE_SESSION_HISTORY view. Not to worry, because you can still use the DBA_HIST_ACTIVE_SESS_HISTORY view to query the older data. The structure of this view is similar to that of the V$ACTIVE_SESSION_HISTORY view. The DBA_HIST_ACTIVE_SESS_HISTORY view shows the history of the contents of the in-memory active session history of recent system activity. You can also query the V$SESSION_WAIT_HISTORY view to examine the last ten wait events for a session, while it's still active. This view offers more reliable information for very recent wait events than the V$SESSION and V$SESSION_WAIT views, both of which show wait information for only the most recent wait. Here's a typical query using the V$SESSION_WAIT_HISTORY view.

```
SQL> select sid from v$session_wait_history
     where wait_time = (select max(wait_time) from v$session_wait_history);
```

Any non-zero values under the WAIT_TIME column represent the time waited by this session for the last wait event. A zero value for this column means that the session is waiting currently for a wait event.

5-18. Analyzing Recent Wait Events in a Database

Problem

You'd like to find out the most important waits in your database in the recent past, as well as the users, SQL statements, and objects that are responsible for most of those waits.

Solution

Query the V$ACTIVE_SESSION_HISTORY view to get information about the most common wait events, and the SQL statements, database objects, and users responsible for those waits. The following are some useful queries you can use.

To find the most important wait events in the last 15 minutes, issue the following query:

```
SQL> select event,
     sum(wait_time +
     time_waited) total_wait_time
     from v$active_session_history
     where sample_time between
     sysdate - 30/2880 and sysdate
     group by event
     order by total_wait_time desc
```

To find out which of your users experienced the most waits in the past 15 minutes, issue the following query:

```
SQL> select s.sid, s.username,
     sum(a.wait_time +
     a.time_waited) total_wait_time
     from v$active_session_history a,
     v$session s
     where a.sample_time between sysdate - 30/2880 and sysdate
     and a.session_id=s.sid
     group by s.sid, s.username
     order by total_wait_time desc;
```

Execute the following query to find out the objects with the highest waits.

```
SQL>select a.current_obj#, o.object_name, o.object_type, a.event,
     sum(a.wait_time +
     a.time_waited) total_wait_time
     from v$active_session_history a,
     dba_objects d
     where a.sample_time between sysdate - 30/2880 and sysdate
```

```
and a.current_obj# = d.object_id
group by a.current_obj#, d.object_name, d.object_type, a.event
order by total_wait_time;
```

You can identify the SQL statements that have been waiting the most during the last 15 minutes with this query.

```
SQL> select a.user_id,u.username,s.sql_text,
       sum(a.wait_time + a.time_waited) total_wait_time
       from v$active_session_history a,
       v$sqlarea s,
       dba_users u
       where a.sample_time between sysdate - 30/2880 and sysdate
       and a.sql_id = s.sql_id
       and a.user_id = u.user_id
       group by a.user_id,s.sql_text, u.username;
```

How It Works

The "Solution" section shows how to join the V$ACTIVE_SESSION_HISTORY view with other views, such as the V$SESSION, V$SQLAREA, DBA_USERS, and DBA_OBJECTS views, to find out exactly what's causing the highest number of wait events or who's waiting the most, in the past few minutes. This information is extremely valuable when troubleshooting "live" database performance issues.

5-19. Identifying Time Spent Waiting Due to Locking

Problem

You want to identify the total time spent waiting by sessions due to locking issues.

Solution

You can use the following query to identify (and quantify) waits caused by locking of a table's rows. Since the query orders the wait events by time waited, you can quickly see which type of wait events accounts for most of the waits in your instance.

```
SQL> select wait_class, event, time_waited / 100 time_secs
  2  from v$system_event e
  3  where e.wait_class <> 'Idle' AND time_waited > 0
  4  union
  5  select 'Time Model', stat_name NAME,
  6  round ((value / 1000000), 2) time_secs
  7  from v$sys_time_model
  8  where stat_name NOT IN ('background elapsed time', 'background cpu time')
  9* order by 3 desc;
```

WAIT_CLASS	EVENT	TIME_SECS
System I/O	log file parallel write	45066.32
System I/O	control file sequential read	23254.41
Time Model	DB time	11083.91
Time Model	sql execute elapsed time	7660.04
Concurrency	latch: shared pool	5928.73
Application	enq: TX - row lock contention	3182.06

...
```
SQL>
```

In this example, the wait event enq: TX - row lock contention reveals the total time due to row lock enqueue wait events. Note that the shared pool latch events are classified under the Concurrency wait class, while the enqueue TX - row lock contention event is classified as an Application class wait event.

How It Works

The query in the "Solution" section joins the V$SYSTEM_EVENT and the V$SYS_TIME_MODEL views to show you the total time waited due to various wait events. In our case, we're interested in the total time waited due to enqueue locking. If you're interested in the total time waited by a specific session, you can use a couple of different V$ views to find out how long sessions have been in a wait state, but we recommend using the V$SESSION view, because it shows you various useful attributes of the blocking and blocked sessions. Here's an example showing how to find out how long a session has been blocked by another session.

```
SQL>select sid, username, event, blocking_session,
    seconds_in_wait, wait_time
    from v$session where state in ('WAITING');
```

The query reveals the following about the session with SID 81, which is in a WAITING state:

```
SID  : 81 (this is the blocked session)
username: SH (user who's being blocked right now)
event: TX - row lock contention (shows the exact type of lock contention)
blocking session: 68 (this is the "blocker")
seconds_in_wait: 3692 (how long the blocked session is in this state)
```

The query reveals that the user SH, with a SID of 81, has been blocked for almost an hour (3,692 seconds). User SH is shown as waiting for a lock on a table that is currently locked by session 68. While the V$SESSION view is highly useful for identifying the blocking and blocked sessions, it can't tell you the SQL statement that's involved in the blocking of the table. Often, identifying the SQL statement that's involved in a blocking situation helps in finding out exactly why the statement is leading to the locking behavior. To find out the actual SQL statement that's involved, you must join the V$SESSION and the V$SQL views, as shown here.

```
SQL> select sid, sql_text
    from v$session s, v$sql q
    where sid in (68,81)
    and (
    q.sql_id = s.sql_id or  q.sql_id = s.prev_sql_id)
SQL> /
```

```
        SID                     SQL_TEXT
 -------------        -------------------------------------------------------
         68           select * from test for update
         81           update hr.test set name='nalapati' where user_id=1111
SQL>
```

The output of the query shows that session 81 is being blocked because it's trying to update a row in a table that has been locked by session 68, using the SELECT … FOR UPDATE statement. In cases such as this, if you find a long queue of user sessions being blocked by another session, you must kill the blocking session so the other sessions can process their work. You'll also see a high active user count in the database during these situations—killing the blocking session offers you an immediate solution to resolving contention caused by enqueue locks. Later on, you can investigate why the blocks are occurring, so as to prevent these situations.

For any session, you can identify the total time waited by a session for each wait class, by issuing the following query:

```
SQL> select wait_class_id, wait_class,
    total_waits, time_waited
    from v$session_wait_class
    where sid = <SID>;
```

If you find, for example, that this session endured a very high number of waits in the application wait class (wait class ID for this class is 4217450380), you can issue the following query using the V$SYSTEM_EVENT view, to find out exactly which waits are responsible:

```
SQL> select event, total_waits, time_waited
    from v$system_event e, v$event_name n
    where n.event_id = e.event_id
    and e.wait_class_id = 4217450380;
```

EVENT	TOTAL_WAITS	TIME_WAITED
enq: TM - contention	82	475

```
...
SQL>
```

In our example, the waits in the application class (ID 4217450380) are due to locking contention as revealed by the wait event enq:TM - contention. You can further use the V$EVENT_HISTOGRAM view, to find out how many times and for how long sessions have waited for a specific wait event since you started the instance. Here's the query you need to execute to find out the wait time pattern for enqueue lock waits:

```
SQL> select wait_time_milli bucket, wait_count
    from v$event_histogram
    where event = 'enq: TX - row lock contention';
```

A high amount of enqueue waits due to locking behavior is usually due to faulty application design. You'll sometimes encounter this when an application executes many updates against the same row or a set of rows. Since this type of high waits due to locking is due to inappropriately designed applications, there's not much you can do by yourself to reduce these waits. Let your application team know why these waits are occurring, and ask them to consider modifying the application logic to avoid the waits.

Any of the following four DML statements can cause locking contention: INSERT, UPDATE, DELETE, and SELECT FOR UPDATE. INSERT statements wait for a lock because another session is attempting to insert a row with an identical value. This usually happens when you have a table that has a primary key or unique constraint, with the application generating the keys. Use an Oracle sequence instead to generate the key values, to avoid these types of locking situations. You can specify the NOWAIT option with a SELECT FOR UPDATE statement to eliminate session blocking due to locks. You can also use the SELECT FOR UPDATE NOWAIT statement to avoid waiting by sessions for locks when they issue an UPDATE or DELETE statement. The SELECT FOR UPDATE NOWAIT statement locks the row without waiting.

5-20. Minimizing Latch Contention

Problem

You're seeing a high number of latch waits, and you'd like to reduce the latch contention.

Solution

Severe latch contention can slow your database down noticeably. When you're dealing with a latch contention issue, start by executing the following query to find out the specific types of latches and the total wait time caused by each wait.

```
SQL> select event, sum(P3), sum(seconds_in_wait) seconds_in_wait
     from v$session_wait
     where event like 'latch%'
     group by event;
```

The previous query shows the latches that are currently being waited for by this session. To find out the amount of time the entire instance has waited for various latches, execute the following SQL statement.

```
SQL> select wait_class, event, time_waited / 100 time_secs
     from v$system_event e
     where e.wait_class <> 'Idle' AND time_waited > 0
     union
     select 'Time Model', stat_name NAME,
     round ((value / 1000000), 2) time_secs
     from v$sys_time_model
     where stat_name not in ('background elapsed time', 'background cpu time')
     order by 3 desc;
```

WAIT_CLASS	EVENT	TIME_SECS
Concurrency	library cache pin	622.24
Concurrency	latch: library cache	428.23
Concurrency	latch: library cache lock	93.24
Concurrency	library cache lock	24.20
Concurrency	latch: library cache pin	60.28

...

The partial output from the query shows the latch-related wait events, which are part of the Concurrency wait class.

You can also view the top five wait events in the AWR report to see if lache contention is an issue, as shown here:

Event	Waits	Time (s)	(ms)	Time	Wait Class
db file sequential read	42,005,780	232,838	6	73.8	User I/0
CPU time		124,672		39.5	Other
latch free	11,592,952	76,746	7	24.3	Other
wait list latch free	107,553	2,088	19	0.7	Other
latch: library cache	1,135,976	1,862	2	0.6	Concurrency

Here are the most common Oracle latch wait types and how you can reduce them.

Shared pool and library latches: These are caused mostly by the database repeatedly executing the same SQL statement that varies slightly each time. For example, a database may execute a SQL statement 10,000 times, each time with a different value for a variable. The solution in all such cases is to use bind variables. An application that explicitly closes all cursors after each execution may also contribute to this type of wait. The solution for this is to specify the CURSOR_SPACE_FOR_TIME initialization parameter. Too small a shared pool may also contribute to the latch problem, so check your SGA size.

Cache buffers LRU chain: These latch events are usually due to excessive buffer cache usage and may be caused both by excessive physical reads as well as logical reads. Either the database is performing large full table scans, or it's performing large index range scans. The usual cause for these types of latch waits is either the lack of an index or the presence of an unselective index. Also check to see if you need to increase the size of the buffer cache.

Cache buffer chains: These waits are due to one or more hot blocks that are being repeatedly accessed. Application code that updates a table's rows to generate sequence numbers, rather than using an Oracle sequence, can result in such hot blocks. You might also see the cache buffer chains wait event when too many processes are scanning an unselective index with similar predicates.

Also, if you're using Oracle sequences, re-create them with a larger cache size setting and try to avoid using the ORDER clause. The CACHE clause for a sequence determines the number of sequence values the database must cache in the SGA. If your database is processing a large number of inserts and updates, consider increasing the cache size to avoid contention for sequence values. By default, the cache is set to 20 values. Contention can result if values are being requested fast enough to frequently deplete the cache. If you're dealing with a RAC environment, using the NOORDER clause will prevent enqueue contention due to the forced ordering of queued sequence values.

How It Works

Oracle uses internal locks called latches to protect various memory structures. When a server process attempts to get a latch but fails to do so, that attempt is counted as a latch free wait event. Oracle doesn't group all latch waits into a single latch free wait event. Oracle does use a generic latch free wait event, but this is only for the minor latch-related wait events. For the latches that are most common, Oracle uses various subgroups of latch wait events, with the name of the wait event type. You can identify the exact type of latch by looking at the latch event name. For example, the latch event `latch: library cache` indicates contention for library cache latches. Similarly, the `latch: cache buffer chains` event indicates contention for the buffer cache.

Oracle uses various types of latches to prevent multiple sessions from updating the same area of the SGA. Various database operations require sessions to read or update the SGA. For example, when a session reads a data block into the SGA from disk, it must modify the buffer cache least recently used chain. Similarly, when the database parses a SQL statement, that statement has to be added to the library cache component of the SGA. Oracle uses latches to prevent database operations from stepping on each other and corrupting the SGA.

A database operation needs to acquire and hold a latch for very brief periods, typically lasting a few nanoseconds. If a session fails to acquire a latch at first because the latch is already in use, the session will try a few times before going to "sleep." The session will re-awaken and try a few more times, before going into the sleep mode again if it still can't acquire the latch it needs. Each time the session goes into the sleep mode, it stays longer there, thus increasing the time interval between subsequent attempts to acquire a latch. Thus, if there's a severe contention for latches in your database, it results in a severe degradation of response times and throughput.

Don't be surprised to see latch contention even in a well-designed database running on very fast hardware. Some amount of latch contention, especially the cache buffers chain latch events, is pretty much unavoidable. You should be concerned only if the latch waits are extremely high and are slowing down database performance.

Contention due to the library cache latches as well as shared pool latches is usually due to applications not using bind variables. If your application can't be recoded to incorporate bind variables, all's not lost. You can set the `CURSOR_SHARING` parameter to force Oracle to use bind variables, even if your application hasn't specified them in the code. You can choose between a setting of `FORCE` or `SIMILAR` for this parameter to force the substituting of bind variables for hard-coded values of variables. The default setting for this parameter is `EXACT`, which means that the database won't substitute bind variables for literal values. When you set the `CURSOR_SHARING` parameter to `FORCE`, Oracle converts all literals to bind variables. The `SIMILAR` setting causes a statement to use bind variables only if doing so doesn't change a statement's execution plan. Thus, the `SIMILAR` setting seems a safer way to go about forcing the database to use bind variables instead of literals. Although there are some concerns about the safety of setting the `CURSOR_SHARING` parameter to `FORCE`, we haven't seen any real issues with using this setting. The library cache contention usually disappears once you set the `CURSOR_SHARING` parameter to `FORCE` or to `SIMILAR`. The `CURSOR_SHARING` parameter is one of the few Oracle silver bullets that'll improve database performance immediately by eliminating latch contention. Use it with confidence when dealing with library cache latch contention.

The cache buffer chains latch contention is usually due to a session repeatedly reading the same data blocks. First identify the SQL statement that's responsible for the highest amount of the cache buffers chain latches and see if you can tune it. If this doesn't reduce the latch contention, you must identify the actual hot blocks that are being repeatedly read.

If a hot block belongs to an index segment, you may consider partitioning the table and using local indexes. For example, a hash partitioning scheme lets you spread the load among multiple partitioned indexes. You can also consider converting the table to a hash cluster based on the indexed columns. This way, you can avoid the index altogether. If the hot blocks belong to a table segment instead, you can still consider partitioning the table to spread the load across the partitions. You may also want to reconsider the application design to see why the same blocks are being repeatedly accessed, thus rendering them "hot."

5-21. Managing Locks from Oracle Enterprise Manager

Problem

You'd like to find out how to handle locking issues through the Oracle Enterprise Manager Database Control GUI interface.

Solution

Instead of issuing multiple SQL queries to identify quickly disappearing locking events, you can use Oracle Enterprise Manager (OEM) DB Control to identify and resolve locking situations. You can find all current locks in the instance, including the blocking and the blocked sessions—you can can also kill the blocking session from OEM.

Here are the ways you can manage locking issues through OEM:

- In the Home page of DB Control, you'll see locking information in the Alerts table. Look for the User Block category to identify blocking sessions. The alert name you must look for is Blocking Session Count. Clicking the message link shown for this alert, such as "Session 68 is blocking 12 other sessions," for example, will take you to the Blocking Session Count page. In the Alert History table on this page, you can view details about the blocking and blocked sessions.

  Also in the Home page, under Related Alerts, you'll find the ADDM Performance table. Locking issues are revealed by the presence of the Row Lock Waits link. Click the Row Lock Waits link to go to the Row Lock Waits page. This page, shown in Figure 5-1, lets you view you all the SQL statements that were found waiting for row locks.

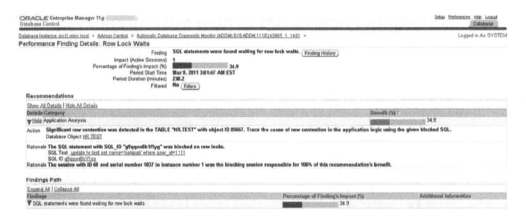

Figure 5-1. *The Row Lock Waits page in OEM*

- You can also view blocking session details by clicking the Performance tab in the Home page. Click Blocking Sessions under the Additional Monitoring Links section to go to the Blocking Sessions page. The Blocking Sessions page contains details for both the blocking as well as the blocked sessions. You can see the exact wait event, which will be enq: TX row lock contention when one session blocks another. You can find out the exact SQL statement that's involved in blocking sessions, by clicking the SQL ID link on this page. You can kill the blocking session from this page by clicking the Kill Session button at the top left side of the page.

- Also in the Additional Monitoring Links section is another link named Instance Locks, which takes you to the Instance Locks page. The Instance Locks page shows the session details for both the blocking and blocked sessions. You can click the SQL ID link to view the current SQL that's being executed by the blocker and the blocked sessions. You can also find out the name of the object that's locked. You can kill the blocking session by clicking the Kill Session button.

How It Works

You don't necessarily have to execute multiple SQL scripts to analyze locking behavior in your database. The SQL code we showed you earlier in various recipes was meant to explain how Oracle locking works. On a day-to-day basis, it's much more practical and efficient to just use OEM to quickly find out who's blocking a session and why.

5-22. Analyzing Waits from Oracle Enterprise Manager

Problem

You'd like to use Oracle Enterprise Manager to manage waits in your database instances.

Solution

The OEM interface lets you quickly analyze current waits in your database, instead of running SQL scripts to do so. In the Home page, the Active Sessions graph shows the relative amounts of waits, I/O, and CPU. Click the Waits link in this graph to view the Active Sessions graph. To the right of the graph, you'll see various links such as Concurrency, Application, Cluster, Administrative, User I/O, etc. Clicking each of these links will take you to a page that shows you all active sessions that are waiting for waits under that wait class. We summarize the wait events under the most important of these wait classes here.

> User I/O: This shows wait events such as db file scattered read, db file sequential read, direct path read, direct path write, and read by other session. You can click any of the links for the various waits to get a graph of the wait events. For example, clicking the "db file scattered read" link will take you to the histogram for the "Wait Event: db file scattered read" page.

> System I/O: This shows waits due to the db file parallel write, log file parallel write, control file parallel write, and the control file sequential read wait events.

> Application: This shows active sessions waiting for events such as enqueue locks.

How It Works

Once you understand the theory behind the Oracle Wait Interface, you can use OEM to quickly analyze current wait events in your database. You can find out not only which wait events are adversely affecting performance, but also which SQL statement and which users are involved. All the details pages you can drill down to from the Active Session page show a graph of the particular wait event class from the time the instance started. The pages also contain tables named Top SQL and Top Users, which show exactly which SQL and users are affected by the wait event.

CHAPTER 6

Analyzing Operating System Performance

Solving database performance issues sometimes requires the use of operating system (OS) utilities. These tools often provide information that can help isolate database performance problems. Consider the following situations:

- You're running multiple databases and multiple applications on one server and want to use OS utilities to identify which database (and corresponding process) is consuming the most operating system resources. This approach is invaluable when one database application is consuming resources to the point of causing other databases on the box to perform poorly.

- You need to verify if the database server is adequately sized for current application workload in terms of CPU, memory, disk I/O, and network bandwidth.

- An analysis is needed to determine at what point the server will not be able to handle larger (future) workloads.

- You've used database tools to identify system bottlenecks and want to double-check the analysis via operating system tools.

In these scenarios, to effectively analyze, tune, and troubleshoot, you'll need to employ OS tools to identify resource-intensive processes. Furthermore, if you have multiple databases and applications running on one server, when troubleshooting performance issues, it's often more efficient to first determine which database and process is consuming the most resources. Operating system utilities help pinpoint whether the bottleneck is CPU, memory, disk I/O, or a network issue. In Linux/Unix environments, once you have the operating system identifier, you can then query the database to show any corresponding database processes and SQL statements.

Take a look at Figure 6-1. This flowchart details the decision-making process and the relevant Linux/Unix operating system tools that a DBA steps through when diagnosing sluggish server performance. For example, when you're dealing with performance problems, one common first task is to log on to the box and quickly check for disk space issues using OS utilities like df and du. A full mount point is a common cause of database unavailability.

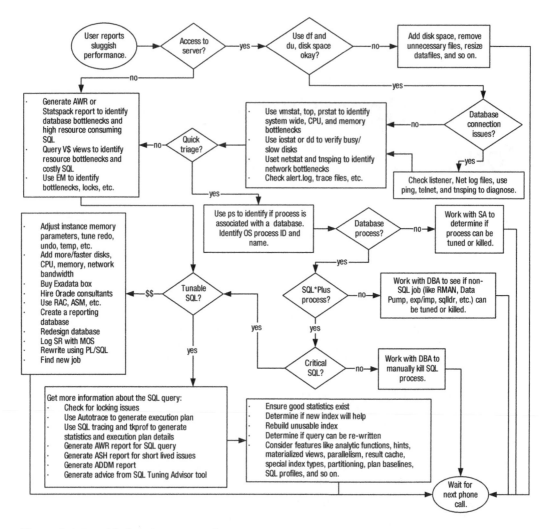

Figure 6-1. *Troubleshooting poor performance*

After inspecting disk space issues, the next task is to use an OS utility such as vmstat, top, or ps to determine what type of bottleneck you have. For example, is sluggish performance related to a disk I/O issue, CPU, memory, or the network? After determining the type of bottleneck, the next step is to determine if a database process is causing the bottleneck.

The ps command is useful for displaying the process name and ID of the resource-consuming session. When you have multiple databases running on one box, you can determine which database is associated with the process from the process name. Once you have the process ID and associated database, you can then log on to the database and run SQL queries to determine if the process is associated with a SQL query. If the problem is SQL-related, then you can identify further details regarding the SQL query and where it might be tuned.

Figure 6-1 encapsulates the difficulty of troubleshooting performance problems. Correctly pinpointing the cause of performance issues and recommending an efficient solution is often easier said than done. When trying to resolve issues, some paths result in relatively efficient and inexpensive solutions, such as terminating a runaway operating system process or regenerating fresh statistics. Other decisions may lead you to conclude that you need to add expensive hardware or redesign the system. Your performance tuning conclusions can have long-lasting financial impact on your company and thus influence your ability to retain a job. Obviously you want to focus on the cause of a performance problem and not just address the symptom. If you can consistently identify the root cause of the performance issue and recommend an effective and inexpensive solution, this will greatly improve your employment opportunities.

The focus of this chapter is to provide detailed examples that show how to use Linux/Unix operating system utilities to identify server performance issues. These utilities are invaluable for providing extra information used to diagnose performance issues outside of tools available within the database. Operating system utilities act as an extra set of eyes to help zero in on the cause of poor database performance.

6-1. Detecting Disk Space Issues

Problem

Users are reporting that they can't connect to a database. You log on to the database server, attempt to connect to SQL*Plus, and receive this error:

```
ORA-09817: Write to audit file failed.
Linux Error: 28: No space left on device
Additional information: 12
```

You want to quickly determine if a mount point is full and where the largest files are within this mount point.

Solution

In a Linux/Unix environment, use the df command to identify disk space issues. This example uses the -h to format the output so that space is reported in megabytes or gigabytes:

```
$ df -h
```

Here is some sample output:

```
Filesystem            Size  Used Avail Use% Mounted on
/dev/mapper/VolGroup00-LogVol00
                       29G   28G     0 100% /
/dev/sda1              99M   19M   75M  20% /boot
```

The prior output indicates that the root (/) file system is full on this server. In this situation, once a full mount point is identified, then use the find command to locate the largest files contained in a directory structure. This example navigates to the ORACLE_HOME directory and then connects the find, ls, sort, and head commands to identify the largest files beneath that directory:

```
$ cd $ORACLE_HOME
$ find . -ls | sort -nrk7 | head -10
```

If you have a full mount point, also consider looking for the following types of files that can be moved or removed:

- Deleting database trace files

- Removing large Oracle Net log files

- Moving, compressing, or deleting old archive redo log files

- Removing old installation files or binaries

- If you have datafiles with ample free space, consider resizing them to smaller sizes

Another way to identify where the disk space is being used is to find the largest space-consuming directories beneath a given directory. This example combines the du, sort, and head commands to show the ten largest directories beneath the current working directory:

```
$ du -S . | sort -nr | head -10
```

The prior command is particularly useful for identifying a directory that might not necessarily have large files in it, but lots of small files consuming space (like trace files).

■ **Note**   On Solaris Unix systems, the prior command will need to use du with the –o option.

How It Works

When you have a database that is hung because there is little or no free disk space, you should quickly find files that can be safely removed without compromising database availability. On Linux/Unix servers, the df, find, and du commands are particularly useful.

When working with production database servers, it's highly desirable to proactively monitor disk space so that you're warned about a mount point becoming full. Listed next is a simple shell script that monitors disk space for a given set of mount points:

```
#!/bin/bash
mntlist="/orahome /oraredo1 /oraarch1 /ora01 /oradump01 /"
for ml in $mntlist
do
echo $ml
usedSpc=$(df -h $ml | awk '{print $5}' | grep -v capacity | cut -d "%" -f1 -)
BOX=$(uname -a | awk '{print $2}')
#
case $usedSpc in
[0-9])
arcStat="relax, lots of disk space: $usedSpc"
;;
[1-7][0-9])
arcStat="disk space okay: $usedSpc"
```

```
;;
[8][0-9])
arcStat="space getting low: $usedSpc"
;;
[9][0-9])
arcStat="warning, running out of space: $usedSpc"
echo $arcStat $ml | mailx -s "space on: $BOX" dkuhn@oracle.com
;;
[1][0][0])
arcStat="update resume, no space left: $usedSpc"
echo $arcStat $ml | mailx -s "space on: $BOX" dkuhn@oracle.com
;;
*)
arcStat="huh?: $usedSpc"
esac
#
BOX=$(uname -a | awk '{print $2}')
echo $arcStat
#
done
#
exit 0
```

You'll have to modify the script to match your environment. For example, the second line of the script specifies the mount points on the box being monitored:

```
mntlist="/orahome /oraredo1 /oraarch1 /ora01 /oradump01 /"
```

These mount points should match the mount points listed in the output of the df -h command. For a Solaris box that this script runs on, here's the output of df:

```
Filesystem          size    used   avail capacity  Mounted on
/                    35G    5.9G    30G    17%      /
/ora01              230G    185G    45G    81%      /ora01
/oraarch1           100G    12G     88G    13%      /oraarch1
/oradump01          300G    56G    244G    19%      /oradump01
/orahome             20G    15G     5.4G   73%      /orahome
/oraredo1            30G    4.9G    25G    17%      /oraredo1
```

Also, depending on what version of Linux/Unix you're using, you'll have to modify this line as well:

```
usedSpc=$(df -h $ml | awk '{print $5}' | grep -v capacity | cut -d "%" -f1 -)
```

The prior line of code depends on the output of the df command, which can vary somewhat depending on the operating system vendor and version. For example, on one Linux system, the output of df might span two lines and reports on Use% instead of capacity, so in this scenario, the usedSpc variable is populated as shown:

```
usedSpc=$(for x in `df -h $ml | grep -v "Use%"` ; do echo $x ; done | \
grep "%" |   cut -d "%" -f1 -)
```

The prior code (broken into two lines to fit on the page) runs several Linux/Unix commands and places the output in the usedSpc variable. The command first runs df -h, which is piped to the awk command. The awk command takes the output and prints out the fifth column. This is piped to the grep command, which uses −v to eliminate the word Use% from the output. This is finally piped to the cut command, which cuts out the "%" character from the output.

On a Linux/Unix system, a shell script such as the prior one can easily be run from a scheduling utility such as cron. For example, if the shell script is named filesp.bsh, here is a sample cron entry:

```
#----------------------------------------------------------------
# Filesystem check
7 * * * * /orahome/oracle/bin/filesp.bsh 1>/orahome/oracle/bin/log/filesp.log 2>&1
#----------------------------------------------------------------
```

The prior entry instructs the system to run the filesp.bsh shell script at seven minutes after the hour for every hour of the day.

6-2. Identifying System Bottlenecks (vmstat)

Problem

You want to determine if a server performance issue is specifically related to disk I/O, CPU, memory, or network.

■ **Note** If you are running under Solaris, see Recipe 6-3 for a specific solution applying to that operating system.

Solution

Use vmstat to determine where the system is resource-constrained. For example, the following command reports on system resource usage every five seconds on a Linux system:

```
$ vmstat 5
```

Here is some sample output:

```
procs -----------memory---------- ---swap-- -----io---- --system-- -----cpu------
 r  b   swpd   free   buff  cache   si   so    bi    bo   in   cs us sy id wa st
 2  0 228816 2036164  78604 3163452    0    0     1    16    0    0 29  0 70  0  0
 2  0 228816 2035792  78612 3163456    0    0     0    59  398  528 50  1 49  0  0
 2  0 228816 2035172  78620 3163448    0    0     0    39  437  561 50  1 49  0  0
```

To exit out of vmstat in this mode, press Ctrl+C. You can also have vmstat report for a specific number of runs. For example, this instructs vmstat to run every six seconds for a total of ten reports:

```
$ vmstat 6 10
```

Here are some general heuristics you can use when interpreting the output of vmstat:

- If the wa (time waiting for I/O) column is high, this is usually an indication that the storage subsystem is overloaded. See Recipe 6-6 for identifying the sources of I/O contention.

- If b (processes sleeping) is consistently greater than 0, then you may not have enough CPU processing power. See Recipes 6-5 and 6-9 for identifying Oracle processes and SQL statements consuming the most CPU.

- If so (memory swapped out to disk) and si (memory swapped in from disk) are consistently greater than 0, you may have a memory bottleneck. See Recipe 6-5 for details on identifying Oracle processes and SQL statements consuming the most memory.

How It Works

The vmstat (virtual memory statistics) tool helps quickly identify bottlenecks on your server. Use the output of vmstat to help determine if the performance bottleneck is related to CPU, memory, or disk I/O. Table 6-1 describes the columns available in the output of vmstat. These columns may vary somewhat depending on your operating system and version.

Table 6-1. *Descriptions of* vmstat *Output Columns*

Column	Description
r	Number of processes waiting for run time
b	Number of processes in uninterruptible sleep
swpd	Amount of virtual memory
free	Amount of idle memory
buff	Amount of buffer memory
cache	Amount of cache memory
inact	Amount of inactive memory (-a option)
active	Amount of active memory (-a option)
si	Amount of memory swapped from disk/second
so	Amount of memory swapped to disk/second
bi	Blocks read/second from disk

Continued

Column	Description
bo	Blocks written/second to disk
in	Number of interrupts/seconds
cs	Number of context switches/second
us	CPU time running non-kernel code
sy	CPU time running kernel code
Id	CPU time idle
wa	CPU time waiting for I/O
st	CPU time taken from virtual machine

OS WATCHER

Oracle provides a collection of operating system scripts that gather and store metrics for CPU, memory, disk I/O, and network usage. The OS Watcher tool suite automates the gathering of statistics using tools such as top, vmstat, iostat, mpstat, netstat, and so on.

You can obtain OS Watcher from the My Oracle Support web site (support.oracle.com). Navigate to the support web site and search for OS Watcher. The OS Watcher User Guide can be found under document ID **301137.1**. This tool is supported on most Linux/Unix systems, and there is also a version for the Windows platform.

6-3. Identifying System Bottlenecks (Solaris)

Problem

You're working on a Solaris system, and irate users are reporting the database application is slow. You have multiple databases running on this box and want to identify which processes are consuming the most CPU resources. Once the resource-consuming processes are identified at the OS, then you want to map them (if possible) to a database process.

■ **Note** If you are not running Solaris, then see the solution in Recipe 6-2.

Solution

On most Solaris systems, the **prstat** utility is used to identify which processes are consuming the most CPU resources. For example, you can instruct the **prstat** to report system statistics every five seconds:

```
$ prstat 5
```

Here is some sample output:

```
  PID USERNAME  SIZE   RSS STATE  PRI NICE      TIME  CPU PROCESS/NLWP
16609 oracle   2364M 1443M cpu2    60    0   3:14:45  20% oracle/11
27565 oracle   2367M 1590M cpu3    21    0   0:11:28  16% oracle/14
23632 oracle   2284M 1506M run     46    2   0:16:18 6.1% oracle/11
 4066 oracle   2270M 1492M sleep   59    0   0:02:52 1.7% oracle/35
15630 oracle   2274M 1482M sleep   48    0  19:40:41 1.2% oracle/11
```

Type **q** or press Ctrl+C to exit **prstat**. In the prior output, process 16609 is consistently showing up as a top CPU-consuming process.

After identifying a top resource-consuming process, you can determine which database the process is associated with by using the **ps** command. This example reports on process information associated with the PID of 16609:

```
$ ps -ef | grep 16609
  oracle 16609  3021  18   Mar 09 ?         196:29 ora_dw00_ENGDEV
```

In this example, the name of the process is **ora_dw00_ENGDEV** and the associated database is **ENGDEV**.

How It Works

If you're working on a Solaris server, the **top** utility is oftentimes not installed. In these environments, the **prstat** command can be used to determine top resource-consuming processes on the system. Table 6-2 describes several of the columns displayed in the default output of **prstat**.

Table 6-2. Column Descriptions of the top Output

Column	Description
PID	Unique process identifier
USERNAME	OS username running the process
SIZE	Virtual memory size of the process
RSS	Resident set size of process
STATE	State of process (running, stopped, and so on)
PRI	Priority of process
NICE	Nice value used to compute priority
TIME	Cumulative execution time
CPU	Percent of CPU consumption
PROCESS	Name of the executed file
NLWP	Number of LWPs in the process

6-4. Identifying Top Server-Consuming Resources (top)

Problem

You have a Linux server that hosts multiple databases. Users are reporting sluggishness with an application that uses one of the databases. You want to identify which processes are consuming the most resources on the server and then determine if the top consuming process is associated with a database.

Solution

The top command shows a real-time display of the highest resource-consuming processes on a server. Here's the simplest way to run top:

```
$ top
```

Listed next is a fragment of the output:

```
top - 04:40:05 up 353 days, 15:16,  3 users,  load average: 2.84, 2.34, 2.45
Tasks: 454 total,   4 running, 450 sleeping,   0 stopped,   0 zombie
Cpu(s): 64.3%us,  3.4%sy,  0.0%ni, 20.6%id, 11.8%wa,  0.0%hi,  0.0%si,  0.0%st
Mem:   7645184k total, 6382956k used, 1262228k free,   176480k buffers
Swap:  4128760k total,      184k used,  4128576k free,  3953512k cached

  PID USER      PR  NI  VIRT  RES  SHR S %CPU %MEM    TIME+  COMMAND
19888 oracle    25   0  148m  13m  11m R 100.1  0.2 313371:45 oracle
19853 oracle    25   0  148m  13m  11m R 99.8  0.2 313375:41 oracle
 9722 oracle    18   0 1095m 287m 150m R 58.6  3.8  0:41.89 oracle
  445 root      11  -5     0    0    0 S  0.3  0.0  8:32.67 kjournald
 9667 oracle    15   0  954m  55m  50m S  0.3  0.7  0:01.03 oracle
    2 root      RT  -5     0    0    0 S  0.0  0.0  2:17.99 migration/0
```

Type **q** or press Ctrl+C to exit **top**. In the prior output, the first section of the output displays general system information such as how long the server has been running, number of users, CPU information, and so on. The second section shows which processes are consuming the most CPU resources (listed top to bottom). In the prior output, the process ID of 19888 is consuming a large amount of CPU. To determine which database this process is associated with, use the **ps** command:

```
$ ps 19888
```

Here is the associated output:

```
PID TTY      STAT   TIME COMMAND
19888 ?        Rs   313393:32 oracleO11R2 (DESCRIPTION=(LOCAL=YES)
```

In the prior output, the fourth column displays the value of **oracleO11R2**. This indicates that this is an Oracle process associated with the **O11R2** database. If the process continues to consume resources, you can next determine if there is a SQL statement associated with the process (see Recipe 6-9) or terminate the process (see Recipe 6-10).

■ **Tip**   If you work in a Solaris operating system environment, use the **prstat** command to view the top CPU-consuming processes (see Recipe 6-3 for details).

How It Works

If installed, the **top** utility is often the first investigative tool employed by DBAs and system administrators to identify resource-intensive processes on a server. If a process is continuously consuming excessive system resources, then you should further determine if the process is associated with a database and a specific SQL statement.

By default, **top** will repetitively refresh (every few seconds) information regarding the most CPU-intensive processes. While **top** is running, you can interactively change its output. For example, if you type **>**, this will move the column that **top** is sorting one position to the right. Table 6-3 lists the most useful hot key features to alter the **top** display to the desired format.

Table 6-3. Commands to Interactively Change the top Output

Command	Function
Spacebar	Immediately refreshes the output
< or >	Moves the sort column one to the left or to the right; by default, top sorts on the CPU column.
d	Changes the refresh time
R	Reverses the sort order
z	Toggles the color output
h	Displays help menu
F or O	Chooses a sort column

Table 6-4 describes several of the columns displayed by top. Use these descriptions to help interpret the output.

Table 6-4. Column Descriptions of the top Output

Column	Description
PID	Unique process identifier
USER	OS username running the process
PR	Priority of the process
NI	Nice value or process; negative value means high priority; positive value means low priority.
VIRT	Total virtual memory used by process
RES	Non-swapped physical memory used
SHR	Shared memory used by process
S	Process status
%CPU	Processes percent of CPU consumption since last screen refresh
%MEM	Percent of physical memory the process is consuming

Column	Description
TIME	Total CPU time used by process
TIME+	Total CPU time, showing hundredths of seconds
COMMAND	Command line used to start a process

6-5. Identifying CPU and Memory Bottlenecks (ps)

Problem

You want to quickly isolate which processes on the server are consuming the most CPU and memory resources.

Solution

The ps (process status) command is handy for quickly identifying top resource-consuming processes. For example, this command displays the top ten CPU-consuming resources on the box:

```
$ ps -e -o pcpu,pid,user,tty,args | sort -n -k 1 -r | head
```

Here is a partial listing of the output:

```
97.8 26902 oracle    ?        oracleO11R2 (DESCRIPTION=(LOCAL=YES)(ADDRESS=(PROTOCOL=beq)))
 0.5 27166 oracle    ?        ora_diag_O11R2
0.0     9 root       ?        [ksoftirqd/2]
```

In the prior output, the process named oracleO11R2 is consuming an inordinate amount of CPU resources on the server. The process name identifies this as an Oracle process associated with the O11R2 database.

Similarly, you can also display the top memory-consuming processes:

```
$ ps -e -o pmem,pid,user,tty,args | sort -n -k 1 -r | head
```

How It Works

The Linux/Unix ps command displays information about currently active processes on the server. The pcpu switch instructs the process status to report the CPU usage of each process. Similarly the pmem switch instructs ps to report on process memory usage. This gives you a quick and easy way to determine which processes are consuming the most resources.

When using multiple commands on one line (such as ps, sort, and head), it's often desirable to associate the combination of commands with a shortcut (alias). Here's an example of creating aliases:

```
$ alias topc='ps -e -o pcpu,pid,user,tty,args | sort -n -k 1 -r | head'
$ alias topm='ps -e -o pmem,pid,user,tty,args | sort -n -k 1 -r | head'
```

Now instead of typing in the long line of commands, you can use the alias—for example:

```
$ topc
```

Also consider establishing the aliases in a startup file (like .bashrc or .profile) so that the commands are automatically defined when you log on to the database server.

6-6. Identifying I/O Bottlenecks

Problem

You are experiencing performance problems and want to determine if the issues are related to slow disk I/O.

Solution

Use the iostat command with the -x (extended) option combined with the -d (device) option to generate I/O statistics. This next example displays extended device statistics every ten seconds:

```
$ iostat -xd 10
```

You need a fairly wide screen to view this output; here's a partial listing:

```
Device:    rrqm/s wrqm/s   r/s   w/s rsec/s  wsec/s   rkB/s   wkB/s avgrq-sz
avgqu-sz   await  svctm  %util
sda         0.01   3.31  0.11  0.31   5.32   28.97    2.66   14.49    83.13
0.06  138.44   1.89   0.08
```

This periodic extended output allows you to view in real time which devices are experiencing spikes in read and write activity. To exit from the previous iostat command, press Ctrl+C. The options and output may vary depending on your operating system. For example, on some Linux/Unix distributions, the iostat output may report the disk utilization as %b (percent busy).

When trying to determine whether device I/O is the bottleneck, here are some general guidelines when examining the iostat output:

- Look for devices with abnormally high blocks read or written per second.

- If any device is near 100% utilization, that's a strong indicator I/O is a bottleneck.

How It Works

The iostat command can help you determine whether disk I/O is potentially a source of performance problems. Table 6-5 describes the columns displayed in the iostat output.

Table 6-5. *Column Descriptions of* `iostat` *Disk I/O Output*

Column	Description
Device	Device or partition name
tps	I/O transfers per second to the device
Blk_read/s	Blocks per second read from the device
Blk_wrtn/s	Blocks written per second to the device
Blk_read	Number of blocks read
Blk_wrtn	Number of blocks written
rrqm/s	Number of read requests merged per second that were queued to device
wrqm/s	Number of write requests merged per second that were queued to device
r/s	Read requests per second
w/s	Write requests per second
rsec/s	Sectors read per second
wsec/s	Sectors written per second
rkB/s	Kilobytes read per second
wkB/s	Kilobytes written per second
avgrq-sz	Average size of requests in sectors
avgqu-sz	Average queue length of requests
await	Average time in milliseconds for I/O requests sent to the device to be served
svctm	Average service time in milliseconds
%util	Percentage of CPU time during which I/O requests were issued to the device. Near 100% indicates device saturation

You can also instruct `iostat` to display reports at a specified interval. The first report displayed will report averages since the last server reboot; each subsequent report shows statistics since the previously generated snapshot. The following example displays a device statistic report every three seconds:

```
$ iostat -d 3
```

You can also specify a finite number of reports that you want generated. This is useful for gathering metrics to be analyzed over a period of time. This example instructs iostat to report every 2 seconds for a total of 15 reports:

```
$ iostat 2 15
```

When working with locally attached disks, the output of the iostat command will clearly show where the I/O is occurring. However, it is not that clear-cut in environments that use external arrays for storage. What you are presented with at the file system layer is some sort of a virtual disk that might also have been configured by a volume manager. In virtualized storage environments, you'll have to work with your system administrator or storage administrator to determine exactly which disks are experiencing high I/O activity.

Once you have determined that you have a disk I/O contention issue, then you can use utilities such as AWR (if licensed), Statspack (no license required), or the V$ views to determine if your database is I/O stressed. For example, the AWR report contains an I/O statistics section with the following subsections:

- IOStat by Function summary

- IOStat by Filetype summary

- IOStat by Function/Filetype summary

- Tablespace IO Stats

- File IO Stats

You can also directly query data dictionary views such as V$SQL to determine which SQL statements are using excessive I/O—for example:

```
SELECT *
FROM
(SELECT
  parsing_schema_name
 ,direct_writes
 ,SUBSTR(sql_text,1,75)
 ,disk_reads
FROM v$sql
ORDER BY disk_reads DESC)
WHERE rownum < 20;
```

To determine which sessions are currently waiting for I/O resources, query V$SESSION:

```
SELECT
 username
,program
,machine
,sql_id
FROM v$session
WHERE event LIKE 'db file%read';
```

To view objects that are waiting for I/O resources, run a query such as this:

```
SELECT
 object_name
,object_type
,owner
FROM v$session   a
    ,dba_objects b
WHERE a.event LIKE 'db file%read'
AND   b.data_object_id = a.row_wait_obj#;
```

Once you have identified queries (using the prior queries in this section), then consider the following factors, which can cause a SQL statement to consume inordinate amounts of I/O:

- Poorly written SQL

- Improper indexing

- Improper use of parallelism (which can cause excessive full table scans)

You'll have to examine each query and try to determine if one of the prior items is the cause of poor performance as it relates to I/O.

6-7. Identifying Network-Intensive Processes

Problem

You're investigating performance issues on a database server. As part of your investigation, you want to determine if there are network bottlenecks on the system.

Solution

Use the netstat (network statistics) command to display network traffic. Perhaps the most useful way to view netstat output is with the -ptc options. These options display the process ID and TCP connections, and they continuously update the output:

```
$ netstat -ptc
```

Press Ctrl+C to exit the previous command. Here's a partial listing of the output:

```
(Not all processes could be identified, non-owned process info
 will not be shown, you would have to be root to see it all.)
Active Internet connections (w/o servers)
Proto Recv-Q Send-Q Local Address  Foreign Address  State       PID/Program name
tcp       0      0 rmug.com:62386 rmug.com:1521    ESTABLISHED 22864/ora_pmon_RMDB
tcp       0      0 rmug.com:53930 rmug.com:1521    ESTABLISHED 6091/sqlplus
tcp       0      0 rmug.com:1521  rmug.com:53930   ESTABLISHED 6093/oracleRMDB1
tcp       0      0 rmug.com:1521  rmug.com:62386   ESTABLISHED 10718/tnslsnr
```

If the `Send-Q` (bytes not acknowledged by remote host) column has an unusually high value for a process, this may indicate an overloaded network. The useful aspect about the previous output is that you can determine the operating system process ID (PID) associated with a network connection. If you suspect the connection in question is an `oracle` session, you can use the techniques described in the "Solution" section of Recipe 6-9 to map an operating system PID to an Oracle process or SQL statement.

How It Works

When experiencing performance issues, usually the network is not the cause. Most likely you'll determine that bad performance is related to a poorly constructed SQL statement, inadequate disk I/O, or not enough CPU or memory resources. However, as a DBA, you need to be aware of all sources of performance bottlenecks and how to diagnose them. In today's highly interconnected world, you must possess network troubleshooting and monitoring skills. The `netstat` utility is a good starting place for monitoring server network connections.

6-8. Troubleshooting Database Network Connectivity

Problem

A user has reported that he or she can't connect to a database. You know there are many components involved with network connectivity and want to figure out the root cause of the problem.

Solution

Use these steps as guidelines when diagnosing Oracle database network connectivity issues:

1. Use the operating system `ping` utility to determine whether the remote box is accessible—for example:

    ```
    $ ping dwdb
    dwdb is alive
    ```

    If `ping` doesn't work, work with your system or network administrator to ensure you have server-to-server connectivity in place.

2. Use `telnet` to see if you can connect to the remote server and port (that the listener is listening on)—for example:

    ```
    $ telnet ora03 1521
    Trying 127.0.0.1...
    Connected to ora03.
    Escape character is '^]'.
    ```

    The prior output indicates that connectivity to a server and port is okay. If the prior command hangs, then contact your SA or network administrator for further assistance.

3. Use `tnsping` to determine whether Oracle Net is working. This utility will verify that an Oracle Net connection can be made to a database via the network—for example:

```
$ tnsping dwrep
..........
Used TNSNAMES adapter to resolve the alias
Attempting to contact (DESCRIPTION = (ADDRESS = (PROTOCOL = TCP)
(HOST = dwdb1.us.farm.com)(PORT = 1521))
(CONNECT_DATA = (SERVER = DEDICATED) (SERVICE_NAME = DWREP)))
OK (500 msec)
```

If `tnsping` can't contact the remote database, verify that the remote listener and database are both up and running. On the remote box, use the `lsnrctl status` command to verify that the listener is up. Verify that the remote database is available by establishing a local connection as a non-SYS account (SYS can often connect to a troubled database when other schemas will not work).

4. Verify that the TNS information is correct. If the remote listener and database are working, then ensure that the mechanism for determining TNS information (like the `tnsnames.ora` file) contains the correct information.

Sometimes the client machine will have multiple TNS_ADMIN locations and `tnsnames.ora` files. One way to verify whether a particular `tnsnames.ora` file is being used is to rename it and see whether you get a different error when attempting to connect to the remote database.

How It Works

Network connectivity issues can be troublesome to diagnose because there are several architectural components that have to be in place for it to work correctly. You need to have the following in place:

- A functional network

- Open ports from point to point

- Oracle Net correctly installed and configured

- Target database and listener up and running

- Correct navigational information from the client to the target database

If you're still having issues, examine the client `sqlnet.log` file and the remote server `listener.log` file. Sometimes these log files will show additional information that will pinpoint the issue.

6-9. Mapping a Resource-Intensive Process to a Database Process

Problem

It's a dark and stormy night, and the system is performing poorly. You identify an operating system–intensive process on the box. You want to map an operating system process back to a database process. If the database process is a SQL process, you want to display the user of the SQL statement and also the SQL.

Solution

In Linux/Unix environments, if you can identify the resource-intensive operating system process, then you can easily check to see if that process is associated with a database process. The process consists of the following:

1. Run an OS command to identify resource-intensive processes and associated IDs.

2. Identify the database associated with the process.

3. Extract details about the process from the database data dictionary views.

4. If it's a SQL statement, get those details.

5. Generate an execution plan for the SQL statement.

For example, suppose you identify the top CPU-consuming queries with the ps command:

```
$ ps -e -o pcpu,pid,user,tty,args|grep -i oracle|sort -n -k 1 -r|head
```

Here is some sample output:

```
16.4 11026   oracle ?     oracleDWREP (DESCRIPTION=(LOCAL=YES)(ADDRESS=(PROTOCOL=beq)))
 0.1  6448   oracle ?     oracleINVPRD (LOCAL=NO)
 0.5  3639   oracle ?     ora_dia0_STAGE
 0.4 28133   oracle ?     ora_dia0_DEVSEM
 0.4  4093   oracle ?     ora_dia0_DWODI
 0.4  3534   oracle ?     ora_dia0_ENGDEV
 0.2  4111   oracle ?     ora_mmnl_DWODI
```

The prior output identifies one operating system process consuming an excessive amount of CPU (16.4%). The process ID is 11026 and name is `oracleDWREP`. From the process name, it's an Oracle process associated with the DWREP database.

You can determine what type of Oracle process this is by querying the data dictionary:

```
SELECT
   'USERNAME   : ' || s.username    || CHR(10) ||
   'SCHEMA     : ' || s.schemaname  || CHR(10) ||
   'OSUSER     : ' || s.osuser      || CHR(10) ||
   'PROGRAM    : ' || s.program     || CHR(10) ||
```

```
 'SPID      : ' || p.spid        || CHR(10) ||
 'SID       : ' || s.sid         || CHR(10) ||
 'SERIAL#   : ' || s.serial#     || CHR(10) ||
 'KILL STRING: ' || '''' || s.sid || ',' || s.serial# || ''''   || CHR(10) ||
 'MACHINE   : ' || s.machine     || CHR(10) ||
 'TYPE      : ' || s.type        || CHR(10) ||
 'TERMINAL  : ' || s.terminal    || CHR(10) ||
 'SQL ID    : ' || q.sql_id      || CHR(10) ||
 'SQL TEXT  : ' || q.sql_text
FROM v$session s
    ,v$process p
    ,v$sql     q
WHERE s.paddr  = p.addr
AND   p.spid   = '&&PID_FROM_OS'
AND   s.sql_id = q.sql_id(+);
```

The prior script prompts you for the operating system process ID. Here is the output for this example:

```
USERNAME    : MV_MAINT
SCHEMA      : MV_MAINT
OSUSER      : oracle
PROGRAM     : sqlplus@dwdb (TNS V1-V3)
SPID        : 11026
SID         : 410
SERIAL#     : 30653
KILL STRING: '410,30653'
MACHINE     : dwdb
TYPE        : USER
TERMINAL    : pts/2
SQL ID      : by3c8848gyngu
SQL TEXT    : SELECT "A1"."REGISTRATION_ID","A1"."PRODUCT_INSTANCE_ID"
,"A1"."SOA_ID","A1"."REG_SOURCE_IP_ADDR","A1"...
```

The output indicates that this is a SQL*Plus process with a database SID of 410 and SERIAL# of 30653. You'll need this information if you decide to terminate the process with the ALTER SYSTEM KILL SESSION statement (see Recipe 6-10 for details).

In this example, since the process is running a SQL statement, further details about the query can be extracted by generating an execution plan:

```
SQL> SELECT * FROM table(DBMS_XPLAN.DISPLAY_CURSOR(('&&sql_id')));
```

You'll be prompted for the sql_id when you run the prior statement (in this example, the sql_id is by3c8848gyngu). Here is a partial listing of the output:

```
SQL_ID  by3c8848gyngu, child number 0
-------------------------------------
SELECT "A1"."REGISTRATION_ID","A1"."PRODUCT_INSTANCE_ID","A1"."SOA_ID","
A1"."REG_SOURCE_IP_ADDR","A1"."REGISTRATION_STATUS","A1"."CREATE_DTT","A
1"."DOMAIN_ID","A1"."COUNT_FLG","A2"."PRODUCT_INSTANCE_ID","A2"."SVC_TAG
Plan hash value: 4286489280
```

```
--------------------------------------------------------------------------------
| Id|Operation                     |Name          | Rows | Bytes | Cost (%CPU)| Time     |
--------------------------------------------------------------------------------
|  0|SELECT STATEMENT              |              |      |       | 64977 (100)|          |
|  1| NESTED LOOPS                 |              |      |       |            |          |
|  2|  NESTED LOOPS                |              |    1 |   499 | 64977  (5) | 00:13:00 |
|  3|   NESTED LOOPS OUTER         |              |    1 |   462 | 64975  (5) | 00:13:00 |
|  4|    NESTED LOOPS OUTER        |              |    1 |   454 | 64973  (5) | 00:13:00 |
|  5|     NESTED LOOPS             |              |    1 |   420 | 64972  (5) | 00:13:00 |
|  6|      NESTED LOOPS OUTER      |              |    1 |   351 | 64971  (5) | 00:13:00 |
|  7|       NESTED LOOPS          |              |    1 |   278 | 64969  (5) | 00:13:00 |
|  8|        NESTED LOOPS OUTER   |              |    1 |   188 | 64967  (5) | 00:13:00 |
|  9|         NESTED LOOPS        |              |    1 |   180 | 64966  (5) | 00:13:00 |
|*10|          TABLE ACCESS FULL |REGISTRATIONS |    1 |    77 | 64964  (5) | 00:13:00 |
--------------------------------------------------------------------------------
```

This output will help you determine the efficiency of the SQL statement and provide insight on how to tune it. Refer to Chapter 9 for details on how to manually tune a query and Chapter 11 for automated SQL tuning.

How It Works

The process described in the "Solution" section of this recipe allows you to quickly identify resource-intensive processes, then map the OS process to a database process, and subsequently map the database process to a SQL statement. Once you know which SQL statement is consuming resources, then you can generate an execution plan to further attempt to determine any possible inefficiencies.

Sometimes the resource-consuming process will not be associated with a database. In these scenarios, you'll have to work with your SA to determine what the process is and if it can be tuned or terminated.

Also, you may encounter resource-intensive processes that are database-specific but not associated with a SQL statement. For example, you might have a long-running RMAN backup process, Data Pump, or PL/SQL jobs running. In these cases, work with your DBA to identify whether these types of processes can be tuned or killed.

ORADEBUG

You can use Oracle's oradebug utility to display top consuming SQL statements if you know the operating system ID. For example, suppose that you have used a utility such as top or ps to identify a high CPU-consuming operating system process, and from the name of the process you determine it's a database process. Now log in to SQL*Plus and use oradebug to display any SQL associated with the process. In this example, the OS process ID is 7853:

```
SQL> oradebug setospid 7853;
Oracle pid: 18, Unix process pid: 7853, image: oracle@xengdb (TNS V1-V3)
```

Now show the SQL associated with this process (if any):

```
SQL> oradebug current_sql;
```

If there is a SQL statement associated with the process, it will be displayed—for example:

```
select
 a.table_name
from dba_tables a, dba_indexes b, .....
```

The oradebug utility can be used in a variety of methods to help troubleshoot performance issues. You can display the name of the trace file associated with the session by issuing the following:

```
SQL> oradebug tracefile_name;
```

Use oradebug help to display all options available.

6-10. Terminating a Resource-Intensive Process

Problem

You have identified a process that is consuming inordinate amounts of system resources (see Recipe 6-9) and determined that it's a runaway SQL statement that needs to be killed.

Solution

There are three basic ways to terminate a SQL process:

- If you have access to the terminal where the SQL statement is running, you can press Ctrl+C and attempt to halt the process.

- Determine the session ID and serial number, and then use the SQL ALTER SYSTEM KILL SESSION statement.

- Determine the operating system process ID, and use the kill utility to stop the process.

If you happen to have access to the terminal from which the resource-consuming SQL statement is running, you can attempt to press Ctrl+C to terminate the process. Oftentimes you don't have access to the terminal and will have to use a SQL statement or an operating system command to terminate the process.

Using SQL to Kill a Session

If it's an Oracle process and you have identified the SID and SERIAL# (see Recipe 6-9), you can terminate a process from within SQL*Plus. Here is the general syntax:

```
alter system kill session 'integer1, integer2 [,integer3]' [immediate];
```

In the prior syntax statement, integer1 is the value of the SID column and integer2 is the value from the SERIAL# column (of V$SESSION). In a RAC environment, you can optionally specify the value of the instance ID for integer3. The instance ID can be retrieved from the GV$SESSION view.

Here's an example that terminates a process with a SID of 1177 and a SERIAL# of 38583:

```
SQL> alter system kill session '1177,38583';
```

If successful, you should see this output:

```
System altered.
```

When you kill a session, this will mark the session as terminated, roll back active transactions (within the session), and release any locks (held by the session). The session will stay in a terminated state until any dependent transactions are rolled back. If it takes a minute or more to roll back the transaction, Oracle reports the session as "marked to be terminated" and returns control to the SQL prompt. If you specify IMMEDIATE (optional), Oracle will roll back any active transactions and immediately return control back to you.

Using the OS Kill Command

If you have access to the database server and access to an operating system account that has privileges to terminate an Oracle process (such as the oracle OS account), you can also terminate a process directly with the kill command.

For example, suppose you run the ps command and have done the associated work to determine that you have a SQL statement that has been running for hours and needs to be terminated. The kill command directly terminates the operating system process. In this example, the process ID of 6254 is terminated:

```
$ kill -9 6254
```

■ **Caution** Ensure that you don't kill the wrong Oracle process. If you accidentally kill a required Oracle background process, this will cause your instance to abort.

How It Works

Sometimes you'll find yourself in a situation where you need to kill hung SQL processes, database jobs, or SQL statements that are consuming inordinate amounts of resources. For example, you may have a test server where a job has been running for several hours, is consuming much of the server resources, and needs to be stopped so that other jobs can continue to process in a timely manner.

Manually killing a SQL statement will cause the transaction to be rolled back. Therefore take care when doing this. Ensure that you are killing the correct process. If you erroneously terminate a critical process, this obviously will have an adverse impact on the application and associated data.

Troubleshooting the Database

Oracle Database 11g offers new ways of diagnosing the health of your database. This chapter contains several recipes that show how to use the database's built-in diagnostic infrastructure to resolve database performance issues. You'll learn how to use ADRCI, the Automatic Diagnostic Repository Command Interpreter, to perform various tasks such as checking the database alert log, creating a diagnostic package for sending to Oracle Support engineers, and running a proactive health check of the database.

Many common Oracle database performance-related issues occur when you have space issues with the temporary tablespace or when you're creating a large index or a large table with the create table as select (CTAS) technique. Undo tablespace space issues are another common source of trouble for many DBAs. This chapter has several recipes that help you proactively monitor, diagnose, and resolve temporary tablespace and undo tablespace–related issues. When a production database seems to hang, there are ways to collect critical diagnostic data for analyzing the causes, and this chapter shows you how to log in to an unresponsive database to collect diagnostic data.

7-1. Determining the Optimal Undo Retention Period

Problem

You need to determine the optimal length of time for undo retention in your database.

Solution

You can specify the length of time Oracle will retain undo data after a transaction commits, by specifying the UNDO_RETENTION parameter. Here is how to set the undo retention to 30 minutes for an instance, by updating the value of the UNDO_RETENTION parameter in the SPFILE.

```
SQl> alter system set undo_retention=1800 scope=both;

System altered.

SQL>
```

To determine the optimal value for the UNDO_RETENTION parameter, you must first calculate the actual amount of undo that the database is generating. Once you know approximately how much undo the database is generating, you can calculate a more precise value for the UNDO_RETENTION parameter. Use the following formula to calculate the value of the UNDO_RETENTION parameter:

UNDO_RETENTION = UNDO SIZE/(DB_BLOCK_SIZE*UNDO_BLOCK_PER_SEC)

You can calculate the actual undo that's generated in your database by issuing the following query:

```
SQL> select sum(d.bytes) "undo"
  2   from v$datafile d,
  3   v$tablespace t,
  4   dba_tablespaces s
  5   where s.contents = 'UNDO'
  6   and s.status = 'ONLINE'
  7   and t.name = s.tablespace_name
  8   and d.ts# = t.ts#;

  UNDO
----------
 104857600
SQL>
```

You can calculate the value of UNDO_BLOCKS_PER_SEC with the following query:

```
SQL> select max(undoblks/((end_time-begin_time)*3600*24))
  2   "UNDO_BLOCK_PER_SEC"
  3   FROM v$undostat;

UNDO_BLOCK_PER_SEC
------------------
           7.625
SQL>
```

You most likely remember the block size for your database—if not, you can look it up in the SPFILE or find it by issuing the command show parameter db_block_size. Let's say the db_block_size is 8 KB (8,192 bytes) for your database. You can then calculate the optimal value for the UNDO_RETENTION parameter using the formula shown earlier in this recipe—for example, giving a result in seconds: 1,678.69 = 104,857,600/(7.625 * 8,192). In this case, assigning a value of 1,800 seconds for the undo_retention parameter is appropriate, because it's a bit more than what is indicated by our formula for computing the value of this parameter.

How It Works

Automatic undo management is the default mode for undo management starting with release 11g. If you create a database with the Database Configuration Assistant (DBCA), Oracle automatically creates an auto-extending undo tablespace named UNDOTBS1. If you're manually creating a database, you specify the undo tablespace in the database creation statement, or you can add the undo tablespace at any point. If a database doesn't have an explicit undo tablespace, Oracle will store the undo records in the SYSTEM tablespace.

Once you set the UNDO_TABLESPACE initialization parameter, Oracle automatically manages undo retention for you. Optionally, you can set the UNDO_RETENTION parameter to specify how long Oracle retains older undo data before overwriting it with newer undo data.

The formula in the "Solution" section shows how to base the undo retention period on current database activity. Note that we rely on the dynamic view V$UNDOSTAT to calculate the value for the undo retention period. Therefore, it's essential that you execute your queries after the database has been running for some time, thus ensuring that it has had the chance to process a typical workload.

If you configure the UNDO_RETENTION parameter, the undo tablespace must be large enough to hold the undo generated by the database within the time you specify with the UNDO_RETENTION parameter. When a transaction commits, the database may overwrite its undo data with newer undo data. The undo retention period is the minimum time for which the database will attempt to retain older undo data. Oracle retains the undo data for both read consistency purposes as well as to support Oracle Flashback operations, for the duration you specify with the UNDO_RETENTION parameter. After it saves the undo data for the period you specified for the UNDO_RETENTION parameter, the database marks that undo data as *expired* and makes the space occupied by that data available to write undo data for new transactions.

By default, the database uses the following criteria to determine how long it needs to retain undo data:

- Length of the longest-running query

- Length of the longest-running transaction

- Longest flashback duration

It's somewhat difficult to understand how the Oracle database handles the retention of undo data. Here's a brief summary of how things work:

- If you don't configure the undo tablespace with the AUTOEXTEND option, the database simply ignores the value you set for the UNDO_RETENTION parameter. The database will automatically tune the undo retention period based on database workload and the size of the undo tablespace. So, make sure you set the undo tablespace to a large value if you're receiving errors indicating that the database is not retaining undo for a long enough time. Typically, the undo retention in this case is for a duration significantly longer than the longest-running active query in the database.

- If you want the database to try to honor the settings you specify for the UNDO_RETENTION parameter, make sure that you enable the AUTOEXTEND option for the undo tablespace. This way, Oracle will automatically extend the size of the undo tablespace to make room for undo from new transactions, instead of overwriting the older undo data. However, if you're receiving ORA-0155 (snapshot too old) errors, say due to Oracle Flashback operations, it means that the database isn't able to dynamically tune the undo retention period effectively. In a case such as this, try increasing the value of the UNDO_RETENTION parameter to match the length of the longest Oracle Flashback operation. Alternatively, you can try going to a larger fixed-size undo tablespace (without the AUTOEXTEND option).

The key to figuring out the right size for the undo tablespace or the correct setting for the UNDO_RETENTION parameter is to understand the nature of the current database workload. In order to understand the workload characteristics, it's important to examine the V$UNDOSTAT view, because it contains statistics showing how the database is utilizing the undo space, as well as information such as the length of the longest-running queries. You can use this information to calculate the size of the undo space for the current workload your database is processing. Note that each row in the V$UNDOSTAT view shows undo statistics for a ten-minute time interval. The table contains a maximum of 576 rows, each for a ten-minute interval. Thus, you can review undo usage for up to four days in the past.

Here are the key columns you should monitor in the V$UNDOSTAT view for the time period you're interested in—ideally, the time period should include the time when your longest-running queries are executing. You can use these statistics to size both the UNDO_TABLESPACE as well as the UNDO_RETENTION initialization parameters.

> begin_time: Beginning of the time interval.

> end_time: End of the time interval.

> undoblks: Number of undo blocks the database consumed in a ten-minute interval; this is what we used in our formula for the estimation of the size of the undo tablespace.

> txncount: Number of transactions executed in a ten-minute interval.

> maxquerylen: This shows the length of the longest query (in seconds) executed in this instance during a ten-minute interval. You can estimate the size of the UNDO_RETENTION parameter based on the maximum value of the MAXQUERYLEN column.

> maxqueryid: Identifier for the longest-running SQL statement in this interval.

> nospaceerrcnt: The number of times the database didn't have enough free space available in the undo tablespace for new undo data, because the entire undo tablespace was being used by active transactions; of course, this means that you need to add space to the undo tablespace.

> tuned_undoretention: The time, in seconds, for which the database will retain the undo data after the database commits the transaction to which the undo belongs.

The following query based on the V$UNDOSTAT view shows how Oracle automatically tunes undo retention (check the TUNED_UNDORETENTION column) based on the length of the longest-running query (MAXQUERYLEN column) in the current instance workload.

```
SQL> select to_char(begin_time,'hh24:mi:ss') BEGIN_TIME,
  2  to_char(end_time,'hh24:mi:ss') END_TIME,
  3  maxquerylen,nospaceerrcnt,tuned_undoretention
  4  from v$undostat;
```

BEGIN_TI	END_TIME	MAXQUERYLEN	NOSPACEERRCNT	TUNED_UNDORETENTION
12:25:35	12:29:30	892	0	1673
12:15:35	12:25:35	592	0	1492
12:05:35	12:15:35	1194	0	2094
11:55:35	12:05:35	592	0	1493
11:45:35	11:55:35	1195	0	2095
11:35:35	11:45:35	593	0	1494
11:25:35	11:35:35	1196	0	2097
11:15:35	11:25:35	594	0	1495
11:05:35	11:15:35	1195	0	2096

```
10:55:35 11:05:35        593         0              1495
10:45:35 10:55:35        1198        0              2098
...
SQL>
```

Note that the value of the TUNED_UNDORETENTION column fluctuates continuously, based on the value of the maximum query length (MAXQUERYLEN) during any interval. You can see that the two columns are directly related to each other, with Oracle raising or lowering the tuned undo retention based on the maximum query length during a given interval (of ten minutes). The following query shows the usage of undo blocks and the transaction count during each ten-minute interval.

```
SQL> select to_char(begin_time,'hh24:mi:ss'),to_char(end_time,'hh24:mi:ss'),
  2  maxquerylen,ssolderrcnt,nospaceerrcnt,undoblks,txncount from v$undostat
  3  order by undoblks
  4  /

TO_CHAR( TO_CHAR( MAXQUERYLEN SSOLDERRCNT NOSPACEERRCNT   UNDOBLKS    TXNCOUNT
-------- -------- ----------- ----------- ------------- ---------- ----------
17:33:51 17:36:49        550         0              0          1          18
17:23:51 17:33:51        249         0              0         33         166
17:13:51 17:23:51        856         0              0         39         520
17:03:51 17:13:51        250         0              0         63         171
16:53:51 17:03:51        850         0              0        191         702
16:43:51 16:53:51        245         0              0        429         561

6 rows selected.

SQL>
```

Oracle provides an easy way to help set the size of the undo tablespace as well as the undo retention period, through the OEM Undo Advisor interface. You can specify the length of time for the advisor's analysis, for a period going back to a week—the advisor uses the AWR hourly snapshots to perform its analysis. You can specify the undo retention period to support a flashback transaction query. Alternatively, you can let the database determine the desired undo retention based on the longest query in the analysis period.

7-2. Finding What's Consuming the Most Undo

Problem

Often, one or two user sessions seem to be hogging the undo tablespaces. You'd like to identify the user and the SQL statement that are using up all that undo space.

Solution

High undo usage often involves a long-running query. Use the following query to find out which SQL statement has run for the longest time in your database.

```
SQL> select s.sql_text from v$sql s, v$undostat u
    where u.maxqueryid=s.sql_id;
```

You can join the **V$TRANSACTION** and the **V$SESSION** views to find out the most undo used by a session for a currently executing transaction, as shown here:

```
SQL> select s.sid, s.username, t.used_urec, t.used_ublk
    from v$session s, v$transaction t
    where s.saddr = t.ses_addr
    order by t.used_ublk desc;
```

You can also issue the following query to find out which session is currently using the most undo in an instance:

```
SQL>select s.sid, t.name, s.value
    from v$sesstat s, v$statname t
    where s.statistic# = t.statistic#
    and t.name = 'undo change vector size'
    order by s.value desc;
```

The query's output relies on the statistic undo change vector size in the **V$STATNAME** view, to show the SID for the sessions consuming the most undo right now. The **V$TRANSACTION** view shows details about active transactions. Here's another query that joins the **V$TRANSACTION**, **V$SQL** and **V$SESSION** views:

```
SQL> select sql.sql_text sql_text, t.USED_UREC Records, t.USED_UBLK Blocks,
(t.USED_UBLK*8192/1024) KBytes from v$transaction t,
  2  v$session s,
  3  v$sql sql
  4  where t.addr = s.taddr
  5  and s.sql_id = sql.sql_id
  6* and s.username ='&USERNAME'
SQL>
```

The column USED_UREC shows the number of undo records used, and the USED_UBLK column shows the undo blocks consumed by a transaction.

How It Works

You can issue the queries described in the "Solution" section to identify the sessions that are responsible for the most undo usage in your database, as well as the users that are responsible for those sessions. You can query the **V$UNDOSTAT** with the appropriate begin_time and end_time values to get the SQL identifier of the longest-running SQL statement during a time interval. The MAXQUERYID column captures the SQL identifier. You can use this ID to query the **V$SQL** view in order to find out the actual SQL statement. Similarly, the **V$TRANSACTION** and the **V$SESSION** views together help identify the users that are consuming the most undo space. If excessive undo usage is affecting performance, you might want to look at the application to see why the queries are using so much undo.

7-3. Resolving an ORA-01555 Error

Problem

You're receiving the ORA-01555 (snapshot too old) errors during nightly runs of key production batch jobs. You want to eliminate these errors.

Solution

While setting a high value for the UNDO_RETENTION parameter can potentially minimize the possibility of receiving "snapshot too old" errors, it doesn't guarantee that the database won't overwrite older undo data that may be needed by a running transaction. You can move long-running batch jobs to a separate time interval when other programs aren't running in the database, to avoid these errors.

Regardless, while you can minimize the occurrence of "snapshot too old" errors with these approaches, you can't completely eliminate such errors without specifying the *guaranteed undo retention* feature. When you configure guaranteed undo retention in a database, no transaction can fail because of the "snapshot too old" error. Oracle will keep new DML statements from executing when you set up guaranteed undo retention. Implementing the guaranteed undo feature is simple. Suppose you want to ensure that the database retains undo for at least an hour (3,600 seconds). First set the undo retention threshold with the alter system command shown here, and then set up guaranteed undo retention by specifying the retention guarantee clause to alter the undo tablespace.

```
SQL> alter system set undo_retention=3600;
System altered.
SQL> alter tablespace undotbs1 retention guarantee;
Tablespace altered.
SQL>
```

You can switch off guaranteed undo retention by executing the alter tablespace command with the retention noguarantee clause.

■ **Tip** You can enable guaranteed undo retention by using the alter system command as shown in this recipe, as well as with the create database and create undo tablespace statements.

How It Works

Oracle uses the undo records stored in the undo tablespace to help roll back transactions, provide read consistency, and to help recover the database. In addition, the database also uses undo records to read data from a past point in time using Oracle Flashback Query. Undo data serves as the underpinning for several Oracle Flashback features that help you recover from logical errors.

Occurrence of the Error

The ORA-01555 error (snapshot too old) may occur in various situations. The following is a case where the error occurs during an export.

```
EXP-00008: ORACLE error 1555 encountered
ORA-01555: snapshot too old: rollback segment number 10 with name "_SYSSMU10$" too small
EXP-00000: Export terminated unsuccessfully
```

And you can receive the same error when performing a flashback transaction:

```
ERROR at line 1:
ORA-01555: snapshot too old: rollback segment number  with name "" too small
ORA-06512: at "SYS.DBMS_FLASHBACK", line 37
ORA-06512: at "SYS.DBMS_FLASHBACK", line 70
ORA-06512: at li
```

The "snapshot too old" error occurs when Oracle overwrites undo data that's needed by another transaction. The error is a direct result of how Oracle's read consistency mechanism works. The error occurs during the execution of a long-running query when Oracle tries to read the "before image" of any changed rows from the undo segments. For example, if a long-running query starts at 1 a.m. and runs until 6 a.m., it's possible for the database to change the data that's part of this query during the period in which the query executes. When Oracle tries to read the data as it appeared at 1 a.m., the query may fail if that data is no longer present in the undo segments.

If your database is experiencing a lot of updates, Oracle may not be able to fetch the changed rows, because the before changes recorded in the undo segments may have been overwritten. The transactions that changed the rows will have already committed, and the undo segments don't have a record of the before change row values because the database overwrote the relevant undo data. Since Oracle fails to return consistent data for the current query, it issues the ORA-01555 error. The query that's currently running requires the before image to construct read-consistent data, but the before image isn't available.

The ORA-01555 error may be the result of one or both of the following: too many updates to the database or too small an undo tablespace. You can increase the size of the undo tablespace, but that doesn't ensure that the error won't occur again.

Influence of Extents

The database stores undo data in undo extents, and there are three distinct types of undo extents:

Active: Transactions are currently using these extents.

Unexpired: These are extents that contain undo that's required to satisfy the undo retention time specified by the UNDO_RETENTION initialization parameter.

Expired: These are extents with undo that's been retained longer than the duration specified by the UNDO_RETENTION parameter.

If the database doesn't find enough expired extents in the undo tablespace or it can't get new undo extents, it'll re-use the unexpired (but never an active undo extent) extents, and this leaves the door open for an ORA-01555, "snapshot too old" error. By default, the database will essentially shrink the undo retention period you specify, if it encounters space pressure to accommodate the undo from new transactions. Since the unexpired undo extents contain undo records needed to satisfy the undo retention period, overwriting those extents in reality means that the database is lowering the undo retention period you've set. Enabling the undo retention guarantee helps assure the success of long-running queries as well as Oracle Flashback operations. The "guarantee" part of the undo retention guarantee is *real*—Oracle will certainly retain undo at least for the time you specify and will never overwrite any of the unexpired undo extents that contain the undo required to satisfy the undo retention period. However, there's a stiff price attached to this guarantee—Oracle will guarantee retention even if it means that DML transactions fail because the database can't find space to record the undo for those transactions. Therefore, you must exercise great caution when enabling the guaranteed undo retention capability.

7-4. Monitoring Temporary Tablespace Usage

Problem

You want to monitor the usage of the temporary tablespace.

Solution

Execute the following query to find out the used and free space in a temporary tablespace.

```
SQL> select * from (select a.tablespace_name,
     sum(a.bytes/1024/1024) allocated_mb
     from dba_temp_files a
     where a.tablespace_name = upper('&&temp_tsname') group by a.tablespace_name) x,
     (select sum(b.bytes_used/1024/1024) used_mb,
     sum(b.bytes_free/1024/1024) free_mb
     from v$temp_space_header b
     where b.tablespace_name=upper('&&temp_tsname') group by b.tablespace_name);

Enter value for temp_tsname: TEMP
...
TABLESPACE_NAME                 ALLOCATED_MB    USED_MB    FREE_MB
------------------------------ ------------ ---------- ----------
TEMP                              52.9921875 52.9921875          0
SQL>
```

Obviously, the temporary tablespace shown in this example is in serious need of some help from the DBA.

How It Works

Oracle uses temporary tablespaces for storing intermediate results from sort operations as well as any temporary tables, temporary LOBs, and temporary B-trees. You can create multiple temporary tablespaces, but only one of them can be the default temporary tablespace. If you don't explicitly assign a temporary tablespace, that user is assigned the default temporary tablespace.

You won't find information about temporary tablespaces in the **DBA_FREE_SPACE** view. Use the **V$TEMP_SPACE_HEADER** as shown in this example to find how much free and used space there is in any temporary tablespace.

7-5. Identifying Who Is Using the Temporary Tablespace

Problem

You notice that the temporary tablespace is filling up fast, and you want to identify the user and the SQL statements responsible for the high temporary tablespace usage.

Solution

Issue the following query to find out which SQL statement is using up space in a sort segment.

```
SQL> select s.sid || ',' || s.serial# sid_serial, s.username,
    o.blocks * t.block_size / 1024 / 1024 mb_used, o.tablespace,
    o.sqladdr address, h.hash_value, h.sql_text
    from v$sort_usage o, v$session s, v$sqlarea h, dba_tablespaces t
    where o.session_addr = s.saddr
    and o.sqladdr = h.address (+)
    and o.tablespace = t.tablespace_name
    order by s.sid;
```

The preceding query shows information about the session that issued the SQL statements well as the name of the temporary tablespace and the amount of space the SQL statement is using in that tablespace.

You can use the following query to find out which sessions are using space in the temporary tablespace. Note that the information is in the summary form, meaning it doesn't separate the various sort operations being run by a session—it simply gives the total temporary tablespace usage by each session.

```
SQL> select s.sid || ',' || s.serial# sid_serial, s.username, s.osuser, p.spid,
    s.module,s.program,
    sum (o.blocks) * t.block_size / 1024 / 1024 mb_used, o.tablespace,
    count(*) sorts
    from v$sort_usage o, v$session s, dba_tablespaces t, v$process p
    where o.session_addr = s.saddr
    and s.paddr = p.addr
    and o.tablespace = t.tablespace_name
    group by s.sid, s.serial#, s.username, s.osuser, p.spid, s.module,
    s.program, t.block_size, o.tablespace
    order by sid_serial;
```

The output of this query will show you the space that each session is using in the temporary tablespace, as well as the number of sort operations that session is performing right now.

How It Works

Oracle tries to perform sort and hash operations in memory (PGA), but if a sort operation is too large to fit into memory, it uses the temporary tablespace to do the work. It's important to understand that even a single large sort operation has the potential to use up an entire temporary tablespace. Since all database sessions share the temporary tablespace, the session that runs the large sort operation could potentially result in other sessions receiving errors due to lack of room in that tablespace. Once the temporary tablespace fills up, all SQL statements that seek to use the temporary tablespace will fail with the ORA-1652: unable to extend temp segment error. New sessions may not be able to connect, and queries can sometimes hang and users may not be able to issue new queries. You try to find any blocking locks, but none exists. If the temporary tablespace fills up, transactions won't complete. If you look in the alert log, you'll find that the temporary tablespace ran out of space.

Operations that use an ORDER BY or GROUP BY clause frequently use the temporary tablespace to do their work. You must also remember that creating an index or rebuilding one also makes use of the temporary tablespace for sorting the index.

Oracle uses the PGA memory for performing the sort and hash operations. Thus, one of the first things you must do is to review the current value set for the PGA_AGGREGATE_TARGET initialization parameter and see if bumping it up will help. Nevertheless, even a larger setting for the PGA_AGGREGATE_TARGET parameter doesn't guarantee that Oracle will perform a huge sort entirely in memory. Oracle allocates each session a certain amount of PGA memory, with the amount it allocates internally determined, based on the value of the PGA_AGGREGATE_TARGET parameter. Once a large operation uses its share of the PGA memory, Oracle will write intermediary results to disk in the temporary tablespace. These types of operations are called *one-pass* or *multi-pass* operations, and since they are performed on disk, they are much slower than an operation performed entirely in the PGA.

If your database is running out of space in the temporary tablespace, you must increase its size by adding a tempfile. Enabling *autoextend* for a temporary tablespace will also help prevent "out of space" errors. Since Oracle allocates space in a temporary tablespace that you have assigned for the user performing the sort operation, you can assign users that need to perform heavy sorting a temporary tablespace that's different from that used by the rest of the users, thus preventing the heavy sorting activity from hurting database performance.

Note that unlike table or index segments, of which there are several for each object, a temporary tablespace has just one segment called the sort segment. All sessions share this sort segment. A single SQL statement can use multiple sort and hash operations. In addition, the same session can have multiple SQL statements executing simultaneously, with each statement using multiple sort and hash operations. Once a sort operation completes, the database immediately marks the blocks used by the operations as free and allocates them to another sort operation. The database adds extents to the sort segment as the sort operation gets larger, but if there's no more free space in the temporary tablespace to allocate additional extents, it issues the ORA-1652:unable to extend temp segment error. The SQL statement that's using the sort operation will fail as a result.

■ **Note** Although you'll receive an ORA-1652 error when a SQL statement performing a huge sort fails due to lack of space in the temporary tablespace, that's not the only reason you'll get this error. You'll also receive this error when performing a table move operation (alter table …move), if the tablespace to which you're moving the table doesn't have room to hold the table. Same is the case sometimes when you're creating a large index. Please see Recipe 7-6 for an explanation of this error.

7-6. Resolving the "Unable to Extend Temp Segment" Error

Problem

While creating a large index, you receive an Oracle error indicating that the database is unable to extend a TEMP segment. However, you have plenty of free space in the temporary tablespace.

Solution

When you get an error such as the following, your first inclination may be to think that there's no free space in the temporary tablespace.

```
ORA-01652: unable to extend temp segment by 1024 in tablespace INDX_01
```

You cannot fix this problem by adding space to the temporary tablespace. The error message clearly indicates the tablespace that ran out of space. In this case, the offending tablespace is INDX_01, and not the TEMP tablespace. Obviously, an index creation process failed because there was insufficient space in the INDX_01 tablespace. You can fix the problem by adding a datafile to the INDX_01 tablespace, as shown here:

```
SQL>alter tablespace INDX_01 add datafile '/u01/app/oracle/data/indx_01_02.dbf'
  2 size 1000m;
```

How It Works

When you receive the ORA-01652 error, your normal tendency is to check the temporary tablespace. You check the DBA_TEMP_FREE_SPACE view, and there's plenty of free space in the default temporary tablespace, TEMP. Well, if you look at the error message carefully, it tells you that the database is unable to extend the temp segment in the INDX_01 tablespace. When you create an index, as in this case, you provide the name of the permanent tablespace in which the database must create the new index. Oracle starts the creation of the new index by putting the new index structure into a temporary segment in the tablespace you specify (INDX_01 in our example) for the index. The reason is that if your index creation process fails, Oracle (to be more specific, the SMON process) will remove the temporary segment from the tablespace you specified for creating the new index. Once the index is successfully created (or rebuilt), Oracle converts the temporary segment into a permanent segment within the INDX_01 tablespace. However, as long as Oracle is still creating the index, the database deems it a temporary segment and thus when an index creation fails, the database issues the ORA-01652 error, which is also the error code for an "out of space" error for a temporary tablespace. The TEMP segment the error refers to is the segment that was holding the new index while it was being built. Once you increase the size of the INDX_01 tablespace, the error will go away.

■ **Tip**   The temporary segment in an ORA-1652 error message may not be referring to a temporary segment in a temporary tablespace.

The key to resolving the ORA-01652 error is to understand that Oracle uses temporary segments in places other than a temporary tablespace. While a temporary segment in the temporary tablespace is for activities such as sorting, a permanent tablespace can also use temporary segments when performing temporary actions necessary during the creation of a table (CTAS) or an index.

■ **Tip**   When you create an index, the creation process uses two different temporary segments. One temporary segment in the TEMP tablespace is used to sort the index data. Another temporary segment in the permanent tablespace holds the index while it is being created. After creating the index, Oracle changes the temporary segment in the index's tablespace into a permanent segment. The same is the case when you create a table with the CREATE TABLE…AS SELECT (CTAS) option.

As the "Solution" section explains, the ORA-01652 error refers to the tablespace where you're rebuilding an index. If you are creating a new index, Oracle uses the temporary tablespace for sorting the index data. When creating a large index, it may be a smart idea to create a large temporary tablespace and assign it to the user who's creating the index. Once the index is created, you can re-assign the user the original temporary tablespace and remove the large temporary tablespace. This strategy helps avoid enlarging the default temporary tablespace to a very large size to accommodate the creation of a large index.

If you specify autoextend for a temporary tablespace, the temp files may get very large, based on one or two large sorts in the database. When you try to reclaim space for the TEMP tablespace, you may get the following error.

```
SQL> alter database tempfile '/u01/app/oracle/oradata/prod1/temp01.dbf' resize 500M;
alter database tempfile '/u01/app/oracle/oradata/prod1/temp01.dbf' resize 500M
*ERROR at line 1:
ORA-03297: file contains used data beyond requested RESIZE value
```

One solution is to create a new temporary tablespace, make that the default temporary tablespace, and then drop the larger temporary tablespace. In Oracle Database 11g, you can simplify matters by using the following alter tablespace command to shrink the temporary tablespace:

```
SQL> alter tablespace temp shrink space;

Tablespace altered.

SQL>
```

In this example, we shrank the entire temporary tablespace, but you can shrink a specific tempfile by issuing the command alter tablespace temp shrink tempfile <file_name>. The command will shrink the tempfile to the smallest size possible.

7-7. Resolving Open Cursor Errors

Problem

You are frequently getting the `Maximum Open Cursors exceeded error`, and you want to resolve the error.

Solution

One of the first things you need to do when you receive the `ORA-01000`: "maximum open cursors exceeded" error is to check the value of the initialization parameter `open_cursors`. You can view the current limit for open cursors by issuing the following command:

```
SQL> sho parameter open_cursors

NAME                                 TYPE        VALUE
------------------------------------ ----------- ---------
open_cursors                         integer     300
SQL>
```

The parameter OPEN_CURSORS sets the maximum number of cursors a session can have open at once. You specify this parameter to control the number of open cursors. Keeping the parameter's value too low will result in a session receiving the `ORA-01000` error. There's no harm in specifying a very large value for the OPEN_CURSORS parameter (unless you expect all sessions to simultaneously max out their cursors, which is unlikely), so you can usually resolve cursor-related errors simply by raising the parameter value to a large number. However, you may sometimes find that raising the value of the `open_cursors` parameter doesn't "fix" the problem. In such cases, investigate which processes are using the open cursors by issuing the following query:

```
SQL> select a.value, s.username,s.sid,s.serial#,s.program,s.inst_id
     from gv$sesstat a,gv$statname b,gv$session s
     where a.statistic# = b.statistic# and s.sid=a.sid
     and b.name='opened cursors current'
```

The GV$OPEN_CURSOR (or the V$OPEN_CURSOR) view shows all the cursors that each user session has currently opened and parsed, or cached. You can issue the following query to identify the sessions with a high number of opened and parsed or cached cursors.

```
SQL> select saddr, sid, user_name, address,hash_value,sql_id, sql_text
     from gv$open_cursor
     where sid in
     (select sid from v$open_cursor
     group by sid having count(*)  > &threshold);
```

The query lists all sessions with an open cursor count greater than the threshold you specify. This way, you can limit the query's output and focus just on the sessions that have opened, parsed, or cached a large number of cursors.

You can get the actual SQL code and the open cursor count for a specific session by issuing the following query:

```
SQl> select sql_id,substr(sql_text,1,50) sql_text, count(*)
     from gv$open_cursor where sid=81
     group by sql_id,substr(sql_text,1,50)
     order by sql_id;
```

The output shows the SQL code for all open cursors in the session with the SID 81. You can examine all SQL statements with a high open cursor count, to see why the session was keeping a large number of cursors open.

How It Works

If your application is not closing open cursors, then setting the OPEN_CURSORS parameter to a higher value won't really help you. You may momentarily resolve the issue, but you're likely to run into the same issue a little later. If the application layer never closes the ref cursors created by the PL/SQL code, the database will simply hang on to the server resources for the used cursors. You must fix the application logic so it closes the cursors—the problem isn't really in the database.

If you're using a Java application deployed on an application server such as the Oracle WebLogic Server, the WebLogic Server's JDBC connection pools provide open database connections for applications. Any prepared statements in each of these connections will use a cursor. Multiple application server instances and multiple JDBC connection pools will mean that the database needs to support all the cursors. If multiple requests share the same session ID, the open cursor problem may be due to implicit cursors. The only solution then is to close the connection after each request.

A *cursor leak* is when the database opens cursors but doesn't close them. You can run a 10046 trace for a session to find out if it's closing its cursors:

```
SQL> alter session set events '10046 trace name context forever, level 12';
```

If you notice that the same SQL statement is associated with different cursors, it means that the application isn't closing its cursors. If the application doesn't close its cursors after opening them, Oracle assigns different cursor numbers for the next SQL statement it executes. If the cursor is closed, instead, Oracle will re-use the same cursor number for the next cursor it assigns. Thus, if you see the item PARSING IN CURSOR #nnnn progressively increase in the output for the 10046 trace, it means that the application is not closing the cursors. Note that while leaving cursors open may be due to a faulty application design, developers may also intentionally leave cursors open to reduce soft parsing, or when they use the session cursor cache.

You can use the SESSION_CACHED_CURSORS initialization parameter to set the maximum number of cached closed cursors for each session. The default setting is 50. You can use this parameter to prevent a session from opening an excessive number of cursors, thereby filling the library cache or forcing excessive hard parses. Repeated parse calls for a SQL statement leads Oracle to move the session cursor for that statement into the session cursor cache. The database satisfies subsequent parse calls by using the cached cursor instead of re-opening the cursor.

When you re-execute a SQL statement, Oracle will first try to find a parsed version of that statement in the shared pool—if it finds the parsed version in the shared pool, a soft parse occurs. Oracle is forced to perform the much more expensive hard parse if it doesn't find the parsed version of the statement in the shared pool. While a soft parse is much less expensive than a hard parse, a large number of soft parses can affect performance, because they do require CPU usage and library cache latches. To reduce the number of soft parses, Oracle caches the recent closed cursors of each session in a local session cache for that session—Oracle stores any cursor for which a minimum of three parse calls were made, thus avoiding having to cache every single session cursor, which will fill up the cursor cache.

The default value of 50 for the SESSION_CACHED_CURSORS initialization parameter may be too low for many databases. You can check if the database is bumping against the maximum limit for session-cached cursors by issuing the following statement:

```
SQL> select max(value) from v$sesstat
  2  where statistic# in (select statistic# from v$statname
  3* where name = 'session cursor cache count');


MAX(VALUE)
----------
        49

SQL>
```

The query shows the maximum number of session cursors that have been cached in the past. Since this number (49) is virtually the same as the default value (or the value you've set) for the SESSION_CACHED_CURSORS parameter, you must set the parameter's value to a larger number. Session cursor caches use the shared pool. If you're using automatic memory management, there's nothing for you to do after you reset the SESSION_CACHED_CURSORS parameter—the database will bump up the shared pool size if necessary. You can find out how many cursors each session has in its session cursor cache by issuing the following query:

```
SQL> select a.value,s.username,s.sid,s.serial#
  2  from v$sesstat a, v$statname b,v$session s
  3  where a.statistic#=b.statistic# and s.sid=a.sid
  4* and b.name='session cursor cache count';
```

7-8. Resolving a Hung Database

Problem

Your database is hung. Users aren't able to log in, and existing users can't complete their transactions. The DBAs with SYSDBA privileges may also be unable to log in to the database. You need to find out what is causing the database to hang, and fix the problem.

Solution

Follow these general steps when facing a database that appears to be hung:

1. Check your alert log to see if the database has reported any errors, which may indicate why the database is hanging.

2. See if you can get an AWR or ASH report or query some of the ASH views, as explained in Chapter 5. You may notice events such as hard parses at the top of the Load Profile section of the AWR report, indicating that this is what is slowing down the database.

3. A single ad hoc query certainly has the potential to bring an entire database to its knees. See if you can identify one or more very poorly performing SQL statements that may be leading to the hung (or a very poorly performing) database.

4. Check the database for blocking locks as well as latch contention.

5. Check the server's memory usage as well as CPU usage. Make sure the sessions aren't stalling because you've sized the PGA too low, as explained in Chapter 3.

6. Don't overlook the fact that a scary-looking database hang may be caused by something as simple as the filling up of all archive log destinations. If the archive destination is full, the database will hang, and new user connections will fail. You can, however, still connect as the SYS user, and once you make room in the archive destination by moving some of the archived redo log files, the database becomes accessible to the users.

7. Check the Flash Recovery Area (FRA). A database also hangs when it's unable to write Flashback Database logs to the recovery area. When the FRA fills up, the database won't process new work and it won't spawn new database connections. You can fix this problem by making the recovery area larger with the `alter system set db_recovery_file_dest_size` command.

If you're still unable to resolve the reasons for the hung database, you most likely have a truly hung database. While you're investigating such a database, you may sometimes find yourself unable to connect and log in. In that case, use the "prelim" option to log in to the database. The prelim option doesn't require a real database connection. Here's an example that shows how to use the prelim option to log into a database:

```
C:\app\ora\product\11.2.0\dbhome_1\bin>sqlplus /nolog

SQL*Plus: Release 11.2.0.1.0 Production on Sun Mar 27 10:43:31 2011

Copyright (c) 1982, 2010, Oracle.  All rights reserved.

SQL> set _prelim on
SQL> connect / as sysdba
Prelim connection established
SQL>
```

Alternatively, you can use the command `sqlplus -prelim "/ as sysdba"` to log in with the `-prelim` option. Note that you use the `nolog` option to open a SQL*Plus session. You can't execute the `set _prelim on` command if you're already connected to the database. Once you establish a `prelim` connection as shown here, you can execute the `oradebug hanganalyze` command to analyze a hung database—for example:

```
SQL> oradebug hanganalyze 3
Statement processed.
SQL>
```

In an Oracle RAC environment, specify the `oradebug hanganalyze` command with additional options, as shown here:

```
SQL> oradebug setinst all
SQL> oradebug -g def hanganalyze 3
```

You can repeat the oradebug hanganalyze command a couple of times to generate dump files for varying process states.

In addition to the dump files generated by the hanganalyze command, Oracle Support may often also request a process state dump, also called a systemstate dump, to analyze hung database conditions. The systemstate dump will report on what the processes are doing and the resources they're currently holding. You can get a systemstate dump from a non-RAC system by executing the following set of commands.

```
SQL> oradebug setmypid
Statement processed.
SQL> oradebug dump systemstate 266
Statement processed.
SQL>
```

Issue the following commands to get a systemstate dump in a RAC environment:

```
SQL> oradebug setmypid
SQL> oradebug unlimit
SQL> oradebug -g all dump systemstate 266
```

Note that unlike the oradebug hanganalyze command, you must connect to a process. The setmypid option specifies the process, in this case your own process. You can also specify a process ID other than yours, in which case you issue the command oradebug setmypid <pid> before issuing the dump systemstate command. If you try to issue the dump systemstate command without setting the PID, you'll receive an error:

```
SQL> oradebug dump systemstate 10
ORA-00074: no process has been specified
SQL>
```

You must take the systemstate dumps a few times, with an interval of about a minute or so in between the dumps. Oracle Support usually requests several systemstate dumps along with the trace files generated by the hanganalyze command.

How It Works

The key thing you must ascertain when dealing with a "hung" database is whether the database is really hung, or just slow. If one or two users complain about a slow-running query, you need to analyze their sessions, using the techniques described in Chapter 5, to see if the slowness is due to a blocking session or to an Oracle wait event. If several users report that their work is going slowly, it could be due to various reasons, including CPU, memory (SGA or PGA), or other system resource issues.

Check the server's CPU usage as one of your first steps in troubleshooting a hung database. If your server is showing 100% CPU utilization, or if it's swapping or paging, the problem may not lie in the database at all. As for memory, if the server doesn't have enough free memory, new sessions can't connect to the database.

■ **Tip**   The "prelim" option shown in the "Solution" section lets you connect to the SGA without opening a session. You can thus "log" in to the hung database even when normal SQL*Plus logins don't work. The oradebug session you start once you connect to the SGA actually analyzes what's in the SGA and dumps it into a trace file.

A true database hang can be due to a variety of reasons, including a system that has exhausted resources such as the CPU or memory, or because several sessions are stuck waiting for a resource such as a lock. While the database can automatically resolve deadlocks between sessions (by killing one of the sessions holding a needed lock), when there's a latch or pin on an internal kernel-level resource, Oracle is sometimes unable to automatically detect and resolve the internal deadlock—and this leads to what Oracle Support calls a "true database hang." A true database hang is thus an internal deadlock or a cyclical dependency among multiple processes. Oracle Support will usually ask you to provide them the hanganalyze trace files and multiple systemstate dumps to enable them to diagnose the root cause of your hang. At times like this, you may not even be able to log into the database. Your first instinct when you realize that you can't even log in to a database is to try shutting down and restarting, often referred to as bouncing the database. Unfortunately, while shutting down and restarting the database may "resolve" the issue, it'll also disconnect all users—and you're no wiser as to what exactly caused the problem. If you do decide to bounce your database, quickly generate a few hanganalyze and systemstate dumps first.

■ **Tip**   As unpleasant as it may be at times, if you find that you simply can't connect to a hung database, then collect any trace dumps you may need, and quickly bounce the database so that users can access their applications. Especially when you're dealing with a database that's hanging because of memory issues, bouncing the instance may get things going again quickly.

If you find that the database is completely unresponsive, and you can't even log in to the database with the SYSDBA privilege, you can use the prelim option to log into the database. The prelim option stands for preliminary connection, and it starts an Oracle process and attaches that process to the SGA shared memory. However, this is not a full or complete connection, but a limited connection where the structures for query execution are not set up—so, you cannot even query the V$ views. However, the prelim option lets you run oradebug commands to get error dump stacks for diagnostic purposes. The output of the hanganalyze command can tell Oracle Support engineers if your database is really hanging, because of sessions waiting for some resource. The command makes internal kernel calls to find out all sessions that are waiting for a resource and shows the relationship between the blocking and waiting sessions. The hanganalyze option that you can specify with either the oradebug command or an alter session statement produces details about hung sessions. Once you get the dump file, Oracle Support personnel can analyze it and let you know the reasons for the database hang.

You can invoke the hanganalyze command at various levels ranging from 1 to 10. Level 3 dumps processes that are in a hanging (IN_HANG) state. You normally don't need to specify a level higher than 3, because higher levels will produce voluminous reports with too many details about the processes.

■ **Note** The dump files you create with the `hanganalyze` and the `systemstate` commands are created in ADR's trace directory.

Note that we issued the **oradebug** command to get a `systemstate` dump with a level of 266. Level 266 (combination of Level 256, which produces short stack information, and Level 10) is for Oracle releases 9.2.0.6 and onward (earlier releases used `systemstate level 10`). Level 266 allows you to dump the short stacks for each process, which are Oracle function calls that help Oracle development teams determine which Oracle function is causing the problem. The short stack information also helps in matching known bugs in the code. On Solaris and Linux systems, you can safely specify level 266, but on other systems, it may take a long time to dump the short stacks. Therefore, you may want to stick with level 10 for the other operating systems.

If you can find out the blocking session, you can also take a dump just for that session, by using the command **oradebug setospid nnnn**, where nnnn is the blocking session's PID, and then invoking the **oradebug** command, as shown here:

```
SQL> oradebug setospid  9999
SQL> oradebug unlimit
SQL> oradebug dump errorstack  3
```

Note that you can generate the `hanganalyze` and `systemstate` dumps in a normal session (as well as in a prelim session), without using the **oradebug** command. You can invoke the `hanganalyze` command with an `alter session` command, as shown here.

```
SQL>alter session set  events 'immediate trace name hanganalyze level 3';
```

Similarly, you can get a `systemstate` dump with the following command:

```
SQL> alter session set events 'immediate trace name SYSTEMSTATE level 10';
Session altered.
SQL>
```

The **oradebug** and `systemstate` dumps are just two of the many dumps you can collect. Use the **oradebug dumplist** command to view the various error dumps you can collect.

```
SQL> oradebug dumplist
TRACE_BUFFER_ON
TRACE_BUFFER_OFF
LATCHES
PROCESSSTATE
SYSTEMSTATE
INSTANTIATIONSTATE
REFRESH_OS_STATS
CROSSIC
CONTEXTAREA
HANGDIAG_HEADER
HEAPDUMP
...
```

Note that while you can read some of the dump files in an editor, these files are mainly for helping Oracle Support professionals troubleshoot a database hang situation. There's not much you can do with the dump files, especially when a database hang situation is due to an Oracle bug or a kernel-level lock, except to send them along to Oracle Support for analysis.

7-9. Invoking the Automatic Diagnostic Repository Command Interpreter

Problem

You'd like to invoke the Automatic Diagnostic Repository Command Interpreter (ADRCI) and work with various components of the Automatic Diagnostic Repository (ADR).

Solution

ADRCI is a tool to help you manage Oracle diagnostic data. You can use ADRCI commands in both an interactive as well as a batch mode.

To start ADRCI in the interactive mode, type **adrci** at the command line, as shown here:

```
$ adrci

ADRCI: Release 11.2.0.1.0 - Production on Mon Mar 14 11:41:41 2011

Copyright (c) 1982, 2009, Oracle and/or its affiliates.  All rights reserved.

ADR base = "c:\app\ora"
adrci>
```

You can issue the adrci command from any directory, so long as the PATH environment variable includes ORACLE_HOME/bin/. You can enter each command at the adrci prompt, and when you're done using the utility, you can type **EXIT** or **QUIT** to exit. You can view all the ADRCI commands available to you by typing **HELP** at the ADRCI command line, as shown here:

```
adrci> HELP

 HELP [topic]
   Available Topics:
        CREATE REPORT
        ECHO
        EXIT
        HELP
        HOST
        IPS
...
        SHOW HOMES | HOME | HOMEPATH
        SHOW INCDIR
        SHOW INCIDENT
        SHOW PROBLEM
```

```
        SHOW REPORT
        SHOW TRACEFILE
        SPOOL
```

There are other commands intended to be used directly by Oracle, type
"HELP EXTENDED" to see the list

adrci>

You can get detailed information for an individual ADRCI command by adding the name of the command as an attribute to the HELP command. For example, here is how to get the syntax for the show tracefile command:

adrci> help *show tracefile*

```
  Usage: SHOW TRACEFILE [file1 file2 ...] [-rt | -t]
                        [-i inc1 inc2 ...] [-path path1 path2 ...]

  Purpose: List the qualified trace filenames.
...
  Options:
  Examples:
...
adrci>
```

You can also execute ADRCI commands in the batch mode by incorporating the commands in a script or batch file. For example, if you want to run the ADRCI commands SET HOMEPATH and SHOW ALERT from within an operating system script, include the following line inside a shell script:

SET HOMEPATH diag/rdbms/orcl/orcl; SHOW ALERT -term

Let's say your script name is myscript.txt. You can then execute this script by issuing the following command inside an operating system shell script or batch file:

$ adrci script=myscript.txt

Note that the parameter SCRIPT tells ADRCI that it must execute the commands within the text file myscript.txt. If the text file is not within the same directory from where the shell script or batch file is running, you must provide the path for the directory where you saved the text file.

To execute an ADRCI command directly at the command line instead of invoking ADRCI first and working interactively with the ADR interface, specify the parameter EXEC with the ADRCI command, as shown here:

$ adrci EXEC="SHOW HOMES; SHOW INCIDENT"

This example shows how to include two ADRCI commands–SHOW HOMES and SHOW INCIDENT—by executing the ADRCI command at the command line.

How It Works

The Automatic Diagnostic Repository is a directory structure that you can access even when the database is down, because it's stored outside the database. The root directory for the ADR is called the *ADR base* and is set by the DIAGNOSTIC_DEST initialization parameter. Each Oracle product or component has its own *ADR home* under the ADR base. The location of each of the ADR homes follows the path diag/product_type/product_id/instance_id. Thus, the ADR home for a database named orcl1 with the instance name orcl1 and the ADR base set to /app/oracle will be /app/oracle/diag/rdbms/orcl1/orcl1. Under each of the ADR homes are the diagnostic data, such as the trace and dump files and the alert log, as well as other diagnostic files, for that instance of an Oracle product.

The ADRCI utility helps you manage the diagnostic data in the ADR. ADRCI lets you perform the following types of diagnostic tasks:

- *View diagnostic data in the ADR (Automatic Diagnostic Repository)*: The ADR stores diagnostic data such as alert logs, dump files, trace files, health check reports, etc.

- *View health check reports*: The diagnosability infrastructure automatically runs health checks to capture details about the error and adds them to other diagnostic data it collects for that error. You can also manually invoke a health check.

- *Package incidents and problem information for transmission to Oracle Support*: A *problem* is a critical database error, and an *incident* is a single occurrence of a specific problem. An incident package is a collection of diagnostic data that you send to Oracle Support for troubleshooting purposes. ADRCI has special commands that enable you to create packages and generate zipped diagnostic packages to send to Oracle Support.

You can view all ADR locations for the current database instance by querying the V$DIAG_INFO view, as shown here.

```
SQL> select * from v$diag_info;
```

INST_ID	NAME	VALUE
1	Diag Enabled	TRUE
1	ADR Base	c:\app\ora
1	ADR Home	c:\app\ora\diag\rdbms\orcl1\orcl1
1	Diag Trace	c:\app\ora\diag\rdbms\orcl1\orcl1\trace
1	Diag Alert	c:\app\ora\diag\rdbms\orcl1\orcl1\alert
1	Diag Incident	c:\app\ora\diag\rdbms\orcl1\orcl1\incident
1	Diag Cdump	c:\app\ora\diag\rdbms\orcl1\orcl1\cdump
1	Health Monitor	c:\app\ora\diag\rdbms\orcl1\orcl1\hm
1	Default Trace File	c:\app\ora…\trace\orcl1_ora_6272.trc
1	Active Problem Count	2
1	Active Incident Count	3

```
11 rows selected.

SQL>
```

The ADR home is the root directory for a database's diagnostic data. All diagnostic files such as the alert log and the various trace files are located under the ADR home. The ADR home is located directly underneath the ADR base, which you specify with the DIAGNOSTIC_DEST initialization parameter. Here's how to find out the location of the ADR base directory:

```
adrci> show base
ADR base is "c:\app\ora"
adrci>
```

You can view all the ADR homes under the ADR base by issuing the following command:

```
adrci> show homes
ADR Homes:
diag\clients\user_salapati\host_3975876188_76
diag\clients\user_system\host_3975876188_76
diag\rdbms\orcl1\orcl1
diag\tnslsnr\miropc61\listener
adrci>
```

You can have multiple ADR homes under the ADR base, and multiple ADR homes can be current at any given time. Your ADRCI commands will work only with diagnostic data in the current ADR home. How do you know which ADR home is current at any point in time? The ADRCI homepath helps determine the ADR homes that are current, by pointing to the ADR home directory under the ADR base hierarchy of directories.

■ **Note** Some ADRCI commands require only one ADR home to be current—these commands will issue an error if multiple ADR homes are current.

You can use either the show homes or the show homepath command to view all ADR homes that are current:

```
adrci> show homepath
ADR Homes:
diag\clients\user_salapati\host_3975876188_76
diag\clients\user_system\host_3975876188_76
diag\rdbms\orcl1\orcl1
diag\tnslsnr\miropc61\listener
adrci>
```

If you want to work with diagnostic data from multiple database instances or components, you must ensure that all the relevant ADR homes are current. Most of the time, however, you'll be dealing with a single database instance or a single Oracle product or component such as the listener, for example. An ADR homepath is always relative to the ADR. If you specify /u01/app/oracle/ as the value for the ADR base directory, for example, all ADR homes will be under the ADR_Base/diag directory. Issue the set homepath command to set an ADR home directory to a single home, as shown here:

```
adrci> set homepath diag\rdbms\orcl1\orcl1

adrci> show homepath

ADR Homes:
diag\rdbms\orcl1\orcl1
adrci>
```

> ■ **Note** Diagnostic data includes descriptions of incidents and problems, health monitoring reports, and traditional diagnostic files such as trace files, dump files, and alert logs.

Note that before you set the homepath with the `set homepath` command, the `show homepath` command shows all ADR homepaths. However, once you set the homepath to a specific home, the `show homepath` command shows just a single homepath. It's important to set the homepath before you execute several ADRCI commands, as they are applicable to only a single ADR home. For example, if you don't set the homepath before issuing the following command, you'll receive an error:

```
adrci> ips create package
DIA-48448: This command does not support multiple ADR homes
adrci>
```

The error occurs because the `ips create package` command is not valid with multiple ADR homes. The command will work fine after you issue the `set homepath` command to set the homepath to a single ADR home. Commands such as the one shown here work only with a single current ADR home, but others work with multiple current ADR homes—there are also commands that don't need a current ADR home. The bottom line is that all ADRCI commands will work with a single current ADR home.

7-10. Viewing an Alert Log from ADRCI

Problem

You want to view an alert log by using ADRCI commands.

Solution

To view an alert log with ADRCI, follow these steps:

1. Invoke ADRCI.

   ```
   $ adrci
   ```

2. Set the ADR home with the `set homepath` command.

   ```
   adrci> set homepath diag\rdbms\orcl1\orcl1
   ```

3. Enter the following command to view the alert log:

   ```
   adrci>show alert

   ADR Home = c:\app\ora\diag\rdbms\orcl1\orcl1:
   *************************************************************************
   Output the results to file: c:\temp\alert_10916_7048_orcl1_1.ado
   ```

The alert log will pop up in your default editor. The ADRCI prompt will return once you close the text file in the editor.

You can also query the `V$DIAG_INFO` view to find the path that corresponds to the Diag Trace entry. You can change the directory to that path and open the `alert_<db_name>.log` file with a text editor.

How It Works

The alert log holds runtime information for an Oracle instance and provides information such as the initialization parameters the instance is using, as well as a record of key changes such as redo log file switches and, most importantly, messages that show Oracle errors and their details. The alert log is critical for troubleshooting purposes, and is usually the first place you'll look when a problem occurs. Oracle provides the alert log as both a text file as well as an XML-formatted file.

The `show alert` command brings up the XML-formatted alert log without displaying the XML tags. You can set the default editor with the `SET EDITOR` command, as shown here:

```
adrci> set editor notepad.exe
```

The previous command changes the default editor to Notepad. The `show alert -term` command shows the alert log contents in the terminal window. If you want to examine just the latest events in the alert log, issue the following command:

```
adrci>show alert -tail 50
```

The `tail` option shows you a set of the most recent lines from the alert log in the command window. In this example, it shows the last 50 lines from the alert log. If you don't specify a value for the `tail` parameter, by default, it shows the last ten lines from the alert log.

The following command shows a "live" alert log, in the sense that it will show changes to the alert log as the entries are added to the log.

```
adrci> show alert -tail -f
```

The previous command shows the last ten lines of the alert log and prints all new messages to the screen, thus offering a "live" display of ongoing additions to the alert log. The CTRL+C sequence will take you back to the ADRCI prompt.

When troubleshooting, it is very useful to see if the database issued any ORA-600 errors. You can issue the following command to trap the ORA-600 errors.

```
adrci> show alert -p "MESSAGE_TEXT LIKE '%ORA-600%'"
```

Although you can view the alert log directly by going to the file system location where it's stored, it's much easier to do so through the ADRCI tool. ADRCI is especially useful for working with the trace files of an instance. The `SHOW TRACEFILE` command shows all the trace files in the trace directory of the instance. You can issue the `SHOW TRACEFILE` command with various filters—the following example looks for trace files that reference the background process mmon:

```
$ adrci> show tracefile %mmon%
    diag\rdbms\orcl1\orcl1\trace\orcl1_mmon_1792.trc
    diag\rdbms\orcl1\orcl1\trace\orcl1_mmon_2340.trc
adrci>
```

This command lists all trace files with the string mmon in their file names. You can apply filters to restrict the output to just the trace files associated with a specific incident number, as shown here:

```
adrci> show tracefile -I 43417
        diag\rdbms\orcl1\orcl1\incident\incdir_43417\orcl1_ora_4276_i43417.trc
adrci>
```

The previous command lists the trace files related to the incident number 43417.

7-11. Viewing Incidents with ADRCI

Problem

You want to use ADRCI to view incidents.

Solution

You can view all incidents in the ADR with the show incident command (be sure to set the homepath first):

```
$ adrci
$ set homepath diag\rdbms\orcl1\orcl1


adrci> show incident

ADR Home = c:\app\ora\diag\rdbms\orcl1\orcl1:
*************************************************************************
INCIDENT_ID          PROBLEM_KEY
 CREATE_TIME
-------------------- --------------------------------------------------
 43417                ORA 600 [kkqctinvvm(2): Inconsistent state space!]
 2010-12-17 09:26:15.091000 -05:00
 43369                ORA 600 [kkqctinvvm(2): Inconsistent state space!]
 2010-12-17 11:08:40.589000 -05:00
 79451                ORA 445
 2011-03-04 03:00:39.246000 -05:00
 84243                ORA 445
 2011-03-14 19:12:27.434000 -04:00
 84244                ORA 445
 2011-03-20 16:55:54.501000 -04:00
5 rows fetched
```

You can specify the detail mode to view details about a specific incident, as shown here:

```
adrci> show incident -mode detail -p "incident_id=43369"

ADR Home = c:\app\ora\diag\rdbms\orcl1\orcl1:
*************************************************************************

INCIDENT INFO RECORD 1
*************************************************************************
   INCIDENT_ID                 43369
   STATUS                      ready
   CREATE_TIME                 2010-12-17 11:08:40.589000 -05:00
   PROBLEM_ID                  1
```

```
CLOSE_TIME                    <NULL>
FLOOD_CONTROLLED              none
ERROR_FACILITY               ORA
ERROR_NUMBER                 600
ERROR_ARG1                   kkqctinvvm(2): Inconsistent state space!
SIGNALLING_COMPONENT         SQL_Transform
PROBLEM_KEY                  ORA 600 [kkqctin: Inconsistent state space!]
FIRST_INCIDENT               43417
FIRSTINC_TIME                2010-12-17 09:26:15.091000 -05:00
LAST_INCIDENT                43369
LASTINC_TIME                 2010-12-17 11:08:40.589000 -05:00
KEY_VALUE                    ORACLE.EXE.3760_3548
KEY_NAME                     PQ
KEY_NAME                     SID
KEY_VALUE                    71.304
OWNER_ID                     1
INCIDENT_FILE                c:\app\ora\diag\rdbms\orcl1\orcl1\trace\orcl1_ora_3548.trc

adrci>
```

How It Works

The show incident command reports on all open incidents in the database. For each incident, the output for this command shows the problem key, incident ID, and the time when the incident occurred. In this example, we first set the ADRCI homepath, so the command shows incidents from just this ADR home. If you don't set the homepath, you'll see incidents from all the current ADR homes.

As mentioned earlier, an incident is a single occurrence of a problem. A problem is a critical error such as an ORA-600 (internal error) or an ORA-07445 error relating to operating system exceptions. The problem key is a text string that shows the problem details. For example, the problem key ORA 600 [kkqctinvvm(2): Inconsistent state space!] shows that the problem is due to an internal error.

When a problem occurs several times, the database creates an incident for each occurrence of the problem, each with a unique incident ID. The database logs the incident in the alert log and sends an alert to the Oracle Enterprise Manager, where they show up in the Home page. The database automatically gathers diagnostic data for the incident, called incident dumps, and stores them in the ADR trace directory.

Since a critical error can potentially generate numerous identical incidents, the fault diagnosability infrastructure applies a "flood control" mechanism to limit the generation of incidents. For a given problem key, the database allows only 5 incidents within one hour and a maximum of 25 incidents in one day. Once a problem triggers incidents beyond these thresholds, the database merely logs the incidents in the alert log and the Oracle Enterprise Manager, but stops generating new incident dumps for them. You can't alter the default threshold settings for the incident flood control mechanism.

7-12. Packaging Incidents for Oracle Support

Problem

You want to send the diagnostic files related to a specific problem to Oracle Support.

Solution

You can package the diagnostic information for one more incidents through either Database Control or through commands that you can execute from the ADRCI interface. In this solution, we show you how to package incidents through ADRCI. You can use various IPS commands to package all diagnostic files related to a specific problem in a zipped format and send the file to Oracle Support. Here are the steps to create an incident package.

1. Create an empty logical package as shown here:

    ```
    adrci> ips create package
    Created package 1 without any contents, correlation level typical
    adrci>
    ```

    In this example, we created an empty package, but you can also create a package based on an incident number, a problem number, a problem key or a time interval. In all these cases, the package won't be empty - it'll include the diagnostic information for the incident or problem that you specify. Since we created an empty package, we need to add diagnostic information to that package in the next step.

2. Add diagnostic information to the logical package with the `ips add incident` command:

    ```
    adrci> ips add incident 43369 package 1
    Added incident 43369 to package 1
    adrci>
    ```

    At this point, the incident 43369 is associated with package 1, but there'sno diagnostic data in it yet.

3. Generate the physical package.

    ```
    adrci> ips generate package 1 in \app\ora\diagnostics
    Generated package 1 in file \app\ora\diagnostics\IPSPKG_20110419131046_COM_1.zip,
    mode complete
    adrci>
    ```

    When you issue the `generate package` command, ADRCI gathers all relevant diagnostic files and adds them to a zip file in the directory you designate.

4. Send the resulting zip file to Oracle Support.

    If you decide to add supplemental diagnostic data to an existing physical package (zipped file), you can do so by specifying the `incremental` option with the `generate package` command:

    ```
    adrci> ips generate package 1 in \app\ora\diagnostics incremental
    ```

    The incremental zip file created by this command will have the term `INC` in the file name, indicating that it is an incremental zip file.

How It Works

A physical package is the zip file that you can send to Oracle Support for diagnosing a problem in your database. Since an incident is a single occurrence of a problem, adding the incident number to the logical package and generating the physical package rolls up all the diagnostic data for that problem (incident) into a single zipped file. In this example, we showed you how to first create an empty logical package and then associate it with an incident number. However, the `ipc create package` command has several options: you can specify the incident number or a problem number directly when you create the logical package, and skip the `add incident` command. You can also create a package that contains all incidents between two points in time, as shown here:

```
adrci> ips create package time '2011-04-12 10:00:00.00 -06:00' to '2011-04-12 23
:00:00.00 -06:00'
Created package 2 based on time range 2011-04-12 12:00:00.000000 -06:00 to 2011-
04-12 23:00:00.000000 -06:00, correlation level typical
adrci>
```

The package generated by the previous command contains all incidents that occurred between 10 a.m. and 11 p.m. on April 12, 2011.

Note that you can also manually add a specific diagnostic file to an existing package. To add a file, you specify the file name in the `ips add file` command—you are limited to adding only those diagnostic files that are within the ADR base directory. Here is an example:

```
adrci> ips add file <ADR_BASE>/diag/rdbms/orcl1/orcl1/trace/orcl_ora12345.trc package 1
```

By default, the `ips generate package` command generates a zip file that includes all files for a package. The incremental option will limit the files to those that the database has generated since you originally generated the zipped file for that package. The `ips show files` command shows all the files in a package and the `ips show incidents` command shows all the incidents in a package. You can issue the `ips remove file` command to remove a diagnostic file from a package.

7-13. Running a Database Health Check

Problem

You'd like to run a comprehensive diagnostic health check on your database. You'd like to find out if there's any data dictionary or file corruption, as well as any other potential problems in the database.

Solution

You can use the database health monitoring infrastructure to run a health check of your database. You can run various integrity checks, such as transaction integrity checks and dictionary integrity checks. You can get a list of all the health checks you can run by querying the V$HM_CHECK view:

```
SQL> select name from v$hm_check where internal_check='N';
```

Once you decide on the type of check, specify the name of the check in the DBMS_HM package's RUN_CHECK procedure, as shown here:

```
SQL> begin
  2   dbms_hm.run_check('Dictionary Integrity Check','testrun1');
  3   end;
  4  /

PL/SQL procedure successfully completed.

SQL>
```

You can also run a health check from the Enterprise Manager. Go to Advisor Central ➤ Checkers, and select the specific checker from the Checkers subpage to run a health check.

How It Works

Oracle automatically runs a health check when it encounters a critical error. You can run a manual check using the procedure shown in the "Solution" section. The database stores all health check findings in the ADR.

You can run most of the health checks while the database is open. You can run the Redo Integrity Check and the DB Structure Integrity Check only when the database is closed—you must place the database in the NOMOUNT state to run these two checks.

You can view a health check's findings using either the DBMS_HM package or through the Enterprise Manager. Here is how to get a health check using the DBMS_HM package:

```
SQL> set long 100000
SQL> set longchunksize 1000
SQL> set pagesize 1000
SQL> set linesize 512
SQL> select dbms_hm.get_run_report('testrun1') from dual;

DBMS_HM.GET_RUN_REPORT('TESTRUN1')
---------------------------------------------------------------
Basic Run Information
 Run Name                   : testrun1
 Run Id                     : 61
 Check Name                 : Dictionary Integrity Check
 Mode                       : MANUAL
 Status                     : COMPLETED
 Start Time                 : 2011-04-19 15:46:50.313000 -04:00
 End Time                   : 2011-04-19 15:46:54.117000 -04:00
 Error Encountered          : 0
 Source Incident Id         : 0
 Number of Incidents Created : 0

Input Paramters for the Run
 TABLE_NAME=ALL_CORE_TABLES
 CHECK_MASK=ALL
```

```
Run Findings And Recommendations

SQL>
```

In this example, fortunately, there are no findings and thus no recommendations, since the dictionary health check didn't find any problems. You can also go to Advisor Central ➤ Checkers and run a report from the Run Detail page for any health check you have run. Use the show hm_run, create report, and show report commands to view health check reports with the ADRCI utility. You can use the views V$HM_FINDING and V$HM_RECOMMENDATION to investigate the findings as well as the recommendations pursuant to a health check.

7-14. Creating a SQL Test Case

Problem

You need to create a SQL test case in order to reproduce a SQL failure on a different machine, either to support your own diagnostic efforts, or to enable Oracle Support to reproduce the failure.

Solution

In order to create a SQL test case, first you must export the SQL statement along with several bits of useful information about the statement. The following example shows how to capture the SQL statement that is throwing an error. In this example, the user SH is doing the export (you can't do the export as the user SYS).

First, connect to the database as SYSDBA and create a directory to hold the test case:

```
SQL> conn / as sysdba
Connected.
SQL> create or replace directory TEST_DIR1 as 'c:\myora\diagnsotics\incidents\';

Directory created.
SQL> grant read,write on directory TEST_DIR1 to sh;

Grant succeeded.
SQL>
```

Then grant the DBA role to the user through which you will create the test case, and connect as that user:

```
SQL> grant dba to sh;

Grant succeeded.

SQL> conn sh/sh
Connected.
```

Issue the SQL command that's throwing the error:

```
SQL> select * from  my_mv  where max_amount_sold >100000 order by 1;
```

Now you're ready to export the SQL statement and relevant information, which you can import to a different system later on. Use the EXPORT_SQL_TESTCASE procedure to export the data, as shown here:

```
SQL> set serveroutput on

SQL> declare mycase clob;
  2  begin
  3  dbms_sqldiag.export_sql_testcase
  4  (directory    =>'TEST_DIR1',
  5  sql_text      => 'select * from my_mv where max_amount_sold >100000 order by 1',
  6  user_name     => 'SH',
  7  exportData    =>  TRUE,
  8  testcase      => mycase
  9  );
 10  end;
 11  /

PL/SQL procedure successfully completed.

SQL>
```

Once the export procedure completes, you are ready to perform the import, either on the same or on a different server. The following example creates a new user named TEST, and imports the test case into that user's schema. Here are the steps for importing the SQL statement and associated information into a different schema.

```
SQL> conn /as sysdba
Connected.
SQL> create or replace directory TEST_DIR2 as 'c:\myora\diagnsotics\incidents\'; /

Directory created.
SQL> grant read,write on directory TEST_dir2 to test;
```

Transfer all the files in the TEST_DIR1 directory to the TEST_DIR2 directory. Then grant the DBA role to user TEST, and connect as that user:

```
SQL> grant dba to test;

Grant succeeded.

SQL> conn test/test
Connected.
```

Perform the import of the SQL data as the user TEST, by invoking the IMPORT_SQL_TESTCASE procedure, as shown here:

```
SQL> begin
  2  dbms_sqldiag.import_sql_testcase
  3  (directory=>'TEST_DIR2',
  4  filename=>'oratcb1_008602000001main.xml',
  5  importData=>TRUE
```

```
6  );
7  end;
8  /
```

PL/SQL procedure successfully completed.

SQL>

The user TEST will now have all the objects to execute the SQL statement that you want to investigate. You can verify this by issuing the original select statement. It should give you the same output as under the SH schema.

How It Works

Oracle offers the SQL Test Case Builder (TCB) to reproduce a SQL failure. You can create a test case through Enterprise Manager or through a PL/SQL package. The "Solution" section of this recipe shows how create a test case using the EXPORT_SQL_TESTCASE procedure of the DBMS_SQLDIAG package. There are several variants of this package, and our example shows how to use a SQL statement as the source for creating a SQL test case. Please review the DBMS_SQLDIAG.EXPORT_TESTCASE procedure in Oracle's PL/SQL Packages manual for details about other options to create test cases.

■ **Note** Remember that you should run the Test Case Builder as any user, other than SYS, who has been granted the DBA role.

Often, you'll find yourself trying to provide a test case for Oracle, without which the Oracle Support personnel won't be able to investigate a particular problem they are helping you with. The SQL Test Case Builder is a tool that is part of Oracle Database 11g, and its primary purpose is to help you quickly obtain a reproducible test case. The SQL Test Case Builder helps you easily capture pertinent information relating to a failed SQL statement and package it in a format that either a developer or an Oracle support person can use to reproduce the problem in a different environment.

You access the SQL Test Case Builder through the DBMS_SQLDIAG package. To create a test case, you must first export the SQL statement, including all the objects that are part of the statement, and all other related information. The export process is very similar to an Oracle export with the EXPDP command, and thus uses a directory, just as EXPDP does. Oracle creates the SQL test case as a script that contains the statements that will re-create the necessary database objects, along with associated runtime information such as statistics, which enable you to reproduce the error. The following are the various types of information captured and exported as part of the test case creation process:

- SQL text for the problem statement

- Table data—this is optional, and you can export a sample or complete data.

- The execution plan

- Optimizer statistics

- PL/SQL functions, procedure, and packages

- Bind variables

- User privileges

- SQL profiles

- Metadata for all the objects that are part of the SQL statement

- Dynamic sampling results

- Runtime information such as the degree of parallelism, for example

In the `DBMS_SQLDIAG` package, the `EXPORT_SQL_TESTCASE` procedure exports a SQL test case for a SQL statement to a directory. The `IMPORT_SQL_TESTCASE` procedure imports the test case from a directory. In the `EXPORT_SQL_TESTCASE` procedure, here is what the attributes stand for:

`DIRECTORY`: The directory where you want to store the test case files

`SQL_TEXT`: The actual SQL statement that's throwing the error

`TESTCASE`: The name of the test case

`EXPORTDATA`: By default, Oracle doesn't export the data. You can set this parameter to `TRUE` in order to export the data. You can optionally limit the amount of data you want to export, by specifying a value for the Sampling Percent attribute. The default value is 100.

The Test Case Builder automatically exports the PL/SQL package specifications but not the package body. However, you can specify that the TCB export the package body as well. The export process creates several files in the directory you specify. Of these files, the file in the format `oratcb1_008602000001main.xml` contains the metadata for the test case.

7-15. Generating an AWR Report

Problem

You'd like to generate an AWR report to analyze performance problems in your database.

Solution

The database automatically takes an AWR snapshot every hour, and saves the statistics in the AWR for eight days. An AWR report contains data captured between two snapshots, which need not be consecutive. Thus, an AWR report lets you examine instance performance between two points in time. You can generate an AWR report through Oracle Enterprise Manager. However, we show you how to create an AWR report using Oracle-provided scripts.

To generate an AWR report for a single instance database, execute the `awrrpt.sql` script as shown here.

```
SQL> @?/rdbms/admin/awrrpt.sql

Current Instance
~~~~~~~~~~~~~~~~~

   DB Id    DB Name      Inst Num Instance
----------- ------------ -------- ------------
 1118243965 ORCL1              1 orcl1
Specify the Report Type
~~~~~~~~~~~~~~~~~~~~~~~~~
Would you like an HTML report, or a plain text report?
Enter 'html' for an HTML report, or 'text' for plain text
Defaults to 'html'
Enter value for report_type: text
```

Type Specified:

Select a text- or an HTML-based report. The HTML report is the default report type, and it provides a nice-looking, well-formatted, easy-to-read report. Press Enter to select the default HTML-type report.

```
Instances in this Workload Repository schema
~~~~~~~~~~~~~~~~~~~~~~~~~~~~~~~~~~~~~~~~~~~~~~

   DB Id     Inst Num DB Name      Instance     Host
----------- -------- ------------ ------------ ------------
* 1118243965        1 ORCL1        orcl1        MIROPC61

Using 1118243965 for database Id
Using            1 for instance number
```

You must specify the DBID for the database at this point. In our example, however, there's only one database and therefore one DBID, so there's no need to enter the DBID.

```
Specify the number of days of snapshots to choose from
~~~~~~~~~~~~~~~~~~~~~~~~~~~~~~~~~~~~~~~~~~~~~~~~~~~~~~~~~
Entering the number of days (n) will result in the most recent
(n) days of snapshots being listed.  Pressing <return> without
specifying a number lists all completed snapshots.
Enter value for num_days: 1
```

Enter the number of days for which you want the database to list the snapshot IDs. In this example, we chose 1 because we want to generate an AWR for a time period that falls in the last day.

```
Listing the last day's Completed Snapshots
                                            Snap
Instance     DB Name        Snap Id   Snap Started      Level
------------ ------------ --------- ------------------ -----
orcl1        ORCL1             1877 17 Apr 2011 00:00     1
                               1878 17 Apr 2011 07:47     1
```

Specify a beginning and an ending snapshot for the AWR report.

```
Specify the Begin and End Snapshot Ids
~~~~~~~~~~~~~~~~~~~~~~~~~~~~~~~~~~~~~~~~~
Enter value for begin_snap: 1877
Begin Snapshot Id specified: 1877

Enter value for end_snap: 1878
End Snapshot Id specified: 1878
```

You can either accept the default name for the AWR report by pressing Enter, or enter a name for the report.

```
Specify the Report Name
~~~~~~~~~~~~~~~~~~~~~~~~~
The default report file name is awrrpt_1_1877_1878.txt.  To use this name,
press <return> to continue, otherwise enter an alternative.

Enter value for report_name:
Using the report name awrrpt_1_1877_1878.html
```

The database generates an AWR report in the same directory from which you invoked the `awrrpt.sql` script. For example, if you choose an HTML-based report, the AWR report will be in the following format: `awrrpt_1_1881_1882.html`.

■ **Tip**   You can generate an AWR report to analyze the performance of a single SQL statement by executing the `awrsqrpt.sql` script.

How It Works

The AWR reports that you generate show performance statistics captured between two points in time, each of which is called a snapshot. You can gain significant insights into your database performance by reading the AWR reports carefully. An AWR report takes less than a minute to run in most cases, and holds a treasure trove of performance information. The report consists of multiple sections. Walking through an AWR report usually shows you the reason that your database isn't performing at peak levels.

To generate an AWR report for all instances in an Oracle RAC environment, use the `awrgrpt.sql` script instead. You can generate an AWR report for a specific instance in a RAC environment by using the `awrrpti.sql` script. You can also generate an AWR report for a single SQL statement by invoking the `awrsqrpt.sql` script and providing the `SQL_ID` of the SQL statement.

You can generate an AWR report to span any length of time, as long as the AWR has snapshots covering that period. By default, the AWR retains its snapshots for a period of eight days.

You can generate an AWR snapshot any time you want, either through the Oracle Enterprise Manager or by using the `DBMS_WORKLOAD_REPOSITORY` package. That ability is useful when, for example, you want to investigate a performance issue from 20 minutes and the next snapshot is 40 minutes away. In that case, you must either wait 40 minutes or create a manual snapshot. Here's an example that shows how to create an AWR snapshot manually:

```
SQL> exec dbms_workload_repository.create_snapshot();

PL/SQL procedure successfully completed.
SQL>
```

Once you create the snapshot, you can run the `awrrpt.sql` script. Then select the previous two snapshots to generate an up-to-date AWR report.

You can generate an AWR report when your user response time increases suddenly, say from one to ten seconds during peak hours. An AWR report can also be helpful if a key batch job is suddenly taking much longer to complete. Of course, you must check the system CPU, I/O, and memory usage during the period as well, with the help of operating system tools such as `sar`, `vmstat`, and `iosat`.

If the system CPU usage is high, that doesn't necessarily mean that it's the CPU that's the culprit. CPU usage percentages are not always a true measure of throughput, nor is CPU usage always useful as a database workload metric. Make sure to generate the AWR report for the precise period that encompasses the time during which you noticed the performance deterioration. An AWR report that spans a 24-hour period is of little use in diagnosing a performance dip that occurred 2 hours ago for only 30 minutes. Match your report to the time period of the performance problem.

7-16. Comparing Database Performance Between Two Periods

Problem

You want to examine and compare how the database performed during two different periods.

Solution

Use the `awrddrpt.sql` script (located in the `$ORACLE_HOME/rdbms/admin` directory) to generate an AWR Compare Periods Report that compares performance between two periods. Here are the steps.

1. Invoke the `awrddrpt.sql` script.

   ```
   SQL> @$ORACLE_HOME/rdbms/admin/awrddrpt.sql
   ```

2. Select the report type (default is text).

   ```
   Enter value for report_type: html
   Type Specified:  html
   ```

3. Specify the number of days of snapshots from which you want to select the beginning and ending snapshots for the first time period.

   ```
   Specify the number of days of snapshots to choose from
   Enter value for num_days: 4
   ```

4. Choose a pair of snapshots over which you want to analyze the first period's performance.

```
Specify the First Pair of Begin and End Snapshot Ids
~~~~~~~~~~~~~~~~~~~~~~~~~~~~~~~~~~~~~~~~~~~~~~~~~~~~~~~~
Enter value for begin_snap: 2092
First Begin Snapshot Id specified: 2092

Enter value for end_snap: 2093
First End   Snapshot Id specified: 2093
```

5. Select the number of days of snapshots from which you want to select the pair of snapshots for the second period. Enter the value 4 so you can select a pair of snapshots from the previous 4 days.

```
Specify the number of days of snapshots to choose from
Enter value for num_days: 4
```

6. Specify the beginning and ending snapshots for the second period.

```
Specify the Second Pair of Begin and End Snapshot Ids
~~~~~~~~~~~~~~~~~~~~~~~~~~~~~~~~~~~~~~~~~~~~~~~~~~~~~~~~
Enter value for begin_snap2: 2134
Second Begin Snapshot Id specified: 2134

Enter value for end_snap2: 2135
Second End   Snapshot Id specified: 2135
```

7. Specify a report name or accept the default name.

```
Specify the Report Name
~~~~~~~~~~~~~~~~~~~~~~~~~
The default report file name is awrdiff_1_2092_1_2134.html  To use this name,
press <return> to continue, otherwise enter an alternative.

Enter value for report_name:
Using the report name awrdiff_1_2092_1_2134.html
Report written to awrdiff_1_2092_1_2134.html
SQL>
```

How It Works

Generating an AWR Compare Periods report is a process very similar to the one for generating a normal AWR report. The big difference is that the report does not show what happened between two snapshots, as the normal AWR report does. The AWR Compare Periods report compares performance between two different time periods, with each time period involving a different pair of snapshots. If you want to compare the performance of your database between 9 a.m. and 10 a.m. today and the same time period three days ago, you can do it with the AWR Compare Periods report. You can run an AWR Compare Periods report on one or all instances of a RAC database.

The AWR Compare Periods report is organized similarly to the normal AWR report, but it shows each performance statistic for the two periods side by side, so you can quickly see the differences (or similarities) in performance. Here's a section of the report showing how you can easily review the differences in performance statistics between the first and the second periods.

	First	Second	Diff
% Blocks changed per Read:	61.48	15.44	-46.04
Recursive Call %:	98.03	97.44	-0.59
Rollback per transaction %:	0.00	0.00	0.00
Rows per Sort:	2.51	2.07	-0.44
Avg DB time per Call (sec):	1.01	0.03	-0.98

7-17. Analyzing an AWR Report

Problem

You've generated an AWR report that covers a period when the database was exhibiting performance problems. You want to analyze the report.

Solution

An AWR report summarizes its performance-related statistics under various sections. The following is a quick summary of the most important sections in an AWR report.

Session Information

You can find out the number of sessions from the section at the very top of the AWR report, as shown here:

```
Snap Id     Snap Time          Sessions Curs/Sess
---------   -----------------  -------- ---------
Begin Snap:    1878 17-Apr-11 07:47:33       38     1.7
  End Snap:    1879 17-Apr-11 09:00:48       34     3.7
  Elapsed:            73.25 (mins)
  DB Time:            33.87 (mins)
```

Be sure to check the Begin Snap and End Snap times, to confirm that the period encompasses the time when the performance problem occurred. If you notice a very high number of sessions, you can investigate if shadow processes are being created—for example, if the number of sessions goes up by 200 between the Begin Snap and End Snap times when you expect the number of sessions to be the same at both times, the most likely cause is an application startup issue, which is spawning all those sessions.

Load Profile

The load profile section shows the per-second and per-transaction statistics for various indicators of database load such as hard parses and the number of transactions.

```
Load Profile                    Per Second      Per Transaction
~~~~~~~~~~~~                    ---------------  ---------------
              DB Time(s):              0.5                  1.4
              DB CPU(s):               0.1                  0.3
              Redo size:           6,165.3             19,028.7
           Logical reads:           876.6              2,705.6
           Block changes:            99.2                306.0
          Physical reads:            10.3                 31.8
         Physical writes:             1.9                  5.9
              User calls:             3.4                 10.4
                 Parses:             10.2                 31.5
            Hard parses:              1.0                  3.0
                 Logons:              0.1                  0.2
           Transactions:              0.3
```

The Load Profile section is one of the most important parts of an AWR report. Of particular significance are the physical I/O rates and hard parses. In an efficiently performing database, you should see mostly soft parses and very few hard parses. A high hard parse rate usually is a result of not using bind variables. If you see a high per second value for logons, it usually means that your applications aren't using persistent connections. A high number of logons or an unusually high number of transactions tells you something unusual is happening in your database. However, the only way you'll know the numbers are unusual is if you regularly check the AWR reports and know what the various statistics look like in a normally functioning database, at various times of the day!

Instance Efficiency Percentages

The instance efficiency section shows several hit ratios as well as the "execute to parse" and "latch hit" percentages.

```
Instance Efficiency Percentages (Target 100%)
~~~~~~~~~~~~~~~~~~~~~~~~~~~~~~~~~~~~~~~~~~~~~~~
              Buffer Nowait %:  100.00      Redo NoWait %:  100.00
              Buffer  Hit   %:   99.10   In-memory Sort %:  100.00
              Library Hit   %:   95.13        Soft Parse %:   90.35
            Execute to Parse %:   70.71        Latch Hit %:   99.97
    Parse CPU to Parse Elapsd %:  36.71     % Non-Parse CPU:   83.60

Shared Pool Statistics         Begin    End
                               ------   ------
              Memory Usage %:   81.08    88.82
      % SQL with executions>1:  70.41    86.92
    % Memory for SQL w/exec>1:  69.60    91.98
```

The *execute to parse ratio* should be very high in a well-running instance. A low value for the % SQL with exec>1 statistic means that the database is not re-using shared SQL statements, usually because the SQL is not using bind variables.

Top 5 Foreground Events

The Top 5 Timed Foreground Events section shows the events that were responsible for the most waits during the time spanned by the AWR report.

```
Top 5 Timed Foreground Events
~~~~~~~~~~~~~~~~~~~~~~~~~~~~~~~
                                              Avg Wait % DB
Event                        Waits   Time(s)  (ms)   time Wait Class
-------------------------- ----------- ----------- ------ ------ ----------
db file sequential read      13,735       475     35   23.4 User I/O
DB CPU                                    429          21.1
latch: shared pool              801        96    120    4.7 Concurrenc
db file scattered read          998        49     49    2.4 User I/O
control file sequential read  9,785        31      3    1.5 System I/O
```

The Top 5 Timed Foreground Events section is where you can usually spot the problem, by showing you why the sessions are "waiting." The Top 5 Events information shows the total waits for all sessions, but usually one or two sessions are responsible for most of the waits. Make sure to analyze the total waits and average waits (ms) separately, in order to determine if the waits are significant. Merely looking at the total number of waits or the total wait time for a wait event could give you a misleading idea about its importance. You must pay close attention to the average wait times for an event as well. In a nicely performing database, you should see CPU and I/O as the top wait events, as is the case here. If any wait events from the concurrent wait class such as latches show up at the top, investigate those waits further. For example, if you see events such as enq: TX - row lock contention, gc_buffer_busy (RAC), or latch free, it usually indicates contention in the database. If you see an average wait of more than 2 ms for the log file sync event, investigate the wait event further (Chapter 5 shows how to analyze various wait events). If you see a high amount of waits due to the db file sequential read or the db file scattered read wait events, there are heavy indexed reads (this is normal) or full table scans going on. You can find out the SQL statement and the tables involved in these read events in the AWR report.

Time Model Statistics

Time model statistics give you an idea about how the database has spent its time, including the time it spent on executing SQL statements as against parsing statements. If parsing time is very high, or if hard parsing is significant, you must investigate further.

```
Time Model Statistics          DB/Inst: ORCL1/orcl1  Snaps: 1878-1879

Statistic Name                        Time (s) % of DB Time
------------------------------------- ------------------- ------------
sql execute elapsed time                1,791.5         88.2
parse time elapsed                        700.1         34.5
hard parse elapsed time                   653.7         32.2
```

Top SQL Statements

This section of the AWR report lets you quickly identify the most expensive SQL statements.

```
SQL ordered by Elapsed Time          DB/Inst: ORCL1/orcl1  Snaps: 1878-1879
-> Captured SQL account for    13.7% of Total DB Time (s):          2,032
-> Captured PL/SQL account for   19.8% of Total DB Time (s):          2,032

     Elapsed                Elapsed Time
     Time (s)   Executions  per Exec (s)  %Total   %CPU   %IO   SQL Id
--------------- ------------ ------------- ------ ------ ------ -------------
      292.4            1        292.41     14.4    8.1   61.2  b6usrg82hwsas
...
```

You can generate an explain plan for the expensive SQL statements using the SQL ID from this part of the report.

PGA Histogram

The PGA Aggregate Target Histogram shows how well the database is executing the sort and hash operations—for example:

```
PGA Aggr Target Histogram            DB/Inst: ORCL1/orcl1  Snaps: 1878-1879
-> Optimal Executions are purely in-memory operations

 Low     High
Optimal Optimal   Total Execs  Optimal Execs  1-Pass Execs M-Pass Execs
------- -------  -------------- --------------  ------------ ------------
  2K      4K        13,957         13,957            0            0
 64K     128K          86             86            0            0
128K     256K          30             30            0            0
```

In this example, the database is performing all sorts and hashes optimally, in the PGA. If you see a high number of one-pass executions and even a few large multi-pass executions, that's an indication that the PGA is too small and you should consider increasing it.

How It Works

Analyzing an AWR report should be your first step when troubleshooting database performance issues such as a slow-running query. An AWR report lets you quickly find out things such as the number of connections, transactions per second, cache-hit rates, wait event information, and the SQL statements that are using the most CPU and I/O. It shows you which of your SQL statements are using the most resources, and which wait events are slowing down the database. Most importantly, probably, the report tells you if the database performance is unusually different from its typical performance during a given time of the day (or night). The AWR report sections summarized in the "Solution" section are only a small part of the AWR report. Here are some other key sections of the report that you must review when troubleshooting performance issues:

- Foreground Wait Events
- SQL Ordered by Gets
- SQL Ordered by Reads
- SQL Ordered by Physical Reads

- Instance Activity Stats

- Log Switches

- Enqueue Activity

- Reads by Tablespace, Datafile, and SQL Statement

- Segments by Table Scans

- Segments by Row Lock Waits

- Undo Segment Summary

Depending on the nature of the performance issue you're investigating, several of these sections in the report may turn out to be useful. In addition to the performance and wait statistics, the AWR report also offers advisories for both the PGA and the SGA. The AWR report is truly your best friend when you are troubleshooting just about any database performance issue. In a matter of minutes, you can usually find the underlying cause of the issue and figure out a potential fix. AWR does most of the work for you—you just need to know what to look for!

Creating Efficient SQL

Structured Query Language is like any other programming language in that it can be coded well, coded poorly, and everywhere in between. Learning to create efficient SQL statements has been discussed in countless books. This chapter zeroes in on basic SQL coding fundamentals, and addresses some techniques to improve performance of your SQL statements. In addition, some emphasis is given to ramifications of poorly written SQL, along with a few common pitfalls to avoid in your SQL statements within your application.

Writing good SQL statements the first time is the best way to get good performance from your SQL queries. Knowing the fundamentals is the key to accomplishing the goal of good performance. This chapter focuses on the basics of the SQL language:

- `SELECT` statement

- `WHERE` clause

- Joining tables

- Subqueries

- Set operators

Then, we'll focus on basic techniques to improve performance of your queries, as well as help ensure your queries are not hindering the performance of other queries within your database. It's important to take the time to write efficient SQL statements the first time, which is easy to say, but tough to accomplish when balancing client requirements, budgets, and project timelines. However, if you adhere to basic coding practices and fundamentals, you can greatly improve the performance of your SQL queries.

Note Several times in this chapter, we make a distinction between ISO syntax and traditional Oracle syntax. Specifically, we do that with respect to join syntax. However, that distinction is a bit mis-stated. With the exception of Oracle's use of the (+) to indicate an outer join, all of Oracle's join syntax complies with the ISO SQL standard, so it is *all* ISO syntax. However, it is common in the field to refer to the more newly implemented syntax as "ISO syntax," and we follow that pattern in this chapter.

8-1. Retrieving All Rows from a Table

Problem

You need to write a query to retrieve all rows from a given table within your database.

Solution

Within the SQL language, you use the SELECT statement to retrieve data from the database. Everything following the SELECT statement tells Oracle what data you need from the database. The first thing you need to determine is from which table(s) you need to retrieve data. Once this has been determined, you have what you need to be able to run a query to get data from the database. If we have an EMPLOYEES table within our Oracle database, we can perform a describe on that table in order to see the structure of the table. By doing this, we can see the column names for the table, and can determine which columns we want to select from the database.

```
SQL> describe employees
 Name                                      Null?    Type
 ----------------------------------------- -------- ----------------------------
 EMPLOYEE_ID                               NOT NULL NUMBER(6)
 FIRST_NAME                                         VARCHAR2(20)
 LAST_NAME                                 NOT NULL VARCHAR2(25)
 EMAIL                                     NOT NULL VARCHAR2(25)
 PHONE_NUMBER                                       VARCHAR2(20)
 HIRE_DATE                                 NOT NULL DATE
 JOB_ID                                    NOT NULL VARCHAR2(10)
 SALARY                                             NUMBER(8,2)
 COMMISSION_PCT                                     NUMBER(2,2)
 MANAGER_ID                                         NUMBER(6)
 DEPARTMENT_ID                                      NUMBER(4)
```

If we want to retrieve a list of all the employees' names from our EMPLOYEES table, we now have all the information we need to assemble a simple query against the EMPLOYEES table in the database. We know we are selecting from the EMPLOYEES table, which is needed for the FROM clause. We also know we want to select the names of the employees, which is needed to satisfy the SELECT clause. At this point, we can issue the following query against the database:

```
SELECT last_name, first_name
FROM employees;

LAST_NAME                 FIRST_NAME
------------------------- --------------------
Abel                      Ellen
Baer                      Hermann
Cabrio                    Anthony
Dilly                     Jennifer
Ernst                     Bruce
```

If we want to select all columns from the EMPLOYEES table, we can list every column from the table in the SELECT clause, or we can substitute listing every column with the asterisk, which indicates that we want to retrieve all the columns:

```
SELECT *
FROM employees;
```

If our manager wants the format of the output to be a comma-delimited list of all the employees' names, we can modify our query to accomplish this task:

```
SELECT last_name || ', ' || first_name AS "Employee Name"
FROM employees;
```

```
Employee Name
---------------------------------------------
Abel, Ellen
Baer, Hermann
Cabrio, Anthony
Dilly, Jennifer
Ernst, Bruce
```

In the foregoing case, we placed the concatenation characters, which are comprised of two vertical bars, in the query to indicate that we are combining the contents of multiple columns into a single output column. At the same time, we are creating a column alias by using the AS clause, and calling the combined last and first names "Employee Name".

How It Works

SELECT is the most fundamental statement needed to retrieve data from an Oracle database. While there are many clauses and features of a SELECT statement, at its most basic, there are really only two clauses needed to first retrieve data out of an Oracle database—and those clauses are the SELECT clause and the FROM clause. Normally, more is required to accurately retrieve the desired result set. You may want only a subset of the columns within a database table, and you may want only a subset of rows from a given table. Furthermore, you may want to perform manipulation on data pulled from the database. All this requires more sophisticated components of the SQL language than the simple SELECT statement. However, the SELECT and FROM clauses are the basic building blocks to assemble a query, from the most simple of queries to the most complex of queries.

■ **Note**   In order to select data from any database table, you need to either own the table or have been given the privilege to select data from the given set of tables.

8-2. Retrieve a Subset of Rows from a Table

Problem

You want to filter the data from a database SELECT query to return only a subset of rows from a database table.

Solution

The WHERE clause gives the user the ability to filter rows and return only the desired result set back from the database. There are various ways to construct a WHERE clause, a few of which will be reviewed within this recipe. The first thing that occurs within a WHERE clause is that one or more columns' values are compared to some other value. See Table 8-1 for a list of comparison operators that can be used within the WHERE clause. One of the more common comparison operators is the equal sign, which denotes an equality condition:

```
SELECT *
FROM EMP
WHERE deptno = 20;
```

In the foregoing query, we are selecting all columns from the EMP table, which is denoted by using the asterisk, and we want only those rows for department 20, which is determined by the WHERE clause.

Table 8-1. Comparison Operators Used in the WHERE Clause

Operator	Description
=	Equal to
!= , <> , ^=	Not equal to
<	Less than
>	Greater than
<=	Less than or equal to
>=	Greater than or equal to
IS NULL IS NOT NULL	Checking for existence of null values
LIKE NOT LIKE	Used to search when entire column value is not known

How It Works

In many SQL statements, there can be multiple conditions in a WHERE clause. Coding multiple conditions is done by using the logical operators OR, AND, and IN. If you have multiple logical operators within your SQL statement, Oracle will first always evaluate all AND clauses prior to any of the OR clauses. If there are matching logical operators in the same statement, they are evaluated from left to right. This can be confusing when constructing a complex WHERE condition. Therefore, when coding multiple conditions within a WHERE clause, delimit each clause with parentheses, else you may not get the results you are expecting. This is good SQL coding practice, and makes SQL code simpler to read and maintain—for example:

```
SELECT last_name, first_name, salary, email
FROM employees
WHERE (department_id = 20
OR department_id = 30)
AND commission_pct > 0;
```

If we have the need for multiple OR logical operators within our statement, we can replace them with the IN logical operator, which can simplify our SQL statement. By rewriting the foregoing query to use the IN logical operator, our query would look like the following:

```
SELECT last_name, first_name, salary, email
FROM employees
WHERE department_id IN (20,30)
AND commission_pct > 0;
```

If you want to find all the same information for all departments except department 20 or 30, the SQL code would look like the following:

```
SELECT last_name, first_name, salary, email
FROM employees
WHERE (department_id != 20
AND department_id <> 30)
AND commission_pct > 0;
```

Note that in the foregoing, for demonstration, we used two of the "not equal" comparison operators. It is generally good coding practice to be consistent, and use the same operators across all of your SQL code. This avoids confusion with others who need to look at or modify your SQL code. Even subtle differences like this can make someone else ponder why one piece of SQL code was done one way, and another piece of SQL code was done a different way. When writing SQL code, writing for efficiency is important, but it is equally important to write the code with an eye on maintainability. If SQL code is consistent, it simply will be easier to read and maintain.

Taking the previous SQL statement, we again will use the logical OR operator, add the NOT operand, and accomplish the same task:

```
SELECT last_name, first_name, salary, email
FROM employees
WHERE department_id NOT IN(20,30)
AND commission_pct > 0;
```

The last two queries both provided the proper results, but in this case, using the IN clause simplified our SQL statement.

8-3. Joining Tables with Corresponding Rows

Problem

Within a single query, you wish to retrieve matching rows from multiple tables. These tables have at least one common column on which to match the data between the tables.

Solution

A join condition within the SQL language is used to combine data from multiple tables within a single query. When there are corresponding rows in all tables involved in the join process, it is called an "inner join." What this means is that based on the common join columns between the tables, only data that matches between the two tables will be returned.

Let's say you want to get the city where all departments in your company are based. There are two different ways to approach this before writing your SQL statement. You can use either traditional Oracle syntax, or the newer ISO syntax. Using traditional Oracle SQL, the syntax would be as follows:

```
SELECT d.location_id, department_name, city
FROM departments d, locations l
WHERE d.location_id = l.location_id;
```

To write the same statement using ISO syntax, there are several methods that can be used:

- Natural Join

- JOIN ... USING clause

- JOIN ... ON clause

If using the NATURAL JOIN clause, you are letting Oracle determine the natural join condition and which columns will be joined on, and therefore there are no join clauses or conditions in the statement:

```
SELECT location_id, department_name, city
FROM departments NATURAL JOIN locations;
```

If tables you are joining have common named join columns, you can specify the JOIN ... USING clause, and you specify this common column within parentheses:

```
SELECT location_id, department_name, city
FROM departments JOIN locations
USING (location_id);
```

It is very common for the join condition between tables to have differently named columns that are needed to complete the join criteria. In these cases, the JOIN ... ON clause is appropriate:

```
SELECT d.loc_id, department_name, city
FROM departments d JOIN locations l
ON l.location_id = d.loc_id;
```

How It Works

When using traditional Oracle SQL, you need to specify all join conditions in the WHERE clause. Therefore, the WHERE clause will contain all join conditions, along with any filtering criteria.

With ISO SQL, a key advantage is that the join conditions are done in the FROM clause, and the WHERE clause is used solely for filtering criteria. This makes SQL statements easier to read and decipher. No longer do you need to determine within a WHERE clause which statements are join conditions and which are filtering criteria. The advantage of this is more evident when you are joining three or more tables. The filtering criteria are solely in the WHERE clause and are easily visible:

```
SELECT last_name, first_name, department_name, city,
state_province state, postal_code zip, country_name
FROM employees
JOIN departments USING (department_id)
JOIN locations USING (location_id)
JOIN countries USING (country_id)
JOIN regions USING (region_id)
WHERE department_id = 20;
```

If you prefer to write SQL statements with traditional Oracle SQL, good practice just for readability and more maintainable SQL code is to place all join conditions first in the WHERE clause, and place all filtering criteria at the end of the WHERE clause. It also makes the code easier to read and maintain if you can simply line up the code. This is an optional practice, but helps anyone else who may need to look at your SQL code:

```
SELECT last_name, first_name, department_name, city,
state_province state, postal_code zip, country_name
FROM employees e, departments d, locations l, countries c, regions r
WHERE e.department_id = d.department_id
  AND d.location_id   = l.location_id
  AND l.country_id    = c.country_id
  AND c.region_id     = r.region_id
  and d.department_id = 20;
```

Also, when using the JOIN ... ON or JOIN ... USING clause, it may be more clear to specify the optional INNER keyword, as it would immediately be known it is an inner join that is being done:

```
SELECT location_id, department_name, city
FROM departments INNER JOIN locations
USING (location_id);
```

8-4. Joining Tables When Corresponding Rows May Be Missing

Problem

You need data from two or more tables, but some of the data is missing in one or more of the tables. For instance, you want to get a list of all of the departments for your company, along with their base locations. For whatever reason, you've been told that there are locations listed within your company that do not map to a single department, in which case there are no department locations listed.

Solution

You need to show all locations, so an inner join will not work in this case. Instead, you can write what is termed an *outer join*. Notice the (+) syntax in the following example:

```
SELECT l.location_id, city, department_id, department_name
FROM locations l, departments d
WHERE l.location_id = d.location_id(+)
ORDER BY 1;
```

```
LOCATION_ID CITY                    DEPARTMENT_ID DEPARTMENT_NAME
----------- --------------------    ------------- ------------------------
       1100 Venice
       1400 Southlake                          60 IT
       1500 South San Francisco                50 Shipping
       1700 Seattle                           170 Manufacturing
       1700 Seattle                           240 Sales
       1700 Seattle                           270 Payroll
       1700 Seattle                           120 Treasury
       1700 Seattle                           110 Accounting
       1700 Seattle                           100 Finance
       1700 Seattle                            30 Purchasing
       1800 Toronto                            20 Marketing
       2000 Beijing
       2400 London                             40 Human Resources
       2700 Munich                             70 Public Relations
       3200 Mexico City
```

To specify an outer join using traditional Oracle SQL, simply place a plus sign within parentheses in the WHERE clause join condition next to a column from the table that you know has missing data. We know in the foregoing case that there are locations that are not assigned to a single department. From the results, we can see the locations that have no departments assigned to them.

To execute the same query using ISO SQL syntax, you use the LEFT OUTER JOIN or RIGHT OUTER JOIN clauses, which can be shortened to LEFT JOIN or RIGHT JOIN—for example:

```
SELECT location_id, city, department_id, department_name
FROM locations LEFT JOIN departments d
USING (location_id)
ORDER BY 1;
```

Now let's say you must execute a query in which either table, on either side of the join, could be missing one or more corresponding rows. One approach is to create a union of two outer join queries:

```
SELECT last_name, first_name, department_name
FROM employees e, departments d
WHERE e.manager_id = d.manager_id(+)
UNION
SELECT last_name, first_name, department_name
FROM employees e, departments d
```

```
WHERE e.manager_id(+) = d.manager_id
ORDER BY department_name, last_name, first_name;
```

```
LAST_NAME                FIRST_NAME           DEPARTMENT_NAME
------------------------ -------------------- -------------------------
Gietz                    William              Accounting
                                              Administration
                                              Benefits
Cambrault                Gerald               Executive
Chen                     John                 Finance
                                              Government Sales
                                              Human Resources
Pataballa                Valli                IT
                                              Manufacturing
Fay                      Pat                  Marketing
                                              Payroll
                                              Public Relations
Tobias                   Sigal                Purchasing
Tucker                   Peter                Sales
                                              Shareholder Services
Sarchand                 Nandita              Shipping
                                              Treasury
Lee                      Linda
Morse                    Steve
```

From the foregoing results, we can see all employees that manage departments, all employees that do not manage departments, as well as those departments with no assigned manager.

In order to do the same query using ISO SQL syntax, use the FULL OUTER JOIN clause, which can be shortened to FULL JOIN:

```
SELECT last_name, first_name, department_name
FROM employees FULL JOIN departments
USING (manager_id);
```

How It Works

There are really three outer joins that can be done based on your circumstances. Table 8-2 describes all the possible join conditions. SQL statements using traditional syntax or ISO SQL syntax are both perfectly acceptable. However, it is generally easier to write, read, and maintain ISO SQL than traditional Oracle SQL.

One of the main advantages of the ISO syntax is that for multiple table joins, all the join conditions are specified in the FROM clause, and are therefore isolated and easy to see. In Oracle SQL, the join conditions are specified in the WHERE clause, along with any other filtering criteria needed for the query. If you inherited poorly structured SQL code, it is simply harder to read longer and more complex SQL statements that have join conditions and filtering criteria interspersed within a single WHERE clause.

One other type of join not already mentioned is the cross join, which is a Cartesian join. While this type of join is rarely useful, it can be occasionally beneficial. As a DBA, let's say you are gathering database size information for your enterprise of databases, and are placing the results in a single spreadsheet. You need to get database and host information for each query. You can execute the following query:

```
SELECT d.name, i.host_name, round(sum(f.bytes)/1048576) megabytes
FROM v$database d
CROSS JOIN v$instance i
CROSS JOIN v$datafile f
GROUP BY d.name, i.host_name;
```

```
NAME      HOST_NAME                       MEGABYTES
--------- ------------------------------- ----------
ORCL      DREGS-PC                             2333
```

In this case, the v$instance and v$database views contain only a single row, so there is no harm in doing a Cartesian join. The foregoing join could also be written with traditional Oracle SQL:

```
SELECT d.name, i.host_name, round(sum(f.bytes)/1048576) megabytes
FROM v$database d, v$instance i, v$datafile f
GROUP BY d.name, i.host_name;
```

Table 8-2. *Oracle Join Conditions*

Join Type	Traditional Join Syntax	ISO Join Syntax	Description
Inner join	WHERE clause, with one clause specified for each join condition	FROM clause, along with: NATURAL JOIN JOIN ... USING JOIN … ON	There are corresponding rows in each table matching the condition.
Left outer join	WHERE clause, the 3-character sequence of (+) placed next to column from table with missing data	FROM clause, along with: LEFT OUTER JOIN LEFT JOIN	There may not be corresponding rows in the table on the right side of the join condition.
Right outer join	WHERE clause, the 3-character sequence of (+) placed next to table with missing data	FROM clause, along with: RIGHT OUTER JOIN RIGHT JOIN	This means there may not be corresponding rows on table on the left side of the join condition.
Full outer join	Two SELECT statements with union condition specified, with one side of the outer join specified on first part of the union, and the other side of the outer join specified on second part of the union	FROM clause, along with: FULL OUTER JOIN FULL JOIN	This means there may not always be corresponding rows in both tables. It cannot be specified natively with traditional Oracle SQL syntax, and must be constructed with a UNION, while ISO SQL has the syntax built in.
Cross join	WHERE clause; there are no join conditions between the joined tables.	FROM clause, along with: CROSS JOIN	This means a Cartesian join is indicated.

8-5. Constructing Simple Subqueries

Problem

You need to retrieve data from the database, but cannot get the data you need using a single query.

Solution

It is common that data needs from a relational database are complex enough that the data cannot be retrieved within a single SQL SELECT statement. Rather than having to run two or more queries serially, it is possible to construct several SQL SELECT statements and place them within a single query. These additional SELECT statements are called subqueries, sub-selects, or nested selects.

Let's say you want to get the name of the employee with the highest salary in your company so you can ask your boss for a raise. Since you don't know what the highest salary is, you first have to run a query to determine the following:

```
SELECT MAX(salary) FROM employees;
```

```
MAX(SALARY)
-----------
      24000
```

Then, knowing what the highest salary is, you could run a second query to get the employee(s) with that salary:

```
SELECT last_name, first_name
FROM employees
WHERE salary = 24000;
```

```
LAST_NAME                FIRST_NAME
------------------------ --------------------
King                     Steven
```

It's very simple to combine the foregoing two queries, and construct a single SQL statement with a subquery to accomplish the same task:

```
SELECT last_name, first_name
FROM employees
WHERE salary =
(SELECT MAX(salary) FROM employees);
```

```
LAST_NAME                FIRST_NAME
------------------------ --------------------
King                     Steven
```

How It Works

Within a SQL statement, a subquery can be placed within the SELECT, WHERE, or HAVING clauses. You can also place a query within the FROM clause, which is also called an inline view, which is addressed in a different recipe. There are several kinds of subqueries that can be constructed:

- Single-row or scalar subquery

- Multiple-row subquery

- Multiple-column subquery

- Correlated subquery (addressed in a different recipe)

The subquery itself is also called an *inner query*. Except for correlated subqueries, the inner query is executed first, and then the results of the inner query are passed to the outer query, which is then executed.

Single-Row Subqueries

Single-row subqueries return a single column of a single row. The example shown in the "Solution" section is a single-row subquery. Use caution and be certain that the subquery can return only a single value; otherwise you can get an error from your subquery:

```
SELECT last_name, first_name
FROM employees
WHERE salary =
(SELECT salary FROM employees WHERE department_id = 30);

(SELECT salary FROM employees WHERE department_id = 30)
   *
ERROR at line 4:
ORA-01427: single-row subquery returns more than one row
```

In the foregoing example, there are multiple employees in department 30, so the subquery would return all of the matching rows.

If you want to see how your salary stacks up against the average salaries of employees in your company, you can issue a subquery in the SELECT clause to accomplish this:

```
SELECT last_name, first_name, salary, ROUND((SELECT AVG(salary) FROM employees)) avg_sal
FROM employees
WHERE last_name = 'King';

LAST_NAME                 FIRST_NAME              SALARY    AVG_SAL
------------------------- ---------------------- ---------- ----------
King                      Steven                   24000      6462
```

Let's say you want to know which departments overall had a higher salary than the average for your company. By placing the subquery in the HAVING clause, you can get the desired results:

```
column avg_sal format 99999.99

SELECT department_id, ROUND(avg(salary),2) avg_sal
```

```
FROM employees
GROUP BY department_id
HAVING avg(salary) > (SELECT AVG(salary) FROM employees)
ORDER BY 2;

DEPARTMENT_ID   AVG_SAL
-------------  ---------
           40   6500.00
          100   8600.00
           80   8955.88
           20   9500.00
           70  10000.00
          110  10150.00
           90  19333.33

8 rows selected.
```

Multiple-Row Subqueries

If you know the desired subquery is going to return multiple rows, you can use the IN, ANY, ALL, and SOME operators. The IN operator is the same as having multiple OR conditions in a select statement. For example, in the following SQL statement, we are getting the DEPARTMENT_NAME for departments 20, 30, and 40.

```
SELECT department_id, department_name
FROM departments
WHERE department_id = 20
OR department_id = 30
OR department_id = 40;

DEPARTMENT_ID DEPARTMENT_NAME
------------- ------------------------------
           20 Marketing
           30 Purchasing
           40 Human Resources
```

Using the IN operator, we can simplify our SQL statement and achieve the same result:

```
SELECT department_id, department_name
FROM departments
WHERE department_id IN (20,30,40);
```

The ANY and SOME operators function identically. They are used to compare a value retrieved from the database to each value shown in the list of values in the query. They are used with the comparison operators =, !=, <>, <, <=, >, or >=. Use care with ANY or SOME, as it evaluates each value separately, without regard to the entire list of values. For example, using the same query to get the department name for departments 20, 30, or 40, if we modify this query to use ANY or SOME, we can see how Oracle evaluates each value in the ANY clause. Because we used the ANY clause, departments 10, 20, and 30 were included in the result, even though departments 20 and 30 were within our ANY clause. This is because each value is evaluated separately before the result set is returned.

```
SELECT department_id, department_name
FROM departments
WHERE department_id < ANY (20,30,40);

SELECT department_id, department_name
FROM departments
WHERE department_id < SOME (20,30,40);

DEPARTMENT_ID DEPARTMENT_NAME
------------- ------------------------------
           10 Administration
           20 Marketing
           30 Purchasing
```

The ALL operator essentially uses a logical AND operator to do the comparison of values shown in the query. While with the ANY operator, each value was compared individually to see if there was a match, the ALL operator needs to compare every value in the list before determining if there is a match. Using our department table as an example, see the following query. In this query, we are retrieving the department names from the table if the DEPARTMENT_ID value is less than or equal to *all* values in the list:

```
SELECT department_id, department_name
FROM departments
WHERE department_id <= ALL (20,30,40);

DEPARTMENT_ID DEPARTMENT_NAME
------------- ------------------------------
           10 Administration
           20 Marketing
```

Multiple-Column Subqueries

At times, you need to match data based on multiple columns. If placed within the WHERE clause, the column list needs to be placed within parentheses. As an example, if you want to get a list of the employees with the highest salary in their respective departments, you can write a multiple-column subquery such as the following:

```
SELECT last_name, first_name, department_id, salary
FROM employees
WHERE (department_id, salary) IN
(SELECT department_id, max(salary)
FROM employees
GROUP BY department_id)
ORDER BY department_id;
```

LAST_NAME	FIRST_NAME	DEPARTMENT_ID	SALARY
Whalen	Jennifer	10	4400
Hartstein	Michael	20	13000
Raphaely	Den	30	11000
Mavris	Susan	40	6500
Fripp	Adam	50	8200

Hunold	Alexander	60	9000
Baer	Hermann	70	10000
Russell	John	80	14000
King	Steven	90	24000
Greenberg	Nancy	100	12000
Higgins	Shelley	110	12000

11 rows selected.

8-6. Constructing Correlated Subqueries

Problem

You are writing a subquery to retrieve data from a given set of tables from your database, but in order to retrieve the proper results, you really need to reference the outer query from inside the inner query.

Solution

The correlated subquery is a powerful component of the SQL language. The reason it is called "correlated" is that it allows you to reference the outer query from within the inner query. For example, we want to see all the jobs each current employee has ever held in the company:

```
SELECT employee_id, job_id
FROM job_history h
WHERE job_id in
(SELECT job_id FROM employees e
WHERE e.job_id = h.job_id)
ORDER BY 1;

EMPLOYEE_ID JOB_ID
----------- ----------
        101 AC_ACCOUNT
        101 AC_MGR
        102 IT_PROG
        114 ST_CLERK
        122 ST_CLERK
        176 SA_REP
        176 SA_MAN
        200 AD_ASST
        200 AC_ACCOUNT
        201 MK_REP

10 rows selected.
```

How It Works

Because you reference the outer query from inside the inner query, the process of executing a correlated subquery is essentially the opposite compared to a simple subquery. In a correlated subquery, the outer query is executed first, as the inner query needs the data from the outer query in order to be able to process the query and retrieve the results. The steps to execute a correlated subquery are as follows. These steps repeat for each row in the outer query:

1. Retrieve row from the outer query.

2. Execute the inner query.

3. The outer query compares the value returned from the inner query.

4. If there is a value match in step 3, the row is returned to the user.

Another type of correlated subquery is to use the EXISTS clause in a subquery. When you use EXISTS, a test is done to see if the inner query returns at least one row. This is the important test that occurs when using the EXISTS operator. As you can see from the following example, the column list of the SELECT clause within the inner query is irrelevant. Something is included there simply to have proper SQL syntax only. If we want to see which of our employees are also managers, we can use the EXISTS operator with a self-join back to the employees table to determine this information:

```
SELECT employee_id, last_name, first_name
FROM employees e
WHERE EXISTS
(SELECT 'ANY LITERAL WILL DO HERE'
FROM employees m
WHERE e.employee_id = manager_id);
```

```
EMPLOYEE_ID LAST_NAME                FIRST_NAME
----------- ------------------------ --------------------
        100 King                     Steven
        101 Kochhar                  Neena
        102 De Haan                  Lex
        103 Hunold                   Alexander
        108 Greenberg                Nancy
        114 Raphaely                 Den
        120 Weiss                    Matthew
        121 Fripp                    Adam
        122 Kaufling                 Payam
        123 Vollman                  Shanta
        124 Mourgos                  Kevin
        145 Russell                  John
        146 Partners                 Karen
        147 Errazuriz                Alberto
        148 Cambrault                Gerald
        149 Zlotkey                  Eleni
        201 Hartstein                Michael
        205 Higgins                  Shelley

18 rows selected.
```

You can also use NOT EXISTS if you want to test the opposite condition within a query. For example, your CEO wants to determine the manager-to-employee ratio within your company. Using the query from the previous example, we can first use the EXISTS operator to determine the number of managers within the company:

```
SELECT count(*)
FROM employees e
WHERE EXISTS
(SELECT 'TESTING 1,2,3'
FROM employees m
WHERE e.employee_id = manager_id);
```

```
  COUNT(*)
----------
        18
```

If we convert EXISTS to NOT EXISTS, we can determine the number of non-managers within the company:

```
SELECT count(*)
FROM employees e
WHERE NOT EXISTS
(SELECT 'X'
FROM employees m
WHERE e.employee_id = manager_id);
```

```
  COUNT(*)
---------
       89
```

8-7. Comparing Two Tables to Finding Missing Rows

Problem

You need to compare data for a subset of columns between two tables. You need to find rows in one table that are missing from the other.

Solution

You can use the Oracle MINUS set operator to compare two sets of data, and show data missing from one of the tables. When using any of the Oracle set operators, the SELECT clauses must be identical in terms of number of columns, and the datatypes of each column.

As an example, you work for a cable television company, and you want to find out what channels are offered free of charge. To test this out, you could first simply get a list of the channels offered by your company:

```
SELECT channel_id FROM channels;

CHANNEL_ID
----------
         2
         3
         4
         5
         9
```

Then, you can run a query to find out which channels have costs associated with them by querying the COSTS table:

```
SELECT DISTINCT channel_id FROM costs
ORDER BY channel_id;

CHANNEL_ID
----------
         2
         3
         4
```

By quickly doing a visual examination of the results, the free channels are channels 5 and 9. By using a set operator, in this case, MINUS, you can get this result from a single query:

```
SELECT channel_id
FROM channels
MINUS
SELECT channel_id
FROM costs;

CHANNEL_ID
----------
         5
         9
```

How It Works

It is also very common to use set operators in queries to get more information about the missing data. For instance, you have gotten the free channel list, but you really need to get more information about those free channels, and would like to accomplish everything within a single query:

```
SELECT channel_id, channel_desc FROM channels
WHERE channel_id IN
(SELECT channel_id
FROM channels
MINUS
SELECT channel_id
FROM costs);
```

```
CHANNEL_ID CHANNEL_DESC
---------- --------------------
         5 Catalog
         9 Tele Sales
```

8-8. Comparing Two Tables to Finding Matching Rows

Problem

You need to compare data for a subset of columns between two tables. You need to see all matching rows from those tables.

Solution

You can use the Oracle INTERSECT set operator to compare two sets of data, and show the matching data between the two tables. Again, when using any of the Oracle set operators, the SELECT clauses must be identical in terms of number of columns, and the datatypes of each column.

   Using the example of the free channels, we now want to see which channels are not free, and have costs associated with them. By using the INTERSECT set operator, we will see only the matching rows between the two tables:

```
SELECT channel_id
FROM channels
INTERSECT
SELECT channel_id
FROM costs;

CHANNEL_ID
----------
         2
         3
         4
```

How It Works

When using INTERSECT, think of it as the overlapping data between two tables, based on the column list in the SELECT statement.

8-9. Combining Results from Similar SELECT Statements

Problem

You need to combine the results between two similar SELECT statements, and would like to accomplish it within a single query.

Solution

You can use the Oracle set operators UNION or UNION ALL to combine results from two like queries. The difference between using UNION and UNION ALL is that UNION will automatically eliminate any duplicate rows, and each row of the result set will be unique. When using UNION ALL, it will show all matching rows, including duplicate rows. Using UNION ALL may yield better performance than UNION, because a sort to eliminate duplicates is avoided. If your application can eliminate duplicates during processing, it may be worth the performance gained from using UNION ALL.

In Oracle's sample schemas, we have the SCOTT.EMP table and the HR.EMPLOYEES table. If we want to see all the employees on both tables, we can use a UNION set operator to get the results:

```
SELECT empno, hiredate FROM scott.emp
UNION
SELECT employee_id, hire_date FROM hr.employees;

    EMPNO HIREDATE
---------- ---------
      100 17-JUN-87
      101 21-SEP-89
      102 13-JAN-93
      ...
     7902 03-DEC-81
     7934 23-JAN-82
     7997 15-AUG-11

122 rows selected.
```

How It Works

You are running two queries where you have a nearly identical column list, but let's say you have one additional column on one table. In this case, we have the COMM column on the SCOTT.EMP table, which is the commission amount an employee has earned. You don't have an equivalent column on the HR.EMPLOYEES table. By using NULL in the missing column, you can still use a set operator such as UNION as long as you account for any missing columns on either side of the operation:

```
SELECT empno, mgr, hiredate, sal, deptno, comm
FROM scott.emp
UNION
SELECT employee_id, manager_id, hire_date, salary, department_id, NULL
FROM hr.employees;
```

EMPNO	MGR	HIREDATE	SAL	DEPTNO	COMM
100		17-JUN-87	24000	90	
101	100	21-SEP-89	17000	90	
102	100	13-JAN-93	17000	90	
...					
7369	7902	17-DEC-80	800	20	
7499	7698	20-FEB-81	1600	30	300
7521	7698	22-FEB-81	1250	30	500
7566	7839	02-APR-81	2975	20	
7654	7698	28-SEP-81	1250	30	1400

After examining the HR.EMPLOYEES table, there is a column named COMMISSION_PCT. We can derive the actual commission based on this column, and add it to the previous query. Also, our manager has told us that he or she wants to see a value in the commission column for all employees, even if they earn no commission:

```
SELECT empno, mgr, hiredate, sal, deptno, nvl(comm,0)
FROM scott.emp
UNION
SELECT employee_id, manager_id, hire_date, salary, department_id,
nvl(salary*commission_pct/100,0)
FROM hr.employees;
```

EMPNO	MGR	HIREDATE	SAL	DEPTNO	NVL(COMM,0)
100		17-JUN-87	24000	90	0
101	100	21-SEP-89	17000	90	0
102	100	13-JAN-93	17000	90	0
...					
147	100	10-MAR-97	12000	80	36
148	100	15-OCT-99	11000	80	33
149	100	29-JAN-00	10500	80	21
...					
7499	7698	20-FEB-81	1600	30	300
7521	7698	22-FEB-81	1250	30	500
7566	7839	02-APR-81	2975	20	0

One point to stress again is that the datatypes for each column also must be the same. For example, we are doing a union between the SCOTT.EMP table and the HR.DEPARTMENTS table, and want to see a combined list of the department numbers, along with their locations. However, based on the datatype list, we cannot use an Oracle set operator such as UNION for this, as the location column for each table is different:

```
SQL> desc scott.dept
 Name                                      Null?    Type
 ----------------------------------------- -------- ------------------------

 DEPTNO                                    NOT NULL NUMBER(2)
 DNAME                                              VARCHAR2(14)
 LOC                                                VARCHAR2(13)

SQL> desc hr.departments
```

```
Name                                      Null?    Type
---------------------------------------- -------- ------------------------

DEPARTMENT_ID                            NOT NULL NUMBER(4)
DEPARTMENT_NAME                          NOT NULL VARCHAR2(30)
MANAGER_ID                                        NUMBER(6)
LOCATION_ID                                       NUMBER(4)

SQL> l
  1  SELECT deptno, loc FROM scott.dept
  2  UNION
  3* select department_id, location_id from hr.departments
SQL> /
SELECT deptno, loc FROM scott.dept
                *
ERROR at line 1:
ORA-01790: expression must have same datatype as corresponding expression
```

8-10. Searching for a Range of Values

Problem

You need to retrieve data from your database based on a range of values for a given column.

Solution

The BETWEEN clause is commonly used to retrieve a range of values from a database. It is most commonly used with dates, timestamps, and numbers, but can also be used with alphanumeric data. It is an efficient way of retrieving data from the database when an exact set of values is not known for a column within the WHERE clause. For instance, if we wanted to see all employees that were hired between the year 2000 and through the year 2010, the query could be written as follows:

```
SELECT last_name, first_name, hire_date
FROM employees
WHERE hire_date BETWEEN '2000-01-01' and '2010-12-31'
ORDER BY hire_date;
```

When using the BETWEEN clause, it is an efficient way to find a range of values for a column, and works for a multitude of datatypes. If you want to get a range of values for a NUMBER datatype as in the SALARY column, a range can be given:

```
SELECT last_name, first_name, salary
FROM employees
WHERE salary BETWEEN 20000 and 30000
ORDER BY salary;
```

If you want to add to the foregoing query and get only those employees whose last names are in the first half of the alphabet, you can supply a range to satisfy this request. In order to guarantee all values, we filled out the possible values to the 25-character length of the last_name column:

```
SELECT last_name, first_name, salary
FROM employees
WHERE salary BETWEEN 20000 and 30000
AND last_name BETWEEN 'Aaaaaaaaaaaaaaaaaaaaaaaaaaa'
AND 'Mzzzzzzzzzzzzzzzzzzzzzzzz'
ORDER BY salary;
```

How It Works

One common pitfall when using the BETWEEN clause is with the use of date-based columns, whether it be the DATE datatype, the TIMESTAMP datatype, or any other date-based datatype. If not constructed carefully, desired rows can be missed from the result set.

One way this occurs is that often queries on dates are done using a combination of year, month, and day. It is important to remember that even though the format of the date-based fields on an Oracle database usually defaults to a year, month, and day type of format, the element of time must always be accounted for, else rows can be missed from a query. In this first example, we have an employee, Sarah Bell, who was hired February 4, 1996:

```
SELECT hire_date FROM employees
WHERE email = 'SBELL';


HIRE_DATE
----------
1996-02-04
```

If we query the database, and don't consider the time element for any date column, we can omit critical rows from our result set. Therefore it is important to know whether the time portion of the column is included in the makeup of the data. In this case, there is indeed a time element present in the hire_date column:

```
SELECT last_name, first_name, hire_date
FROM employees
WHERE hire_date = '1996-02-04';


no rows selected
```

Sometimes, when rows are inserted into the database, the time portion of a date or timestamp can be truncated. However, when coding efficient SQL, it is important to always assume there is a time element present for any and all date-based columns. Based on that assumption, we can modify the foregoing query to consider the time element in the hire_date column:

```
SELECT last_name, first_name, to_char(hire_date,'yyyy-mm-dd:hh24:mi:ss') hire_date
FROM employees
WHERE hire_date
BETWEEN TO_DATE('1996-02-04:00:00:00','yyyy-mm-dd:hh24:mi:ss')
AND TO_DATE('1996-02-04:23:59:59','yyyy-mm-dd:hh24:mi:ss');


LAST_NAME                 FIRST_NAME            HIRE_DATE
-----------------------   --------------------  -------------------
Bell                      Sarah                 1996-02-04:12:30:46
```

Here is a similar case, where we are performing a SELECT to retrieve all data for a given month specified in the query. In this case, we are retrieving all employees who were hired in the month of September, 1997. If we omit the time element from the BETWEEN clause, we can actually omit data that meets the criteria for our query:

```
SELECT last_name, first_name, hire_date
FROM employees
WHERE hire_date
BETWEEN '1997-09-01' and '1997-09-30';
```

```
LAST_NAME                FIRST_NAME           HIRE_DATE
------------------------  --------------------  ----------
Chen                     John                 1997-09-28
```

```
SELECT last_name, first_name, hire_date
FROM employees
WHERE hire_date
BETWEEN TO_DATE('1997-09-01:00:00:00','yyyy-mm-dd:hh24:mi:ss')
AND TO_DATE('1997-09-30:23:59:59','yyyy-mm-dd:hh24:mi:ss');
```

```
LAST_NAME                FIRST_NAME           HIRE_DATE
------------------------  --------------------  ----------
Chen                     John                 1997-09-28
Sciarra                  Ismael               1997-09-30
```

If you are using a BETWEEN clause in your query, and there is an index on the column specified in the WHERE clause, the Oracle optimizer can use the index to retrieve the data. You would need to perform an explain plan to validate if this is the case, but using BETWEEN means an index can often be used if one is present, and can be an efficient manner of selecting data from the database using a range of values:

```
SELECT last_name, first_name, salary
FROM employees
WHERE last_name between 'Ba' and 'Bz'
ORDER BY salary;
```

```
-----------------------------------------------------------
| Id  | Operation                     | Name        |
-----------------------------------------------------------
|   0 | SELECT STATEMENT              |             |
|   1 |  SORT ORDER BY                |             |
|   2 |   TABLE ACCESS BY INDEX ROWID| EMPLOYEES   |
|   3 |    INDEX RANGE SCAN           | EMP_NAME_IX |
-----------------------------------------------------------
```

8-11. Handling Null Values

Problem

You have null values in some of your database data, and need to understand the ramifications of dealing with null values in data. You also need to write queries to correctly deal with such nulls.

Solution

Null values have to be dealt with in a certain manner, depending on whether you are searching for null values in your data in the SELECT clause, or you are attempting to make a determination of what to do when a null value is found in the WHERE clause.

Handling Nulls in the SELECT Clause

Within the SELECT clause, if you are dealing with data within a column that contains null values, there are two Oracle-provided functions you can use within SQL to transform a null value into a more usable form. The two functions are NVL and NVL2.

■ **Note**   Actually, there are more than just the two functions NVL and NVL2. However, those are widely used, and are a good place to begin.

With NVL, you simply pass in the column name, along with the value you want to give the output based on whether that value is null in the database. For instance, in our employees table, not all employees get a commission based on their jobs, and the value in that column for these employees is null:

```
SELECT ename , sal , comm
FROM emp
ORDER BY ename;

ENAME           SAL       COMM
---------- ---------- ----------
ADAMS          1100
ALLEN          1600        300
BLAKE          2850
KING           5000
MARTIN         1250       1400
```

If we simply want to see a zero in the commission column for employees not eligible for a commission, we can use the NVL function to accomplish this:

```
SELECT ename , sal , NVL(comm,0) comm
FROM emp
ORDER BY ename;
```

```
ENAME           SAL      COMM
----------  ----------  ----------
ADAMS          1100         0
ALLEN          1600       300
BLAKE          2850         0
KING           5000         0
MARTIN         1250      1400
```

If we decide to perform arithmetic on a null value, the result will always be null; therefore if we want to compute "Total Compensation" as salary plus commission, we must apply the NVL function to properly compute this with consideration of the null values. In the following example, we compute the sum of these columns, both with and without the NVL function. Without using NVL, we get an incorrect result, which can be seen in the TOTAL_COMP_NO_NVL output field:

```
SELECT ename , sal , nvl(comm,0) comm, sal+comm total_comp_no_nvl,
       sal+NVL(comm,0) total_comp_nvl
FROM emp
ORDER BY ename;
```

```
ENAME           SAL      COMM TOTAL_COMP_NO_NVL TOTAL_COMP_NVL
----------  ----------  ---------- ----------------- --------------
ADAMS          1100         0                          1100
ALLEN          1600       300              1900        1900
BLAKE          2850         0                          2850
KING           5000         0                          5000
MARTIN         1250      1400              2650        2650
```

The NVL2 is similar to NVL, except that NVL2 takes in three arguments—the value or column, the value to return if the column is not null, and finally the value to return if the column is null. For instance, if we use the same foregoing example when determining if an employee gets a commission, we simply want to assign a value to each employee stating whether he or she is a "commissioned" or "non-commissioned" employee. We can accomplish this with the NVL2 function:

```
SELECT ename , sal ,
NVL2(comm,'Commissioned','Non-Commissioned') comm_status
FROM emp
ORDER BY ename;
```

```
ENAME           SAL COMM_STATUS
----------  ---------- ----------------
ADAMS          1100 Non-Commissioned
ALLEN          1600 Commissioned
BLAKE          2850 Non-Commissioned
KING           5000 Non-Commissioned
MARTIN         1250 Commissioned
```

Handling Nulls in the WHERE Clause

Within the WHERE clause, if you simply want to check a column to see if it contains a null value, use IS NULL or IS NOT NULL as the comparison operator—for example:

```
SELECT ename , sal
FROM emp
WHERE comm IS NULL
ORDER BY ename;

ENAME          SAL
---------- ----------
ADAMS         1100
BLAKE         2850
KING          5000


SELECT ename , sal
FROM emp
WHERE comm IS NOT NULL
ORDER BY ename;

ENAME          SAL
---------- ----------
ALLEN         1600
MARTIN        1250
```

You can also use the NVL or NVL2 function in the WHERE clause just as it was used in the SELECT statement:

```
SELECT ename , sal
FROM emp
WHERE NVL(comm,0) = 0
ORDER BY ename;

ENAME          SAL
---------- ----------
ADAMS         1100
BLAKE         2850
KING          5000
```

How It Works

It is best to always explicitly handle the possibility of null values, so if a column of a table is nullable, assume nulls exist, else output results can be undesired or unpredictable. One quick check that can be made to determine if a column has null values is to compare a count of rows in the table (COUNT *) to a count of rows for that column (COUNT <column_name>). A count on a nullable column will count only those rows that do not have null values. Here's an example:

```
SELECT count(*) FROM emp;

  COUNT(*)
----------
        14

SELECT count(comm) FROM emp;

COUNT(COMM)
-----------
          4
```

This technique of comparing row count to a count of values in a column is a handy way to check if nulls exist in a column.

Another very useful function that can be used in the handling of null values is the COALESCE function. With COALESCE, you can pass in a series of values, and the function will return the first non-NULL value. If all values within COALESCE are NULL, a NULL value is returned. Here is a simple example:

```
SELECT coalesce(NULL,'ABC','DEF') FROM dual;

COA
---
ABC
```

Let's say you wanted to get the shipping address for your customers, and if none were present, you would then get the billing address. Using COALESCE, you could achieve this as shown in the following example:

```
SELECT COALESCE(
(SELECT shipping_address FROM customers
WHERE cust_id = 9342),
(SELECT billing_address FROM customers
WHERE cust_id = 9342))
FROM dual;
```

All arguments used in a statement with COALESCE must be with the same datatype, else you will receive an error, as shown here:

```
SELECT coalesce(NULL,123,'DEF') FROM dual;
                         *
ERROR at line 1:
ORA-00932: inconsistent datatypes: expected NUMBER got CHAR
```

8-12. Searching for Partial Column Values

Problem

You need to search for a string from a column in the database, but do not know the exact value of the column data.

Solution

When you are unsure of the data values in the columns you are filtering on in your WHERE clause, you can utilize the LIKE operator. Unlike the normal comparison operators such as the equal sign, the BETWEEN clause, or the IN clause, the LIKE operator allows you to search for matches based on a partial string of the column data. When you use the LIKE clause, you need to also use the "%" symbol or the "_" symbol within the data itself in order to search for the data you need. The percent sign is used to replace one to many characters. For example, if you want to see the list of employees that were hired in 1995, regardless of the exact date, the LIKE clause can be used to search for any matches within hire_date that contain the string 1995. When using LIKE with a date or timestamp datatype, you need to ensure that the date format you are using is compatible with your search criteria in your LIKE statement. For instance, if the default date format for your database is DD-MON-YY, then the string 1995 is not compatible with that format and a match would never be found. In order to search in this manner, set your date format within your session before issuing your query:

```
alter session set nls_date_format = 'yyyy-mm-dd';

Session altered.

SELECT employee_id, last_name, first_name, hire_date
FROM employees
WHERE hire_date LIKE '%1995%'
ORDER BY hire_date;

EMPLOYEE_ID LAST_NAME                  FIRST_NAME            HIRE_DATE
----------- -------------------------- --------------------- ----------
        122 Kaufling                   Payam                 1995-05-01
        115 Khoo                       Alexander             1995-05-18
        137 Ladwig                     Renske                1995-07-14
        141 Rajs                       Trenna                1995-10-17
```

An easy way to remedy having to worry about the date format of your session is to simply use the TO_CHAR function within the query. The advantage of this method is it is very easy to code, without having to worry about your session's date format. See the following example:

```
SELECT employee_id, last_name, first_name, hire_date
FROM employees
WHERE to_char(hire_date,'yyyy') = '1995'
ORDER BY hire_date;
```

The underscore symbol ("_") is used to replace exactly one character. Let's say you were looking for an employee that had a last name of "Olsen" or "Olson," but were unsure of the spelling. In a single query, you can use the underscore in conjunction with the LIKE clause to find all employees with that name variation in your database:

```
SELECT last_name, first_name, phone_number
FROM employees
WHERE last_name like 'Ols_n';

LAST_NAME                  FIRST_NAME            PHONE_NUMBER
-------------------------- --------------------- --------------------
Olsen                      Christopher           011.44.1344.498718
Olson                      TJ                    650.124.8234
```

How It Works

The LIKE clause is extremely useful for finding data within your database when you are unsure of the exact column values stored within the data. There are performance ramifications that need to be considered when using the LIKE clause. The primary consideration is that when the LIKE clause is used, the chances of the optimizer using an index to aid in retrieving the data are reduced. Since an index is based on a complete value for a column, having to search for only a portion of the complete value of a column is problematic for the optimizer to be able to use an index.

Using our foregoing example of finding employees that started during the year 1995, here is the explain plan for that query:

```
----------------------------------------
| Id  | Operation        | Name        |
----------------------------------------
|  0  | SELECT STATEMENT |             |
|  1  |  TABLE ACCESS FULL| EMPLOYEES  |
----------------------------------------
```

Since an index is based on an entire value, the optimizer can recognize that an index can be used if the first part of the value is intact in the search criteria. By placing the percent signs on both sides of the value, it is the same as saying "contains." If we place the percent sign on only the trailing end of the value, it is the same as "starts with." Since the leading edge of the value is intact, the optimizer will be able to effectively compare the value based on the value in the LIKE clause with an existing index, and can therefore use such an index, if one is present on that column:

```
SELECT employee_id, last_name, first_name, hire_date
FROM employees
WHERE hire_date LIKE '1995%';
```

```
EMPLOYEE_ID LAST_NAME              FIRST_NAME            HIRE_DATE
----------- ---------------------- -------------------- ----------
        115 Khoo                   Alexander            1995-05-18
        122 Kaufling               Payam                1995-05-01
        137 Ladwig                 Renske               1995-07-14
        141 Rajs                   Trenna               1995-10-17
```

```
-------------------------------------------------------
| Id  | Operation                  | Name            |
-------------------------------------------------------
|  0  | SELECT STATEMENT           |                 |
|  1  |  TABLE ACCESS BY INDEX ROWID| EMPLOYEES      |
|  2  |   INDEX RANGE SCAN         | EMP_NAME_IX     |
-------------------------------------------------------
```

Sometimes it is very possible for an underscore to be part of the data that is being searched. In these cases, it is important to preface the underscore with the escape character. If you are a DBA, and are searching for a tablespace name in your database, which easily can contain the underscore character, make sure you consider that underscore is a wildcard symbol, and must be considered. See the following example:

```
SELECT tablespace_name FROM dba_tablespaces
WHERE tablespace_name like '%EE_DATA';
```

```
TABLESPACE_NAME
------------------------------
EMPLOYEE_DATA
EMPLOYEE1DATA
```

It is very possible that the underscore is searched as data, not as a substitution character for the LIKE clause. If you insert an escape character within the query, you can avoid getting undesired results. By inserting the escape character directly in front of the underscore, then the underscore will be considered as part of the data, rather than a substitution character:

```
SELECT tablespace_name FROM dba_tablespaces
WHERE tablespace_name LIKE '%EE^_DATA' ESCAPE '^';
```

```
TABLESPACE_NAME
------------------------------
EMPLOYEE_DATA
```

The benefit of the LIKE clause is the flexibility it gives you in finding data based on a partial value of the column data. The likely trade-off is performance. Queries using the LIKE clause are often much less likely to use an index. As an alternative to LIKE, the BETWEEN clause, although not as simple to code within your SQL statement, can generally be more likely to use an index. Sometimes, however, the LIKE clause can be perceived as a clause to avoid because of the performance ramifications, but if the leading percent sign is avoided, often the optimizer will use an index, if available.

In the TO_CHAR example of the "Solution" section, you will note that the TO_CHAR function is placed on the left side of the comparison operator. Generally, when this occurs, it means no index on the filtering column will be used (see Recipe 8-14 for more discussion on this topic). However, with certain Oracle functions and the manner in which they are translated, an index still may be used. The only way to be certain is to simply run an explain plan on your query. For our foregoing query using TO_CHAR, it still used an index even though the function was placed on the left side of the comparison operator:

```
SELECT employee_id, last_name, first_name, hire_date
FROM employees
WHERE to_char(hire_date,'yyyy') = '1995'
ORDER BY hire_date;
```

```
-------------------------------------------------------
| Id | Operation                    | Name         |
-------------------------------------------------------
|  0 | SELECT STATEMENT             |              |
|  1 |   TABLE ACCESS BY INDEX ROWID| EMPLOYEES    |
|  2 |    INDEX FULL SCAN           | EMPLOYEES_I1 |
-------------------------------------------------------
```

8-13. Re-using SQL Statements Within the Shared Pool

Problem

You are getting an excessive amount of hard-parsing for your SQL statements, and want to lower the number of SQL statements that go through the hard parse process.

Solution

Implementing bind variables within an application can tremendously improve the efficiency and performance of queries. Essentially, bind variables are called substitution variables, and replace literals within a query. By placing bind variables within your SQL statements, the statements can be re-used in memory, and do not have to go through the entire expensive SQL parsing process.

Here is an example of a normal SQL statement, with literal values shown in the WHERE clause:

```
SELECT employee_id, last_name || ', ' || first_name employee_name
FROM employees
WHERE employee_id = 115;

EMPLOYEE_ID EMPLOYEE_NAME
----------- ------------------------
        115 Khoo, Alexander
```

There are a couple of ways to define bind variables within Oracle. First, you can simply use SQL Plus. To accomplish this within SQL Plus, you first need to define a variable, along with a datatype to the variable. Then, you can use the exec command, which actually will run a PL/SQL command to populate the variable with the desired value. Notice that when referencing a bind variable in SQL Plus, it is prefaced with a colon:

```
SQL> variable g_emp_id number
SQL> exec :g_emp_id := 115;

PL/SQL procedure successfully completed.
```

After you have defined a variable and assigned a value to it, you can simply substitute the variable name within your SQL statement. Again, since it is a bind variable, you need to preface it with a colon:

```
SELECT employee_id, last_name || ', ' || first_name employee_name
FROM employees
WHERE employee_id = :g_emp_id;

EMPLOYEE_ID EMPLOYEE_NAME
----------- ------------------------
        115 Khoo, Alexander
```

You can also assign variables within PL/SQL. The nice advantage of PL/SQL is that just by using variables in PL/SQL, they are automatically bind variables, so there is no special coding required. And, unlike SQL Plus, no colon is required when referencing a variable that was defined within the PL/SQL block:

```
SQL> set serveroutput on
  1  DECLARE
  2    v_emp_id employees.employee_id%TYPE := 200;
  3    v_last_name employees.last_name%TYPE;
  4    v_first_name employees.first_name%TYPE;
  5  BEGIN
  6    SELECT last_name, first_name
  7    INTO v_last_name, v_first_name
  8    FROM employees
  9    WHERE employee_id = v_emp_id;
 10  dbms_output.put_line('Employee Name = ' || v_last_name || ', ' || v_first_name);
 11* END;
SQL> /
Employee Name = Whalen, Jennifer
```

How It Works

When bind variables are used, their use increases the likelihood that a SQL statement can be re-used within the shared pool. Oracle uses a hashing algorithm to assign a value to every unique SQL statement. If literals are used within a SQL statement, the hash values between two otherwise identical statements will be different. By using the bind variables, the statements will have the same hash value within the shared pool, and part of the expensive parsing process can be avoided.

Re-use Is Efficient

Re-use is efficient because Oracle does not have to go through the entire parsing process for those SQL statements. If you do not use bind variables within your SQL statements, and instead use literals, the statements need to be completely parsed.

See Table 8-3 for a review of the steps taken to process a SQL statement. A statement that is "hard-parsed" must execute all of the steps. If a statement is "soft parsed," the optimizer generally does not execute the optimization and row source generation steps.

Table 8-3. *Steps to Execute a SQL Statement*

Step	Description
Syntax checking	Determines if SQL statement is syntactically correct
Semantic checking	Determines if objects referenced in SQL statement exist and user has proper privileges to those objects
Check shared pool	Oracle uses hashing algorithm to generate hash value for SQL statement and checks shared pool for existence of that statement in the shared pool.
Optimization	The Oracle optimizer chooses what it perceives as the best execution plan for the SQL statement based on gathered statistics.

Continued

Step	Description
Row source generation	This is an Oracle program that received the execution plan from the optimization step and generates a query plan. When you generate an explain plan for a statement, it shows the detailed query plan.
Execution	Each step of the query plan is executed, and the result set is returned to the user.

Hard-Parsing Can Be Avoided

By using bind variables, a hard parse can be avoided and can help the performance of SQL queries, as well as reduce the amount of memory thrashing that can occur in the shared pool. The TKPROF utility is one way to verify whether SQL statements are being re-used in the shared pool. Later, there are examples of PL/SQL code that use bind variables, and PL/SQL code that does not use bind variables.

By using the TKPROF utility, we can see how these statements are processed. In order to see this information with the TKPROF utility, we first must turn tracing on within our session:

```
alter session set sql_trace=true;
```

The trace file gets generated in the location specified by the diagnostic_dest or user_dump_dest parameter settings. The following PL/SQL block updates the employees table and gives all employees a 3% raise. Since all PL/SQL variables are treated as bind variables, we can see with the TKPROF output that the update statement was parsed only once, but executed 107 times:

```
BEGIN
FOR i IN 100..206
LOOP
UPDATE employees
SET salary=salary*1.03
WHERE employee_id = i;
END LOOP;
COMMIT;
END;
```

Here is an excerpt from the TKPROF-generated report, which summarizes information about the session on which tracing was enabled:

```
SQL ID : f7mtnudzhm2py
UPDATE EMPLOYEES SET SALARY=SALARY*1.03
WHERE
 EMPLOYEE_ID = :B1
```

call	count	cpu	elapsed	disk	query	current	rows
Parse	1	0.00	0.00	0	0	0	0
Execute	107	0.01	0.00	0	107	112	107
Fetch	0	0.00	0.00	0	0	0	0
total	108	0.01	0.00	0	107	112	107

In the following example, we do the same thing using dynamic SQL with the execute immediate command:

```
BEGIN
FOR i IN 100..206
LOOP
execute immediate 'UPDATE employees SET salary=salary*1.03 WHERE employee_id = ' || i;
END LOOP;
COMMIT;
END;
```

Since the entire statement is assembled together prior to execution, the variable is converted to a literal before execution. We can see with the TKPROF output that the statement was parsed with each execution:

```
SQL ID : 67776qbqqz5wc
UPDATE employees SET salary=salary*:"SYS_B_0"
WHERE
 employee_id = :"SYS_B_1"
```

call	count	cpu	elapsed	disk	query	current	rows
Parse	107	0.00	0.00	0	0	0	0
Execute	107	0.00	0.04	0	107	112	107
Fetch	0	0.00	0.00	0	0	0	0
total	214	0.00	0.05	0	107	112	107

Bind Variables Are Usable with EXECUTE IMMEDIATE

If we want to use the execute immediate command more efficiently, we can convert that execute immediate command to use a bind variable with the USING clause, and specify a bind variable within the execute immediate statement. The result shows that the statement was parsed only one time:

```
BEGIN
FOR i IN 100..206
LOOP
execute immediate 'UPDATE employees SET salary=salary*1.03 WHERE employee_id = :empno' USING
i;
END LOOP;
COMMIT;
END;
```

```
SQL ID : 4y09bqzjngvq4
update employees set salary=salary*1.03
where
 employee_id = :empno
```

call	count	cpu	elapsed	disk	query	current	rows
Parse	1	0.00	0.00	0	0	0	0
Execute	107	0.01	0.01	0	107	112	107
Fetch	0	0.00	0.00	0	0	0	0
total	108	0.01	0.01	0	107	112	107

■ **Tip**   Hard-parsing always occurs for DDL statements.

8-14. Avoiding Accidental Full Table Scans

Problem

You have queries that should be using indexes, but instead are doing full table scans. You want to avoid doing full table scans when the optimizer could be using an index to retrieve the data.

Solution

When constructing a SQL statement, a fundamental rule to try to always observe, if possible, is to avoid using functions on the left side of the comparison operator. A function essentially turns a column into a literal value, and therefore the Oracle optimizer does not recognize that converted value as a column any longer, but as a value instead.

Here, we're trying to get a list of all the employees that started since the year 1999. Because we placed a function on the left side of the comparison operator, the optimizer is forced to do a full table scan, even though the HIRE_DATE column is indexed:

```
SELECT employee_id, salary, hire_date
FROM employees
WHERE TO_CHAR(hire_date,'yyyy-mm-dd') >= '2000-01-01';
```

```
----------------------------------------
| Id  | Operation        | Name      |
----------------------------------------
|   0 | SELECT STATEMENT |           |
|   1 |  TABLE ACCESS FULL| EMPLOYEES |
----------------------------------------
```

By moving the function to the right side of the comparison operator and leaving `HIRE_DATE` as a pristine column in the `WHERE` clause, the optimizer can now use the index on `HIRE_DATE`:

```
SELECT employee_id, salary, hire_date
FROM employees
WHERE hire_date >= TO_DATE('2000-01-01','yyyy-mm-dd');
```

```
-------------------------------------------------
| Id  | Operation                   | Name      |
-------------------------------------------------
|  0  | SELECT STATEMENT            |           |
|  1  |   TABLE ACCESS BY INDEX ROWID| EMPLOYEES |
|  2  |    INDEX RANGE SCAN         | EMP_I5    |
-------------------------------------------------
```

How It Works

Functions are wonderful tools to convert a value or return the desired value based on what you need from the database, but they can be a performance killer if used incorrectly within a SQL statement. Make sure all functions are on the right side of the comparison operator, and the optimizer will be able to use any indexes on columns specified in the `WHERE` clause. This rule holds true for any function. In certain cases, it is possible Oracle will still use an index even if a function is on the left side of the comparison operator, but this is usually the exception. See Recipe 8-12 for an example of this.

Keep in mind that the datatype for a given column in the `WHERE` clause may change how the SQL statement needs to be modified to move the function to the right side of the comparison operator. With the following example, we had to change the comparison operator in order to effectively move the function:

```
SELECT last_name, first_name
FROM employees
WHERE SUBSTR(phone_number,1,3) = '515';
```

```
--------------------------------------------
| Id  | Operation          | Name      |
--------------------------------------------
|  0  | SELECT STATEMENT   |           |
|  1  |   TABLE ACCESS FULL| EMPLOYEES |
--------------------------------------------
```

In order to effectively get all numbers in the 515 area code, we can use a `BETWEEN` clause and capture all possible values. We can also use a `LIKE` clause, as long as the wildcard character is on the trailing end of the condition. By using either of these methods, the optimizer changed the execution plan to use an index:

```
SELECT last_name, first_name
FROM employees
WHERE phone_number BETWEEN '515.000.0000' and '515.999.9999';
```

```
SELECT last_name, first_name
FROM employees
WHERE phone_number LIKE'515%';
```

```
--------------------------------------------------
| Id  | Operation                  | Name         |
--------------------------------------------------
|   0 | SELECT STATEMENT           |              |
|   1 |  TABLE ACCESS BY INDEX ROWID| EMPLOYEES   |
|   2 |   INDEX RANGE SCAN         | EMP_I6       |
--------------------------------------------------
```

8-15. Creating Efficient Temporary Views

Problem

You need a table or a view of data that does not exist to construct a needed query, and do not have the authority to create such a table or view on your database.

Solution

At times, within a single SQL statement, you want to create a table "on the fly" that is used solely for your query, and will never be used again. In the FROM clause of your query, you normally place the name of your table or view on which to retrieve the data. In cases where a needed view of the data does not exist, you can create a temporary view of that data with what is called an "inline view," where you specify the characteristics of that view right in the FROM clause of your query:

```
SELECT last_name, first_name, department_name dept, salary
FROM employees e join
        ( SELECT department_id, max(salary) high_sal
          FROM employees
          GROUP BY department_id ) m
USING (department_id) join departments
USING (department_id)
WHERE e.salary = m.high_sal
ORDER BY SALARY desc;
```

LAST_NAME	FIRST_NAME	DEPT	SALARY
King	Steven	Executive	24000
Russell	John	Sales	14000
Hartstein	Michael	Marketing	13000
Greenberg	Nancy	Finance	12000
Higgins	Shelley	Accounting	12000
Raphaely	Den	Purchasing	11000
Baer	Hermann	Public Relations	10000
Hunold	Alexander	IT	9000

Fripp	Adam	Shipping	8200
Mavris	Susan	Human Resources	6500
Whalen	Jennifer	Administration	4400

In the foregoing query, we are getting the employees with the highest salary for each department. There isn't such a view in our database. Moreover, there isn't a way to directly join the employees table to the departments table to retrieve this data within a single query. Therefore, the inline view is created as part of the SQL statement, and holds only the key information we needed—it has the high salary and department information, which now can easily be joined to the employees table based on the employee with that matching salary.

How It Works

Inline views, as with many components of the SQL language, need to be used carefully. While extremely useful, if misused or overused, inline views can cause database performance issues, especially in terms of the use of the temporary tablespace. Since inline views are created and used only for the duration of a query, their results are held in the program global memory area, and if too large, the temporary tablespace. Before using an inline view, the following questions should be considered:

1. Most importantly, how often will the SQL containing the inline view be run? (If only once or rarely, then it might be best to simply execute the query and not worry about any potential performance impact).

2. How many rows will be contained in the inline view?

3. What will the row length be for the inline view?

4. How much memory is allocated for the pga_aggregate_target or memory_target setting?

5. How big is the temporary tablespace that is used by your Oracle user or schema?

If you have a simple ad hoc query you are doing, this kind of analysis may not be necessary. If you are creating a SQL statement that will run in a production environment, it is important to perform this analysis, as if all the temporary tablespace is consumed by an inline view, it affects not only the completion of that query, but also the successful completion of any processing for any user that may use that specific temporary tablespace. In many database environments, there is only a single temporary tablespace. Therefore, if one user process consumes all the temporary space with a single operation, this affects the operations for every user in the database.

Consider the following query:

```
WITH service_info AS
(SELECT
product_id,
geographic_id,
sum(qty) quantity
FROM services
GROUP BY
product_id,
geographic_id),
product_info AS
(SELECT product_id, product_group, product_desc
```

```
FROM products
WHERE source_sys = 'BILLING'),
billing_info AS
(SELECT journal_date, billing_date, product_id
FROM BILLING
WHERE journal_date = TO_DATE('2011-08-15', 'YYYY-MM-DD'))
SELECT
product_group,
product_desc,
journal_date,
billing_date,
sum(service_info.quantity)
FROM service_info JOIN product_info
ON service_info.product_id = product_info.product_id JOIN billing_info
ON  service_info.product_id = billing_info.product_id
WHERE
service_info.quantity > 0
GROUP BY
product_group,
product_desc,
journal_date,
billing_date;
```

In this query, there are three inline views created: the SERVICE_INFO view, the PRODUCT_INFO view, and the BILLING_INFO view. Each of these queries will be processed and the results stored in the program global area or the temporary tablespace before finally processing the true end-user query, which starts with the final SELECT statement shown in the query. While efficient in that the desired results can be done by executing a single query, the foregoing query, depending on the size of the data within the tables, can be tremendously inefficient to process, as storing potentially millions of rows in the temporary tablespace uses critical resources needed by an entire community of users that use the database. In examples such as these, it is generally more efficient at the database level to create tables that hold the data defined by the inline views—in this case, three separate tables. Then, the final query can be extracted from joining the three permanent tables to generate the results. While this may be more upfront work by the development team and the DBA, it could very well pay dividends if the query is run on a regular basis. Furthermore, as complexity increases with a SQL statement, ease of maintenance decreases. So, overall, it is more efficient, and usually more maintainable, to break a complex statement into chunks.

Inline views provide great benefit. However, do the proper analysis and investigation prior to implementing the use of such a view in a production environment.

■ **Caution** Large inline views can easily consume a large amount of temporary tablespace

---

8-16. Avoiding the NOT Clause

Problem

You have queries that use the NOT clause that are not performing adequately, and wish to modify them to improve performance.

Solution

Just as often as we query our database for equality conditions, we will query our database for non-equality conditions. It is the nature of retrieving data from a database and the nature of the SQL language to allow users to do this.

There are performance drawbacks in using the NOT clause within your SQL statements, as they trigger full table scans. Here's an example query from a previous recipe:

```
SELECT last_name, first_name, salary, email
FROM employees_big
WHERE department_id NOT IN(20,30)
AND commission_pct > 0;
```

```
--------------------------------------------------------------------------
| Id  | Operation          | Name          | Rows  | Bytes | Cost (%CPU)| Time     |
--------------------------------------------------------------------------
|   0 | SELECT STATEMENT   |               |  697K |   21M |  4480   (1)| 00:00:54 |
|*  1 |  TABLE ACCESS FULL | EMPLOYEES_BIG |  697K |   21M |  4480   (1)| 00:00:54 |
--------------------------------------------------------------------------
```

Even though we have an index on the department_id column, by using the NOT clause we cause Oracle to bypass the use of that index in order to properly search and ensure all rows were not those in department 20 or 30. Note the overall cost of 4480 that Oracle assigned to this query.

It is possible to enable the use of the index by rewriting the query. For instance, let's issue a subquery to get a list of all the department_id values that are not 20 or 30, and then pass that list to the parent query. By doing this, we are moving the NOT clause to the much smaller departments table, so the table scan on that table will be fast. Those values get passed the parent query, and the parent query can use an index because it no longer needs the NOT clause.

Here's the new query, and the resulting execution plan.

```
SELECT last_name, first_name, salary, email
FROM employees_big
WHERE department_id IN
(SELECT department_id FROM departments
WHERE department_id NOT IN (20,30))
AND commission_pct > 0;
```

```
-----------------------------------------------------------------------------
| Id  | Operation          | Name      | Rows | Bytes | Cost (%CPU)| Time     |
-----------------------------------------------------------------------------
|   0 | SELECT STATEMENT   |           |   33 |  1188 |    3   (0)| 00:00:01 |
|   1 |  NESTED LOOPS      |           |   33 |  1188 |    3   (0)| 00:00:01 |
|*  2 |   TABLE ACCESS FULL| EMPLOYEES |   34 |  1088 |    3   (0)| 00:00:01 |
|*  3 |   INDEX UNIQUE SCAN| DEPT_ID_PK|    1 |     4 |    0   (0)| 00:00:01 |
-----------------------------------------------------------------------------
```

Note now that after our change, the query now uses an index, and the overall cost that Oracle assigned dropped from 4480 to 3.

How It Works

You can effectively use the NOT clause several ways:

- Comparison operators ('<>', '!=', '^=')

- NOT IN

- NOT LIKE

By using NOT, each of the following queries has the same basic effect in that it will negate the use of any possible index on the columns to which NOT applies:

```
SELECT last_name, first_name, salary, email
FROM employees
WHERE department_id != 20
AND commission_pct > 0;

SELECT last_name, first_name, salary, email
FROM employees
WHERE department_id NOT IN(20,30)
AND commission_pct > 0;

SELECT last_name, first_name, salary, email
FROM employees
WHERE hire_date NOT LIKE '2%'
AND commission_pct > 0;
```

```
-----------------------------------------
| Id  | Operation          | Name      |
-----------------------------------------
|   0 | SELECT STATEMENT   |           |
|   1 |  TABLE ACCESS FULL| EMPLOYEES |
-----------------------------------------
```

At times, a full table scan is simply required. Even if an index is present, if you need to read more than a certain percentage of rows of a table, the Oracle optimizer may perform a full table scan regardless of whether an index is present. Still, if you simply try to avoid using NOT where possible, you may be able to improve performance on your queries.

All this said, you can try to use NOT EXISTS as an alternative that may improve performance in these conditions. Using the foregoing query and modifying it to use NOT EXISTS, you can still use an index to improve performance of the query:

```
SELECT last_name, first_name, salary, email
FROM employees
WHERE NOT EXISTS
(SELECT department_id FROM departments
WHERE department_id in(20,30))
AND commission_pct > 0;
```

```
-----------------------------------------
| Id | Operation          | Name        |
-----------------------------------------
|  0 | SELECT STATEMENT   |             |
|  1 |  FILTER            |             |
|  2 |   TABLE ACCESS FULL | EMPLOYEES  |
|  3 |   INLIST ITERATOR  |             |
|  4 |    INDEX UNIQUE SCAN| DEPT_ID_PK |
-----------------------------------------
```

8-17. Controlling Transaction Sizes

Problem

You are performing a series of DML activities, and want to better manage the units of work and the recoverability of your transactions.

Solution

With the use of savepoints, you can split up transactions more easily into logical chunks, and can manage them more effectively upon failure. With the use of savepoints, you can roll back a series of DML statements to an incremental savepoint you have created. Within your SQL session, simply create a savepoint at an appropriate place during your processing that allows you to more easily isolate a "logical unit of work." The following is an example showing how to create a savepoint:

```
SQL> savepoint A;

Savepoint created.
```

If you have an online bookstore, for instance, and you have a customer placing an online order, when he or she submits an order, a logical unit of work for this transaction would be as follows:

- Adding a row to the orders table

- Adding one to many rows to the orderitems table

When processing this online order, you will want to commit all the information for the order and all items for an order as one transaction. This represents multiple database DML statements, but needs to be processed one at a time to preserve the integrity of a customer order; therefore it can be regarded as one "logical unit of work." By using savepoints, you can more easily process multiple DML statements as logical units of work. When a savepoint is created, it is essentially creating an alias based on a system change number (SCN). After creating a savepoint, you then have the luxury to roll back a transaction to that SCN based on the savepoint you created.

How It Works

Let's say your company has established two new departments, as well as employees for those departments. You need to insert rows in the corresponding DEPT and EMP tables, but you need to do this in one transaction per department. In case of an error, you can roll back to the point the last logical transaction completed. First, we can see a current picture of the DEPT table:

```
SELECT * FROM dept;

    DEPTNO DNAME          LOC
---------- -------------- -------------
        10 ACCOUNTING     NEW YORK
        20 RESEARCH       DALLAS
        30 SALES          CHICAGO
        40 OPERATIONS     BOSTON
```

We first insert the information for the first department into the DEPT and EMP tables, and then create a savepoint:

```
INSERT INTO dept VALUES (50,'PAYROLL','LOS ANGELES');

1 row created.

INSERT INTO emp VALUES (7997,'EVANS','ACCTNT',7566,'2011-08-15',900,0,50);

1 row created.

savepoint A;

Savepoint created.
```

We then start processing information for the second department. Let's say in the middle of the transaction, an unknown error occurs between the insert into the DEPT table and the insert into the EMP table. In this case, we know this transaction of inserting the information into the recruiting department must be rolled back. At the same time, we wish to commit the transaction to the payroll department. Using the savepoint we created, we can commit a portion of the transaction, while rolling back the portion of the transaction we do not want to keep:

```
INSERT INTO dept VALUES (60,'RECRUITING','DENVER');

1 row created.

ROLLBACK to savepoint A;
```

Rollback complete.

COMMIT;

Commit complete.

Because of the savepoint, our rollback rolled back the incomplete transaction only for department 60, and the subsequent commit wrote the complete transaction for department 50 to the database in both the DEPT and EMP tables:

SELECT * FROM dept;

```
    DEPTNO DNAME          LOC
---------- -------------- -------------
        10 ACCOUNTING     NEW YORK
        20 RESEARCH       DALLAS
        30 SALES          CHICAGO
        40 OPERATIONS     BOSTON
        50 PAYROLL        LOS ANGELES
```

SELECT * FROM emp
WHERE empno = 7997;

```
     EMPNO ENAME       JOB              MGR HIREDATE    SAL       COMM DEPTNO
---------- ----------- ---------- ---------- ---------- ---- ---------- -------
      7997 EVANS       ACCTNT          7566 2011-08-15  900          0     50
```

There are many similar mechanisms or coding techniques you can use in programming languages such as PL/SQL. The SAVEPOINT command in the SQL language is a simple way to manage transactions without having to code more complex programming structures.

CHAPTER 9

Manually Tuning SQL

It has been said many times in books, articles, and other publications that over 90% of all performance problems on a database are due to poorly written SQL. Often, database administrators are given the task of "fixing the database" when queries are not performing adequately. The database administrator is often guilty before proven innocent—and often has the task of proving that a performance problem is not the database itself, but rather, simply, SQL statements that are not written efficiently. The goal, of course, is to have SQL statements written efficiently the first time. This chapter's focus is to help monitor and analyze existing queries to help show why they may be underperforming, as well as show some steps to improve queries.

If you have SQL code that you are maintaining or that needs help to improve performance, some of the questions that need to be asked first include the following:

- Has the query run before successfully?

- Was the query performance acceptable in the past?

- Are there any metrics on how long the query has run when successful?

- How much data is typically returned from the query?

- When was the last time statistics were gathered on the objects referenced in the query?

Once these questions are answered, it helps to direct the focus to where the problem may lie. You then may want to run an explain plan for the query to see if the execution plan is reasonable at first glance. The skill of reading an explain plan takes time and improves with experience. Sometimes, especially if there are views on top of the objects being queried, an explain plan can be lengthy and intimidating. Therefore, it's important to simply know what to look for first, and then dig as you go.

At times, poorly running SQL can expose database configuration issues, but normally, poorly performing SQL queries occur due to poorly written SQL statements. Again, as a database administrator or database developer, the best approach is to take time up front whenever possible to tune the SQL statements prior to ever running in a production environment. Often, a query's elapsed time is a benchmark for efficiency, which is an easy trap in which to fall. Over time, database characteristics change, more historical data may be stored for an application, and a query that performed well on initial install simply doesn't scale as an application matures. Therefore, it's important to take the time to do it right the first time, which is easy to say, but tough to accomplish when balancing client requirements, budgets, and project timelines.

9-1. Displaying an Execution Plan for a Query

Problem

You want to quickly retrieve an execution plan from within SQL Plus for a query.

Solution

From within SQL Plus, you can use the AUTOTRACE feature to quickly retrieve the execution plan for a query. This SQL Plus utility is very handy at getting the execution plan, along with getting statistics for the query's execution plan. In the most basic form, to enable AUTOTRACE within your session, execute the following command within SQL Plus:

```
SQL> set autotrace on
```

Then, you can run a query using AUTOTRACE, which will show the execution plan and query execution statistics for your query:

```
SELECT last_name, first_name
FROM employees NATURAL JOIN departments
WHERE employee_id = 101;
```

```
LAST_NAME                    FIRST_NAME
---------------------------  --------------------
Kochhar                      Neena
```

Id	Operation	Name	Rows	Bytes	Cost (%CPU)	Time
0	SELECT STATEMENT		1	33	2 (0)	00:00:01
1	NESTED LOOPS		1	33	2 (0)	00:00:01
2	TABLE ACCESS BY INDEX ROWID	EMPLOYEES	1	26	1 (0)	00:00:01
* 3	INDEX UNIQUE SCAN	EMP_EMP_ID_PK	1		0 (0)	00:00:01
* 4	TABLE ACCESS BY INDEX ROWID	DEPARTMENTS	11	77	1 (0)	00:00:01
* 5	INDEX UNIQUE SCAN	DEPT_ID_PK	1		0 (0)	00:00:01

```
Statistics
-----------------------------------------------------------
          0  recursive calls
          0  db block gets
          4  consistent gets
          0  physical reads
          0  redo size
        490  bytes sent via SQL*Net to client
        416  bytes received via SQL*Net from client
          2  SQL*Net roundtrips to/from client
          0  sorts (memory)
          0  sorts (disk)
          1  rows processed
```

How It Works

There are several options to choose from when using AUTOTRACE, and the basic factors are as follows:

1. Do you want to execute the query?

2. Do you want to see the execution plan for the query?

3. Do you want to see the execution statistics for the query?

As you can see from Table 9-1, you can abbreviate each command, if so desired. The portions of the words in brackets are optional.

Table 9-1. *Options of AUTOTRACE Within SQL Plus*

AUTOTRACE Option	Execution Plan Shown	Statistics Shown	Query Executed
AUTOT[RACE] OFF	No	No	Yes
AUTOT[RACE] ON	Yes	Yes	Yes
AUTOT[RACE] ON EXP[LAIN]	Yes	No	Yes
AUTOT[RACE] ON STAT[ISTICS]	No	Yes	Yes
AUTOT[RACE] TRACE[ONLY]	Yes	Yes	Yes, but query output is suppressed.
AUTOT[RACE] TRACE[ONLY] EXP[LAIN]	Yes	No	No

The most common use for AUTOTRACE is to get the execution plan for the query, without running the query. By doing this, you can quickly see whether you have a reasonable execution plan, and can do this without having to execute the query:

```
SQL> set autot trace exp

SELECT l.location_id, city, department_id, department_name
  FROM locations l, departments d
  WHERE l.location_id = d.location_id(+)
  ORDER BY 1;
```

```
-------------------------------------------------------------------------------
| Id | Operation             | Name        | Rows | Bytes | Cost (%CPU)| Time     |
-------------------------------------------------------------------------------
|  0 | SELECT STATEMENT      |             |   27 |   837 |    8  (25)| 00:00:01 |
|  1 |  SORT ORDER BY        |             |   27 |   837 |    8  (25)| 00:00:01 |
|* 2 |   HASH JOIN OUTER     |             |   27 |   837 |    7  (15)| 00:00:01 |
|  3 |    TABLE ACCESS FULL| LOCATIONS   |   23 |   276 |    3   (0)| 00:00:01 |
|  4 |    TABLE ACCESS FULL| DEPARTMENTS |   27 |   513 |    3   (0)| 00:00:01 |
-------------------------------------------------------------------------------
```

For the foregoing query, if you wanted to see only the execution statistics for the query, and did not want to see all the query output, you would do the following:

```
SQL> set autot trace stat
SQL> /

43 rows selected.
```

```
Statistics
----------------------------------------------------------
          0  recursive calls
          0  db block gets
         14  consistent gets
          0  physical reads
          0  redo size
       1862  bytes sent via SQL*Net to client
        438  bytes received via SQL*Net from client
          4  SQL*Net roundtrips to/from client
          1  sorts (memory)
          0  sorts (disk)
         43  rows processed
```

Once you are done using AUTOTRACE for a given session and want to turn it off and run other queries without using AUTOTRACE, run the following command from within your SQL Plus session:

```
SQL> set autot off
```

The default for each SQL Plus session is AUTOTRACE OFF, but if you want to check to see what your current AUTOTRACE setting is for a given session, you can do that by executing the following command:

```
SQL> show autot
autotrace OFF
```

9-2. Customizing Execution Plan Output

Problem

You want to configure the explain plan output for your query based on your specific needs.

Solution

The Oracle-provided PL/SQL package DBMS_XPLAN has extensive functionality to get explain plan information for a given query. There are many functions within the DBMS_XPLAN package. The DISPLAY function can be used to quickly get the execution plan for a query, and also to customize the information that is presented to meet your specific needs. The following is an example that invokes the basic display functionality:

```
explain plan for
SELECT last_name, first_name
FROM employees JOIN departments USING(department_id)
WHERE employee_id = 101;

Explained.

SELECT * FROM table(dbms_xplan.display);

PLAN_TABLE_OUTPUT
--------------------------------------------------------------------------------
Plan hash value: 1833546154


--------------------------------------------------------------------------------
| Id  | Operation                    | Name         | Rows  | Bytes | Cost (%CPU)| Time     |
--------------------------------------------------------------------------------
|   0 | SELECT STATEMENT             |              |     1 |    22 |     1   (0)| 00:00:01|
|*  1 |  TABLE ACCESS BY INDEX ROWID| EMPLOYEES    |     1 |    22 |     1   (0)| 00:00:01|
|*  2 |   INDEX UNIQUE SCAN          | EMP_EMP_ID_PK|     1 |       |     0   (0)| 00:00:01|
--------------------------------------------------------------------------------

Predicate Information (identified by operation id):
---------------------------------------------------

   1 - filter("EMPLOYEES"."DEPARTMENT_ID" IS NOT NULL)
   2 - access("EMPLOYEES"."EMPLOYEE_ID"=101)
```

The DBMS_XPLAN.DISPLAY procedure is very flexible in configuring how you would like to see output. If you wanted to see only the most basic execution plan output, using the foregoing query, you could configure the DBMS_XPLAN.DISPLAY function to get that output:

```
SELECT * FROM table(dbms_xplan.display(null,null,'BASIC'));


------------------------------------------------------
| Id  | Operation                    | Name         |
------------------------------------------------------
|   0 | SELECT STATEMENT             |              |
|   1 |  TABLE ACCESS BY INDEX ROWID| EMPLOYEES    |
|   2 |   INDEX UNIQUE SCAN          | EMP_EMP_ID_PK|
------------------------------------------------------
```

How It Works

The DBMS_XPLAN.DISPLAY function has a lot of built-in functionality to provide customized output based on your needs. The function provides four basic levels of output detail:

- BASIC
- TYPICAL (default)
- SERIAL
- ALL

Table 9-2 shows the format options that are included within each level of detail option.

Table 9-2. DBMS_XPLAN.DISPLAY *Options*

Format Option	BASIC	TYPICAL	SERIAL	ALL	Description
Basic (ID, Operation, Object Name	X	X	X	X	
ALIAS (Section)				X	Information on object aliases and query block information
BYTES (Column)		X	X	X	Estimated bytes
COST (Column)		X	X	X	Displays optimizer cost
NOTE (Section)		X	X	X	Shows NOTE section of the explain plan
PARALLEL (Detail within plan)		X		X	Show parallelism information related to the explain plan
PARTITION (Columns)		X	X	X	Displays partition pruning information
PREDICATE (Section)		X	X	X	Shows PREDICATE section of the explain plan
PROJECTION (Section)				X	Shows PROJECTION section of the explain plan
REMOTE (Detail within plan)				X	Shows information for distributed queries
ROWS (Column)		X	X	X	Shows estimated number of rows

If you simply want the default output format, there is no need to pass in any special format options:

```
SELECT * FROM table(dbms_xplan.display);
```

If you want to get all available output for a query, use the ALL level of detail format output option:

```
SELECT * FROM table(dbms_xplan.display(null,null,'ALL'));
```

```
---------------------------------------------------------------------------------------------
| Id  | Operation                     | Name          | Rows  | Bytes | Cost (%CPU)| Time     |
---------------------------------------------------------------------------------------------
|   0 | SELECT STATEMENT              |               |     1 |    22 |     1   (0)| 00:00:01 |
|*  1 |  TABLE ACCESS BY INDEX ROWID  | EMPLOYEES     |     1 |    22 |     1   (0)| 00:00:01 |
|*  2 |   INDEX UNIQUE SCAN           | EMP_EMP_ID_PK |     1 |       |     0   (0)| 00:00:01 |
---------------------------------------------------------------------------------------------

Query Block Name / Object Alias (identified by operation id):
-------------------------------------------------------------

   1 - SEL$38D4D5F3 / EMPLOYEES@SEL$1
   2 - SEL$38D4D5F3 / EMPLOYEES@SEL$1

Predicate Information (identified by operation id):
---------------------------------------------------

   1 - filter("EMPLOYEES"."DEPARTMENT_ID" IS NOT NULL)
   2 - access("EMPLOYEES"."EMPLOYEE_ID"=101)

Column Projection Information (identified by operation id):
----------------------------------------------------------

   1 - "EMPLOYEES"."FIRST_NAME"[VARCHAR2,20], "EMPLOYEES"."LAST_NAME"[VARCHAR2,25]
   2 - "EMPLOYEES".ROWID[ROWID,10]

Note
-----
   - rule based optimizer used (consider using cbo)
```

One of the very nice features of the DBMS_XPLAN.DISPLAY function is after deciding the base level of detail you need, you can add individual options to be displayed in addition to the base output for that level of detail. For instance, if you want just the most basic output information, but also want to know cost information, you can format the DBMS_XPLAN.DISPLAY as follows:

```
SELECT * FROM table(dbms_xplan.display(null,null,'BASIC +COST'));
```

```
--------------------------------------------------------------------------------
| Id | Operation                    | Name                         | Cost (%CPU)|
--------------------------------------------------------------------------------
|  0 | SELECT STATEMENT             |                              |    1   (0)|
|  1 |  RESULT CACHE                | 0fnzzb94z0dj2b5vzkmq4f4xcu   |           |
|  2 |   TABLE ACCESS BY INDEX ROWID| EMPLOYEES                    |    1   (0)|
|  3 |    INDEX UNIQUE SCAN         | EMP_EMP_ID_PK                |    0   (0)|
--------------------------------------------------------------------------------
```

You can also do the reverse, that is, subtract information you do not want to see. If you wanted to see the output using the TYPICAL level of output, but did not want to see the ROWS or BYTES information, you could issue the following query to display that level of output:

```
SELECT * FROM table(dbms_xplan.display(null,null,'TYPICAL -BYTES -ROWS'));
```

```
---------------------------------------------------------------------------------
| Id | Operation                    | Name          | Cost (%CPU)| Time     |
---------------------------------------------------------------------------------
|  0 | SELECT STATEMENT             |               |    1   (0)| 00:00:01 |
|* 1 |  TABLE ACCESS BY INDEX ROWID | EMPLOYEES     |    1   (0)| 00:00:01 |
|* 2 |   INDEX UNIQUE SCAN          | EMP_EMP_ID_PK |    0   (0)| 00:00:01 |
---------------------------------------------------------------------------------
```

9-3. Graphically Displaying an Execution Plan

Problem

You want to quickly view an execution plan without having to run SQL statements to retrieve the execution plan. You would like to use a GUI to view the plan, so that you can just click your way to it.

Solution

From within Enterprise Manager, you can quickly find the execution plan for a query. In order to use this functionality, you will have to have Enterprise Manager configured within your environment. This can be either Database Control, which manages a single database, or Grid Control, which manages an enterprise of databases. In order to see the execution plan for a given query, you will need to navigate to the Top Sessions screen of Enterprise Manager. (Refer to the Oracle Enterprise Manager documentation for your specific release.) Once on the Top Sessions screen, you can drill down into session specific information. First, find your session. Then, click the SQL ID shown under Current SQL. From there, you can click Plan, and the execution plan will appear, such as the one shown in Figure 9-1.

Figure 9-1. Sample execution plan output from within Enterprise Manager

How It Works

Using Enterprise Manager makes it very easy to find the execution plan for currently running SQL operations within your database. If a particular SQL statement isn't performing as expected, this method is one of the fastest ways to determine the execution plan for a running query or other SQL operation. In order to use this feature, you must be licensed for the Tuning Pack of Enterprise Manager.

9-4. Reading an Execution Plan

Problem

You have run an explain plan for a given SQL statement, and want to understand how to read the plan.

Solution

The execution plan for a SQL operation tells you step-by-step exactly how the Oracle optimizer will execute your SQL operation. Using AUTOTRACE, let's get an explain plan for the following query:

```
set autotrace trace explain

SELECT ename, dname
FROM emp JOIN dept USING (deptno);
```

```
-------------------------------------------------------------------------------------
| Id  | Operation                    | Name    | Rows  | Bytes | Cost (%CPU)| Time     |
-------------------------------------------------------------------------------------
|   0 | SELECT STATEMENT             |         |    14 |   308 |    6  (17)| 00:00:01 |
|   1 |  MERGE JOIN                  |         |    14 |   308 |    6  (17)| 00:00:01 |
|   2 |   TABLE ACCESS BY INDEX ROWID| DEPT    |     4 |    52 |    2   (0)| 00:00:01 |
|   3 |    INDEX FULL SCAN           | PK_DEPT |     4 |       |    1   (0)| 00:00:01 |
|*  4 |   SORT JOIN                  |         |    14 |   126 |    4  (25)| 00:00:01 |
|   5 |    TABLE ACCESS FULL         | EMP     |    14 |   126 |    3   (0)| 00:00:01 |
-------------------------------------------------------------------------------------
```

```
Predicate Information (identified by operation id):
---------------------------------------------------

   4 - access("EMP"."DEPTNO"="DEPT"."DEPTNO")
       filter("EMP"."DEPTNO"="DEPT"."DEPTNO")
```

```
Note
-----
   - automatic DOP: Computed Degree of Parallelism is 1 because of parallel threshold
```

Once you have an explain plan to interpret, you can tell which steps are executed first because the innermost or most indented steps are executed first, and are executed from the inside out, in top-down order. In the foregoing query, we are joining the EMP and DEPT tables. Here are the steps of how the query is processed based on the execution plan:

1. The PK_DEPT index is scanned (ID 3).

2. All EMP table rows are scanned (ID 5).

3. Rows are retrieved from the DEPT table based on the matching entries in the PK_DEPT index (ID 2).

4. Resulting data from the EMP table is sorted (ID 4).

5. Data from the EMP and DEPT tables are then joined via a MERGE JOIN (ID 1).

6. The resulting data from the query is returned to the user (ID 0).

How It Works

When first looking at an explain plan and wanting to quickly get an idea of the steps in which the query will be executed, do the following:

1. Look for the most indented rows in the plan (the right-most rows). These will be executed first.

2. If multiple rows are at the same level of indentation, they will be executed in top-down fashion in the plan, with the highest rows in the plan first moving downward in the plan.

3. Look at the next most indented row or rows and continue working your way outward.

4. The top of the explain plan corresponds with the least indented or left-most part of the plan, and usually is where the results are returned to the user.

Once you have an explain plan for a query, and can understand the sequence of how the query will be processed, you then can move on and perform some analysis to determine if the explain plan you are looking at is efficient. When looking at your explain plan, answer these questions and consider these factors when determining if you have an efficient plan:

- What is the access path for the query (is the query performing a full table scan or is the query using an index)?

- What is the join method for the query (if a join condition is present)?

- Look at the columns within the filtering criteria found within the WHERE clause of the query, and determine if they are indexed.

- Get the volume or number of rows for each table in the query. Are the tables small, medium-sized, or large? This may help you determine the most appropriate join method. See Table 9-3 for a synopsis of the types of join methods.

- When were statistics last gathered for the objects involved in the query?

- Look at the COST column of the explain plan to get a starting cost.

By looking at our original explain plan, we determined that the EMP table is larger in size, and also that there is no index present on the DEPTNO column, which is used within a join condition between the DEPT and EMP tables. By placing an index on the DEPTNO column on the EMP table and gathering statistics on the EMP table, the plan now uses an index:

```
---------------------------------------------------------------------------------
| Id  | Operation                    | Name   | Rows  | Bytes | Cost (%CPU)| Time     |
---------------------------------------------------------------------------------
|   0 | SELECT STATEMENT             |        |    14 |   280 |     6  (17)| 00:00:01 |
|   1 |  MERGE JOIN                  |        |    14 |   280 |     6  (17)| 00:00:01 |
|   2 |   TABLE ACCESS BY INDEX ROWID| EMP    |    14 |    98 |     2   (0)| 00:00:01 |
|   3 |    INDEX FULL SCAN           | EMP_I2 |    14 |       |     1   (0)| 00:00:01 |
|*  4 |   SORT JOIN                  |        |     4 |    52 |     4  (25)| 00:00:01 |
|   5 |    TABLE ACCESS FULL         | DEPT   |     4 |    52 |     3   (0)| 00:00:01 |
---------------------------------------------------------------------------------
```

Table 9-3. *Join Methods*

Method	Description
Hash	Most appropriate if at least one table involved in the query is large
Nested loop	Appropriate for smaller tables
Sort merge	Appropriate for pre-sorted data
Cartesian	Signifies either no join condition or a missing join condition; usually signifies an unwanted condition and query needs to be scrutinized to ensure there is a join condition for each and every table in the query

For information on parallel execution plans, see Chapter 15.

■ **Tip**   One of the most common reasons for a sub-optimal explain plan is the lack of current statistics on one or more objects involved in a query.

9-5. Monitoring Long-Running SQL Statements

Problem

You have a SQL statement that runs a long time, and you want to be able to monitor the progress of the statement and find out when it will finish.

Solution

By viewing information for a long-running query in the V$SESSION_LONGOPS data dictionary view, you can gauge about when a query will finish. Let's say you are running the following query, with join conditions, against a large table:

```
SELECT last_name, first_name FROM employees_big
WHERE last_name = 'EVANS';
```

With a simple query against the V$SESSION_LONGOPS view, you can quickly get an idea of how long the query will execute, and when it will finish:

```
SELECT username, target, sofar blocks_read, totalwork total_blocks,
round(time_remaining/60) minutes
FROM v$session_longops
WHERE sofar <> totalwork
and username = 'HR';

USERNAME     TARGET               BLOCKS_READ TOTAL_BLOCKS  MINUTES
-----------  -------------------- ----------- ------------  ----------
HR           HR.EMPLOYEES_BIG          81101      2353488          10
```

As the query progresses, you can see the BLOCKS_READ column increase, as well as the MINUTES column decrease. It is usually necessary to place the WHERE clause to eliminate rows that have been completed, which is why in the foregoing query it asked for rows where the SOFAR column did not equal TOTALWORK.

How It Works

In order to be able to monitor a query within the V$SESSION_LONGOPS view, the following requirements apply:

- The query must run for six seconds or greater.

- The table being accessed must be greater than 10,000 database blocks.

- TIMED_STATISTICS must be set or SQL_TRACE must be turned on.

- The objects within the query must have been analyzed via DBMS_STATS or ANALYZE.

This view can contain information on SELECT statements, DML statements such as UPDATE, as well as DDL statements such as CREATE INDEX. Some common operations that find themselves in the V$SESSION_LONGOPS view include table scans, index scans, join operations, parallel operations, RMAN backup operations, sort operations, and Data Pump operations.

9-6. Identifying Resource-Consuming SQL Statements That Are Currently Executing

Problem

You have contention issues within your database, and want to identify the SQL statement consuming the most system resources.

■ **Note**   Recipe 9-9 shows how to examine the historical record to find resource-consuming SQL statements that have executed in the past, but that are not currently executing.

Solution

Look at the V$SQLSTATS view, which gives information about currently or recently run SQL statements. If you wanted to get the top five recent SQL statements that performed the highest disk I/O, you could issue the following query:

```
SELECT sql_text, disk_reads FROM
  (SELECT sql_text, buffer_gets, disk_reads, sorts,
   cpu_time/1000000 cpu, rows_processed, elapsed_time
   FROM v$sqlstats
   ORDER BY disk_reads DESC)
WHERE rownum <= 5;
```

If you wanted to see the top five SQL statements by CPU time, sorts, loads, invalidations, or any other column, simply replace the disk_reads column in the foregoing query with your desired column. The SQL_TEXT column can make the results look messy, so another alternative is to substitute the SQL_TEXT column with SQL_ID, and then, based on the statistics shown, you can run a query to simply get the SQL_TEXT based on a given SQL_ID.

How It Works

The V$SQLSTATS view is meant to help more quickly find information on resource-consuming SQL statements. V$SQLSTATS has the same information as the V$SQL and V$SQLAREA views, but V$SQLSTATS has only a subset of columns of the other views. However, data is held within the V$SQLSTATS longer than either V$SQL or V$SQLAREA.

Sometimes, there are SQL statements that are related to the database background processing of keeping the database running, and you may not want to see those statements, but only the ones related to your application. If you join V$SQLSTATS to V$SQL, you can see information for particular users. See the following example:

```
SELECT schema, sql_text, disk_reads, round(cpu,2) FROM
  (SELECT s.parsing_schema_name schema, t.sql_id, t.sql_text, t.disk_reads,
   t.sorts, t.cpu_time/1000000 cpu, t.rows_processed, t.elapsed_time
   FROM v$sqlstats t join v$sql s on(t.sql_id = s.sql_id)
   WHERE parsing_schema_name = 'SCOTT'
   ORDER BY disk_reads DESC)
WHERE rownum <= 5;
```

Keep in mind that V$SQL represents SQL held in the shared pool, and is aged out faster than the data in V$SQLSTATS, so this query will not return data for SQL that has been already aged out of the shared pool.

9-7. Seeing Execution Statistics for Currently Running SQL

Problem

You want to view execution statistics for SQL statements that are currently running.

Solution

You can use the V$SQL_MONITOR view to see real-time statistics of currently running SQL, and see the resource consumption used for a given query based on such statistics as CPU usage, buffer gets, disk reads, and elapsed time of the query. Let's first find a current executing query within our database:

```
SELECT sid, sql_text FROM v$sql_monitor
WHERE status = 'EXECUTING';
```

```
       SID SQL_TEXT
---------- ------------------------------------------------------------
       100 select department_name, city, avg(salary)
           from employees_big join departments using(department_id)
           join locations using (location_id)
           group by department_name, city
           having avg(salary) > 2000
           order by 2,1
```

For the foregoing executing query found in V$SQL_MONITOR, we can see the resource utilization for that statement as it executes:

```
SELECT sid, buffer_gets, disk_reads, round(cpu_time/1000000,1) cpu_seconds
FROM v$sql_monitor
WHERE SID=100
AND status = 'EXECUTING';
```

```
       SID BUFFER_GETS DISK_READS CPU_SECONDS
---------- ----------- ---------- -----------
       100      149372       4732        39.1
```

The V$SQL_MONITOR view contains currently running SQL statements, as well as recently run SQL statements. If you wanted to see the top five most CPU-consuming queries in your database, you could issue the following query:

```
SELECT * FROM (
  SELECT sid, buffer_gets, disk_reads, round(cpu_time/1000000,1) cpu_seconds
  FROM v$sql_monitor
  ORDER BY cpu_time desc)
WHERE rownum <= 5;
```

```
       SID BUFFER_GETS DISK_READS CPU_SECONDS
---------- ----------- ---------- -----------
        20     1332665      30580       350.5
       105      795330      13651       269.7
        20      259324       5449        71.6
        20      259330       5485        71.3
       100      259236       8188        67.9
```

How It Works

SQL statements are monitored in V$SQL_MONITOR under the following conditions:

- Automatically for any parallelized statements

- Automatically for any DML or DDL statements

- Automatically if a particular SQL statement has consumed at least five seconds of CPU or I/O time

- Monitored for any SQL statement that has monitoring set at the statement level

To turn monitoring on at the statement level, a hint can be used. See the following example:

```
SELECT /*+ monitor */ ename, dname
FROM emppart JOIN dept USING (deptno);
```

If, for some reason, you do not want certain statements monitored, you can use the NOMONITOR hint in the statement to prevent monitoring from occurring for a given statement.

Statistics in V$SQL_MONITOR are updated near real-time, that is, every second. Any currently executing SQL statement that is being monitored can be found in V$SQL_MONITOR. Completed queries can be found there for at least one minute after execution ends, and can exist there longer, depending on the space requirements needed for newly executed queries. One key advantage of the V$SQL_MONITOR view is it has detailed statistics for each and every execution of a given query, unlike V$SQL, where results are cumulative for several executions of a SQL statement. In order to drill down, then, to a given execution of a SQL statement, you need three columns from V$SQL_MONITOR:

1. SQL_ID

2. SQL_EXEC_START

3. SQL_EXEC_ID

If we wanted to see all executions for a given query (based on the SQL_ID column), we can get that information by querying on the three necessary columns to drill to a given execution of a SQL query:

```
SELECT * FROM (
  SELECT sql_id, to_char(sql_exec_start,'yyyy-mm-dd:hh24:mi:ss') sql_exec_start,
         sql_exec_id, sum(buffer_gets) buffer_gets,
         sum(disk_reads) disk_reads, round(sum(cpu_time/1000000),1) cpu_secs
  FROM v$sql_monitor
  WHERE sql_id = 'fcg00hyh7qbpz'
  GROUP BY sql_id, sql_exec_start, sql_exec_id
  ORDER BY 6 desc)
WHERE rownum <= 5;
```

```
SQL_ID        SQL_EXEC_START      SQL_EXEC_ID BUFFER_GETS DISK_READS CPU_SECS
------------- ------------------- ----------- ----------- ---------- --------
fcg00hyh7qbpz 2011-05-21:12:28:10    16777222      259324       5449     71.6
fcg00hyh7qbpz 2011-05-21:12:29:24    16777223      259330       5485     71.3
fcg00hyh7qbpz 2011-05-21:12:26:08    16777220      213823       4502     58.4
fcg00hyh7qbpz 2011-05-21:12:27:09    16777221      211752       4579     58.1
fcg00hyh7qbpz 2011-05-21:12:25:37    16777219      107973       2414     29.4
```

Keep in mind that if a statement is running in parallel, one row will appear for each parallel thread for the query, including one for the query coordinator. However, they will share the same SQL_ID, SQL_EXEC_START, and SQL_EXEC_ID values. In this case, you could perform an aggregation on a particular statistic, if desired. See the following example for a parallelized query, along with parallel slave information denoted by the PX_SERVER# column:

```
SELECT sql_id, sql_exec_start, sql_exec_id, px_server# px#, disk_reads,
       cpu_time/1000000 cpu_secs, buffer_gets
FROM v$sql_monitor
WHERE status = 'EXECUTING'
ORDER BY px_server#;
```

SQL_ID	SQL_EXEC_S	SQL_EXEC_ID	PX#	DISK_READS	CPU_SECS	BUFFER_GETS
0gzf8010xdasr	2011-05-21	16777216	1	4306	38.0	136303
0gzf8010xdasr	2011-05-21	16777216	2	4625	40.6	146497
0gzf8010xdasr	2011-05-21	16777216	3	4774	41.6	149717
0gzf8010xdasr	2011-05-21	16777216	4	4200	37.6	132167
0gzf8010xdasr	2011-05-21	16777216		6	92.2	53

Then, to perform a simple aggregation for a given query, in this case, our parallelized query, the aggregation is done on the three key columns that make up a single execution of a given SQL statement:

```
SELECT sql_id,sql_exec_start, sql_exec_id, sum(buffer_gets) buffer_gets,
       sum(disk_reads) disk_reads, round(sum(cpu_time/1000000),1) cpu_seconds
FROM v$sql_monitor
WHERE sql_id = '0gzf8010xdasr'
GROUP BY sql_id, sql_exec_start, sql_exec_id;
```

SQL_ID	SQL_EXEC_S	SQL_EXEC_ID	BUFFER_GETS	DISK_READS	CPU_SECONDS
0gzf8010xdasr	2011-05-21	16777216	642403	20351	283.7

If you wanted to perform an aggregation for one SQL statement, regardless of the number of times is has been executed, simply run the aggregate query only on the SQL_ID column, as shown here:

```
SELECT sql_id, sum(buffer_gets) buffer_gets,
       sum(disk_reads) disk_reads, round(sum(cpu_time/1000000),1) cpu_seconds
FROM v$sql_monitor
WHERE sql_id = '0gzf8010xdasr'
GROUP BY sql_id;
```

■ **Note** Initialization parameter STATISTICS_LEVEL must be set to TYPICAL or ALL, and CONTROL_MANAGEMENT_PACK_ACCESS must be set to DIAGNOSTIC+TUNING for SQL monitoring to occur.

9-8. Monitoring Progress of a SQL Execution Plan

Problem

You want to see the progress a query is making from within the execution plan used.

Solution

There are a couple of ways to get information to see where a query is executing in terms of the execution plan. First, by querying the **V$SQL_PLAN_MONITOR** view, you can get information for all queries that are in progress, as well as recent queries that are complete. If we are joining two tables to get employee and department information, our query would look like this:

```
SELECT ename, dname
FROM emppart JOIN dept USING (deptno);
```

```
-------------------------------------------
| Id  | Operation              | Name      |
-------------------------------------------
|   0 | SELECT STATEMENT       |           |
|   1 |  PX COORDINATOR        |           |
|   2 |   PX SEND QC (RANDOM)   | :TQ10001  |
|   3 |    HASH JOIN           |           |
|   4 |     BUFFER SORT        |           |
|   5 |      PX RECEIVE        |           |
|   6 |       PX SEND BROADCAST | :TQ10000 |
|   7 |        TABLE ACCESS FULL| DEPT     |
|   8 |      PX BLOCK ITERATOR  |          |
|   9 |       TABLE ACCESS FULL | EMPPART  |
-------------------------------------------
```

To see information for the foregoing query while it is currently running, you can issue a query like the one shown here (some rows have been removed for conciseness):

```
column operation format a25
column plan_line_id format 9999 heading 'LINE'
column plan_options format a10 heading 'OPTIONS'
column status format a10
column output_rows heading 'ROWS'
break on sid on sql_id on status

SELECT sid, sql_id, status, plan_line_id,
plan_operation || ' ' || plan_options operation, output_rows
FROM v$sql_plan_monitor
WHERE status not like '%DONE%'
ORDER BY 1,4;
```

```
       SID SQL_ID         STATUS        LINE OPERATION                         ROWS
---------- -------------- ----------    ----- -------------------------- ----------
        18 36bdwxutr5n75  EXECUTING        0 SELECT STATEMENT              3929326
                                           1 PX COORDINATOR                3929326
        27 36bdwxutr5n75  EXECUTING        0 SELECT STATEMENT                    0
                                           2 PX SEND QC (RANDOM)           1752552
                                           3 HASH JOIN                     1752552
                                           8 PX BLOCK ITERATOR             1752552
                                           9 TABLE ACCESS FULL             1752552
       101 36bdwxutr5n75  EXECUTING        0 SELECT STATEMENT                    0
                                           2 PX SEND QC (RANDOM)           2148232
                                           3 HASH JOIN                     2148232
                                           8 PX BLOCK ITERATOR             2148232
                                           9 TABLE ACCESS FULL             2148232
```

In this particular example, the EMPPART table has a parallel degree of 2, and we can see that for SIDs 27 and 101, these are the parallel slaves that are getting the data. As these processes pass data back to the query coordinator and then back to the user, we can see that when we look at SID 18. If we simply run subsequent queries against the V$SQL_PLAN_MONITOR view, we can see the progress of the query as it is executing. In the foregoing example, we simply see the output row values increasing as the query progresses.

Another method of seeing the progress of a query via the execution plan is by using the DBMS_SQLTUNE.REPORT_SQL_MONITOR function. If we use the same query against the EMPPART and DEPT tables used in the previous example, we can run the REPORT_SQL_MONITOR function to get a graphical look at the progress. See the following example of how to generate the file that would produce the HTML file that could be, in turn, used to view our progress. Figure 9-2 shows portions of the resulting report.

```
set pages 9999
set long 1000000
SELECT DBMS_SQLTUNE.REPORT_SQL_MONITOR(sql_id=> '36bdwxutr5n75',type=>'HTML') FROM dual;
```

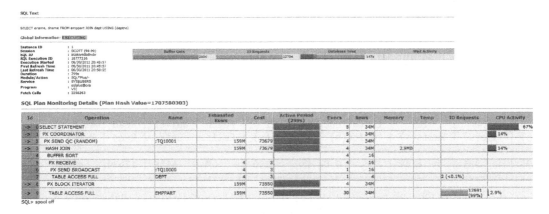

Figure 9-2. Sample HTML report from DBMS_SQLTUNE.REPORT_SQL_MONITOR

How It Works

The **V$SQL_PLAN_MONITOR** is populated from the **V$SQL_MONITOR** view (see Recipe 9-7). Both of these views are new as of Oracle 11g, and are updated every second that a statement executes. The **V$SQL_MONITOR** view is populated each time a SQL statement is monitored.

The **DBMS_SQLTUNE.REPORT_SQL_MONITOR** function can be invoked in several ways. The level of detail, as well as the type of detail you wish to see in the report, can be changed based on the parameters passed into the function. The output can be viewed in several formats, including plain text, HTML, and XML. The default output format is plain text. As an example, let's say we wanted to see the output for our join against the **EMPPART** and **DEPT** tables. In this instance, we want the output in text format. We want the detail aggregated, and we want to see just the most basic level of detail. Our query would then be run as follows:

```
SELECT DBMS_SQLTUNE.REPORT_SQL_MONITOR
(sql_id=>'36bdwxutr5n75',event_detail=>'NO',report_level=>'BASIC') FROM dual;

SQL Monitoring Report

SQL Text
-------------------------------
select ename, dname from emppart join dept using (deptno)

Global Information
-------------------------------
  Status              :  EXECUTING
  Instance ID         :  1
  Session             :  SCOTT (27:229)
  SQL ID              :  36bdwxutr5n75
  SQL Execution ID    :  16777225
  Execution Started   :  05/15/2011 14:56:16
  First Refresh Time  :  05/15/2011 14:56:16
  Last Refresh Time   :  05/15/2011 15:09:47
  Duration            :  812s
  Module/Action       :  SQL*Plus/-
  Service             :  SYS$USERS
  Program             :  sqlplus@ora
  Fetch Calls         :  6131367

Global Stats
========================================================================================================
| Elapsed | Cpu     | IO       | Concurrency | Other    | Fetch | Buffer | Read  | Read  |
| Time(s) | Time(s) | Waits(s) | Waits(s)    | Waits(s) | Calls | Gets   | Reqs  | Bytes |
========================================================================================================
|     398 |     235 |     6.45 |        0.04 |      156 |    6M |   556K | 17629 |   4GB |
========================================================================================================
```

Refer to the Oracle PL/SQL Packages and Types Reference for a complete list of all the parameters that can be used to execute the **REPORT_SQL_MONITOR** function. It is a very robust function, and there are a myriad of permutations to report on, based on your specific need.

9-9. Identifying Resource-Consuming SQL Statements That Have Executed in the Past

Problem

You want to view information on previously run SQL statements to aid in identifying resource-intensive operations.

■ **Note** Recipe 9-6 shows how to identify *currently executing* statements that are resource-intensive.

Solution

The DBA_HIST_SQLSTAT and DBA_HIST_SQLTEXT views are two of the views that can be used to get historical information on SQL statements and their resource consumption statistics. For example, to get historical information on what SQL statements are incurring the most disk reads, you can issue the following query against DBA_HIST_SQLSTAT:

```
SELECT * FROM (
  SELECT sql_id, sum(disk_reads_delta) disk_reads_delta,
              sum(disk_reads_total) disk_reads_total,
              sum(executions_delta) execs_delta,
              sum(executions_total) execs_total
  FROM dba_hist_sqlstat
  GROUP BY sql_id
  ORDER BY 2 desc)
WHERE rownum <= 5;
```

SQL_ID	DISK_READS_DELTA	DISK_READS_TOTAL	EXECS_DELTA	EXECS_TOTAL
36bdwxutr5n75	6306401	10933153	13	24
0bx1z9rbm10a1	1590538	1590538	2	2
0gzf8010xdasr	970292	1848743	1	3
1gtkxf53fk7bp	969785	969785	7	7
4h81qj5nspx6s	869588	869588	2	2

Since the actual text of the SQL isn't stored in DBA_HIST_SQLSTAT, you can then look at the associated DBA_HIST_SQLTEXT view to get the SQL text for the query with the highest number of disk reads:

```
SELECT sql_text FROM dba_hist_sqltext
WHERE sql_id = '36bdwxutr5n75';
```

```
SQL_TEXT
-----------------------------------------
select ename, dname
from emppart join dept using (deptno)
```

How It Works

There are many useful statistics to get from the DBA_HIST_SQLSTAT view regarding historical SQL statements, including the following:

- CPU utilization

- Elapsed time of execution

- Number of executions

- Total disk reads and writes

- Buffer get information

- Parallel server information

- Rows processed

- Parse calls

- Invalidations

Furthermore, this information is separated by two views of the data. There is a set of "Total" information in one set of columns, and there is a "Delta" set of information in another set of columns. The "Total" set of columns is calculated based on instance startup. The "Delta" columns are based on the values seen in the BEGIN_INTERVAL_TIME and END_INTERVAL_TIME columns of the DBA_HIST_SNAPSHOT view.

If you want to see explain plan information for historical SQL statements, there is an associated view available to retrieve that information for a given query. You can access the DBA_HIST_SQL_PLAN view to get the explain plan information for historical SQL statements. See the following example:

```
SELECT id, operation || ' ' || options operation, object_name, cost, bytes
FROM dba_hist_sql_plan
WHERE sql_id = '0gzf8010xdasr'
ORDER BY 1;


        ID OPERATION                   OBJECT_NAME       COST      BYTES
---------- ------------------------- ------------ ---------- ----------
         0 SELECT STATEMENT                                73679
         1 PX COORDINATOR
         2 PX SEND QC (RANDOM)         :TQ10001          73679 3506438144
         3 HASH JOIN                                     73679 3506438144
         4 BUFFER SORT
         5 PX RECEIVE                                         3         52
         6 PX SEND BROADCAST           :TQ10000              3         52
         7 TABLE ACCESS FULL           DEPT                  3         52
         8 PX BLOCK ITERATOR                             73550 1434451968
         9 TABLE ACCESS FULL           EMPPART           73550 1434451968

10 rows selected.
```

9-10. Comparing SQL Performance After a System Change

Problem

You are making a system change, and want to see the impact that change will have on performance of a SQL statement.

Solution

By using the Oracle SQL Performance Analyzer, and specifically the `DBMS_SQLPA` package, you can quantify the performance impact a system change will have on one or more SQL statements. A system change can be an initialization parameter change, a database upgrade, or any other change to your environment that could affect SQL statement performance.

Let's say you are going to be performing a database upgrade, and want to see the impact the upgrade is going to have on a series of SQL statements run within your database. Using the `DBMS_SQLPA` package, the basic steps to get the information needed to perform the analysis generally are as follows:

1. Create an analysis task based on a single or series of SQL statements.

2. Run an analysis for those statements based on your current configuration.

3. Perform the given change to your environment (like a database upgrade).

4. Run an analysis for those statements based on the new configuration.

5. Run a "before and after" comparison to determine what impact the change has on the performance of your SQL statement(s).

6. Generate a report to view the output of the comparison results.

Using the foregoing steps, see the following example for a single query. First, we need to create an analysis task. For the database upgrade example, this would be done on an appropriate test database that is Oracle 11g. In this case, within SQL Plus, we will do the analysis for one specific SQL statement:

```
variable g_task varchar2(100);

EXEC :g_task := DBMS_SQLPA.CREATE_ANALYSIS_TASK(sql_text => 'select ename, dname from emppart
join dept using(deptno)');
```

In order to properly simulate this scenario, on our Oracle 11g database, we then set the `optimizer_features_enable` parameter back to Oracle 10g. We then run an analysis for our query using the "before" conditions—in this case, with a previous version of the optimizer:

```
alter session set optimizer_features_enable='10.2.0.4';

EXEC DBMS_SQLPA.EXECUTE_ANALYSIS_TASK(task_name=>:g_task,execution_type=>'test
execute',execution_name=>'before_change');
```

After completing the before analysis, we set the optimizer to the current version of our database, which, for this example, represents the version to which we are upgrading our database:

```
alter session set optimizer_features_enable='11.2.0.1';

EXEC DBMS_SQLPA.EXECUTE_ANALYSIS_TASK(task_name=>:g_task,execution_type=>'test
execute',execution_name=>'after_change');
```

Now that we have created our analysis task based on a given SQL statement, and have run "before" and "after" analysis tasks for that statement based on the changed conditions, we can now run an analysis task to compare the results of the two executions of our query. There are several metrics that can be compared. In this case, we are comparing "buffer gets":

```
EXEC DBMS_SQLPA.EXECUTE_ANALYSIS_TASK(task_name=>:g_task,execution_type=>'COMPARE
PERFORMANCE',execution_name=>'compare change',execution_params =>
dbms_advisor.arglist('comparison_metric','buffer_gets'));
```

Finally, we can now use the REPORT_ANALYSIS_TASK function of the DBMS_SQLPA package in order to view the results. In the following example, we want to see output only if the execution plan has changed. The output can be in several formats, the most popular being HTML and plain text. For our example, we produced text output:

```
set long 100000 longchunksize 100000 linesize 200 head off feedback off echo off
spool compare_report.txt

SELECT DBMS_SQLPA.REPORT_ANALYSIS_TASK(:g_task, 'TEXT', 'CHANGED_PLANS', 'ALL')
FROM DUAL;

General Information
-------------------------------------------------------------------------------
 Task Information:                          Workload Information:
--------------------------------------     ------------------------------------
  Task Name    : TASK_1383
  Task Owner   : SCOTT
  Description  :

Execution Information:
-------------------------------------------------------------------------------
  Execution Name  : compare change      Started           : 05/28/2011 17:28:07
  Execution Type  : COMPARE PERFORMANCE  Last Updated      : 05/28/2011 17:28:08
  Description     :                     Global Time Limit : UNLIMITED
  Scope           : COMPREHENSIVE       Per-SQL Time Limit : UNUSED
  Status          : COMPLETED           Number of Errors  : 0

Analysis Information:
-------------------------------------------------------------------------------
 Comparison Metric: BUFFER_GETS
 ------------------
 Workload Impact Threshold: 1%
 -------------------------
 SQL Impact Threshold: 1%
 ---------------------
```

Before Change Execution:

```
------------------------------------------------
 Execution Name      : before_change
 Execution Type      : TEST EXECUTE
 Description         :
 Scope               : COMPREHENSIVE
 Status              : COMPLETED
 Started             : 05/28/2011 17:19:47
 Last Updated        : 05/28/2011 17:23:37
 Global Time Limit   : UNLIMITED
 Per-SQL Time Limit  : UNUSED
 Number of Errors    : 0
------------------------------------------------
```

After Change Execution:

```
------------------------------------------------
 Execution Name      : after_change
 Execution Type      : TEST EXECUTE
 Description         :
 Scope               : COMPREHENSIVE
 Status              : COMPLETED
 Started             : 05/28/2011 17:23:43
 Last Updated        : 05/28/2011 17:28:07
 Global Time Limit   : UNLIMITED
 Per-SQL Time Limit  : UNUSED
 Number of Errors    : 0
------------------------------------------------
```

Execution Statistics:

Stat Name	Impact on Workload	Value Before	Value After	Impact on SQL	% Workload Before	% Workload After
elapsed_time	-12.24%	230.819	259.072	-12.24%	100%	100%
parse_time	-4100%	0	.041	-4.1%	0%	100%
cpu_time	-1.62%	198.948	202.177	-1.62%	100%	100%
buffer_gets	0%	16882239	16882239	0%	100%	100%
cost	0%	16812553	16812553	0%	100%	100%
reads	-34.9%	77791	104939	-34.9%	100%	100%
writes	0%	0	0	0%	0%	0%
rows	%	16777222	16777222	%	%	%

Findings (1):
----
1. The structure of the SQL execution plan has changed.

Execution Plan Before Change:

Id	Operation	Name	Rows	Bytes	Cost	Time
0	SELECT STATEMENT		16777222	671088880	16793338	
1	NESTED LOOPS		16777222	671088880	16793338	
2	PARTITION RANGE ALL		16777222	335544440	16116	
3	TABLE ACCESS FULL	EMPPART	16777222	335544440	16116	
4	TABLE ACCESS BY INDEX ROWID	DEPT	1	20	1	
* 5	INDEX UNIQUE SCAN	PK_DEPT	1			

Execution Plan After Change:

```
-----------------------------------------------------------------------------------
| Id  | Operation                      | Name    | Rows     | Bytes     | Cost     | Time     |
-----------------------------------------------------------------------------------
|   0 | SELECT STATEMENT               |         | 16777222 | 352321662 | 16812553 |  6:02:31 |
|   1 |  NESTED LOOPS                  |         |          |           |          |          |
|   2 |   NESTED LOOPS                 |         | 16777222 | 352321662 | 16812553 | 56:02:31 |
|   3 |    PARTITION RANGE ALL         |         | 16777222 | 150994998 |    29013 | 00:05:49 |
|   4 |     TABLE ACCESS FULL          | EMPPART | 16777222 | 150994998 |    29013 | 00:05:49 |
| * 5 |     INDEX UNIQUE SCAN          | PK_DEPT |        1 |           |        0 | 00:00:01 |
|   6 |    TABLE ACCESS BY INDEX ROWID | DEPT    |        1 |        12 |        1 | 00:00:01 |
-----------------------------------------------------------------------------------
```

In the foregoing example output, we can see the before and after execution statistics, as well as the before and after execution plans. We can also see an estimated workload impact and SQL impact percentages, which are very useful in order to see, at a quick glance, if there is a large impact by making the system change being made. In this example, we can see there would be a 1% change, and by looking at the execution plans, we see a negligible difference. So, for the foregoing query, the database upgrade will essentially have minimal or no impact on the performance of our query. If you see an impact percentage of 10% or greater, it may mean more analysis and tuning need to occur to proactively tune the query or the system prior to making the change to your production environment. In order to get an accurate comparison, it is also recommended to export production statistics and import them into your test environment prior to performing the analysis using DBMS_SQLPA.

■ **Tip**   In SQL Plus, remember to SET LONG and SET LONG CHUNKSIZE in order for output to be displayed properly.

How It Works

The SQL Performance Analyzer and the DBMS_SQLPA package can be used to analyze a SQL workload, which can be defined as any of the following:

- A SQL statement

- A SQL ID stored in cache

- A SQL tuning set (see Chapter 11 for information on SQL tuning sets)

- A SQL ID based on a snapshot from the Automatic Workload Repository (see Chapter 4 for more information)

In normal circumstances, it is easiest to gather information on a series of SQL statements, rather than one single statement. Getting information via Automatic Workload Repository (AWR) snapshots or via SQL tuning sets is the easiest way to get information for a series of statements. The AWR snapshots will contain information based on a specific time period, while SQL tuning sets will contain information on a specifically targeted set of SQL statements. Some of the possible key reasons to consider doing a "before and after" performance analysis include the following:

- Initialization parameter changes

- Database upgrades

- Hardware changes

- Operating system changes

- Application schema object additions or changes

- The implementation of SQL baselines or profiles

There is an abundance of information available for comparison. When reporting on the information gathered in your analysis, it may be beneficial to show only the output for SQL statements affected adversely by the system change. For instance, you may want to narrow down the information shown from the REPORT_ANALYSIS_TASK function to show information only on SQL statements such as the following:

- Those statements that show regressed performance

- Those statements with a changed execution plan

- Those statements that show errors in the SQL statements

It may be beneficial to flush the shared_pool and/or the buffer_cache prior to gathering information on each of your tasks, which will aid in getting the best possible information for comparison. Information on analysis tasks is stored in the data dictionary. You can reference any of the data dictionary views prefaced with "DBA_ADVISOR" to get information on performance analysis tasks you have created, executions performed, as well as execution statistics, execution plans, and report information. Refer to the Oracle PL/SQL Packages and Types Reference for your version of the database for a complete explanation of the DBMS_SQLPA package, which is new as of version Oracle 11g.

■ **Note** The ADVISOR system privilege is needed to perform the analysis tasks using DBMS_SQLPA.

CHAPTER 10

Tracing SQL Execution

Tracing session activity is at the heart of most SQL performance tuning exercises. Oracle provides a rich set of tools to trace SQL activity. This chapter introduces the Oracle SQL trace facility and shows you how to set up SQL tracing in your environment. Oracle provides numerous "events" that help you perform various types of traces.

Although there are several tracing methods available, Oracle now recommends that you use the DBMS_MONITOR package for most types of tracing. The chapter contains several recipes that explain how to use this package to generate traces. In addition, we show how to trace sessions by setting various Oracle events, the setting of which is often requested by Oracle Support. You'll learn how to trace a single SQL statement, a session as well as an entire instance, as well as how to trace parallel queries. There are recipes that show how to trace another user's session and how to use a trigger to start a session trace. You'll also learn how to trace the Oracle optimizer's execution path.

Oracle provides the TKPROF utility as well as the freely downloadable profiler named Oracle Trace Analyzer. This chapter shows how to use both of these profilers to analyze the raw trace files you generate.

10-1. Preparing Your Environment

Problem

You want to make sure your database is set up correctly for tracing SQL sessions.

Solution

You must do three things before you can start tracing SQL statements:

1. Enable timed statistics collection.
2. Specify a destination for the trace dump file.
3. Adjust the trace dump file size.

You can enable the collection of timed statistics by setting the timed_statistics parameter to true. Check the current value of this parameter first:

```
SQL> sho parameter statistics

NAME                                TYPE        VALUE
----------------------------------- ----------- -----------
...
statistics_level                    string      TYPICAL
timed_statistics                    boolean     TRUE
SQL>
```

If the value of the timed_statistics parameter is false, you set it to true with the following statement.

```
SQL> alter system set timed_statistics=true scope=both;

System altered.

SQL>
```

You can also set this parameter at the session level with the following statement:

```
SQL> alter session set timed_statistics=true
```

You can find the location of the trace directory (which was referred to as the user dump directory in pre-Oracle Database 11g releases) with the following command:

```
SQL> select name,value from v$diag_info
  2* where name='Diag Trace'
SQL> /

NAME                                         VALUE
---------------------------                  ----------------------------------------

Diag Trace                                   c:\app\ora\diag\rdbms\orcl1\orcl1\trace


SQL>
```

In Oracle Database 11g, the default value of the max_dump_file_size parameter is unlimited, as you can verify by issuing the following command:

```
SQL> sho parameter dump

NAME                                TYPE        VALUE
----------------------------------- ----------- ----------
...
max_dump_file_size                  string      unlimited
```

An unlimited dump file size means that the file can grow as large as the operating system permits

How It Works

Before you can trace any SQL sessions, ensure that you've set the timed_statistics initialization parameter to true. If the value for this parameter is false, SQL tracing is disabled. Setting the timed_statistics parameter to true enables the database to collect statistics such as the CPU and elapsed times and store them in various dynamic performance tables. The default value of this parameter, starting with the Oracle 11.1.0.7.0 release, depends on the value of the initialization parameter statistics_level. If you set the statistics_level parameter to basic, the default value of the timed_statistics parameter is false. If you set statistics_level to the value typical or all, the default value of the timed_statistics parameter is true. The timed_statistics parameter is dynamic, meaning you don't have to restart the database to turn it on—you can turn this parameter on for the entire database without a significant overhead. You can also turn the parameter on only for an individual session.

When you trace a SQL session, Oracle generates a trace file that contains diagnostic data that's very useful in troubleshooting SQL performance issues. Starting with Oracle Database 11g, the database stores all diagnostic files under a dedicated diagnostic directory that you specify through the diagnostic_dest initialization parameter. The structure of the diagnostic directory is as follows:

```
<diagnostic_dest>/diag/rdbms/<dbname>/<instance>
```

The diagnostic directory is called the ADR Home. If your database name is prod1 and the instance name is prod1 as well, then the ADR home directory will be the following:

```
<diagnostic_dest>/diag/rdbms/prod1/prod1
```

The ADR home directory contains trace files in the <ADR Home>/trace subdirectory. Trace files usually have the extension .trc. You'll notice that several trace files have a corresponding trace map file with the .trm extension. The .trm files contain structural information about trace files, which the database uses for searching and navigation. You can view the diagnostic directory setting for a database with the following command:

```
SQL> sho parameter diagnostic_dest

NAME                                 TYPE        VALUE
------------------------------------ ----------- -----------
diagnostic_dest                      string      C:\APP\ORA
SQL>
```

The V$DIAG_INFO view shows the location of the various diagnostic directories, including the trace directory, which is listed in this view under the name Diag Trace. Although the new database diagnosability infrastructure in Oracle Database 11g ignores the user_dump_dest initialization parameter, the parameter still exists, and points to the same directory as the $ADR_BASE\diag\rdbms\<database>\<instance>\trace directory, as the following command shows:

```
SQL> show parameter user_dump_dest

NAME                                 TYPE        VALUE
------------------------------------ ----------- ------------------------------
user_dump_dest                       string      c:\app\ora\diag\rdbms\orcl1\or
                                                 cl1\trace
SQL>
```

In Oracle Database 11g, you don't have to set the max_dump_file_size parameter to specify the maximum size of a trace file.

10-2. Tracing a Specific SQL Statement

Problem

You want to trace a specific SQL statement, in order to find out where the database is spending its time during the execution of the statement.

Solution

In an Oracle 11.1or higher release, you can use the enhanced SQL tracing interface to trace one or more SQL statements. Here are the steps to tracing a set of SQL statements.

1. Issue the `alter session set events` statement, as shown here, to set up the trace.

   ```
   SQL> alter session set events 'sql_trace level 12';

   Session altered.
   SQL>
   ```

2. Execute the SQL statements.

   ```
   SQL> select count(*) from sales;
   ```

3. Set tracing off.

   ```
   SQL> alter session set events 'sql_trace off';

   Session altered.

   SQL>
   ```

You can choose to trace specific SQL statements by specifying the SQL ID of a statement in the `alter session set events` statement. Here are the steps:

1. Find the SQL ID of the SQL statement by issuing this statement:

   ```
   SQL> select sql_id,sql_text
        from v$sql
        where sql_text='select sum(quantity_sold) from sales';

   SQL_ID                   SQL_TEXT
   ----------------         -----------------------------------
   fb2yuOp1kgvhr            select sum(quantity_sold) from sales

   SQL>
   ```

2. Set tracing on for the specific SQL statement whose SQL ID you've retrieved.

```
SQL> alter session set events 'sql_trace [sql:fb2yu0p1kgvhr] level 12';

Session altered.

SQL>
```

3. Execute the SQL statement.

```
SQL> select sum(quantity_sold) from sales;

SUM(QUANTITY_SOLD)
------------------
            918843
```

4. Turn off tracing.

```
SQL> alter session set events 'sql_trace[sql:fb2yu0p1kgvhr] off';

Session altered.

SQL>
```

You can trace multiple SQL statements by separating the SQL IDs with the pipe (|) character, as shown here:

```
SQL> alter session set events 'sql_trace [sql: fb2yu0p1kgvhr|4v433su9vvzsw]';
```

You can trace a specific SQL statement running in a different session by issuing an alter system set events statement:

```
SQL> alter system set events 'sql_trace[sql:fb2yu0p1kgvhr] level 12';

System altered.
SQL>
```

You can get the SQL ID for the statement by querying the V$SQL view as shown earlier in this recipe, or you can get it through the Oracle Enterprise Manager. Once the user in the other session completes executing the SQL statement, turn off tracing with the following command:

```
SQL> alter system set events 'sql_trace[sql:fb2yu0p1kgvhr] off';

System altered.

SQL>
```

How It Works

In Oracle Database 11g, you can set the Oracle event SQL_TRACE to trace the execution of one or more SQL statements. You can issue either an alter session or an alter system statement for tracing a specific SQL statement. Here's the syntax of the command:

```
alter session/system set events 'sql_trace [sql:<sql_id>|<sql_id>] … event specification';
```

Even if you execute multiple SQL statements before you turn the tracing off, the trace file will show just the information pertaining to the SQL_ID or SQL_IDs you specify.

10.3. Enabling Tracing in Your Own Session

Problem

You want to trace your own session.

Solution

Normal users can use the DBMS_SESSION package to trace their sessions, as shown in this example:

```
SQL>execute dbms_session.session_trace_enable(waits=>true, binds=> false);
```

To disable tracing, the user must execute the session_trace_disable procedure, as shown here:

```
SQL> execute dbms_session.session_trace_disable();
```

How It Works

The DBMS_MONITOR package, which Oracle recommends for all tracing, is executable only by a user with the DBA role. If you don't have the DBA role, you can use the dbms_session.session_trace_enable procedure to trace your own session.

10-4. Finding the Trace Files

Problem

You'd like to find a way to easily identify your trace files.

Solution

Issue the following statement to set an identifier for your trace files, before you start generating the trace:

```
SQL> alter session set tracefile_identifier='MyTune1';
```

To view the most recent trace files the database has created, in Oracle Database 11.1 and newer releases, you can query the Automatic Diagnostic Repository (ADR) by executing the following command (see Chapter 5 for details on the adrci utility):

```
adrci> show tracefile -t
08-MAY-11 19:01:48   diag\rdbms\orcl1\orcl1\trace\orcl1_p000_8652_MyTune1.trc
08-MAY-11 19:01:48   diag\rdbms\orcl1\orcl1\trace\orcl1_p001_6424_MyTune1.trc
08-MAY-11 19:01:48   diag\rdbms\orcl1\orcl1\trace\orcl1_p002_5980_MyTune1.trc
adrci>
```

To find out the path to your current session's trace file, issue the following command:

```
SQL>  select value from v$diag_info
        where name = 'Default Trace File';

VALUE
--------------------------------------------------------------------

c:\app\ora\diag\rdbms\orcl1\orcl1\trace\orcl1_ora_11248_My_Tune1.trc

SQL>
```

To find all trace files for the current instance, issue the following query:

```
SQL> select value from v$diag_info where name = 'Diag Trace'
```

How It Works

Often, it's hard to find the exact trace file you're looking for, because there may be a bunch of other trace files in the trace directory, all with similar-looking file names. A best practice during SQL tracing is to associate your trace files with a unique identifier. Setting an identifier for the trace files you're going to generate makes it easy to identify the SQL trace files from among the many trace files the database generates in the trace directory.

You can confirm the value of the trace identifier with the following command:

```
SQL> sho parameter tracefile_identifier
NAME                                 TYPE        VALUE
------------------------------------ ----------- ---------------
tracefile_identifier                 string      MyTune1
SQL>
```

The column TRACEID in the V$PROCESS view shows the current value of the tracefile_identifier parameter as well. The trace file identifier you set becomes part of the trace file name, making it easy to pick the correct file name for a trace from among a large number of trace files in the trace directory. You can modify the value of the tracefile_identifier parameter multiple times for a session. The trace file names for a process will contain information to indicate that they all belong to the same process.

Once you set the tracefile_identifier parameter, the trace files will have the following format, where sid is the Oracle SID, pid is the process ID, and traceid is the value you've set for the tracefile_identifier initialization parameter.

```
sid_ora_pid_traceid.trc
```

10-5. Examining a Raw SQL Trace File

Problem

You want to examine a raw SQL trace file.

Solution

Open the trace file in a text editor to inspect the tracing information. Here are portions of a raw SQL trace generated by executing the dbms_monitor.session_trace_enable procedure:

```
PARSING IN CURSOR #3 len=490 dep=1 uid=85 oct=3 lid=85 tim=269523043683 hv=672110367
ad='7ff18986250' sqlid='bqasjasn0z5sz'

PARSE #3:c=0,e=647,p=0,cr=0,cu=0,mis=1,r=0,dep=1,og=1,plh=0,tim=269523043680
EXEC #3:c=0,e=1749,p=0,cr=0,cu=0,mis=1,r=0,dep=1,og=1,plh=3969568374,tim=269523045613
WAIT #3: nam='Disk file operations I/O' ela= 15833 FileOperation=2 fileno=4 filetype=2 obj#=-1
tim=269523061555
FETCH #3:c=0,e=19196,p=0,cr=46,cu=0,mis=0,r=1,dep=1,og=1,plh=3969568374,tim=269523064866
STAT #3 id=3 cnt=12 pid=2 pos=1 obj=0 op='HASH GROUP BY (cr=46 pr=0 pw=0 time=11 us cost=4
size=5317 card=409)'
STAT #3 id=4 cnt=3424 pid=3 pos=1 obj=89079 op='TABLE ACCESS  FULL DEPT (cr=16 pr=0 pw=0
time=246 us cost=3 size=4251 card=327)'
```

As you can see from this excerpt of the raw trace file, you can glean useful information, such as parse misses, waits, and the execution plan of the SQL statement.

How It Works

The usual practice after getting a session trace file is to analyze it using a tool such as TKPROF. However, you can examine a trace file by visually reading the trace output. The raw trace files capture information for each of the following three steps of SQL statement processing:

Parse: During this stage, the database converts the SQL statement into an execution plan, and checks for authorization and the existence of tables and other objects.

Execute: The database executes the SQL statement during this phase. For a SELECT statement, the execute phase identifies the rows the database must retrieve. The database modifies the data for DML statements such as insert, update, and delete.

Fetch: This step applies only for a SELECT statement. During this phase, the database retrieves the selected rows.

A SQL trace file will contain detailed statistics for each of the three phases of execution, in addition to wait event information. You usually format the raw trace files with a utility such as TKPROF. However, there are times when a raw trace file can show you useful information very quickly, by a simple scroll through the file. A locking situation is a good example where you can visually inspect a raw trace file. TKPROF doesn't provide you details about latches and locks (enqueues). If you suspect that a query was waiting on a lock, digging deep into a raw trace file shows you exactly where and why a query was waiting. In the WAIT line, the elapsed time (ela) shows the amount of time waited (in microseconds). In our example, elapsed wait time for "Disk file operations I/O" is 15,833 microseconds. Since 1 second=1,000,000 microseconds, this is not a significant wait time. The raw trace file clearly shows if an I/O wait event, as is true in this case, or another type of wait event held up the query. If the query was waiting on a lock, you'll see something similar to the following: WAIT #2: nam='enqueue ela-300….

We've purposefully kept the discussion short in this recipe, because tools such as TKPROF and the Oracle Trace Analyzer provide you sophisticated diagnostic information by profiling the raw trace files.

10-6. Analyzing Oracle Trace Files

Problem

You want to know how to analyze an Oracle trace file.

Solution

There are multiple ways to interpret a SQL trace file. Here are the different approaches:

- Read the raw SQL trace file in a text editor.

- Use the Oracle-provided TKPROF (Trace Kernel Profiler) utility.

- Use Oracle Trace Analyzer, a free product you can download from Oracle Support.

- Use third-party tools.

How It Works

Getting a SQL trace is often the easy part—analyzing it is, of course, more of a task than collecting the trace. Sometimes, if you're particularly adept at it, you can certainly directly view the source trace file itself, but in most cases, you need a tool to interpret and profile the huge amount of data that a trace file can contain. Note that the TKPROF or other profiling tools show the elapsed times for various phases of query execution, but not the information for locks and latches. If you're trying to find out if any locks are slowing down a query, look at the raw trace files to see if there are any enqueue waits in the WAIT lines of the raw file.

You can easily read certain trace files such as the trace file for event 10053, since the file doesn't contain any SQL execution statistics (such as parsing, executing, and fetching statistics), and no wait event analysis—it mostly consists of a trace of the execution path used by the cost-based optimizer (CBO). However, for any SQL execution trace files, such as those you generate with the event 10046, a visual inspection of the trace file, while technically possible, is not only time-consuming, but the raw data is not in a summary form and key events are often described in obscure ways. Therefore, using a profiler such as the TKPROF utility is really your best option.

The TKPROF utility is an Oracle-supplied profiling tool that most Oracle DBAs use on a routine basis. Recipes 10-7 and 10-8 show how to use TKPROF.

Oracle's Trace Analyzer is free (you have to download it from Oracle Support), easy to install and use, and produces clear reports with plenty of useful diagnostic information. You do have to install the tool first, but it takes only a few minutes to complete the installation. Thereafter, you just pass the name of the trace file to a script to generate the formatted output. Recipe 10-9 shows how to install and use the Oracle Trace Analyzer.

There are also third-party profiling tools that offer features not found in the TKPROF utility. Some of these tools generate pretty HTML trace reports and some include charts as well to help you visually inspect the details of the execution of the SQL statement that you've traced. Note that in order to use some of these products, you'll have to upload your trace files for analysis. If your trace files contain sensitive data or security information, this may not work for you.

10-7. Formatting Trace Files with TKPROF

Problem

You've traced a session, and you want to use TKPROF to format the trace file.

Solution

You run the TKPROF utility from the command line. Here's an example of a typical tkprof command for formatting a trace file.

```
$ tkprof user_sql_001.trc user1.prf explain=hr/hr table=hr.temp_plan_table_a sys=no
  sort=exeela,prsela,fchela
```

In the example shown here, the tkprof command takes the user_sql_001.trc trace file as input and generates an output file named user1.prf. The "How it Works" section of this recipe explains key optional arguments of the TKPROF utility.

How It Works

TKPROF is a utility that lets you format any extended trace files that you generate with the event 10046 or through the DBMS_MONITOR package. You can use this tool to generate reports for analyzing results of the various types of SQL tracing explained in this chapter. You can run TKPROF on a single trace file or a set of trace files that you've concatenated with the trcsess utility. TKPROF shows details of various aspects of SQL statement execution, such as the following:

- SQL statement text

- SQL trace statistics

- Number of library cache misses during the parse and execute phases

- Execution plans for all SQL statements

- Recursive SQL calls

You can view a list of all the arguments you can specify issuing the tkprof command without any arguments, as shown here:

```
$ tkprof
Usage: tkprof tracefile outputfile [explain= ] [table= ]
              [print= ] [insert= ] [sys= ] [sort= ]
...
```

Here's a brief explanation of the important arguments you can specify with the tkprof command:

filename1: Specifies the name of the trace file

filename2: Specifies the formatted output file

waits: Specifies whether the output file should record a summary of the wait events; default is *yes*.

sort: By default, TKPROF lists the SQL statements in the trace file in the order they were executed. You can specify various options with the sort argument to control the order in which TKPROF lists the various SQL statements.

- prscpu: CPU time spent parsing

- prsela: Elapsed time spent parsing

- execpu: CPU time spent executing

- exeela: Elapsed time spent executing

- fchela: Elapsed time spent fetching

print: By default TKPROF will list all traced SQL statements. By specifying a value for the print option, you can limit the number of SQL statements listed in the output file.

sys: By default TKPROF lists all SQL statements issued by the user SYS, as well as recursive statements. Specify the value no for the sys argument to make TKPROF omit these statements.

explain: Writes execution plans to the output file; TKPROF connects to the database and issues explain plan statements using the username and password you provide with this parameter.

table: By default, TKPROF uses a table named PLAN_TABLE in the schema of the user specified by the explain parameter, to store the execution plans. You can specify an alternate table with the table parameter.

width: This is an integer that determines the output line widths of some types of output, such as the explain plan information.

10-8. Analyzing TKPROF Output

Problem

You've formatted a trace file with TKPROF, and you now want to analyze the TKPROF output file.

CHAPTER 10 ■ TRACING SQL EXECUTION

Solution

Invoke the TKPROF utility with the tkprof command as shown here:

```
c:\>tkprof orcl1_ora_6448_mytrace1.trc ora6448.prf explain=hr/hr sys=no
sort=prsela,exeela,fchela

TKPROF: Release 11.2.0.1.0 - Development on Sat May 14 11:36:35 2011

Copyright (c) 1982, 2009, Oracle and/or its affiliates.  All rights reserved.

c:\app\ora\diag\rdbms\orcl1\orcl1\trace>
```

In this example, orcl1_ora_6448_mytrace1.trc is the trace file you want to format. The ora6448.prf file is the TKPROF output file. The "How it Works" section that follows shows how to interpret a TKPROF output file.

How It Works

In our example, there's only a single SQL statement. Thus, the sort parameters (prsecla, exeela, fchela) don't really matter, because they come into play only when TKPROF needs to list multiple SQL statements. Here's a brief description of the key sections in a TKPROF output file.

Header

The header section shows the trace file name, the sort options, and a description of the terms used in the output file.

```
Trace file: orcl1_ora_6448_mytrace1.trc
Sort options: prsela  exeela  fchela
********************************************************************************
count    = number of times OCI procedure was executed
cpu      = cpu time in seconds executing
elapsed  = elapsed time in seconds executing
disk     = number of physical reads of buffers from disk
query    = number of buffers gotten for consistent read
current  = number of buffers gotten in current mode (usually for update)
rows     = number of rows processed by the fetch or execute call
********************************************************************************
```

Execution Statistics

TKPPROF lists execution statistics for each SQL statement in the trace file. TKPROF lists the execution statistics for the three steps that are part of SQL statement processing: parse, execute, and fetch.

call	count	cpu	elapsed	disk	query	current	rows
Parse	1	0.01	0.03	0	64	0	0
Execute	1	0.00	0.00	0	0	0	0
Fetch	5461	0.29	0.40	0	1299	0	81901
total	5463	0.31	0.43	0	1363	0	81901

The following is what the SQL execution statistics in the table stand for:

count: The number of times the database parsed, executed, or fetched this statement

cpu: The CPU time used for the parse/execute/fetch phases

elapsed: Total elapsed time (in seconds) for the parse/execute/fetch phases

disk: Number of physical block reads for the parse/execute/fetch phases

query: Number of data blocks read with logical reads from the buffer cache in consistent mode for the parse/fetch/execute phases (for a select statement)

current: Number of data blocks read and retrieved with logical reads from the buffer cache in current mode (for insert, update, delete, and merge statements)

rows: Number of fetched rows for a select statement or the number of rows inserted, deleted, or updated, respectively, for an insert, delete, update, or merge statement

Row Source Operations

The next section of the report shows the number of misses in the library cache, the current optimizer mode, and the row source operations for the query. Row source operations show the number of rows that the database processes for each operation such as joins or full table scans.

```
Misses in library cache during parse: 1
Optimizer mode: ALL_ROWS
Parsing user id: 85  (HR)


Rows     Row Source Operation
-------  --------------------------------------------------
  81901  HASH JOIN  (cr=1299 pr=0 pw=0 time=3682295 us cost=22 size=41029632 card=217088)
   1728    TABLE ACCESS FULL DEPT (cr=16 pr=0 pw=0 time=246 us cost=6 size=96768 card=1728)
   1291    TABLE ACCESS FULL EMP (cr=1283 pr=0 pw=0 time=51213 us cost=14 size=455392
card=3424)
```

The "Misses in library cache during parse" indicates the number of hard parses during the parse and execute database calls. In the Row Source Operation column, the output includes several statistics for each row source operation. These statistics quantify the various types of work performed during a row source operation. The following is what the different statistics stand for (you may not see all of these for every query):

cr: Blocks retrieved through a logical read in the consistent mode

pr: Number of blocks read through a physical disk read

pw: Number of blocks written with a physical write to a disk time: Total time (in milliseconds) spent processing the operation

cost: Estimated cost of the operation

size: Estimated amount of data (bytes) returned by the operation

card: Estimated number of rows returned by the operation

The Execution Plan

If you specified the explain parameter when issuing the tkprof command, you'll find an execution table showing the execution plan for each SQL statement.

```
Rows     Execution Plan
-------  ----------------------------------------
      0  SELECT STATEMENT    MODE: ALL_ROWS
  81901    HASH JOIN
   1728      TABLE ACCESS (FULL) OF 'DEPT' (TABLE)
   1291      TABLE ACCESS (FULL) OF 'EMP' (TABLE)
```

In our example, the execution plan shows that there were two full table scans, and a hash join following it.

Wait Events

You'll see the wait events section only if you've specified waits=>true in your trace command. The wait events table summarizes waits during the trace period:

```
Elapsed times include waiting on following events:
  Event waited on                           Times    Max. Wait  Total Waited
  ------------------------------------      Waited   ---------  ------------
  SQL*Net message from client               5461      112.95        462.81
  db file sequential read                      1        0.05          0.05

********************************************************************************
```

In this example, the SQL*Net message to client waits account for most of the waits, but these are idle waits. If you see wait events such as the db file sequential read event or the db file scattered read event with a significant number of waits (and/or total wait time), you need to investigate those wait events further.

Note that the TKPROF output doesn't show you information about any bind variables. It also doesn't show any waits due to enqueue locks.

10-9. Analyzing Trace Files with Oracle Trace Analyzer

Problem

You want to use the Oracle Trace Analyzer to analyze trace files.

Solution

The Oracle Trace Analyzer, also known as TRCANLZR or TRCA, is a SQL trace profiling tool that's an alternative to the TKPROF utility. You must download the TRCA from Oracle Support. Once you download TRCA, unzip the files and install TRCA by executing the /trca/install/trcreate.sql script.

Once you install TRCA, you must log in as a user with the SYSDBA privilege to execute the tacreate.sql script. The tacreate.sql generates the formatted output files for any traces you've generated. The script asks you for information relating to the location of the trace files, the output file, and the tablespace where you want TRCA to store its data.

Here are the steps for installing and running TRCA.

1. Installing TRCA is straightforward, so we just show you a summary of the installation here:

```
SQL> @tacreate.sql
Uninstalling TRCA, please wait
TADOBJ completed.
SQL>
SQL> WHENEVER SQLERROR EXIT SQL.SQLCODE;
SQL> REM If this DROP USER command fails that means a session is connected wi
this user.
SQL> DROP USER trcanlzr CASCADE;
SQL> WHENEVER SQLERROR CONTINUE;
SQL>
SQL> SET ECHO OFF;
TADUSR completed.
TADROP completed.

Creating TRCA$ INPUT/BDUMP/STAGE Server Directories
...

TACREATE completed. Installation completed successfully.
SQL>
```

2. Set up tracing.

```
SQL> alter session set events '10046 trace name context forever, level 12';

System altered.

SQL>
```

3. Execute the SQL statement you want to trace.

```
SQL> select …
```

4. Turn off tracing.

```
SQL> alter session set events '10046 trace name context off';
System altered.

SQL>
```

5. Run the /trca/run/trcanlzr script (START trcanlzr.sql) to profile the trace you've just generated. You must pass the trace file name as input to this script:

```
c:\trace\trca\trca\run>sqlplus hr/hr
SQL> START trcanlzr.sql orcl1_ora_7460_mytrace7.trc
Parameter 1:
Trace Filename or control_file.txt (required)
Value passed to trcanlzr.sql:
~~~~~~~~~~~~~~~~~~~~~~~~~~~~~~~
TRACE_FILENAME: orcl1_ora_7460_mytrace7.trc
Analyzing orcl1_ora_7460_mytrace7.trc
... analyzing trace(s) ...
Trace Analyzer completed.
Review first trcanlzr_error.log file for possible fatal errors.
TKPROF: Release 11.2.0.1.0 - Development on Sat May 14 15:59:13 2011
    ...
    233387  05/14/2011 15:59   trca_e21106.html
    115885  05/14/2011 15:59   trca_e21106.txt
File trca_e21106.zip has been created
TRCANLZR completed.
SQL>
c:\trace\trca\trca\run>
```

You can now view the profiled trace data in text or HTML format—TRCA provides both of these in the ZIP file that it creates when it completes profiling the trace file. TRCA places the ZIP file in the directory from which you run the /trca/run/trcanlzr.sql script.

How It Works

Oracle Support Center of Expertise (CoE) provides the TRCA diagnostic tool. Although many DBAs are aware of the TRCA, few use it on regular basis. Some of us have used it in response to a request by Oracle Support. As you learned in the "Solution" section, the TRCA tool accepts a SQL trace generated by you and outputs a diagnostic report in both text and HTML formats. The TRCA tool also provides you a TKPROF report (it executes the tkprof command as part of its diagnostic data collection). Since TRCA provides a rich set of diagnostic information, consider using it instead of TKPROF.

Apart from the data normally collected by the TKPROF utility, TRCA also identifies expensive SQL statements and gathers their explain plans. It also shows the optimizer statistics and configuration parameters that have a bearing on the performance of the SQL statements in the trace.

■ **Tip**   Use TRCA instead of TKPROF for analyzing your trace files—it provides you a wealth of diagnostic information, besides giving you a TKPROF output file as part of the bargain.

In our example, we used TRCA to format a trace file on the same system where we generated the trace. However, if you can't install TRCA in a production system, not to worry. TRCA can also analyze production traces using a different system. The details are in the trca_instructions HTML document, which is part of the TRCA download ZIP file.

Here are the major sections of a TRCA report, and as you can see already, the report offers a richer set of diagnostic information than that offered by TKPROF.

Summary: Provides a breakdown of elapsed time, response time broken down into CPU and non-idle wait time, and other response time-related information

Non-Recursive Time and Totals: Provides a breakdown of response time and elapsed time during the parse, execute, and fetch steps; the report also contains a table that provides total and average waits for each idle and non-idle wait event.

Top SQL: Provides detailed information about SQL statements that account for the most response time, elapsed time, and CPU time, as shown in the following extract from the report:

```
There are 2 SQL statements with "Response Time Accounted-for" larger than threshold of
10.0% of the "Total Response Time Accounted-for".
These combined 2 SQL statements are responsible for a total of 99.3% of the "Total
Response Time Accounted-for".

There are 3 SQL statements with "Elapsed Time" larger than threshold of 10.0% of the
"Total Elapsed Time".
These combined 3 SQL statements are responsible for a total of 75.5% of the "Total Elapsed
Time".

There is only one SQL statement with "CPU Time" larger than threshold of 10.0% of the
"Total CPU Time".
```

Individual SQL: This is a highly useful section, as it lists all SQL statements and shows their elapsed time, response time, and CPU time. It provides the hash values and SQL IDs of each statement.

SQL Self - Time, Totals, Waits, Binds and Row Source Plan: Shows parse, execute, and fetch statistics for each statement, similar to the TKPROF utility; it also shows the wait event breakdown (average and total times) for each statement. There's also a very nice explain plan for each statement, which shows the time and the cost of each execution step.

Tables and Indexes: Shows the number of rows, partitioning status, the sample size, and the last time the object was analyzed; for indexes, it additionally shows the clustering factor and the number of keys.

Summary: Shows I/O related wait (such as the db file sequential read event) information including average and total waits, for tables and indexes

Hot I/O Blocks: Shows the list of blocks with the largest wait time or times waited

Non-default Initialization Parameters: Lists all non-default initialization parameters

As this brief review of TRCA shows, it's a far superior tool than TKPROF. Besides, if you happen to love TKPROF reports, it includes them as well in its ZIP file. So, what are you waiting for? Download the TRCA and benefit from its rich diagnostic profiling of problem SQL statements.

10-10. Tracing a Parallel Query

Problem

You'd like to trace a parallel query.

Solution

You can get an event 10046 trace for a parallel query in the same way as you would for any other query. The only difference is that the 10046 event will generate as many trace files as the number of parallel query servers. Here's an example:

```
SQL>alter session set tracefile_identifier='MyTrace1';

SQL> alter session set events '10046 trace name context forever, level 12';

Session altered.

SQL> select /*+ full(sales) parallel (sales 6) */ count(quantity_sold) from
    sales;

COUNT(QUANTITY_SOLD)
--------------------
            918843

SQL> alter session set events '10046 trace name context off';

Session altered.

SQL>
```

You'll now see a total of seven trace files with the trace file identifier MyTrace1 in the trace directory. Depending on what you're looking for, you can analyze each of the trace files separately, or consolidate them into one big trace file with the trcsess utility before analyzing it with TKPROF or another profiler such as the Oracle Trace Analyzer. You'll also find several files with the suffix .trm in the trace directory—you can ignore these files, as they are for use by the database.

How It Works

The only real difference between getting an extended trace for a single query and one for a parallel query is that you'll have multiple trace files, one for each parallel query server. When a user executes a parallel query, Oracle creates multiple parallel query processes to process the query, with each process getting its own session. That's the reason Oracle creates multiple trace files for a parallel query.

Once you turn off the trace, go to the trace directory and execute the following command to find all the trace files for the parallel query:

```
$ find . -name '*MyTrace1*'
```

The find command lists all the trace files for your parallel query (ignore the files ending with .trm in the trace directory). You can move the trace files to another directory and use the trcsess utility to consolidate those files, as shown here:

```
$ trcsess output=MyTrace1.trc clientid='px_test1' orcl1_ora_8432_mytrace1.trc
orcl1_ora_8432_mytrace2.trc
```

You're now ready to use the TKPROF utility to profile the parallel query.

When you issue a parallel query, the parallel execution coordinator/query coordinator (QC) controls the execution of the query. The parallel execution servers/slaves (QS) do the actual work. The parallel execution server *set* is the set of all the query servers that execute an operation. The query coordinator and each of the execution servers generate their own trace files. For example, if one of the slave processes waits for a resource, the database records the resulting wait events in that slave process's trace file, but not in the query coordinator's trace file.

Note that if you're using a 10.2 or an older release, the trace files for the user process will be created in the user dump directory and the background processes (slaves) will generate trace files in the background dump directory. In 11.1 and newer databases, the trace files for both background and user processes are in the same directory (trace). You can find the trace file names by issuing the show tracefile -t command after invoking ADRCI, or by querying the V$DIAG_INFO view from SQL*Plus.

10-11. Tracing Specific Parallel Query Processes

Problem

You want to trace one or more specific parallel query processes.

Solution

Identify the parallel query processes you want to trace with the following command.

```
SQL> select inst_id,p.server_name,
     p.status as p_status,
     p.pid as p_pid,
     p.sid as p_sid
     from  gv$px_process p
     order by p.server_name;
```

Let's say you decide to trace the processes p002 and p003. Issue the following alter system set events command to trace just these two parallel processes.

```
SQL> alter system set events 'sql_trace  {process: pname = p002 | p003}';
```

Once you're done tracing, turn off the trace by issuing the following command:

```
SQL> alter system set events 'sql_trace  {process: pname = p002 | p003} off';
```

How It Works

Tracing parallel processes is always tricky. One of the improvements made to the tracing infrastructure in the Oracle Database 11g release is the capability to trace a specific statement or a set of statements. This capability comes in handy when there are a large number of SQL statements being executed by a session and you're sure about the identity of the SQL statement whose execution you want to trace.

10-12. Tracing Parallel Queries in a RAC System

Problem

You're tracing a parallel query in a RAC environment, but aren't sure in which instance the trace files are located.

Solution

Finding the trace files for the server (or thread or slave) processes is sometimes difficult in a RAC environment, because you aren't sure on which node or node(s) the database has created the trace files. Here are the steps to follow to make it easier to find the trace files on the different nodes.

1. Set the px_trace with an alter session command, to help identify the trace files, as shown here:

    ```
    SQL> alter session set tracefile_identifier='10046';
    SQL> alter session set  "_px_trace" = low , messaging;
    SQL> alter session set events '10046 trace name context forever,level 12';
    ```

2. Execute your parallel query.

    ```
    SQL> alter table bigsales (parallel 4);
    SQL> select count(*) from bigsales;
    ```

3. Turn all tracing off.

    ```
    SQL> alter session set events '10046 trace name context off';
    SQL> alter session set "_px_trace" = none;
    ```

Specifying px_trace will cause the query coordinator's trace file to include information about the slave processes that are part of the query, and the instance each slave process belongs to. You can then retrieve the trace files from the instances listed in the query coordinator's trace file.

How It Works

The _px_trace (px trace) parameter is an undocumented, internal Oracle parameter that has existed since the 9.2 release. Once you run the trace commands as shown in the "Solution" section of this recipe, the trace file for the query coordinator (QC) process will show within it the name of each of the slave processes and the instances the processes have run on—for example:

```
Acquired 4 slaves on 1 instances avg height=4 in 1 set q serial:2049
        P000 inst 1 spid 7512
        P001 inst 1 spid 4088
        P002 inst 1 spid 7340
        P003 inst 1 spid 9256
```

In this case, you know that Instance 1 is where you must look to get the trace files for the slave processes P000, P001, P002, and P003. On Instance 1, in the ADR trace subdirectory, look for file names that contain the words P000 (or P001/P002/P003), to identify the correct trace files.

10-13. Consolidating Multiple Trace Files

Problem

You have generated multiple trace files for a session in order to tune performance, and you want to consolidate those files into a single trace file.

Solution

Use the `trcsess` command to merge multiple trace files into a single trace file. Here's a simple example:

```
c:\trace> trcsess output=combined.trc session=196.614 orcl1_ora_8432_mytrace1.trc
orcl1_ora_8432_mytrace2.trc
C:\trace>
```

The `trcsess` command shown here combines two trace files generated for a session into a single trace file. The session parameter identifies the session with a session identifier, consisting of the session index and session serial number, which you can get from the **V$SESSION** view.

How It Works

The `trcsess` utility is part of the Oracle database and helps by letting you consolidate multiple trace files during performance tuning and debugging exercises. Here's the syntax of the `trcsess` command:

```
trcsess [output=output_file_name]
        [session=session_id]
        [client_id=cleint_id]
        [service=service_name]
        [action=action_name]
        [module=module_name]
        [trace_files]
```

You must specify one of these five options when issuing the `trcess` command: `session`, `client_id`, `service`, `action`, and `module`. For example, if you issue the command in the following manner, the command includes all the trace files in the current directory for a session and combines them into a single file:

```
$ trcsess output=main.trc session=196.614
```

In our example, we specified the name of the consolidated trace file with the `output` option. If you don't specify the output option, `trcsess` prints the output to standard out. Once you use `trcsess` to combine the output of multiple trace files into one consolidated file, you can use the `TKPROF` utility to analyze the file, just as you'd do in the case of a single trace file.

10-14. Finding the Correct Session for Tracing

Problem

You want to initiate a session trace for a user from your own session, and you would like to find out the correct session to trace.

Solution

You must have the `SID` and the serial number for the user whose session you want to trace. You can find these from the `V$SESSION` view, of course, once you know the user's name. However, you must get several other details about the user's session to identify the correct session, since the user may have multiple sessions open. Use the following query to get the user's information:

```
SQL> select a.sid, a.serial#, b.spid, b.pid,
     a.username, a.osuser, a.machine
     from
     v$session a,
     v$process b
     where a.username IS NOT NULL
     and a.paddr=b.addr;
```

The query provides several attributes such as `USERNAME`, `OSUSER`, and `MACHINE`, which help you unambiguously select the correct session.

How It Works

You can't always rely on the first set of `SID` and serial number you manage to find for the user whose session you want to trace. Together, the `SID` and serial number uniquely identify a session. However, you may find multiple `SID` and serial number combinations for the same user, because your database may be using common user logins. Therefore, querying the `V$SESSION` view for other information such as `OSUSER` and `MACHINE` besides the `SID` and serial number helps to identify the correct user session.

`V$SESSION` view columns such as `COMMAND`, `SERVER`, `LOGON_TIME`, `PROGRAM`, and `LAST_CALL_ET` help identify the correct session to trace. If you still can't find the correct session, you may want to join the `V$SESSION` and `V$SQLAREA` views to identify the correct session.

10-15. Tracing a SQL Session

Problem

You want to turn on SQL tracing for a session to diagnose a performance problem.

Solution

There are multiple ways to trace a session, but the Oracle-recommended approach is to use the DBMS_MONITOR package to access the SQL tracing facility. To trace a session, first identify the session with the following command, assuming you know either the username or the SID for the session:

```
SQL> select sid, serial#, username from v$session;
```

Once you get the SID and SERIAL# from the previous query, invoke the session_trace_enable procedure of the DBMS_MONITOR package, as shown here:

```
SQL> execute dbms_monitor.session_trace_enable(session_id=>138,serial_num=>242,
waits=>true,binds=>false);
PL/SQL procedure successfully completed.
SQL>
```

▨ **Caution** SQL tracing does impose an overhead on the database—you need to be very selective in tracing sessions in a production environment, as a trace can fill up a disk or affect CPU usage adversely.

In this example, we chose to trace the wait information as well, but it's optional. Once you execute this command, have the user execute the SQL statements that you're testing (in a dev or test environment). In a production environment, wait for a long enough period to make sure you've captured the execution of the SQL statements, before turning the tracing off. Invoke the session_trace_disable procedure to disable the SQL tracing for the session, as shown here:

```
SQL> execute dbms_monitor.session_trace_disable();
PL/SQL procedure successfully completed.
SQL>
```

Once you complete tracing the session activity, you can get the trace file for the session from the trace directory and use the TKPROF utility (or a different profiler) to get a report. The trace file will have the suffix mytrace1, the value you set as the trace file identifier.

To trace the current user session, use the following pair of commands:

```
SQL> execute dbms_monitor.session_trace_enable();
SQL> execute dbms_monitor.session_trace_disable();
```

How It Works

Tracing an entire session is expensive in terms of resource usage and you must do so only when you haven't identified a poorly performing SQL statement already. A session trace gathers the following types of information.

- Physical and logical reads for each statement that's running in the session

- CPU and elapsed times

- Number of rows processed by each statement

- Misses in the library cache

- Number of commits and rollbacks

- Row operations that show the actual execution plan for each statement

- Wait events for each SQL statement

■ **Note** You need the DBA role to execute procedures and functions in the DBMS_MONITOR package.

You can specify the following parameters for the session_trace_enable procedure:

session_id: Identifies the session you want to trace (SID); if you omit this, your own session will be traced.

serial_num: Serial number for the session

waits: Set it to true if you want to capture wait information (default = false).

binds: Set it to true to capture bind information (default=false).

plan_stat: Determines the frequency with which the row source statistics (execution plan and execution statistics) are dumped

All the parameters for the session_trace_enable procedure are self-evident, except the plan_stat parameter. You can set the following values for this parameter:

never: The trace file won't contain any information about row source operations.

first_execution (same as setting the plan_stat parameter to the value null): Row source information is written once, after the first execution of a statement.

all_executions: Execution plan and execution statistics are written for each execution of the cursor, instead of only when the cursor is closed.

Since an execution plan for a statement can change during the course of a program run, you may want to set the plan_stat parameter to the value all_executions if you want to capture all possible execution plans for a statement.

10-16. Tracing a Session by Process ID

Problem

You want to identify and trace a session using an operating system process ID.

Solution

Execute the `alter session` (or `alter system`) `set events` command to trace a session by its operating system process ID, which is shown by the `SPID` column in the `V$PROCESS` view. The general format of this command is as follows:

```
alter session set events 'sql_trace {process:pid}'
```

Here are the steps to tracing a session by its OS PID.

1. Get the OS process ID by querying the `V$PROCESS` view.

   ```
   SQL> select spid,pname from v$process;
   ```

2. Once you identify the SPID of the user, issue the following statement to start the trace for that session:

   ```
   SQL> alter session set events 'sql_trace {process:2714}';
   Session altered.
   SQL>
   ```

3. Turn off tracing the following way:

   ```
   SQL> alter session set events 'sql_trace {process:2714} off';
   Session altered.
   SQL>
   ```

   You can also execute the `set events` command in the following manner, to concatenate two processes:

   ```
   SQL> alter system set events 'sql_trace {process:2714|2936}';
   System altered.
   SQL> alter system set events 'sql_trace {process:2714|2936} off';
   System altered.
   SQL>
   ```

When you concatenate two processes, the database generates two separate trace files, one for each process, as shown here:

```
orcl1_ora_2714.trc
orcl1_ora_2936.trc
```

How It Works

In Oracle Database 11g, the `alter session set events` command has been enhanced to allow you to trace a process by specifying the process ID (PID), process name (PNAME), or the Oracle Process ID

(ORAPID). You can also use an `alter system` command with the same general syntax as well. Here's the syntax of the command:

```
alter session set events 'sql_trace {process : pid = <pid>, pname = <pname>, orapid =
<orapid>} rest of event specification'
```

The `V$PROCESS` view contains information about all currently active processes. In the `V$PROCESS` view, the following columns help you identify the three process-related values:

```
PID: the Oracle process identifier
SPID: the Operating System process identifier
PNAME: name of the process
```

In this recipe, we showed how to generate a trace file using the OS process identifier (`SPID` column in the `V$PROCESS` view). You can use the general syntax shown here to generate a trace using the PID or the process name.

10-17. Tracing Multiple Sessions

Problem

You want to trace multiple SQL sessions that belong to a single user.

Solution

You can trace multiple sessions that belong to a user by using the `client_id_trace_enable` procedure from the `DBMS_MONITOR` package. Before you can execute the `dbms_monitor.client_id_trace_enable` procedure, you must set the `client_identifier` for the session by using the `DBMS_SESSION` package, as shown here:

```
SQL> execute dbms_session.set_identifier('SH')
```

Once you set the client identifier as shown here, the `client_identifier` column in the `V$SESSION` view is populated. You can confirm the value of the `client_identifier` column by executing the following statement:

```
SQL> select sid, serial#,username from v$session where client_identifier='SH';
```

Now you can execute the `dbms_monitor.client_id_trace_enable` procedure:

```
SQL> execute dbms_monitor.client_id_trace_enable(client_id=>'SH', waits=>true, binds=>false);
```

You can disable the trace with the following command:

```
SQL> execute dbms_monitor.client_id_trace_disable(client_id=>'SH');
```

How It Works

Setting the `client_identifier` column lets you enable the tracing of multiple sessions, when several users may be connecting as the same Oracle user, especially in applications that use connection pools. The `client_id_trace_enable` procedure collects statistics for all sessions with a specific client ID.

Note that the `client_id` that you must specify doesn't have to belong to a currently active session. By default, the waits and binds parameters are set to `false` and you can set the tracing of both waits and binds by adding those parameters when you execute the `client_id_trace_enable` procedure:

```
SQL> exec dbms_monitor.client_id_trace_enable('SH',true,true);
```

PL/SQL procedure successfully completed.

You can query the `DBA_ENABLED_TRACES` view to find the status of a trace that you executed with a client identifier. In this view, the column `TRACE_TYPE` shows the value `CLIENT_ID` and the `PRIMARY_ID` shows the value of the client identifier.

```
SQL> select trace_type, primary_id,waits,binds from dba_enabled_traces;
```

TRACE_TYPE	PRIMARY_ID	WAITS	BINDS
CLIENT_ID	SH	TRUE	TRUE

10-18. Tracing an Instance or a Database

Problem

You want to trace the execution of all SQL statements in the entire instance or database.

Solution

Use the `dbms_monitor.database_trace_enable` procedure to trace a specific instance or an entire database. Issue the following pair of commands to start and stop tracing for an *individual instance*.

```
SQL> execute dbms_monitor.database_trace_enable(instance_name=>'instance1');
SQL> execute dbms_monitor.database_trace_disable(instance_name=>'instance1');
```

You can optionally specify the waits and binds attributes. The following commands enable and disable SQL tracing at the *database level*:

```
SQL> execute dbms_monitor.database_trace_enable();
SQL> execute dbms_monitor.database_trace_disable();
```

You can also set the `sql_trace` initialization parameter to `true` to turn on and turn off SQL tracing, but this parameter is deprecated. Oracle recommends that you use the `dbms_monitor` (or the `dbms_session`) package for SQL tracing.

How It Works

Obviously, instance-level and database-level SQL tracing is going to impose a serious overhead, and may well turn out to be another source of performance problems! You normally don't ever have to do this—use the session-level tracing instead to identify performance problems. If you must trace an entire instance, because you don't know from which session a query may be executed, turn off tracing as soon as possible, to reduce the overhead.

10-19. Generating an Event 10046 Trace for a Session

Problem

You want to get an Oracle event 10046 trace for a session.

Solution

You can get an Oracle event 10046 trace, also called an extended trace, by following these steps:

1. Set your trace file identifier.

    ```
    SQL> alter session set tracefile_identifier='10046';
    ```

2. Issue the following statement to start the trace.

    ```
    SQL> alter session set events '10046 trace name context forever, level 12'
    ```

3. Execute the SQL statement(s) that you want to trace.

    ```
    SQL> select sum(amount_sold) from sales;
    ```

4. Turn tracing off with the following command:

    ```
    SQL> alter session set events '10046 trace name context off';
    ```

You'll find the trace dump file in the trace directory that's specified by the `diagnostic_dest` parameter (`$DIAG_HOME/rdbms/db/inst/trace`). You can analyze this trace file with `TKPROF` or another utility such as the Oracle Trace Analyzer.

How It Works

Here's what the various keywords in the syntax for setting a 10046 trace mean:

`set events`: Sets a specific Oracle event, in this case, the event 10046

`10046`: Specifies when an action should be taken

`trace`: The database must take this action when the event (10046) occurs.

`name`: Indicates the type of dump or trace

`context`: Specifies that Oracle should generate a context-specific trace; if you replace `context` with `errorstack`, the database will not trace the SQL statement. It dumps the error stack when it hits the 10046 event.

`forever`: Specifying the keyword `forever` tells the database to invoke the action (trace) every time the event (10046) is invoked, until you disable the 10046 trace. If you omit the keyword `forever`, the action is invoked just once, following which the event is automatically disabled.

`level 12`: Specifies the trace level—in this case, it captures both bind and wait information.

While the Oracle event 10046 has existed for several years, this trace is identical to the trace you can generate with the `session_trace_enable` procedure of the `DBMS_MONITOR` package:

```
SQL> execute dbms_monitor.session_trace_enable(session_id=>99,
serial_num=>88,waits=>true,binds=>true);
```

Both the 10046 event and the `dbms_monitor.session_trace_enable` procedure shown here generate identical tracing information, called extended tracing because the trace includes wait and bind variable data.

If you aren't using the new diagnostic infrastructure (ADR) introduced in Oracle Database 11g, make sure you set the dump file size to the value `unlimited`, as the 10046 trace often produces very large trace files, and the database will truncate the dump file if there isn't enough space in the trace dump directory.

The level of tracing you specify for the 10046 trace determines which types of information is gathered by the trace. The default level is 1, which collects basic information. Level 4 allows you to capture the bind variable values, which are shown as `:bi`, `:b2`, and so on. You can see the actual values that Oracle substitutes for each of the bind variables. Level 8 provides all the information from a Level 1 trace plus details about all the wait events during the course of the execution of the SQL query. A Level 12 trace is a combination of the Level 4 and Level 8 traces, meaning it'll include both bind variable and wait information. Level 16 is new in Oracle Database 11g, and provides STAT line dumps for each execution of the query. Note that this is the same as setting the value `all_executions` for the `plan_level` parameter when you trace with the `dbms_monitor.session_trace_enable` procedure.

■ **Tip**   If the session doesn't close cleanly before you disable tracing, your trace file may not include important trace information.

While getting a 10046 trace and analyzing it does provide valuable information regarding the usage of bind variables and the wait events, you need to be careful about when to trace sessions. If the instance as a whole is poorly performing, your tracing might even make performance worse due to overhead imposed by running the trace. In addition, it takes time to complete the trace, run it through `TKPROF` or some other profiler, and go through the dozens of SQL statements in the report. Here is a general strategy that has worked for us in our own work:

If you're diagnosing general performance problems, a good first step would be to get an AWR report, ideally taking several snapshots spaced 1–15 minutes apart. Often, you can identify the problem from a review of the AWR report. The report will highlight things such as inefficient SQL statements, contention of various types, memory issues, latching, and full table scans that are affecting performance. You can get all this information without running a 10046 trace.

Run a 10046 trace when a user reports a problem and you can't identify a problem through the AWR reports. If you've clearly identified a process that is performing poorly, you can trace the relevant session. You can also run this trace in a development environment to help developers understand the query execution details and tune their queries.

10-20. Generating an Event 10046 Trace for an Instance

Problem

You want to trace a problem SQL query, but you can't identify the session in advance. You would like to trace all SQL statements executed by the instance.

Solution

You can turn on tracing at the instance level with the following `alter system` command, after connecting to the instance you want to trace.

```
SQL> alter system set events '10046 trace name context forever,level 12';
```

The previous command enables the tracing of all sessions that start after you issue the command—it won't trace sessions that are already connected.

You disable the trace by issuing the following command:

```
SQL> alter system set events '10046 trace name context off';
```

This command disables tracing for all sessions.

How It Works

Instance-wide tracing helps in cases where you know a problem query is running, but there's no way to identify the session ahead of time. Make sure that you enable instance-wide tracing only when you have no other alternative, and turn it off as soon as you capture the necessary diagnostic information. Any instance-wide tracing is going to not only generate very large trace files in a busy environment, but also contribute significantly to the system workload.

10-21. Setting a Trace in a Running Session

Problem

You want to set a trace in a session, but the session has already started.

■ **Note** A user who phones to ask for help with a long-running query is a good example of a case in which you might want to initiate a trace in a currently executing session. Some business-intelligence queries, for example, run for dozens of minutes, even hours, so there is time to initiate a trace mid-query and diagnose a performance problem.

Solution

You can set a trace in a running session using the operating system process ID (PID), with the help of the oradebug utility. Once you identify the PID of the session you want to trace, issue the following commands to trace the session.

```
SQL> connect / as sysdba
SQL> oradebug setospid <SPID>
SQL> oradebug unlimit
SQL> oradebug event 10046 trace name context forever,level 12
SQL> oradebug event 10046 trace name context off
```

In the example shown here, we specified Level 12, but as with the 10046 trace you set with the alter session command, you can specify the lower tracing levels 4 or 8.

How It Works

The oradebug utility comes in handy when you can't access the session you want to trace, or when the session has already started before you can set tracing. oradebug lets you attach to the session and start the SQL tracing. If you aren't sure about the operating system PID (or SPID) associated with an Oracle session, you can find it with the following query.

```
SQL> select p.PID,p.SPID,s.SID
  2  from v$process p,v$session s
  3  where s.paddr = p.addr
  4* and s.sid = &SESSION_ID
```

oradebug is only a facility that allows you to set tracing—it's not a tracing procedure by itself. The results of the 10046 trace you obtain with the oradebug command are identical to those you obtain with a normal event 10046 trace command.

In the example shown in the "Solution" section, we use the OS PID of the Oracle users. You can also specify the Oracle Process Identifier (PID) to trace a session, instead of the OS PID.

```
SQL> connect / as sysdba
SQL> oradebug setorapid 9834
SQL> oradebug unlimit
SQL> oradebug event 10046 trace name context forever,level 12
```

In an Oracle RAC environment, as is the case with all other types of Oracle tracing, make sure you connect to the correct instance before starting the trace. As an alternative to using oradebug, you can use the dbms_system.set_sql_trace_in_session procedure to set a trace in a running session. Note that DBMS_SYSTEM is an older package, and the recommended way to trace sessions starting with the Oracle Database 10g release is to use the DBMS_MONITOR package.

10-22. Enabling Tracing in a Session After a Login

Problem

You want to trace a user's session, but that session starts executing queries immediately after it logs in.

Solution

If a session immediately begins executing a query after it logs in, it doesn't give you enough time to get the session information and start tracing the session. In cases like this, you can create a *logon trigger* that automatically starts tracing the session once the session starts. Here is one way to create a logon trigger to set up a trace for sessions created by a specific user:

```
SQL> create or replace trigger trace_my_user
  2     after logon on database
  3     begin
  4      if user='SH' then
  5      dbms_monitor.session_trace_enable(null,null,true,true);
  6      end if;
  8*    end;
SQL> /

Trigger created.

SQL>
```

Before creating the logon trigger, make sure that you grant the user the `alter session` privileges, as shown here:

```
SQL> grant alter session to sh,hr;

Grant succeeded.
SQL>
```

How It Works

Often, you find it hard to trace session activity because the session already starts executing statements before you can set up the trace. This is especially so in a RAC environment, where it is harder for the DBA to identify the instance and quickly set up tracing for a running session. A logon trigger is the perfect solution for such cases. Note that in a RAC environment, the database generates the trace files in the trace directory of the instance to which a user connected.

A logon trigger for tracing sessions is useful for tracing SQL statements issued by a specific user, by setting the trace as soon as the user logs in. From that point on, the database traces all SQL statements issued by that user. Make sure you disable the tracing and drop the logon trigger once you complete tracing the SQL statements you are interested in. Remember to revoke the `alter session` privilege from the user as well.

10-23. Tracing the Optimizer's Execution Path

Problem

You want to trace the cost-based optimizer (CBO) to examine the execution path for a SQL statement.

Solution

You can trace the optimizer's execution path by setting the Oracle event 10053. Here are the steps.

1. Set the trace identifier for the trace file.

```
SQL> alter session set tracefile_identifier='10053_trace1'
Session altered.
SQL>
```

2. Issue the `alter session set events` statement to start the trace.

```
SQL> alter session set events '10053 trace name context forever,level 1';
Session altered.
SQL>
```

3. Execute the SQL statement whose execution path you want to trace.

```
SQL> select * from users
  2  where user_id=88 and
  3  account_status='OPEN'
  4  and username='SH';
...
SQL>
```

4. Turn the tracing off.

```
SQL> alter session set events '10053 trace name context off';
Session altered.
SQL>
```

You can examine the raw trace file directly to learn how the optimizer went about its business in selecting the execution plan for the SQL statement.

How It Works

An event 10053 trace gives you insight into the way the optimizer does its job in selecting the optimal execution plan for a SQL statement. For example, you may wonder why the optimizer didn't use an index in a specific case—the event 10053 trace shows you the logic used by the optimizer in skipping that index. The optimizer considers the available statistics for all objects in the query and evaluates various join orders and access paths. The event 10053 trace also reveals all the evaluations performed by the optimizer and how it arrived at the best join order and the best access path to use in executing a query.

You can set either Level 1 or Level 2 for the event 10053 trace. Level 2 captures the following types of information:

- Column statistics

- Single access paths

- Table joins considered by the optimizer

- Join costs

- Join methods considered by the optimizer

A Level 1 trace includes all the foregoing, plus a listing of all the default initialization parameters used by the optimizer. You'll also find detailed index statistics used by the optimizer in determining the best execution plan. The trace file captures the amazing array of statistics considered by the cost optimizer, and explains how the CBO creates the execution plan. Here are some of the important things you'll find in the CBO trace file.

- List of all internal optimizer-related initialization parameters

- Peeked values of the binds in the SQL statement

- Final query after optimizer transformations

- System statistics (CPUSPEEDNW, IOTFRSPEED, IOSEEKTIM, MBRC)

- Access path analysis for all objects in the query

- Join order evaluation

Unlike a raw 10046 event trace file, a 10053 event trace file is quite easy (and interesting) to read. Here are key excerpts from our trace file. The trace file shows the cost-based query transformations applied by the optimizer:

```
OBYE:   Considering Order-by Elimination from view SEL$1 (#0)
OBYE:     OBYE performed.
```

In this case, the optimizer eliminated the **order by** clause in our SQL statement. After performing all its transformations, the optimizer arrives at the "final query after transformations," which is shown here:

```
select channel_id,count(*)
from sh.sales
group by channel_id
```

Next, the output file shows the access path analysis for each of the tables in your query.

```
Access path analysis for SALES
***************************************
SINGLE TABLE ACCESS PATH
  Single Table Cardinality Estimation for SALES[SALES]
  Table: SALES  Alias: SALES
    Card: Original: 918843.000000  Rounded: 918843  Computed: 918843.00  Non Adjusted:
918843.00
  Access Path: TableScan
    Cost:   495.47  Resp: 495.47  Degree: 0
      Cost_io: 481.00  Cost_cpu: 205554857
      Resp_io: 481.00  Resp_cpu: 205554857
  Access Path: index (index (FFS))
    Index: SALES_CHANNEL_BIX
    resc_io: 42.30  resc_cpu: 312277
    ix_sel: 0.000000  ix_sel_with_filters: 1.000000
  Access Path: index (FFS)
    Cost:   42.32  Resp: 42.32  Degree: 1
      Cost_io: 42.30  Cost_cpu: 312277
      Resp_io: 42.30  Resp_cpu: 312277
  ****** trying bitmap/domain indexes ******
  Access Path: index (FullScan)
```

```
    Index: SALES_CHANNEL_BIX
    resc_io: 75.00  resc_cpu: 552508
    ix_sel: 1.000000  ix_sel_with_filters: 1.000000
    Cost: 75.04  Resp: 75.04  Degree: 0
  Access Path: index (FullScan)
    Index: SALES_CHANNEL_BIX
    resc_io: 75.00  resc_cpu: 552508
    ix_sel: 1.000000  ix_sel_with_filters: 1.000000
    Cost: 75.04  Resp: 75.04  Degree: 0
  Bitmap nodes:
    Used SALES_CHANNEL_BIX
      Cost = 75.038890, sel = 1.000000
  Access path: Bitmap index - accepted
    Cost: 75.038890 Cost_io: 75.000000 Cost_cpu: 552508.000000 Sel: 1.000000
    Believed to be index-only
  ****** finished trying bitmap/domain indexes ******
******** Begin index join costing ********
******** End index join costing ********
  Best:: AccessPath: IndexFFS
  Index: SALES_CHANNEL_BIX
        Cost: 42.32  Degree: 1  Resp: 42.32  Card: 918843.00  Bytes: 0
```

In this case, the optimizer evaluates various access paths and shows the optimal access path as an Index Fast Full Scan (IndexFFS).

The optimizer then considers various permutations of join orders and estimates the cost for each join order it considers:

```
Considering cardinality-based initial join order.
Join order[1]:  SALES[SALES]#0
GROUP BY sort
GROUP BY adjustment factor: 1.000000
      Total IO sort cost: 0      Total CPU sort cost: 834280255
      Best so far:  Table#: 0  cost: 101.0459  card: 918843.0000  bytes: 2756529
Number of join permutations tried: 1
GROUP BY adjustment factor: 1.000000
GROUP BY cardinality:  4.000000, TABLE cardinality:  918843.000000
      Total IO sort cost: 0      Total CPU sort cost: 834280255
  Best join order: 1
  Cost: 101.0459  Degree: 1  Card: 918843.0000  Bytes: 2756529
```

As our brief review of the 10053 trace output shows, you can get answers to puzzling questions such as why exactly the optimizer chose a certain join order or an access path, and why it ignored an index. The answers are all there!

10-24. Generating Automatic Oracle Error Traces

Problem

You want to create an automatic error dump file when a specific Oracle error occurs.

Solution

You can create error dumps to diagnose various problems in the database, by specifying the error number in a `hanganalyze` or `systemstate` command. For example, diagnosing the causes for deadlocks is often tricky. You can ask the database to dump a trace file when it hits the `ORA-00060: Deadlock detected` error. To do this, specify the event number 60 with the `hanganalyze` or the `systemstate` command:

```
SQL> alter session set events '60 trace name hanganalyze level 4';

Session altered.

SQL> alter session set events '60 trace name systemstate level 266';

Session altered.

SQL>
```

Both of these commands will trigger the automatic dumping of diagnostic data when the database next encounters the `ORA-00060` error. You can use the same technique in an Oracle RAC database. For example, you can issue the following command to generate automatic `hanganalyze` dumps:

```
SQL>alter session set events '60 trace name hanganalyze_global level 4';
```

This `alter session` statement invokes the `hanganalyze` command in any instance in which the database encounters the `ORA-00060` error.

How It Works

Setting event numbers for an error will ensure that when the specified error occurs the next time, Oracle automatically dumps the error information for you. This comes in very handy when you're diagnosing an error that occurs occasionally and getting a current `systemstate` dump or a `hanganalyze` dump is unhelpful. Some events such as deadlocks have a text alias, in which case you can specify the alias instead of the error number. For the `ORA-00060` error, the text alias is `deadlock`, and so you can issue the following command for tracing the error:

```
SQL> alter session set events 'deadlock trace name systemstate level 266';

Session altered.

SQL>
```

Similarly, you can use text aliases wherever they're available, for other error events.

10-25. Tracing a Background Process

Problem

You want to trace a background process.

Solution

If you aren't sure of the correct name of the background process you want to trace, you can list the exact names of all background processes by issuing the following command:

```
SQL> select name,description from v$bgprocess;
```

Suppose you want to trace the dbw0 process. Issue the following commands to start and stop the trace.

```
SQL> alter system set events 'sql_trace {process:pname=dbw0}';
System altered.
SQL> alter system set events 'sql_trace {process:pname=dbw0} off';
System altered.
SQL>
```

You can trace two background processes at the same time by specifying the pipe (|) character to separate the process names:

```
SQL> alter system set events 'sql_trace {process:pname=dbw0|dbw1}';
System altered.

SQL> alter system set events 'sql_trace {process:pname=dbw0|dbw1} off';
System altered.
SQL>
```

How It Works

The Oracle Database 11g release offers several improvements to the SQL tracing facility. One of them is the new capability that allows you to issue an `alter system set events` command to trace a process (or a set of processes) or a specific SQL statement (or a set of statements). This recipe shows how to trace a background process by specifying the process name.

10-26. Enabling Oracle Listener Tracing

Problem

You want to trace the Oracle listener for diagnostic purposes.

Solution

To generate a trace for the Oracle listener, add the following two lines in the `listener.ora` file, which is by default located in the `$ORACLE_HOME/network/admin` directory.

```
trace_level_listener=support
trace_timestamp_listener=true
```

You can optionally specify a file name for the listener trace by adding the line
`trace_file_listener=<file_name>`. Reload the listener with the `lsnrctl reload` command, and then
check the status of the listener with the `lsnrctl status` command. You should see the trace file listed in
the output:

```
C:\>lsnrctl reload

The command completed successfully

C:\>lsnrctl status
...

Listener Parameter File   C:\app\ora\product\11.2.0\dbhome_1\network\admin\liste
ner.ora
Listener Log File         c:\app\ora\diag\tnslsnr\MIROPC61\listener\alert\log.xm
l
Listener Trace File       c:\app\ora\diag\tnslsnr\MIROPC61\listener\trace\ora_86
40_9960.trc
...
  Instance "orcl1", status READY, has 1 handler(s) for this service...
Service "orcl1XDB.miro.local" has 1 instance(s).
  Instance "orcl1", status READY, has 1 handler(s) for this service...
The command completed successfully

C:>
```

The output shows the listener trace file you've just configured.

■ **Note**   This and the next recipe don't have anything to with SQL tracing, which is the focus of this chapter.
However, we thought we'd add these two recipes because they're useful, and there's no better chapter to put
them in!

How It Works

You can specify various levels for listener tracing. You can specify Level 4 (**user**) for user trace
information and Level 10 (**admin**) for administrative trace information. Oracle Support may request Level
16 (**support**) for troubleshooting Oracle listener issues.

If you can't reload or restart the listener, you can configure the tracing dynamically by issuing the
following commands:

```
C:>lsnrctl

LSNRCTL> set current_listener listener
Current Listener is listener
LSNRCTL> set trc_level 16
```

```
Connecting to (DESCRIPTION=(ADDRESS=(PROTOCOL=IPC)(KEY=EXTPROC
listener parameter "trc_level" set to support
The command completed successfully
LSNRCTL>
```

You can turn off listener tracing by issuing the command set trc_level off, which is the default value for this parameter:

```
LSNRCTL> set trc_level off
Connecting to (DESCRIPTION=(ADDRESS=(PROTOCOL=IPC)(KEY=EXTPROC1521)))
LISTENER parameter "trc_level" set to off
The command completed successfully
LSNRCTL>
```

You'll notice that the lsnrctl status command doesn't show the listener trace file any longer. Note that the trace file for the listener will not be in the $ORACLE_HOME\rdbms\network\admin directory. Rather, the database stores the trace file in the diag directory of the database diagnosability infrastructure (ADR), under the tnslsnr directory, as shown here:

```
Listener Trace File        c:\app\ora\diag\tnslsnr\myhost\listener\trace\ora_86
                               40_9960.trc
```

10-27. Setting Archive Tracing for Data Guard

Problem

You want to trace the creation and transmission of the archive logs in a Data Guard environment.

Solution

You can trace the archive logs on either the primary or the standby database by setting the log_archive_trace initialization parameter:

```
log_archive_trace=trace_level(integer)
```

For example, if you want to set tracing at Level 15 on the primary server, you'd set this parameter as follows:

```
SQL> alter system set log_archive_trace=15
```

By default the log_archive_trace parameter is set to zero, meaning archive log tracing is disabled.

How It Works

Although archive log tracing is disabled when you leave the log_archive_trace parameter at its default level of zero, the database will still record error conditions in the trace files and the alert log. When you set the log_archive_trace parameter to a non-zero value, Oracle writes the appropriate trace output generated by the archive log process to an audit trail. The audit trail is the same trace directory as that for the SQL trace files—the *trace* directory in the ADR (this is the same as the user dump directory specified by the user_dump_dest initialization parameter).

On the primary database, the `log_archive_trace` parameter controls the output of the ARC*n* (archiver), FAL (fetch archived log), and the LGWR (log writer) background processes. On the standby databases, it traces the work of the ARC*n*, RFS (remote file server), and the FAL processes.

You can specify any of 15 levels of archive log tracing. Here's what the important tracing levels mean:

Level 1: Tracks the archiving of log files

Level 2: Tracks archive log status by destination

Level 4: Tracks archive operational phase

Level 8: Tracks archive log destination activity

Level 128: Tracks LGWR redo shipping network activity

Level 4096: Tracks real-time apply activity

Level 8192: Tracks redo apply activity (media recovery or physical standby)

When you specify a higher level of tracing, the trace will include information from all lower tracing levels. For example, if you specify Level 15, the trace file will include trace information from Levels 1, 2, 4, and 8.

CHAPTER 11

Automated SQL Tuning

Prior to Oracle Database 11g, accurately identifying poorly performing SQL queries and recommending solutions was mainly the purview of veteran SQL tuners. Typically one had to know how to identify high-resource SQL statements and bottlenecks, generate and interpret execution plans, extract data from the dynamic performance views, understand wait events and statistics, and then collate this knowledge to produce good SQL queries. As you'll see in this chapter, the Oracle SQL tuning paradigm has shifted a bit.

With the advent of automated SQL tuning features, anybody from novice to expert can generate and recommend solutions for SQL performance problems. This opens the door for new ways to address problematic SQL. For example, imagine your boss coming to you each morning with tuning recommendations and asking what the plan is to implement enhancements. This is different.

The automated SQL tuning feature is not a panacea for SQL performance angst. If you are an expert SQL tuner, there's no need to fear your skills are obsolete or your job is lost. There will always be a need to verify recommendations and successfully implement solutions. A human is still required to review the automated SQL tuning output and confirm the worthiness of fixes.

Still, there's been a change in the way SQL performance problems can be identified and solutions can be recommended. Some old-school folks may disagree and argue that you can't allow just anybody to generate SQL tuning advice. Regardless, Oracle has made these automated tools accessible and usable by the general population (for a fee). Therefore you need to understand the underpinnings of these features and how to use them.

This chapter focuses on the following automated SQL tuning tools:

- Automatic SQL Tuning
- SQL tuning sets (STS)
- SQL Tuning Advisor
- Automatic Database Diagnostic Monitor (ADDM)

Starting with Oracle Database 11g, *Automatic SQL Tuning* is a preset background database job that by default runs every day. This task examines high resource-consuming statements in the Automatic Workload Repository (AWR). It then invokes the SQL Tuning Advisor and generates tuning advice (if any) for each statement analyzed. As part of automated SQL tuning, you can configure characteristics such as the automatic acceptance of some recommendations such as SQL profiles (see Chapter 12 for details on SQL profiles).

A *SQL tuning set* (STS) is a database object that contains one or more SQL statements *and* the associated execution statistics. You can populate a SQL tuning set from multiple sources, such as SQL recorded in the AWR and SQL in memory, or you can provide specific SQL statements. It's critical that you be familiar with SQL tuning sets. This feature is used as an input to several of Oracle's performance tuning and management tools, such as the SQL Tuning Advisor, SQL Plan Management, SQL Access Advisor, and SQL Performance Advisor.

The *SQL Tuning Advisor* is central to Oracle's Automatic SQL Tuning feature. This tool runs automatically on a periodic basis and generates tuning advice for high resource-consuming SQL statements found in the AWR. You can also run the SQL Tuning Advisor manually and provide as input specific snapshot periods in the AWR, high resource-consuming SQL in memory, or user-provided SQL statements. This tool can be invoked via the `DBMS_SQLTUNE` package, SQL Developer, or Enterprise Manager.

The *Automatic Database Diagnostic Monitor* (ADDM) analyzes information in the AWR and provides recommendations on database performance issues including high resource-consuming SQL statements. The main goal of ADDM is to help you reduce the overall time (the DB time metric) spent by the database processing user requests. This tool can be invoked from an Oracle-provided SQL script, the `DBMS_ADDM` package, or Enterprise Manager.

All of the prior listed tools require an extra license from Oracle. You may not have a license to run these tools. Even if you don't have one, we still recommend that you know how these tools function. For example, you might have a manager asking if these automated tools are worth the cost, or you might be working with a developer who is investigating the use of these tools in a test environment. As a SQL tuning guru, you need to be familiar with these tools, as you will sooner or later encounter these automated features.

Before investigating the recipes in this chapter, please take a long look at Figure 11-1. This diagram demonstrates how the various automated tools interact and in what scenarios you would use a particular feature. Refer back to this diagram as you work through the recipes in this chapter. Particularly notice that you can easily use SQL statements found in the AWR or SQL currently in memory as input for various Oracle tuning tools. This allows you to systematically identify and use high-resource SQL statements as the target for various performance tuning activities.

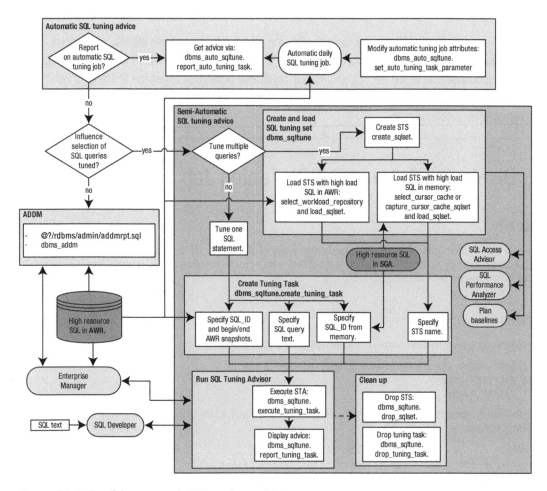

Figure 11-1. *Oracle's automatic SQL tuning tools*

The first several recipes in this chapter deal with the Automatic SQL Tuning feature. You'll be shown how to determine if and when the automated job is running and how to modify its characteristics. The middle section of this chapter focuses on how to create and manage SQL tuning sets. SQL tuning sets are used widely as input to various Oracle performance tuning tools. Lastly, the chapter shows you how to manually run the SQL Tuning Advisor and ADDM to generate performance recommendations for SQL statements.

■ **Note** In the examples in this chapter, we focus on showing you how to use features via SQL and built-in PL/SQL packages. While we do show some screenshots from Enterprise Manager, we don't focus on the graphical tool usage. You should be able to use the SQL and PL/SQL regardless of whether Enterprise Manager is installed. Furthermore, the manual approach allows you to understand each piece of the process and will help you to diagnose issues when problems arise.

11-1. Displaying Automatic SQL Tuning Job Details

Problem

You have an Oracle Database 11g environment and want to determine if the Automatic SQL Tuning job is enabled and regularly running. If the job is enabled, you want to display other aspects, such as when it starts and how long it executes.

Solution

Use the following query to determine if any Automatic SQL Tuning jobs are enabled:

```
SELECT client_name, status, consumer_group, window_group
FROM dba_autotask_client
ORDER BY client_name;
```

The following output shows that there are three enabled automatic jobs running, one of which is the SQL Tuning Advisor:

```
CLIENT_NAME                        STATUS    CONSUMER_GROUP             WINDOW_GROUP
-------------------------------    --------  ------------------------   --------------------
sql tuning advisor                 ENABLED   ORA$AUTOTASK_SQL_GROUP     ORA$AT_WGRP_SQ
auto space advisor                 ENABLED   ORA$AUTOTASK_SPACE_GROUP   ORA$AT_WGRP_SA
auto optimizer stats collection    ENABLED   ORA$AUTOTASK_STATS_GROUP   ORA$AT_WGRP_OS
```

Run the following query to view the last several times the Automatic SQL Tuning Advisor job has run:

```
SELECT task_name, status, TO_CHAR(execution_end,'DD-MON-YY HH24:MI')
FROM dba_advisor_executions
WHERE task_name='SYS_AUTO_SQL_TUNING_TASK'
ORDER BY execution_end;
```

Here is some sample output:

```
TASK_NAME                        STATUS      TO_CHAR(EXECUTION_END
-------------------------------  ----------  ---------------------
SYS_AUTO_SQL_TUNING_TASK         COMPLETED   30-APR-11 06:00
SYS_AUTO_SQL_TUNING_TASK         COMPLETED   01-MAY-11 06:02
```

How It Works

When you create a database in Oracle Database 11g or higher, Oracle automatically implements three automatic maintenance jobs:

- Automatic SQL Tuning Advisor

- Automatic Segment Advisor

- Automatic Optimizer Statistics Collection

These tasks are automatically configured to run in maintenance windows. A maintenance window is a specified time and duration for the task to run. You can view the maintenance window details with this query:

```
SELECT window_name,TO_CHAR(window_next_time,'DD-MON-YY HH24:MI:SS')
,sql_tune_advisor, optimizer_stats, segment_advisor
FROM dba_autotask_window_clients;
```

Here's a snippet of the output for this example:

```
WINDOW_NAME       TO_CHAR(WINDOW_NEXT_TIME SQL_TUNE OPTIMIZE SEGMENT_
----------------  ------------------------ -------- -------- --------
THURSDAY_WINDOW   28-APR-11 22:00:00       ENABLED  ENABLED  ENABLED
FRIDAY_WINDOW     29-APR-11 22:00:00       ENABLED  ENABLED  ENABLED
SATURDAY_WINDOW   30-APR-11 06:00:00       ENABLED  ENABLED  ENABLED
SUNDAY_WINDOW     01-MAY-11 06:00:00       ENABLED  ENABLED  ENABLED
```

There are several data dictionary views related to the automatically scheduled jobs. See Table 11-1 for descriptions of these views.

Table 11-1. *Automatic Maintenance Task View Descriptions*

View Name	Description
DBA_AUTOTASK_CLIENT	Statistical information about automatic jobs
DBA_AUTOTASK_CLIENT_HISTORY	Window history of job execution
DBA_AUTOTASK_CLIENT_JOB	Currently running automatic scheduled jobs
DBA_AUTOTASK_JOB_HISTORY	History of automatic scheduled job runs
DBA_AUTOTASK_SCHEDULE	Schedule of automated tasks for next 32 days
DBA_AUTOTASK_TASK	Information regarding current and past tasks
DBA_AUTOTASK_OPERATION	Operations for automated tasks
DBA_AUTOTASK_WINDOW_CLIENTS	Displays windows that belong to the MAINTENANCE_WINDOW_GROUP

11-2. Displaying Automatic SQL Tuning Advice

Problem

You're aware that Oracle automatically runs a daily job that generates SQL tuning advice. You want to view the advice.

Solution

If you're using Oracle Database 11g Release 2 or higher, here's the quickest way to display automatically generated SQL tuning advice:

```
SQL> SET LINESIZE 80 PAGESIZE 0 LONG 100000
SQL> SELECT DBMS_AUTO_SQLTUNE.REPORT_AUTO_TUNING_TASK FROM DUAL;
```

■ **Note** Starting with Oracle Database 11g Release 2, the DBMS_AUTO_SQLTUNE package should be used (instead of DBMS_SQLTUNE) for administrating automatic SQL tuning features. If you are using an older release of Oracle, use DBMS_SQLTUNE.REPORT_AUTO_TUNING_TASK to view automated SQL tuning advice.

Depending on the activity in your database, there may be a great deal of output. Here's a small sample of output from a very active database:

```
GENERAL INFORMATION SECTION
-------------------------------------------------------------------------------
Tuning Task Name                     : SYS_AUTO_SQL_TUNING_TASK
Tuning Task Owner                    : SYS
Workload Type                        : Automatic High-Load SQL Workload
Execution Count                      : 30
Current Execution                    : EXEC_3483
Execution Type                       : TUNE SQL
Scope                                : COMPREHENSIVE
.....
Completion Status                    : COMPLETED
Started at                           : 04/10/2011 06:00:01
Completed at                         : 04/10/2011 06:02:41
Number of Candidate SQLs             : 103
Cumulative Elapsed Time of SQL (s)   : 49124
-------------------------------------------------------------------------------
```

```
SUMMARY SECTION
--------------------------------------------------------------------------
                     Global SQL Tuning Result Statistics
--------------------------------------------------------------------------
Number of SQLs Analyzed                      : 103
Number of SQLs in the Report                 : 8
Number of SQLs with Findings                 : 8
Number of SQLs with Alternative Plan Findings: 1
Number of SQLs with SQL profiles recommended : 1
--------------------------------------------------------------------------
    SQLs with Findings Ordered by Maximum (Profile/Index) Benefit, Object ID
--------------------------------------------------------------------------
object ID  SQL ID       statistics profile(benefit) index(benefit) restructure
---------- ------------ ---------- ---------------- -------------- -----------
      9130 crx9h7tmwwv67                 51.44%
```

AUTOMATICALLY E-MAILING SQL OUTPUT

On Linux/Unix systems, it's quite easy to automate the e-mailing of output from a SQL script. First encapsulate the SQL in a shell script, and then use a utility such as cron to automatically generate and e-mail the output. Here's a sample shell script:

```
#!/bin/bash
if [ $# -ne 1 ]; then
  echo "Usage: $0 SID"
  exit 1
fi
# source oracle OS variables
. /var/opt/oracle/oraset $1
#
BOX=`uname -a | awk '{print$2}'`
OUTFILE=$HOME/bin/log/sqladvice.txt
#
sqlplus -s <<EOF
mv_maint/foo
SPO $OUTFILE
SET LINESIZE 80 PAGESIZE 0 LONG 100000
SELECT DBMS_AUTO_SQLTUNE.REPORT_AUTO_TUNING_TASK FROM DUAL;
EOF
cat $OUTFILE | mailx -s "SQL Advice: $1 $BOX" larry@oracle.com
exit 0
```

Here's the corresponding cron entry that runs the report on a daily basis:

```
#-------------------------------------------------------------------
# SQL Advice report from SQL auto tuning
16 11 * * * /orahome/oracle/bin/sqladvice.bsh DWREP
   1>/orahome/oracle/bin/log/sqladvice.log 2>&1
#-------------------------------------------------------------------
```

In the prior cron entry, the command was broken into two lines to fit on a page within this book.

How It Works

The "Solution" section describes a simple method to display in-depth tuning advice for high-load queries in your database. Depending on the activity and load on your database, the report may contain no suggestions or may provide a great deal of advice. The Automatic SQL Tuning job uses the high-workload SQL statements identified in the AWR as the target SQL statements to report on. The advice report consists of one or more of the following general subsections:

- General information
- Summary
- Details
- Findings
- Explain plans
- Alternate plans
- Errors

The general information section contains high-level information regarding the start and end time, number of SQL statements considered, cumulative elapsed time of the SQL statements, and so on.

The summary section contains information regarding the SQL statements analyzed—for example:

```
                   Global SQL Tuning Result Statistics
-------------------------------------------------------------------------------
Number of SQLs Analyzed                       : 26
Number of SQLs in the Report                  : 5
Number of SQLs with Findings                  : 5
Number of SQLs with Alternative Plan Findings : 1
Number of SQLs with SQL profiles recommended  : 5
Number of SQLs with Index Findings            : 2
-------------------------------------------------------------------------------
   SQLs with Findings Ordered by Maximum (Profile/Index) Benefit, Object ID
-------------------------------------------------------------------------------
object ID  SQL ID         statistics profile(benefit) index(benefit) restructure
---------- -------------  ---------- ---------------- -------------- -----------
     1160  31q9w59vpt86t                      98.27%          99.90%
     1167  3u8xd0vf2pnhr                      98.64%
```

The detail section contains information describing specific SQL statements, such as the owner and SQL text. Here is a small sample:

```
DETAILS SECTION
-------------------------------------------------------------------------------
 Statements with Results Ordered by Maximum (Profile/Index) Benefit, Object ID
-------------------------------------------------------------------------------
Object ID  : 1160
Schema Name: CHN_READ
SQL ID     : 31q9w59vpt86t
SQL Text   : SELECT "A2"."UMID","A2"."ORACLE_UNIQUE_ID","A2"."PUBLIC_KEY","A2"
             ."SERIAL_NUMBER",:1||"A1"."USER_NAME","A1"."USER_NAME",NVL("A2"."
             CREATE_TIME_DTT",:2),NVL("A2"."UPDATE_TIME_DTT",:3) FROM
             "COMPUTER_SYSTEM" "A2","USERS" "A1" WHERE
```

The findings section contains recommendations such as accepting a SQL profile or creating an index—for example:

```
FINDINGS SECTION
-------------------------------------------------------------------------------
1- SQL Profile Finding (see explain plans section below)
-------------------------------------------------------
  A potentially better execution plan was found for this statement.
  Recommendation (estimated benefit: 98.27%)
  -----------------------------------------
  - Consider accepting the recommended SQL profile to use
parallel execution for this statement.
    execute dbms_sqltune.accept_sql_profile(task_name =>
             'SYS_AUTO_SQL_TUNING_TASK', object_id => 1160, task_owner =>
             'SYS', replace => TRUE, profile_type => DBMS_SQLTUNE.PX_PROFILE);
.................
2- Index Finding (see explain plans section below)
-------------------------------------------------
The execution plan of this statement can be improved by creating
one or more indices.
  Recommendation (estimated benefit: 99.9%)
  -----------------------------------------
  - Consider running the Access Advisor to improve the physical schema design
    or creating the recommended index.
    create index CHAINSAW.IDX$$_90890002 on
    CHAINSAW.COMPUTER_SYSTEM("UPDATE_TIME_DTT");
```

Where appropriate, the original execution plan for a query is displayed along with a suggested fix and new execution plan. This allows you to see the before and after plan differences. This is very useful when determining if the findings (such as adding an index) would improve performance.

Lastly, there is an error section of the report. For most scenarios, there typically will not be an error section in the report.

The "Solution" section showed how to execute the REPORT_AUTO_TUNING_TASK function from a SQL statement. This function can also be called from an anonymous block of PL/SQL. Here's an example:

```
VARIABLE tune_report CLOB;
BEGIN
  :tune_report := DBMS_AUTO_SQLTUNE.report_auto_tuning_task(
    begin_exec  => NULL
   ,end_exec    => NULL
   ,type        => DBMS_AUTO_SQLTUNE.type_text
```

```
    ,level        => DBMS_AUTO_SQLTUNE.level_typical
    ,section      => DBMS_AUTO_SQLTUNE.section_all
    ,object_id    => NULL
    ,result_limit => NULL);
END;
/
--
SET LONG 1000000
PRINT :tune_report
```

The parameters for the REPORT_AUTO_TUNING_TASK function are described in detail in Table 11-2. These parameters allow you a great deal of flexibility to customize the advice output.

Table 11-2. Parameter Details for the REPORT_AUTO_TUNING_TASK Function

Parameter Name	Description
BEGIN_EXEC	Name of beginning task execution; NULL means the most recent task is used.
END_EXEC	Name of ending task; NULL means the most recent task is used.
TYPE	Type of report to produce; TEXT specifies a text report.
LEVEL	Level of detail; valid values are BASIC, TYPICAL, and ALL.
SECTION	Section of the report to include; valid values are ALL, SUMMARY, FINDINGS, PLAN, INFORMATION, and ERROR.
OBJECT_ID	Used to report on a specific statement; NULL means all statements.
RESULT_LIMIT	Maximum number of SQL statements to include in report

11-3. Generating a SQL Script to Implement Automatic Tuning Advice

Problem

You've reported on the automatic tuning advice. Now you want to generate a SQL script that can be used to implement tuning advice.

Solution

Use the `DBMS_SQLTUNE.SCRIPT_TUNING_TASK` function to generate the SQL statements to implement the advice of a tuning task. You need to provide as input the name of the automatic tuning task. In this example, the name of the task is `SYS_AUTO_SQL_TUNING_TASK`:

```
SET LINES 132 PAGESIZE 0 LONG 10000
SELECT DBMS_SQLTUNE.SCRIPT_TUNING_TASK('SYS_AUTO_SQL_TUNING_TASK') FROM dual;
```

Here is a small snippet of the output for this example:

```
execute dbms_stats.gather_index_stats(ownname => 'STAR2', indname => 'F_CONFIG_P
ROD_INST_FK1', estimate_percent => DBMS_STATS.AUTO_SAMPLE_SIZE);
create index NSESTAR.IDX$$_17F5F0004 on NSESTAR.D_DATES("FISCAL_YEAR","FISCAL_WE
EK_NUMBER_IN_YEAR","DATE_DTT");
```

How It Works

The `SCRIPT_TUNING_TASK` function generates the SQL to implement the advice recommended by the Automatic SQL Tuning job. If the tuning task doesn't have any advice to give, then there won't be any SQL statements generated in the output. `SYS_AUTO_SQL_TUNING_TASK` is the default name of the Automatic SQL Tuning task. If you're unsure of the details regarding this task, then query the `DBA_ADVISOR_LOG` view:

```
select task_name, execution_start from dba_advisor_log
where task_name='SYS_AUTO_SQL_TUNING_TASK'
order by 2;
```

Here's some sample output for this example:

```
TASK_NAME                      EXECUTION
------------------------------ ---------
SYS_AUTO_SQL_TUNING_TASK       19-APR-11
```

11-4. Modifying Automatic SQL Tuning Features

Problem

You've noticed that sometimes the Automatic SQL Tuning advice job recommends that a SQL profile be applied to a SQL statement (see Chapter 12 for details on SQL profiles). The default behavior of the tuning advice job is to not automatically accept SQL profile recommendations. You want to modify this behavior and have the Automatic SQL Tuning job automatically place any SQL profiles that it recommends into an accepted state.

Solution

Use the `DBMS_AUTO_SQLTUNE.SET_AUTO_TUNING_TASK_PARAMETER` procedure to modify the default behavior of Automatic SQL Tuning. For example, if you want SQL profiles to be automatically accepted, you can do so as follows:

```
BEGIN
  DBMS_AUTO_SQLTUNE.SET_AUTO_TUNING_TASK_PARAMETER(
    parameter => 'ACCEPT_SQL_PROFILES', value => 'TRUE');
END;
/
```

You can verify that auto SQL profile accepting is enabled via this query:

```
SELECT parameter_name, parameter_value
FROM dba_advisor_parameters
WHERE task_name = 'SYS_AUTO_SQL_TUNING_TASK'
AND  parameter_name ='ACCEPT_SQL_PROFILES';
```

Here is some sample output:

```
PARAMETER_NAME                    PARAMETER_VALUE
-----------------------------     -----------------------------
ACCEPT_SQL_PROFILES               TRUE
```

To disable automatic acceptance of SQL profiles, pass a FALSE value to the procedure:

```
BEGIN
  DBMS_AUTO_SQLTUNE.SET_AUTO_TUNING_TASK_PARAMETER(
    parameter => 'ACCEPT_SQL_PROFILES', value => 'FALSE');
END;
/
```

■ **Note** Starting with Oracle Database 11g Release 2, the DBMS_AUTO_SQLTUNE package should be used (instead of DBMS_SQLTUNE) for administrating Automatic SQL Tuning features.

How It Works

The DBMS_AUTO_SQLTUNE.SET_AUTO_TUNING_TASK_PARAMETER procedure allows you to modify the default behavior of the Automatic SQL Tuning job. You can view all of the current settings for Automatic SQL Tuning via this query:

```
SELECT parameter_name ,parameter_value
FROM dba_advisor_parameters
WHERE task_name = 'SYS_AUTO_SQL_TUNING_TASK'
AND  parameter_name IN ('ACCEPT_SQL_PROFILES',
                        'MAX_SQL_PROFILES_PER_EXEC',
                        'MAX_AUTO_SQL_PROFILES',
                        'EXECUTION_DAYS_TO_EXPIRE');
```

Here's some sample output:

```
PARAMETER_NAME                    PARAMETER_VALUE
-----------------------------     -----------------------------
ACCEPT_SQL_PROFILES               FALSE
EXECUTION_DAYS_TO_EXPIRE          30
```

```
MAX_SQL_PROFILES_PER_EXEC      20
MAX_AUTO_SQL_PROFILES          10000
```

The prior parameters are described in Table 11-3.

Table 11-3. Description of SET_AUTO_TUNING_TASK_PARAMETER Parameters

Parameter Name	Description
ACCEPT_SQL_PROFILE	Determines if SQL profiles are automatically accepted
EXECUTION_DAYS_TO_EXPIRE	Number of days to save task history
MAX_SQL_PROFILES_PER_EXEC	Limit of SQL profiles accepted per execution of tuning task
MAX_AUTO_SQL_PROFILES	Maximum limit of SQL profiles automatically accepted

You can also use Enterprise Manager to manage the features regarding Automatic SQL Tuning. From the main database page, navigate to the Advisor Central page. Next, click the SQL Advisors link. Now click the Automatic SQL Tuning Results page. You should be presented with a screen similar to Figure 11-2.

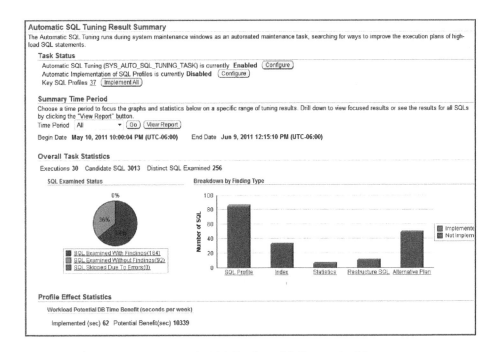

Figure 11-2. Managing Automatic SQL Tuning with Enterprise Manager

From this screen, you can configure, view results, disable, and enable various aspects of Automatic SQL Tuning.

11-5. Disabling and Enabling Automatic SQL Tuning

Problem

You want to completely disable and later re-enable the Automatic SQL Tuning job.

Solution

Use the DBMS_AUTO_TASK_ADMIN.DISABLE procedure to disable the Automatic SQL Tuning job. This example disables the Automatic SQL Tuning Advisor job.

```
BEGIN
  DBMS_AUTO_TASK_ADMIN.DISABLE(
  client_name => 'sql tuning advisor',
  operation => NULL,
  window_name => NULL);
END;
/
```

To re-enable the job, use the ENABLE procedure as shown:

```
BEGIN
  DBMS_AUTO_TASK_ADMIN.ENABLE(
  client_name => 'sql tuning advisor',
  operation => NULL,
  window_name => NULL);
END;
/
```

You can report on the status of the automatic tuning job via this query:

```
SELECT client_name ,status ,consumer_group
FROM dba_autotask_client
ORDER BY client_name;
```

Here's some sample output:

```
CLIENT_NAME                      STATUS          CONSUMER_GROUP
-------------------------------- --------------- ------------------------------
auto optimizer stats collection  ENABLED         ORA$AUTOTASK_STATS_GROUP
auto space advisor               ENABLED         ORA$AUTOTASK_SPACE_GROUP
sql tuning advisor               ENABLED         ORA$AUTOTASK_SQL_GROUP
```

How It Works

You might want to disable the Automatic SQL Tuning job because you have a very active database and want to ensure that this job doesn't impact the overall performance of the database. The DBMS_AUTO_TASK_ADMIN.ENABLE/DISABLE procedures allow you to turn on and off the Automatic SQL Tuning job. These procedures take three parameters (see Table 11-4 for details). The behavior of the procedures varies depending on which parameters you pass in:

- If CLIENT_NAME is provided and both OPERATION and WINDOW_NAME are NULL, then the client is disabled.

- If OPERATION is provided, then the operation is disabled.

- If WINDOW_NAME is provided, and OPERATION is NULL, then the client is disabled in the provided window name.

The prior parameters allow you to control at a granular detail the schedule of the automatic task. Given the prior rules, you would disable the Automatic SQL Tuning job during the Tuesday maintenance window as follows:

```
BEGIN
  dbms_auto_task_admin.disable(
  client_name => 'sql tuning advisor',
  operation => NULL,
  window_name => 'TUESDAY_WINDOW');
END;
/
```

You can verify that the window has been disabled via this query:

```
SELECT window_name,TO_CHAR(window_next_time,'DD-MON-YY HH24:MI:SS')
,sql_tune_advisor
FROM dba_autotask_window_clients;
```

Here is a snippet of the output:

```
WINDOW_NAME      TO_CHAR(WINDOW_NEXT_TIME SQL_TUNE
---------------- ------------------------ --------
TUESDAY_WINDOW   03-MAY-11 22:00:00       DISABLED
```

Table 11-4. *Parameter Descriptions for* DBMS_AUTO_TASK_ADMIN.ENABLE *and* DISABLE *Procedures*

Parameter	Description
CLIENT_NAME	Name of client; query DBA_AUTOTASK_CLIENT for details.
OPERATION	Name of operation; query DBA_AUTOTASK_OPERATION for details.
WINDOW_NAME	Operation name of the window

11-6. Modifying Maintenance Window Attributes

Problem

You realize that the automatic tasks (such as the Automatic SQL Tuning job) run during regularly scheduled maintenance windows. You want to modify the length of time associated with a maintenance window.

Solution

Here's an example that changes the duration of the Sunday maintenance window to two hours:

```
BEGIN
  dbms_scheduler.set_attribute(
  name => 'SUNDAY_WINDOW',
  attribute => 'DURATION',
  value => numtodsinterval(2, 'hour'));
END;
/
```

You can confirm the changes to the maintenance window with this query:

```
SELECT window_name, next_start_date, duration
FROM dba_scheduler_windows;
```

Here is a snippet of the output:

```
WINDOW_NAME       NEXT_START_DATE                            DURATION
----------------  -----------------------------------------  --------------------
SATURDAY_WINDOW   07-MAY-11 06.00.00.000000 AM US/MOUNTAIN   +000 20:00:00
SUNDAY_WINDOW     08-MAY-11 06.00.00.000000 AM US/MOUNTAIN   +000 02:00:00
```

How It Works

The key to understanding how to modify a maintenance window is that it is an attribute of the database job scheduler and therefore must be maintained via the DBMS_SCHEDULER package. When you install Oracle Database 11g, by default three automatic maintenance jobs are configured:

- Automatic SQL Tuning

- Statistics gathering

- Segment advice

These jobs automatically execute in preconfigured daily maintenance windows. A maintenance window consists of a day of the week and the length of time the job runs.

You can view the future one month's worth of scheduled jobs via this query:

```
SELECT window_name, to_char(start_time,'dd-mon-yy hh24:mi'), duration
FROM dba_autotask_schedule
ORDER BY start_time;
```

Here is a small sample of the output:

```
WINDOW_NAME           TO_CHAR(START_TIME,'D DURATION
--------------------  -------------------- --------------------
SATURDAY_WINDOW       14-may-11 06:00      +000 20:00:00
SUNDAY_WINDOW         15-may-11 06:00      +000 02:00:00
```

■ **Tip**   See Oracle's Database Administrator's Guide (available on the Oracle Technology Network web site) for further details on managing scheduled jobs.

11-7. Creating a SQL Tuning Set Object

Problem

You're working on a performance issue that requires that you analyze a group of SQL statements. Before you process the SQL statements as a set, you need to create a SQL tuning set object.

Solution

Use the DBMS_SQLTUNE.CREATE_SQLSET procedure to create a SQL tuning set object—for example:

```
BEGIN
  DBMS_SQLTUNE.CREATE_SQLSET(
  sqlset_name => 'HIGH_IO',
  description => 'High disk read tuning set');
END;
/
```

The prior code creates a tuning set with the name of HIGH_IO. At this point, you have created a named tuning set object. The tuning set does not contain any SQL statements.

How It Works

A SQL tuning set object must be created before populating a tuning set with SQL statements (see Recipes 11-9 through 11-11 for details on adding SQL statements to an STS). You can view any defined SQL tuning sets in the database by querying the DBA_SQLSET view:

```
SQL> select id, name, created, statement_count from dba_sqlset;
```

Here is some sample output:

```
        ID NAME                           CREATED   STATEMENT_COUNT
---------- ------------------------------ --------- ---------------
         5 HIGH_IO                        26-APR-11               0
```

If you need to drop a SQL tuning set object, then use the DBMS_SQLTUNE.DROP_SQLSET procedure to drop a tuning set. The following example drops a tuning set named MY_TUNING_SET:

```
SQL> EXEC DBMS_SQLTUNE.DROP_SQLSET(sqlset_name => 'MY_TUNING_SET' );
```

11-8. Viewing Resource-Intensive SQL in the AWR

Problem

Before populating a SQL tuning set, you want to view high-load SQL statements in the AWR. You want to eventually use SQL contained in the AWR as input for populating a SQL tuning set.

Solution

The DBMS_SQLTUNE.SELECT_WORKLOAD_REPOSITORY function can be used to extract SQL stored in the AWR. This particular query selects queries in the AWR between snapshots 8200 and 8201 ordered by the top 10 in the disk reads usage category:

```
SELECT
 sql_id
,substr(sql_text,1,20)
,disk_reads
,cpu_time
,elapsed_time
FROM table(DBMS_SQLTUNE.SELECT_WORKLOAD_REPOSITORY(8200,8201,
           null, null, 'disk_reads',null, null, null, 10))
ORDER BY disk_reads DESC;
```

Here is a small snippet of the output:

```
SQL_ID          SUBSTR(SQL_TEXT,1,20 DISK_READS    CPU_TIME  ELAPSED_TIME
--------------  -------------------- ---------- ------------- -------------
achffburdff9j   delete from "MVS"."     101145     814310000     991574249
5vku5ap6g6zh8   INSERT /*+ BYPASS_RE     98172      75350000      91527239
```

How It Works

Before you work with SQL tuning sets, it's critical to understand you can use the DBMS_SQLTUNE.SELECT_WORKLOAD_REPOSITORY function to retrieve high resource-usage SQL from the AWR. The result sets retrieved by this PL/SQL function can be used as input for populating SQL tuning sets. See Table 11-5 for a description of the SELECT_WORKLOAD_REPOSITORY function parameters.

You have a great deal of flexibility in how you use this function. A few examples will help illustrate this. Say you want to retrieve SQL from the AWR that was not parsed by the SYS user. Here is the SQL to do that:

```
SELECT sql_id, substr(sql_text,1,20)
,disk_reads, cpu_time, elapsed_time, parsing_schema_name
FROM table(
```

```
DBMS_SQLTUNE.SELECT_WORKLOAD_REPOSITORY(8200,8201,
'parsing_schema_name <> ''SYS''',
NULL, NULL,NULL,NULL, 1, NULL, 'ALL'));
```

The following example retrieves the top ten queries ranked by buffer gets for non-SYS users:

```
SELECT
 sql_id
,substr(sql_text,1,20)
,disk_reads
,cpu_time
,elapsed_time
,buffer_gets
,parsing_schema_name
FROM table(
DBMS_SQLTUNE.SELECT_WORKLOAD_REPOSITORY(
 begin_snap => 21730
,end_snap => 22900
,basic_filter => 'parsing_schema_name <> ''SYS'''
,ranking_measure1 => 'buffer_gets'
,result_limit => 10
));
```

In the prior queries, the SYS keyword is enclosed by two single quotes (in other words, those aren't double quotes around SYS).

Table 11-5. Parameter Descriptions of the SELECT_WORKLOAD_REPOSITORY Function

Parameter	Description
BEGIN_SNAP	Non-inclusive beginning snapshot ID
END_SNAP	Inclusive ending snapshot ID
BASELINE_NAME	Name of AWR baseline
BASIC_FILTER	SQL predicate to filter SQL statements from workload; if not set, then only SELECT, INSERT, UPDATE, DELETE, MERGE, and CREATE TABLE statements are captured.
OBJECT_FILTER	Not currently used
RANKING_MEASURE(n)	Order by clause on selected SQL statement(s), such as elapsed_time, cpu_time, buffer_gets, disk_reads, and so on; N can be 1, 2, or 3.
RESULT_PERCENTAGE	Filter for choosing top N% for ranking measure

Continued

Parameter	Description
RESULT_LIMIT	Limit of the number of SQL statements returned in the result set.
ATTRIBUTE_LIST	List of SQL statement attributes (TYPICAL, BASIC, ALL, and so on)
RECURSIVE_SQL	Include/exclude recursive SQL (HAS_RECURSIVE_SQL or NO_RECURSIVE_SQL)

11-9. Viewing Resource-Intensive SQL in Memory

Problem

Before populating a SQL tuning set, you want to view high-load SQL statements in the cursor cache in memory. You want to eventually use SQL contained in memory as input for populating a SQL tuning set.

Solution

Use the DBMS_SQLTUNE.SELECT_CURSOR_CACHE function to view current high resource-consuming SQL statements in memory. This query selects SQL statements in memory that have required more than a million disk reads:

```
SELECT
 sql_id
,substr(sql_text,1,20)
,disk_reads
,cpu_time
,elapsed_time
FROM table(DBMS_SQLTUNE.SELECT_CURSOR_CACHE('disk_reads > 1000000'))
ORDER BY sql_id;
```

Here is some sample output:

```
SQL_ID          SUBSTR(SQL_TEXT,1,20 DISK_READS   CPU_TIME ELAPSED_TIME
------------- -------------------- ---------- ---------- ------------
0s6gq1c890p4s delete from "MVS"."    3325320 8756130000   1.0416E+10
b63h4skwvpshj BEGIN dbms_mview.ref   9496353 1.4864E+10   3.3006E+10
```

How It Works

Before you work with SQL tuning sets, it's critical to understand you can use the
`DBMS_SQLTUNE.SELECT_CURSOR_CACHE` function to retrieve high resource-usage SQL from memory. The
result set retrieved by this PL/SQL function can be used as input for populating SQL tuning sets. See
Table 11-6 for a description of the `SELECT_CURSOR_CACHE` function parameters.

You have a great deal of flexibility in how you use this function. Here's an example that selects SQL
in memory, but excludes statements parsed by the SYS user and also returns statements with an elapsed
time greater than 100,000:

```
SELECT sql_id, substr(sql_text,1,20)
,disk_reads, cpu_time, elapsed_time
FROM table(DBMS_SQLTUNE.SELECT_CURSOR_CACHE('parsing_schema_name <> ''SYS''
                                             AND elapsed_time > 100000'))
ORDER BY sql_id;
```

In the prior query, the SYS keyword is enclosed by two single quotes (in other words, those aren't
double quotes around SYS). The SQL_TEXT column is truncated to 20 characters so that the output can be
displayed on the page more easily. Here is some sample output:

```
SQL_ID        SUBSTR(SQL_TEXT,1,20 DISK_READS   CPU_TIME ELAPSED_TIME
------------- -------------------- ---------- ---------- ------------
byzwu34haqmh4 SELECT /* DS_SVC */           0     140000       159828
```

Once you have identified a SQL_ID for a resource-intensive SQL statement, you can view all of its
execution details via this query:

```
SELECT *
FROM table(DBMS_SQLTUNE.SELECT_CURSOR_CACHE('sql_id = ''byzwu34haqmh4'''));
```

Note that the SQL_ID in the prior statement is enclosed by two single quotes (not double quotes).
This next example selects the top ten queries in memory in terms of CPU time for non-SYS users:

```
SELECT
 sql_id
,substr(sql_text,1,20)
,disk_reads
,cpu_time
,elapsed_time
,buffer_gets
,parsing_schema_name
FROM table(
DBMS_SQLTUNE.SELECT_CURSOR_CACHE(
 basic_filter => 'parsing_schema_name <> ''SYS'''
,ranking_measure1 => 'cpu_time'
,result_limit => 10
));
```

Table 11-6. *Parameter Descriptions of the SELECT_CURSOR_CACHE Function*

Parameter	Description
BASIC_FILTER	SQL predicate to filter SQL in the cursor cache
OBJECT_FILTER	Currently not used
RANKING_MEASURE(n)	ORDER BY clause for the SQL returned
RESULT_PERCENTAGE	Filter for the top N percent queries for the ranking measure provided; invalid if more than one ranking measure provided
RESULT_LIMIT	Top number of SQL statements filter
ATTRIBUTE_LIST	List of SQL attributes to return in result set
RECURSIVE_SQL	Include recursive SQL

11-10. Populating SQL Tuning Set from High-Resource SQL in AWR

Problem

You want to create a SQL tuning set and populate it with the top I/O-consuming SQL statements found in the AWR.

Solution

Use the following steps to populate a SQL tuning set from high resource-consuming statements in the AWR:

1. Create a SQL tuning set object.

2. Determine begin and end AWR snapshot IDs.

3. Populate the SQL tuning set with high-resource SQL found in AWR.

The prior steps are detailed in the following subsections.

Step 1: Create a SQL Tuning Set Object

Create a SQL tuning set. This next bit of code creates a tuning set named IO_STS:

```
BEGIN
  dbms_sqltune.create_sqlset(
    sqlset_name => 'IO_STS'
    description => 'STS from AWR');
END;
/
```

Step 2: Determine Begin and End AWR Snapshot IDs

If you're unsure of the available snapshots in your database, you can run an AWR report or select the SNAP_ID from DBA_HIST_SNAPSHOTS:

```
select snap_id, begin_interval_time
from dba_hist_snapshot order by 1;
```

Step 3: Populate the SQL Tuning Set with High-Resource SQL Found in AWR

Now the SQL tuning set is populated with the top 15 SQL statements ordered by disk reads. The begin and end AWR snapshot IDs are 26800 and 26900 respectively:

```
DECLARE
  base_cur dbms_sqltune.sqlset_cursor;
BEGIN
  OPEN base_cur FOR
    SELECT value(x)
    FROM table(dbms_sqltune.select_workload_repository(
      26800,26900, null, null,'disk_reads',
      null, null, null, 15)) x;
  --
  dbms_sqltune.load_sqlset(
    sqlset_name => 'IO_STS',
    populate_cursor => base_cur);
END;
/
```

The prior code populates the top 15 SQL statements contained in the AWR ordered by disk reads. The DBMS_SQLTUNE.SELECT_WORKLOAD_REPOSITORY function is used to populate a PL/SQL cursor with AWR information based on a ranking criterion. Next the DBMS_SQLTUNE.LOAD_SQLSET procedure is used to populate the SQL tuning set using the cursor as input.

How It Works

The DBMS_SQLTUNE.SELECT_WORKLOAD_REPOSITORY function can be used in a variety of ways to populate a SQL tuning set using queries in the AWR. You can instruct it to load SQL statements by criteria such as disk reads, elapsed time, CPU time, buffer gets, and so on. See Table 11-5 for descriptions for parameters to this function. When designating the AWR as input, you can use either of the following:

- Begin and end AWR snapshot IDs
- An AWR baseline that you've previously created

You can view the details of the SQL tuning set (created in the "Solution" section) via this query:

```
SELECT
 sqlset_name
,elapsed_time
,cpu_time
,buffer_gets
,disk_reads
,sql_text
FROM dba_sqlset_statements
WHERE sqlset_name = 'IO_STS';
```

11-11. Populating a SQL Tuning Set from Resource-Consuming SQL in Memory

Problem

You want to populate a tuning set from high resource-consuming SQL statements that are currently in the memory.

Solution

Use the DBMS_SQLTUNE.SELECT_CURSOR_CACHE function to populate a SQL tuning set with statements currently in memory. This example creates a tuning set and populates it with high-load resource-consuming statements not belonging to the SYS schema and having disk reads greater than 1,000,000:

```
-- Create the tuning set
EXEC DBMS_SQLTUNE.CREATE_SQLSET('HIGH_DISK_READS');
-- populate the tuning set from the cursor cache
DECLARE
  cur DBMS_SQLTUNE.SQLSET_CURSOR;
BEGIN
  OPEN cur FOR
  SELECT VALUE(x)
  FROM table(
  DBMS_SQLTUNE.SELECT_CURSOR_CACHE(
  'parsing_schema_name <> ''SYS'' AND disk_reads > 1000000',
  NULL, NULL, NULL, NULL, 1, NULL,'ALL')) x;
--
  DBMS_SQLTUNE.LOAD_SQLSET(sqlset_name => 'HIGH_DISK_READS',
    populate_cursor => cur);
END;
/
```

In the prior code, notice that the SYS user is bookended by sets of two single quotes (not double quotes). The SELECT_CURSOR_CACHE function loads the SQL statements into a PL/SQL cursor, and the LOAD_SQLSET procedure populates the SQL tuning set with the SQL statements.

How It Works

The `DBMS_SQLTUNE.SELECT_CURSOR_CACHE` function (see Table 11-6 for function parameter descriptions) allows you to extract from memory SQL statements and associated statistics into a SQL tuning set. The procedure allows you to filter SQL statements by various resource-consuming criteria, such as the following:

- `ELAPSED_TIME`
- `CPU_TIME`
- `BUFFER_GETS`
- `DISK_READS`
- `DIRECT_WRITES`
- `ROWS_PROCESSED`

This allows you a great deal of flexibility on how to filter and populate the SQL tuning set.

11-12. Populating SQL Tuning Set with All SQL in Memory

Problem

You want to create a SQL tuning set and populate it with all SQL statements currently in memory.

Solution

Use the `DBMS_SQLTUNE.CAPTURE_CURSOR_CACHE_SQLSET` procedure to efficiently capture all of the SQL currently stored in the cursor cache (in memory). This example creates a SQL tuning set named `PROD_WORKLOAD` and then populates by sampling memory for 3,600 seconds (waiting 20 seconds between each polling event):

```
BEGIN
  -- Create the tuning set
  DBMS_SQLTUNE.CREATE_SQLSET(
    sqlset_name => 'PROD_WORKLOAD'
   ,description => 'Prod workload sample');
  --
  DBMS_SQLTUNE.CAPTURE_CURSOR_CACHE_SQLSET(
    sqlset_name      => 'PROD_WORKLOAD'
   ,time_limit       => 3600
   ,repeat_interval => 20);
END;
/
```

How It Works

The DBMS_SQLTUNE.CAPTURE_CURSOR_CACHE_SQLSET procedure allows you to poll for queries and memory and use any queries found to populate a SQL tuning set. This is a powerful technique that you can use when it's required to capture a sample set of all SQL statements executing.

You have a great deal of flexibility on instructing DBMS_SQLTUNE.CAPTURE_CURSOR_CACHE_SQLSET to capture SQL statements in memory (see Table 11-7 for details on all parameters). For example, you can instruct the procedure to capture a cumulative set of statistics for each SQL statement by specifying a CAPTURE_MODE of DBMS_SQLTUNE.MODE_ACCUMULATE_STATS.

```
BEGIN
  DBMS_SQLTUNE.CAPTURE_CURSOR_CACHE_SQLSET(
    sqlset_name     => 'PROD_WORKLOAD'
    ,time_limit      => 60
    ,repeat_interval => 10
    ,capture_mode    => DBMS_SQLTUNE.MODE_ACCUMULATE_STATS);
END;
/
```

This is more resource-intensive than the default settings, but produces more accurate statistics for each SQL statement.

Table 11-7. CAPTURE_CURSOR_CACHE_SQLSET Parameter Descriptions

Parameter	Description	Default Value
SQLSET_NAME	SQL tuning set name	none
TIME_LIMIT	Total time in seconds to spend sampling	1800
REPEAT_INTERVAL	While sampling, amount of time to pause in seconds before polling memory again	300
CAPTURE_OPTION	Either INSERT, UPDATE, or MERGE statements when new statements are detected	MERGE
CAPTURE_MODE	When capture option is UPDATE or MERGE, either replace statistics or accumulate statistics. Possible values are MODE_REPLACE_OLD_STATS or MODE_ACCUMULATE_STATS.	MODE_REPLACE_OLD_STATS
BASIC_FILTER	Filter type of statements captured	NULL
SQLSET_OWNER	SQL tuning set owner; NULL indicates the current user.	NULL
RECURSIVE_SQL	Include (or not) recursive SQL; possible values are HAS_RECURSIVE_SQL, NO_RECURSIVE_SQL.	HAS_RECURSIVE_SQL

11-13. Displaying the Contents of a SQL Tuning Set

Problem

You have populated a SQL tuning set and want to verify its characteristics such as the SQL statements and corresponding statistics.

Solution

You can determine the name and number of SQL statements for SQL tuning sets in your database via this query:

```
SELECT name, created, statement_count
FROM dba_sqlset;
```

Here is some sample output:

```
NAME                             CREATED     STATEMENT_COUNT
-------------------------------  ---------   ---------------
test1                            19-APR-11                29
```

Use the following query to display the SQL text and associated statistical information for each query within the SQL tuning set:

```
SELECT sqlset_name, elapsed_time, cpu_time, buffer_gets, disk_reads, sql_text
FROM dba_sqlset_statements;
```

Here is a small snippet of the output. The SQL_TEXT column has been truncated in order to fit the output on the page:

```
SQLSET_NAME     ELAPSED_TIME   CPU_TIME  BUFFER_GETS DISK_READS SQL_TEXT
---------------  ------------  ---------- ----------- ---------- -----------------------------
test1               235285363   45310000      112777       3050 INSERT ......
test1                52220149   22700000      328035      18826 delete from.....
```

How It Works

Recall that a SQL tuning set consists of one or more SQL statements and the corresponding execution statistics. This information is viewable from the DBA_SQLSET_* views. Table 11-8 describes the type of SQL tuning set information contained within each of these views.

Table 11-8. Views Containing SQL Tuning Set Information

View Name	Description
DBA_SQLSET	Displays information regarding SQL tuning sets
DBA_SQLSET_BINDS	Displays bind variable information associated with SQL tuning sets
DBA_SQLSET_PLANS	Shows execution plan information for queries in a SQL tuning set
DBA_SQLSET_STATEMENTS	Contains SQL text and associated statistics
DBA_SQLSET_REFERENCES	Shows whether a SQL tuning set is active

You can also use the DBMS_SQLTUNE.SELECT_SQLSET function to retrieve information about SQL tuning sets—for example:

```
SELECT
 sql_id
,elapsed_time
,cpu_time
,buffer_gets
,disk_reads
,sql_text
FROM TABLE(DBMS_SQLTUNE.SELECT_SQLSET('&&sqlset_name'));
```

Whether you use the DBMS_SQLTUNE.SELECT_SQLSET function or directly query the data dictionary views depends entirely on your personal preference or business requirement.

11-14. Selectively Deleting Statements from a SQL Tuning Set

Problem

You want to prune SQL statements from an STS that don't meet a performance measure, such as queries that have less than 2,000,000 disk reads.

Solution

First view the existing SQL information associated with an STS:

```
select sqlset_name, disk_reads, cpu_time, elapsed_time, buffer_gets
from dba_sqlset_statements;
```

Here is some sample output:

```
SQLSET_NAME                      DISK_READS   CPU_TIME ELAPSED_TIME BUFFER_GETS
-----------------------------    ---------- ---------- ------------ -----------
IO_STS                             3112941 3264960000   7805935285     2202432
IO_STS                             2943527 3356460000   8930436466     1913415
IO_STS                             2539642 2310610000   5869237421     1658465
IO_STS                             1999373 2291230000   6143543429     1278601
IO_STS                             1993973 2243180000   5461607976     1272271
IO_STS                             1759096 1930320000   4855618689     1654252
```

Now use the DBMS_SQLTUNE.DELETE_SQLSET procedure to remove SQL statements from the STS based on the specified criterion. This example removes SQL statements that have less than 2,000,000 disk reads from the SQL tuning set named IO_STS:

```
BEGIN
  DBMS_SQLTUNE.DELETE_SQLSET(
    sqlset_name  => 'IO_STS'
    ,basic_filter => 'disk_reads < 2000000');
END;
/
```

How It Works

The key to understanding is that a SQL tuning set consists of the following:

- One or more SQL statements
- Associated metrics/statistics for each SQL statement

Because the metrics/statistics are part of the STS, you can remove SQL statements from a SQL tuning set based on characteristics of the associated metrics/statistics. You can use the DBMS_SQLTUNE.DELETE_SQLSET procedure to remove statements from the STS based on statistics such as the following:

- ELAPSED_TIME
- CPU_TIME
- BUFFER_GETS
- DISK_READS
- DIRECT_WRITES
- ROWS_PROCESSED

If you want to delete all SQL statements from a SQL tuning set, then don't specify a filter—for example:

```
SQL> exec  DBMS_SQLTUNE.DELETE_SQLSET(sqlset_name  => 'IO_STS');
```

11-15. Transporting a SQL Tuning Set

Problem

You've identified some resource-intensive SQL statements in a production environment. You want to transport these statements and associated statistics to a test environment, where you can tune the statements without impacting production.

Solution

The following steps are used to copy a SQL tuning set from one database to another:

1. Create a staging table in source database.

2. Populate the staging table with STS data.

3. Copy the staging table to the destination database.

4. Unpack the staging table in the destination database.

The prior steps are elaborated on in the following subsections.

Step 1: Create a Staging Table in the Source Database

Use the DBMS_SQLTUNE.CREATE_STGTAB_SQLSET procedure to create a table that will be used to contain the SQL tuning set metadata. This example creates a table named STS_TABLE:

```
BEGIN
  dbms_sqltune.create_stgtab_sqlset(
  table_name => 'STS_TABLE'
 ,schema_name => 'MV_MAINT');
END;
/
```

Step 2: Populate Staging Table with STS Data

Now populate the staging table with STS metadata using DBMS_SQLTUNE.PACK_STGTAB_SQLSET:

```
BEGIN
  dbms_sqltune.pack_stgtab_sqlset(
  sqlset_name          => 'IO_STS'
 ,sqlset_owner          => 'SYS'
 ,staging_table_name   => 'STS_TABLE'
 ,staging_schema_owner => 'MV_MAINT');
END;
/
```

If you're unsure of the names of the STS you want to transport, run the following query to get the details:

```
SELECT name, owner, created, statement_count
FROM dba_sqlset;
```

Step 3: Copy the Staging Table to the Destination Database

You can copy the table from one database to the other via Data Pump, the old `exp`/`imp` utilities, or by using a database link. This example creates a database link in the destination database and then copies the table from the source database:

```
create database link source_db
connect to mv_maint
identified by foo
using 'source_db';
```

In the destination database, the table can be copied directly from the source with the `CREATE TABLE AS SELECT` statement:

```
SQL> create table STS_TABLE as select * from STS_TABLE@source_db;
```

Step 4: Unpack the Staging Table in the Destination Database

Use the `DBMS_SQLTUNE.UNPACK_STGTAB_SQLSET` procedure to take the contents of the staging table and populate the data dictionary with the SQL tuning set metadata. This example unpacks all SQL tuning sets contained within the staging table:

```
BEGIN
DBMS_SQLTUNE.UNPACK_STGTAB_SQLSET(
  sqlset_name        => '%'
 ,replace            => TRUE
 ,staging_table_name => 'STS_TABLE');
END;
/
```

How It Works

A SQL tuning set consists of one or more queries and corresponding execution statistics. You will occasionally have a need to copy a SQL tuning set from one database to another. For example, you might be having performance problems with a production database but want to capture and move the top resource-consuming statements to a test database where you can diagnose the SQL (within the STS) without impacting production.

Keep in mind that an STS can be used as input for any of the following tools:

- SQL Tuning Advisor

- SQL Access Advisor

- SQL Plan Management

- SQL Performance Analyzer

The prior tools are used extensively to troubleshoot and test SQL performance. Transporting a SQL tuning set from one environment to another allows you to use these tools in a testing or development environment.

■ **Note**   SQL tuning sets can be transported to Oracle Database 10g R2 or higher versions of the database only.

11-16. Creating a Tuning Task

Problem

You realize that as part of manually running the SQL Tuning Advisor, you need to first create a tuning task.

■ **Tip**   Refer to Figure 11-1 for the details on the flow of processes required when manually running the SQL Tuning Advisor.

Solution

Use the DBMS_SQLTUNE.CREATE_TUNING_TASK procedure to create a SQL tuning task. You can use the following as inputs when creating a SQL tuning task:

- Text for a specific SQL statement

- SQL identifier for a specific SQL statement from the cursor cache in memory

- Single SQL statement from the AWR given a range of snapshot IDs

- SQL tuning set name (see Recipes 11-7 through 11-11 for details on how to create a SQL tuning set)

Examples of the prior techniques for creating a SQL tuning task are described in the following subsections.

■ **Note**   The user creating the tuning task needs the ADMINISTER SQL MANAGEMENT OBJECT system privilege.

Text for a Specific SQL Statement

This example provides the text of a SQL statement when creating the tuning task:

```
DECLARE
  tune_task VARCHAR2(30);
  tune_sql  CLOB;
BEGIN
  tune_sql := 'select count(*) from mgmt_db_feature_usage_ecm';
  tune_task := DBMS_SQLTUNE.CREATE_TUNING_TASK(
    sql_text     => tune_sql
   ,user_name    => 'MV_MAINT'
   ,scope        => 'COMPREHENSIVE'
   ,time_limit   => 60
   ,task_name    => 'tune_test'
   ,description => 'Provide SQL text'
);
END;
/
```

SQL ID for a Specific SQL Statement from the Cursor Cache

First identify the SQL_ID by querying V$SQL:

```
SELECT sql_id, sql_text
FROM v$sql where sql_text like '%&&mytext%';
```

Once you have the SQL_ID, you can provide it as input to DBMS_SQLTUNE.CREATE_TUNING_TASK:

```
DECLARE
  tune_task VARCHAR2(30);
  tune_sql  CLOB;
BEGIN
  tune_task := DBMS_SQLTUNE.CREATE_TUNING_TASK(
    sql_id       => '98u3gf0xzq03f'
   ,task_name    => 'tune_test2'
   ,description => 'Provide SQL ID'
);
END;
/
```

Single SQL Statement from the AWR Given a Range of Snapshot IDs

Here's an example of creating a SQL tuning task by providing a SQL_ID and range of AWR snapshot IDs:

```
DECLARE
  tune_task VARCHAR2(30);
  tune_sql  CLOB;
```

```
BEGIN
  tune_task := DBMS_SQLTUNE.CREATE_TUNING_TASK(
    sql_id      => '1tbu2jp7kv0pm'
   ,begin_snap  => 21690
   ,end_snap    => 21864
   ,task_name   => 'tune_test3'
);
END;
/
```

If you're not sure which SQL_ID (and associated query) to use, then run this query:

```
SQL> select sql_id, sql_text from dba_hist_sqltext;
```

If you're unaware of the available snapshot IDs, then run this query:

```
SQL> select snap_id from dba_hist_snapshot order by 1;
```

■ **Tip** By default, the AWR contains only high resource-consuming queries. You can modify this behavior and ensure that a specific SQL statement is included in every snapshot (regardless of its resource consumption) by adding it to the AWR via the following:

```
SQL> exec dbms_workload_repository.add_colored_sql('98u3gf0xzq03f');
```

SQL Tuning Set Name

If you have the requirement of running the SQL Tuning Advisor against multiple SQL queries, then a SQL tuning set is required. To create a tuning task using a SQL tuning set as input, do so as follows:

```
SQL> variable mytt varchar2(30);
SQL> exec :mytt := DBMS_SQLTUNE.CREATE_TUNING_TASK(sqlset_name => 'IO_STS');
SQL> print :mytt
```

How It Works

Before manually executing the SQL Tuning Advisor, you first need to define what SQL statements will be used as input. You do this by creating a SQL tuning task. Oracle provides a great deal of flexibility on how you add SQL statements to a tuning task. As shown in the "Solution" section, you can do the following:

- Hard-code the text for a specific SQL query

- Use a SQL query in memory

- Use a SQL query in the AWR

- Define a SQL tuning set when tuning multiple queries

The prior techniques provide a variety of ways to identify SQL statements to be analyzed by the SQL Tuning Advisor. Once you've created a tuning task, you can view its details via this query:

```
select owner, task_name, advisor_name, created
from dba_advisor_tasks
order by created;
```

Once you have created a tuning task, you can now manually execute the SQL Tuning Advisor (Recipe 11-17). If you need to drop the tuning task, you can do so as follows:

```
SQL> exec dbms_sqltune.drop_tuning_task(task_name => '&&task_name');
```

11-17. Manually Running SQL Tuning Advisor

Problem

You want to manually execute SQL Tuning Advisor and get tuning advice for a SQL statement.

Solution

Use the following steps to manually run the SQL Tuning Advisor:

1. Create a tuning task (see Recipe 11-16 for complete details); this defines which SQL statements will be tuned. This can be a single SQL statement or several SQL statements within a SQL tuning set.

2. Execute the tuning task.

3. Display the results of the tuning task.

This example runs the SQL Tuning Advisor for a single SQL statement. First a tuning task is created.

```
DECLARE
  tune_task VARCHAR2(30);
  tune_sql  CLOB;
BEGIN
  tune_sql := 'select a.emp_id, b.dept_name ' ||
              'from emp a, dept b ' ||
              'where a.dept_id = b.dept_id';
  --
  tune_task := DBMS_SQLTUNE.CREATE_TUNING_TASK(
    sql_text    => tune_sql
   ,user_name   => 'MV_MAINT'
   ,scope       => 'COMPREHENSIVE'
   ,time_limit  => 60
   ,task_name   => 'tune_test'
   ,description => 'Tune a SQL statement.'
);
END;
/
```

Next the tuning task is executed:

```
SQL> exec dbms_sqltune.execute_tuning_task(task_name => 'tune_test');
```

Lastly, a report is generated that displays the tuning advice:

```
SQL> set long 10000 longchunksize 10000
SQL> set linesize 132 pagesize 200
SQL> select dbms_sqltune.report_tuning_task('tune_test') from dual;
```

Here is some sample output:

```
1- Statistics Finding
---------------------
  Table "MV_MAINT"."DEPT" was not analyzed.
  Recommendation
  --------------
  - Consider collecting optimizer statistics for this table.
....
2- Index Finding (see explain plans section below)
--------------------------------------------------
  The execution plan of this statement can be improved by creating one or more
  indices.
  Recommendation (estimated benefit: 97.98%)
  ------------------------------------------
  - Consider running the Access Advisor to improve the physical schema design
    or creating the recommended index.
    create index MV_MAINT.IDX$$_21E10001 on MV_MAINT.EMP("DEPT_ID");
```

The prior output has specific recommendations on generating statistics for a table in the query and adding an index. You'll need to test the recommendations to ensure that performance does improve before implementing them in a production environment.

OPTIMIZER TUNING MODES

The optimizer operates in two different modes: normal and tuning. When a SQL statement executes, the optimizer operates in normal mode and quickly identifies a reasonable execution plan. In this mode, the optimizer spends only a fraction of a second to try to determine the best plan.

When the SQL Tuning Advisor analyzes a query, it runs the optimizer in tuning mode. In this mode, the optimizer can take several minutes to analyze each step of the execution plan and generate an execution plan that is potentially much more efficient than the plan generated under normal mode.

This is somewhat similar to a computer chess game. When you allow the chess software to spend only a second or less on each move, it's easy to beat the game. However, if you allow the chess game to spend a minute or more on each move, in this mode the game makes much more optimal decisions.

How It Works

The SQL Tuning Advisor helps automate the task of tuning poorly performing queries. The tool is fairly easy to use, and it provides suggestions on how to tune a query, such as the following:

- Rewriting the SQL
- Adding indexes
- Implementing a SQL profile or plan baselines
- Generating statistics

You can also manually run the SQL Tuning Advisor from either SQL Developer or Enterprise Manager. Running the SQL Tuning Advisor from these tools is briefly described in the next two subsections.

Running SQL Tuning Advisor from SQL Developer

If you have access to SQL Developer 3.0 or higher, then it's very easy to run the SQL Tuning Advisor for a query. Follow these simple steps:

1. Open a SQL worksheet.
2. Type in the query.
3. Click the button associated with the SQL Tuning Advisor.

You will be presented with any findings and recommendations. If you have access to SQL Developer (it's a free download), this is the easiest way to run the SQL Tuning Advisor.

■ **Note** Before running SQL Tuning Advisor, ensure the user that you're connected to has the ADVISOR system privilege granted to it.

Running SQL Tuning Advisor from Enterprise Manager

You can also run the advisor from within Enterprise Manager. Log into Enterprise Manager and follow these steps:

1. From the main database page, click the Advisor Central link (near the bottom).
2. Under the Advisors section, click the SQL Advisors link.
3. Click the SQL Tuning Advisor link.

You should be presented with a page similar to the one shown in Figure 11-3.

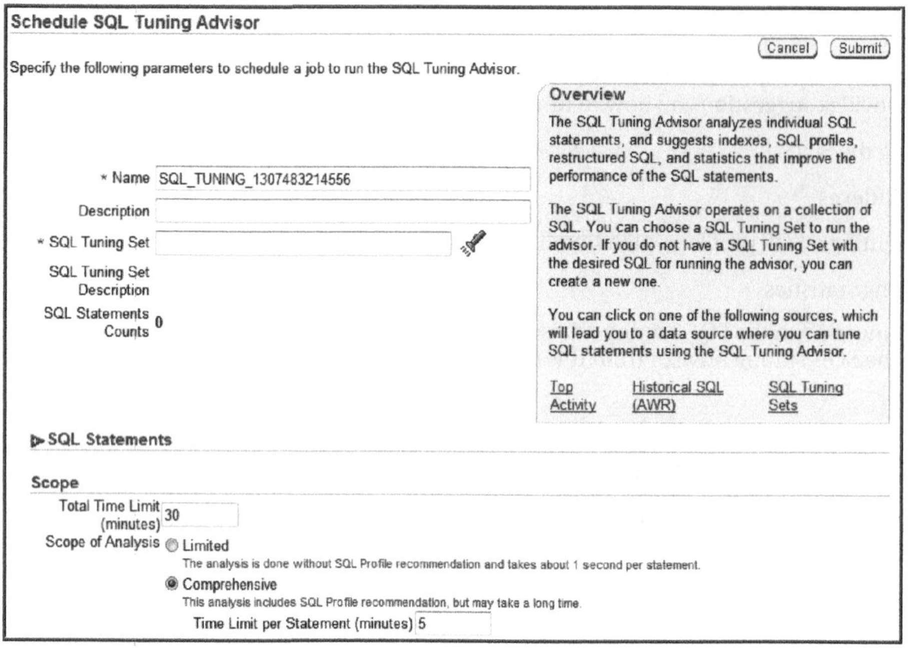

Figure 11-3. Scheduling SQL Tuning Advisor jobs from Enterprise Manager

From here you can run a SQL Tuning Advisor tuning task on the top SQL statements or SQL in the AWR, or provide a SQL tuning set as input.

11-18. Getting SQL Tuning Advice from the Automatic Database Diagnostic Monitor

Problem

You want to get advice on problem SQL statements from the Automatic Database Diagnostic Monitor (ADDM).

Solution

You can view an ADDM report from the following tools:

- SQL*Plus script

- DBMS_ADDM package

- Enterprise Manager

These techniques are elaborated on in the following subsections.

SQL Approach

You can run the ADDM report manually as shown:

```
SQL> @?/rdbms/admin/addmrpt.sql
```

You'll be prompted to specify a beginning and ending snapshot. Here's some sample output:

```
Instance     DB Name         Snap Id   Snap Started        Level
------------ ------------ --------- ------------------- -----
DWREP        DWREP           26482 09 Apr 2011 08:00        1
                            26483 09 Apr 2011 09:00        1
                            26484 09 Apr 2011 10:00        1
                            26485 09 Apr 2011 11:00        1
                            26486 09 Apr 2011 12:00        1


Specify the Begin and End Snapshot Ids
~~~~~~~~~~~~~~~~~~~~~~~~~~~~~~~~~~~~~~~~
Enter value for begin_snap:
```

You'll then be prompted for a report name:

```
The default report file name is addmrpt_1_26468_26486.txt. To use this name,
press <return> to continue, otherwise enter an alternative.
Enter value for report_name:
```

After the report executes, you can inspect the output. There's a Top SQL Statements section that reports on tuning recommendations for the top resource-consuming SQL statement. Here's some sample output:

```
Finding 1: Top SQL Statements
Impact is .79 active sessions, 72.17% of total activity.
-------------------------------------------------------
SQL statements consuming significant database time were found. These
statements offer a good opportunity for performance improvement.
   Recommendation 1: SQL Tuning
   Estimated benefit is .58 active sessions, 53.07% of total activity.
   ----------------------------------------------------------------
   Action
      Investigate the INSERT statement with SQL_ID "2nw0mmysuma43" for
      possible performance improvements. You can supplement the information
      given here with an ASH report for this SQL_ID.
      Related Object
         SQL statement with SQL_ID 2nw0mmysuma43.
         INSERT INTO bling
         ( registration_id,company
         ,soa_id,product_name
```

DBMS_ADDM Package

The DBMS_ADDM package is available with Oracle Database 11g R2 or higher. When using the DBMS_ADDM package, you must pass in a valid range of begin and end AWR snapshot IDs—for example:

```
var task_name varchar2(30);
exec DBMS_ADDM.ANALYZE_DB(:task_name, 8020, 8050);
print :task_name
```

Here is some sample output displaying the task name:

```
TASK_NAME
--------------------------------
TASK_8676
```

Query the DBA_HIST_SNAPSHOT view if you're not sure of what snapshots are available. Next the ADDM report is displayed:

```
SET LONG 1000000 PAGESIZE 0;
SELECT DBMS_ADDM.GET_REPORT('TASK_8676') FROM DUAL;
```

The output can be quite lengthy. Here is a small snippet recommending that you run the SQL Tuning Advisor for a specific SQL statement:

```
Action
   Run SQL Tuning Advisor on the DELETE statement with SQL_ID
   "0s6gq1c890p4s".
   Related Object
      SQL statement with SQL_ID 0s6gq1c890p4s.
      delete from "MVS"."MGMT_DB_FEAT_USE_ECM_LATEST"
Rationale
   The SQL spent 98% of its database time on CPU, I/O and Cluster waits.
   This part of database time may be improved by the SQL Tuning Advisor.
```

Enterprise Manager

First, log into Enterprise Manager. From the main login page, you can access the ADDM reports in Enterprise Manager as follows:

1.   From the main database page, click the Advisor Central link (near the bottom).

2.   Under the Advisors section, click the ADDM link.

You should be presented with a page similar to the one shown in Figure 11-4.

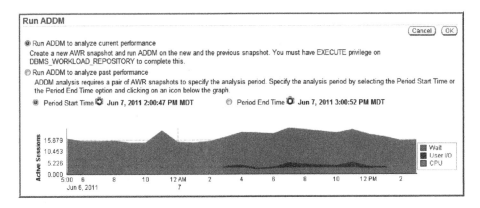

Figure 11-4. *Running ADDM from Enterprise Manager*

From this page, you can run ADDM to analyze current performance or investigate past performance issues.

How It Works

The ADDM analyzes AWR snapshots every hour (by default) and produces performance recommendations. The suggestions are ranked by the expected benefit of implementing a recommendation. Listed next are the types of recommendations you can expect from ADDM:

- Expensive SQL statements

- Expensive PL/SQL

- RAC issues

- CPU bottlenecks

- Memory sizing recommendations

- Database configuration recommendations

- I/O bottlenecks

If you are having database performance issues, the ADDM report is an excellent place to first look for bottlenecks and problem areas of the database. The ADDM also details top resource-consuming SQL statements and makes recommendations on how to tune these queries.

CHAPTER 12

Execution Plan Optimization and Consistency

An execution plan describes how Oracle will retrieve the data to satisfy the results of a query. When you submit a SQL statement, the query optimizer quickly produces several execution plans and will determine which plan is most efficient. In most scenarios, the prior behavior results in a well-performing execution plan. However, you will encounter situations where you know additional details about your environment and need to adjust the optimizer's choice of an execution plan. Listed next are features you can use to influence the decision path the optimizer uses when selecting a plan:

- Initialization parameters

- Statistics

- Hints

- SQL profiles

- SQL plan management (plan baselines)

- Stored outlines (deprecated in favor of plan baselines)

It's critical you understand how these features affect the optimizer's choice of an execution plan. When troubleshooting SQL performance problems, you must determine which of the prior features are enabled and how they influence query behavior. The performance of a SQL statement can vary drastically depending on which feature is implemented and the impact of the various combinations of features.

Initialization parameters (that impact the optimizer) and statistics gathering are detailed in Chapter 13. Using hints is the emphasis of Chapter 14. The focus of this chapter is SQL profiles and plan baselines.

SQL profiles are optionally generated corrections and improvements to statistics. The recommendation (and code) to implement a SQL profile is manifested through the output of the SQL Tuning Advisor. You can manually enable SQL profiles or configure them to be automatically accepted. SQL profiles help the optimizer derive better execution plans.

SQL plan management allows you to store and manage execution plans within tables in the database. *Plan baselines* consist of one or more stored execution plans that have been accepted for a SQL query. When you run a query, and if a plan baseline exists for the query, the optimizer will give precedence to execution plans within the plan baseline. *Plan history* is the super set of both accepted and unaccepted execution plans for a query. You can manually change the state of an unaccepted plan to accepted (this moves it to the plan baseline). This is known as *evolving a plan baseline.*

Plan baselines help ensure that the optimizer consistently chooses the same execution plan, regardless of changes in the database environment. Plan baselines provide the following benefits:

- Preserving performance when upgrading from one database version to another; in other words, helping ensure that the same execution plan is used for a query before and after the upgrade

- Keeping performance stable and consistent when data changes, or statistics are updated, or new SQL profiles become available

- Providing a mechanism for accepting more efficient executions plans as they become available (like a new index is added or a SQL profile becomes available)

Figure 12-1 displays the flow of choices that the optimizer makes when choosing an execution plan. Please take a few minutes to analyze this diagram and ensure you grasp how the various features influence the optimizer's behavior. As you view the diagram, keep in mind the following:

- Hints are the only feature that requires a physical modification to the SQL query. All of the other techniques can be used to improve performance without changing the query.

- Initialization parameters, statistics, hints, SQL profiles, and plan baselines can all operate independently of each other. No one feature is dependent on the existence of another feature.

- The optimizer works fine with out-of-the-box settings. You don't need any of these features (hints, SQL profiles, and so on) to be explicitly enabled. However, to get the maximum performance from SQL queries, we highly recommend you know when and how to use these features to help the query optimizer make optimal decisions.

As you look at the skep-shaped diagram, to help understand how the optimizer chooses between the low-cost plan and a plan baseline plan, consider the general steps taken when formulating an execution plan:

1. The optimizer first considers initialization parameters, hints, and SQL profiles when choosing the lowest-cost plan.

2. Regardless of the plan arrived at in step 1, if a plan baseline exists for the query, the optimizer will choose the lowest-cost plan from the plan baseline. Additionally, the optimizer will give preference to plans that have a fixed state in the plan baseline.

3. If the accepted plans in the plan baseline are not reproducible (say an index has been dropped that all of the plan baseline plans depend on), then the optimizer chooses the lowest-cost plan generated in step 1. Lowest cost in this situation means using the least amount of database resources such as CPU, I/O, and memory.

4.   If a plan baseline exists for a query, and if the low-cost plan (from step 1) has a lower cost than the plan from the plan baseline, then the low-cost plan is automatically added to the plan history for the query in an unaccepted state. You can choose to move plans from the plan history into the plan baseline so that the optimizer will consider them when choosing an execution plan. This provides you the flexibility to use better plans as they become available (evolving the plan).

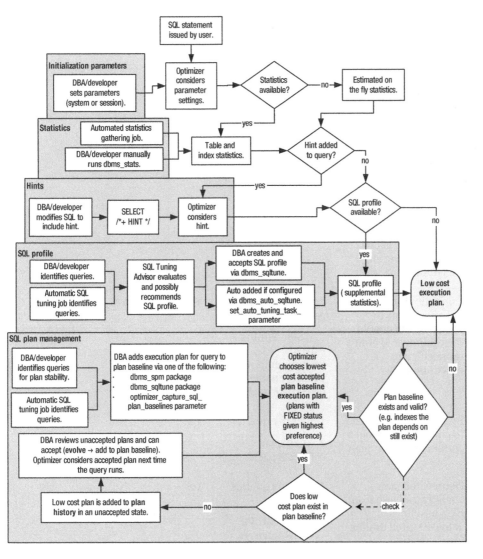

Figure 12-1. Oracle database features influencing optimizer's choice of execution plan

Features such as initialization parameters and hints don't require an extra license and are available with all editions of the Oracle database. Other features such as SQL profiles require an extra license and ship only with the Enterprise Edition. Table 12-1 summarizes the characteristics of each query optimizer-influencing feature.

Table 12-1. *Oracle Features Influencing the Generation of an Execution Plan*

Feature	Purpose	How to Enable	Enterprise Edition Required?	Extra License Required?	Require Change to SQL?
Initialization parameters	Influence aspects such as efficiently delivering query result sets to the client application	ALTER SYSTEM or SESSION statement	No	No	No
Statistics	Provide optimizer with characteristics of the table, data, and indexes so as to better generate execution plans	Statistics are automatically enabled and gathered, and can also be manually collected.	No	No	No
Hints	Suggestions coded into the query to influence optimizer decisions when choosing an execution plan	Add a SQL hint to the query	No	No	Yes
SQL profiles	Corrections and enhancements to statistics that enable the optimizer to craft a more efficient execution plan	1. Run SQL Tuning Advisor. 2. If SQL Tuning Advisor recommends a profile, enable via DBMS_TUNE package.	Yes	Yes	No
Plan baselines	Instructs the optimizer to consistently select a certain execution plan	1. Identify queries. 2. Enable via DBMS_SPM package.	Yes	No	No
Stored Outlines	Deprecated plan stability tool; use fixed plan baselines to achieve stored outline functionality.	1. Identify queries. 2. CREATE OR REPLACE OUTLINE ... FOR <query>.	Yes	No	No

The first part of this chapter focuses on managing SQL profiles. The rest of the chapter deals with the implementation and use of plan baselines. We describe practical and real-world examples of the use of these tools. Where appropriate, we also have added instructions on how to use a given feature via Enterprise Manager.

12-1. Creating and Accepting a SQL Profile

Problem

You have a poorly performing query, and you want to get advice from the SQL Tuning Advisor. You realize that the SQL Tuning Advisor may recommend that a SQL profile be applied to the problem query as part of the tuning recommendation.

Solution

Run the SQL Tuning Advisor for the problem query. Keep in mind that the SQL Tuning Advisor may or may not recommend a SQL profile as a solution for performance issues. To run the SQL Tuning Advisor manually, perform the following steps:

1. Use DBMS_SQLTUNE to create a tuning task.

2. Execute the tuning task.

3. Generate the tuning advice report.

4. If SQL profile is part of the tuning advice output, then create and accept.

The following example follows the prior steps. In this scenario, the SQL Tuning Advisor recommends that a SQL profile be applied to the given query.

■ **Tip**   See Chapter 11 for complete details on creating SQL tuning tasks. Chapter 11 covers topics such as using the AWR, memory, or SQL tuning sets as the source of SQL for a tuning task.

Step 1: Use DBMS_SQLTUNE to Create a Tuning Task

The first step is to create a tuning task that is associated with the problem SQL statement. In the following code, the SQL text is hard-coded as input to the **tune_sql** variable:

```
DECLARE
  tune_sql  CLOB;
  tune_task VARCHAR2(30);
BEGIN
  tune_sql := 'select count(*) from mgmt_db_feature_usage_ecm2';
  tune_task := DBMS_SQLTUNE.CREATE_TUNING_TASK(
    sql_text   => tune_sql
```

```
      ,user_name  => 'STAGING'
      ,scope      => 'COMPREHENSIVE'
      ,time_limit => 60
      ,task_name  => 'TUNE1'
      ,description => 'Calling SQL Tuning Advisor for one statement'
);
END;
/
```

The prior code is placed in a file named `sqltune.sql`, and executed as follows:

```
SQL> @sqltune.sql
```

If you need to later drop the tuning task, you can use the `DBMS_SQLTUNE.DROP_TUNING_TASK` procedure. Obviously don't drop the tuning task at this point because you'll need it for the next several steps.

■ **Note** When working with tuning advice and SQL profiles, ensure that the database account you're using has the `ADMINISTER SQL MANAGEMENT OBJECT` system privilege granted to it. This privilege contains all of the privileges required to manage tuning tasks and SQL profiles.

Step 2: Execute the Tuning Task

This step runs the SQL Tuning Advisor to generate advice regarding any queries associated with the tuning task (created in step 1):

```
SQL> exec dbms_sqltune.execute_tuning_task(task_name=>'TUNE1');
```

Step 3: Run Tuning Advice Report

Now use `DBMS_SQLTUNE` to extract any tuning advice generated in step 2:

```
set long 10000
set longchunksize 10000
set lines 132
set pages 200
select dbms_sqltune.report_tuning_task('TUNE1') from dual;
```

For this example, the SQL Tuning Advisor recommends creating a SQL profile. Here is a snippet from the output that contains the recommendation and the code required to create the SQL profile:

```
Recommendation (estimated benefit: 86.11%)
------------------------------------------
  - Consider accepting the recommended SQL profile to use parallel execution
    for this statement.
    execute dbms_sqltune.accept_sql_profile(task_name => 'TUNE1', task_owner
            => 'SYS', replace => TRUE, profile_type =>
            DBMS_SQLTUNE.PX_PROFILE);
```

```
Executing this query parallel with DOP 8 will improve its response time
86.11% over the original plan. However, there is some cost in enabling
parallel execution...
```

Step 4: Create and Accept SQL Profile

To actually create the SQL profile, you need to run the code recommended by the SQL Tuning Advisor (from step 3)—for example:

```
begin
-- This is the code from the SQL Tuning Advisor
dbms_sqltune.accept_sql_profile(
    task_name => 'TUNE1',
    task_owner => 'SYS',
    replace => TRUE,
    profile_type => DBMS_SQLTUNE.PX_PROFILE);
--
end;
/
```

When the prior code is run, it creates and enables the SQL profile. Now whenever the associated SQL query is executed, the SQL profile will be considered by the optimizer when formulating an execution plan.

■ **Tip**   How do you know if a SQL profile is being used by the optimizer? Set AUTOTRACE on and view the execution plan with the profile enabled and then disabled. You should see a lower-cost execution plan being used when the profile is enabled. Additionally, consider inspecting the SQL_PROFILE column of V$SQL.

How It Works

The only Oracle-supported method for creating a SQL profile is to run the SQL Tuning Advisor and if recommended, create a SQL profile using the Tuning Advisor's output. In other words, the SQL Tuning Advisor determines if a SQL profile will help, and if so generates the code required to create a SQL profile for a given query.

The "Solution" section detailed how to manually run the SQL Tuning Advisor. Keep in mind that as of Oracle Database 11g, this tuning task job automatically runs on a regularly scheduled basis. See Chapter 11 for details on automatic SQL tuning features. You can easily review the output of the automatic tuning job via this query:

```
SQL> SELECT DBMS_AUTO_SQLTUNE.REPORT_AUTO_TUNING_TASK FROM DUAL;
```

We recommend that you review the output of the automatic tuning job on a regular basis. The SQL Tuning Advisor will provide the code to create and accept SQL profiles as part of the output.

■ **Tip**   See Recipe 12-2 for details on how to configure the automatic acceptance of SQL profiles.

As noted in the "Solution" section, a SQL profile is created and accepted via the DBMS_SQLTUNE.ACCEPT_SQL_PROFILE procedure. There are many options available when using this procedure (see Table 12-2 for details).

Table 12-2. *Parameters for the ACCEPT_SQL_PROFILE Procedure*

Parameter Name	Description
TASK_NAME	Mandatory name of tuning task
OBJECT_ID	The identifier of the advisor object representing the SQL statement
NAME	Name of SQL profile (case-sensitive)
DESCRIPTION	Description of SQL profile
CATEGORY	Category name that must match the session value of the SQLTUNE_CATEGORY initialization parameter
TASK_OWNER	Tuning task owner
REPLACE	Specify TRUE to replace profile if it already exists
FORCE_MATCH	Specify TRUE for SQL statement matching after normalization of literal values into bind values
PROFILE_TYPE	REGULAR_PROFILE specifies no change to parallel execution; PX_PROFILE changes regular profile to parallel execution.

The FORCE_MATCH parameter of ACCEPT_SQL_PROFILE requires further explanation. Recall that a SQL profile is associated with a SQL statement. The SQL statement is identified via a hash function (SQL signature). The hash function is generated after converting the SQL text and removing extra white space. When setting FORCE_MATCH to TRUE, this additionally normalizes literal values into bind values. This is similar to the algorithm generated via the FORCE option of the CURSOR_SHARING database initialization parameter.

For example, with FORCE_MATCH set to TRUE, the following two SQL statements will generate the same SQL signature:

```
SQL> select value from my_table where value = 'AA';
SQL> select value from my_table where value = 'bb';
```

This allows SQL statements that use literal values to share the same SQL profile. If there is a combination of literal values and bind variables in a SQL statement, then literal values are not normalized.

SQL PROFILE VS. DATABASE PROFILE

It's puzzling that Oracle would choose the name of "profile" and apply it to two diverse database features, namely SQL profiles and database profiles. Perhaps in a future release, Oracle might consider renaming SQL profiles to something like SQL Optional More Intelligent Statistics That Make Your Queries Run Faster. Regardless, ensure you don't confuse a SQL profile with a database profile.

Briefly, a SQL profile is associated with a SQL statement and contains corrections to statistics that help the optimizer generate a more efficient execution plan. The SQL Tuning Advisor recommends and generates the code required to create and accept a SQL profile, whereas a database profile is an object assigned to a user that constrains database resource usage and also enforces password security. A database profile is created with the CREATE PROFILE statement.

12-2. Automatically Accepting SQL Profiles

Problem

You realize that the Automatic SQL Tuning job runs on a daily basis (in Oracle Database 11g or higher). You determine that the automatic tuning job generates reasonable SQL profiles for problematic queries and now want to enable the automatic acceptance of SQL profiles generated by the automatic tuning job.

■ **Tip**   See Chapter 11 for full details on modifying the Automatic SQL Tuning job.

Solution

Use the DBMS_AUTO_SQLTUNE.SET_AUTO_TUNING_TASK_PARAMETER procedure to enable the automatic acceptance of SQL profiles recommended by the Automatic SQL Tuning task—for example:

```
BEGIN
DBMS_AUTO_SQLTUNE.SET_AUTO_TUNING_TASK_PARAMETER(
  parameter => 'ACCEPT_SQL_PROFILES', value => 'TRUE');
END;
/
```

If you want to disable the automatic acceptance of SQL profiles, then do so as follows (using the FALSE parameter):

```
BEGIN
DBMS_AUTO_SQLTUNE.SET_AUTO_TUNING_TASK_PARAMETER(
  parameter => 'ACCEPT_SQL_PROFILES', value => 'FALSE');
END;
/
```

■ **Note** The DBMS_AUTO_SQLTUNE package requires the DBA role or that EXECUTE on the package has been granted explicitly to a user. This package is available in Oracle Database 11g R2 or higher. If you are using a lower version of the database, then use the DBMS_SQLTUNE package.

How It Works

In Oracle Database 11g or higher, an automatically configured job runs the SQL Tuning Advisor on a periodic basis (determined by a configured maintenance window). This job identifies high resource-consuming SQL statements from performance metrics contained in the AWR. When the automatic tuning job runs, it will occasionally recommend that a SQL profile be implemented for a poorly performing SQL statement. Oracle will automatically accept the profile if the following conditions are true:

- Automatic acceptance has been configured via DBMS_AUTO_SQLTUNE.SET_AUTO_TUNING_TASK_PARAMETER.

- With the SQL profile, the performance gain is determined (by the SQL Tuning Advisor) to be at least three times more (than without the profile).

You can report on the details of the automatic tuning task configuration via this query:

```
SELECT
 parameter_name
,parameter_value
FROM dba_advisor_parameters
WHERE task_name = 'SYS_AUTO_SQL_TUNING_TASK'
AND   parameter_name
  IN ('ACCEPT_SQL_PROFILES',
      'MAX_SQL_PROFILES_PER_EXEC',
      'MAX_AUTO_SQL_PROFILES',
      'EXECUTION_DAYS_TO_EXPIRE');
```

Here is some sample output:

```
PARAMETER_NAME            PARAMETER_VALUE
------------------------- --------------------
EXECUTION_DAYS_TO_EXPIRE  30
ACCEPT_SQL_PROFILES       TRUE
MAX_SQL_PROFILES_PER_EXEC 20
MAX_AUTO_SQL_PROFILES     10000
```

■ **Tip** SQL profiles that have automatically been implemented display the value of AUTO in the TYPE column of the DBA_SQL_PROFILES view.

You can also use Enterprise Manager to configure the automatic acceptance of SQL profiles. From the main database page, navigate to the Advisor Central page. Next, click the SQL Advisors link. Now click the Automatic SQL Tuning Results page. Next click the configure button of Automatic Implementation of SQL Profiles. You should see a page similar to Figure 12-2.

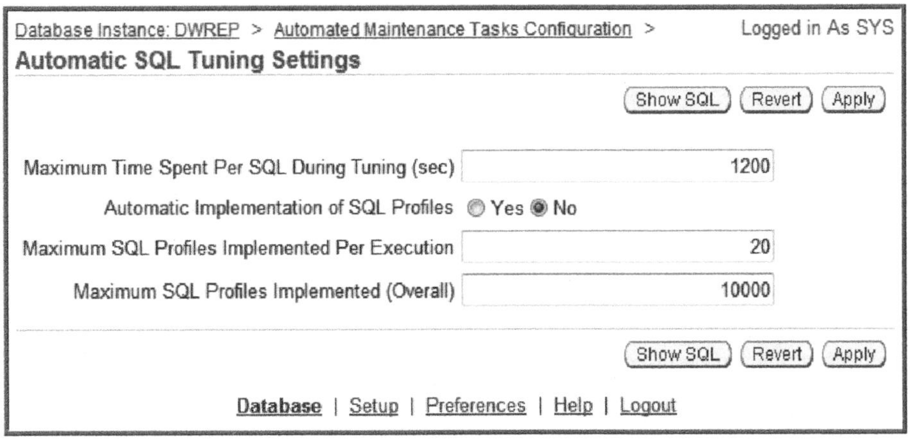

Figure 12-2. Configuring automatic acceptance of SQL profiles

From this screen, you can manage features such as the automatic acceptance of SQL profiles, maximum time for a tuning session, and so on.

12-3. Displaying SQL Profile Information

Problem

You have created and accepted several SQL profiles and now want to view information related to these database objects.

Solution

Use the DBA_SQL_PROFILES view to display information about SQL profiles. Here's an example that selects the most interesting columns:

```
SQL> select name, type, status, sql_text from dba_sql_profiles;
```

Here is a snippet of the output:

```
NAME                             TYPE     STATUS    SQL_TEXT
-----------------------------    ------   --------  ------------------------------
SYS_SQLPROF_012eda58a1be0001     MANUAL   ENABLED   SELECT ecm_snapshot_id AS id...
SYS_SQLPROF_012ea20305980000     MANUAL   ENABLED   SELECT * FROM inv_maint...
SYS_SQLPROF_012edf0316930003     MANUAL   ENABLED   SELECT /* + parallel(mgmt_db_f...
```

For this database, there are several manually enabled SQL profiles (as shown in the prior output).

■ **Note** Since a SQL profile is associated with a specific SQL statement (and not a user), there are no ALL- or USER-level views associated with SQL profiles.

How It Works

Recall that a SQL profile contains improvements to existing statistics. The DBA_SQL_PROFILES view is the best source for viewing the SQL profile name, attributes, and associated SQL text.

To view the internal SQL profile hint-related information, you can additionally query the DBMSHSXP_SQL_PROFILE_ATTR view—for example:

```
SELECT
 a.name
,b.comp_data
FROM dba_sql_profiles       a
    ,dbmshsxp_sql_profile_attr b
WHERE a.name = b.profile_name;
```

Here is some sample output:

```
SYS_SQLPROF_0130520c90dc0002
<outline_data><hint><![CDATA[OPT_ESTIMATE(@"SEL$2",
NLJ_INDEX_SCAN, "FS"@"SEL$2", ("MAP"@"SEL$2"), "DB_FEAT_OPT_112_SUM_MV_IDX3",
SCALE_ROWS=0.3369001041)]]></h
```

The prior output gives you an indication of the types of hints within a SQL profile. This information is used by the optimizer to better estimate the cardinality of each execution step. This data allows the optimizer to make better decisions when generating an execution plan.

You can also view this internal SQL profile information by querying the SQLOBJ$ and SQLOBJ$DATA views. The data in these views is in XML format, and therefore you must format the output with Oracle XML functions when querying—for example:

```
SELECT
  extractvalue(value(a), '.') sqlprofile_hints
FROM sqlobj$     o
    ,sqlobj$data d
    ,table(xmlsequence(extract(xmltype(d.comp_data),'/outline_data/hint'))) a
WHERE o.name    = '&&profile_name'
AND   o. plan_id = d.plan_id
AND   o.signature = d.signature
```

```
AND    o.category = d.category
AND    o.obj_type = d.obj_type;
```

Here is a small sample of the output:

```
OPT_ESTIMATE(@"SEL$EFOEO5FC", INDEX_SCAN, "MGMT_TARGETS"@"SEL$4",
"MIDX3", SCALE_ROWS=50.68489486)
OPT_ESTIMATE(@"SEL$EFOEO5FC", NLJ_INDEX_FILTER,
"MGMT_ECM_GEN_SNAPSHOT"@"SEL$3", ("MGMT_TARGETS"@"SEL$4"),
"IDX$$_1197C0001", SCALE_ROWS=0.4308705)
```

Again, these profile statistics don't force the optimizer to use a certain execution plan. Rather these statistics provide the optimizer the flexibility to choose a more efficient execution plan.

■ **Note**   If you're using Oracle Database 10g, then use the SQLPROF$ and SQLPROF$ATTR views.

12-4. Disabling a SQL Profile

Problem

You think that a SQL profile is no longer required for a query. You want to manually disable (not drop) the SQL profile.

Solution

First verify the name of the SQL profile that you want to disable:

```
SQL> select name, status from dba_sql_profiles;
```

Here's a partial snippet of the output:

```
NAME                             STATUS
------------------------------   --------
SYS_SQLPROF_012eda58a1be0001     ENABLED
```

Now use the DBMS_SQLTUNE.ALTER_SQL_PROFILE procedure to modify the status of the profile to disabled:

```
BEGIN
  DBMS_SQLTUNE.ALTER_SQL_PROFILE(
    name => 'SYS_SQLPROF_012eda58a1be0001',
    attribute_name => 'STATUS',
    value => 'DISABLED');
END;
/
```

How It Works

The status of a SQL profile is one of several modifiable attributes. You can also modify characteristics such as the name, description, and category. See Table 12-3 for a description of the modifiable attributes.

■ **Note** You need the ALTER ANY SQL PROFILE privilege to alter a SQL profile.

Table 12-3. Modifiable SQL Profile Attributes

Attribute Name	Possible Values	Description
STATUS	ENABLED or DISABLED	Enable or disable the use of an existing SQL profile
NAME	Valid unique identifier	Used to reset the name of the profile
DESCRIPTION	Character string up to 500 characters	Description of the SQL profile
CATEGORY	Valid category name	Used to reset the category name

The category of a SQL profile has some interesting implications. A category allows you to control the use of a SQL profile through the setting of the SQLTUNE_CATEGORY initialization parameter (this parameter can be set at the session or system level). When a query is executed, if a SQL profile is available, the optimizer will check to ensure that the category assigned to the SQL profile is the same as the system- or session-level setting of SQLTUNE_CATEGORY. If the category of the SQL profile matches the setting of SQLTUNE_CATEGORY, then the optimizer will consider using the SQL profile.

The default category for a SQL profile is DEFAULT. Also the default value for SQLTUNE_CATEGORY is DEFAULT. Therefore, unless you alter the SQL profile category or modify the SQLTUNE_CATEGORY parameter, the SQL profile will be used as input by the optimizer.

You can alter the category to something other than DEFAULT. This means that only sessions that modify the initialization parameter of SQLTUNE_CATEGORY to the value of the category for the SQL profile will be able to use the profile. For example, say you modify the SQL profile to have a category of TEST1:

```
BEGIN
  DBMS_SQLTUNE.ALTER_SQL_PROFILE(
    name => 'SYS_SQLPROF_012eda58a1be0001',
    attribute_name => 'CATEGORY',
    value => 'TEST1');
END;
/
```

Now the only sessions that can see and use the profile are those that have SQLTUNE_CATEGORY set to TEST1:

```
SQL> alter session set sqltune_category=TEST1;
```

This allows you to isolate a profile's use to only those sessions that have the SQLTUNE_CATEGORY set to match the category of the SQL profile. This allows you to test the impact of implementing a SQL profile and back it out quickly, simply by altering either the session-level or system-level setting of SQLTUNE_CATEGORY.

You can also manage many aspects of a SQL profile from Enterprise Manager. From the main database page, navigate to the Server tab. In the Query Optimizer section, click the SQL Plan Control tab. You should be presented with a screen similar to Figure 12-3.

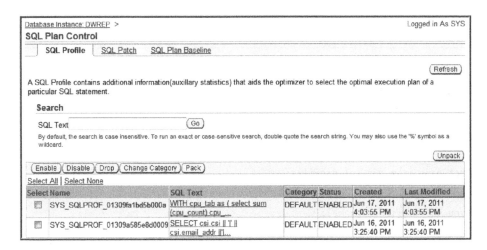

Figure 12-3. *Managing SQL profiles*

From this screen, you can manage features such as enabling, disabling, changing the category, and dropping a SQL profile.

12-5. Dropping a SQL Profile

Problem

You've tested a query with and without a SQL profile attached to the query. You determine the query performance is not significantly better with the SQL profile. You want to drop the SQL profile so you're not cluttering up the data dictionary with unnecessary and obsolete information.

Solution

Use the DBMS_SQLTUNE.DROP_SQL_PROFILE procedure to drop a SQL profile. Pass in the name of the SQL profile you want to drop—for example:

```
SQL> exec dbms_sqltune.drop_sql_profile('SYS_SQLPROF_012edef0d0a70002');
```

If successful, you should see the following:

```
PL/SQL procedure successfully completed.
```

How It Works

It's fairly easy to drop a SQL profile. You might want to do this if you're cleaning up a database or if you want to remove profiles from a testing environment. If you're unsure of the SQL profile name, you can query DBA_SQL_PROFILES for more information (see Recipe 12-3 for details).

■ **Note**   You need the DROP ANY SQL PROFILE privilege to drop a SQL profile.

If you want to drop all profiles in a database, you can use PL/SQL to loop through all profiles and drop them:

```
declare
  cursor c1 is select name from dba_sql_profiles;
begin
  for r1 in c1 loop
    dbms_sqltune.drop_sql_profile(r1.name);
  end loop;
end;
/
```

12-6. Moving a SQL Profile

Problem

You have a test database and want to extract all of the SQL profiles from the test database and move them to a production database.

Solution

Listed next are the steps involved with transporting a SQL profile from one database to another:

1. Create a staging table.

2. Populate the staging table.

3. Move the table from the source database to the destination database (Data Pump or database link).

4. On the destination database, extract information from the staging table to populate the data dictionary with SQL profile information.

These steps are detailed in the following subsections.

Step 1: Create a Staging Table

Use the DBMS_SQLTUNE.CREATE_STGTAB_SQLPROF procedure to create the staging table. This example creates a table named PROF_STAGE owned by the MV_MAINT user:

```
BEGIN
  dbms_sqltune.create_stgtab_sqlprof(
    table_name => 'PROF_STAGE',
    schema_name => 'MV_MAINT' );
END;
/
```

Step 2: Populate the Staging Table

Use the DBMS_SQLTUNE.PACK_STGTAB_SQLPROF procedure to populate the table created in step 1 with SQL profile information. This example populates the table with information regarding a specific SQL profile:

```
BEGIN
  dbms_sqltune.pack_stgtab_sqlprof(
    profile_name => 'SYS_SQLPROF_012edf84806e0004',
    staging_table_name => 'PROF_STAGE',
    staging_schema_owner => 'MV_MAINT' );
END;
/
```

■ **Tip**   The PROFILE_NAME parameter can include wildcard characters. For example, if you want to transport all SQL profiles in a database, you can use '%' for the PROFILE_NAME.

Step 3: Copy the Staging Table to the Destination Database

You can copy the table from one database to the other via Data Pump, the old exp/imp utilities, or by using a database link. This example creates a database link in the destination database and then copies the table from the source database:

```
create database link source_db
connect to mv_maint
identified by foo
using 'source_db';
```

Once the database link has been created, the table can be copied directly from the source with the CREATE TABLE...AS SELECT statement:

```
SQL> create table PROF_STAGE as select * from PROF_STAGE@source_db;
```

Step 4: Load the Contents of the Staging Table into the Destination Database

Now in the destination database, unpack the table to load profile information into the database:

```
BEGIN
  DBMS_SQLTUNE.UNPACK_STGTAB_SQLPROF(
    replace => TRUE,
    staging_table_name => 'PROF_STAGE');
END;
/
```

If no profile name is specified, the default is the % wildcard character (meaning all profiles in the table will be loaded into the destination database).

How It Works

It's fairly easy to copy SQL profiles from one database to another. You simply have to create a special table to hold the profile information, then populate the table, copy the table to the destination database, and lastly unpack the table's contents. Table 12-4 describes all of the parameters for the profile packing procedure.

Table 12-4. Parameters for the `DBMS_SQLTUNE.PACK_STGTAB_SQLPROF` *Procedure*

Parameter Name	Description	Default Value
PROFILE_NAME	Name of profile (% wildcard characters can be used)	%
PROFILE_CATEGORY	Name of category, can use % wildcards in name	DEFAULT
STAGING_TABLE_NAME	Name of the staging table to store profile information	No default value.
STAGING_SCHEMA_OWNER	Owner of staging table (NULL means use current schema)	NULL

The `DBMS_SQLTUNE.UNPACK_STGTAB_SQLPROF` procedure takes the same parameters as the packing procedure with an additional `REPLACE` parameter. The `REPLACE` parameter specifies whether to replace profiles if they already exist (can be `TRUE` or `FALSE`).

12-7. Automatically Adding Plan Baselines

Problem

You want to automatically create plan baselines for every SQL query that repeatedly executes in your database.

Solution

Listed next are the steps for automatically creating plan baselines for SQL statements that execute more than once:

1. Set the `OPTIMIZER_CAPTURE_SQL_PLAN_BASELINES` parameter to `TRUE` (either at the session or system level).

2. Execute two times or more the queries for which you want plan baselines captured.

3. Set the `OPTIMIZER_CAPTURE_SQL_PLAN_BASELINES` to `FALSE`.

This next example illustrates the process for adding a plan baseline (for a query) using the prior steps. First set the specified initialization parameter at the session level:

```
SQL> alter session set optimizer_capture_sql_plan_baselines=true;
```

Now a query is executed twice. Oracle will automatically create a plan baseline for a query that is run two or more times while the `OPTIMIZER_CAPTURE_SQL_PLAN_BASELINES` parameter is set to `TRUE`:

```
SQL> select emp_id from emp where emp_id=3000;
SQL> select emp_id from emp where emp_id=3000;
```

Now set the initialization parameter back to `FALSE`.

```
SQL> alter session set optimizer_capture_sql_plan_baselines=false;
```

The query now should have an entry in the `DBA_SQL_PLAN_BASELINES` view showing that it has an enabled plan baseline associated with it—for example:

```
SELECT
 sql_handle, plan_name, enabled, accepted,
 created, optimizer_cost, sql_text
FROM dba_sql_plan_baselines;
```

Here is a partial listing of the output:

```
SQL_HANDLE          PLAN_NAME                      ENA ACC...
------------------- ------------------------------ --- ---...
SQL_790bd425fe4a0125 SQL_PLAN_7k2yn4rz4n095d8a279cc YES YES...
```

How It Works

Enabling `OPTIMIZER_CAPTURE_SQL_PLAN_BASELINES` allows you to automatically capture plan baselines for queries running repeatedly (more than once) in your database. The "Solution" section described how to use this feature at the session level. You can also set the parameter so that all repeating queries in the database have plan baselines generated—for example:

```
SQL> alter system set optimizer_capture_sql_plan_baselines=true;
```

From this point, any query in the database that runs more than once will automatically have a plan baseline created for it. We wouldn't recommend that you do this in a production environment unless you have first carefully tested this feature and ensured that there will be no adverse side effects (from storing a plan baseline for every query). However, you may have a test environment where you want to purposely create a plan baseline for every SQL statement that is repeatedly run.

■ **Note** By default, the `OPTIMIZER_CAPTURE_SQL_PLAN_BASELINES` parameter is `FALSE`.

You can also manage the use of plan baselines from Enterprise Manager. From the main database page, navigate to the Server tab. In the Query Optimizer section, click the SQL Plan Control tab. Next, click the SQL Plan Baseline tab. You should see a screen similar to Figure 12-4.

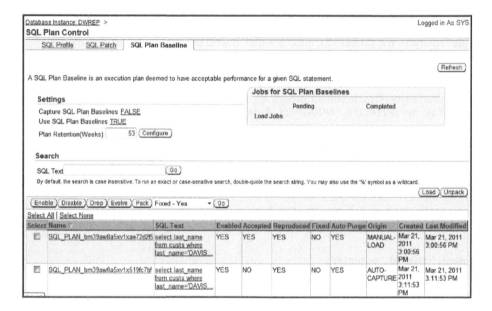

Figure 12-4. Managing plan baselines

From this screen, you can manage tasks such as enabling, disabling, dropping, and evolving plan baselines.

12-8. Creating a Plan Baseline for One SQL Statement

Problem

You want to create a plan baseline for a specific SQL statement that you're currently executing.

Solution

The procedure for manually associating a plan baseline with a SQL statement is as follows:

1. Identify the SQL statement(s) for which you want plan baselines.

2. Provide an identifier such as the SQL_ID as input to the DBMS_SPM package to create a plan baseline for the SQL statement.

For example, suppose you have a SQL statement you've been working with such as the following:

```
SQL> select emp_id from emp where emp_id = 100;
```

Now query the V$SQL view to determine the SQL_ID for the query:

```
select
 sql_id
,sql_text
from v$sql
where sql_text
  like 'select emp_id from emp where emp_id = 100';
```

Here is a snippet of the output:

```
SQL_ID         SQL_TEXT
-------------- ------------------------------------------------------------
0qgmjf9krq285 select emp_id from emp where emp_id = 100
```

Now that the SQL_ID has been identified, use it as input to the DBMS_SPM.LOAD_PLANS_FROM_CURSOR_CACHE function to create a plan baseline for the given query—for example:

```
DECLARE
  plan1 PLS_INTEGER;
BEGIN
  plan1 := DBMS_SPM.LOAD_PLANS_FROM_CURSOR_CACHE(sql_id => '0qgmjf9krq285');
END;
/
```

The query now should have an entry in the DBA_SQL_PLAN_BASELINES view showing that it has an enabled plan baseline associated with it—for example:

```
SQL> select sql_handle, plan_name, sql_text from dba_sql_plan_baselines;
```

Here's a small snippet of the output:

```
SQL_HANDLE                PLAN_NAME                                 SQL_TEXT
------------------------- ----------------------------------------- ----------------------
SQL_f34ef255797c4713      SQL_PLAN_g6mrkapwrsjsmd8a279cc            select emp_id.....
```

How It Works

The "Solution" section described how to identify a single SQL statement for which you want to create a plan baseline (based on the SQL_ID) using a query in the cursor cache. There are many methods for creating a plan baseline for a query, such as using the SQL text, schema, module, and so on. For example, next a plan baseline is loaded based on a partial SQL string:

```
DECLARE
  plan1 PLS_INTEGER;
BEGIN
  plan1 := DBMS_SPM.LOAD_PLANS_FROM_CURSOR_CACHE(
             attribute_name => 'sql_text'
            ,attribute_value => 'select emp_id from emp%');
END;
/
```

See Table 12-5 for details on input parameters available with the
DBMS_SPM.LOAD_PLANS_FROM_CURSOR_CACHE function.

■ **Note**   See Recipe 12-9 for an example of how to create plan baselines for SQL statements contained in a SQL
tuning set.

Table 12-5. *Parameters for the LOAD_PLANS_FROM_CURSOR_CACHE Function*

Parameter Name	Description
SQL_ID	SQL statement identifier
PLAN_HASH_VALUE	Plan identifier; if NULL, then capture all plans for the given SQL_ID.
SQL_TEXT	Text used for identifying plan baseline into which plans are loaded
SQL_HANDLE	SQL handle used for identifying plan baseline into which plans are loaded
FIXED	Value of NO means plans are not loaded in a fixed state. YES means plans are loaded as fixed. Fixed plan baselines are given preference over non-fixed.
ATTRIBUTE_NAME	One of the following: SQL_TEXT, PARSING_SCHEMA_NAME, MODULE, ACTION
ATTRIBUTE_VALUE	Value of the attribute; when using SQL_TEXT attribute, the value can contain wildcard values.
ENABLED	Plans are loaded in an enabled state (default is YES).

12-9. Creating Plan Baselines for SQL Contained in SQL Tuning Set

Problem

You have the following scenario:

- You're upgrading a database to a new version.

- You know from past experience that upgrading to newer versions of Oracle can sometimes cause SQL statements to perform poorly because the optimizer in the upgraded version of the database is choosing a less efficient (worse) execution plan than the optimizer from the prior version of the database.

- You want to ensure that SQL statements execute with acceptable performance after the upgrade.

In essence, you are upgrading and would prefer that the optimizer choose the same execution plans both before and after the upgrade. You don't want the upgrade to result in new plans that risk degrading performance.

Solution

To deal with this problem, use the most resource-intensive SQL queries in the AWR as candidates for the creation of plan baselines. This solution uses the technique of creating an AWR baseline. An AWR baseline is a snapshot of activity in the AWR designated by begin/end snapshot IDs. Listed next are the steps for creating and populating a SQL tuning set with high resource-consuming SQL statements found in an AWR baseline and then creating plan baselines for those queries:

1. Create an AWR baseline.

2. Create a SQL tuning set object.

3. Populate the SQL tuning set with the queries found in the AWR baseline.

4. Use the tuning set as input to DBMS_SPM to create a plan baseline for each query contained in the SQL tuning set.

■ **Note** You have a great deal of flexibility on how to populate a SQL tuning set with high resource-consuming queries in the AWR or memory. See Chapter 11 for complete details on working with SQL tuning sets.

Step 1: Create an AWR Baseline

The first step is to create an AWR baseline. For example, suppose you knew you had high-load queries running between two snapshots in your database. The following creates an AWR baseline using two snapshot IDs:

```
BEGIN
  DBMS_WORKLOAD_REPOSITORY.create_baseline (
    start_snap_id => 26632,
    end_snap_id   => 26635,
    baseline_name => 'peak_baseline_apr15_11');
END;
/
```

If you're unsure of the available snapshots in your database, you can run an AWR report or select the SNAP_ID from DBA_HIST_SNAPSHOTS:

```
select snap_id, begin_interval_time
from dba_hist_snapshot order by 1;
```

Step 2: Create a SQL Tuning Set Object

Now create a SQL tuning set. This next bit of code creates a tuning set named test1:

```
BEGIN
  dbms_sqltune.create_sqlset(
    sqlset_name => 'test1'
   ,description => 'STS from AWR');
END;
/
```

Step 3: Populate the SQL Tuning Set with High-Resource Queries Found in AWR Baseline

Now the SQL tuning set (created in step 2) is populated with any queries found within the AWR baseline (created in step 1):

```
DECLARE
  base_cur dbms_sqltune.sqlset_cursor;
BEGIN
  OPEN base_cur FOR
    SELECT value(x)
    FROM table(dbms_sqltune.select_workload_repository(
      'peak_baseline_apr15_11', null, null,'elapsed_time',
      null, null, null, 15)) x;
  --
```

```
  dbms_sqltune.load_sqlset(
    sqlset_name => 'test1',
    populate_cursor => base_cur);
END;
/
```

In the prior lines of a code, the AWR baseline name is passed to the DBMS_SQLTUNE package. The queries within the baseline are select by the elapsed time, and the top 15 are specified.

Step 4: Use the Tuning Set As Input to DBMS_SPM to Create Plan Baselines for Each Query Contained in the SQL Tuning Set

Now the tuning set (populated in step 3) is provided as input to the DBMS_SPM package:

```
DECLARE
  test_plan1 PLS_INTEGER;
BEGIN
  test_plan1 := dbms_spm.load_plans_from_sqlset(
                  sqlset_name=>'test1');
END;
/
```

Any queries contained in the tuning set should now have entries in the DBA_SQL_PLAN_BASELINES view.

How It Works

The technique shown in the "Solution" section is a very powerful method for creating plan baselines for the most resource-consuming queries running in your database. The key to this recipe is understanding that you can use as input (to the DBMS_SPM package) queries contained in a SQL tuning set. A SQL tuning set can be populated from high resource-consuming statements found in the AWR and memory. This allows you to easily create plan baselines for the most problematic queries.

Having plan baselines in place for resource-intensive queries helps ensure that the same execution plan is used after there are changes to your system, such as a database upgrades, changes in statistics, different data sets, and so on.

Keep in mind that it's possible to have more than one accepted execution plan within the plan baseline. If you have a specific plan that you want the optimizer to always use, then consider altering the plan to a FIXED state. See Recipe 12-10 for details on altering a plan baseline to a FIXED state.

12-10. Altering a Plan Baseline

Problem

You have several accepted plan baseline execution plans for one query. You want to specifically instruct the optimizer to give preference to one of the accepted plans.

Solution

The optimizer will give preference to plan baselines with a FIXED state. Use the DBMS_SPM package and ALTER_SQL_PLAN_BASELINE function to alter a current plan baseline execution plan to FIXED. Here's an example:

```
DECLARE
 pf PLS_INTEGER;
BEGIN
  pf := dbms_spm.alter_sql_plan_baseline(
    plan_name => 'SQL_PLAN_1wskqhvrwf8g60e23be79'
    ,attribute_name => 'fixed'
    ,attribute_value => 'YES');
END;
/
```

You can query the FIXED column of DBA_SQL_PLAN_BASELINES to verify that it is now baseline-neutered. Listed next is such a query:

```
SELECT
 sql_handle, plan_name, enabled, accepted, fixed
FROM dba_sql_plan_baselines;
```

Here is some sample output:

```
SQL_HANDLE          PLAN_NAME                         ENA ACC FIX
------------------- ----------------------------- --- --- ---
SQL_457bf2f82571bd38 SQL_PLAN_4ayzkz0kr3g9s90e466fd YES YES NO
SQL_790bd425fe4a0125 SQL_PLAN_7k2yn4rz4n095d8a279cc YES YES YES
```

How It Works

You can think of fixing a plan baseline as a way of establishing a preference hierarchy for how the optimizer chooses a plan baseline. The optimizer will give first priority to any accepted *and* fixed plan baselines. If none is available, then accepted non-fixed plan baselines are considered. Execution plans that are added to a plan baseline that already contains a fixed plan baseline will be considered secondary (unless you add them as fixed).

Table 12-6 describes the parameters available with ALTER_SQL_PLAN_BASELINE. You can specify either the SQL_HANDLE or PLAN_NAME or both. If the SQL_HANDLE is NULL, then a PLAN_NAME must be specified and vice versa.

Table 12-6. *Parameters for the* ALTER_SQL_PLAN_BASELINE *Function*

Parameter	Description
SQL_HANDLE	SQL handle identifier for the SQL statement in the plan baseline
PLAN_NAME	Unique identifier for a plan baseline
ATTRIBUTE_NAME	Name of the attribute being modified
ATTRIBUTE_VALUE	Attribute value being modified

The ATTRIBUTE_NAME and ATTRIBUTE_VALUE parameters consist of a name/value pairing that can be used to alter various attributes of a plan baseline. See Table 12-7 for a complete description of the possible pairings.

▓ **Tip**　Use the ENABLED attribute of ALTER_SQL_PLAN_BASELINE to either disable or re-enable a plan baseline for use.

Table 12-7. *Values for* ATTRIBUTE_NAME *and* ATTRIBUTE_VALUE

Attribute Name	Possible Attribute Values	Description
ENABLED	YES or NO	YES means the plan is available for use. The plan may or may not have been accepted.
FIXED	YES or NO	YES means the plan is fixed.
AUTOPURGE	YES or NO	YES means the plan can be purged if the plan isn't used within a time period. NO means the plan is never purged.
PLAN_NAME	String up to 30 characters	Name of plan
DESCRIPTION	String up to 500 characters	Description of plan

12-11. Determining If Plan Baselines Exist

Problem

You recently implemented a plan baseline for a query. You want to verify the configuration of a plan baseline.

Solution

Run the following query to view details regarding any plan baselines that have been configured:

```
set pages 100
set linesize 132
col sql_handle form a20
col plan_name form a30
col sql_text form a20
col created form a20
--
SELECT sql_handle, plan_name, enabled
,accepted, created, optimizer_cost, sql_text
FROM dba_sql_plan_baselines;
```

The output from the prior query is very wide and has been modified to fit within the page width:

```
SQL_HANDLE            PLAN_NAME                       ENA ACC
-------------------- ------------------------------- --- ---
SQL_b98d2ae2145eec3d SQL_PLAN_bm39aw8a5xv1xae72d2f5 YES YES
CREATED              OPTIMIZER_COST SQL_TEXT
-------------------- -------------- --------------------
21-MAR-11 10.53.29.0              2 select last_name from custs...
```

In the output, there are two key columns: the SQL_HANDLE and PLAN_NAME. Each query has an associated SQL_HANDLE that is an identifier for a query. Each execution plan has a unique PLAN_NAME. The PLAN_NAME will be unique within DBA_SQL_PLAN_BASELINES, whereas there could be multiple rows with the same SQL_HANDLE (but different PLAN_NAME).

How It Works

The DBA_SQL_PLAN_BASELINES view provides a quick and easy way to determine if plan baselines exist and are in use. If a plan is enabled and accepted, then the query has a plan baseline in use.

■ **Note** There is no ALL or USER-level data dictionary views for plan baselines. This is because the plan baseline is associated with a specific SQL statement and not a user.

If you have doubts about whether a plan baseline is being considered by the optimizer, then set AUTOTRACE on and view the output—for example:

```
SQL> set autotrace trace explain;
SQL> select emp_id from emp where emp_id = 100;
```

Here is a partial listing of the output indicating that a SQL plan baseline execution plan is used for this query:

```
Execution Plan
-------------------------------------------------------
Plan hash value: 2872589290
---------------------------------------------------------------------
..................
- SQL plan baseline "SQL_PLAN_g6mrkapwrsjsmd8a279cc" used for this statement
```

12-12. Displaying Plan Baseline Execution Plans

Problem

You want to quickly view details regarding an existing plan baseline, such as the associated execution plan.

Solution

Use the DBMS_XPLAN.DISPLAY_SQL_PLAN_BASELINE function to display the execution plan and corresponding plan baseline details. This example reports details for a specific plan:

```
SELECT *
FROM TABLE(
DBMS_XPLAN.DISPLAY_SQL_PLAN_BASELINE(plan_name=>'SQL_PLAN_bm39aw8a5xv1xae72d2f5'));
```

Here is some sample output:

```
--------------------------------------------------------------------------
SQL handle: SQL_b98d2ae2145eec3d
SQL text: select last_name from custs where last_name='DAVIS'
--------------------------------------------------------------------------

--------------------------------------------------------------------------
Plan name: SQL_PLAN_bm39aw8a5xv1xae72d2f5     Plan id: 2926760693
Enabled: YES     Fixed: NO     Accepted: YES     Origin: MANUAL-LOAD
--------------------------------------------------------------------------
Plan hash value: 1824334906

---------------------------------------------------------------------------
| Id  | Operation          | Name  | Rows  | Bytes | Cost (%CPU)| Time     |
---------------------------------------------------------------------------
|   0 | SELECT STATEMENT   |       |     2 |    54 |     2   (0)| 00:00:01 |
|*  1 |  TABLE ACCESS FULL | CUSTS |     2 |    54 |     2   (0)| 00:00:01 |
---------------------------------------------------------------------------
```

How It Works

The `DBMS_XPLAN.DISPLAY_SQL_PLAN_BASELINE` function allows you to display one or more execution plans in a plan baseline. The return type for this function is a PL/SQL table type. This function takes three parameters (described in Table 12-8).

Table 12-8. Parameters for the DISPLAY_SQL_PLAN_BASELINE Function

Parameter	Description
SQL_HANDLE	Identifier for the SQL statement; instructs function to display all plans for the SQL statement
PLAN_NAME	Instructs function to display a specific plan for a SQL statement
FORMAT	Determines the detail of information displayed; takes values of BASIC, TYPICAL, and ALL

If you want to display all plans for a SQL statement, then use as input the `SQL_HANDLE` parameter—for example:

```
SELECT *
FROM TABLE(
DBMS_XPLAN.DISPLAY_SQL_PLAN_BASELINE(sql_handle=>'SQL_b98d2ae2145eec3d'));
```

Here is a partial listing of the output showing there are multiple plans in the plan baseline for this SQL query:

```
--------------------------------------------------------------------
Plan name: SQL_PLAN_bm39aw8a5xv1x519fc7bf      Plan id: 1369425855
Enabled: YES     Fixed: NO     Accepted: NO     Origin: AUTO-CAPTURE
--------------------------------------------------------------------
Plan hash value: 16205770
--------------------------------------------------------------------
| Id  | Operation       | Name      | Rows  | Bytes | Cost (%CPU)| Time     |
--------------------------------------------------------------------
|   0 | SELECT STATEMENT |          |    2  |   54  |    1   (0)| 00:00:01 |
|*  1 |   INDEX RANGE SCAN| CUSTS_IDX1 |    2  |   54  |    1   (0)| 00:00:01 |
--------------------------------------------------------------------
Predicate Information (identified by operation id):
--------------------------------------------------
   1 - access("LAST_NAME"='DAVIS')
--------------------------------------------------------------------
Plan name: SQL_PLAN_bm39aw8a5xv1xae72d2f5      Plan id: 2926760693
Enabled: YES     Fixed: NO     Accepted: YES     Origin: MANUAL-LOAD
--------------------------------------------------------------------
Plan hash value: 1824334906
```

```
---------------------------------------------------------------------
| Id | Operation        | Name  | Rows  | Bytes | Cost (%CPU)| Time     |
---------------------------------------------------------------------
|  0 | SELECT STATEMENT |       |     2 |    54 |     2  (0)| 00:00:01 |
|* 1 |  TABLE ACCESS FULL| CUSTS |     2 |    54 |     2  (0)| 00:00:01 |
---------------------------------------------------------------------
```

12-13. Adding a New Plan to Plan Baseline (Evolving)

Problem

You have the following scenario:

- You have an existing plan baseline for the query.

- You have recently added an index that the query can use.

- The optimizer determines a new lower-cost plan is now available for the query and adds the new plan to the plan history in an unaccepted state.

- You notice the new plan either from a recommendation by the SQL Tuning Advisor or by querying the DBA_SQL_PLAN_BASELINES view.

- You have examined the new execution plan, have run the query in a test environment, and are confident that the new plan will result in better performance.

You want to evolve the low-cost plan in the history so that it's moved to an accepted plan in the baseline. You realize that once the plan is accepted in the baseline, the optimizer will use it (if it's the lowest-cost plan in the baseline).

Solution

First verify that there are plans in the unaccepted state for the query in question (see Recipes 12-11 and 12-12 for more details). Here's a quick example:

```
SELECT sql_handle, plan_name, enabled, accepted, optimizer_cost
FROM dba_sql_plan_baselines
WHERE sql_text like '%select emp_id from emp where emp_id = 100%';
```

Here is the output indicating there are two plans, one unaccepted but with a much lower cost:

```
SQL_HANDLE          PLAN_NAME                      ENA ACC OPTIMIZER_COST
------------------- ------------------------------ --- --- --------------
SQL_f34ef255797c4713 SQL_PLAN_g6mrkapwrsjsm01205c23 YES NO               1
SQL_f34ef255797c4713 SQL_PLAN_g6mrkapwrsjsmd8a279cc YES YES              7
```

Use the DBMS_SPM.EVOLVE_SQL_PLAN_BASELINE function to move a plan from the history to the baseline (evolve the plan). In this example, the SQL handle (unique SQL string associated with a SQL statement) is used to evolve a plan:

```
SET SERVEROUT ON SIZE 1000000
SET LONG 100000
DECLARE
  rpt CLOB;
BEGIN
  rpt := DBMS_SPM.EVOLVE_SQL_PLAN_BASELINE(
    sql_handle => 'SQL_f34ef255797c4713');
  DBMS_OUTPUT.PUT_LINE(rpt);
END;
/
```

If Oracle determines that there is an unaccepted plan with a lower cost, then you'll see output similar to this indicating that the plan has been moved to the accepted state (evolved):

```
-------------------------------------------------------------------------------
                        Evolve SQL Plan Baseline
Report
-------------------------------------------------------------------------------

Inputs:
-------
  SQL_HANDLE =
SQL_f34ef255797c4713
  PLAN_NAME   =
  TIME_LIMIT = DBMS_SPM.AUTO_LIMIT
  VERIFY     = YES
  COMMIT     = YES

Plan:
SQL_PLAN_4fpttm0b55uwr918dd295
-------------------------------------
  Plan was verified: Time used .09 seconds.
  Plan passed
performance criterion: 11.56 times better than baseline plan.
  Plan was changed to an accepted plan.
```

You can quickly verify that the new plan baseline is now in use by setting AUTOTRACE on and running the query—for example:

```
SQL> set autotrace trace explain;
SQL> select emp_id from emp where emp_id = 100;
```

Here's a small snippet of the output indicating the new plan baseline is in use:

```
SQL plan baseline "SQL_PLAN_g6mrkapwrsjsm01205c23" used for this statement
```

How It Works

One key feature of SQL plan management is that when a new low-cost plan is generated by the query optimizer, if the new low-cost plan has a lower cost than the accepted plan(s) in the plan baseline, the new low-cost plan will automatically be added to the query's plan history in an unaccepted state.

You can choose to accept this new low-cost plan, which then moves it into the plan baseline as accepted. Moving an unaccepted execution plan from the plan history to the plan baseline (ENABLED and ACCEPTED) is known as *evolving the plan baseline*.

Why would a new plan ever be generated by the optimizer? There are several factors that would cause the optimizer to create a new execution plan that doesn't match an existing one in the plan baseline:

- New statistics are available.

- A new SQL profile has been assigned to the query.

- An index has been added or dropped.

This gives you a powerful technique to manage and use new plans as they become available. You can use the DBMS_SPM.EVOLVE_SQL_PLAN_BASELINE function in the following modes:

- Specify the name of the plan to evolve.

- Provide a list of plans to evolve.

- Run it with no value, meaning that Oracle will evolve all non-accepted plans contained within the plan baseline repository.

Table 12-9 describes the parameters used in the DBMS_SPM.EVOLVE_SQL_PLAN_BASELINE function.

Table 12-9. *Parameters for the EVOLVE_SQL_PLAN_BASELINE Function*

Parameter	Description	Default Value
SQL_HANDLE	SQL statement ID; NULL means consider all statements with unaccepted plans.	NULL
PLAN_NAME	Plan name; NULL means consider all unaccepted plans in plan baseline.	NULL
PLAN_LIST	List of plan names	DBMS_SPM.NAME_LIST
TIME_LIMIT	Time limit in minutes to verify plans; valid only if VERIFY=YES. DBMS_SPM.AUTO_LIMIT lets Oracle choose the time limit; DBMS_SPM.NO_LIMIT means no time limit.	DBMS_SPM.AUTO_LIMIT
VERIFY	Verify that performance will be improved before accepting the plan	YES
COMMIT	Updates accepted status from NO to YES	YES

12-14. Disabling Plan Baselines

Problem

You're working with a test database that has many SQL statements with associated plan baselines. You want to determine what the performance difference would be without the plan baselines enabled and therefore want to temporarily disable the use of plan baselines.

Solution

To disable the use of any SQL plan baselines within the database, set the OPTIMIZER_USE_SQL_PLAN_BASELINES initialization parameter to FALSE:

```
SQL> alter system set optimizer_use_sql_plan_baselines=false scope=both;
```

The prior line disables the use of the plan baselines at the SYSTEM level and records the value in memory and in the server parameter file. To re-enable the use of plan baselines, set the value back to TRUE.

You can also set the OPTIMIZER_USE_SQL_PLAN_BASELINES at the session level. This disables the use of plan baselines for the duration of the session for the currently connected user:

```
SQL> alter session set optimizer_use_sql_plan_baselines=false;
```

How It Works

The default value for OPTIMIZER_USE_SQL_PLAN_BASELINES is TRUE, which means by default, if plan baselines are available, they will be used. When enabled, the optimizer will look for a valid plan baseline execution plan for the given SQL query and choose the one with the lowest cost. This gives you a quick and easy way to disable/enable the use of plan baselines within your entire database or specific to a session.

If you want to disable the use of one specific plan baseline, then alter its state to DISABLED:

```
DECLARE
 pf PLS_INTEGER;
BEGIN
  pf := dbms_spm.alter_sql_plan_baseline(
    plan_name => 'SQL_PLAN_4ayzkz0kr3g9s6afbe2b3'
    ,attribute_name => 'ENABLED'
    ,attribute_value => 'NO');
END;
/
```

■ **Tip** See Recipe 12-10 for more details on how to alter plan baselines.

12-15. Removing Plan Baseline Information

Problem

You have several plan baselines that you no longer want to use and therefore want to remove them.

Solution

You can drop a single plan baseline. This removes a single plan baseline using the PLAN_NAME parameter:

```
DECLARE
  plan_name1 PLS_INTEGER;
BEGIN
  plan_name1 := DBMS_SPM.DROP_SQL_PLAN_BASELINE(
                        plan_name => 'SQL_PLAN_bm39aw8a5xv1x519fc7bf');
END;
/
```

You can also drop all plans associated with a SQL statement. This example removes all plans associated with a SQL statement using the SQL_HANDLE parameter:

```
DECLARE
  sql_handle1 PLS_INTEGER;
BEGIN
  sql_handle1 := DBMS_SPM.DROP_SQL_PLAN_BASELINE(
                        sql_handle => 'SQL_b98d2ae2145eec3d');
END;
/
```

How It Works

You may occasionally want to remove SQL plan baselines for the following reasons:

- You have old plans that aren't used anymore because more efficient plans (evolved) are available for a SQL statement.

- You have plans that were never accepted and now want to remove them.

- You have plans that were created for testing environments that are no longer needed.

As shown in the "Solution" section, you can remove a specific plan baseline via the PLAN_NAME parameter. This will remove one specific plan. If you have several plans associated with one SQL statement, you can remove all plan baselines for that SQL statement via the SQL_HANDLE parameter.

If you have a database where you want to clear out all plans, then you can encapsulate the call DBMS_SPM.DROP_SQL_PLAN_BASELINE within a PL/SQL block that drops all plans by looping through any plan found in DBA_SQL_PLAN_BASELINES:

```
SET SERVEROUT ON SIZE 1000000
DECLARE
  sql_handle1 PLS_INTEGER;
  CURSOR c1 IS
    SELECT sql_handle
    FROM dba_sql_plan_baselines;
BEGIN
  FOR r1 IN c1 LOOP
    sql_handle1 := DBMS_SPM.DROP_SQL_PLAN_BASELINE(sql_handle => r1.sql_handle);
    DBMS_OUTPUT.PUT_LINE('PB dropped for SH: ' || r1.sql_handle);
  END LOOP;
END;
/
```

12-16. Transporting Plan Baselines

Problem

You have a test environment, and you want to ensure that all of the plan baselines in the test system are moved to a production database.

Solution

Follow these steps to transport plan baselines:

1. Create a table using the DBMS_SPM package and CREATE_STGTAB_BASELINE procedure.

2. Populate the table with plan baselines using the DBMS_SPM.PACK_STGTAB_BASELINE function.

3. Copy the staging table to the destination database using a database link or Data Pump.

4. Import the plan baseline information using the DBMS_SPM.UNPACK_STGTAB_BASELINE function.

This example first uses the DBMS_SPM package to create a table named EXP_PB:

```
BEGIN
  DBMS_SPM.CREATE_STGTAB_BASELINE(table_name => 'exp_pb');
END;
/
```

■ **Note** You cannot create the staging table in the SYS user.

Next the EXP_PB table is populated with plan baselines created by the database user MV_MAINT:

```
DECLARE
  pbs NUMBER;
BEGIN
  pbs := DBMS_SPM.PACK_STGTAB_BASELINE(
          table_name => 'exp_pb',
          enabled => 'yes',
          creator => 'MV_MAINT');
END;
/
```

The prior code populates the table with all plan baselines created by a user. You can also populate the table by PLAN_NAME, SQL_HANDLE, SQL_TEXT, or various other criteria. The only mandatory parameter is the name of the table to be populated.

Now copy the staging table to the destination database. You can use a database link, Data Pump, or the old exp/imp utilities to accomplish this.

Lastly, on the destination database, use the DBMS_SPM.UNPACK_STGTAB_BASELINE function to take the contents of the EXP_PB table and create plan baselines:

```
DECLARE
  pbs NUMBER;
BEGIN
  pbs := DBMS_SPM.UNPACK_STGTAB_BASELINE(
          table_name => 'exp_pb',
          enabled => 'yes');
END;
/
```

You should now have all of the plan baselines transferred to your target database. You can query DBA_SQL_PLAN_BASELINES to verify this.

How It Works

It's a fairly easy process to create a table, populate it with plan baseline information, copy the table, and the import its contents into the destination database. As shown in step 2 of the "Solution" section of this recipe, the PACK_STGTAB_BASELINE function is used (see Table 12-10). This function allows quite a bit of flexibility in what types of plan baselines you want exported. You can limit the plan baselines extracted to a specific user, or enabled, or accepted, and so on.

Likewise, the DBMS_SPM.UNPACK_STGTAB_BASELINE function allows you a great deal of flexibility on what types of plan baselines are extracted from the staging table and loaded into the destination database. The input parameters for UNPACK_STGTAB_BASELINE are the same as the parameters used for PACK_STGTAB_BASELINE (described in Table 12-10).

Table 12-10. *Parameters for the* PACK_STGTAB_BASELINE *Function*

Parameter Name	Description
TABLE_NAME	Mandatory name of table to be populated with plan baseline information
TABLE_OWNER	Staging table owner; NULL specifies current user.
SQL_HANDLE	Uniquely identifies a SQL statement
PLAN_NAME	Uniquely identifies a specific plan baseline; % wildcards valid as input
SQL_TEXT	Identifies SQL queries by text; % wildcards valid as input
CREATOR	User who created plan baseline
ORIGIN	Origin of plan baseline; valid values are: MANUAL-LOAD, AUTO_CAPTURE, MANUAL_SQLTUNE, or AUTO_SQLTUNE.
ENABLED	Specifies enabled plan baselines; YES and NO are valid values.
ACCEPTED	Specifies accepted plan baselines; YES and NO are valid values.
FIXED	Specifies fixed plan baselines; YES and NO are valid values.
MODULE	Module name
ACTION	Action name

CHAPTER 13

Configuring the Optimizer

The cost optimizer determines the most efficient execution plan for a SQL statement. The optimizer depends heavily on the statistics that you (or the database) gather. This chapter explains how to set the optimizer goal and how to control the behavior of the optimizer. You'll learn how to enable and disable automatic statistics collection by the database and when to collect statistics manually. You'll learn how to set preferences for statistics collection as well as how to validate new statistics before making them available to the optimizer. The chapter explains how to lock statistics, export statistics, gather system statistics, restore older versions of statistics, and how to handle missing statistics.

Bind peeking behavior, wherein the optimizer looks at the bind variable values when parsing a SQL statement, can have unpredictable effects on execution plans. The chapter explains adaptive cursor sharing, which is designed to produce execution plans based on the specific values of bind variables.

Collecting statistics on large tables is always problematic, and the chapter shows how to use the incremental statistics gathering feature to speed up statistics collection for large partitioned tables. You'll also learn how to use the new concurrent statistics collection feature to optimize statistics collection for large tables.

Collecting extension statistics for expressions and column groups improves optimizer performance, and you'll learn how to collect these types of statistics. The chapter also explains how to let the database tell you which columns in a table are candidates for creating a column group.

13-1. Choosing an Optimizer Goal

Problem

You want to set the cost optimizer goal for your database.

Solution

You can influence the behavior of the cost optimizer by setting an optimizer goal. The optimizer will collect appropriate statistics based on the goal you set. You set the optimizer goal with the optimizer_mode initialization parameter. You can set the parameter to the values ALL_ROWS or FIRST_ROWS_n, as shown here:

```
optimizer_mode=all_rows
optimizer_mode=first_rows_n          /* n can be 1,10,100 or 1000 */
```

The default value for the optimizer_mode parameter is ALL_ROWS.

How It Works

The default value for the optimizer_mode parameter, ALL_ROWS, has the goal of maximizing throughput—it minimizes resource use to complete the processing of the entire statement and get all the requested rows. The alternate value of FIRST_ROWS_*n* uses the goal of response time, which is the time it takes to return the first *n* number of rows.

If you set the optimizer_mode parameter to FIRST_ROWS_*n*, all sessions will use the optimizer goal of best response time. However, you can change the optimizer goal just at the session level by executing a SQL statement such as the following:

```
SQL> alter session set optimizer_mode=first_rows_1;
```

Note that the ALL_ROWS optimizer mode setting has built-in bias toward full table scans, because its goal is to minimize resource usage. The FIRST_ROWS_n setting, on the other hand, favors index accesses because its goal is minimizing response time, and thus returns the requested number of rows as fast as possible.

In addition to the optimizer_mode parameter, you can also set the following parameters to influence the behavior of the optimizer:

- optimizer_index_caching

- optimizer_index_cost_adj

- db_file_multiblock_read_count

In general, changing these parameters at the database level can lead to unexpected optimizer behavior, including potential performance deterioration for some queries. The recommended practice is to leave these parameters at their default levels. We, however, do show (Recipe 13-11) how to use one of these parameters (optimizer_index_cost_adj) at the session level, to improve the performance of a long-running query by forcing the optimizer to use an index.

13-2. Enabling Automatic Statistics Gathering

Problem

You want to enable automatic statistics gathering in your database.

■ **Tip**   Oracle recommends the enabling of automatic optimizer statistics collection.

Solution

You enable automatic statistics collection by using the enable procedure in the DBMS_AUTO_TASK_ADMIN package. Check the status of the auto optimizer stats collection task in the following way:

```
SQL> select client_name,status from dba_autotask_client;

CLIENT_NAME                                                     STATUS
-------------------------------------------------------------- --------
auto optimizer stats collection                                DISABLED
auto space advisor                                             ENABLED
sql tuning advisor                                            ENABLED
SQL>
```

Execute the dbms_auto_task_admin.enable procedure to enable the automatic statistics collection task:

```
SQL> begin dbms_auto_task_admin.enable(
  2  client_name=>'auto optimizer stats collection',
  3  operation=>NULL,
  4  window_name=>NULL);
  5  end;
  6  /

PL/SQL procedure successfully completed.
```

Check the status of the *auto optimizer stats collection* task:

```
SQL>  SELECT client_name,status from dba_autotask_client;

CLIENT_NAME                                                     STATUS
-------------------------------------------------------------- --------
auto optimizer stats collection                                ENABLED
auto space advisor                                             ENABLED
sql tuning advisor                                            ENABLED

SQL>
```

You can disable the statistics collection task by using the dbms_auto_task_admin.disable procedure:

```
SQL> begin
  2  dbms_auto_task_admin.disable(
  3  client_name=> 'auto optimizer stats collection',
  4  operation=> NULL,
  5  window_name=> NULL);
  6  end;
  7  /

PL/SQL procedure successfully completed.

SQL>
```

How It Works

Automatic optimizer statistics collection is enabled by default when you create a database with the DBCA. If you've disabled automatic statistics collection, you can enable it by executing the procedure shown in the "Solution" section. Once you enable automatic statistics collection, the database collects statistics whenever they get stale—the database determines this based on the changes made to the tables and indexes. Automating statistics collection eliminates all the work involved in collecting statistics yourself.

When you enable automatic optimizer statistics collection, the "auto optimizer stats collection" task calls the DBMS_STATS.GATHER_DATABASE_STATS_JOB_PROC procedure. This procedure is virtually identical to the DBMS_STATS.GATHER_DATABASE_STATS procedure—the big difference is that the database will collect the statistics only during the maintenance window that you specify. If you don't specify a maintenance window, the database uses the default maintenance window, which opens every night from 10 p.m. to 6 a.m. and all day on weekends. The "auto optimizer stats collection" job collects statistics first for those objects that need the new statistics the most. Thus, the auto statistics collection job will first collect statistics for objects that don't have any statistics, or objects that underwent substantial modifications (usually about 10% of the rows). This way, if the statistics collection job doesn't complete before the end of the maintenance window, the database ensures that objects with the stalest statistics are refreshed for sure.

You can query the DBA_OPTSTAT_OPERATIONS view to find out the beginning and ending times for the automatic statistics collection job, as shown here:

```
SQL> select operation,target,start_time,end_time from dba_optstat_operations
2*  where operation='gather_database_stats(auto)';

OPERATION                     START_TIME                        END_TIME
--------------------          ----------------------------      ----------------------------
gather_database_stats         26-APR-11 10.00.02.970000 PM      26-APR-11 10.03.11.671000 PM
...
SQL>
```

■ **Tip**   Automatic statistics collection works very well with OLTP databases whose data changes moderately on a day-to-day basis, but not for most data warehouses that perform nightly data loading from ETL jobs.

The DBA_TAB_MODIFICATIONS view stores information about the inserts, deletes, and updates to a table. By default, the OPTIONS parameter for the GATHER_DATABASE_STATS procedure is set to the value GATHER AUTO. What this means is that once you enable automatic statistics collection, the database will collect statistics for all tables where more than 10% of the rows have been affected by insert, delete, and update operations.

Automatic statistics collection by the database works well for most OLTP databases. However, in a data warehouse environment, you may run into issues because the automatic statistics collection job runs during the nightly maintenance window. If your ETL or ELT jobs load data into a table after the auto job has already collected statistics for that table, you could end up with unrepresentative statistics for that table. In a data warehouse environment, it's a good idea to collect statistics manually right after the load process completes and disable the default automatic statistics collection job.

Note that in addition to collecting statistics for all schema objects, the auto stats job also gathers dictionary statistics (for the SYS and SYSTEM schemas).

13-3. Setting Preferences for Statistics Collection

Problem

You want to set default values for the parameters used by the DBMS_STATS procedures that gather various types of statistics.

Solution

Use the appropriate DBMS_STATS.SET_*_PREFS procedure to change the default values for parameters that control statistics collection. Use the following procedures for changing the default values of the parameters used at various levels of statistics collection:

- SET_TABLE_PREFS: Lets you specify default parameters to be used by the DBMS_STATS.GATHER_*_STATS procedures for a specific table

- SET_SCHEMA_PREFS: Lets you change the default parameters to be used by the DBMS_STATS.GATHER_*_STATS procedures for all objects in a specific schema

- SET_DATABASE_PREFS: Lets you change the default parameters to be used by the DBMS_STATS.GATHER_*_STATS procedures for the entire database, including all user schemas and system schemas such as SYS and SYSTEM

- SET_GLOBAL_PREFS: Sets global statistics preferences; this procedure lets you change the default statistic collection parameters for any object in the database that doesn't have an existing preference at the table level. If you don't set table-level preferences or you don't set any parameter explicitly in the DBMS_STATS.GATHER_*_STATS procedure, the parameters default to their global settings.

Here's an example that shows how to set default preferences at the database level by invoking the SET_DATABASE_PREFS procedure:

```
SQL> execute dbms_stats.set_database_prefs('ESTIMATE_PERCENT','20');
```

Once you set a preference for a parameter at the database level, it applies to all tables in the database. Note that the SET_*_PREFS procedures accept three parameters:

- pname refers to the name of the preference, such as the ESTIMATE_PERCENT preference used in the previous example.

- pvalue lets you specify a value for the preference. If you specify NULL as the value for the pvalue parameter, the preference's value will be set to the Oracle default values.

- add_sys is an optional parameter that, if set to TRUE, will also include all Oracle-owned tables in the statistics collection process.

How It Works

All DBMS_STATS.GATHER_*_STATS procedures use default values for the various parameters. There are two ways you can handle the specification of values for the various parameters that are part of the procedures in the DBMS_STATS package such as the GATHER_TABLE_STATS procedure. You can specify the preference values when you execute a procedure such as GATHER_TABLE_STATS to collect statistics. Alternatively, you can change the default values of the preferences at the table, schema, database, or global level with the appropriate DBMS_STATS.SET_*_PREFS procedure, as shown in the "Solution" section. If you don't specify a value for any of the statistics gathering parameters, the database uses the default value for that parameter.

You can find the default value of any preference by executing the DBMS_STATS.GET_PREFS procedure. The following example shows how to find the value of the current setting of the STALE_PERCENT parameter:

```
SQL> select dbms_stats.get_prefs ('STALE_PERCENT','SH') stale_percent from dual;

STALE_PERCENT
-------------------------------------------------------------------------------

10

SQL>
```

You specify similar preferences when you collect statistics at the table, schema, or database level. Here is a description of the various preferences you can specify to control the way the database gathers statistics.

CASCADE

This specifies whether the database should collect index statistics along with the table statistics. By default, the database automatically collects statistics (cascade=true) for all of a table's indexes.

DEGREE

This specifies the degree of parallelism the database must use when gathering statistics. Oracle recommends using the default setting of the constant DBMS_STATS.AUTO_DEGREE. Oracle chooses the correct degree of parallelism based on the object and the parallelism-related initialization parameters. When you use the default DBMS_STATS.AUTO_DEGREE setting, Oracle determines the degree of parallelism based on the size of the object. If the object is small enough, Oracle collects statistics serially, and if the object is large, Oracle uses the default degree of parallelism based on the number of CPUs. Note that the default degree is NULL, which means that the database collects statistics using parallelism only if you set the degree of parallelism at the table level with the DEGREE clause.

ESTIMATE_PERCENT

This specifies the percentage of rows the database must use to estimate the statistics. For large tables, estimation is the only way to complete the statistics collection process within a reasonable time—statistics collection is not a trivial process—it's resource-intensive and consumes a lot of time for large tables. You can set a value between 0 and 100 for the estimate_percent parameter. A rule of thumb here is that the more uniform a table's data, the smaller the sample size can be. On the other hand, if a table's data is highly skewed, you should use a higher sample size to capture the variations in the data distribution. Of course, setting this parameter to 100 means that the database isn't doing an estimation—it will collect statistics for each row in a table. Often, DBAs set the estimate_percent parameter too high, because they've had bad experiences with a table when they set a small sample size. If you think the data is uniformly distributed, even a 1 or 2% sample will get you very accurate statistics, and save you a bunch of time and processing overhead.

■ **Tip**　In Oracle Database 11g, the NDV (number of distinct values) count, which is a key statistic calculated by setting the estimate_percent parameter to DBMS_STATS.AUTO_SAMPLE_SIZE, is statistically identical to the NDV count calculated by a 100% complete statistics collection. The best practice is to start with the AUTO_SAMPLE_SIZE and set your own sample size only if you have to.

It's not easy to select the best size for the estimate_percent parameter—if you set it too high, it'll take a long time to collect statistics. If you set it too low, you can gather the statistics quickly all right, but those statistics can very well be inaccurate. By default, the database uses the constant DBMS_STATS.AUTO_SAMPLE_SIZE to determine the best sample size. You specify the AUTO value for the estimate_percent parameter in the following way:

```
SQL> exec dbms_stats.gather_table_stats(NULL, 'MASSIVE_TABLE', estimate_percent=>
dbms_stats.auto_sample_size)
```

When you set the AUTO value for the estimate_percent parameter, not only does the database automatically determine the sampling size, but it also adjusts the size of the sample as the data distribution changes. NDV is a good criterion to calculate the accuracy of the statistics collected with varying samples sizes. The NDV of a column is defined as follows:

```
accuracy rate = 1 - (estimated NDV - actual NDV) /actual NDV
```

The accuracy rate can range over 0 to 100%. A 100% sample size will always give you a 100% accuracy rate—what is significant is that in Oracle 11g, auto sampling provides accuracy rates that are very close to 100%, and take a fraction of the time it takes to collect complete statistics for a large table.

METHOD_OPT

You can specify two things with the METHOD_OPT parameter: the columns for which the database will collect statistics, and the columns on which the database will create histograms. You can also specify the number of the buckets in the histograms. You can specify one of the following options for this parameter:

```
FOR ALL [INDEXED  |  HIDDEN]  COLUMNS  [size_clause]
FOR COLUMNS [size_clause]  column  [size_clause]  [,COLUMN  [size_clause]…]
```

The FOR ALL option lets you specify that the database must collect statistics for all columns, or only for the indexed columns. If you specify the INDEXED COLUMNS option, the database will collect statistics only for those columns that have an index on them. Be careful with this option, as the database will not collect statistics on the table's columns, instead using basic default statistics for the columns. Using the FOR ALL INDEXED COLUMNS in a data warehouse environment could be especially problematic, as indexes aren't heavily used in that environment.

The FOR COLUMNS option lets you specify one or more columns on which the database must gather statistics, instead of on all columns in a table, which is the default behavior. Here's how to specify the column clause in this context:

```
column:= column_name  |  extension name  |  extension
```

The column_name clause refers to the name of the column, and extension can be either a column group (in the format column_name, column_name [,…]) or an expression.

The key clause for both the FOR ALL and the FOR COLUMNS options is the size_clause. The size_clause determines whether the database should collect histograms for a column, and under what conditions. One option is to supply an integer value indicating the number of histogram buckets—in the range 1 through 254—that you would like—for example:

```
SQL> exec dbms_stats.gather_table_stats('HR','EMPLOYEES',method_opt=> 'for columns size 254
job_id')

PL/SQL procedure successfully completed.
SQL>
```

When you execute this procedure, the database collects histograms, and there will be 254 histogram buckets.

■ **Note** A value of 1 for the integer clause (for example, 'FOR ALL COLUMNS SIZE 1') won't really create any histograms on the columns, because all the data is placed into a single bucket. Also, if there's already a histogram(s) on a table, setting the value 1 for the integer clause will remove the histogram(s).

Another option for the size_clause is to specify one of the following three values:

REPEAT: Specifies that the database must collect histograms on only those columns that already have histograms collected for them; setting the value *repeat* instead of the integer 1 value ensures that you retain any useful histograms.

AUTO: Lets the database determine for which columns it should collect histograms, based on each column's data distribution (whether it's uniform or skewed) and the actual column usage statistics

SKEWONLY: Lets the database determine for which columns it should collect histograms, based on each column's data distribution

Here is an example that specifies SKEWONLY:

```
SQL> exec dbms_stats.gather_table_stats('HR','EMPLOYEES',method_opt=> 'for all columns size
skewonly')
PL/SQL procedure successfully completed.
SQL>
```

When you specify SKEWONLY, the database will look at the data distribution for each column to determine if the data is skewed enough to warrant the creation of a histogram.

The default value for the METHOD_OPT parameter is FOR ALL COLUMNS SIZE AUTO. That is, the database will collect statistics for all columns in a table, and it automatically selects the columns for which it should create histograms.

NO_INVALIDATE

You can set three different values for this parameter. The value TRUE means that the database doesn't invalidate the dependent cursors of the table for which it's collecting statistics. The value FALSE means that the database immediately invalidates the dependent cursors. Finally, you can set this parameter to the value DBMS_STATS.AUTO_INVALIDATE, to let Oracle decide to invalidate the cursors—this is also the default value for the NO_INVALIDATE parameter.

GRANULARITY

This parameter determines how the database handles statistics gathering for partitioned tables. Here are the various options you can specify for the GRANULARITY parameter:

ALL: Gathers subpartition-, partition-, and global-level statistics; this setting provides a very accurate set of table statistics, but is extremely resource-intensive and takes much longer to complete than a statistics collection job with the other options.

GLOBAL: Gathers just global statistics for a table

PARTITION: Gathers only partition-level statistics—the partition-level statistics are rolled up at the table level, and may not be very accurate at the table level.

GLOBAL AND PARTITION: Gathers the global- and partition-level statistics, but not the subpartition-level statistics

SUBPARTITION: Gathers only subpartition statistics

AUTO: This is the default value for the GRANULARITY parameter and determines the granularity based on the partitioning type.

Note that the ALL setting could take a long time to complete besides using up a lot of resources. It's not really necessary to gather statistics at the subpartition level for composite partitioned tables. In most cases, the default setting of AUTO works well. The ALL setting is definitely overkill, and isn't necessary in most, probably all situations.

PUBLISH

By default, the database publishes all statistics right after it completes the statistics gathering process. You can specify that the database keep newly collected statistics as pending statistics by setting the PUBLISH parameter to FALSE.

INCREMENTAL

The INCREMENTAL preference determines whether the database maintains a partitioned table's statistics without having to perform a full table scan. The default value of this parameter is FALSE, meaning the database does a full table scan to maintain global statistics. Recipe 13-19 discusses incremental statistics collection in detail.

STALE_PERCENT

The STALE_PERCENT preference determines the proportion of a table's rows that must change before the database considers the table's statistics as "stale" and starts gathering fresh statistics. By default, the STALE_PERCENT parameter is set to 10%. Don't collect statistics on tables that haven't changed at all, or have changed very little, as you'd be collecting unnecessary statistics.

AUTOSTATS_TARGET

This preference is valid only for auto stats collection, and you specify it when setting global statistics preferences with the SET_GLOBAL_STATS procedure. You can set the following values for this preference:

ALL: Collects statistics for all objects in the database

ORACLE: Collects statistics for all Oracle-owned objects

AUTO: The database determines for which objects it should collect statistics.

The default value for the AUTOSTATS_TARGET parameter is AUTO. Note that currently the ALL and the AUTO (default) settings work the same way. Oracle recommends that you set the AUTOSTATS_TARGET preference to the value ORACLE, to ensure that the database collects fresh dictionary statistics (for objects owned by SYS and SYSTEM).

We've incorporated several Oracle best practices for statistics collection in this recipe. Try to stick with the default settings for the preferences unless you have strong reasons to do otherwise. Remember that if you're creating a new table, you can load the data first and collect statistics just for the table. Create the indexes afterward, because the database automatically computes statistics for the indexes during index creation time.

13-4. Manually Generating Statistics

Problem

You're trying to determine if you should let the database automatically collect the optimizer statistics, or if you must manually collect the statistics.

Solution

In most cases, the automatic statistics collection task is good enough to collect the optimizer statistics. In fact, there are many production databases that automate statistics collection as shown in Recipe 13-2 and never use a manual statistic collection process. However, there are cases where manual statistic collection may be necessary. Here are two cases when you must manually collect statistics.

Volatile Tables

If your database contains volatile tables that experience numerous deletes (or even truncates) throughout the day, then an automatic stats collection job that runs during the nightly maintenance window isn't adequate. There are a couple of strategies you can use in this type of situation, where a table's data keeps fluctuating throughout the day:

- Collect the statistics when the table has the number of rows that represent its "typical" state. Once you do this, lock the statistics to prevent the automatic statistics collection job from collecting fresh statistics for this table during the nightly maintenance window.

- The other option is to make the statistics of the table null.

You make the statistics of a table null by deleting the statistics first and then locking the table's statistics right after that, as shown in the following example:

```
SQL> execute dbms_stats.delete_table_stats('OE','ORDERS');

PL/SQL procedure successfully completed.

SQL> execute dbms_stats.lock_table_stats('OE','ORDERS');

PL/SQL procedure successfully completed.

SQL>
```

Bulk Loaded Tables

For tables that you bulk load data into, you must collect statistics immediately after loading the data. If you don't collect statistics right after bulk loading data into a table, the database can still use dynamic sampling to estimate the statistics, but these statistics aren't as comprehensive as the statistics that you collect.

How It Works

Before Oracle introduced the automatic optimizer statistics collection feature in the Oracle Database 10g release, every DBA collected scripts using the recommended DBMS_STATS package (or even the older analyze table command). With automatic statistics collection, DBAs don't have to collect optimizer statistics by scheduling DBMS_STATS jobs. However, you may still run into situations where automatic statistics collection isn't appropriate. The "Solution" section describes two such cases, and how to handle them by manually collecting the statistics.

You can manually collect statistics at the table, schema, or database level, by using the appropriate DBMS_STATS.GATHER_*_STATS procedure.

When you're manually gathering the optimizer statistics, it's a good idea to stick with the default settings for the various parameters that control how the database collects the statistics. Often, performance of the statistics gathering job (how fast) and the quality of the statistics itself improve when you revert to the default settings. For example, many DBAs set too high a sample size with the estimate_percent parameter, rather than letting the database use the appropriate sample size based on the DBMS_STATS.AUTO_SAMPLE_SIZE constant.

13-5. Locking Statistics

Problem

You want to lock the statistics for a table or a schema, to freeze the statistics.

Solution

You can lock a table or a schema's statistics by executing the appropriate DBMS_STATS.LOCK_* procedures. For example, you can lock a table's statistics with the LOCK_TABLE_STATS procedure in the DBMS_STATS package:

```
SQL> execute dbms_stats.lock_table_stats(ownname=>'SH',tabname=>'SALES');

PL/SQL procedure successfully completed.
SQL>
```

You can unlock the table's statistics by executing the following procedure:

```
SQL> execute dbms_stats.unlock_table_stats(ownname=>'SH',tabname=>'SALES');

PL/SQL procedure successfully completed.

SQL>
```

You can lock a schema's statistics with the DBMS_STATS.LOCK_SCHEMA_STATS procedure, as shown here:

```
SQL> execute dbms_stats.lock_schema_stats('SH');

PL/SQL procedure successfully completed.
SQL>
```

Unlock the statistics with the UNLOCK_SCHEMA_STATS procedure:

```
SQL> execute dbms_stats.unlock_schema_stats('SH');

PL/SQL procedure successfully completed.

SQL>
```

How It Works

You may want to lock a table's statistics to freeze the current set of statistics. You may also lock the statistics after you delete the existing statistics first—in this case, you are forcing the database to use dynamic sampling to estimate the table's statistics. Deleting a table's statistics and then locking the statistics is in effect the same as setting the statistics on a table to null. You have the option of setting the force argument with the GATHER_TABLE__STATS procedure to override a table's lock on its statistics.

■ **Note**   Locking a table also locks all statistics that depend on that table, such as index, histogram and column statistics.

13-6. Handling Missing Statistics

Problem

Certain tables in your database are missing statistics, because the tables have had data loaded into them outside the nightly batch window. You can't collect statistics on the table during the day when the database is handling other workload.

Solution

Oracle uses dynamic sampling to compensate for missing statistics. The database will scan a random sample of data blocks in a table when you enable dynamic sampling. You enable/disable dynamic sampling in the database by setting the `optimizer_dynamic_sampling` initialization parameter. Dynamic sampling is enabled by default, as you can see from the following:

```
SQL> sho parameter dynamic

NAME                                TYPE        VALUE
----------------------------------- ----------- -----
optimizer_dynamic_sampling          integer     2
SQL>
```

The default level of dynamic sampling is 2—setting it to 0 disables dynamic sampling. You can modify the default value by setting a different sampling level as shown here:

```
SQL> alter system set optimizer_dynamic_sampling=4 scope=both;
System altered.

SQL>
```

How It Works

Ideally, you should gather optimizer statistics with the `DBMS_STATS` package (manually or through automatic statistics collection). In cases where you don't have a chance to collect statistics for a newly created or newly loaded table, the table won't have any statistics until the database automatically generates the statistics through its automatic stats collection job or when you schedule a manual statistics collection job. Even if you don't collect any statistics, the database uses some basic statistics such as table and index block counts to estimate the selectivity of the predicates in a query. Dynamic sampling goes a step further, augmenting these basic statistics by dynamically gathering additional statistics at compile time. Dynamic sampling is of particular help when dealing with frequently executed queries that involve tables with no statistics.

■ **Note** Oracle doesn't perform dynamic sampling for external tables.

There's a cost to dynamic sampling, because the database uses resources to gather statistics during query compilation. If you don't execute these queries many times, the database incurs an overhead each time it executes a query involving table(s) for which it must dynamically collect statistics. For dynamic sampling to really pay off, it must help queries that are executed frequently.

It's important to understand the significance of the dynamic sampling levels, which can range from 0 to 10. Note that the sample size used for dynamic sampling at various sampling levels is in terms of data blocks, not rows. Here is a brief description of the various dynamic sampling levels.

Level 1: Uses dynamic sampling for all tables that don't have statistics, provided there's at least one non-partitioned table without statistics in the query; the table must also not have any indexes and it must be larger than 32 blocks, which is the sample size for this level.

Level 2: Uses dynamic sampling if at least one table in the query has no statistics; sample size is 64 blocks.

Level 3: Uses dynamic sampling if the query meets the Level 2 criteria and it has one or more expressions in a WHERE clause predicate; sample size is 64 blocks.

Level 4: Uses dynamic sampling if the query meets all Level 3 criteria, and in addition it uses complex predicates such as an OR/AND operator between multiple predicates; sample size is 64 blocks.

Levels 5–9: Use dynamic sampling if the statement meets the Level 4 criteria; each of these levels differs only in the sample size, which ranges from 128 to 4086 blocks.

Level 10: The most comprehensive level—it uses dynamic sampling for all statements, and the sample it uses isn't really a sample, because it checks all data blocks to get the statistics.

Dynamic sampling is a complement to the statistics collected by the DBMS_STATS package's procedures. Oracle doesn't expect you to use this in general, due to the additional overhead for gathering optimizer statistics during the generation of an execution plan. Dynamic sampling does help in getting better cardinality estimates, but is more suitable for longer-running queries in a data warehouse or a decision support system, rather than for queries in an OLTP database, due to the overhead involved. You must also keep in mind that the statistics collected through dynamic sampling are by no means the same as the statistics collected through the DBMS_STATS procedures. Dynamic sampling merely collects rudimentary statistics such as the number of data blocks and the high and low values of columns. If you must set a dynamic sampling level, do so at the session level with an alter session statement, rather than setting it database-wide.

13-7. Exporting Statistics

Problem

You want to export a set of statistics from your production database to a much smaller test database.

Solution

You can export optimizer statistics from one database to another by using the
`DBMS_STATS.EXPORT_*_STATS` procedures. These procedures let you export optimizer statistics from a
source table, schema, or database. Once you complete the export of the statistics, you must execute one
of the `DBMS_STATS.IMPORT_*_STATS` procedures to import the statistics into a different database. You can
export statistics at the table, schema, or database level. Here's an example that explains how to export
statistics from a table.

1. Create a table to hold the exported statistics:

   ```
   SQL> execute dbms_stats.create_stat_table(ownname=>'SH',stattab=>'mytab',
                                              tblspace=>'USERS')

   PL/SQL procedure successfully completed.

   SQL>
   ```

2. Export the statistics for the table `SH.SALES` from the data dictionary into the
   `mytab` table, using the `DBMS_STATS.EXPORT_*STATS` procedure.

   ```
   SQL> exec dbms_stats.export_table_stats(ownname=> 'SH',tabname=>'SALES',stattab=
   >'mytab')

   PL/SQL procedure successfully completed.

   SQL>
   ```

3. In a different database, import the statistics using the
   `DBMS_STATS.IMPORT_*STATS` procedure.

   ```
   SQL> exec dbms_stats.import_table_stats(ownname=>'SH',tabname=>'SALES',stattab=>
   'MyTab',no_invalidate=>true);

   PL/SQL procedure successfully completed.

   SQL>
   ```

How It Works

The `EXPORT_TABLE_STATS` procedure exports the current statistics for a table from the data dictionary and
stores them in a table that you create. Note that this procedure doesn't generate fresh statistics and the
database will continue to use the current statistics for the table (`SH.SALES` in our example). By default, the
`cascade` option is `true`, meaning the procedure will export statistics for all indexes in the `SH.SALES` table
along with the column statistics.

   You can make the optimizer use the exported statistics only after you import them into the data
dictionary, in the same or a different database. The `IMPORT_TABLE_STATS` procedure imports the statistics
you've exported earlier, into the data dictionary. Setting the `no_invalidate` parameter to `true` (default is
`false`) ensures that any dependent cursors aren't invalidated. By default, you can't import a table's
statistics when the statistics are locked. You can override this property by setting the `force` parameter to
`true`. If you're importing the statistics into a different database from the one from which you exported
the statistics, you must export the table in which you stored the statistics to the target database. You

must then import the table into the target database before you can execute the IMPORT_TABLE_STATS procedure.

Exporting and importing statistics is an ideal way to present the same statistics to the optimizer in a test system as those in a production system, to ensure consistent explain plans. It's also a good strategy when you want to preserve a known set of good statistics for a longer period than what is allowed by the "restore statistics" feature explained in Recipe 13-8. The ability to export and import statistics enables you to test different sets of statistics before deciding which set of parameters is the best for your database.

In this recipe, we showed you how to export and import table-level statistics. The DBMS_STATS package also contains procedures to export and import statistics at the column, index, schema, and database level. In addition, there are procedures for exporting and importing dictionary statistics, statistics for fixed objects, and system statistics.

13-8. Restoring Previous Versions of Statistics

Problem

Performance of certain queries has deteriorated suddenly after collecting fresh statistics. You want to see if you can use an older set of statistics that you knew worked well.

Solution

Use the DBMS_STATS.RESTORE_STATS procedure to revert to an older set of optimizer statistics. Before you restore older statistics, check how far back you can go to restore older statistics:

```
SQL> select dbms_stats.get_stats_history_availability from dual;

GET_STATS_HISTORY_AVAILABILITY
---------------------------------------------------------------------
19-APR-11 07.49.26.718000000 AM -04:00

SQL>
```

The output of this query shows that you can restore statistics to a timestamp that's more recent than the timestamp shown, which is 19-APR-11 07.49.26.718000000 AM -04:00.

Execute the RESTORE_*_STATS procedures of the DBMS_STATS package to revert to statistics from an earlier period. The following example shows how to restore statistics at the schema level.

```
SQL> exec dbms_stats.restore_schema_stats(ownname=>'SH',as_of_timestamp=>'19-MAY
-11 01.30.31.323000 PM -04:00',no_invalidate=>false)

PL/SQL procedure successfully completed.

SQL>
```

How It Works

When the database collects fresh statistics, it doesn't get rid of the previous set of statistics. Instead, it retains the older versions for a set number of days. You have the ability to restore older statistics by executing the DBMS_STATS.RESTORE_*_STATS procedures, which replace the current statistics with the statistics from the time you specify. Restore statistics when you want the optimizer to use the same execution plans as it did when it had access to an older set of statistics. By default, the database manages the retention and purging of historical statistics. Here's how to find out how many days' worth of statistics the database retains by default.

```
SQL> select dbms_stats.get_stats_history_retention from dual;

GET_STATS_HISTORY_RETENTION
---------------------------
                         31
SQL>
```

The database automatically purges statistics it has collected more than 31 days ago (provided newer statistics exist!). You can manually purge all old versions of statistics by executing the DBMS_STATS.PURGE_STATS procedure. You can change the number of days the database retains statistics by executing the following command:

```
SQL> exec dbms_stats.alter_stats_history_retention(retention=>60);

PL/SQL procedure successfully completed.

SQL>
```

The command tells the database to save historical statistics for a period of 60 days.

In the example shown in the "Solution" section, we showed how to restore statistics for a schema. You can similarly restore statistics for a database with the RESTORE_DATABASE_STATS procedure or for a table with the RESTORE_TABLE_STATS procedure. You can also restore dictionary stats with the RESTORE_DICTIONARY_STATS procedure and system stats with the RESTORE_SYSTEM_STATS procedure.

13-9. Gathering System Statistics

Problem

You know the optimizer uses I/O and CPU characteristics of a system during the selection of an execution plan. You'd like to ensure that the optimizer is using accurate system statistics.

Solution

You can collect two types of system statistics to capture your system's I/O and CPU characteristics. You can collect *workload statistics* or *noworkload statistics* to enable the optimizer to better estimate the true I/O and CPU costs, which are a critical part of query optimization.

When the database gathers noworkload statistics, it simulates a workload. Here's how you collect noworkload statistics, using the DBMS_STATS.GATHER_SYSTEM_STATS procedure:

```
SQL> execute dbms_stats.gather_system_stats()

PL/SQL procedure successfully completed.

SQL>
```

You can also gather system statistics while the database is processing a typical workload. These system statistics, called workload statistics, are more representative of actual system I/O and CPU characteristics and present a more accurate system hardware picture to the optimizer. You can collect workload system statistics by executing the DBMS_STATS.GATHER_SYSTEM_STATS procedure with the "start" and "stop" options:

```
SQL> execute dbms_stats.gather_system_stats('start')

PL/SQL procedure successfully completed.
SQL>
```

You can execute the previous command before the beginning of the workload window. Once the workload window ends, stop the system statistics gathering by executing the following command:

```
SQL> execute dbms_stats.gather_system_stats('stop')

PL/SQL procedure successfully completed.

SQL>
```

You can also execute the GATHER_SYSTEM_STATS procedure with an interval parameter, to instruct the database to collect workload system statistics over a period of time that you specify and automatically stop the statistics gathering process at the end of the period. Here's an example:

```
SQL> execute dbms_stats.gather_system_stats('interval',90);
PL/SQL procedure successfully completed.
SQL>
```

The previous command collects workload statistics for 90 minutes.

Once you collect noworkload or workload system statistics, you can check the values captured for the various system statistics in the sys.aux_stats$ view, shown in the next section.

■ **Tip** Oracle highly recommends the gathering of system statistics in order to provide more accurate CPU and I/O cost estimates to the optimizer.

How It Works

Accurate system statistics are critical for the optimizer's evaluation of alternative execution plans. It's through its estimates of various system performance characteristics such as I/O speed and CPU speed that the optimizer calculates the cost of, say, a full table scan vs. an indexed read.

You can pass up to nine optimizer system statistics to the optimizer, by collecting system statistics. The database gathers the first three statistics during a noworkload simulated statistics gathering process.

It gathers all nine system statistics during a workload mode system statistics collection. Here's a summary of the nine system statistics:

cpuspeedNW: Shows the noworkload CPU speed, in terms of the average number of CPU cycles per second

ioseektim: The sum of seek time, latency time, and OS overhead time

iotfrspeed: Stands for I/O transfer speed and tells the optimizer how fast the database can read data in a single read request

cpuspeed: Stands for CPU speed during a workload statistics collection

maxthr: The maximum I/O throughput

slavethr: Average parallel slave I/O throughput

sreadtim: The Single Block Read Time statistic shows the average time for a random single block read.

mreadtim: The Multiblock Read Time statistic shows the average time (in seconds) for a sequential multiblock read.

mbrc: The Multi Block Read Count statistic shows the average multiblock read count in blocks.

When you collect the noworkload system statistics, the database captures only the cpuspeedNW, ioseektim, and iotfrspeed system statistics. Here's a query that shows the default system statistics in an Oracle 11g database (on a Windows system).

```
SQL> select pname, pval1 from sys.aux_stats$ where sname = 'SYSSTATS_MAIN';

PNAME                            PVAL1
------------------------------   ----------
CPUSPEED
CPUSPEEDNW                       1183.90219
IOSEEKTIM                                10
IOTFRSPEED                             4096
MAXTHR
MBRC
MREADTIM
SLAVETHR
SREADTIM

9 rows selected.

SQL>
```

The database uses noworkload systems statistics by default, with the values of the three noworkload statistics—I/O transfer speed (IOTFRSPEED), I/O seek time (IOSEEKTIM), and CPU speed (CPUSPEEDNW)—initialized to default values when you start the instance. Once you collect the noworkload statistics as shown in the "Solution" section, some or all of the three noworkload system statistics may change. In our case, once we collected the noworkload statistics, the value of CPUSPEEDNW changed to 2039.06 and the value of the IOSEEKTIM statistic changed to 14.756. However, the value of the IOTFRSPEED statistic remained constant at 4096.

If you notice that the `sys.aux_stats$` view continues to show the default values for noworkload statistics even after you manually gather the statistics a few times, you can manually set the statistics values to known specifications of your I/O or CPU system by using the `DBMS_STATS.SET_SYSTEM_STATS` procedure. You can use this procedure to set values for any of the nine system statistics.

When you gather system statistics in the workload mode, you'll see values for some or all of the remaining six system statistics. In our example, these are the system statistics collected by running the `GATHER_SYSTEM_STATS` procedure in the workload mode.

```
SQL>  select pname, pval1 from sys.aux_stats$ where sname = 'SYSSTATS_MAIN';

PNAME                              PVAL1
---------------------------   ----------
CPUSPEED                             2040
CPUSPEEDNW                        2039.06
IOSEEKTIM                          14.756
IOTFRSPEED                           4096
MAXTHR
MBRC                                    7
MREADTIM                        46605.947
SLAVETHR
SREADTIM                        51471.538

9 rows selected.

SQL>
```

If the database performs any full table scans during the workload statistics collection period, Oracle uses the value of the `mbrc` and the `mreadtim` statistics to estimate the cost of a full table scan. In the absence of these two statistics, the database uses the value of the `db_file_multiblock_read_count` parameter to estimate the cost of full table scans.

You can delete all system statistics by executing the `DELETE_SYSTEM_STATS` procedure:

```
SQL> execute dbms_stats.delete_system_stats()

PL/SQL procedure successfully completed.

SQL>
```

According to Oracle, collecting workload statistics doesn't impose an additional overhead on your system. However, ensure that you specify a specific interval or stop the statistics collection after a brief period, to avoid potential overhead.

13-10. Validating New Statistics

Problem

You're collecting new statistics, but you don't want the database to automatically use those statistics until you validate them.

Solution

In this example, we'll show how to keep the database from automatically publishing new statistics for a table. Here are the procedures you must follow to do this.

1. Execute the following statement to keep the database from automatically publishing new statistics it collects for the SH.SALES table.

    ```
    SQL> execute dbms_stats.set_table_prefs('SH','SALES','PUBLISH','false');

    PL/SQL procedure successfully completed.

    SQL>
    ```

    The statement sets the preference for the PUBLISH parameter to false (default=true) for the SH.SALES table. From here on, the database won't automatically publish the statistics you collect for the SH.SALES table. Rather, it keeps those statistics in abeyance, pending your approval. These statistics are called pending statistics, because the database hasn't made them available to the optimizer yet.

2. Collect new statistics for the SH.SALES table:

    ```
    SQL> exec dbms_stats.gather_table_stats('sh','sales');

    PL/SQL procedure successfully completed.
    SQL>
    ```

3. Tell the optimizer to use the newly collected pending statistics, so you can test your queries with those statistics:

    ```
    SQL>  alter session set optimizer_use_pending_statistics=true;

    Session altered.

    SQL>
    ```

4. Perform your tests by running a workload against the SH.SALES table and checking the performance and the execution plans.

5. If you're happy with the new set of (pending) statistics, make them public by executing this statement:

    ```
    SQL> execute dbms_stats.publish_pending_stats('SH','SALES');

    PL/SQL procedure successfully completed.

    SQL>
    ```

6. If you want to delete the new statistics instead, execute the following command:

```
SQL> exec dbms_stats.delete_pending_stats('SH','SALES');

PL/SQL procedure successfully completed.

SQL>
```

How It Works

By default the database immediately starts using all statistics it gathers. However, you can specify that the database not automatically use the new statistics it collects until you decide that the statistics are going to improve or at least don't degrade current execution plans. You do this by keeping the new statistics in a *pending* state. Making the statistics available to the optimizer so it can use them in figuring out execution plans is called *publishing* the statistics. The database stores published statistics in its data dictionary. If you aren't sure about the efficacy of a new set of statistics, you can keep the database from automatically publishing statistics until you complete testing them first. When you keep statistics in the pending state, the database won't store them in the data dictionary—instead, it stores them in a private area, and makes those statistics available to the optimizer only if you set the optimizer_use_pending_statistics parameter to true.

After specifying that the database must keep newly collected statistics in the pending status, you can choose to either publish the new statistics or delete them. Use the publish_pending_stats procedure to publish the statistics and the delete_pending_stats procedure to delete the statistics. If you delete the pending statistics for an object, the database will use existing statistics for that object.

In this example, we showed how to change the PUBLISH setting for statistics at the table level. You can also do this at the schema level, but not at the database level. If working at the schema level, you need to run the following statements instead (the schema name is SH).

```
SQL> execute dbms_stats.set_schema_prefs('SH','PUBLISH','false');
SQL> execute dbms_stats.publish_pending_stats(null,null);
SQL> execute dbms_stats.delete_pending_stats('SH');
```

13-11. Forcing the Optimizer to Use an Index

Problem

You know that using a certain index on a column is going to speed up a query, but the optimizer doesn't use the index in its execution plans. You want to force the optimizer to use the index.

Solution

You can force the optimizer to use an index when it isn't doing so, by adjusting the optimizer_index_cost_adj initialization parameter. You can set this parameter at the system or session level. Here's an example that shows how to set this parameter at the session level:

```
SQL> alter session set optimizer_index_cost_adj=50;

Session altered.
SQL>
```

The default value for the `optimizer_index_cost_adj` parameter is 100, and you can set the parameter to a value between 0 and 10000. The lower the value of the parameter, the more likely it is for the optimizer to use an index.

How It Works

The `optimizer_index_cost_adj` parameter lets you adjust the cost of an index access. The optimizer uses a default value of 100 for this parameter, which means that it evaluates an indexed access path based on the normal costing model. Based on the optimizer's estimate of the cost of performing an indexed read, it makes the decision of whether to use the index. Usually this works fine. However, in some cases, the optimizer doesn't use an index even if it leads to a better execution plan, because the optimizer's estimates of the cost of the indexed access path may be off. Since it uses a default value of 100 for the `optimizer_index_cost_adj` parameter, you make the index cost seem lower to the optimizer by setting this parameter to a smaller value. Any value less than 100 makes the use of an index look cheaper (in terms of the cost of an indexed read) to the optimizer. Often, when you do this, the optimizer starts using the index you want it to use. In our example, we set the `optimizer_index_cost_adj` parameter to 50, making the cost of an index access path appear half as expensive as its normal cost (100). The lower you set the value of this parameter, the cheaper an index cost access path appears to the optimizer, and the more likely it will be to prefer an index access path to a full table scan.

We recommend that you set the `optimizer_index_cost_adj` parameter only at the session level for a specific query, because it has the potential to change the execution plans for many queries if you set it at the database level. By default, if you set the `ALL_ROWS` optimizer goal, there's a built-in preference for full table scans by the optimizer. By setting the `optimizer_index_cost_adj` parameter to a value less than 100, you're inducing the optimizer to prefer an index scan over a full table scan. Use the `optimizer_index_cost_adj` parameter with confidence, especially in an OLTP environment, where you can experiment with low values such as 5 or 10 for the parameter to force the optimizer to use an index.

By default, the optimizer assumes that the cost of a multiblock read I/O associated with a full table scan and the single block read cost associated with an indexed read are identical. However, a single block read is likely to be less expensive than a multiblock read. The `optimizer_index_cost_adj` parameter lets you adjust the cost of a single block read associated with an index read more accurately to reflect the true cost of an index read vis-à-vis the cost of a full table scan. The default value of 100 means that a single block read is 100% of a multiblock read—so it's telling the optimizer to treat the cost of an indexed read as identical to the cost of a multiblock I/O full table scan. When you set the parameter to a value of 50, you're telling the optimizer that the cost of a single block I/O (index read) is only half the cost of a multiblock I/O. This makes the optimizer choose the indexed read over a full table scan.

Note that accurate system statistics (`mbrc`, `mreadtim`, `sreadtim`, etc.) have a bearing on the use of indexes vs. full table scans. Ideally, you should collect workload system statistics and leave the `optimizer_index_cost_adj` parameter alone. You can also calculate the relative costs of a single block read and a multiblock read and set the `optimizer_index_cost_adj` parameter value based on those calculations. However, the best strategy is to simply use the parameter at the session level for a specific statement and not at the database level. Simply experiment with various levels of the parameter until the optimizer starts using the index.

You can also use a more "scientific" way to figure out the correct setting for the `optimizer_index_cost_adj` parameter, by setting it to a value that reflects the "true" difference between single and multiblock reads. You can simply compare the average wait times for the `db file sequential read` wait event (represents a single block I/O) and the `db file scattered read` wait event (represents multiblock I/O), to arrive at an approximate value for the `optimizer_index_cost_adj` parameter. Issue the following query to view the average wait times for both of the wait events.

```
SQL> select event, average_wait from v$system_event
     where event like 'db file s%read';
EVENT                                                            AVERAGE_WAIT
---------------------------------------------------------------- ------------
db file sequential read                                                  .91
db file scattered read                                                  1.41

SQL>
```

Based on the output of this query, single block sequential reads take roughly 75% of the time it takes to perform a multiblock (scattered) read. This indicates that the `optimizer_cost_index_adj` parameter should be set to somewhere around 75. However, as we mentioned earlier, setting the parameter at the database level isn't recommended—instead, use this parameter sparingly for specific statements where you want to force the use of an index.

13-12. Enabling Query Optimizer Features

Problem

You've upgraded your database, but you want to ensure the query plans don't change due to new optimizer features in the new release.

Solution

By default, the database enables all query optimizer features in the current database version. You can control the set of optimizer features enabled in a database by setting the `optimizer_features_enable` initialization parameter. For example, if you're running an Oracle Database 11g Release 2 database, the optimizer features are set to the 11.2 release, as shown here:

```
SQL> show parameter optimizer_features_enable

NAME                                 TYPE         VALUE
------------------------------------ ----------- ----------
optimizer_features_enable            string       11.2.0.1
SQL>
```

You can set the optimizer features of a database to an earlier release by setting the `optimizer_features_enable` parameter to a different value from its default value (same as the database release). For example, in an 11.x release, you can do this:

```
SQL> alter system set optimizer_features_enable='10.2.0.5';
```

```
System altered.
SQL>
```

You can now check the current value of the parameter:

```
SQL> show  parameter optimizer_features_enable
```

```
NAME                                 TYPE         VALUE
------------------------------------ ------------ --------------
optimizer_features_enable            string       10.2.0.5
SQL>
```

You can set the `optimizer_features_enable` parameter to any past major release or a point release, all the way back to the Oracle Database 8.0 release.

How It Works

Setting the `optimizer_features_enable` parameter to the value of the previous database release ensures that when you upgrade the database, the optimizer will behave exactly the same way as it did before the upgrade. This is a strategy that DBAs commonly use to ensure that query plans don't suddenly deteriorate following an upgrade. Once you understand the new optimizer features better, you can set the value of the `optimizer_features_enable` parameter to the same value as the upgraded database release.

Of course, you won't be able to take advantage of any of the new optimizer features when you set the `optimizer_features_enable` parameter to a lower value than the current release—but you aren't going to be surprised by any sudden changes in the execution plans either. Optimizer features don't change drastically between releases, but it all depends on the database release. For example, there are six major new optimizer features in the 11.1.0.6 release that weren't in the 10.2.0.2 release. These include the enhanced bind peeking feature and the ability to use extended statistics to estimate selectivity. Different applications will behave differently following the introduction of a new optimizer feature—that's where the ability to retain the current optimizer feature set during an upgrade provides you a safety net. You get the opportunity to fully test and understand the implications of the new optimizer features before enabling them in a production database.

The example shown in the "Solution" section shows how to set the optimizer features level for an entire database. You can, however, enable it just at the session level (`alter session …`) to test for regressions in execution plans following an upgrade. You can also specify the release number with a hint, so you can test a query with optimizer features from a specific release, as shown here in an 11.2 release database.

```
SQL>  select /*+ optimizer_features_enable ('11.1.0.6')  */ sum(sales) from sales
    order by product_id;
```

This `SELECT` statement was executed in an 11.2 release database, but uses optimizer features from the 11.1 release.

13-13. Keeping the Database from Creating Histograms

Problem

You think that the presence of a histogram on a particular column is leading to sub-optimal execution plans. You'd like the database not to use any histograms on that column.

Solution

You need to do two things if you want to keep Oracle from using the histogram it's automatically collecting on a column:

1. Drop the histogram by executing the DELETE_COLUMN_STATS procedure:

```
SQL> begin
  2  dbms_stats.delete_column_stats(ownname=>'SH',tabname=>'SALES',
  3  colname=>'PROD_ID',col_stat_type=>'HISTOGRAM');
  4  end;
  5  /

PL/SQL procedure successfully completed.

SQL>
```

2. Once you drop the histogram, tell Oracle not to create a histogram on the PROD_ID column by executing the following SET_TABLE_PREFS procedure:

```
SQL> begin
  2  dbms_stats.set_table_prefs('SH','SALES','METHOD_OPT','FOR  ALL COLUMNS SIZE
     AUTO,
     FOR COLUMNS  SIZE 1 PROD_ID');
  3  end;
  4  /

PL/SQL procedure successfully completed.

SQL>
```

How it Works

For various reasons, DBAs often would sometimes like to keep the optimizer from using a histogram on a column, If there's already a histogram on a column, you must first get rid of it and then use the dbms_stats.set_table_prefs procedure to keep the database from creating a histogram on that column. In the Oracle Database 10g release, you drop the histogram first, freeze the statistics (with the lock_table_stats procedure) and then manually collect statistics on the table, specifying that the database must not collect statistics for the column for which you dropped the histogram. Because you locked the statistics, you must also specify the force=true option when executing the dbms_stats.gather_table_stats procedure to manually collect statistics on a table. As you can see, the dbms_stats.set_table_prefs procedure in the 11g release makes things a lot simpler.

In the command shown in the Solution section, `FOR ALL COLUMNS SIZE AUTO` option tells the database to create histograms on any column that Oracle deems skewed. However, the `FOR COLUMNS SIZE 1 PROD_ID` tells the database not to create a histogram for the column `PROD_ID` in the `SH.SALES` table. The `SIZE` column accepts values 1–254, with the integer number you specify representing the number of buckets in the histogram. Telling the database to use just a single bucket (N=1) means that all data will be in a single bucket—i.e., the database won't create a histogram on that column.

13-14. Improving Performance When Not Using Bind Variables

Problem

For various reasons, your developers didn't specify bind variables in the code. You notice heavy latch contention and poor response times due to the non-use of bind variables. You want to improve the performance of the database in a situation like this, where you can't change existing code.

Solution

If your applications aren't using bind variables, there will be an increase in expensive hard-parsing in the database. To avoid this, you need to set the `cursor_sharing` initialization parameter to a non-default value. The default value for this parameter is `EXACT`. You can set the `cursor_sharing` parameter to either `FORCE` or `SIMILAR` to determine which SQL statements can share the same cursors.

Here's how you can set the `cursor_sharing` parameter to `force` or `similar`.

```
SQL> alter system set cursor_sharing=force;
SQL> alter system set cursor_sharing=similar;
```

Setting the `cursor_sharing` parameter to a non-default value has several implications, as the next section explains.

How It Works

The best practice in writing SQL code is to use bind variables so the SQL statements are shareable. During the parse stage, the optimizer will compare a SQL statement's text with the texts of existing statements that are stored in the shared pool. The database considers the current statement *identical* to another statement only if it matches the other statement in all respects, including each character, space, and even case. When you leave the `cursor_sharing` parameter at its default value of `EXACT`, Oracle will reuse the shared SQL area when it reexecutes a SQL statement that uses bind variables. There's no need for hard-parsing the new statement because a parsed version already exists in the shared pool. The new statement can use an existing cursor (thus it's called a shared cursor) and not create its own parent cursor.

If the code doesn't use bind variables, but the new SQL statement the database is parsing is the same in all respects to a previously parsed statement in the shared pool, the statement is considered *similar* to the previous statement.

By default, the database shares cursors when SQL statements are identical, but not when they are similar. The database will perform a heavy amount of hard-parsing if applications use literal values instead of bind variables, and in a busy system, it could put enormous pressure on the shared pool and the cursor cache. You can make the database share cursors when the new statement is similar (but not identical) to an existing parsed statement, by setting the cursor_sharing parameter to either FORCE or SIMILAR. Setting the cursor_sharing parameter to either FORCE or SIMILAR lets the database replace the literal values with system-generated bind variables. The goal here is to reduce the number of parent cursors in the shared pool. Sharing cursors even when the application doesn't use bind variables relieves the pressure on the shared pool by reducing the number of parent cursors in the cursor cache (in the shared pool). Leaving the cursor_sharing parameter at its default value will make the database perform a hard parse if the statement it's parsing isn't identical to an existing statement in the shared pool. However, if you set the parameter to FORCE or SIMILAR, the database will perform the much cheaper soft parse when it finds a similar statement in the shared pool.

When to Set CURSOR_SHARING to a Non-default Value

Ideally, you should leave the cursor_sharing parameter at its default value of EXACT. However, if your response time is suffering due to a heavy amount of library cache misses, and the SQL statements aren't using bind variables, consider setting the cursor_sharing parameter to FORCE or SIMILAR. If the application doesn't use bind variables, your hands are tied—the fixes will be long in coming, and meanwhile, you have a slow-performing database on your hands. Go ahead and change the cursor_sharing parameter from its default setting under these circumstances. There are really no issues with setting the cursor_sharing parameter to a non-default value, except minor drawbacks such as the non-support for star transformation, for example.

■ **Tip** Oracle recommends using the FORCE setting for the CURSOR_SHARING parameter, in an OLTP environment.

Oracle recommends that, if possible, you should leave the cursor_sharing parameter at its default value of EXACT, and use shareable SQL by employing bind variables in your code instead of literal values. If you do decide to change the default setting to SIMILAR or FORCE due to pressure in the shared pool and latch contention, be aware that there are some performance implications in doing so. If you set the cursor_sharing parameter to FORCE, the database uses system-generated bind values, uses the same execution plan for each execution of a statement, and uses one parent cursor and one child cursor for each distinct SQL statement. If you set the parameter to SIMILAR and there are no histograms on the column for which the database generates bind values, the behavior is the same as with the FORCE setting. If there are histograms, on the other hand, the SIMILAR setting will result in a different plan based on the value of the bind variable, and thus there'll be a different child cursor for each execution. When there's no histogram, the database acts as if bind variables are not used, under the SIMILAR setting.

Although Oracle has historically recommended the SIMILAR setting for the cursor_sharing parameter, in Oracle Database 11g, unless you're in a DSS environment, Oracle recommends that you set the cursor_sharing parameter to FORCE, because it limits the growth of child cursors when compared to setting the parameter to the SIMILAR value.

Implications of Setting CURSOR_SHARING to a Non-default Value

Both the FORCE and the SIMILAR settings can help you get around the non-use of bind variables in an application, by letting the database generate bind values (system-generated bind values, as opposed to user-specified)). However, you should be aware of the differences in the behavior of the optimizer when you set the cursor_sharing parameter to FORCE as opposed to the SIMILAR setting. The key thing to understand here is that there's a conflict between query performance and the space used in the shared pool by multiple executions of a query. Here is a summary of the performance implications of setting the cursor_sharing parameter to EXACT, FORCE, and SIMILAR. Let's assume the following query, which contains a literal:

```
select * from employees where job = 'Clerk'
```

Note that if the query were to use bind variables instead of literals, it would be of the following form:

```
select * from employees where job=:b
```

EXACT: The database doesn't replace any literals, and the optimizer sees the query as it's presented to the optimizer. The optimizer generates a different plan for each execution of the statement, based on the literal values in the statement. The plan would thus be an optimal one, but each statement has its own parent cursor, and therefore a statement that's executed numerous times can use a considerable amount of space in the shared pool. This could potentially lead to latch contention and a slowdown in performance.

FORCE: Regardless of whether there's a histogram, the optimizer will replace the literal values with a bind value and optimize this query as if it were in the following form:

```
select * from employees where job=:b
```

The optimizer uses a single plan for each SQL statement, regardless of the literal values. Thus, the execution plan won't be optimal, as the plan is generic, and not based on the literal values. If a query uses literal values, the optimizer will use those values to find the most efficient execution plan. If there are no literals in the SQL statement, it's very hard for the optimizer to figure out the best execution plan. By "peeking" at the value of the bind variables, the optimizer can get a better idea of the selectivity of the where clause condition—it is almost as if literals had been used in the SQL statement. The optimizer peeks at the bind values during the hard parse state. Since the execution plan is based on the specific value of the bind variable that the optimizer happened to peek at, the execution plan may not be optimal for all possible values of the bind variable.

In this example, the optimizer uses bind peeking based on the specific value of the JOB column it sees. In this case, the optimizer uses the value Clerk to estimate the cardinality for the query. When it executes the same statement (with a different value in the JOB column, say, Manager), the optimizer will use the same plan that it generated the first time (JOB=Clerk). Since there is only one parent cursor and just child cursors for the distinct statements, there's less pressure on the shared pool. Note that a child cursor uses far less space in the shared pool than a parent cursor. Often, setting the cursor_sharing parameter to FORCE immediately resolves serious latch contention in the database, making this one of the few magic bullets that can help you quickly reduce latch contention.

SIMILAR (without a histogram on the JOB column): The database will use literal replacement—it uses a system-generated bind value instead of the literal value for the JOB column (Clerk). This is because the absence of a histogram on the JOB column tells the optimizer that the data in the JOB column isn't skewed, and therefore the optimizer chooses the same plan for each execution of the statement, even though the literal values are different. The optimizer thinks it shouldn't make any changes to the execution plans for the statements that differ only in literal values because the data is uniformly distributed. The SIMILAR setting without a histogram on the columns in a query provides the same query performance and a similar impact on the shared pool as when you specify the FORCE setting.

SIMILAR (with a histogram on the JOB column): When the optimizer sees the histogram in the JOB column, it realizes that the column is skewed—this tells the optimizer that the results of the query may vary widely depending on the literal value of the JOB column. Consequently, the optimizer generates a different plan for each statement based on the literal values—thus the plans are very efficient, as in the case when you specify the EXACT setting. The SIMILAR option with a histogram in place does use more space in the shared pool, but not as much as when you use the EXACT setting. The reason for this is that each statement has its own child cursor instead of a parent cursor.

The choice among the various settings of the cursor_sharing parameter really boils down to an assessment of what's more critical to database performance: using the default EXACT setting or SIMILAR (with a histogram on the relevant column) does provide better query performance but leads to the generation of numerous parent cursors (EXACT setting) or child cursors (SIMILAR setting). If there's a severe pressure in the shared pool, and consequent latch contention, the entire database will perform poorly. Under these circumstances, you're better off implementing a system-wide solution by setting the cursor_sharing parameter to FORCE, as this guarantees that there's only a single child cursor for each SQL statement. If you're concerned about the impact of a single SQL statement, just drop the histogram on the relevant columns used in the SQL statement and set the cursor_sharing parameter to FORCE—this will ensure that the optimizer uses system-generated bind values for the column(s) and ensures that the SQL statement uses much less space in the shared pool. As you'll see in the next section, Oracle Database 11g's adaptive cursor sharing offers an even better solution, if you set the cursor_sharing parameter to FORCE and keep the histograms on the columns.

13-15. Understanding Adaptive Cursor Sharing

Problem

Your database uses user-defined bind variables. You want to know if there's anything you can do to optimize database behavior so it doesn't "blindly" use the same execution plan for all bind variable values.

Solution

In prior releases, Oracle used a single execution plan for each execution of a SQL statement, regardless of the values of the bind variables. In Oracle Database 11g, the database feature called *adaptive cursor sharing* enables a SQL statement with bind variables to use multiple execution plans, with each execution plan based on the values of the bind variable(s). Adaptive cursor sharing is enabled by default, and you can't disable it.

How It Works

The adaptive cursor-sharing feature is designed to improve the execution plans for SQL queries that contain bind variables. To understand how adaptive cursor sharing helps, it's important to understand how Oracle's bind peeking feature works. Bind peeking (introduced in Oracle 9i) lets the optimizer peek at the value of a bind variable when the database invokes the cursor for the first time. The optimizer uses the "peeked value" to determine the selectivity of the WHERE clause.

The problem with using user-defined bind variables is that the execution plan doesn't have an accurate measure of the selectivity of the WHERE clause. Bind peeking helps improve matters by letting the optimizer act as if it were actually using a literal value instead of the bind variable, thus helping it generate better execution plans for SQL statements with bind variables. Bind peeking works well when the values of the column in the WHERE clause have a uniform distribution. If the column values are skewed, the plan the optimizer chooses by peeking at the value of the user-defined bind variable may not necessarily be good for all possible values of the bind variable. You thus end up with a situation where the execution plan will be very efficient if the SQL statement has the bind variable value that the optimizer has peeked at—and inefficient execution plans for all other possible values of the bind variable.

Let's learn how adaptive cursor sharing works, with the help of an example that involves a column with skewed data.

Our test table, DEMO, has 78,681 rows. The data has three columns, which are all skewed. Thus, when we gathered statistics for this table, we created histograms on the three columns, as shown here.

```
SQL> select column_name,table_name,histogram from user_TAB_COLUMNS
    where table_name='DEMO';

COLUMN_NAME                          TABLE_NAME                          HISTOGRAM
------------------------------------ ----------------------------------- ----------------
RNUM                                 DEMO                                HEIGHT BALANCED
RNAME                                DEMO                                HEIGHT BALANCED
STATUS                               DEMO                                FREQUENCY
```

Note that when the optimizer notices that there's a histogram on a table, it marks the data in that column as skewed. The column STATUS has two values: Coarse and Fine. Only 157 rows have the value of Coarse, and 78,524 rows have the value Fine, making the data extremely skewed.

Let's perform a sequence of operations to illustrate how adaptive cursor sharing works. Issue a query with the bind variable set to the value Coarse. Since very few rows in the DEMO table have this value, we expect the database to use an index range scan, which is exactly what the optimizer does. Here is our query and its execution:

```
SQL> var b varchar2(6)
SQL> exec :b:='Coarse';

PL/SQL procedure successfully completed.

SQL> select /*+ ACS */ count(*) from demo where status = :b;
  COUNT(*)
----------
       157

SQL> select * from table(dbms_xplan.display_cursor);

PLAN_TABLE_OUTPUT
--------------------------------------------------------------------------------
SQL_ID  cxau3vvabpzd0, child number 0
-------------------------------------
select /*+ ACS */ count(*) from demo where status = :b
```

```
Plan hash value: 3478245284
----------------------------------------------------------------------
| Id  | Operation          | Name      | Rows  | Bytes | Cost (%CPU)| Time     |
----------------------------------------------------------------------
|   0 | SELECT STATEMENT   |           |       |       | 1 (100)|          |
|   1 |   SORT AGGREGATE   |           |     1 |     6 |        |          |
```

PLAN_TABLE_OUTPUT

```
----------------------------------------------------------------------
|*  2 |    INDEX RANGE SCAN| IDX01_DEMO |   157 |   942 |    1   (0)| 00:00:52 |
----------------------------------------------------------------------
Predicate Information (identified by operation id):
---------------------------------------------------
   2 - access("STATUS"=:B)
19 rows selected.
```

Next issue the following statement to check whether the database has marked the STATUS column as bind-sensitive or bind-aware or both:

```
SQL> select child_number, executions, buffer_gets, is_bind_sensitive as
  2  "BIND_SENSI", is_bind_aware as "BIND_AWARE", is_shareable as "BIND_SHARE"
  3  from v$SQL
  4* where sql_text like 'select /*+ ACS */%'
SQL> /
CHILD_NUMBER EXECUTIONS BUFFER_GETS BIND_SENSI  BIND_AWARE  BIND_SHARE
------------ ---------- ----------- ----------- ----------- -----------
           0          1          43 Y           N           Y

SQL>
```

Note that the database marks the STATUS column as bind-sensitive, because there's a histogram on the column STATUS. Each time you execute the query with a different value for the bind variable, the database compares the execution statistics with those from the prior execution. If the execution statistics differ significantly, it marks the column as bind-aware. One of the inputs the database uses in deciding whether to mark a statement as bind-aware is the number of rows processed. Once a cursor is marked bind-aware, the optimizer will choose an execution plan based on the value of the bind variable. Here, the IS_BIND_AWARE column is marked N, because there are no prior execution statistics to compare. The BIND_SHAREABLE column is marked Y.

Issue the query again, with the bind variable set to the value Fine. Since almost all of the rows have the STATUS column set to the value Fine, we expect the optimizer to prefer a full table scan. However, the optimizer picks exactly the same plan as before (INDEX RANGE SCAN). The reason for this is that the database is using the same execution plan from the first execution—for example:

```
SQL> exec :b := 'Fine';

PL/SQL procedure successfully completed.

SQL> select /*+ ACS */ count(*) from demo where status = :b;
```

```
  COUNT(*)
----------
     78524

SQL> select * from table(dbms_xplan.display_cursor);

PLAN_TABLE_OUTPUT
--------------------------------------------------------------------------------
SQL_ID  cxau3vvabpzd0, child number 0
-------------------------------------
select /*+ ACS */ count(*) from demo where status = :b

Plan hash value: 3478245284
--------------------------------------------------------------------------------
| Id  | Operation           | Name       | Rows  | Bytes | Cost (%CPU)| Time      |
--------------------------------------------------------------------------------
|   0 | SELECT STATEMENT    |            |       |       |   1 (100)|           |
|   1 |  SORT AGGREGATE     |            |     1 |     6 |          |           |

PLAN_TABLE_OUTPUT
--------------------------------------------------------------------------------
|*  2 |   INDEX RANGE SCAN| IDX01_DEMO |   157 |   942 |     1   (0)| 00:00:52 |

--------------------------------------------------------------------------------
Predicate Information (identified by operation id):
---------------------------------------------------
   2 - access("STATUS"=:B)

19 rows selected.
```

Since the cursor for the SQL statement is marked bind-sensitive, the optimizer uses the same execution plan (INDEX RANGE SCAN) as before. Note in the following example that the BIND_AWARE column is still marked N. The optimizer is using the same cursor as before (child_number 0).

```
SQL> select child_number, executions, buffer_gets, is_bind_sensitive as
  2  "BIND_SENSI", is_bind_aware as "BIND_AWARE", is_shareable as "BIND_SHARE"
  3  from v$sql
  4  WHERE sql_text like 'select /*+ ACS */%';

CHILD_NUMBER EXECUTIONS BUFFER_GETS BIND_SENSI  BIND_AWARE  BIND_SHARE
------------ ---------- ----------- ----------- ----------- -----------
           0          2         220 Y           N           Y

SQL>
```

Execute the query again, with the same value for the STATUS column as in the previous query ('Fine'). Voila! The optimizer now uses an INDEX FAST FULL SCAN, instead of the INDEX RANGE SCAN. The change in execution plans is automatic—it is as if the optimizer is learning as it goes along and modifies the plan when it's certain that the new plan is more efficient. Here is the execution and the new plan:

```
SQL> exec :b := 'Fine';
PL/SQL procedure successfully completed.

SQL> select /*+ ACS */ count(*) from demo where status = :b;
  COUNT(*)
----------
     78524

SQL> select * from table(dbms_xplan.display_cursor);
PLAN_TABLE_OUTPUT
--------------------------------------------------------------------------------
SQL_ID  cxau3vvabpzd0, child number 1
-------------------------------------
select /*+ ACS */ count(*) from demo where status = :b

Plan hash value: 2683512795

--------------------------------------------------------------------------------
| Id  | Operation            | Name      | Rows  | Bytes | Cost (%CPU)| Time     |

PLAN_TABLE_OUTPUT
--------------------------------------------------------------------------------
|   0 | SELECT STATEMENT     |           |       |       |    45 (100)|          |
|     |
|   1 |  SORT AGGREGATE      |           |     1 |     6 |            |          |
|     |
|*  2 |   INDEX FAST FULL SCAN| IDX01_DEMO | 78524 |   460K|    45   (0)| 00:38:  |
PLAN_TABLE_OUTPUT
--------------------------------------------------------------------------------
37 |
--------------------------------------------------------------------------------
Predicate Information (identified by operation id):
---------------------------------------------------
   2 - filter("STATUS"=:B)
19 rows selected.
```

Note that the BIND_AWARE column now shows the value Y. When we execute the query with the same bind variable value (Fine) the second time, since the query is marked as bind-sensitive, the database evaluates the execution statistics from the previous execution. Since the statistics are different, it marks the cursor as bind-aware. The optimizer then decides a new plan is more optimal and thus performs a hard parse and generates a new execution plan that uses an INDEX FAST FULL SCAN instead of an INDEX RANGE SCAN. The following query shows details about the child cursors as well as whether the query is bind-sensitive or bind-aware.

```
SQL> select child_number, executions, buffer_gets, is_bind_sensitive as
  2  "BIND_SENSI", is_bind_aware as "BIND_AWARE", is_shareable as "BIND_SHARE"
  3  from v$sql
  4  WHERE sql_text like 'select /*+ ACS */%';
```

CHILD_NUMBER	EXECUTIONS	BUFFER_GETS	BIND_SENSI	BIND_AWARE	BIND_SHARE
0	2	220	Y	N	Y
1	1	184	Y	Y	Y

SQL>

Note that the IS_BIND_AWARE column shows the value Y now. Notice also that there is a new child cursor (child_number 1) that represents the new execution plan containing the INDEX FAST FULL SCAN—this new cursor is marked bind-aware.

We execute the query again, but this time with the original bind variable value Coarse. The optimizer will choose the correct execution plan, by performing an INDEX RANGE SCAN. Here's the information about the child cursors, as well as whether the query is bind-sensitive or bind-aware.

```
SQL> select child_number, executions, buffer_gets, is_bind_sensitive as
  2  "BIND_SENSI", is_bind_aware as "BIND_AWARE", is_shareable as "BIND_SHARE"
  3  from v$sql
  4  where sql_text like 'select /*+ ACS */%';
```

CHILD_NUMBER	EXECUTIONS	BUFFER_GETS	BIND_SENSI	BIND_AWARE	BIND_SHARE
0	2	220	Y	N	N
1	1	184	Y	Y	Y
2	1	2	Y	Y	Y

SQL>

The database creates a new child cursor (child_number=2) for this query and marks the original cursor (child_cursor=0) as not being bind-aware. Eventually the database will remove this cursor from the shared pool.

In our example, we used only two values for the bind variable in our tests. What happens if there are dozens of different bind variable values? Oracle doesn't always perform a hard parse for each distinct bind variable value. Initially it performs a hard parse for some values of the bind variable, during which it determines the relationships between various bind variables and the associated execution plan. After the initial mapping of the bind variable values and the associated execution plans, Oracle is smart enough to simply pick the optimal child cursor from the cache without performing a hard parse for other bind values.

Adaptive cursor sharing is a new feature introduced in the Oracle Database 11g release. In earlier releases, DBAs often flushed the shared pool (and worse, sometimes restarted the database) when confronted with situations where the database apparently started using an inappropriate execution plan for a SQL statement, due to the bind peeking effect. In the 11g release, you don't have to do anything—the optimizer automatically changes execution plans when it encounters skewed data. With adaptive cursor sharing, the database uses multiple execution plans for a statement that uses bind variables, ensuring that the best execution plan is always used, depending on the value of the bind variable. Adaptive cursor sharing means that when different bind variable values indicate different amounts of data to be handled by the query, Oracle adapts its behavior by using different execution plans for the query instead of sticking to the same plan for all bind values. Since adaptive cursor sharing works only where literal values are replaced with binds, Oracle encourages you to use the FORCE setting for the cursor_sharing parameter. If you set the parameter to SIMILAR and you have a histogram on a column, the optimizer doesn't perform a literal replacement with bind variables, and thus adaptive cursor sharing won't take place. You must set the cursor_sharing parameter to FORCE for adaptive cursor sharing to work, thus letting the optimizer select the optimal execution plan for different values of the bind variable.

13-16. Creating Statistics on Expressions

Problem

You want to create statistics on an expression such as an user-created function.

Solution

Execute the GATHER_TABLE_STATS procedure of the DBMS_STATS package in the following way, to gather statistics on an expression. In this example, we're gathering statistics for the lower function, which transforms the cust_state_province column.

```
SQL> execute dbms_stats.gather_table_stats('sh','customers',-
   > method_opt =>'for all columns size skewonly -
   > for columns(lower(cust_state_province)) size skewonly');

PL/SQL procedure successfully completed.

SQL>
```

Alternatively, you can collect expression statistics by invoking the create_extended_stats function—for example:

```
SQL> select
  2  dbms_stats.create_extended_stats(null,'customers','(lower(cust_state_province))')
  3  from dual;
```

Note that (lower (cust_state_province)) is called an *extension*, because collecting statistics on functions is a type of Oracle extended statistics. Any statistics you collect for expressions and column groups (see Recipe 13-17) are called "extended statistics."

How It Works

The optimizer knows the selectivity of a table's column and uses the selectivity estimates for creating optimal execution plans. However, applying a function to a column in the WHERE clause of a query throws the optimizer off, because it can't estimate the selectivity of the underlying column. Here's an example of a function that makes the optimizer's job harder:

```
SQL> select count(*) from customers
     where lower(cust_state_province) = 'CA';
```

Expression statistics on functions enable the optimizer to obtain a vastly more accurate selectivity value for predicates that involve expressions.

You can issue the following query to find details about expression statistics on a table's columns:

```
SQL> select extension_name, extension
     from user_stat_extensions
     where table_name='CUSTOMERS';
```

```
EXTENSION_NAME                            EXTENSION
-----------------------------------       ------------------------------
SYS_STUBPHJSBRKOIK9O2YV3W8HOUE            (LOWER("CUST_STATE_PROVINCE"))
SQL>
```

You can delete expression statistics you've collected on a table by using the drop_extended_stats function:

```
SQL> exec dbms_stats.drop_extended_stats(null,'customers','(lower(cust_state_pro
vince))');
```

```
PL/SQL procedure successfully completed.
```

```
SQL>
```

Note that extended statistics include both statistics on expressions such as a function and statistics gathered for a column group that consists of two or more related columns. Recipe 13-17 shows how to collect statistics on column groups.

13-17. Creating Statistics for Related Columns

Problem

You're aware that certain columns from a table that are part of a join condition are correlated. You want to make the optimizer aware of this relationship.

Solution

In order to generate statistics for two or more related columns, you must first create a *column group* and then collect fresh statistics for the table so the optimizer can use the newly generated "extended statistics." Use the DBMS_STATS.CREATE_EXTENDED_STATS function to define a column group that consists of two or more columns from a table. Here's how you execute this function to create a column group that consists of the COUNTRY_ID and CUST_STATE_PROVINCE columns in the table SH.CUSTOMERS.

```
SQL> select dbms_stats.create_extended_stats(null,'CUSTOMERS', '(country_id,cust
_state_province)') from dual;
```

```
DBMS_STATS.CREATE_EXTENDED_STATS(NULL,'CUSTOMERS','(COUNTRY_ID,CUST_STATE_PROVIN
-------------------------------------------------------------------------------

SYS_STUJGVLRVH5USVDU$XNV4_IR#4
SQL>
```

Once you create the column group, gather fresh statistics for the CUSTOMERS table to generate statistics for the new column group.

```
SQL> exec dbms_stats.gather_table_stats(null,'customers');

PL/SQL procedure successfully completed.

SQL>
```

How It Works

Often, values in one column of a table influence the values of another column in that table, due to natural relationships that exist between the data stored in the two columns. For example, the values of the CUST_STATE_PROVINCE column in the SH.CUSTOMERS table are influenced by the values of the COUNTRY_ID column. You can find a CUST_STATE_PROVINCE value of Florida only in the United States. The optimizer doesn't know about real-life relationships and thus tends to produce wrong estimates of the all-important cardinality statistic when multiple related columns appear in the WHERE clause of a query or in a group_by key. Column group statistics help the optimizer capture the correlation among a table's columns. If a query includes the predicates CUST_STATE_PROVINCE ='Florida' and COUNTRY_ID=U.S., Oracle can derive a better estimate of the combined selectivity of these two predicates by looking up the statistics for the column group instead of using separate statistics for the two columns.

The statistics the database gathers on the column groups that you create are called extended statistics. These statistics provide much more accurate cardinality estimates to the optimizer, which helps the optimizer produce more efficient execution plans. When you create extended statistics, Oracle maintains a subset of statistics for the column groups that you create, including the number of distinct values, nulls, and histograms for the group. Even if a query contains columns in addition to the columns that are part of a column group, the optimizer takes advantage of the extended stats that are available to it. For example, suppose you've created a column group as shown in this recipe, using the CUST_STATE_PROVINCE and the COUNTRY_ID columns. If the WHERE clause for a query includes these two columns as well as the CUST_CITY column, Oracle will still take advantage of the extended statistics on the CUST_STATE_PROVINCE and COUNTRY_ID columns.

13-18. Automatically Creating Column Groups

Problem

You know that creating extended statistics by generating statistics on correlated table columns helps generate better execution plans. You want to find out how to select candidate column groups for creating extended statistics.

Solution

In Oracle Database 11.2.0.2 and later releases, you can use the *Auto Column Group Creation* feature to let the database tell you which column groups you must create. You can use this feature only for creating column groups, but not for collecting extended statistics for columns with expressions (see Recipe 13-16).

In order to use the Auto Column Group Creation capability and let the database provide advice on which column groups to create in the database, you must let the database monitor the workload in the database. Begin by executing the DBMS_STATS.SEED_COL_USAGE procedure to determine the appropriate column groups that you must create:

```
SQl> begin
    dbms_stats.seed_col_usage(null,null,900);
    end;
    /
```

By executing this procedure, you're telling the database to monitor the workload for 15 minutes (900 seconds) to determine if you need to create any column groups. The procedure captures the column usage information and stores it in the **sys.col_group_usage$** view.

Next run some queries to create the workload. If the queries are long-running, you can just run explain plan statements for the queries so the database can capture the column group information. Once the monitoring period (15 minutes) is over, review the captured column usage information by using the following query:

```
SQL> select dbms_stats.report_col_usage(user,'customers') from dual;
```

The REPORT_COL_USAGE procedure shows a column usage report for the CUSTOMERS table, based on the queries you've executed, and the explain plans that you ran. The column usage shows how the database used each column of the CUSTOMERS table, and lists column usage in the following format:

- Equality predicates (EQ): If a column was used in an equality predicate such as in the clause where COUNTRY_ID='US', that column was used independently. No extension statistics are called for in this case.

- FILTER: If a set of columns was used in a SELECT statement that contained one or more of those columns in a GROUP BY clause, all columns in the SELECT statement are recorded as a column group filter.

- GROUP_BY: All columns used together in a GROUP_BY clause.

Once you view the column usage report, you can let Oracle automatically create the column groups for the columns used in the filter predicates and the columns used in the GROUP_BY clause. Do that by executing the following procedure:

```
SQL>select dbms_stats.create_extended_stats(user,'customers') from dual;
```

Alternatively, you can create column groups only for columns that you specify, by issuing the following command:

```
SQL> select dbms_stats.create_extended_stats(null,'CUSTOMERS', '(cust_city,cust_
state_province,country_id)') from dual
SQL> /
DBMS_STATS.CREATE_EXTENDED_STATS(NULL,'CUSTOMERS','(CUST_CITY,CUST_STATE_PROVINC
```

```
-------------------------------------------------------------------------
SYS_STUMZ$C3AIHLPBROI#SKA58H_N
SQL>
```

At this point, you've created the column group, but there are no statistics on the column group. Regather statistics for the CUSTOMERS table to generate statistics for the new column group—for example:

```
SQL> exec dbms_stats.gather_table_stats(user,'customers')
PL/SQL procedure successfully completed.
SQL>
```

How It Works

Letting Oracle point out potential column groups based on the actual column usage during a workload is far more efficient than your trying to figure out the appropriate column groups for each table. Once you run the workload, you can view the column usage report and ask the database to create all proposed column groups for an entire schema at the same time, by executing the dbms_stats.create_extended_stats function and passing the value NULL for the table_name parameter.

13-19. Maintaining Statistics on Partitioned Tables

Problem

You load data into one or more partitions frequently, and the maintenance of global statistics is a problem. You want to collect new global statistics without having to go through a time- and resource-consuming process.

Solution

You can use the *incremental statistics maintenance* feature in the Oracle 11g release to maintain global statistics after each load into a new partition. For example, if you want to maintain global statistics for the SH.SALES table, here are the steps to follow:

1. Turn on incremental statistics collection for the SH.SALES table:

    ```
    SQL> exec dbms_stats.set_table_prefs('SH','SALES','INCREMENTAL','TRUE');

    PL/SQL procedure successfully completed.

    SQL>
    ```

2. After each load into a partition, gather global table-level statistics as shown here:

    ```
    SQL> exec dbms_stats.gather_table_stats('SH','SALES');

    PL/SQL procedure successfully completed.

    SQL>
    ```

In order to set the incremental statistics collection feature for partitioned tables, you must specify the AUTO_SAMPLE_SIZE value for the ESTIMATE_PERCENT parameter and the AUTO value for the GRANULARITY parameter.

How It Works

The incremental statistics collection feature is disabled by default. You enable the feature by setting the INCREMENTAL preference. In our example, we showed how to set the INCREMENTAL preference at the table level, but you can also set it at the schema or database level.

When dealing with a partitioned table, the optimizer uses both global statistics (statistics for the entire table) and statistics for the individual partitions to select the optimal execution plan. By default, following a change in a partition's data, the database uses a two-pass scanning technique to maintain accurate table statistics. Under this two-pass technique, the database will do the following:

- Scan the entire table to gather the global statistics during the first pass.

- Scan the changed partitions in the second pass, to gather the partition statistics.

When you load data into (or delete data from) a partition(s) as part of a nightly batch job, for example, the database will scan the partition(s) to gather the partition-level statistics. In addition, it scans the entire table to gather the table-level global statistics. The database scans not only the changed partitions, but also all the other partitions in the table as well. As you can tell, this full scan of the table each time a partition's data changes is an expensive process, especially when dealing with very large tables.

Once you turn the incremental statistics collection feature on, Oracle uses a far more efficient technique to maintain a partitioned table's statistics. When a partition's data changes, the database gathers just the statistics for that partition and derives the global table statistics without scanning any of the other partitions. How does the database maintain the global statistics without scanning the entire table? Oracle can derive some global statistics from partition-level statistics—for example, it derives the total number of rows by just adding up the rows in each partition. For deriving the number of distinct values (NDVs), Oracle makes use of a structure called a synopsis, which is something like a sample of the NDVs in a column. Oracle derives the global NDV by merging all partition synopses. In summary, when you implement incremental statistics collection, Oracle skips the default full table scan to gather the table's statistics and instead does the following:

1. Gathers statistics for the partition you loaded and creates synopses for that partition

2. Creates a global synopsis by merging all the partition-level synopses

3. Computes the global statistics from the partition-level statistics and the global synopses

Incremental statistics collection is extremely efficient and something you must consider using when dealing with large partitioned tables, especially when you're loading data into one or more empty partitions frequently, as is the case in many data warehouses.

13-20. Concurrent Statistics Collection for Large Tables

Problem

You want to minimize the amount of time it takes to gather statistics by taking advantage of your multi-processor environment.

Solution

In Oracle Database 11g Release 2 (11.2.0.2), you can specify the *concurrent statistics gathering mode* to gather statistics on multiple tables and multiple partitions (and subpartitions) within a table concurrently. By doing this, you can take advantage of your multi-processor environment and complete the statistics collection process much faster.

By default, concurrent statistics gathering is disabled. You enable it by executing the SET_GLOBAL_PREFS procedure. Follow these steps to enable concurrent statistics gathering.

1. Set the job_queue_processes parameter to at least 4.

   ```
   SQL>alter system set job_queue_processes=4;
   ```

   If you don't plan on using parallel execution for gathering statistics (see the following section), but want to fully utilize your system resources, you must set the job_queue_processes parameter to two times the number of CPU cores on the server.

2. Enable concurrent statistics gathering.

   ```
   SQL> begin
        dbms_stats.set_global_prefs('CONCURRENT','TRUE');
        end;
        /
   ```

Make sure the user executing this command has the CREATE JOB, MANAGE SCHEDULER, and the MANAGE ANY QUEUE privileges.

How It Works

The goal of concurrent statistics gathering is to reduce the statistics gathering time for large tables and partitions. When you enable concurrent statistics gathering, Oracle uses the job scheduler and advanced queuing capabilities of the database to create multiple concurrent statistics gathering jobs. The job_queue_processes parameter determines the maximum number of concurrent statistics gathering jobs. In a RAC environment, you must set this parameter on each node. Concurrent statistics gathering works somewhat differently depending on the level of statistics gathering (table level or not), as explained here.

If you execute the DBMS_STATS.GATHER_TABLE_STATS procedure to collect statistics on a partitioned table, Oracle will create a separate statistics collection job for each partition (and subpartition) in the table. The scheduler determines how many jobs to run concurrently, and how many jobs it must queue, based on the system capacity.

■ **Note** The value of the job_queue_processes parameter determines the maximum number of concurrent statistics collection jobs.

If you execute the GATHER_DATABASE_STATS, GATHER_SCHEMA_STATS, or the GATHER_DICTIONARY_STATS procedures, Oracle creates a separate statistics collection job for each table and each partition in a partitioned table. To prevent potential deadlocking issues, Oracle won't process multiple partitioned tables concurrently. Oracle creates a coordinator job for each partitioned table, to manage the partition statistics collection jobs. Each job is either a coordinator for a table's partition-level jobs (if the table is partitioned), or is an actual statistics gathering job. If you have multiple partitioned tables, the database queues all partitioned tables except one; as it finishes gathering statistics for each partitioned table, it dequeues and starts another job for a partitioned table. This queuing behavior doesn't apply to non-partitioned tables.

Using a Parallel Execution Strategy

If you're gathering statistics for very large tables, you can enable parallel execution of the individual statistics gathering jobs. To do this, you must disable the **parallel_adaptive_multi_user** initialization parameter as shown here:

```
SQL> alter system set parallel_adaptive_multi_user=false;
```

Although not necessary, Oracle also recommends that you enable parallel statement queuing by activating the resource manager, creating a temporary resource plan, and enable queuing for the consumer group OTHER _GROUPS. Here's a simple example that shows how to create a temporary resource plan and enable the resource manager:

```
begin
  dbms_resource_manager.create_pending_area();
  dbms_resource_manager.create_plan('parallel_test', 'parallel_test');
  dbms_resource_manager.create_plan_directive(
        'parallel_test',
        'OTHER_GROUPS',
        'OTHER_GROUPS directive for parallel test',
        parallel_target_percentage => 90);
  dbms_resource_manager.submit_pending_area();
end;
/
ALTER SYSTEM SET RESOURCE_MANAGER_PLAN = 'parallel_test' SID='*';
```

Monitoring Concurrent Stats Collection Jobs

Use the DBA_SCHEDULER_JOBS view to monitor the concurrent statistics gathering jobs. You can view all the concurrent statistics collection jobs in your database by issuing the following statement:

```
SQL> select job_name,state,comments
     from dba_scheduler_jobs
     where job_class like 'CONC%';
```

If you want to limit the output to currently executing jobs, add the line "and state='RUNNING'" to the previous query. Similarly, you can add the line "and state='SCHEDULED'" to view only the scheduled jobs that are waiting to run. You can check the elapsed time for the currently executing statistics gathering jobs by issuing the following query:

```
SQL> select job_name,elapsed_time
     from dba_scheduler_running_jobs
     where job_name like 'ST$%';
```

CHAPTER 14

Implementing Query Hints

Placing hints in SQL is a common and simple approach to improve performance. Hints influence Oracle's optimizer to take a specific path to accomplish a given task, overriding the default path the optimizer may have chosen. Hints can also be viewed as a double-edged sword. If not implemented and maintained properly, they can hurt performance in the long run.

The most popular reason to use hints is simply to get data out of the database faster, and many of the available hints are geared for that purpose. The Oracle database supports more than 60 hints, so it is apparent that hints can be placed in SQL for a multitude of reasons. The purpose of this chapter is to categorize these hints into subsets, and then to show specific examples of some of the popular and most performance-impacting hints.

Some of the reasons to place hints in SQL are to change the access path to the database, change the join order or join type for queries that are doing joins, hints for DML, and hints for data warehouse–specific operations, to name a few. In addition, there are new Oracle 11g hints to take advantage of some of the new features of Oracle 11g.

14-1. Writing a Hint

Problem

You want to place a hint into a SQL statement.

Solution

Place your hint into the statement using the /*+ hint */ syntax—for example:

```
SELECT /*+ full(emp) */ * FROM emp;
```

Be sure to leave a space following the plus sign. The /*+ sequence is exactly three characters long, with no spaces. Generally, you want to place your hint immediately following the SQL verb beginning the statement. While it is not required to place this sequence of characters after the SQL verb, it is customary to do this.

How It Works

Hints are delimited by special characters placed within your SQL statement. Each hint starts with a forward slash, followed by the star and plus characters. They end with a star and forward slash:

```
SELECT /*+ full(emp) */ * FROM emp;
```

Table 14-1 breaks down many of the most popular hints into specific categories. This table is meant to make it easier to zero in on a hint based on your specific need, so keep in mind that some of these hints actually can fit into multiple categories. Another thing to remember about hints is that for many of them, you can enable a particular feature or aspect, and you can disable that same feature or aspect. For example, there is an `INDEX` hint to enable the use of an index. There is also a `NO_INDEX` hint, which disables the use of an index. This is true for many of the available hints within the Oracle database.

For a complete listing of hints, refer to the Oracle Database Performance Tuning Guide for your version of the database.

Table 14-1. Hints by Category

Category	Hint Names
Access path (table)	FULL HASH CLUSTER
Access path (index)	INDEX / NO_INDEX INDEX_ASC / INDEX_DESC INDEX_FFS / NO_INDEX_FFS INDEX_SS / NO_INDEX_SS INDEX_SS_ASC / INDEX_SS_DESC INDEX_COMBINE / INDEX_JOIN
Join order	ORDERED LEADING
Join method	USE_HASH USE_NL USE_MERGE
Data warehousing	STAR_TRANSFORMATION FACT REWRITE
Optimizer hints	FIRST_ROWS ALL_ROWS OPTIMIZER_FEATURES_ENABLE GATHER_PLAN_STATISTICS

Category	Hint Names
Parallelism	PARALLEL / NO_PARALLEL PARALLEL_INDEX / NO_PARALLEL_INDEX PQ_DISTRIBUTE
DML-related hints	APPEND APPEND_VALUES
Oracle 11g-related hints	RESULT_CACHE STATEMENT_QUEUING
Miscellaneous hints	CACHE DRIVING_SITE DYNAMIC_SAMPLING CURSOR_SHARING_EXACT

14-2. Changing the Access Path

Problem

You have a query that you have determined is not taking the access path you desire.

Solution

You can change the access path of your SQL statement by placing an access path hint in your query. The two most common access path hints to place in a query tell the Oracle optimizer to do a full table scan, or use an index. Often, the optimizer does a good job of choosing the best or at least a reasonable path to the data needed for a query. Sometimes, though, because of the specific makeup of data in a table, the statistics for the objects, or the specific configuration of a given database, the optimizer doesn't necessarily make the best choice. In these cases, you can influence the optimizer by placing a hint in your query.

By the time you decide to place a hint in a query, you should already know that the optimizer isn't making the choice you want. Let's say you want to place a hint in your query to tell the optimizer to modify the access path to either perform a full table scan, or change how the optimizer will access the data from table. Full table scans are appropriate if your query will be returning a large number of rows. For example, if you want to perform a full table scan on your table, your hint will appear as follows:

```
SELECT /*+ full(emp) */ empno, ename
FROM emp
WHERE DEPTNO = 20;
```

The foregoing hint instructs the optimizer to bypass the use of any possible indexes on the EMP table, and simply scan the entire table in order to retrieve the data for the query.

Conversely, let's say you are retrieving a much smaller subset of data from the EMP table, and you want to get the average salary for those employees in department 20. You can tell the optimizer to use an index on a given table in the query:

```
SELECT /*+ index(emp emp_i2) */ avg(sal)
FROM emp
WHERE deptno = 20;
```

■ **Tip**   Hints with incorrect or improper syntax are ignored by the optimizer.

How It Works

Access path hints, like many hints, are placed in your query because you already know what access path the optimizer is going to take for your query, and you believe it will be more efficient using the method you specify with the hint. It is very important that before you use a hint, you validate that you are not getting the access path you desire or think you should be getting. You can also gauge the potential performance gain by analyzing the optimizer's cost of the query with and without the hint.

For example, you want to compare your salary to other jobs in your company, so you write the following query to get, by job title, the minimum, average, and maximum salary.

```
SELECT job, min(sal), avg(sal), max(sal)
FROM emp
WHERE deptno=20
GROUP BY job;
```

```
--------------------------------------------------
| Id  | Operation                    | Name   |
--------------------------------------------------
|   0 | SELECT STATEMENT             |        |
|   1 |  HASH GROUP BY               |        |
|   2 |   TABLE ACCESS BY INDEX ROWID| EMP    |
|   3 |    INDEX RANGE SCAN          | EMP_I2 |
--------------------------------------------------
```

If you want to bypass the use of the index in the query, placing the FULL hint in the query will instruct the optimizer to bypass the use of the index:

```
SELECT /*+ full(emp) */ job, min(sal), avg(sal), max(sal)
FROM emp
WHERE deptno=20
GROUP BY job;
```

```
------------------------------------------
| Id  | Operation         | Name |
------------------------------------------
|   0 | SELECT STATEMENT  |      |
|   1 |  HASH GROUP BY     |      |
|   2 |   TABLE ACCESS FULL| EMP  |
------------------------------------------
```

Another way you can tell the optimizer to bypass the use of an index is by telling the optimizer to not use indexes to retrieve the data for a given query. In this particular case, it has the same effect as the FULL hint:

```
SELECT /*+ no_index(emp) */ job, min(sal), avg(sal), max(sal)
FROM emp
WHERE deptno=20
GROUP BY job;
```

You can also explicitly state the name of the index you wish to bypass:

```
SELECT /*+ no_index(emp emp_i2) */ job, min(sal), avg(sal), max(sal)
FROM emp
WHERE deptno=20
GROUP BY job;
```

In both of the foregoing cases, the result is a full table scan. In a different case, you may have a query that could possibly use different indexes. For instance, on our EMP table, we have an index on the DEPTNO column, and we also have an index on the HIREDATE column. If we wanted to execute a query to get the employees that started in the year 1980 for department 20, our query would look like this:

```
SELECT empno, ename
FROM emp
WHERE DEPTNO = 20
AND hiredate
BETWEEN to_date('1980-01-01','yyyy-mm-dd')
AND to_date('1980-12-31','yyyy-mm-dd');
```

```
---------------------------------------------
| Id  | Operation                  | Name   |
---------------------------------------------
|   0 | SELECT STATEMENT           |        |
|   1 |   TABLE ACCESS BY INDEX ROWID| EMP  |
|   2 |    INDEX RANGE SCAN        | EMP_I1 |
---------------------------------------------
```

In this case, the optimizer chose the EMP_I1 index, which is the index on the HIREDATE column. We can instruct the optimizer to bypass the use of that index:

```
SELECT /*+ no_index(emp emp_i1) */ job, min(sal), avg(sal), max(sal)
FROM emp
WHERE deptno=20
GROUP BY job;
```

In this case, we don't necessarily know what the optimizer is going to do next. It may decide to use our other index on the DEPTNO column, or it could choose to perform a full table scan. It is good practice in using hints to be as specific as possible when instructing the optimizer what to do. Therefore, if we place an index hint to tell the optimizer to use the index on the DEPTNO column, we can see that the optimizer now uses that index:

```
SELECT /*+ index(emp emp_i2) */ empno, ename
FROM emp
WHERE DEPTNO = 20
AND hiredate
BETWEEN to_date('1980-01-01','yyyy-mm-dd')
AND to_date('1980-12-31','yyyy-mm-dd');
```

```
-----------------------------------------------
| Id  | Operation                   | Name   |
-----------------------------------------------
|   0 | SELECT STATEMENT            |        |
|   1 |  TABLE ACCESS BY INDEX ROWID| EMP    |
|   2 |   INDEX RANGE SCAN          | EMP_I2 |
-----------------------------------------------
```

Other examples of index hints are the INDEX_FFS for an index fast full scan, and the INDEX SS for an index skip scan. The INDEX_SS hint is appropriate if you have a table with composite, multi-column indexes. It is possible to have Oracle use the index, even if the query does not use the leading column of the index. At times, the INDEX_SS hint can be beneficial to retrieve data fast, even if the column noted in the WHERE clause isn't the leading column of an index. For example, if we want to get the names of all employees that received a commission, our query would look like this:

```
SELECT ename, comm FROM emp
WHERE comm > 0;
```

```
-----------------------------------
| Id  | Operation        | Name |
-----------------------------------
|   0 | SELECT STATEMENT |      |
|   1 |  TABLE ACCESS FULL| EMP |
-----------------------------------
```

As noted in the explain plan, no index is used. We happen to know there is a composite index on the SAL and COMM columns of our EMP table. We can add a hint to use this index to gain the benefit of having an index on the COMM column, even though it is not the leading column of the index:

```
SELECT /*+ index_ss(emp emp_i3) */ ename, comm FROM emp
WHERE comm > 0;
```

```
-----------------------------------------------
| Id  | Operation                   | Name   |
-----------------------------------------------
|   0 | SELECT STATEMENT            |        |
|   1 |  TABLE ACCESS BY INDEX ROWID| EMP    |
|   2 |   INDEX SKIP SCAN           | EMP_I3 |
-----------------------------------------------
```

■ **Note** Hints influence the optimizer, but the optimizer may still choose to ignore any hints specified in the query.

14-3. Changing the Join Order

Problem

You have a performance issue with a query where you are joining multiple tables, and the Oracle optimizer is not choosing the join order you desire.

Solution

There are two hints—the ORDERED hint, and the LEADING hint—that can be used to influence the join order used within a query.

Using the ORDERED Hint

You are running a query to join two tables, EMP and DEPT, as you want to get the department names for each employee. By placing an ORDERED hint into the query, you can see how the hint alters the execution access path—for example:

```
SELECT ename, deptno
FROM emp JOIN dept USING(deptno);
```

```
----------------------------------------
| Id  | Operation         | Name      |
----------------------------------------
|   0 | SELECT STATEMENT  |           |
|   1 |  HASH JOIN        |           |
|   2 |   INDEX FULL SCAN | PK_DEPT   |
|   3 |   TABLE ACCESS FULL| EMP      |
----------------------------------------
```

```
SELECT /*+ ordered */ ename, deptno
FROM emp JOIN dept USING(deptno);
```

```
----------------------------------------
| Id  | Operation         | Name      |
----------------------------------------
|   0 | SELECT STATEMENT  |           |
|   1 |  NESTED LOOPS     |           |
|   2 |   TABLE ACCESS FULL| EMP      |
|   3 |   INDEX UNIQUE SCAN| PK_DEPT  |
----------------------------------------
```

Using the LEADING Hint

As with the example using the ORDERED hint, you have the same control to specify the join order of the query. The difference with the LEADING hint is that you specify the join order from within the hint itself, while with the ORDERED hint, it is specified in the FROM clause of the query. Here's an example:

```
SELECT /*+ leading(dept, emp) */ ename, deptno
FROM emp JOIN dept USING(deptno);

-----------------------------------------
| Id  | Operation          | Name        |
-----------------------------------------
|   0 | SELECT STATEMENT   |             |
|   1 |  NESTED LOOPS      |             |
|   2 |   TABLE ACCESS FULL| EMP         |
|   3 |   INDEX UNIQUE SCAN| PK_DEPT     |
-----------------------------------------
```

From the foregoing query, we can see that the table order specified in the FROM clause is irrelevant, as the order specified in the LEADING hint itself specifies the join order for the query.

How It Works

The main purpose of specifying either of these hints is for multi-table joins where the most optimal join order is known. This is usually known from past experience with a given query, based on the makeup of the data and the tables. In these cases, specifying either of these hints will save the optimizer the time of having to process all of the possible join orders in determining the optimal join order. This can improve query performance, especially as the number of tables to join within a query increases.

When using either of these hints, you instruct the optimizer about the join order of the tables. Because of this, it is critically important that you know that the hint will improve the query's performance. Oracle recommends, where possible, to use the LEADING hint over the ORDERED hint, as the LEADING hint has more versatility built in. When specifying the ORDERED hint, you specify the join order from the list of tables in the FROM clause, while with the LEADING hint, you specify the join order within the hint itself.

14-4. Changing the Join Method

Problem

You have a query where the optimizer is choosing a non-optimal join type for your query, and you wish to override the join type by placing the appropriate hint in the query.

Solution

There are three possible types of joins: nested loops, hash, and sort merge. Depending on the size of your tables, certain join types perform better than others. You can use hints to specify the join order that you prefer.

Nested Loops Join Hint

To invoke a nested loops join, use the USE_NL hint, and place both tables needing the join within parentheses inside the USE_NL hint:

```
SELECT /*+ use_nl(emp, dept)  */ ename, dname
FROM emp JOIN dept USING (deptno);
```

```
---------------------------------------------------
| Id  | Operation                   | Name   |
---------------------------------------------------
|   0 | SELECT STATEMENT            |        |
|   1 |  NESTED LOOPS               |        |
|   2 |   NESTED LOOPS              |        |
|   3 |    TABLE ACCESS FULL        | DEPT   |
|   4 |    INDEX RANGE SCAN         | EMP_I2 |
|   5 |   TABLE ACCESS BY INDEX ROWID| EMP   |
---------------------------------------------------
```

The nested loops join is usually best when joining small tables together. In a nested loops join, one table is considered the "driving" table. This is the outer table in the join. For each row in the outer, driving table, each row in the inner table is searched for matching rows. In the execution plan for the foregoing statement, the EMP table is the driving, outer table, and it is seen in the execution plan as the outermost part of the plan. The DEPT table is the inner table, and is shown as the innermost part of the execution plan.

Hash Join Hint

To invoke a hash join, use the USE_HASH hint, and place both tables needing the join within parentheses inside the USE_HASH hint:

```
SELECT /*+ use_hash(emp_all, dept)  */ ename, dname
FROM emp_all JOIN dept USING (deptno);
```

```
----------------------------------------------------
| Id  | Operation            | Name    | Rows  |
----------------------------------------------------
|   0 | SELECT STATEMENT     |         | 1037K |
|   1 |  HASH JOIN           |         | 1037K |
|   2 |   TABLE ACCESS FULL  | DEPT    |     4 |
|   3 |   TABLE ACCESS FULL  | EMP_ALL | 1037K |
----------------------------------------------------
```

For the optimizer to use a hash join, it must be an equijoin condition. Hash joins are best used when joining large amounts of data or where a large percentage of rows from a table is needed. The smaller of the two tables is used by the optimizer to build a hash table on the join key between the two tables. In the foregoing example, the DEPT table is the smaller table, and will be used to build the hash table. For best performance, the hash table completely resides in memory.

Sort Merge Join Hint

To invoke a sort merge join, use the USE_MERGE hint, and place both tables needing the join within parentheses inside the USE_MERGE hint:

```
SELECT /*+ use_merge(emp, dept) */ ename, dname
FROM emp JOIN dept USING (deptno)
WHERE deptno != 20;
```

```
-------------------------------------------------
| Id | Operation                    | Name    |
-------------------------------------------------
|  0 | SELECT STATEMENT             |         |
|  1 |  MERGE JOIN                  |         |
|  2 |   TABLE ACCESS BY INDEX ROWID| DEPT    |
|  3 |    INDEX FULL SCAN           | PK_DEPT |
|  4 |   SORT JOIN                  |         |
|  5 |    TABLE ACCESS FULL         | EMP     |
-------------------------------------------------
```

Sort merge joins, like hash joins, are used to join a large volume of data. Unlike the hash join, the sort merge join is used when the join condition between the tables is not an equijoin. The hash join will generally perform better than the sort merge join, unless the data is already sorted on the two tables. During this operation, the input data from both tables is sorted on the join key, and then merged together.

Join Hints When Querying Multiple Tables

If you are joining several tables, and wish to invoke a specific join method between all of the associated tables in the query, you must add a hint for each join condition—for example:

```
SELECT /*+ use_hash(employees, department) use_hash(departments, locations) */
last_name, first_name, department_name,  city, state_province
FROM employees JOIN departments USING (department_id)
JOIN locations USING (location_id);
```

```
-----------------------------------------------------------
| Id | Operation               | Name               |
-----------------------------------------------------------
|  0 | SELECT STATEMENT         |                    |
|  1 |  HASH JOIN               |                    |
|  2 |   HASH JOIN              |                    |
|  3 |    TABLE ACCESS FULL     | LOCATIONS          |
|  4 |    TABLE ACCESS FULL     | DEPARTMENTS        |
|  5 |   VIEW                   | index$_join$_001   |
|  6 |    HASH JOIN             |                    |
|  7 |     INDEX FAST FULL SCAN | EMP_NAME_IX        |
|  8 |     INDEX FAST FULL SCAN | EMP_DEPARTMENT_IX  |
-----------------------------------------------------------
```

How It Works

Table 14-2 summarizes the hints available for each of the different join methods. Hints to instruct the optimizer to choose a join method are sometimes necessary because of several factors:

- Status of statistics on the table

- Size of the PGA

- If the data is sorted at join time

- An unexplained choice of the optimizer

Oracle advises against using hints as much as possible, as over time what was optimal at one moment under one circumstance and one version of the database software may not be optimal the next time. However, sometimes these hints can simply be helpful in fulfilling the short-term need or simply may be the only way to get the optimizer to do what you want it to do.

Table 14-2. *Join Methods and Their Hints*

Method	Hint	Description
Nested loops	`USE_NL /` `NO_USE_NL /` `USE_NL_WITH_INDEX`	Nested loops joins are efficient when processing a small number of rows. The optimizer chooses a driving table, which is the "outer" table in the join. For each row in the outer table, each row in the inner table is searched.
Hash	`USE_HASH /` `NO_USE_HASH`	Hash joins are efficient when processing a large number of rows. Hash joins are used only for equijoins.
Sort merge	`USE_MERGE /` `NO_USE_MERGE`	A sort merge join is ideal for pre-sorted rows and full table scans. The sort merge join is used for non-equality joins. Both tables are sorted on the join key, and then merged. It outperforms nested loops joins for large sets of rows.

■ **Tip**   The size of your PGA can affect which join method the optimizer uses for your query.

14-5. Changing the Optimizer Version

Problem

You have upgraded to a newer version of Oracle, and you are having query performance problems related to the newer version of Oracle. The problem is isolated to a small number of queries, so you want to place a hint in these queries to use the previous version of the optimizer's rules and features.

Solution

In order to specify a version of the optimizer for a given query, you specify the version of the optimizer you desire within the `optimizer_features_enable` hint. Within parentheses, place the desired version of the database within single quotes.

```
SELECT /*+ optimizer_features_enable('10.2') */ *
FROM EMP JOIN DEPT USING(DEPTNO);
```

This method is mostly used as an interim measure to improve performance immediately following an upgrade, until analysis can be done and a resolution found with the query and the upgraded version of the database.

How It Works

You can modify the version of the optimizer for a given query. This can be done via the `optimizer_features_enable` hint, and will be in effect only for a given query. The primary reason this hint is used is that a query that performed well under one specific version of Oracle has seen performance degrade immediately following an Oracle database version upgrade.

There is an Oracle initialization parameter, `optimizer_features_enable`, that can be changed for the entire database instance, and it is an option when widespread performance problems occur within queries immediately after you've upgraded your database. Often, however, changing this parameter at the database instance level is not feasible, nor even desired, as the primary reason for upgrading is to take advantage of new features. So, unless there are significant and widespread performance issues, it is not recommended to change the `optimizer_features_enable` parameter for an entire database instance.

If you have a given query or a small subset of critical queries that are performing at a substandard performance level after an upgrade, a quick method to return to the pre-upgrade performance is to use the `optimizer_features_enable` hint to point to a specific version of the optimizer for a given query.

14-6. Choosing Between a Fast Response and Overall Optimization

Problem

When you execute a query, you can choose between two goals:

- *Fast, initial response*: Get to the point of returning some rows as quickly as possible.

- *Overall optimization*: Minimize overall cost at the expense of upfront processing time.

Your instance will have a default goal configured for it. You can specify hints on a query-by-query basis to override the default goal and get the behavior that you want for a given query.

Solution

There are hints that can be used to override the optimization goal of your database instance. Before using any of the hints related to the optimizer_mode, you first want to validate what your database instance is currently set to. If you have the SELECT ANY DICTIONARY system privilege, you can see what value is set for the optimizer_mode parameter.

```
SQL> show parameter optimizer_mode

NAME                  TYPE                 VALUE
-------------------- -------------------- --------------------
optimizer_mode        string               ALL_ROWS
```

If we run an explain plan for an example query, we can see what the execution plan is by using the default optimizer_mode setting for our database instance.

```
SELECT *
FROM employees NATURAL JOIN departments;
```

```
-------------------------------------------
| Id | Operation        | Name        |
-------------------------------------------
|  0 | SELECT STATEMENT |             |
|  1 |  HASH JOIN       |             |
|  2 |   TABLE ACCESS FULL| DEPARTMENTS |
|  3 |   TABLE ACCESS FULL| EMPLOYEES   |
-------------------------------------------
```

Since the foregoing query is doing full table scans against the tables, and we want to see some rows as soon as possible, but not necessarily the full result set, we can pass in a FIRST_ROWS hint to accomplish this task. It is apparent that this changes the optimizer's execution plan in order to provide results as soon as possible.

```
SELECT /*+ first_rows */ *
FROM employees NATURAL JOIN departments;
```

```
----------------------------------------------------
| Id | Operation                  | Name        |
----------------------------------------------------
|  0 | SELECT STATEMENT           |             |
|  1 |  NESTED LOOPS              |             |
|  2 |   NESTED LOOPS            |             |
|  3 |    TABLE ACCESS FULL        | EMPLOYEES   |
|  4 |    INDEX UNIQUE SCAN        | DEPT_ID_PK  |
|  5 |   TABLE ACCESS BY INDEX ROWID| DEPARTMENTS |
----------------------------------------------------
```

If we needed the reverse situation, and the database's default optimizer_mode was set to FIRST_ROWS, we can supply an ALL_ROWS hint to tell the optimizer to use that mode when determining the execution plan:

```
SQL> alter system set optimizer_mode=first_rows scope=both;

System altered.

SQL> show parameter optimizer_mode

NAME                   TYPE                  VALUE
-------------------    -------------------   --------------------
optimizer_mode         string                FIRST_ROWS

SELECT /*+ all_rows */ *
FROM employees NATURAL JOIN departments;

-------------------------------------------
| Id  | Operation           | Name         |
-------------------------------------------
|   0 | SELECT STATEMENT    |              |
|   1 |  HASH JOIN          |              |
|   2 |   TABLE ACCESS FULL | DEPARTMENTS  |
|   3 |   TABLE ACCESS FULL | EMPLOYEES    |
-------------------------------------------
```

How It Works

The fast, initial response goal is often a good choice for queries when a user is awaiting results. It causes the database engine to make choices that allow rows to begin coming back from the query almost immediately. For example, optimizing for initial response often results in a nested loops join, because such a join can begin returning rows from the very beginning. The trade-off is possibly a longer overall execution time.

The goal of reducing overall query cost is usually a good choice for batch processes. No live, human user is awaiting results, so it is acceptable to spend more time on upfront processing in order to reduce overall query cost. An example might be to execute a hash join, which can't begin returning rows until the join is done, but which might execute in less overall time than a nested loops join.

You can use either the FIRST_ROWS or the ALL_ROWS hint in your query in order to change the optimizer mode, which controls which of the preceding two goals applies to a given query.

To check what the current optimizer mode is for your database instance, check the value of the optimizer_mode initialization parameter. By specifying an optimizer goal hint, it overrides the optimizer mode set at the database instance level, as well as any settings at the session level.

The FIRST_ROWS hint is very popular, as it can quickly return the first possible rows back from a query. The FIRST_ROWS hint is also very common because ALL_ROWS is the default value for the optimizer_mode parameter. It's thus unusual to need to specify ALL_ROWS.

14-7. Performing a Direct-Path Insert

Problem

You are doing a DML INSERT statement, and it is performing slower than needed. You want to optimize the INSERT statement to use a direct-path insert technique.

Solution

By using the APPEND or APPEND_VALUES hint, you can significantly speed up the process of performing an insert operation on the database. Here is an example of the performance savings using the APPEND hint. First, we have a query that does a conventional insert between two tables:

```
INSERT INTO emp_dept
SELECT * FROM emp_ctas_new;

19753072 rows created.
```

Elapsed: 00:01:17.86

```
-------------------------------------------------
| Id  | Operation                | Name          |
-------------------------------------------------
|   0 | INSERT STATEMENT         |               |
|   1 |   LOAD TABLE CONVENTIONAL | EMP_DEPT      |
|   2 |    TABLE ACCESS FULL      | EMP_CTAS_NEW  |
-------------------------------------------------
```

If we place the APPEND hint inside of the same INSERT statement, we see a considerable gain in performance:

```
INSERT /*+ append */ INTO emp_dept
SELECT * FROM emp_ctas_new;

19753072 rows created.
```

Elapsed: 00:00:12.15

```
-----------------------------------------------
| Id  | Operation            | Name           |
-----------------------------------------------
|   0 | INSERT STATEMENT     |                |
|   1 |   LOAD AS SELECT      | EMP_DEPT       |
|   2 |    TABLE ACCESS FULL  | EMP_CTAS_NEW   |
-----------------------------------------------
```

The APPEND hint works with an INSERT statement only with a subquery; it does not work with an INSERT statement with a VALUES clause. For that, you need to use the APPEND_VALUES hint. Here are two examples of an INSERT statement with a VALUES clause, and we can see the effect the hint has on the execution plan:

```
INSERT INTO emp_dept
VALUES (15867234,'Smith, JR','Sales',1359,'2010-01-01',200,5,20);
```

```
---------------------------------------------
| Id  | Operation                | Name      |
---------------------------------------------
|   0 | INSERT STATEMENT         |           |
|   1 |   LOAD TABLE CONVENTIONAL | EMP_DEPT  |
---------------------------------------------
```

```
INSERT /*+ append_values */ INTO emp_dept
VALUES (15867234,'Smith, JR','Sales',1359,'2010-01-01',200,5,20);
```

```
--------------------------------------------
| Id  | Operation              | Name       |
--------------------------------------------
|   0 | INSERT STATEMENT       |            |
|   1 |   LOAD AS SELECT        | EMP_DEPT   |
|   2 |     BULK BINDS GET      |            |
--------------------------------------------
```

How It Works

The APPEND hint works within statements performing DML insert operations from another table, that is, using a subquery from within an INSERT SQL statement. This is appropriate for when you need to copy a large volume of rows between tables. By bypassing the Oracle database buffer cache blocks and appending the data directly to the segment above the high water mark, it saves significant overhead. This is a very popular method for inserting rows into a table very quickly.

When you specify one of these hints, Oracle will perform a direct-path insert. In a direct-path insert, the data is appended at the end of a table, rather than using free space that is found within current allocated blocks for that table. The APPEND and APPEND_VALUES hints, when used, automatically convert a conventional insert operation into a direct-path insert operation. In addition, if you are using parallel operations during an insert, the default mode of operation is to use the direct-path mode. If you want to bypass performing direct-path operations, you can use the NOAPPEND hint.

Keep in mind that if you are running with either of these hints, there is a risk of contention if you have multiple application processes inserting rows into the same table. If two append operations are inserting rows at the same time, performance will suffer, as since the insert append operation appends the data above the high water mark for a segment, only one operation should be done at one time. However, if you have partitioned objects, you can still run several concurrent append operations, as long as each insert operates on separate partitions for a given table.

14-8. Placing Hints in Views

Problem

You are creating a view, and want to place a hint in the view's query in order to improve performance on any queries that access the view.

Solution

Hints can be placed in views, as a view is simply a stored query in the database. Depending on the type of hint used, as well as the type of view that is being queried, you can determine if your hint will be used. It is important to understand what type of view you have so you can determine what impacts hints will have on that view. To understand this, you first need to determine which of the following describes your view:

- Mergeable or non-mergeable view

- Simple or complex view

A simple view is a view that references only one table, and there are not any grouping functions or expressions:

```
CREATE view emp_high_sal
AS SELECT /*+ use_index(employees) */ employee_id, first_name, last_name, salary
FROM employees
WHERE salary > 10000;
```

A complex view can reference multiple tables, or it will have grouping clauses, or use functions and expressions:

```
CREATE or replace view dept_sal
AS SELECT /*+ full(employees) */ department_id, department_name,
departments.manager_id, SUM(salary) total_salary, AVG(salary) avg_salary
FROM employees JOIN departments USING(department_id)
GROUP BY department_id, department_name, departments.manager_id;
```

A mergeable view is simply one in which the optimizer can replace the query calling the view with the query within the view definition itself. For example, we simply want to query all the rows from our EMP_HIGH_SAL view. The optimizer simply has to go directly to the EMPLOYEES table:

```
SELECT * FROM emp_high_sal;
```

```
----------------------------------------
| Id  | Operation         | Name        |
----------------------------------------
|   0 | SELECT STATEMENT  |             |
|   1 |  TABLE ACCESS FULL| EMPLOYEES   |
----------------------------------------
```

The optimizer has simply replaced the query with the query that defined the view:

```
SELECT /*+ full(employees) */ department_id, department_name,
departments.manager_id, SUM(salary) total_salary, AVG(salary) avg_salary
FROM employees JOIN departments USING(department_id)
GROUP BY department_id, department_name, departments.manager_id;
```

With a mergeable view, the hint inside the view is preserved because the essential structure of the view definition is intact based on the query calling the view. See Table 14-3 for the guidelines for hints regarding mergeable views.

Table 14-3. *Rules for Using Hints in Mergeable Views*

Hint Category	Placing Hints Inside Views	Placing Hints in Queries Accessing a View
Access path /join	Used only if the query referencing the view does not reference any other tables or views	Ignored unless single-table view; if so, hint applied to the single table inside the view
Optimizer mode hints	Are used unless there are conflicting hints inside the view, in which case they are all ignored	Hints used regardless of hints inside the views

For a non-mergeable view, the optimizer must break the work up into two pieces. It first must execute the query that defines the view, and then must execute the top-level query. Because of this, the hints defined within the view itself are preserved. For instance, we are querying our DEPT_SAL view. We can see from the explain plan that the query is broken up into pieces:

```
SELECT manager_id, sum(total_salary)
FROM dept_sal
GROUP BY manager_id;
```

```
---------------------------------------------------------
| Id | Operation                     | Name         |
---------------------------------------------------------
|  0 | SELECT STATEMENT              |              |
|  1 |  HASH GROUP BY                |              |
|  2 |   VIEW                        | DEPT_SAL     |
|  3 |    HASH GROUP BY              |              |
|  4 |     MERGE JOIN                |              |
|  5 |      TABLE ACCESS BY INDEX ROWID| DEPARTMENTS |
|  6 |       INDEX FULL SCAN         | DEPT_ID_PK   |
|  7 |      SORT JOIN                |              |
|  8 |       TABLE ACCESS FULL       | EMPLOYEES    |
---------------------------------------------------------
```

See Table 14-4 for the guidelines for hints regarding non-mergeable views.

Table 14-4. *Rules for Using Hints in Non-mergeable Views*

Hint Category	Placing Hints Inside Views	Placing Hints in Queries Accessing a View
Access path	Preserved	Ignored
Join	Preserved	Preserved
Optimizer mode hints	Ignored	They are used, if present.

It can be confusing to understand all the possible scenarios with hints and views, so they need to be used sparingly, and only when other means of tuning have not met the needed requirements.

How It Works

Since a view, as mentioned, is simply a stored query, hints can be placed easily inside the view as they would be inside any query. The type of hint placed in the view will determine how and if a hint can be used within the view. Much like performing DML on a view, there are limitations on when hints are used or ignored.

As a rule of thumb, the simpler a view is, the more likely hints can be effective. Because of the uniqueness of each application, each query, and each view, the only true way to know if a hint will be used is to simply try the hint and perform an explain plan to validate whether a given hint is used.

Oracle does not recommend placing hints in views, as since the underlying objects can change over time, you can expect unpredictable execution plans. Also, views can be created for one specific use, but could be used for other purposes later, and any hints in the views may not help every scenario. In addition, hints placed within views are managed differently than if you were simply executing the query itself. Before any hint placed inside a view is used, the optimizer needs to determine if the view can be merged with the query calling the view.

You can also consider placing hints within queries that access views. It is important to understand the rules of precedence when hints are placed within queries that access the views that have hints within themselves. This especially underlines the need for caution before placing a hint within a view.

■ **Tip**   Hints in queries that reference a complex view are ignored.

14-9. Caching Query Results

Problem

You want to improve the performance on a given set of often-used queries, and want to use Oracle's result cache to store the query results, so they can be retrieved quickly for future use when the same query has been executed.

Solution

The result cache is new to Oracle 11g, and was created in order to store results from often-used queries in memory for quick and easy retrieval. If you run an explain plan on a given query, you can see if the results will be stored in the result cache:

```
SELECT /*+ result_cache */
job_id, min_salary, avg(salary) avg_salary, max_salary
FROM employees JOIN jobs USING (job_id)
GROUP BY job_id, min_salary, max_salary;
```

```
---------------------------------------------------------------
| Id  | Operation                       | Name                 |
---------------------------------------------------------------
|   0 |  SELECT STATEMENT               |                      |
|   1 |   RESULT CACHE                  | 5t4cc5n1gdyfh46jdhfttnhx4g |
|   2 |    HASH GROUP BY                |                      |
|   3 |     NESTED LOOPS                |                      |
|   4 |      NESTED LOOPS               |                      |
|   5 |       TABLE ACCESS FULL         | EMPLOYEES            |
|   6 |       INDEX UNIQUE SCAN         | JOB_ID_PK           |
|   7 |      TABLE ACCESS BY INDEX ROWID| JOBS                |
---------------------------------------------------------------
```

If you then query the V$RESULT_CACHE_OBJECTS view, you can validate whether the results of a query are stored in the result cache by looking at the cache ID value from the explain plan.

```
SELECT ID, TYPE, to_char(CREATION_TIMESTAMP,'yyyy-mm-dd:hh24:mi:ss') cr_date,
BLOCK_COUNT blocks, COLUMN_COUNT columns, PIN_COUNT pins, ROW_COUNT "ROWS"
FROM   V$RESULT_CACHE_OBJECTS
WHERE  CACHE_ID = '5t4cc5n1gdyfh46jdhfttnhx4g';
```

```
       ID TYPE    CR_DATE              BLOCKS  COLUMNS  PINS      ROWS
---------- ------- ------------------- ------- -------- ----- ----------
        4 Result  2011-03-19:15:20:43       1        4     0         19
```

If for some reason your database is set with a default mode of FORCE at the database or table level, you can use the NO_RESULT_CACHE hint to bypass the result cache. If we run our previous query with the result cache mode set to FORCE, it is evident that the result cache is used automatically.

```
SQL> show parameter result_cache_mode
```

```
NAME                 TYPE                 VALUE
-------------------- -------------------- --------------------
result_cache_mode    string               FORCE
```

```
select job_id, min_salary, avg(salary) avg_salary, max_salary
from employees join jobs using (job_id)
group by job_id, min_salary, max_salary;
```

```
---------------------------------------------------------------
| Id  | Operation                       | Name                 |
---------------------------------------------------------------
|   0 |  SELECT STATEMENT               |                      |
|   1 |   RESULT CACHE                  | 5t4cc5n1gdyfh46jdhfttnhx4g |
|   2 |    HASH GROUP BY                |                      |
|   3 |     NESTED LOOPS                |                      |
|   4 |      NESTED LOOPS               |                      |
|   5 |       TABLE ACCESS FULL         | EMPLOYEES            |
|   6 |       INDEX UNIQUE SCAN         | JOB_ID_PK           |
|   7 |      TABLE ACCESS BY INDEX ROWID| JOBS                |
---------------------------------------------------------------
```

If we then rerun with the NO_RESULT_CACHE hint, the result cache is not used and the statement is executed:

```
SELECT /*+ no_result_cache */ job_id, min_salary, avg(salary) avg_salary, max_salary
FROM employees JOIN jobs USING (job_id)
GROUP BY job_id, min_salary, max_salary;
```

```
----------------------------------------------------
| Id | Operation                      | Name       |
----------------------------------------------------
|  0 | SELECT STATEMENT               |            |
|  1 |  HASH GROUP BY                 |            |
|  2 |   NESTED LOOPS                 |            |
|  3 |    NESTED LOOPS                |            |
|  4 |     TABLE ACCESS FULL          | EMPLOYEES  |
|  5 |     INDEX UNIQUE SCAN          | JOB_ID_PK  |
|  6 |    TABLE ACCESS BY INDEX ROWID | JOBS       |
----------------------------------------------------
```

The following query was run twice, first not using the result cache, and the second time using the result cache, and the performance difference is significant:

```
SELECT /*+ no_result_cache */
j.job_id, min_salary, avg(salary) avg_salary, max_salary, department_name
FROM employees_big e, jobs j, departments d
WHERE e.department_id = d.department_id
AND e.job_id = j.job_id
AND salary BETWEEN 5000 AND 9000
GROUP BY j.job_id, min_salary, max_salary, department_name;
```

```
JOB_ID     MIN_SALARY AVG_SALARY MAX_SALARY DEPARTMENT_NAME
---------- ---------- ---------- ---------- ------------------------------
ST_MAN           5500       7280       8500 Shipping
SA_REP           6000       7494      12000 Sales
HR_REP           4000       6500       9000 Human Resources
AC_ACCOUNT       4200       8300       9000 Accounting
IT_PROG          4000       7500      10000 IT
FI_ACCOUNT       4200       7920       9000 Finance
MK_REP           4000       6000       9000 Marketing

7 rows selected.
```

Elapsed: 00:00:21.80

```
SELECT /*+ result_cache */
j.job_id, min_salary, avg(salary) avg_salary, max_salary, department_name
FROM employees_big e, jobs j, departments d
WHERE e.department_id = d.department_id
AND e.job_id = j.job_id
AND salary BETWEEN 5000 AND 9000
GROUP BY j.job_id, min_salary, max_salary, department_name;
```

Elapsed: 00:00:00.08

How It Works

The result cache hint, if placed in a query, will override any database-level, table-level, or session-level result cache settings. Before using hints in your queries, you need to determine the configuration of the result cache on your database. There are two separate result caches to look at: the server-side result cache and the client-side result cache. The server-side result cache is part of the shared pool of the SGA, and stores SQL query results and PL/SQL function results. Query time can be improved significantly, as query results are checked within the result cache first, and if the results exist, they are simply pulled from memory, and the query is not executed. The result cache is most appropriately used for often-run queries that produce the same results.

The result cache can be configured at several levels. As Table 14-5 indicates, it can be configured at the database level, the session level, the table level, or the statement level. The statement level is where hints are specified. If you decide to configure the result cache in your database, there are several initialization parameters that need to be configured. Table 14-6 reviews these parameters. Some are specific parameters for the result cache, while the remaining memory-related parameters need to be analyzed to see if they need to be changed to accommodate the result cache.

Table 14-5. *Result Cache Configuration Hierarchy*

Configuration Level	How to Configure Result Cache
Database level	Configured via initialization parameters (see Table 14-6)
Table level	Configured with the CREATE TABLE or ALTER TABLE statements—for example, ALTER TABLE EMPLOYEES RESULT_CACHE (MODE FORCE)
Session level	Configured via the ALTER SESSION statement—for example, ALTER SESSION SET RESULT_CACHE_MODE=FORCE
Statement level	Configured via the RESULT_CACHE or NO_RESULT_CACHE hints

Table 14-6. *Result Cache Initialization Parameters*

Key Result Cache Initialization Parameters	Description
RESULT_CACHE_MODE	Indicates if result cache is active for all activity or only for manually run activities; MANUAL is the default, which means the result cache is not used unless specified at the table, session, or statement level. FORCE means it will be enabled for all queries for a database instance.
RESULT_CACHE_MAX_SIZE	Determines memory allocated for server-side result cache for database
RESULT_CACHE_MAX_RESULT	Determines maximum size for single result for server-side result cache
CLIENT_RESULT_CACHE_SIZE	Determines maximum size for each client-side session result cache
MEMORY_TARGET	By default, 0.25% of total is allocated for result cache if this parameter is configured.
SGA_TARGET	By default, 0.5% of total is allocated for result cache if this parameter is configured.
SHARED_POOL_SIZE	By default, 1% of total is allocated for result cache if this parameter is configured.

14-10. Directing a Distributed Query to a Specific Database

Problem

You are joining two or more tables together that exist on different databases, and want to direct the work to take place on a particular database, as the remote database is where most of the data resides.

Solution

By default, when you are joining tables that exist on different databases, the database where the query originated is where the majority of the work takes place. You can change this behavior and tell the optimizer which database will do the work:

```
SELECT /*+ driving_site(employees) */ first_name, last_name, department_name
FROM employees@to_emp_link JOIN departments USING(department_id);
```

Specifying the remote site as the driver is most appropriate if the volume on the remote site is large, or if you are querying many tables on the remote site. In order to process a distributed query, the optimizer first has to bring rows from remote tables over to the local site, before processing the overall query. This can be very resource-intensive on the temporary tablespace(s) on the local database. Therefore, by instructing the optimizer to perform the work at the site where the biggest percentage of the data resides, you can drastically improve your query performance.

When specifying the hint, you simply need to specify the remote table or table alias within your hint to direct the optimizer to the site that will do the work. There is no need to specify any hint if you wish the optimizer to do the work on the local database; the hint needs to be specified when you want to direct the work to a remote database.

How It Works

Distributed queries can be a blessing and a curse. By being able to join tables from remote databases, it gives users the impression of data transparency, that is, that the data they need to retrieve appears to be in one place, as they can assemble a single query to retrieve data, when in fact the data may reside on two or more databases. This simplicity in assembling queries is a key advantage of being able to perform distributed queries. The key disadvantage is that optimization of distributed queries is difficult. Essentially, the originating or local database where the query is initiated becomes the "driver" database by default. The optimizer at the local site has no knowledge of the makeup or volume of data at the remote site, and therefore the work is split up into pieces, and the query is not, by default, optimized as a single unit. Therefore, it is important to understand the makeup of the data on each database, in order to attempt to best optimize the query. The key decision you need to make with a distributed query is which database you want to be the "driving" site. The biggest factors in determining which site should be the driving site are as follows:

- How many tables are in the distributed query?

- How many databases are involved in the distributed query?

- Which database contains the most tables involved in the query?

- Which database contains the greatest volume of data?

In essence, if a majority of tables or a large volume of data resides remotely, it may be beneficial to use a remote database as the driving site. Let's say we are joining three tables together, and we want to get employee information along with the department they work in, and their work address. In this scenario, the employee table, being the largest, resides on one database, while two smaller tables, the department and location tables, reside on our local database:

```
SELECT first_name, last_name, department_name, street_address, city
FROM employees@to_emp_link JOIN departments USING(department_id)
JOIN locations USING (location_id);
```

```
----------------------------------------
| Id  | Operation          | Name        |
----------------------------------------
|   0 | SELECT STATEMENT   |             |
|   1 |  HASH JOIN         |             |
|   2 |   HASH JOIN        |             |
|   3 |    TABLE ACCESS FULL| LOCATIONS   |
|   4 |    TABLE ACCESS FULL| DEPARTMENTS |
|   5 |   REMOTE           | EMPLOYEES   |
----------------------------------------
```

From the execution plan, we can see that the EMPLOYEES table is the remote table. What this means is before the join to the employee data can occur, all of that employee data must be brought over to the local database before the query can be completed. In this case, the employee data is by far the largest table of the three. There are far more employees than there are departments or locations, and therefore a large volume of data will be brought over to the local database before the remainder of the query can be processed. So, in this case, performance many improve by having the work done on the database where the employee data resides:

```
SELECT /*+ driving_site(employees) */
first_name, last_name, department_name, street_address, city
FROM employees@to_emp_link JOIN departments USING(department_id)
JOIN locations USING (location_id);
```

```
-----------------------------------------------------------
| Id  | Operation              | Name                       |
-----------------------------------------------------------
|   0 | SELECT STATEMENT REMOTE |                            |
|   1 |  HASH JOIN             |                            |
|   2 |   VIEW                 | index$_join$_001           |
|   3 |    HASH JOIN           |                            |
|   4 |     INDEX FAST FULL SCAN| EMP_DEPARTMENT_IX         |
|   5 |     INDEX FAST FULL SCAN| EMP_NAME_IX               |
|   6 |   HASH JOIN            |                            |
|   7 |    REMOTE             | DEPARTMENTS                |
|   8 |    REMOTE             | LOCATIONS                  |
-----------------------------------------------------------
```

Now the explain plan shows the two smaller tables as remote tables, since the database where the EMPLOYEES table resides is now the driving site for the query. Sometimes you may simply need to determine this by trial and error, when it is not obvious which site should be the driving site.

Another easy way to determine this is simply by determining which query returns faster. If we want to get the average salary for each department and location, the query would look like the following:

```
SELECT department_name, city, avg(salary)
FROM employees_big@to_emp_link JOIN departments USING(department_id)
JOIN locations USING (location_id)
GROUP BY department_name, city
ORDER BY 2,1;
```

```
DEPARTMENT_NAME              CITY                     AVG(SALARY)
---------------------------  -----------------------  -----------
Human Resources              London                          6500
Public Relations             Munich                         10000
Sales                        Oxford                     8955.88235
Accounting                   Seattle                        10150
Administration               Seattle                         4400
Executive                    Seattle                    19333.3333
Finance                      Seattle                         8600
Purchasing                   Seattle                         4150
Shipping                     South San Francisco        3475.55556
IT                           Southlake                       5760
Marketing                    Toronto                         9500

11 rows selected.
```

Elapsed: 00:00:42.87

Since no driving site hint is specified, the local site is the driving site. If we issue the same query specifying the remote and larger table to be the driving site, we see a benefit simply from the time the query takes to execute:

```
SELECT /*+ driving_site(employees_big) */ department_name, city, avg(salary)
FROM employees_big@to_emp_link JOIN departments USING(department_id)
JOIN locations USING (location_id)
GROUP BY department_name, city
ORDER BY 2,1;
```

Elapsed: 00:00:22.24

One more way you can try to determine which site should be the driving site is by figuring out exactly what work is being performed on each site. For example, using the foregoing query as an example, if we do not use the hint, perform the following:

1. Retrieve an explain plan for the query.

2. On the remote database, determine what part of the query is running remotely.

First, we can see the execution plan of our query. Again, we are not using the `driving_site` hint.

```
-------------------------------------------------
| Id  | Operation           | Name              |
-------------------------------------------------
|   0 | SELECT STATEMENT    |                   |
|   1 |  SORT GROUP BY      |                   |
|   2 |   HASH JOIN         |                   |
|   3 |    HASH JOIN        |                   |
|   4 |     TABLE ACCESS FULL| LOCATIONS        |
|   5 |     TABLE ACCESS FULL| DEPARTMENTS      |
|   6 |    REMOTE           | EMPLOYEES_BIG     |
-------------------------------------------------
```

Second, we can determine that the operation occurring on the remote database is the SELECT statement and columns for the remote EMPLOYEES_BIG table. You can retrieve this information directly from the data dictionary on the remote database, or a tool such as Enterprise Manager.

```
SELECT "SALARY","DEPARTMENT_ID"
FROM "EMPLOYEES_BIG" "EMPLOYEES_BIG"
```

If we repeat the foregoing two steps with the same query, only this time we insert a driving_site hint for the EMPLOYEES table, we get the following results. First, we can get the execution plan of our query with the driving_site hint:

```
-------------------------------------------------------------
| Id | Operation              | Name                        |
-------------------------------------------------------------
|  0 | SELECT STATEMENT REMOTE|                             |
|  1 |  RESULT CACHE          | 326m75n1yb5kt2qysx7f37cy2y  |
|  2 |   SORT GROUP BY        |                             |
|  3 |    HASH JOIN           |                             |
|  4 |     HASH JOIN          |                             |
|  5 |      REMOTE            | LOCATIONS                   |
|  6 |      REMOTE            | DEPARTMENTS                 |
|  7 |      TABLE ACCESS FULL | EMPLOYEES_BIG               |
-------------------------------------------------------------
```

Second, we can see which part of the query is being performed on the remote site. In this case, the data was retrieved from Enterprise Manager:

```
SELECT "A2"."DEPARTMENT_NAME","A1"."CITY",AVG("A3"."SALARY")
FROM "EMPLOYEES_BIG" "A3","DEPARTMENTS"@! "A2","LOCATIONS"@! "A1"
WHERE "A2"."LOCATION_ID"="A1"."LOCATION_ID" AND "A3"."DEPARTMENT_ID"="A2"."DEPARTMENT_ID"
GROUP BY "A2"."DEPARTMENT_NAME","A1"."CITY" ORDER BY "A1"."CITY","A2"."DEPARTMENT_NAME"
```

Without the driving site hint, we had to move all rows for the EMPLOYEES_BIG table for the SALARY and DEPARTMENT_ID columns. After transporting this data, the query results could be processed.

With the driving_site hint, we had to move all rows for all columns of the DEPARTMENTS and LOCATIONS table to the remote database. Then, the query results could be processed. And, because we used the driving_site hint, after the query results were compiled, the complete result set had to be transported to the local database. Therefore, you need to factor in not only the data moving between databases for the query itself, but also, if you are using the driving_site hint, the results themselves being transported back to the local database where the query originated.

14-11. Gathering Extended Query Execution Statistics

Problem

You want to gather extended explain plan statistics for a specific query, and do not want to adversely affect performance for an entire database instance while gathering this information.

Solution

You can use the GATHER_PLAN_STATISTICS hint, which, if placed within a query at runtime, will generate extended runtime statistics. It is a two-step process:

1. Execute the query with the gather_plan_statistics hint.

2. Use dbms_xplan.display_cursor to display the results.

See the following example:

```
SELECT /*+ gather_plan_statistics */
city, round(avg(salary)) avg, min(salary) min, max(salary) max
FROM employees JOIN departments USING (department_id)
JOIN locations USING (location_id)
GROUP BY city;
```

CITY	AVG	MIN	MAX
London	6500	6500	6500
Seattle	8844	2500	24000
Munich	10000	10000	10000
South San Francisco	3476	2100	8200
Toronto	9500	6000	13000
Southlake	5760	4200	9000
Oxford	8956	6100	14000

Then, you can use dbms_xplan to display the extended query statistics. Ensure that the SQL Plus setting SERVEROUTPUT is set to OFF, else results will not be properly displayed.

```
SELECT * FROM table(dbms_xplan.display_cursor(format=>'ALLSTATS LAST'));
```

Id	Operation	Name	Starts	E-Rows	A-Rows	Buffers
0	SELECT STATEMENT		2		14	23
1	HASH GROUP BY		0	23	0	23
* 2	HASH JOIN		0	106	0	23
* 3	HASH JOIN		0	27	0	16
4	VIEW	index$_join$_4	0	23	0	8
* 5	HASH JOIN		0		0	8
6	INDEX FAST FULL SCAN	LOC_CITY_IX	0	23	0	4
7	INDEX FAST FULL SCAN	LOC_ID_PK	0	23	0	4
8	VIEW	index$_join$_2	0	27	0	8
* 9	HASH JOIN		0		0	8
10	INDEX FAST FULL SCAN	DEPT_ID_PK	0	27	0	4
11	INDEX FAST FULL SCAN	DEPT_LOC_IX	0	27	0	4
12	TABLE ACCESS FULL	EMPLOYEES	0	107	0	7

There are many other options available using the DISPLAY_CURSOR procedure; refer to the Oracle PL/SQL Packages and Types Reference Guide for a more complete listing of these options.

How It Works

The GATHER_PLAN_STATISTICS hint gathers runtime statistics; therefore the query needs to be executed in order to gather these statistics. If you already have a query that is performing at a substandard optimization level, it may be useful to run your query with the GATHER_PLAN_STATISTICS hint. This can quickly give you information that you simply do not have with a normal explain plan, as it shows you estimated and actual information regarding query statistics. From this, you can determine if the optimizer is optimally executing the SQL, and you can determine if any optimization is needed.

Keep in mind that it does take some resources in order to gather these extra runtime statistics, so use this option with care. It may even be worthwhile to test the runtime differences in some cases. One key benefit of this hint is that the extra statistics are gathered only for the specific query. That way, the scope is limited and has no effect on other processes in the database, or even a particular session. If you wanted a more global setting to gather extended statistics, you can set STATISTICS_LEVEL=ALL at the session or instance level. One quick set of columns to review are the E-Rows and A-Rows columns. By looking at these columns, you can quickly tell if the optimizer is executing the query based on accurate statistics. If there is a large discrepancy between these columns, it is a sign of an inefficient execution plan. The one needed calculation for an accurate analysis is for the E-Rows column. You need to multiply the Starts column with E-Rows to accurately compare the total with A-Rows.

14-12. Enabling Query Rewrite

Problem

You have materialized views in your database environment, and want to have queries that access the source tables that make up the materialized views go against the materialized views directly to retrieve the results.

Solution

The REWRITE hint can be used to direct the optimizer to use a materialized view. The materialized view must have query rewrite enabled, and statistics for the materialized view and the associated objects should be current to increase the likelihood for a query to be rewritten. See the following example:

```
SELECT /*+ rewrite(dept_sal_mv) */ department_id,
sum(nvl(salary+(salary*commission_pct),salary)) total_compensation
FROM employees
GROUP BY department_id
having sum(nvl(salary+(salary*commission_pct),salary)) > 10000
ORDER by 2;
```

We can see here that the optimizer used the materialized view in the execution plan, rather than processing the entire query and recalculating the summary:

```
-----------------------------------------------------------
| Id | Operation                      | Name        |
-----------------------------------------------------------
|  0 | SELECT STATEMENT               |             |
|  1 |  SORT ORDER BY                 |             |
|  2 |   MAT_VIEW REWRITE ACCESS FULL| DEPT_SAL_MV |
-----------------------------------------------------------
```

How It Works

Materialized views are very commonly used to store the result set for often-executed queries. While regular views are simply stored queries in the data dictionary, materialized views are essentially tables that store the result for these queries. Usually, they are created when there are complex joins, summaries, or aggregations occurring within a query. The following example is a materialized view that is calculating the total compensation for each department for a company. Let's say this query is often used by executives of this company to determine how their particular department is doing in terms of distributing compensation to its employees:

```
CREATE MATERIALIZED VIEW DEPT_SAL_MV
ENABLE QUERY REWRITE
AS
SELECT department_id,
sum(nvl(salary+(salary*commission_pct),salary)) total_compensation
FROM employees
GROUP BY department_id;
```

Since the results are stored in the database, there is no need for the optimizer to reprocess the query to retrieve the data. The end-user community does not have to execute a complex join or aggregation over and over, so it is a considerable performance benefit. Some users may not be aware of the materialized views in your environment, and may be executing the raw queries against the star schema or other tables. It is here that the REWRITE hint may help in improving performance on queries that could use a materialized view.

If you enable query rewrite for a materialized view, and if a query executes where the results can be found in that materialized view, the optimizer may choose to "rewrite" the query to go directly against the materialized view, rather than process the query itself. Generally, no hint is required, because if query rewrite is enabled, the optimizer will attempt to rewrite the query. However, it's possible the optimizer may not choose to rewrite the query to use the materialized view, even though that is the desired outcome. In those instances, you can place a hint within your query to have the optimizer use the materialized view, regardless of the execution cost. You can place the actual view name within the hint, or place the hint without the view name:

```
SELECT /*+ rewrite */ department_id,
sum(nvl(salary+(salary*commission_pct),salary)) total_compensation
FROM employees
GROUP BY department_id
having sum(nvl(salary+(salary*commission_pct),salary)) > 10000
ORDER by 2;
```

Conversely, you can also use a NOREWRITE hint if, for some reason, you do not want the optimizer to use the materialized view. One possible reason is that the data in the materialized view is stale compared to the source table(s), and you want to ensure you are getting the most current data. Here we can see that the optimizer bypassed the use of the materialized view and resummarized the data directly from the EMPLOYEES table:

```
SELECT /*+ norewrite */ department_id,
sum(nvl(salary+(salary*commission_pct),salary)) total_compensation
FROM employees
GROUP BY department_id
having sum(nvl(salary+(salary*commission_pct),salary)) > 10000
ORDER by 2;
```

```
-------------------------------------------
| Id  | Operation            | Name        |
-------------------------------------------
|   0 | SELECT STATEMENT     |             |
|   1 |  SORT ORDER BY       |             |
|   2 |   FILTER             |             |
|   3 |    HASH GROUP BY     |             |
|   4 |     TABLE ACCESS FULL| EMPLOYEES   |
-------------------------------------------
```

14-13. Improving Star Schema Query Performance

Problem

You work in a data warehouse environment that contains star schemas, and you want to improve the performance of queries.

Solution

Oracle has a specific solution called "star transformation," which was designed to help improve performance against star schemas in the data warehouse environment. Oracle has the STAR_TRANSFORMATION and FACT hints to help improve query performance using star schemas. In your queries, you can use the STAR_TRANSFORMATION or the FACT hint, or you can use both. The following query is an example of how to use these hints:

```
SELECT /*+ star_transformation */ pr.prod_category, c.country_id,
t.calendar_year, sum(s.quantity_sold), SUM(s.amount_sold)
FROM sales s, times t, customers c, products pr
WHERE s.time_id = t.time_id
AND    s.cust_id = c.cust_id
AND    pr.prod_id = s.prod_id
AND    t.calendar_year = '2011'
GROUP BY pr.prod_category, c.country_id, t.calendar_year;
```

To use just the FACT hint, simply place the fact table name or alias within parentheses in the hint:

`SELECT /*+ fact(s) */ pr.prod_category, c.country_id,`

At times, the optimizer will be more likely to perform star transformation when both hints are present:

`SELECT /*+ star_transformation fact(s) */ pr.prod_category, c.country_id,`

Here is a typical explain plan that has undergone star transformation:

```
---------------------------------------------------------------------
| Id  | Operation                           | Name                   |
---------------------------------------------------------------------
|   0 | SELECT STATEMENT                    |                        |
|   1 |  HASH GROUP BY                      |                        |
|   2 |   HASH JOIN                         |                        |
|   3 |    HASH JOIN                        |                        |
|   4 |     HASH JOIN                       |                        |
|   5 |      PARTITION RANGE ALL            |                        |
|   6 |       TABLE ACCESS BY LOCAL INDEX ROWID| SALES               |
|   7 |        BITMAP CONVERSION TO ROWIDS  |                        |
|   8 |         BITMAP AND                  |                        |
|   9 |          BITMAP MERGE               |                        |
|  10 |           BITMAP KEY ITERATION      |                        |
|  11 |            BUFFER SORT              |                        |
|  12 |             TABLE ACCESS FULL       | CUSTOMERS              |
|  13 |            BITMAP INDEX RANGE SCAN   | SALES_CUST_BIX         |
|  14 |          BITMAP MERGE               |                        |
|  15 |           BITMAP KEY ITERATION      |                        |
|  16 |            BUFFER SORT              |                        |
|  17 |             VIEW                    | index$_join$_016       |
|  18 |              HASH JOIN              |                        |
|  19 |               INDEX FAST FULL SCAN  | PRODUCTS_PK            |
|  20 |               INDEX FAST FULL SCAN  | PRODUCTS_PROD_CAT_IX   |
|  21 |             BITMAP INDEX RANGE SCAN  | SALES_PROD_BIX         |
|  22 |     TABLE ACCESS FULL               | TIMES                  |
|  23 |     TABLE ACCESS FULL               | CUSTOMERS              |
|  24 |    VIEW                             | index$_join$_004       |
|  25 |     HASH JOIN                       |                        |
|  26 |      INDEX FAST FULL SCAN           | PRODUCTS_PK            |
|  27 |      INDEX FAST FULL SCAN           | PRODUCTS_PROD_CAT_IX   |
---------------------------------------------------------------------
```

Note

- **star transformation used for this statement**

How It Works

Before you start running star queries, there are two key configuration elements that need to be taken care of before star transformation can occur:

- Ensure the `star_transformation_enabled` parameter is set to TRUE.

- Ensure that on the fact table, there is a bitmap index on every dimension foreign key column.

If you are at a point to want to use a hint within a star schema, be it the FACT hint or the STAR_TRANSFORMATION hint, it is assumed you have a properly configured environment, else these hints will not be used by the optimizer. These hints are not required for star transformation, but by using either or these hints, the optimizer will look to do transformation. Even with the hint, however, the optimizer may choose to ignore the request, based on what it thinks the best execution plan will be for the query. Star queries are very efficient and perform very well, because the transformation is designed to operate specifically with star schemas.

If, for some reason, you want to avoid the use of star transformation for your query, simply use the `no_star_transformation` hint, and the optimizer will bypass the use of star transformation:

```
SELECT /*+ no_star_transformation */ pr.prod_category, c.country_id,
t.calendar_year, sum(s.quantity_sold), SUM(s.amount_sold)
FROM sales s, times t, customers c, products pr
WHERE s.time_id = t.time_id
AND    s.cust_id = c.cust_id
AND    pr.prod_id = s.prod_id
AND    t.calendar_year = '2011'
GROUP BY pr.prod_category, c.country_id, t.calendar_year;
```

From the explain plan, we can see that the optimizer did not transform our query:

```
-----------------------------------------------------------
| Id  | Operation                      | Name         |
-----------------------------------------------------------
|   0 | SELECT STATEMENT               |              |
|   1 |  HASH GROUP BY                 |              |
|   2 |   NESTED LOOPS                 |              |
|   3 |    NESTED LOOPS                |              |
|   4 |     NESTED LOOPS               |              |
|   5 |      NESTED LOOPS              |              |
|   6 |       PARTITION RANGE ALL      |              |
|   7 |        TABLE ACCESS FULL       | SALES        |
|   8 |        TABLE ACCESS BY INDEX ROWID| PRODUCTS  |
|   9 |         INDEX UNIQUE SCAN      | PRODUCTS_PK  |
|  10 |       TABLE ACCESS BY INDEX ROWID | CUSTOMERS |
|  11 |        INDEX UNIQUE SCAN       | CUSTOMERS_PK |
|  12 |      INDEX UNIQUE SCAN         | TIMES_PK     |
|  13 |     TABLE ACCESS BY INDEX ROWID | TIMES       |
-----------------------------------------------------------
```

At times, it can be tricky to get the star transformation to take place. It is critically important that you have properly configured the star schema with all the appropriate bitmap indexes. Even having one missing bitmap index can affect the ability to have star transformation occur for your queries, so it is important to be very thorough and validate the configuration, especially regarding the bitmap indexes. Some star schemas also employ the use of bitmap join indexes between the fact and dimension tables to aid in achieving star transformation.

Executing SQL in Parallel

Parallelism can help improve performance on particular operations simply by assigning multiple resources to a task. Parallelism is best used on systems with multiple CPUs, as the multiple processes used (that is, the parallel processes) will use those extra CPU resources to more quickly complete a given task.

As a general rule, parallelism is also best used on large tables or indexes, and on databases with large volumes of data. It is ideal for use in data warehouse environments, which are large by their nature. Parallelism is not well suited for OLTP environments, just because of the transactional nature of those systems.

In order to use parallelism properly, there are several important factors to understand:

- The number of CPUs on your system

- Proper configuration of the related initialization parameters

- The key SQL statements that you want to tune for parallelization

- The degree of parallelism (DOP) configured on your database

- The actual performance vs. expected performance of targeted SQL operations

One of the most common pitfalls of parallelism is overuse. It is sometimes seen as a magic bullet to tune and speed up SQL operations. In turn, parallelism can actually lead to poorer rather than better performance. Therefore, it is critically important for the DBA to understand the physical configuration of his or her system, and configure parallelism-related parameters to best suit the system. Educating developers and users of your database about basic questions will increase the success rate of parallel operations. When is it appropriate to use parallelism? How do you properly enable parallelism in SQL operations? What type of operations can be parallelized? Parallelism is a powerful tool to aid in drastically improving performance of database operations, but with that power comes responsibility.

This chapter focuses on the methods to properly configure your database for parallelism, key operations that can be parallelized, how to induce parallelism in your SQL, and some tools to use to see if parallel operations are running optimally.

15-1. Enabling Parallelism for a Specific Query

Problem

You have a slow-running query accessing data from a large table. You want to see if you can speed up the query by instructing Oracle to use multiple processes to retrieve the data.

Solution

There are two distinct types of hints to place in your SQL to try to speed up your query by using multiple processes, or parallelism. One type of hint is for data retrieval itself, and the other is to help speed the process of reading the indexes on a table.

Parallel Hints for Tables

First, you need to determine the degree of parallelism (DOP) desired for the query. This instructs Oracle how many processes it will use to retrieve the data. Second, place a parallel hint inside of the query specifying the table(s) on which to execute parallel SQL, as well the degree of parallelism to use for the query—for example:

```
SELECT /*+ parallel(emp,4) */  empno, ename
FROM emp;
```

If you use a table alias in your query, you must use it in your hint, else the Oracle optimizer will ignore the hint.

```
SELECT/*+ parallel(e,4) */  empno, ename
FROM emp e;
```

The hints in the preceding two queries result in four processes dividing the work of reading rows from the EMP table. Four processes working together will get the job done faster in terms of wall-clock time than one process doing all the work by itself.

Optionally, you can omit specifying a degree of parallelism within the hint. If you specify only the table name or alias in the hint, Oracle will derive the degree of parallelism based on the database initialization parameters, which may or may not give you the desired degree of parallelism:

```
SELECT/*+ parallel(e) */  empno, ename
FROM emp e;
```

Parallel Hints for Indexes

Specify the `parallel_index` hint to control parallel access to indexes. You can generally access an index in parallel only when the index is a locally partitioned index. In that case, you can apply the `parallel_index` hint. Here's an example:

```
SELECT /*+ parallel_index(emp, emp_i4 ,4) */ empno, ename
FROM emp
WHERE deptno = 10;
```

There are two arguments to the `parallel_index` hint: table name and index name. As with specifying the degree of parallelism on tables, if you omit the degree of parallelism from within an index hint, the database itself will compute the degree of parallelism for the query.

If you alias your tables, then you must use the alias names in your hints. See the preceding section on "Parallel Hints for Tables" for an example.

How It Works

In order to effectively use parallel hints, you need to take the following items into consideration:

- The number of tables in your query

- The size of table(s) in your query

- The number of CPUs on your system

- The filtering columns in your `WHERE` clause

- What columns are indexed, if any

You also must analyze and understand three key components of your system prior to using parallel hints in queries:

- System configuration, such as amount of memory and CPUs, and even disk configuration

- Database configuration parameters related to parallelism

- The DOP specified on the objects themselves (tables and indexes)

Parallel SQL must be used with caution, as it is common to overuse, and can cause an over-utilization of system resources, which ultimately results in *slower* rather than faster performance. Overuse is a very common mistake in the use of parallelism.

Depending on the number of tables in your query, you may want to place parallelism on one or more of the tables—depending on their size. A general rule of thumb is that if a table contains more than 10 million rows, or is at least 2 gigabytes in size, it may be a viable candidate for using parallelism.

The degree of parallelism (DOP) should be directly related to the number of CPUs on your system. If you have a single-CPU system, there is little, if any, benefit of using parallel SQL, and the result could very well be returned slower than if no parallelism was used at all.

To help determine if you can use parallelism on any indexes, you need to first determine if any of the filtering columns in your `WHERE` clause are indexed. If so, check to see if the table is partitioned. Typically, then, for a query on a large table, a `parallel_index` hint may help the speed of your query. Overall, when trying to determine whether to use parallelism for your query, it's helpful to perform an explain plan to determine if parallelism will be used. Also, there may be parallelism already specified for an object within your query, so it is also a good idea to check the `DEGREE` column in the `USER_TABLES` or `USER_INDEXES` view prior to checking the degree of parallelism within a hint.

Table 15-1 shows the different parallel hints that can be used.

Table 15-1. *Types of Parallel Hints*

Table Head	Parameters
PARALLEL	Table name, DOP
PARALLEL_INDEX	Table name, index name, DOP
NO_PARALLEL	--
NO_PARALLEL_INDEX	--
PQ_DISTRIBUTE	Table name, distribution value

There are many options Oracle gives you to help you determine a proper DOP, and whether you want to specify it yourself, or you want Oracle to determine the DOP for your query. Table 15-2 briefly describes these options.

Table 15-2. *Degree of Parallelism Options*

Hint Name	Description
PARALLEL	Statement always runs in parallel.
PARALLEL (DEFAULT)	Same as PARALLEL
PARALLEL (AUTO)	Optimizer computes DOP to be used.
PARALLEL (MANUAL)	Parallelism is based on object parallelism.
PARALLEL (integer)	The DOP used is specified by the integer.

Parallel Hints for Tables

In order to determine if parallelism is being used in your query, first perform an explain plan on your query. The following are a simple query and its associated execution plan:

```
select * from emp;
```

```
----------------------------------------------------------------
| Id  | Operation         | Name | Rows | Bytes | Cost (%CPU)| Time     |
----------------------------------------------------------------
|   0 | SELECT STATEMENT  |      |   14 |  1218 |    3   (0)| 00:00:01 |
|   1 |  TABLE ACCESS FULL| EMP  |   14 |  1218 |    3   (0)| 00:00:01 |
----------------------------------------------------------------
```

If parallelism isn't being used, you can insert the parallel hint, and then rerun the explain plan to verify that the optimizer will use parallelism in the execution plan—for example:

```
select /*+ parallel(emp,4) */ * from emp;
```

```
-------------------------------------------------------------------------
| Id  | Operation               | Name    |  TQ   |IN-OUT| PQ Distrib |
-------------------------------------------------------------------------
|   0 | SELECT STATEMENT        |         |       |      |            |
|   1 |  PX COORDINATOR         |         |       |      |            |
|   2 |   PX SEND QC (RANDOM)   | :TQ10000| Q1,00 | P->S | QC (RAND)  |
|   3 |    PX BLOCK ITERATOR    |         | Q1,00 | PCWC |            |
|   4 |     TABLE ACCESS FULL   | EMP     | Q1,00 | PCWP |            |
-------------------------------------------------------------------------
```

■ **Note** The proper database initialization parameters need to be properly set in order for parallelism to be enabled via the use of hints.

Parallel Hints for Indexes

Although it is far less common to parallelize index-based queries, it may be of benefit in certain circumstances. For example, you may want to parallelize the query against a local index that is part of a partitioned table. The following is an example query and the resulting execution plan:

```
SELECT /*+ parallel_index(emp, emp_i3) */ empno, ename
FROM emp
WHERE hiredate between '2010-01-01' and '2010-12-31';
```

```
----------------------------------------------------------------------------------------
| Id  | Operation                          | Name    |  TQ   |IN-OUT| PQ Dist|
----------------------------------------------------------------------------------------
|   0 | SELECT STATEMENT                   |         |       |      |         |
|   1 |  PX COORDINATOR                    |         |       |      |         |
|   2 |   PX SEND QC (RANDOM)              | :TQ10000| Q1,00 | P->S |         |
|   3 |    PX PARTITION RANGE ITERATOR     |         | Q1,00 | PCWC |         |
|   4 |     TABLE ACCESS BY LOCAL INDEX ROWID| EMP   | Q1,00 | PCWP |         |
|   5 |      INDEX RANGE SCAN              | EMP_I3  | Q1,00 | PCWP |         |
----------------------------------------------------------------------------------------
```

When formatting the hint, you can specify all the parameters that tell the optimizer exactly which index to use, and what DOP you desire. In the following query, we're telling the optimizer that we want to use the EMP_I3 index, with a DOP of 4.

```
SELECT /*+ parallel_index(emp, emp_i3, 4) */ empno, ename
FROM emp
WHERE hiredate between '2010-01-01' and '2010-12-31';
```

If you omit the DOP from the hint, the optimizer determines the DOP based on the initialization parameter settings. For instance, in the following example, the table name and index name are specified in the hint, but the DOP is not specified. Oracle will compute the DOP for us in these cases.

```
SELECT /*+ parallel_index(emp, emp_i3) */ empno, ename
FROM emp
WHERE hiredate between '2010-01-01' and '2010-12-31';
```

You can also simply place the table name in the hint, and the optimizer will also determine which index, if any, can be used. If the optimizer determines that no index is suitable, then no index will be used. In the following example, only the table name is used in the hint:

```
SELECT /*+ parallel_index(emp) */ empno, ename
FROM emp
WHERE hiredate between '2010-01-01' and '2010-12-31';
```

■ **Note** As of Oracle 11g Release 2, the NOPARALLEL and NOPARALLEL_INDEX hints have been deprecated. Instead, use NO_PARALLEL and NO_PARALLEL_INDEX.

15-2. Enabling Parallelism at Object Creation

Problem

You have new tables to create in your database that will be growing to a very large size, and you want speed the queries against those tables.

Solution

Having a higher than default DOP on a table or index is an easy way to set a more consistent and fixed method of enabling multiple processes on tables and indexes. Enabling parallelism on tables or indexes is done within DDL commands. You can enable parallelism within the CREATE statement when creating a table or an index.

For a new table, if you are expecting to have consistent queries that can take advantage of multiple processes, it may be easier to set a fixed DOP on your object, rather than having to place hints in your SQL, or let Oracle set the DOP for you. In the following example, we've specified a DOP of 4 on the EMP table:

```
CREATE TABLE EMP
(
 EMPNO NUMBER(4) CONSTRAINT PK_EMP PRIMARY KEY,
 ENAME VARCHAR2(10),
 JOB VARCHAR2(9),
 MGR NUMBER(4),
```

```
HIREDATE DATE,
SAL NUMBER(7,2),
COMM NUMBER(7,2),
DEPTNO NUMBER(2) CONSTRAINT FK_DEPTNO REFERENCES DEPT
)
PARALLEL(DEGREE 4);
```

By placing a static DOP of 4 on the table, any user accessing the EMP table will get a DOP of 4 for each query executed.

```
select * from emp;
```

```
--------------------------------------------------------------------
| Id  | Operation            | Name    |   TQ  |IN-OUT| PQ Distrib |
--------------------------------------------------------------------
|   0 | SELECT STATEMENT     |         |       |      |            |
|   1 |  PX COORDINATOR      |         |       |      |            |
|   2 |   PX SEND QC (RANDOM)| :TQ10000|  Q1,00| P->S | QC (RAND)  |
|   3 |    PX BLOCK ITERATOR |         |  Q1,00| PCWC |            |
|   4 |     TABLE ACCESS FULL| EMP     |  Q1,00| PCWP |            |
--------------------------------------------------------------------
```

You can also specify a default DOP when creating an index. There are circumstances where it may be beneficial to create an index with a higher DOP. With large partitioned tables, it is common to have secondary locally partitioned indexes on often-used columns in the WHERE clause. Some queries that use these indexes may benefit from increasing the DOP. In the following DDL, we've created this index with a DOP of 4:

```
CREATE INDEX EMP_I1
ON EMP (HIREDATE)
LOCAL
PARALLEL(DEGREE 4);
```

How It Works

Placing parallelism on objects themselves helps multiple processes complete the task at hand sooner—whether it be to speed up queries, or to help speed up the creation of an index. In order to be able to assess the proper DOP to place on an object, you should know the access patterns of the data. If less information is known about the objects, the more conservative the DOP should be. Placing a high DOP on a series of objects can hurt performance just as easily as it can help, so enabling DOP on objects needs to be done with careful planning and consideration.

■ **Tip**   If automatic DOP is enabled and configured properly (PARALLEL_DEGREE_POLICY=AUTO), then the parallelism that you set on objects is ignored, and the optimizer chooses the degree of parallelism to be used. See Recipe 15-10 for details on enabling automatic DOP.

15-3. Enabling Parallelism for an Existing Object

Problem

You have a series of slow-running queries accessing a set of existing database tables, and you want to take steps to reduce the execution time of the queries.

Solution

Setting a higher DOP on an existing table or index is an easy way to have a more consistent and fixed method of enabling multiple processes on tables and indexes. Setting the DOP for tables or indexes is done within DDL commands. You can change the DOP on a table or index by using the ALTER statement. For instance, if you have an existing table that needs to have the DOP changed to accommodate user queries that want to take advantage of multiple processes, they can be added easily to the table, which takes effect immediately. The following example alters the default DOP for a table:

```
ALTER TABLE EMP
PARALLEL(DEGREE 4);
```

If, after a time, you wish to reset the DOP on your table, you can also do that with the ALTER statement. See the following two examples on how to reset the DOP for a table:

```
ALTER TABLE EMP
PARALLEL(DEGREE 1);
```

```
ALTER TABLE EMP
NOPARALLEL;
```

If you have an already existing index that you think will benefit from a higher DOP, it can also easily be changed. As with tables, the change takes effect immediately. The following example shows how to change the default DOP for an index:

```
ALTER INDEX EMP_I1
PARALLEL(DEGREE 4);
```

As with tables, you can reset the DOP on an index either of the following two ways:

```
ALTER INDEX EMP_I4
PARALLEL(DEGREE 1);
```

```
ALTER INDEX EMP_I4
NOPARALLEL;
```

How It Works

Increasing the DOP on an existing object is a sign that you already have a performance issue for queries accessing tables within your database. Monitoring parallelism performance is a key factor in knowing if the DOP set for an object or set of objects is appropriate. Examine data in the V$PQ_TQSTAT to assist in determining the DOP that has been used, or V$SYSSTAT to assist in the extent that parallelism is being used on your database. Refer to Recipe 15-12 for some examples of using these data dictionary views.

15-4. Implementing Parallel DML

Problem

You want to induce parallelism when performing DML operations (INSERT, UPDATE, MERGE, DELETE) in order to speed performance and reduce transaction time.

Solution

If operating within a data warehouse environment or an environment with large tables that require a high volume of bulk transactions, parallel DML can help speed up processing and reduce the time it takes to perform these operations. Parallel DML is disabled by default on a database, and must be explicitly enabled with the following statement:

```
ALTER SESSION ENABLE PARALLEL DML;
```

By specifying the foregoing statement, it truly *enables* parallel DML to be possible in a session, but does not guarantee it. Parallel DML operations will occur only under certain conditions:

- Hints are specified in a DML statement.

- Tables with a parallel attribute are part of a DML statement.

- The DML operations meet the appropriate rules for a statement to run in parallel. Key restrictions for using parallel DML are noted later in the recipe.

You may desire, in certain circumstances, to force parallel behavior, regardless of the parallel degree you have placed on an object, or regardless of any hints you've placed in your DML. So, alternatively, you can force parallel DML with the following statement:

```
ALTER SESSION FORCE PARALLEL DML;
```

As a general rule, it is not good practice to force parallel DML in your regularly run DML, as it can quickly consume system resources to a point where performance begins to suffer. It is best used sparingly, and can help with occasional large DML operations.

How It Works

Parallel DML can work for any DML operation—INSERT, UPDATE, MERGE, and DELETE. The rules vary slightly depending on which DML operation you are running. If you want to run an INSERT statement in parallel, for instance, first enable parallelism for your session, and then execute your INSERT statement with the appropriate mechanism in order for the DML to run in parallel:

```
ALTER SESSION ENABLE PARALLEL DML;

INSERT /*+ PARALLEL(DEPT,4) */ INTO DEPT
SELECT /*+ PARALLEL(DEPT_COPY,4) */ * FROM DEPT_COPY;
```

With the foregoing statement, we put a parallel hint into the INSERT statement, and also put a parallel HINT into the SELECT portion of the statement. A very important thing to remember is that even if parallelism is in effect for your DML statement, it does not directly impact any parallelism on a related query within the same statement. For instance, the following statement's DML operation can run in parallel, but the corresponding SELECT statement will run in serial mode, as no parallelism is specified on the query itself.

```
ALTER SESSION ENABLE PARALLEL DML;

INSERT /*+ PARALLEL(DEPT,4) */ INTO DEPT
SELECT * FROM DEPT_COPY;
```

In order to take full advantage of parallel capabilities, try to parallelize all portions of a statement. If you parallelize the INSERT but not the SELECT, the SELECT portion becomes a bottleneck for the INSERT, and the INSERT performance suffers.

Parallel DML operations can also occur on UPDATE, MERGE, and DELETE statements. Let's say your company was generous and decided to give everyone in the accounting department a 1% raise:

```
UPDATE /*+ PARALLEL(EMP,4) */ EMP
SET SAL = SAL*1.01
WHERE DEPTNO=10;
```

Then, after a period of months, your company decides to lay off those employees they gave raises to in accounting:

```
DELETE /*+ PARALLEL(EMP,4) */ FROM EMP
WHERE DEPTNO=10;
```

Another way to parallelize a DML transaction within your database is to use the DBMS_PARALLEL_EXECUTE PL/SQL package. Although more complex to configure, there are some key advantages of using this package to run your parallelized transactions:

- The overall transaction is split into pieces, each of which has its own commit point.

- Transactions are restartable.

- Locks are done only on affected rows.

- Undo utilization is reduced.

- You have more control over how the work is divided. You can divide the work in several ways:

  - By column

  - By ROWID

  - By SQL statement

The obvious benefits of using the DBMS_PARALLEL_EXECUTE package are greater control over how large transactions are run, increased functionality, and more efficient use of database resources. The key trade-off with using this package is it is simply more complex to configure, set up, and run—but may be well worth it when processing large volumes of data.

■ **Tip**   You must execute the `ALTER SESSION ENABLE | FORCE PARALLEL DML` statement in order for parallel DML to occur for your transaction.

Restrictions on Parallel DML

There are plenty of restrictions in using parallel DML, and you need to understand that even if dealing with a large volume of data, parallel DML may not be possible in certain circumstances:

- Individual inserts of rows (using `VALUES` clause) cannot be run in parallel.

- You can modify a table only one time within a transaction.

- Cannot be run for tables with triggers

- Tables with certain constraints may not be eligible.

- There is limited parallel DML functionality on tables with objects or LOB columns.

- There is limited parallel DML functionality on temporary tables.

- Distributed transactions cannot be parallelized.

Degree of Parallelism

Once you submit a parallelized DML operation for execution, Oracle determines, based on a set of precedence rules, what DOP will be used for the entire statement being submitted. It is important to understand these rules so you get the desired DOP you are expecting for your transaction.

For DML transactions, Oracle applies the following base rules of precedence to determine DOP:

1. Checks to see if an hint is specified on `INSERT`, `UPDATE`, `MERGE`, or `DELETE` statements

2. Checks to see if there are any session-level instructions

3. Checks the object-level parallelism on the target object

4. Chooses maximum DOP specified between the queried table or any associated indexes for the query portion of the statement (insert only)

After choosing the appropriate DOP for the insert and query portions of the statement, the query is executed. Note that the DOP chosen for each portion of the statement can be different.

Other Considerations

Using parallel DML can be complex, as there are many permutations of possibilities of the type of objects involved: whether they are partitioned, the DOP specified on the objects, the hints specified in statements, and the parallel parameter settings, just to name a few.

Here are some other factors that need to be considered when using parallel DML:

- For parallelized insert transactions, direct-path loads are performed.

- When deciding whether to use parallel DML, you must weigh the performance gain you will achieve with the space usage for that operation. Parallelized INSERT statements are fast, but cost you more space. If you have specified a DOP of 4 for an insert transaction, 4 extents will be allocated for that operation. You must determine based on your requirements what is more important.

- If objects are partitioned, it can affect how a parallel DML transaction runs.

15-5. Creating Tables in Parallel

Problem

You need to quickly create a table from an existing large table, and want to employ the use of multiple processes to help speed up the creation of the table.

Solution

If you are administering very large databases (VLDBs) or have to rebuild a large table, parallel DDL is fast and has advantages over running parallel DML. Speed is the biggest factor in choosing to use parallel DDL to create a table from an existing large table. Within your specific DDL command, there is a PARALLEL clause that determines if operations are to be performed in parallel. This is done by using the CREATE TABLE ... AS SELECT operation:

```
CREATE TABLE EMP_COPY
PARALLEL(DEGREE 4)
AS
SELECT * FROM EMP;
```

```
-------------------------------------------------------------------
| Id  | Operation              | Name     |  TQ  |IN-OUT| PQ Distrib |
-------------------------------------------------------------------
|   0 | CREATE TABLE STATEMENT |          |      |      |            |
|   1 |  PX COORDINATOR        |          |      |      |            |
|   2 |   PX SEND QC (RANDOM)   | :TQ10000 | Q1,00| P->S | QC (RAND)  |
|   3 |    LOAD AS SELECT       | EMP_COPY | Q1,00| PCWP |            |
|   4 |     PX BLOCK ITERATOR   |          | Q1,00| PCWC |            |
|   5 |      TABLE ACCESS FULL  | EMP      | Q1,00| PCWP |            |
-------------------------------------------------------------------
```

How It Works

The reason parallel DDL is popular is that it is a fast way to perform operations on a large amount of data. The work is divided up in several pieces and done concurrently. Let's say you just bought a new house, and are in the process of moving. If you are loading a large moving truck with boxes, it will simply be faster with four people loading rather than one. Moreover, parallel DDL is an attractive way to perform DML-type operations under the covers of DDL commands.

The most common reasons to use the CREATE TABLE ... AS SELECT include the following:

- The table structure has changed and you need to rebuild the table.

- You are creating a like structure for some specific application purpose.

- You are deleting a large number of rows from the table.

- You need to drop multiple columns from a large table.

Some of the foregoing operations could also be strictly handled with parallel DML, but using parallel DDL has a distinct advantage over parallel DML. Since DDL operations cannot be rolled back, undo is not generated for these operations, and it is simply a more efficient operation.

The DOP for a parallel DDL operation is determined by the object DOP. This also includes the query portion of the statement. If you choose to, you can override the DOP of the objects by issuing the following command:

```
ALTER SESSION FORCE PARALLEL DDL;
```

If you have a very large table from which you need to delete many rows, consider using CREATE TABLE ... AS SELECT rather than using a DML DELETE statement. Deleting rows is an expensive operation. In large data warehouse environments, in scenarios where a large volume of rows needs to be deleted, the cost and time of doing the delete can quickly become unmanageable. Because of the nature of delete, it is very resource-intensive for the database as far as the amount of redo and undo generation it takes to perform the operation. One good rule of thumb to use is that if you are deleting as little as 5–10% of the rows of a large table, it can be simply faster to create a new table with all the rows you want to keep.

Here is an example where we are deleting about 20% of the rows from our EMP table of 1,234,568 rows:

```
delete /*+ parallel(emp,4) */ from emp
 where empno > 1000000
SQL> /

234568 rows deleted.

Elapsed: 00:00:09.94
```

```
-------------------------------------------------------------------------
| Id  | Operation               | Name    |   TQ  |IN-OUT| PQ Distrib |
-------------------------------------------------------------------------
|   0 | DELETE STATEMENT        |         |       |      |            |
|   1 |  PX COORDINATOR         |         |       |      |            |
|   2 |   PX SEND QC (RANDOM)    | :TQ10001| Q1,01 | P->S | QC (RAND) |
|   3 |    INDEX MAINTENANCE     | EMP     | Q1,01 | PCWP |            |
|   4 |     PX RECEIVE           |         | Q1,01 | PCWP |            |
|   5 |      PX SEND RANGE       | :TQ10000| Q1,00 | P->P | RANGE     |
|   6 |       DELETE             | EMP     | Q1,00 | PCWP |            |
|   7 |        PX BLOCK ITERATOR |         | Q1,00 | PCWC |            |
|   8 |         TABLE ACCESS FULL| EMP     | Q1,00 | PCWP |            |
-------------------------------------------------------------------------
```

This delete took 9.94 seconds to run. If we now run a `CREATE TABLE ... AS SELECT` statement to achieve the same result, we can see the difference in performance.

```
create table emp_ctas_new2
parallel(degree 4)
nologging
as select /*+ parallel(a,4) */ * from emp_ctas
where empno <= 1000000
SQL> /
Elapsed: 00:00:01.70
```

Id	Operation	Name	TQ	IN-OUT	PQ Distrib
0	CREATE TABLE STATEMENT				
1	PX COORDINATOR				
2	PX SEND QC (RANDOM)	:TQ10001	Q1,01	P->S	QC (RAND)
3	LOAD AS SELECT	EMP_CTAS_NEW	Q1,01	PCWP	
4	PX RECEIVE		Q1,01	PCWP	
5	PX SEND ROUND-ROBIN	:TQ10000		S->P	RND-ROBIN
6	TABLE ACCESS BY INDEX ROWID	EMP_CTAS			
7	INDEX RANGE SCAN	EMP_CTAS_PK			

Creating the table took 1.7 seconds, over 5 times faster than performing the same operation with a `DELETE` statement. If you have indexes on the table, however, you need to consider that as a factor before choosing this method, because if you re-create a table, you must also re-create the associated indexes for that table. It's still likely to be faster, however, as you can re-create any indexes in parallel as well.

Keep in mind that, even though the foregoing example uses parallel DDL on these statements, this concept holds true even if you are running in serial mode. When you need to delete a large number of rows from a table, the `CREATE TABLE ... AS SELECT` can be compared favorably to `DELETE` with parallel-executed DDL or non-parallel, serial-executed DDL.

One potential drawback of creating tables in parallel is that the space allocations for these operations may leave the table more fragmented than if you created the table serially. This is a trade-off that should be considered when creating tables in parallel. The DOP that is specified in the operation spawns that number of parallel threads, and one extent is allocated for each thread. So, if you have specified a DOP of 4 for your parallel operation, there will be a minimum of 4 extents allocated for the operation. Depending on the `MINIMUM EXTENT` size for the tablespace, Oracle does attempt to trim unused space at the end of the operation. You should expect, though, that parallel create table operations are simply less space-efficient than operations run serially.

15-6. Creating Indexes in Parallel

Problem

You need to create indexes for a large table as quickly as possible and want to employ the use of multiple processes to help speed up the index creation.

Solution

Any time you have a large table, it is a good idea to always create any associated index for that table using parallel DDL, even if you want the DOP on the index to be non-parallelized for queries. The major benefit of creating an index in parallel is that it simply takes much less time to create the index. It always makes sense to create an index for a large table in parallel, and then optionally choose to reset the DOP used for queries after the create operation is complete. In the following example, we are creating the index with a DOP of 4, which will be used during the process of creating the index:

```
CREATE INDEX EMP_COPY_I1
ON EMP_COPY (HIREDATE)
PARALLEL(DEGREE 4);
```

Then, after the index has been created, we can choose to reset the DOP to a different value for use by queries, using either of the following examples:

```
ALTER INDEX EMP_COPY_I1 NOPARALLEL;
ALTER INDEX EMP_COPY_I1 PARALLEL(DEGREE 1);
```

How It Works

The primary reason you want to run parallel DDL on an index is to either create or rebuild a large, existing index. Some of the reasons you may have to do this include the following:

- Adding an index to an already existing large table

- Rebuilding an index that has become fragmented over time

- Rebuilding an index after a large, direct-path load of data

- You want to move an index to a different tablespace

- The index is in an unusable state due to a partition-level operation on the associated table

As with tables, if you wish to bypass the parallelism specified on the index, you can "force" the issue by running the following command:

```
ALTER SESSION FORCE PARALLEL DDL;
```

15-7. Rebuilding Indexes in Parallel

Problem

You have an existing index that needs to be rebuilt quickly, and you want to use multiple processes to speed up the index rebuild process.

Solution

Situations may arise where you may need to rebuild an index, for many of the same reasons to re-create an index. To rebuild an index in parallel, use the ALTER INDEX command:

```
ALTER INDEX EMP_COPY_I1
REBUILD
PARALLEL(DEGREE 4);
```

```
-------------------------------------------------------------------------------
| Id | Operation                   | Name        |    TQ  |IN-OUT| PQ Distrib |
-------------------------------------------------------------------------------
|  0 | ALTER INDEX STATEMENT       |             |        |      |            |
|  1 |  PX COORDINATOR             |             |        |      |            |
|  2 |   PX SEND QC (ORDER)        | :TQ10001    | Q1,01  | P->S | QC (ORDER) |
|  3 |    INDEX BUILD NON UNIQUE   | EMP_COPY_I1 | Q1,01  | PCWP |            |
|  4 |     SORT CREATE INDEX       |             | Q1,01  | PCWP |            |
|  5 |      PX RECEIVE             |             | Q1,01  | PCWP |            |
|  6 |       PX SEND RANGE         | :TQ10000    | Q1,00  | P->P | RANGE      |
|  7 |        PX BLOCK ITERATOR    |             | Q1,00  | PCWC |            |
|  8 |         INDEX FAST FULL SCAN| EMP_COPY_I1 | Q1,00  | PCWP |            |
-------------------------------------------------------------------------------
```

If you need to rebuild a partition of a large local index, you can also use parallelism to perform this operation. See the following example:

```
ALTER INDEX emppart_i1
REBUILD PARTITION emppart2001_p
PARALLEL(DEGREE 4);
```

```
----------------------------------------------------------------------------------------
| Id | Operation                   | Name        | Pstart| Pstop |IN-OUT| PQ Distrib |
----------------------------------------------------------------------------------------
|  0 | ALTER INDEX STATEMENT       |             |       |       |      |            |
|  1 |  PX COORDINATOR             |             |       |       |      |            |
|  2 |   PX SEND QC (ORDER)        | :TQ10001    |       |       | P->S | QC ORDER)  |
|  3 |    INDEX BUILD NON UNIQUE   | EMPPART_I1  |       |       | PCWP |            |
|  4 |     SORT CREATE INDEX       |             |       |       | PCWP |            |
|  5 |      PX RECEIVE             |             |       |       | PCWP |            |
|  6 |       PX SEND RANGE         | :TQ10000    |       |       | P->P | RANGE      |
|  7 |        PX BLOCK ITERATOR    |             |   2   |   2   | PCWC |            |
|  8 |         INDEX FAST FULL SCAN| EMPPART_I1  |   2   |   2   | PCWP |            |
----------------------------------------------------------------------------------------
```

How It Works

Rebuilding an index has a key advantage over re-creating an index from scratch, as well as a key disadvantage. The advantage of rebuilding an index is that the existing index is in place until the rebuild operation is complete, so it can therefore be used by queries that are run concurrently with the rebuild process. The main disadvantage of the index rebuild process is that you will need space for both indexes, which is required during the rebuild process. Some of the key reasons to rebuild an index include the following:

- Rebuilding an index that has become fragmented over time

- Rebuilding an index after a large, direct-path load of data

- You want to move an index to a different tablespace

- The index is in an unusable state due to a partition-level operation on the associated table.

15-8. Moving Partitions in Parallel

Problem

You need to move a table partition to a different tablespace, and wish to employ the use of multiple processes to accomplish this task.

Solution

Let's say you want to move a table partition to another tablespace. For instance, you've created a tablespace on slower, cheaper storage, and you want to move older data there in order to reduce the overall cost of storage on your database. To alter a table to rebuild a partition in parallel, you would issue a command such as the one here:

```
ALTER TABLE EMP
MOVE PARTITION P2
TABLESPACE EMP_S
PARALLEL(DEGREE 4);
```

How It Works

The `ALTER TABLE` statement to move a partition is an easy, efficient way to move data around for a partitioned table. As with some of the other parallel DDL operations shown within this chapter, there are several reasons to need to move a table partition to a different tablespace:

- You are moving older data to cheaper, slower storage.

- You are consolidating a series of partitions to a single tablespace.

- You are moving certain partitions to separate tablespaces to logically group types of data.

Table partitioning is often done to store historical data. Over time, partition maintenance often needs to occur for partitioned tables. By enabling the use of parallelism when moving partitions for a table within your database, it can simply be done faster. With maintenance windows shrinking and data access needs growing, this helps perform necessary partition movements faster, while reducing downtime for your database tables.

15-9. Splitting Partitions in Parallel

Problem

You have a partition with a large amount of data, and want to split that larger partition into two or more smaller partitions.

Solution

As a DBA, at times the need arises to split partitions, and this operation can also be done in parallel. For instance, let's say you have a partitioned table that has a default high-end partition with a large amount of data, and you want to split that data into multiple partitions. In cases such as these, you can split that default partition in parallel to speed up the partition split process. Here is an example of splitting a partition using parallelism:

```
ALTER TABLE EMP
SPLIT PARTITION PMAX at ('2011-04-01') INTO
(PARTITION P4 TABLESPACE EMP_S,
PARTITION PMAX TABLESPACE EMP_S)
PARALLEL(DEGREE 4);
```

How It Works

Adding parallelism can speed up the process of splitting a partition with a large amount of data. Here is an example of a partition with over 16 million rows, and enabling parallelism for the split operation reduced the time of the split operation. First, the split was performed in parallel:

```
ALTER TABLE EMPPART SPLIT PARTITION emppart2000_p AT ('2000-01-01')
INTO (PARTITION emppart1990_p, PARTITION emppart2000_p)
PARALLEL(DEGREE 4);
```

```
Table altered.
```

```
Elapsed: 00:00:53.61
```

The same split was then performed on a similar table, to see the performance impact of doing the split serially:

```
ALTER TABLE EMPPART2 SPLIT PARTITION emppart2000_p AT ('2000-01-01')
INTO (PARTITION emppart1990_p, PARTITION emppart2000_p);
```

```
Table altered.
```

```
Elapsed: 00:01:05.36
```

Again, keep in mind that for parallel operations, an extent needs to be allocated for each parallel operation. For the foregoing partition split operation, the table that used parallelism has a significantly higher number of extents allocated:

```
SELECT segment_name, partition_name, extents
FROM dba_segments
WHERE segment_name LIKE '%EMP%'
AND owner = 'SCOTT'
ORDER BY 2,1;
```

SEGMENT_NAME	PARTITION_NAME	EXTENTS
EMPPART	EMPPART1990_P	335
EMPPART2	EMPPART1990_P	121
EMPPART	EMPPART2000_P	338
EMPPART2	EMPPART2000_P	125

15-10. Enabling Automatic Degree of Parallelism

Problem

You want to allow Oracle to automatically determine if a SQL statement should execute in parallel and what DOP it should use.

Solution

Set the PARALLEL_DEGREE_POLICY to AUTO to allow Oracle to determine whether a statement runs in parallel. You can set this either at the system level or session level. To set it for all SQL statements, run the following command:

```
alter system set parallel_degree_policy=auto scope=both;
```

To set it for a single SQL statement, you can alter your session to enable automatic DOP:

```
alter session set parallel_degree_policy=auto;
```

How It Works

By default, Oracle executes a statement in parallel only when the DOP is set for the table or the parallel hint is used. You can instruct Oracle to automatically consider using parallelism for a statement via the PARALLEL_DEGREE_POLICY initialization parameter. Oracle takes the following steps when a SQL statement is issued when PARALLEL_DEGREE_POLICY is set to AUTO:

1. Statement is parsed.

2. The `PARALLEL_MIN_TIME_THRESHOLD` parameter is checked:

   • If execution time is less than the threshold set, then the statement runs
     without parallelism.

   • If execution time is greater than the threshold set, then the statement runs
     in parallel depending on the automatic DOP that is calculated by the
     optimizer.

The `PARALLEL_DEGREE_POLICY` can be set to three different values: `AUTO`, `LIMITED`, and `MANUAL`. `MANUAL` is
the default and turns off the automatic degree of parallelism. `LIMITED` instructs Oracle to use automatic
DOP only on those objects with parallelism explicitly set. The `AUTO` setting gives Oracle full control over
setting automatic DOP. One prerequisite of using automatic DOP is to run the
`DBMS_RESOURCE_MANAGER.CALIBRATE_IO` procedure. This procedure needs to be run only once, and gathers
information on the hardware characteristics of your system.

With automatic DOP, there is a shift away from downgrading parallel operations based on available
parallel slaves, to use a new feature in Oracle 11g R2 called statement queuing. With statement queuing,
statements will not be downgraded, and will always be run with the query's specified DOP. If there are
not enough slaves to meet that DOP, the statement will be queued until that DOP is available. While it
may appear that queuing could actually degrade the performance of queries in your database because
some statements may have to wait for the specified DOP to be available, it is designed to improve the
overall parallelism performance on the database, as running fewer statements with the specified DOP
will outperform running more statements, some with a downgraded DOP. There are many other
parameters that can be set related to parallelism. Table 15-3 lists other parallel parameters you may
want to consider for your application.

Table 15-3. *Oracle Parallelism-Related Initialization Parameters*

Parameter	Description
parallel_degree_limit	Automatic DOP is determined either by the number of CPUs on the system, the I/O requirements of a given query, or by a set integer value. In order to use the IO value, you must run the `DBMS_RESOURCE_MANAGER.CALIBRATE_IO` procedure.
parallel_degree_policy	Determines whether automatic DOP, statement queuing, and in-memory query execution are enabled. The `MANUAL` setting disables automatic DOP. The `AUTO` setting gives Oracle full control over setting automatic DOP. The `LIMITED` value exercises automatic DOP only on those objects with parallelism explicitly set.
parallel_max_servers	This specifies the maximum number of parallel processes (from 0 to 3600) for a database instance.

Parameter	Description
parallel_min_servers	This specifies the minimum number of parallel processes for a database instance. Setting to a nonzero value keeps that minimum number of parallel processes alive and ready to accept new requests. This saves startup costs of these processes, but costs more in memory utilization.
parallel_servers_target	Setting this parameter tells the database how many parallel processes can run at one time before query statements requiring parallel execution begin to be queued for execution.

15-11. Examining Parallel Explain Plans

Problem

You want to understand how to read parallel explain plans.

Solution

When reading your explain plan, interpret it from the innermost to outermost levels, and from the bottom going up. For instance, here again is our parallel execution plan from using a parallel hint against the EMP table:

```
select /*+ parallel(emp,4) */ * from emp;
```

```
-------------------------------------------------------------------
| Id | Operation             | Name    |   TQ  |IN-OUT| PQ Distrib |
-------------------------------------------------------------------
|  0 | SELECT STATEMENT      |         |       |      |            |
|  1 |  PX COORDINATOR       |         |       |      |            |
|  2 |   PX SEND QC (RANDOM)| :TQ10000 | Q1,00 | P->S | QC (RAND)  |
|  3 |    PX BLOCK ITERATOR  |         | Q1,00 | PCWC |            |
|  4 |     TABLE ACCESS FULL| EMP      | Q1,00 | PCWP |            |
-------------------------------------------------------------------
```

Looking at the foregoing plan starting at the bottom, we are doing a full table scan of the EMP table. The PX BLOCK INTERATOR just above the table scan is responsible for taking that request for a full table scan, and breaking it up into chunks based on the DOP specified. The PX SEND processes pass the data to the consuming processes. Finally, the PX COORDINATOR is the process used by the query coordinator to receive the data from a given parallel process and return to the SELECT statement.

If you look at the IN-OUT column of your explain plan, you can see the execution flow of the operation, and determine if there are any bottlenecks, or any parts of the plan that are not parallelized, which may cause a decrease in the expected performance. As can be seen in Table 15-5, the operation that normally shows that there may be a bottleneck is the PARALLEL_FROM_SERIAL operation, because it means parallel processes are being spawned from a serial operation, which denotes an inefficiency in the process.

For instance, you have a series of employee tables by region of the country, and a user is performing a query to get information from several of these tables. However, the makeup of the query is such that a bottleneck occurs.

```
select /*+ parallel(emp_north,4) */ * from emp_north
union
select * from emp_south;
```

```
---------------------------------------------------------------------------
| Id  | Operation                | Name      |   TQ  |IN-OUT| PQ Distrib |
---------------------------------------------------------------------------
|   0 | SELECT STATEMENT         |           |       |      |            |
|   1 |  PX COORDINATOR          |           |       |      |            |
|   2 |   PX SEND QC (RANDOM)    | :TQ10002  | Q1,02 | P->S | QC (RAND)  |
|   3 |    SORT UNIQUE           |           | Q1,02 | PCWP |            |
|   4 |     PX RECEIVE           |           | Q1,02 | PCWP |            |
|   5 |      PX SEND HASH        | :TQ10001  | Q1,01 | P->P | HASH       |
|   6 |       BUFFER SORT        |           | Q1,01 | PCWP |            |
|   7 |        UNION-ALL         |           | Q1,01 | PCWP |            |
|   8 |         PX BLOCK ITERATOR|           | Q1,01 | PCWC |            |
|   9 |          TABLE ACCESS FULL | EMP_NORTH | Q1,01 | PCWP |         |
|  10 |         BUFFER SORT      |           | Q1,01 | PCWC |            |
|  11 |          PX RECEIVE      |           | Q1,01 | PCWP |            |
|  12 |           PX SEND ROUND-ROBIN | :TQ10000 |    | S->P |RND-ROBIN  |
|  13 |            TABLE ACCESS FULL | EMP_SOUTH |   |      |            |
---------------------------------------------------------------------------
```

You can tell from the foregoing explain plan output that the PX SEND process is serial, and is sending data back to be fed into a parallel process. This represents a bottleneck in this query. If we change all aspects of the query to run in parallel, we see an improvement in the execution plan:

```
select /*+ parallel(emp_north,4) */ * from emp_north
union
select /*+ parallel(emp_south,4) */ * from emp_south;
```

```
---------------------------------------------------------------------------
| Id  | Operation                | Name      |   TQ  |IN-OUT| PQ Distrib |
---------------------------------------------------------------------------
|   0 | SELECT STATEMENT         |           |       |      |            |
|   1 |  PX COORDINATOR          |           |       |      |            |
|   2 |   PX SEND QC (RANDOM)    | :TQ10001  | Q1,01 | P->S | QC (RAND)  |
|   3 |    SORT UNIQUE           |           | Q1,01 | PCWP |            |
|   4 |     PX RECEIVE           |           | Q1,01 | PCWP |            |
|   5 |      PX SEND HASH        | :TQ10000  | Q1,00 | P->P | HASH       |
|   6 |       UNION-ALL          |           | Q1,00 | PCWP |            |
|   7 |        PX BLOCK ITERATOR |           | Q1,00 | PCWC |            |
|   8 |         TABLE ACCESS FULL| EMP_NORTH | Q1,00 | PCWP |            |
|   9 |        PX BLOCK ITERATOR |           | Q1,00 | PCWC |            |
|  10 |         TABLE ACCESS FULL| EMP_SOUTH | Q1,00 | PCWP |            |
---------------------------------------------------------------------------
```

How It Works

Tables 15-4 and 15-5 delineate the fundamental information that can be used to determine the execution plan for a parallel operation. In order to understand the basics of interpreting your explain plan output, you should be aware of two aspects:

- The possible parallel execution steps (Table 15-4)

- The parallel operations that occur within each step (Table 15-5)

The execution steps are the aspects of a parallelized plan, while the operations that occur within your parallel execution plan can help you determine if you have an optimized plan, or one that needs tuning and improvement.

As with non-parallel operations, the explain plan utility is a very useful tool in determining what the optimizer is planning to do to complete the task at hand. When executing operations in parallel, there are specific aspects of the explain plan related to parallelism. These are important to understand, so you can determine if the operation is running as optimized as possible. One of the key aspects of analyzing a parallel explain plan is to determine if there are any aspects of the plan that are being run serially, as this bottleneck can reduce the overall performance of a given operation. That it is why it is critical to understand aspects of the explain plan that relate to parallel operations, with the end goal being that all aspects of the operation are parallelized.

Table 15-4. Parallel Execution Steps

Operation	Description
PX BLOCK ITERATOR	In this step, the work to be done is split into pieces, which in turn will be done by the parallel slaves specified.
PX COORDINATOR	Much like a project manager, this process coordinates and schedules the parallel slaves' work, as well as being responsible for getting data back from the parallel slaves once they complete their tasks.
PX RECEIVE	These processes are consumer slaves of the data written via the producers of the PX SEND processes.
PX SEND	These processes are the producer slaves of getting a portion of the data, and writing to areas to be read by the consumers.

Table 15-5. Parallel Operations

PLAN_TABLE Operation (Other_Tag Column)	Explain Plan In/Out Tag	Description
PARALLEL_FROM_SERIAL	S->P	This denotes that a serial process with the operation is passing information to a parallel process. This is a sign of a bottleneck and an area of potential improvement.
PARALLEL_TO_PARALLEL	P->P	This means that both the producer and the consumer are parallelized. This is the most desired execution flow.
PARALLEL_TO_SERIAL	P->S	This step, although hinting at a bottleneck, is fairly normal. It is toward the top (that is, the end) of an operation, and denotes that results from a parallel process are being fed to the query coordinator at the end of the process.
PARALLEL_COMBINED_WITH PARENT	PCWP	This means a step is being combined with its parent step and run simultaneously (for example, a sort/merge operation).
PARALLEL_COMBINED_WITH CHILD	PCWC	This is the same as PCWP, except it means that a child step/slave process is being run simultaneously with the child process from the execution plan.

15-12. Monitoring Parallel Operations

Problem

You want to quickly get information regarding the performance of your parallel operations from the database.

Solution

If you look at the V$SYSSTAT view, which gives information on system-level statistics in your database, including parallelism-related statistics, you can see, at a quick glance, if the DOP requested was actually used, and if any of those operations were downgraded:

```
SELECT name , value
FROM v$sysstat
WHERE name LIKE '%Parallel%';
```

```
-----------------------------------------------------------  ----------
Parallel operations not downgraded                                10331
Parallel operations downgraded to serial                              0
Parallel operations downgraded 75 to 99 pct                           0
Parallel operations downgraded 50 to 75 pct                           0
Parallel operations downgraded 25 to 50 pct                           0
Parallel operations downgraded 1 to 25 pct                            1
```

6 rows selected.

If you look at the V$PQ_SYSSTAT view, you can see parallel slave activity on your database. From looking at these statistics, you can quickly see if parallelism is properly configured on your database, just by looking at the parallel slave activity. For instance, if you see that the Servers Shutdown and Servers Started values are high, it can be an indication that the PARALLEL_MIN_SERVERS parameter is set too low, as there is overhead occurring to consistently start and stop parallel processes.

```
SELECT * FROM v$pq_sysstat
WHERE statistic LIKE 'Server%';
```

```
STATISTIC                        VALUE
------------------------------  ----------
Servers Busy                         0
Servers Idle                         0
Servers Highwater                    4
Server Sessions                      8
Servers Started                      4
Servers Shutdown                     4
Servers Cleaned Up                   0
```

7 rows selected.

If you are looking for session-level statistics regarding a parallel operation, looking at the V$PQ_TQSTAT view is very useful in determining exactly how the work was split up among the parallel slaves, as well as giving you information about the actual DOP used based on the information within V$PQ_TQSTAT. Let's rerun our parallel query against the EMP table with a hint specifying a DOP of 4.

```
SELECT /*+ parallel(emp,4) */ * FROM emp;
```

After completion of the query, but also within the same session, we can query the V$PQ_TQSTAT to get information about the parallel operations used for that query:

```
SELECT dfo_number, tq_id, server_type, process, num_rows, bytes
FROM v$pq_tqstat
ORDER BY dfo_number DESC, tq_id, server_type DESC , process;
```

DFO_NUMBER	TQ_ID	SERVER_TYP	PROCESS	NUM_ROWS	BYTES
1	0	Producer	P000	298629	13211118
1	0	Producer	P001	302470	13372088
1	0	Producer	P002	315956	13978646
1	0	Producer	P003	317512	14052340
1	0	Consumer	QC	1234567	54614192

We can see that between the four producer parallel slaves, the work was divided fairly evenly between them. We can also validate that the actual DOP used for this query was 4, as specified in the query hint.

How It Works

One of the quickest methods to analyze performance of parallel operations within your database is to analyze the dynamic performance views. These views give you a glimpse of how parallelism is performing overall within your database, which can indicate how well-tuned or badly tuned your database is for parallelism. It can also give you very session-specific details, such as how the work was split up between slaves, and information on the actual DOP used for a given operation. Table 15-6 gives you an overview of the parallelism-related dynamic performance views.

Table 15-6. Key Dynamic Performance Views Related to Parallel Operations

View Name	Description
V$PQ_SESSTAT	Shows parallelism-related statistics for the current session, including number of parallel slaves used
V$PQ_SYSSTAT	Shows parallelism-related statistics for the database instance, including number of parallel slaves used
V$PQ_TQSTAT	Contains statistics on parallel operations across the database instance, including the DOP used and rows processed for each slave of a given operation
V$SYSSTAT	Contains at-a-glance statistics on downgraded parallel-related operations
V$PX_SESSION	Contains information about sessions running parallel operations, and information about the DOP requested and used
V$PQ_SLAVE	Contains information about the current parallel slaves being used by a database instance
V$PX_PROCESS	Contains information about parallel processes and status

15-13. Finding Bottlenecks in Parallel Processes

Problem

You have some parallel processes that are underperforming, and you want to do analysis to find the bottlenecks.

Solution

There are many wait events related to parallelism. Many of these events are considered "idle" wait events—that is, they don't usually indicate a problem. If you query the V$SYSTEM_EVENT view, you can get an idea of the parallelism-related waits that have occurred in your database instance. The following query results show some of the common wait events that can occur:

```
SELECT event, wait_class, total_waits
FROM v$session_event
WHERE event LIKE 'PX%';
```

EVENT	WAIT_CLASS	TOTAL_WAITS
PX Deq Credit: need buffer	Idle	6667936
PX Deq Credit: send blkd	Other	8161247
PX Deq: Execute Reply	Idle	490827
PX Deq: Execution Msg	Idle	685175
PX Deq: Join ACK	Idle	26312
PX Deq: Msg Fragment	Idle	67
PX Deq: Parse Reply	Idle	20891
PX Deq: Signal ACK	Other	25729
PX Deq: Table Q Get Keys	Other	3141
PX Deq: Table Q Normal	Idle	25120970
PX Deq: Table Q Sample	Idle	11124
PX Deq: Table Q qref	Other	1705216
PX Idle Wait	Idle	241116
PX qref latch	Other	1208472

How It Works

Table 15-7 describes some of the key parallelism-related wait events. If you are having significant performance issues, it may be worthwhile to browse these wait events to see if you have excessive waits or wait times. If so, it may indicate an issue with the processing occurring with the parallel slaves. Again, events that are "idle" *generally* do not indicate a problem.

Table 15-7. *Parallelism Wait Events That Could Signify a Tuning Issue*

View Name	Description
PX Deq: Execute Reply	Denotes that the query coordinator (QC) is waiting for results from parallel slaves; this can be a sign of badly tuned SQL. If high waits, analyze the execution plan for efficiency.
PX Deq: Parse Reply	Denotes that parallel slaves are parsing SQL statements; high wait times may point to library cache contention.

Continued

View Name	Description
PX Deq: qref latch	This wait can indicate that the producer slaves are processing too fast, and the consumer slaves cannot keep up.
PX Deq: Table Q Normal	This may indicate that some producer slaves are slow, and that the consumer slaves are waiting.

15-14. Getting Detailed Information on Parallel Sessions

Problem

You have some underperforming parallel processes, and need more detailed information on the sessions.

Solution

By turning on session tracing, you can get detailed trace information on your parallel sessions. This is essentially a four-step process:

1. Set the event in your session.
2. Execute your SQL statement.
3. Turn off your session tracing.
4. Analyze your trace file output.

For example, you are again executing a parallel query against our EMP table. In order to gather trace information, you would do the following:

```
alter session set events '10391 trace name context forever, level 128';

select /*+ parallel(emp,4) */ * from emp;

alter session set events '10391 trace name context off';
```

Then, within the trace file, you can analyze the parallel-related information, such as the following:

```
kxfrDmpUpdSys
        allocated slave set: nsset:1 nbslv:4
          Slave set 0: #nodes:1
          Min # slaves 4: Max # slaves:4
            List of Slaves:
                slv 0 nid:0
                slv 1 nid:0
                slv 2 nid:0
                slv 3 nid:0
            List of Nodes:
                node 0
```

How It Works

As with other session tracing, the trace file can be found in the destination specified under the user_dump_dest parameter. The trace file shows granular information for the parallel processes. If you are experiencing significant performance issues with parallelism, and you wish to delve further into investigating the results of the trace files generated by this event, it may be beneficial to simply create a service request with Oracle in order to get the most detailed information. Reading and understanding these trace files can be difficult and cumbersome, and it may be more expedient to simply send the files to Oracle support for analysis. Yet another way to validate the DOP used for a parallel operation is to use the _px_trace facility, which also generates a trace file:

```
alter session set "_px_trace"="compilation","execution","messaging";
```

```
select /*+ parallel(emp,4) */ * from emp;
```

Then, within the trace file, you can evaluate the DOP requested and used:

```
kkscscid_pdm_eval
        pdml_allowed=0, cursorPdmlMode=0,                  sessPdmlMode=0
        select /*+ parallel(emp,4) */ * from emp

kxfrDefaultDOP
        DOP Trace -- compute default DOP
            # CPU     = 2
            Threads/CPU = 2 ("parallel_threads_per_cpu")
            default DOP = 4 (# CPU * Threads/CPU)

kxfpAdaptDOP
        Requested=4 Granted=4 Target=8 Load=2 Default=4 users=0 sets=1
        load adapt num servers requested to = 4 (from kxfpAdaptDOP())
```

Index

■ P

Lightning Source UK Ltd.
Milton Keynes UK
UKOW06f0409181014

240252UK00008B/165/P